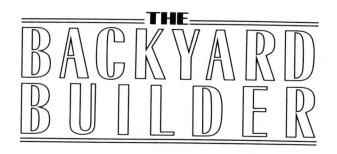

THE BACKYARD BUILDER

Project Director: Ray Wolf
Editor: John Warde
Assistant Editor: Roger Moyer
Writers: Larry McClung
      Roger Rawlings
Illustrator: Frank Rohrbach

Rodale Design Group:
    Manager of Design: Fred Matlack
    Designers: Phil Gehret
            Dennis Kline
            John Kline
            Ed Wachter

Photography Coordinator:
    Mitchell T. Mandel
Photographers: Alison Miksch
          Anthony Rodale
          Mitchell T. Mandel
          and the staff of the
            Rodale Press
            Photography
            Department

Book Design: Barbara Field
Book Layout: Darlene Schneck
Copy Editor: Dolores Plikaitis
Project Coordinator: Kim Miller

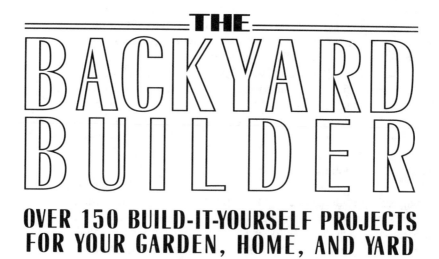

THE BACKYARD BUILDER

OVER 150 BUILD-IT-YOURSELF PROJECTS FOR YOUR GARDEN, HOME, AND YARD

Edited by John Warde

Illustrated by Frank Rohrbach

WINGS BOOKS

New York • Avenel, New Jersey

This 1994 edition is published by Wings Books, distributed by Random House Value Publishing, Inc., 40 Engelhard Avenue, Avenel, New Jersey 07001, by arrangement with Rodale Press, Inc.

Random House
New York • Toronto • London • Sydney • Auckland

Printed and bound in the United States of America

Library of Congress Cataloging-in-Publication Data

The Backyard builder: over 150 build-it-yourself projects for your
    garden, home, and yard / edited by John Warde ; illustrated by Frank
    Rohrbach.
            p.   cm.
        ISBN 0-517-10035-5
        1. Garden structures--Design and construction--Amateurs' manuals.
    I. Warde, John.
    TH4961.B33 1994
        690'.89--dc20   93-28710
                                                                              CIP

8 7 6 5 4 3 2

Contents

Building for the Outdoors x

Projects for the Patio and Yard

Porch Swing 2
Gym-in-a-Yard 8
Bird-Feeding Station 14
Suet Holder 16
Finch Feeder 17
Bird Feeder 20
Redwood Hanging Bird Station 23
Lawn Chair 26
Garden Chair 33
Phone-Pole Garden Bench 36
Wooden Garden Bench 39
Wooden Garden Bench with Back 42
Garden Bench with Wrought-Iron Legs 45
Garden Bench with Wrought-Iron Legs and Arms 49
Tree Bench 52
Plant Steps 56
Stacking Strawberry Box 59
Wooden Window Box 62
Planter Trellis 67

v

Window Trellis 72
Gateway Arbor 77
Sun Trellis 81
Decorative Block Mold 88
Wood and Cement Block Planter 92
Wood and Cement Block Patio Bench 96
Cement Block Charcoal Grill 99
Outdoor Cooking Center 102

Projects for the Garden

Soil Mixer 112
Easy-Dumping Soil Sifter 117
Hanging Soil Sifter 122
Wheelbarrow Flat Carrier/Soil Sifter 125
Insulated Propagation Box 130
Propagation Tray 134
Raised-Bed Gardening System 138
Cold Frame for Raised-Bed Gardening System 142
Sunshade for Raised-Bed Gardening System 147
Trellis for Raised-Bed Gardening System 151
Fence Panels for Raised-Bed Gardening System Compost Bin 154
Big Box Garden 158
Cabin-Jointed Planter 161
Patio Planter 164
Measuring Wheel 168
Row Marker 170
Planting Guide 174
Gardener's Seed Planter 176
Parallelogram Planting Guide 179
Garden Stakes 182
Modular Tunnel Cloche 186
Triangular Cloche 190
Cubical Plant Covers 192
Cloche and Trellis System 195
Tried and True Cold Frame 200
Window-Sash Cold Frame 205
French Double Cold Frame 215
Indoor-Outdoor Greenhouse 220
Tomato-Frame Greenhouse 225

Cantaloupe Fence 233
Snow-Fence Trellis 238
Cucumber Trellis 240
Bean Trellis 242
Super Trellis 245
Redwood Tomato Trellis 247
PVC Trellis 249
Top-Hat Trellis System 253
Garden-Row Bird Screen 258
Removable Garden Fence 261
Sectional Garden Fence 264
Modular Garden Fence 268
Total Garden-Enclosing System 271
Four Garden Gates 276
Fence-Frame Compost Bins 282
Compost Drum 286
Manure-Tea Brewer 292
Feedigator 296
Slatted Compost-Tea Sieve 298
Trickle-Hose Take-Up Reel 301
Double Digger for Raised-Bed Gardening 305
Bicycle Hoe Cultivator 309
Garden Cultivator 313
Gardener's Rolling Cricket 317
The Baksaver 320
Garden Sink 324
Orchard Ladder 329
Apple Picker 336
Herb Drying Rack 338

Projects for Indoor Gardeners

Propagation Bed 342
Plastic-Enclosed Flat 344
Plant Carrier 346
Window-Mounted Seed Starter 348
Hanging Log Basket 353
Hanging Wood and Copper Planter 355
Hanging Planter for Three Plants 358
Three-Tiered Hanging Plant Shelf 361

Hanging Plant Window Extender 364
Slat-Style Window Extender 366
Window Extender with Glass Shelves 369
Freestanding Window Box and Shelves 372
Plant Display Cart 375
Mobile Herb Planter 378
Adjustable Plant Pole 383

Wood-Heating Accessories

Ax Rack 388
Woodcutter's Tote 391
Wood Harvester 394
Five-Bay Sawbuck 399
Firewood Cutting Jig 402
Wood Vault Stairs 406
Firewood Chute 409
Attached Woodbox 412
Firewood Rack 418
Swing-Set Wood Rack 421
Hoop-Style Firewood Rack 424
Firewood Platform 427
Fuel-Storage Bin 430
Traditional Firewood Box 435
Firewood Cart 440
Dustless Ash Container 444
Ash Hoe 447

Storage, Sheds, and Outbuildings

Root-Cellar Storage Boxes 452
Vegetable Bin 455
Jelly Cupboard 461
Under-Stair Storage Shelves 465
Closet Cupboard 469
Adjustable Storage Shelves 475
Freestanding Shelves 478
Ladder-Type Bike Rack 482
Triangular Bike Rack 485
Trash-Can Shed 489

PVC Woodshed 496
Mini-Greenhouse Shed 499
Arched Greenhouse 504
Attached Greenhouse 510
Garden Slat House 521
Potting Shed–Slat House 525
A-Frame Wood and Storage Shed 534
Root Cellar 541
Garden Shed with Wood-Storage Area 549

Projects for Household and Lawn Care

Garden Tool Cart 564
Hose-Reel Cart 569
Trash-Can Dolly 574
Leaf-Bag Frame 576
Wet Broom 578
Auto-Cleanout Caddy 580
Auto-Tool Cart 583
Small-Tool Carrier 589
General-Purpose Stool 593
Kitchen Utility Table 595
Multipurpose Table 599
Folding Utility Table 604
Recycling Unit 607
Collapsible Wheelbarrow 611
Low-Loader Wheelbarrow 615
Heavy-Duty Garden Cart 619
Garden Trailer 622
Tractor Cart 627

BUILDING FOR THE OUTDOORS

Sturdiness. That's the watchword for outdoor projects. A garden cart, porch swing, compost bin—nearly all of the projects presented in this book—must be able to stand up to heavy use and inclement weather. In this chapter, we'll tell you how to be sure that your projects can withstand the hardships of outdoor life. We'll give you advice on how to select the right lumber for outdoor projects. We'll fill you in on the proper woodworking techniques to use. And we'll tell you what sorts of hardware and finishes work best outdoors. All in all, the information in this chapter will help ensure that your projects will last for many years.

LUMBER

Most people use a very straightforward method for choosing lumber. They go down to the local lumberyard or home building center and buy whatever the salesman recommends. If you're lucky enough to deal with a salesman who is both honest and knowledgeable, this technique can work well enough. But if your luck doesn't hold, you may wind up with a load of wood that is badly flawed.

To help you avoid these problems, here's a brief lumber buyer's guide.

Softwood—In general, we recommend No. 2 pine, otherwise known as standard pine. It is good-quality wood, widely available, and is less expensive than Select or top-of-the-line, construction-grade No. 1 pine.

Hardwood—We specify hardwoods for only a few of the projects in this book. You will not normally need hardwood for outdoor projects unless great structural strength is called for or appearance is extremely important. The best hardwood for most purposes is luan mahogany, which is grown in the Philippines (no mahogany trees grow in the United States). Despite mahogany's reputation as a luxurious wood—people often associate it with expensive antique furnishings or the dashboards of luxury automobiles—the luan variety is actually rather moderately priced and is available in

LUMBER GRADES

Softwood

Class	Grade	Characteristics
Select	B and Better (or B & Btr, or Clear)	Practically clear on both sides; no knots; virtually no blemishes.
	C	Slightly more blemishes than B & Btr; perhaps a few very small knots.
	D	One side finish quality; recognizable defects on back.
Common	No. 1 (or Construction)	Smooth grain; evenly distributed knots no more than 2 inches in diameter; no knots near edge.
	No. 2 (or Standard)	Similar to No. 1, except knots up to 3 inches in diameter in wide boards.
	No. 3 (or Utility)	Some coarse or loose knots, or other major blemishes; sometimes a single defect surrounded by good wood.
	No. 4 (or Economy)	Numerous knots, knotholes, and other defects; some usable wood.
	No. 5 (or Economy)	Poor quality; use only if neither appearance nor strength is required.

Hardwood

Grade	Characteristics
Firsts and Seconds (FAS)	Usually at least 6 inches wide and 8 feet long; over 81 percent clear on both sides.
Select	At least 4 inches wide and 6 feet long; one side as good as FAS.
No. 1 Common	Narrower and shorter than Select; 66 percent clear.
No. 2 Common	50 percent clear.
No. 3A Common	33 percent clear.
No. 3B Common	25 percent clear.

most parts of the country. For a hardwood, it is also easy to work with.

Lumber Grades—The table above lists the basic grades for softwood and hardwood. The information it contains should be adequate for most of the lumber you'll want to buy. If you're ever in a situation where the grades on the table do not apply, simply tell the lumber salesman whether you want the top grade, an intermediate grade, or an economy grade, and then inspect the lumber he selects for you before laying down your money.

Inspecting Lumber—We strongly urge you to inspect all the lumber you intend to buy, whether or not you are acquainted with the grading system used at that particular lumberyard. Here's a rundown of the defects to look out for (illustration A):

1. Knots, especially if they occur in the middle section of a piece of lumber, can present problems. They weaken the wood, and they are hard to saw, plane, and sand. Ideally, you should get wood with few knots, and the maximum size of any knots that are present should be no more than one-third the width of the wood.

2. Various insects and fungi attack wood, causing it to decay. If the lumber is riddled with wormholes or if portions of it seem spongy, you should reject it.

3. *Warped wood* is extremely difficult to work with. All surfaces of a piece of lumber should be straight. Run your eye along the edges of at least a few representative pieces before buying a load of lumber.

4. *Checks, shakes,* and *splits* are various types of cracks. No need to worry much about the differences among them— you don't want any of them. You may have to accept a few short cracks in the ends of some pieces of lumber. Consider buying slightly longer lengths to compensate. If there are cracks in the middle portion of a piece, reject it.

5. Some pieces of lumber have bits of bark along one edge, or one edge may be ragged instead of smooth and straight. This defect, called *wane*, merits rejection.

6. Sometimes resin or pitch accumulates between the rings in a tree. These flaws, called *pitch pockets,* weaken a piece of lumber. If the wood you inspect has wide, discolored areas between the grain lines, reject it.

7. Lumber is strongest if the grain in each piece runs parallel to the long edges of the piece. Otherwise, the piece is said to suffer from *cross grain.* Reject it.

Treated Lumber—We mentioned decay as one of the defects to avoid when buying new wood. Decay is also a problem you need to contend with after buying lumber. Wood-eating bugs and fungi can attack your

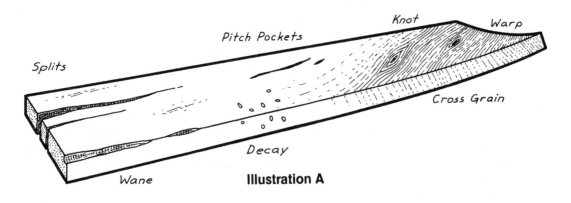

Illustration A

lumber, particularly if it will be in contact with the ground. So for those parts of your projects that will touch the ground, you should use lumber that resists the attacks of both bugs and fungi.

The heartwood of some trees is naturally resistant. Among them are redwood, inland red cedar, western red cedar, walnut, black locust, and both red and white oak. Using lumber cut from the heartwood of these trees can be a good move. Prices can be steep, however, and obtaining supplies can be difficult.

For most outdoor projects, use pressure-treated lumber. This is ordinary lumber that has been impregnated with chemicals to fend off bugs and fungi.

Several types of chemicals are used to treat lumber. The best are chromated copper arsenates (CCA). These are mixtures of chrome, copper, and arsenic compounds that have proven to be effective, odorless, and paintable. And, as preservative chemicals go, CCAs are relatively safe. The chemicals are fixed to the wood fibers during the treatment process, so they will not leach out. Still, any chemical that is toxic to fungi and bugs is likely to be at least potentially harmful to human beings, so you should take certain precautions when working with pressure-treated wood. We discuss these precautions later in this chapter in the section on Safety.

Be sure to get pressure-treated lumber that contains enough CCA for your purposes. Look for the quality stamp that should appear on all pressure-treated lumber you buy. Wood marked LP-2 contains 0.25 pound of wood preservative per cubic foot—it is fine for use aboveground, but it should not come in contact with the ground.

Wood marked LP-22 contains 0.4 pound of preservative per cubic foot—it is suitable for contact with the ground.

Pressure treatment creates a shell of protection around a piece of lumber—the outermost half inch or so of the wood is impregnated with wood preservative, but the center of the wood has little or none. For this reason, if you cut a piece of pressure-treated wood, you should apply wood preservative to the surfaces exposed by the cut. See the discussion of wood preservatives later in this chapter in the section on Finishes.

Plywood—For many projects, you'll find plywood to be indispensable. Traditionally, plywood has been sold in exterior and interior grades. Exterior plywood uses waterproof glue; interior plywood doesn't. Recently, interior plywood has all but disappeared. Still, you should check to be sure that any plywood you buy for outdoor projects is intended for outdoor use.

You can get plywood made of either softwood or hardwood. Among the softwood plywoods, there are five groups, ranked according to the stiffness and strength of the woods used. Group 1 (including such woods as Douglas fir, American beech, and loblolly pine) is strongest; group 5 (including basswood, balsam fir, and balsam poplar) is weakest.

The quality of the outermost layers of wood—the layers you can see—is indicated by a lettering system (see the table on p. xiv).

Hardwood plywood is graded in three categories. A sheet marked 1-2, for example, has a good-quality face (grade 1) with carefully matched grains and a somewhat lower-quality back (grade 2) with unmatched

PLYWOOD VENEER GRADES
(SOFTWOOD)

N	Highest quality — "natural finish," smooth veneer. Select; either all heartwood or all sapwood. Free of open defects. Suitable for decorative work.
A	Smooth, paintable. Not more than 18 neatly made repairs, parallel to grain. May be used for natural finish or for decorative projects that are to be painted.
B	Solid surface. Shims, circular repair plugs, and knots up to 1 inch in diameter; some minor splits. Usable for most projects, except where appearance is an uppermost consideration.
C Plugged	Splits up to ⅛ inch wide; knotholes and borer holes up to ¼ × ½ inch. Some broken grains. Synthetic repairs permitted. Sometimes acceptable as a lower-cost substitute for B.
C	Knots and knotholes up to 1½ inches. Some splits, discoloration, sanding defects. Synthetic and wood repairs. Usable for heavy-duty projects where appearance is unimportant.
D	Lowest quality. Knots and knotholes up to 3 inches in diameter. Splits, stitching. Not for outdoor use.

grains. A grade 3 sheet is generally sound, but it contains noticeable defects and patching.

For both softwood and hardwood sheets, the symbols G2S (good on two sides) and G1S (you guessed it, good on one side) are also used.

Tips on Buying Lumber — Here are a few additional bits of advice you should bear in mind when selecting lumber. By following these suggestions, you'll ensure that you get exactly the lumber you need, and you'll save money in the process.

1. Rough (unsmoothed) stock is perfectly adequate for many outdoor projects, and it can be as much as 20 percent cheaper than dressed (smoothed) lumber. If your lumberyard doesn't have rough lumber, scout around for a lumber mill. Visiting a mill in a pickup truck or station wagon can be well worth your while.

2. If you buy dressed lumber, bear in mind that the planing process reduces the size of each piece of wood. See the table on p. xv for a comparison of nominal vs. actual sizes.

3. Long lumber is usually cheaper than short lumber. For example, if you need two 8-foot-long 2 × 10s, you'll save money if you buy a 16-foot-long 2 × 10 and cut it yourself, instead of buying two 8-footers. There are a couple of exceptions to this rule, however: Very long lumber — 24 feet or more — can be exorbitantly expensive because it must be cut from very tall trees, which have gotten to be rare. Also, very short lumber can often be obtained from the lumberyard's

DRESSED SOFTWOOD SIZES

Nominal	Actual
1 × 2	¾″ × 1½″
1 × 3	¾″ × 2½″
1 × 4	¾″ × 3½″
1 × 5	¾″ × 4½″
1 × 6	¾″ × 5½″
1 × 8	¾″ × 7¼″
1 × 10	¾″ × 9¼″
1 × 12	¾″ × 11¼″
2 × 2	1½″ × 1½″
2 × 4	1½″ × 3½″
2 × 6	1½″ × 5½″
2 × 8	1½″ × 7¼″
2 × 10	1½″ × 9¼″
2 × 12	1½″ × 11¼″

rare, but looking for it can be worthwhile, especially for any wide boards you intend to use. Edge-grain boards will swell, shrink, and twist much less than flat-grain boards.

6. As a general rule, you should always buy about 10 percent more wood than you think you'll need. There's always a certain amount of waste, due to splits at the ends of some boards, knots that show up at exactly the wrong place, and so forth. The extra 10 percent should compensate for these difficulties.

7. You can save money by buying green lumber. This is wood that has not been dried, so it still contains sap. It is almost always significantly cheaper than dried lumber. But green lumber will shrink and perhaps warp. For this reason, it is only suitable for rough-hewn construction where twisted wood and slightly inexact

bargain bin. The bin usually contains cutoffs from longer pieces, and often you can find bits of high-grade wood there for very low prices.

4. Before buying lumber of any particular grade, take a look at the next lowest grade. For example, you may decide that you want No. 2 pine. But before buying it, look over the lumberyard's No. 3 pine. Sometimes the differences in quality can be very small. If you're lucky, you will have stumbled on a lumberyard that sells No. 3 pine that is virtually indistinguishable from No. 2. Buy the No. 3—you'll save anywhere from a few cents to several dollars.

5. If possible, you should buy lumber that has edge grain rather than flat grain (illustration B). Such wood is relatively

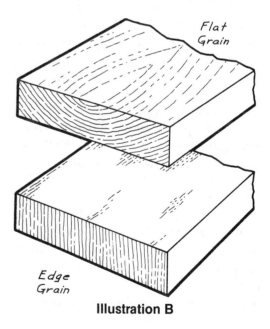

Illustration B

joints are acceptable.

8. Be sure that any pressure-treated wood you buy was dried after the wood preservative chemicals were applied to it. Like green wood, wet pressure-treated wood may warp if the preservative chemicals remain in a liquid state. Such wood is also heavier and may develop surface mold. You can determine the nature of a sheet of plywood by looking at the quality stamp that should appear on it. The stamp will also tell you what preservative chemicals were used on the sheet, whether the sheet can be used in contact with the ground, what year the sheet was treated, and similar related information.

RECYCLED WOOD

We've been talking as if the only way to get lumber is to visit a lumberyard or mill. But actually, you have another option: scavenging. Collecting old lumber may take some work, but the financial payoff can be great, since scavenged lumber is often perfectly usable and very inexpensive. Sometimes, in fact, it's free.

Demolition contractors are often willing to sell molding, studs, joists, and other pieces of wood from buildings that they have been hired to tear down. Occasionally they will actually give the stuff away. Now and then you can find lumber for sale at auctions or flea markets. And, of course, there's always the option of tearing down an old building yourself. Many farmers, homeowners, and businessmen have unused sheds, garages, and other outbuildings on their properties, which they may want to get rid of. Frequently, you can negotiate a deal with them. A common arrangement is to do all of the demolition work in exchange for keeping all of the usable materials in the building.

Inspection — No matter where you find it, scavenged lumber calls for even closer inspection than lumber bought from a lumberyard or sawmill. Eyeball the wood carefully, and use an ice pick or screwdriver to prod here and there, testing for decay. In some cases you'll get lucky: Old lumber was often cut from slower-growing trees than today's lumber, which means it was extremely sturdy when it was new. If it has been protected from the weather, it may still be sturdier than much new lumber that today is cut from fast-growing softwood trees.

More commonly, scavenged lumber will contain numerous defects. There may be cracks and knotholes. The wood may have become brittle with age. (One way to test for this is to place one end of a board on a stack of three or four bricks and then step on the middle of the board to see how much flex it has.) The surface may be weatherbeaten.

A close inspection will tell you whether or not a particular load of wood is worth scavenging. It will also let you start the process of dividing the wood into categories. Normally, you will probably divide a load of scavenged wood into three piles: the best wood, usable for finishing work; slightly marred wood, usable for rough construction; and seriously flawed wood probably best consigned to your wood stove.

Use your tape measure to determine the dimensions of the lumber. Old standard-dimension lumber tends to be larger than that recently produced. For example, a 2 × 4 that was cut before World War II probably measures 2×4 inches, not $1\frac{1}{2} \times 3\frac{1}{2}$ inches like newer 2×4s.

Using Scavenged Wood—Working with secondhand lumber calls for special care. Old boards may contain nails or other metal fasteners, often buried inside. For your own safety and the protection of your tools, inspect scavenged wood carefully before using it. Take pains to remove all such fasteners before setting to work.

Old lumber may also require cleaning. Often, the lumber will have been in contact with the ground or it may have been left outdoors where debris could accumulate on it. In either case, all dirt should be scraped or brushed from the lumber before you work with it. Otherwise, the dirt may damage your tools, and it may promote decay in the wood.

Try to avoid cutting into the knots in old wood. As lumber ages, the knots in it tend to become very hard and brittle. Attempting to cut through a knot may dull the teeth of your saw, may cause sharp chips to fly from the knot, or may cause the knot to fall out of the wood altogether. The best policy is to give knots in old lumber a wide berth.

Beware of splinters from old wood. Because the wood is often weather-beaten and brittle, it tends to splinter readily. You should wear thick work gloves, and you may want to get a tetanus booster shot before handling quantities of scavenged wood.

WEATHER-WISE WOODWORK

The sturdiness and weather resistance of outdoor projects will depend to a large extent on how the projects are put together. You may use strong, weather-resistant wood, but the items you build won't hold up unless you employ the proper techniques for fastening the pieces of wood to each other. You should use construction techniques that will enable the finished projects to stand up to heavy use, moisture, and temperature extremes. Here are some recommendations.

Joints

The primary rule to remember is that each joint used in an outdoor project should either be shielded from the weather, or it should be oriented so that it will shed water. If a joint must be left exposed to the weather, seal it with a high-quality caulking compound.

Remember, also, that a joint will only be as good as the fasteners and glues you use with it. (See the following sections of this chapter.)

The most common joint is the *butt joint*, which consists of the end of one piece of wood attached to a face of another (illustration C). Butt joints are easy to make, but they are weak because the grain at the end of a piece of wood does not firmly grip nails or other fasteners. Sometimes it's a good idea to strengthen butt joints with wood glue and dowels.

For many purposes *half-lap joints* are the best choice (illustration D). They consist of two pieces of wood that are notched and overlapped. A half-lap joint gains its strength from the fact that the overlapping portions of the pieces of wood provide protection and reinforcement for the joint. The easiest way to cut a half-lap joint is to use the dado head on a bench saw or radial-arm saw. Careful sawing with a

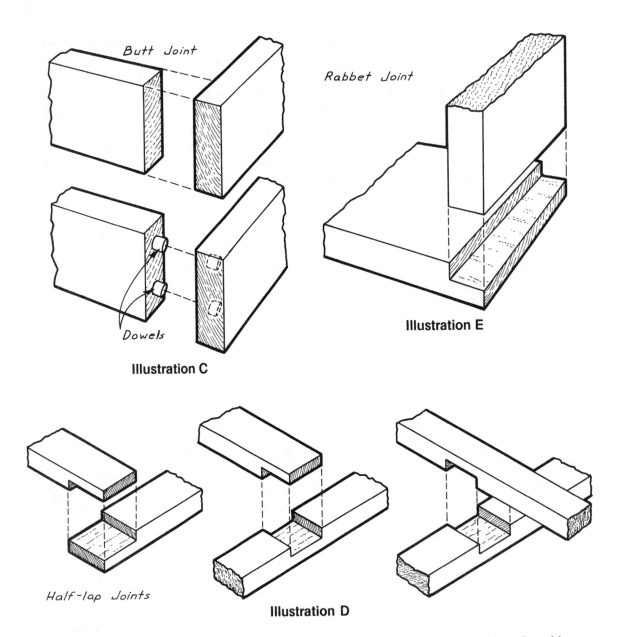

Butt Joint

Dowels

Illustration C

Rabbet Joint

Illustration E

Half-lap Joints

Illustration D

handsaw or portable circular saw followed by paring with a sharp chisel works just as well.

Rabbet joints are useful in simple box-and-case construction. A rabbet is an L-shaped notch cut along the edge or end of a piece of wood. The joint is formed by

fitting a second piece of wood into the rabbet (illustration E). Not only is the end grain of the second piece of wood protected from the weather, but also the rabbet tends to prevent both pieces from twisting.

Mortise-and-tenon joints are fairly hard to make, but they are extremely strong. A mortise is a slot or recess cut in a piece of wood and a tenon is the end of another piece of wood cut to fit snugly into the mortise (illustration F).

Miter joints are not inherently strong, but they are often used for decorative effect and to protect vulnerable end grain. To make the joint, the ends of two pieces of wood are cut at an angle, then joined along the cuts (illustration G). Miter joints can be reinforced by the use of dowels, splines, or metal fasteners.

Glues

Despite manufacturers' claims, few glues are able to withstand the havoc wrought by weather. Until recently, in fact, it was almost unthinkable to use any glue in an outdoor project.

Today, the situation is a little better. A few glues are now available that provide significant aid for the carpenter who is building objects that will be used outdoors. Here are the glues we recommend:

Carpenter's wood glue, also known as yellow glue, is usually sold in squeeze bottles. An aliphatic resin, it dries quickly, is easy to sand, and is quite strong. It can be used in a wide range of temperatures. However, it only offers slight to moderate water resistance, so it should only be used on those parts of a project that will be protected from water.

Resorcinol is a wholly waterproof glue that comes in two containers. One container

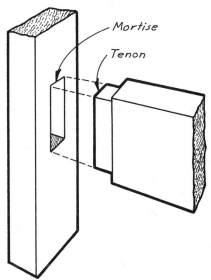

Mortise - and - Tenon Joint
Illustration F

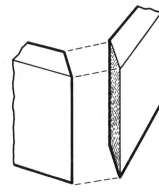

Miter Joints

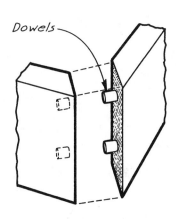

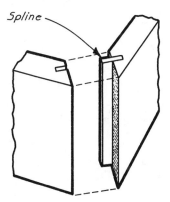

Illustration G

holds a liquid resin that you mix with the powdered catalyst that comes in the second container. Originally intended for use on the hulls of wooden boats, resorcinol is very strong, and it offers reliable protection against water damage. Resorcinol's main drawback is that it stains wood a reddish brown where it is applied.

Epoxy, like resorcinol, comes in two containers. It is an extremely strong but brittle glue that cures rapidly. It is highly waterproof. One special advantage of epoxy is that it bonds dissimilar materials. You can glue wood to metal, glass, or plastic. Epoxy can be used in a wide range of temperatures. Besides serving as a glue, epoxy can also be used as a crack filler.

Fasteners

Most joints depend on metal fasteners (illustration H) to give them much of their strength. For this reason you should select nails, screws, and bolts as carefully as you select the lumber. For outdoor use fasteners should not only grip the wood well, but they must also resist corrosion.

Fasteners made of pure iron are highly resistant, but they are hard to find nowadays. Most so-called iron fasteners are actually made of mild steel (iron with a little carbon mixed in). If you buy mild steel fasteners, make sure they are galvanized or plated in some other manner, so that the steel is entirely encased in a protective coating. Otherwise, rust is sure to result.

You still could have a problem if any of the protective coating chips off. For example, when you drive coated nails into wood, the coating may chip off the nail heads. To avoid this, buy "hot dipped" galvanized nails.

Mild steel fasteners are by far the more easily obtainable. But for use at or below ground level, you should buy fasteners made of more corrosion-resistant metals. The best choices are bronze and brass. Copper and aluminum are too soft for some uses, and stainless steel is not as rust resistant as these other metals.

The fasteners you'll use most often, of course, are *nails.* Smooth-shanked common nails are fine for most purposes, but if an outdoor project will be subjected to temperature extremes, or if it will go through

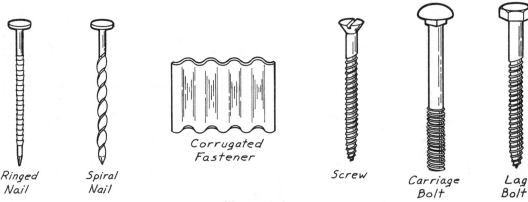

Ringed Nail   Spiral Nail   Corrugated Fastener   Screw   Carriage Bolt   Lag Bolt

Illustration H

frequent wet and dry cycles, then use ringed or spiral nails. The ridges on the shanks of these nails grip the wood more firmly.

A special variety of nail is the *corrugated fastener*. It is used on butt joints and miter joints. The fastener spans the two pieces of wood being joined, and the corrugations help hold the pieces of wood together.

Screws are especially helpful when joining end grain. As we said earlier, nails tend to readily pull out of end grain. Screws grip the wood more firmly. Flathead screws are generally best for outdoor projects. They are usually countersunk so that their heads lie below the surface.

Bolts tend to be the strongest fasteners of all. For most purposes, we recommend carriage bolts. They have necks that are specially designed to grip wood. Carriage bolts extend all the way through the two pieces of wood that are being joined. Though their wide heads often do not require washers, you must always use washers at the other end, where the bolt receives a nut.

Lag bolts (also known as lag screws and sill screws) should be used when joining two pieces of wood that are so thick a carriage bolt cannot pass all the way through them. Essentially, a lag bolt is nothing but a huge screw with a square or hexagonal head that you turn with a wrench. The pilot hole for the unthreaded part of the bolt should be the same diameter as that part of the bolt. However, the pilot hole for the threaded part should be two-thirds of the diameter if you're using softwood or three-quarters of the diameter if you're using hardwood. Always use large washers with lag bolts to keep the head from crushing the wood.

Finishes

A quality finish can extend the life of your handiwork by years. If you have used decay-resistant or pressure-treated wood to build an outdoor project, you may decide not to apply any finish. However, with ordinary wood you'll find it wise to put a finish on the projects you build. Your options include varnish, exterior paint, and wood preservative. Avoid lacquer or shellac —these will not hold up to the weather.

A wide array of *varnishes* is available, including polyurethanes. Most of the varnishes now being sold are synthetic; they are easier to apply than natural varnishes, and they tend to offer better protection. The best choice for outdoor projects is marine varnish, available at boat stores. It's not necessary to apply a primer before brushing on varnish. Simply thin the first coat with the thinner prescribed on the label. Try to find a clean, bug-free area to do your varnishing. Since drying time is several hours, you can end up with lots of debris and small insects stuck on the surface of your project if you don't select the right place to work.

Latex *paints* have always been easier to work with than oil-based paints, and the new latex formulas are virtually as long-lasting. Before applying any paint to bare wood, it's essential to put down one or even two coats of primer. Primer is thin, so it soaks into the wood, thereby giving a large measure of protection. To make sure the paint itself gives maximum weather resistance, select a gloss-finish marine paint. This type sheds water readily and is easy to clean.

The surest defense against weather is provided by *wood preservatives.* As we said earlier, pressure-treated wood comes with wood preservatives in it. Using pressure-treated wood is the preferred option for any part of a project that will be in contact with the ground or that will get wet continually. You can, however, buy wood preservatives that you yourself can apply to bare wood.

Among your options are creosote, pentachlorophenol (penta, for short), and copper or zinc naphthenate. We recommend the naphthenates. Creosote and penta are both highly toxic; moreover, creosote stains wood a dark brown and cannot be painted over, while penta is hard to mix and permeates all the wood. Copper naphthenate will stain wood a pale green, though zinc naphthenate dries clear. Both can be difficult to paint over. However, the naphthenates are considered benign enough for use around edible plants and are safe as well as easy to apply.

The best way to apply wood preservative is to partially fill a container with preservative and then immerse the wood in it. This way, the liquid will be able to soak into all the tiny cracks and crevices in the surface of the wood. Of course, if you're working with large pieces of lumber, you may not be able to immerse all of the wood. But you should be able to immerse at least those portions of the wood that will touch the ground—the ends of a picnic table's legs, for example.

If you can't use the immersion technique, use a natural bristle brush to apply the preservative. (Natural bristles hold preservatives better than synthetic bristles do.) Don't be miserly about it; brush the liquid on heavily so that it will seep deeply into the wood. Regardless of which method you use, do the work in the shade so the pre-

servative won't dry before it has penetrated the wood.

Dipping wood in copper naphthenate should protect it for about 5 years; applying copper naphthenate with a brush should give about 3½ years' worth of protection. After that time, you'll have to reapply it. All other apply-it-yourself wood preservatives also need reapplication after a few years.

Safety

Working outdoors can be hazardous. A shop has level floors, steady workbenches, and convenient storage areas for all tools. There are also safe electrical outlets and controlled lighting. Yards usually have none of these things. Here are steps you can take to improve the situation:

1. Arrange level and stable work surfaces. If you use sawhorses, for example, place them on level ground, or, if you absolutely must work on ground that is uneven, put large, well-anchored shims under the sawhorses to make them level. In either case, select an area that is free of rocks and other toe-stubbers.

2. Set up a separate work table to hold your tools. Don't set any tools on the ground where you could trip over them.

3. When using power tools, pay constant attention to your extension cord. Ideally, you should be close to an outlet and use a short cord. The loops and coils of long cords can trip you up, entangle your work, and (with potentially disastrous effects) get cut by a whirling saw blade.

4. You might think that the sun provides great light for outdoor work. As a general rule, you're right. But clouds

passing in front of the sun or the long shadows of early morning or late afternoon can play odd tricks with the light. If the light gets bad while you're working, quit and wait for it to improve, or rig up an outdoor work lamp.

5. Wear all the proper safety equipment, including safety goggles, work gloves, and steel-toed shoes. When using power tools, wear sound-mufflers or use earplugs. Wear a wide-brimmed cap to shade your eyes when working in the sun.

6. Backyard builders often attract crowds. If members of your family, neighbors, or the neighborhood dogs gather around you, put down your tools and wait for your visitors to leave before getting back to work. Mistakes are easy enough to make when you're devoting all of your attention to your work. When you're distracted, the chances for error (and for injury) rise dramatically. If you invite anyone to stay to help you while you work, make sure they have the same sort of safety equipment you have.

7. Take special precautions when working with pressure-treated lumber or with wood preservatives. Wear heavy overalls, a long-sleeved shirt, nonporous gloves, and a dust mask or respirator. Don't let preservatives touch your skin, eyes, or—if you can help it—your clothes. Wash your clothing separately from other laundry after you have finished working. Throw away the dust mask. Dispose of treated scrap lumber by taking it to an approved dump. Never burn scraps of treated lumber: This releases poisonous chemicals into the air.

PROJECTS FOR THE PATIO AND YARD

PORCH SWING

This version of the traditional porch swing, with slatted seat, dowel backrest, and overall smooth lines, has up-to-the minute style and grace. If you take care cutting the joints and other details and do a good job of finishing, you will produce a swing to grace any porch for a long time to come. By adding special touches such as turned spindles and brass hardware, you can add even more sparkle to this all-time favorite.

You will be building the swing in four sections. First, construct the seat frame and add the slats. Next make the backrest, then the arms, and last, fasten the assembled sections together. After finishing, you are ready to hang your swing from the porch ceiling or nearest tree limb, and enjoy it.

SHOPPING LIST

Lumber
2 pcs. 2 × 4 × 8′
5 pcs. 2 × 3 × 8′
5 pcs. 1 × 3 × 6′
Dowels
12 pcs. ¾″ × 3′ hardwood
Hardware
8 brass roundhead wood screws #10 × 3″
24 brass roundhead wood screws
    #12 × 1¼″
4 lag bolts ¼″ × 3″
4 eyebolts ⁵⁄₁₆″ × 3½″ with nuts
4 carriage bolts ⁵⁄₁₆″ × 3½″ with nuts
12 flat washers ⁵⁄₁₆″
36 brass flat washers ¼″
1 pc. twist-link chain or nylon rope
    ½″ × 25′
¼ pound finishing nails 8d
1 pint waterproof glue

CONSTRUCTION

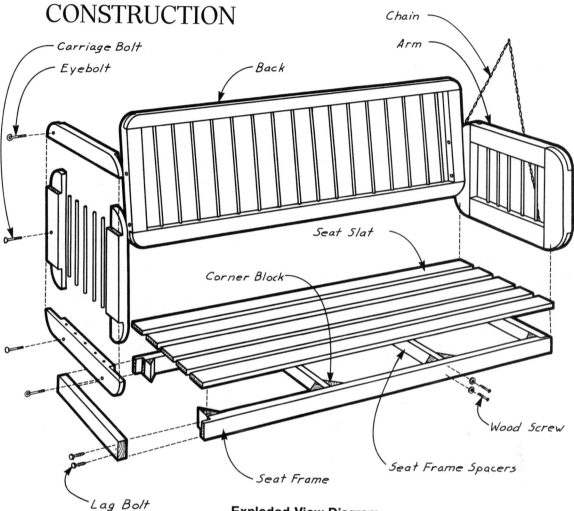

Carriage Bolt
Eyebolt
Back
Chain
Arm
Seat Slat
Corner Block
Wood Screw
Seat Frame Spacers
Seat Frame
Lag Bolt

Exploded-View Diagram

1. Cut two pieces of 2 × 3 (1½″ × 2½″) stock to 57 inches each for the seat frame's front and back. Also cut two pieces of 2 × 3 to 16¼ inches each for the seat frame's sides.

2. Cut rabbets 1⅛ inches deep × 1½ inches wide, as shown in illustration A, across ends of the front and back pieces. The rabbets help to hide the end grain of the side pieces when the seat frame is fitted together, and add strength to the assembled seat.

3. Trim the side pieces so they taper from 2½ inches in front to 2 inches in back. This will cause the back of the seat to angle downward about 2 degrees when assembled, enough to keep the occupants of the swing from shifting forward.

4. Rip the back piece of the seat frame down to 2 inches wide, to match the back end of the side pieces.

5. Drill and counterbore two ¾-inch-diameter by ½-inch-deep holes in the ends of each side piece, as shown in illustration A. Drill

3

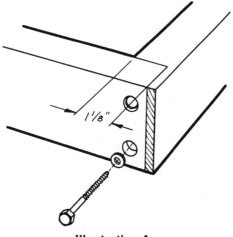

1⅛"

Illustration A

¼-inch shank holes through the center of the counterbored holes. Then, assemble the four frame pieces by drilling ³⁄₁₆-inch-diameter pilot holes through the center of the counterbored holes and into the ends of the front and back pieces. Apply water-proof glue to the joint area. Fit ¼-inch flat washers to ¼ × 3-inch lag bolts and tighten the bolts into the drilled holes to pull the corners tightly together. Be sure the bottom of the frame is flat and that the bevel on the end pieces is up and angled to the back.

6. Cut two pieces of 2 × 3 stock to 14 inches each for the two frame spacers. Hold the pieces to the inside of the frame against the side pieces and mark them to cut a taper to match the side pieces. Do not mark the taper by measuring as you did for the side pieces, since the spacers are 2¼ inches shorter than the side pieces.

7. Position the frame spacers 19 inches on center from each end of the seat frame. Drill ³⁄₁₆-inch-diameter pilot holes, two per spacer, through the front and back pieces and into the spacers, holding the spacers in place. Insert 3-inch #10 brass round-head wood screws fitted with ¼-inch brass flat washers in each hole and tighten them.

LUMBER CUTTING LIST

Size	Piece	Quantity
2 × 4		
1½″ × 3½″ × 22″	Arm section tops and bottoms	4
1½″ × 3½″ × 15½″	Arm section ends	4
2 × 3		
1½″ × 2½″ × 57″	Back section top and bottom	2
1½″ × 2½″ × 57″	Seat frame front and back	2
1½″ × 2½″ × 18″	Back section sides	2
1½″ × 2½″ × 16¼″	Seat frame sides	2
1½″ × 2½″ × 14″	Seat frame spacers	2
1½″ × 1½″ × 2⅛″ × 2½″	Triangular corner blocks	12
1 × 3		
¾″ × 2½″ × 57″	Seat slats	5
Dowels		
¾″ × 14¾″	Backrest	16
¾″ × 10½″	Arm sections	10

8. Cut triangular corner blocks from 2×3 stock and use waterproof glue to fasten them in all 12 inside corners of the seat frame. Clamp, wedge, or nail the blocks to hold them in place until the glue sets.

9. Trim and bevel the top of the corner blocks and frame pieces, where needed, so that the seat frame is evenly tapered front to back.

10. Cut five pieces of 1×3 ($\frac{3}{4}'' \times 2\frac{1}{2}''$) stock to 57 inches each for the seat slats. Sand the slats to remove all sharp edges.

11. Position the rear slat flush with the seat frame's back piece. Maintain a $1\frac{1}{4}$-inch space between the slats by using scrap-wood spacers. Drill $\frac{1}{16}$-inch-diameter pilot holes through the slats and secure them to the seat frame with 8d finishing nails, two per joint. Fasten the front slat so it extends $\frac{1}{2}$ inch beyond the front frame piece. Sink the nail heads below the slat faces.

12. Cut two pieces of 2×3 stock to 57 inches each for the backrest top and bottom pieces. Cut two pieces of 2×3 stock to 18 inches each for the backrest side pieces.

13. Position the four pieces so that the top and bottom pieces overlap the side pieces.

Square the pieces and mark the ends of all pieces for half-lap joints. Cut the half-laps carefully, and check the fit of the joints. Trim the joints as necessary to achieve a close fit.

14. Lay the top and bottom pieces on edge, side-by-side and with the ends flush so that you can mark off the dowel hole locations for the backrest dowels. Center the first holes 6 inches from the ends on the top and bottom pieces. Mark off the remaining holes 3 inches on center and drill the $\frac{3}{4}$-inch-diameter holes 1 inch deep.

15. Drill and counterbore two $\frac{3}{4}$-inch-diameter holes 1 inch deep through each of the backrest side pieces, as shown in illustration B. In the center of each hole, drill a $\frac{5}{16}$-inch-diameter pilot hole, also as shown. These holes will be used in the final assembly (see step 27).

16. Cut 16 pieces of $\frac{3}{4}$-inch-diameter hardwood dowels to $14\frac{3}{4}$ inches each and insert them in the holes drilled in the backrest bottom. No glue is necessary unless the dowels are very loose.

17. Assemble the top piece onto the dowels by starting at one end and working to the other end, one dowel at a time.

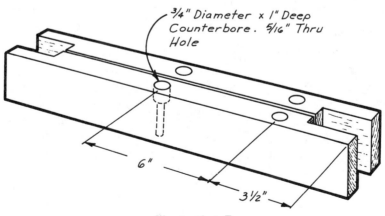

¾" Diameter x 1" Deep Counterbore. 5/16" Thru Hole

6"

3½"

Illustration B

18. Apply waterproof glue to the joint areas and fit the side pieces to the top and bottom pieces. Be sure the counterbored holes face inward. Clamp each corner and drill ⅛-inch-diameter pilot holes, as shown in illustration C. Be sure to have the screw heads on the rear face of the back. Secure the corners with 1¼-inch #12 brass round-head wood screws fitted with ¼-inch brass flat washers. Be sure the frame is in square before drilling the corners.

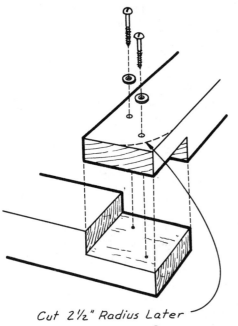

Cut 2½" Radius Later

Illustration C

19. Cut four pieces of 2 × 4 (1½″ × 3½″) stock to 22 inches each and four pieces to 15½ inches each for the arm sections.

20. Lay out the pieces in the positions shown in the exploded-view diagram. Square the corners and mark the pieces for the half-laps. Cut the half-laps, keeping the pieces in order so that the joints can be matched when assembled.

21. Mark dowel hole locations, centered on the edge of each set of longer arm pieces, at 5, 8, 11, 14, and 17 inches. Drill ¾-inch-diameter × 1-inch-deep holes at the positions marked for the dowels.

22. Cut 10 pieces of ¾-inch-diameter hardwood dowels to 10½ inches each for the arm sections. Assemble the arm sections by inserting all the dowels first in one piece and then working the other piece down onto the dowels.

23. Fasten the half-lap joints of the arm section by applying waterproof glue and clamping the corners together. Drill ⅛-inch-diameter pilot holes and secure the corners with 1¼-inch #12 brass round-head wood screws fitted with ¼-inch brass flat washers.

24. Round off the corners of the back and arm sections with 2½-inch radius curves.

25. Sand the pieces, including the seat, and apply whatever finish you desire before the sections are assembled.

26. Assemble the arm sections and seat frame by centering the seat frame against one arm section and drilling a 5/16-inch-diameter pilot hole through the arm section and seat frame 4½ inches from the front edge and 1 inch above the bottom edge, as shown in illustration D. Insert a 5/16 × 4½-inch eyebolt fitted with a 5/16-inch washer through the hole. Secure the bolt with a second washer and a nut. Drill a second 5/16-inch-diameter pilot hole 17½ inches from the front edge and 1 inch above the bottom edge. Insert and secure a 5/16 × 3½-inch carriage bolt in the hole. Repeat the above procedure for the second arm section.

27. Clamp the backrest section in place at a 7-degree angle to the arm sections, as shown in illustration E. Maintain a ¾-inch gap between the backrest and seat frame by using ¾-inch-wide scrap-wood spacers.

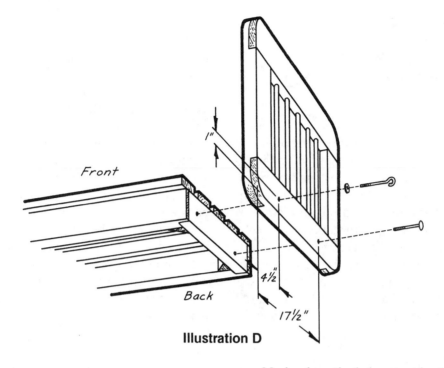

Front

Back

Illustration D

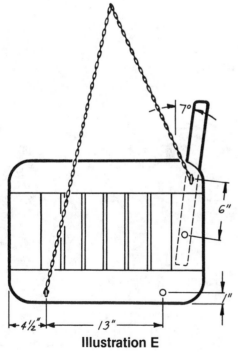

Illustration E

Mark where the holes must be drilled in the arm sections, and drill $5/16$-inch-diameter pilot holes into the arm sections to match the pilot holes in the back section's side pieces. Insert a $5/16 \times 3\frac{1}{2}$-inch eyebolt in the top hole and $5/16 \times 3\frac{1}{2}$-inch carriage bolt in the bottom hole. Fit washers and nuts to the bolts and tighten the bolts in the counterbored holes.

28. Hang the swing with rope or chain fastened to the eyebolts. Pry open the eye loops slightly, if necessary, and close them again after inserting a chain link or rope loop. Angle the chains or rope away from the swing so they will not pinch anyone's fingers or rub against the swing's arm sections.

GYM-IN-A-YARD

This sturdy structure can be built in a backyard to provide the center for a family fitness program. It was designed by members of the Rodale Design Group for use in a circuit training program — intervals of running alternating with stationary muscle-toning exercises. To perform the circuit, you run measured loops, through the neighborhood, for example, and intersperse exercises performed at various stations on the gym in between. Our design aims to make the best use of a compact space. It can, of course, be altered for installing accessories needed for other exercises one might wish to practice.

For our gym-in-a-yard we cut all nine posts to a length that would allow us to sink them 36 inches below grade for maximum stability and to avoid the potential for damage from frost heave. If the frost depth is shallow or not a problem where you live, sink your posts only as deep as is needed for stability. A rule of thumb to follow is that the length of post below grade should be at least one-third the length above grade. Determine the overall length of each post you need and the best way to derive them from stock lengths, then purchase your materials accordingly.

8

SHOPPING LIST

Lumber
9 pcs. 4 × 4 × 12'
1 pc. 4 × 4 × 8 '
1 pc. 4 × 4 × 6'
1 pc. 2 × 10 × 10'
1 pc. 1 × 2 × 4'

Hardware
4 eyebolts ⅜'' × 4'' with two nuts on each
2 eyebolts 5/16'' × 1½'' with two nuts on each
10 lag bolts ¼'' × 3'' with flat washers
4 carriage bolts ¼'' × 5½'' with washers and nuts
19 carriage bolts ¼'' × 4'' with washers and nuts
8 carriage bolts ¼'' × 2½'' with washers and nuts
4 tarp and rope hooks ⅜'' × 2½''
4 pcs. welded link chain (3/16'' thickness) 4'
2 chain lap links ¼'' × 2½''
2 welded rings ½'' × 4''
3 pcs. galvanized pipe 1'' I.D. × 8'
1 pc. galvanized pipe 1'' I.D. × 3'
12 pcs. galvanized pipe 1'' I.D. × 34''
7 pcs. galvanized pipe 1'' I.D. × 25''
1 pc. galvanized pipe 1'' I.D. × 23½''

CONSTRUCTION

1. Use two pieces of 4 × 4 (3½'' × 3½'') stock, each 144 inches in length, for the main parallel beams that will enclose the horizontal ladder at the top of the gym structure. Label one beam front, the other rear. Use six additional pieces of 4 × 4 stock, each 96 inches plus the length needed below grade, for the posts that will support the parallel beams. Label the posts A through F and mark the grade level on each for later reference.

2. Cut half-lap joints on the inside faces of all six posts and on the outside faces of the two beams, in order to join them together, as shown in the exploded-view diagram. Note that posts C and D are not the same distance respectively from posts E and F.

3. Use one piece of 4 × 4 stock, 96 inches in length, for the balance beam. Cut a second piece of 4 × 4 stock to 15 inches plus the length needed below grade, for the balance beam support post. Cut a half-lap joint on the upper end of the support and on one end of the balance beam for joining them, as shown in the exploded-view diagram. Then cut a tenon, 2½ inches long and 1¼ inches wide, at the center of the other end of the balance beam and a matching mortise in the back of post B, beginning 11½ inches above grade level.

4. Cut two pieces of 4 × 4 stock to 46 inches each, plus the length needed below grade, for the parallel bar support posts. Label these posts G and H and mark the grade level on each. Center and drill 1⅜-inch-diameter holes, 2½ inches deep, 43½ inches above grade level on the front faces of these two posts and on the rear faces of posts D and F to receive the ends of the parallel bars. Center and drill a second hole 14 inches below the first on posts F and H only, to receive the ends of the stretch rail. Finally, center and drill similar holes 8 inches above grade level on the inside faces of posts G and H to receive the ends of the step-up rung, as shown in the exploded-view diagram.

5. Center and drill a series of 1⅜-inch-diameter holes 2½ inches deep into the inside faces of the front and rear main beams, to receive the ends of the horizontal ladder rungs. Begin the series 6 inches from one end and space the holes 12 inches apart on center, as shown in illustration A.

6. Drill a series of 1⅜-inch-diameter holes

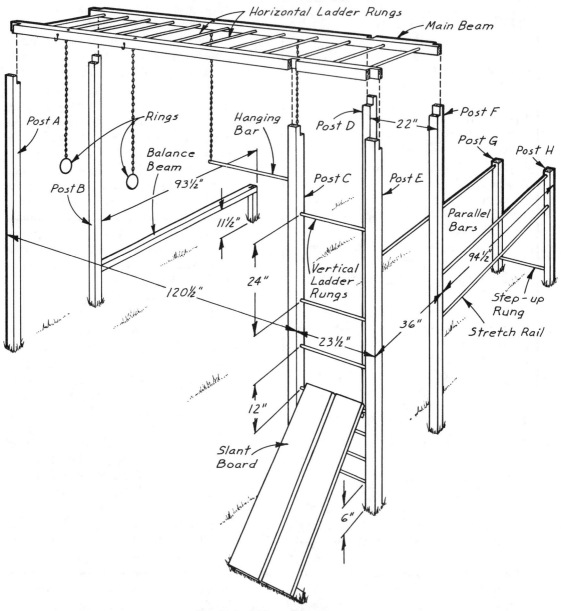

Exploded-View Diagram

2½ inches deep into the inside faces of posts C and E to receive the ends of the vertical ladder rungs. Center the first hole 6 inches above grade level and then drill three additional holes on 6-inch centers, moving up each post, as shown in the exploded-view diagram. Space the next two holes in each series 12 inches on center and the final hole 24 inches on center, as shown in the diagram.

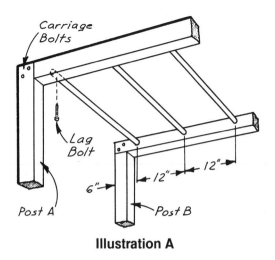

Illustration A

7. Drill a ⅜-inch-diameter hole down through the center of the front beam at a point approximately 28 inches from the end nearest post A to accept one of the eyebolts for suspending the hanging rings. Drill a matching hole 30 inches farther along the beam to accept the other eyebolt. Drill a similar pair of holes in the rear beam for eyebolts to suspend the hanging bar. Locate the first hole midway between the fifth and sixth horizontal ladder rungs, counting from the end nearest post B, and the second hole 34½ inches farther along the beam.

8. Cut 12 pieces of 1-inch-I.D. galvanized pipe, each 34 inches in length, for the horizontal ladder rungs. Cut 7 additional pieces, each 25 inches in length, for the vertical ladder rungs, along with 1 piece 23½ inches long for the step-up rung that will connect posts G and H. Then cut 3 pieces of 1-inch pipe, each 96 inches in length, for the parallel bars and the stretch rail, and 1 piece 36 inches long for the hanging bar.

9. Drill ⁵/₁₆-inch-diameter pilot holes centered ¾ inch from the ends of three horizontal ladder rungs to allow lag bolts to pass through (see step 14). Make each pair of holes parallel. Drill a similar set of holes through the ends of the two parallel bars and the hanging bar.

10. Drill three ¼-inch-diameter pilot holes into the bottom face of each parallel beam for lag bolts. Center these holes 1¾ inches from the inside edges of the beams and locate them so they will pass through the centers of the first, seventh, and last holes drilled in each beam, to receive ladder rungs, as shown in illustration A. Stop the pilot holes when they enter the rung holes. Then drill ¼-inch-diameter holes through the center of the sides of posts D, F, G, and H, to receive carriage bolts. Locate these holes 43½ inches above grade level, where they will pass through the center of the holes drilled to receive the ends of the parallel bars.

11. Drill four ¼-inch-diameter pilot holes for lag bolts into the outside faces of the front and rear main beams. The bolts are needed to attach height-adjusting hooks for the hanging rings and bar (see step 18). Space the hooks the same distance apart as the eyebolts for the rings and bar, as shown in the exploded-view diagram.

12. Fit the post-and-beam joints together temporarily while drilling ¼-inch-diameter pilot holes for carriage bolts. Drill two holes through each of the half-lap joints following the diagonal pattern shown in illustration A, and drill a single hole through the mortise and tenon joining the balance beam and post B. Cut a ¼-inch radius on the edges of all posts and beams except where they will be located inside half-lap joints.

13. Lay out and dig holes for the nine posts following the spacing shown in the exploded-view diagram. Dig the holes for the six main posts approximately 40 inches deep, or deeper if necessary to get below the

LUMBER CUTTING LIST

Size	Piece	Quantity
4 × 4		
3½″ × 3½″ × 144″	Main beams	2
3½″ × 3½″ × 96″ (plus length below grade)	Main posts	6
3½″ × 3½″ × 96″	Balance beam	1
3½″ × 3½″ × 46″ (plus length below grade)	Parallel bar support posts	2
3½″ × 3½″ × 19″	Slant board support cleat	1
3½″ × 3½″ × 15″ (plus length below grade)	Balance beam support post	1
2 × 10		
1½″ × 9¼″ × 60″	Slant board planks	2
1 × 2		
¾″ × 1½″ × 19″	Slant board positioning cleats	2

frost line in your area. Make the holes for the three shorter posts as deep as needed for stability. Place a few inches of gravel in the bottom of each hole to aid drainage. Insert the vertical ladder rungs between posts C and E, then fasten posts A, C, and E to the front beam and posts B, D, and F to the rear beam using ¼ × 4-inch carriage bolts with washers and nuts.

14. Stand both assembled sections of the gym structure upright in their postholes. Fit the rungs of the horizontal ladder between the parallel beams, making sure the pre-drilled rungs are located to align with the pilot holes drilled in the beams in step 9. Insert a ¼ × 3-inch lag bolt with washer into each of those pilot holes and advance it until it makes contact with a rung. Adjust the rungs as needed to allow the lag bolts to pass through and be tightened. Plumb all six posts and make sure the horizontal ladder is level in both directions. Temporarily brace the structure, then backfill around all the posts and tamp the dirt firmly.

15. Stand posts G and H upright in their holes, fitting the step-up rung between them. Fit the stretch rail and the parallel bars between these posts and posts D and F. Work a ¼ × 3-inch lag bolt with washer into each pilot hole on the four posts and through the ends of the parallel bars. Tighten the lag bolts and plumb posts G and H, making sure the parallel bars are level. Backfill around the posts, tamping the dirt firmly as you proceed.

16. Stand the balance beam support post upright in its hole. Fit the tenoned end of the balance beam into the mortise on the back of post B, and fasten the half-lapped end of the beam to the support post with ¼ × 4-inch carriage bolts, washers, and nuts. Plumb the post and level the beam, then backfill around the post, tamping the dirt firmly.

17. Cut four pieces of ³⁄₁₆-inch welded link chain to 48 inches each to support the hanging rings and bar. Fasten the lower ends of two chains to the hanging bar using ⁵⁄₁₆ × 1½-inch eyebolts with two

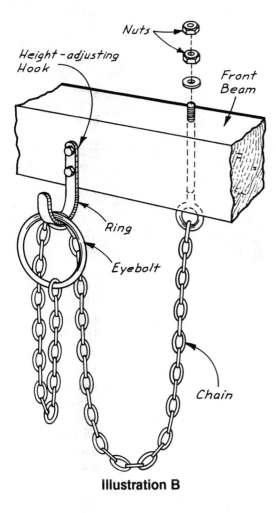

Illustration B

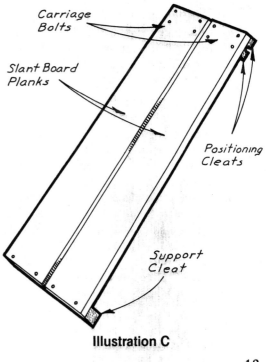

height-adjusting hooks in step 11, using ¼ × 3-inch lag bolts.

19. Cut two pieces of 2 × 10 (1½″ × 9¼″) stock to 60 inches each for planks to form the body of the slant board. Then cut one piece of 4 × 4 to 19 inches for the support cleat, to be positioned beneath the lower end of the slant board, and two pieces of 1 × 2 (¾″ × 1½″) stock to 19 inches each, for positioning cleats to fit beneath the upper end of the slant board in the positions shown in illustration C. Align the outside edges of the plank with the ends of the three cleats and drill a pair of ¼-inch-diameter pilot holes through each meeting of plank and cleat. Fasten the upper ends of the planks to the positioning cleats using ¼ × 2½-inch carriage bolts, washers, and nuts. Fasten the lower ends of the planks to the support cleat using ¼ × 5½-inch carriage bolts, washers, and nuts.

nuts on the end of each. Tighten the nuts against each other to lock them. Fasten the lower ends of the other two chains to ½ × 4-inch welded rings using ¼ × 2½-inch chain lap links.

18. Suspend the hanging rings from the front beam and the hanging bar from the rear beam using ⅜ × 4-inch eyebolts, as shown in illustration B. Use two nuts to lock each eyebolt in place. Also fasten ⅜ × 2½-inch tarp and rope hooks in the four positions where pilot holes were drilled for

Illustration C

13

BIRD-FEEDING STATION

What do you do if you have no convenient tree from which to hang your bird feeder? Build this simple artificial one! The Rodale Design Group came up with the idea and it works wonderfully. You may make yours the same as the one shown here or change the configuration of the support arm and cross arms to suit your individual taste. Naturally, you may add more arms, as desired.

The bird-feeding station pictured is

made of pressure-treated pine. Cedar or redwood—both of which are durable in outdoor applications—is a good alternative.

CONSTRUCTION

1. Cut one piece of 4 × 4 (3½" × 3½") stock to 108 inches for the post. Cut a second piece of the same stock to 36 inches for the support arm.

2. Cut two pieces of 2 × 2 (1½" × 1½") stock to 48 inches each for the cross arms.

3. Lay out and cut a half-lap joint in the post and support arm where they intersect, as shown in the exploded-view diagram. To lay out the joint, place the support arm at a right angle across the post, exactly as it wil be in its finished position. Scribe the width of each piece onto the piece it rests against, and also mark the depth each notch should be: one-half the thickness of each piece. Remove the waste wood between the scribed lines of each piece using a circular saw, or handsaw and chisel.

4. Cut a 1½-inch-deep notch 1½ inches wide across the end of the post nearest the notch

cut in the previous step. The two notches should be parallel, as shown in the exploded-view diagram.

5. Halfway between the two notches in the post, cut a third notch (actually a dado) at a right angle to them, as shown in the exploded-view diagram. Like the notch at the end of the post, this notch should measure 1½ inches deep by 1½ inches wide and extend across the full thickness of the post.

6. If you wish, miter all four faces of the support arm and both cross arms to form points at each end.

7. Sink the post into the ground to a depth of approximately 30 inches. (Be sure not to sink the notched end!) Repack the soil firmly around the base of the post.

8. Fasten the support arm and cross arms to the post in the locations shown in the exploded-view diagram. Use 12d galvanized common nails.

Exploded-View Diagram

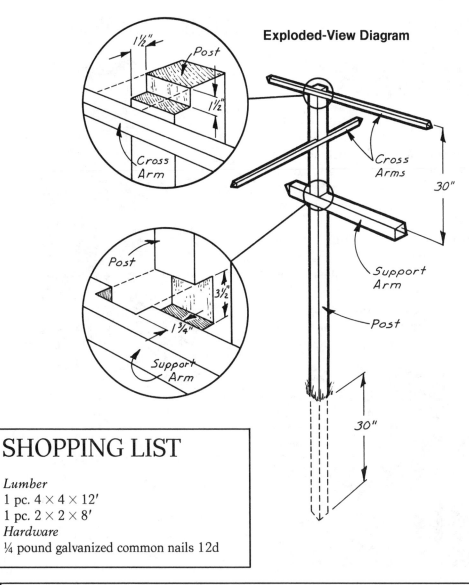

SHOPPING LIST

Lumber
1 pc. 4 × 4 × 12'
1 pc. 2 × 2 × 8'
Hardware
¼ pound galvanized common nails 12d

LUMBER CUTTING LIST

Size	Piece	Quantity
4 × 4		
3½'' × 3½ × 108''	Post	1
3½'' × 3½'' × 36''	Support arm	1
2 × 2		
1½'' × 1½'' × 48''	Cross arms	2

SUET HOLDER

This small holder from the Rodale Design Group can contain approximately one pound of suet sandwiched between two pieces of heavy screen (hardware cloth). Ordinary dime-store key rings hold the sides of the holder together and determine its capacity.

Rubber bands work well to keep the sides of the holder closed securely. Twist ties (the kind that accompany plastic storage bags) also work well and are often easier to use since they do not have to be stretched tightly over the sharp ends of the hardware cloth to fasten them into place.

SHOPPING LIST

Hardware
1 eyescrew 1''
2 key rings ⅞'' diameter
1 pc. ½-inch mesh hardware cloth 4'' × 1'
1 pc. soft wire 10''
2 heavy rubber bands or twist ties

CONSTRUCTION

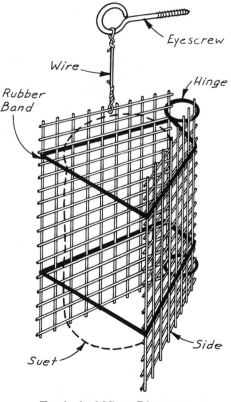

Exploded-View Diagram

1. Cut two pieces of ½-inch mesh hardware cloth to 4 × 6 inches each for the sides of the holder.

2. Join the sides together using two ⅞-inch-diameter key rings for hinges.

3. Cut one piece of soft wire to 10 inches for hanging the holder.

4. Attach one end of the wire to one of the holder sides and the other to a 1-inch eyescrew.

5. Hang the holder by installing the eyescrew in a tree limb, roof eave, or other location. To fill the holder, place a slab of suet between the sides, then fasten the sides closed using two strong rubber bands or twist ties.

FINCH FEEDER

This simple-to-build bird feeder is especially designed to attract finches and other small birds, chiefly by discouraging larger ones. A product of the Rodale Design Group, the feeder's small feed holes and narrow perches are entirely intentional. In addition, the feeder is made to swing freely in the breeze or under the weight of birds clinging to it. Large birds seem to dislike movement while feeding. Finches, however, rarely seem to mind.

The major parts of the feeder are made from PVC pipe. Cedar is used for the wooden parts because of its durability even when left unfinished, as it is here. The

SHOPPING LIST

Lumber
1 pc. cedar 1 × 4 × 3′
Hardware
3 brass roundhead screws #4 × 1″
1 pc. bronze brazing rod ⅛″ × 18″
1 pc. PVC pipe 3″ I.D. × 12″
1 pc. PVC pipe ¾″ I.D. × 3″
1 PVC cap 3″
waterproof panel adhesive
PVC cement

handle is bent to shape from the length of ordinary bronze brazing rod (inexpensive and available at most hardware stores). Like the brass screws that are also used, the brazing rod will not rust.

CONSTRUCTION

1. Cut one piece of 3-inch-diameter PVC pipe to 12 inches in length for the feeder body.
2. From a piece of 1 × 4 (¾″ × 1½″) cedar stock at least 22 inches long rip five strips each ³⁄₁₆ inch thick. Crosscut the strips into 10½-inch lengths for the side pieces of the feeder. Discard the remaining stock or else crosscut it and edge-glue the pieces to make the disks for the bottom plug and perch (see step 7).

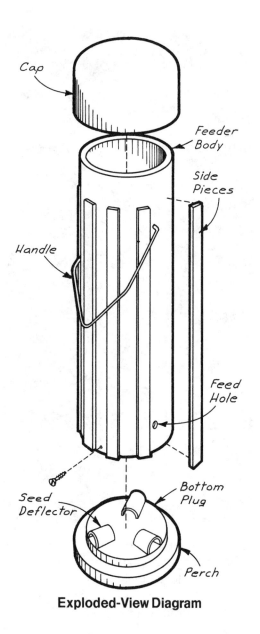

Exploded-View Diagram

3. Glue the strips around the perimeter of the feeder body, as shown in the exploded-view diagram, using waterproof panel adhesive. Space the strips at even intervals, keeping the ends flush with the lower end of the feeder body.

4. Lay out and drill three $7/16$-inch-diameter holes in the feeder body for feed holes. Locate the holes equidistant from each other, at least $1\frac{1}{4}$ inches from the lower end of the feeder body, as shown in the exploded-view diagram.

5. Drill three $1/8$-inch-diameter holes equidistant from each other, approximately $3/8$ inch from the lower end of the feeder body, for fastening the bottom plug (see step 8). Then drill two $3/16$-inch-diameter holes in the upper end of the feeder body to accept the ends of the handle. These upper holes should be exactly opposite each other and be located at least $2\frac{1}{4}$ inches from the end of the feeder body to allow room for the cap (see step 10).

6. Cut two pieces of $3/4$-inch-diameter PVC pipe each $7/8$ inch long, then split each piece in half lengthwise. Discard one piece (only three are needed) and use the others for the seed deflectors. With a sharp knife and some sandpaper shape one end of each deflector to fit against the inside surface of the feeder body, as shown in illustration A. Glue the deflectors in place above the feed holes using PVC cement. The deflectors will prevent the feed from spilling out of the feed holes.

7. Cut two disks, one 3 inches in diameter, the other $4\frac{3}{16}$ inches in diameter, from 1×4 cedar stock or glued-up scrap. Center one disk on top of the other and glue the two together, using waterproof panel adhesive, to make the bottom plug and perch.

8. Insert the plug into the lower end of the feeder body and fasten it in place using 1-inch #4 brass roundhead screws installed through the holes drilled in the feeder body in step 5.

9. Bend the handle to shape from an 18-inch length of $1/8$-inch-diameter brazing rod,

LUMBER CUTTING LIST

Size	Piece	Quantity
1 × 4		
³/₁₆″ × ¾″ × 10½″	Side pieces	10
¾″ × 4³/₁₆″ diameter	Perch	1
¾″ × 3″ diameter	Bottom plug	1

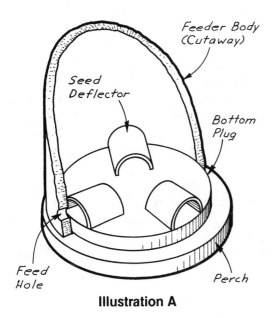

Illustration A

then install the ends in the two holes drilled in the upper part of the feeder body. Brazing rod is soft enough to be bent by hand using a vise or pliers. Bend the rod in half first, then bend it at the midpoint of each segment, and finally bend it at the ends to assure symmetry. Install the handle as gently as possible, then re-shape if necessary.

10. Install a 3-inch-diameter PVC cap on the upper end of the feeder body. You may have to sand the body slightly until a smooth fit is obtained. When you are ready to hang the feeder, remove the cap, fill the feeder body with seed, then replace the cap.

BIRD FEEDER

The Rodale Design Group modeled their plans for this bird feeder on a tried and true design. The feeder is comprised of a tray wide enough so that birds may

SHOPPING LIST

Lumber
1 pc. 1 × 10 × 4'
1 pc. 1 × 2 × 6'
Hardware
2 cotter pins ⅛" × 1½"
2 key rings ⅞" diameter
¼ pound cement-coated common nails 4d
2 pcs. reinforced fiberglass glazing
    7¼" × 11¼"

perch while they feast, a feed bin with transparent sides so the quantity of food may be readily seen, and a top that can quickly be removed when filling the bin. The feeder can either be mounted on a post or suspended from a porch beam or tree limb.

The feeder pictured is made out of cedar and reinforced fiberglass for durability. Other materials may be used, but chemical finishes should be avoided. Keep the feeder natural for the health and happiness of its users.

CONSTRUCTION

1. Cut one piece of 1 × 10 (¾" × 9¼") cedar stock to 12 inches, then rip it to 8 inches in width, for the feed tray. Trim about ½ inch off each corner at a 45-degree angle to provide drainage for the tray.
2. Cut two pieces of 1 × 2 (¾" × 1½") cedar stock to 12 inches each and two more pieces to 9½ inches each for edge bands. Fasten the longer pieces to the sides of the tray and the shorter pieces across the ends using 4d cement-coated common nails. Keep the bottom edges of the tray and edge bands flush while nailing.

3. Cut two pieces of 1 × 10 cedar stock to 8 inches each, then rip them each to 5½ inches in width, for the ends of the feeder. Cut two grooves, each ⅛ inch wide and ⅜ inch deep, on the inside face of each piece, as shown in illustration A, to accept the glazing. Save the rippings from the feeder ends for use in the next step.
4. Rip a piece of cedar scrap into two pieces, each ⅝ inch wide, then trim each to 5½ inches in length, for glazing supports. Center the feeder ends (with their glazing grooves turned inward) against the inside faces of

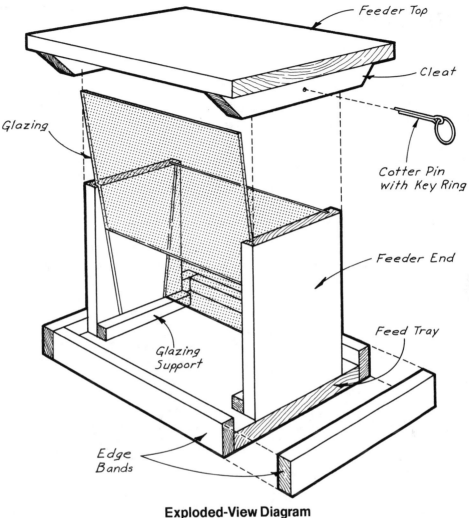

Feeder Top

Cleat

Glazing

Cotter Pin
with Key Ring

Feeder End

Feed Tray

Glazing
Support

Edge
Bands

Exploded-View Diagram

the tray's end edge bands. Fasten with 4d cement-coated common nails. Place the glazing supports on the tray against the inside faces of the feeder ends. Fasten with nails driven at an angle through the supports into the tray.

5. Cut two pieces of reinforced fiberglass glazing, each 7¼ × 11¼ inches, for the

sides of the feeder bin. Slide the glazing into the grooves cut into the feeder ends until each piece rests on the glazing supports.

6. Cut one piece of 1 × 10 cedar stock to 15 inches for the feeder top. Then cut two pieces of 1 × 2 cedar stock to 9¼ inches each for cleats. Miter both ends of

21

LUMBER CUTTING LIST

Size	Piece	Quantity
1 × 10		
¾" × 9¼" × 15"	Feeder top	1
¾" × 8" × 12"	Feed tray	1
¾" × 5½" × 8"	Feeder ends	2
⅝" × ¾" × 5½"	Glazing supports	2
1 × 2		
¾" × 1½" × 12"	Edge bands	2
¾" × 1½" × 9½"	Edge bands	2
¾" × 1½" × 9¼"	Cleats	2

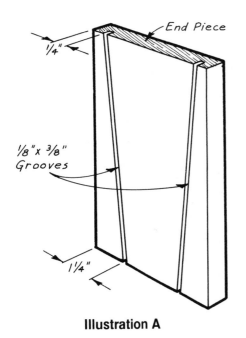

Illustration A

each cleat, then space the cleats 12 inches apart on the underside of the feeder top so their mitered ends face down, as shown in the exploded-view diagram. Fasten the cleats in place with 4d cement-coated common nails.

7. Place the top in position over the feeder bin and drill a 5/32-inch hole through each cleat and the feeder end behind it to accept a hold-down pin. Insert a 1½-inch cotter pin fitted with a ⅞-inch-diameter key-ring handle through each set of holes to secure the feeder top.

8. For the health of the birds, leave the feeder unfinished. Just mount it in a suitable location and fill it with feed.

REDWOOD HANGING BIRD STATION

SHOPPING LIST

Lumber
1 pc. redwood $1 \times 10 \times 4'$
Hardware
4 brass flathead wood screws #6 $\times$ 2''
6 brass flathead wood screws #6 $\times$ 1⅝''
2 brass eyebolts 3/16'' $\times$ 1½'' with washers
    and nuts
wire staples ⅜''
1 brass S-hook ⅝''
8 eyescrews ½''
2 corrugated fasteners ⅜'' $\times$ 1''
1 pc. brass chain (⅛'' thickness) 20''
4 pcs. brass chain (⅛'' thickness) 5¾''
1 small box aluminum nails 1½''
1 small box wire nails #18 $\times$ ¾''
1 pc. aluminum window screen
    11⅞'' $\times$ 15⅜''
boiled linseed oil
varnish

This spacious bird-feeding station designed by the Rodale Design Group is easy both to load and clean. Constructed of redwood and brass for durable good looks, the station consists of a screen-bottomed feeding tray suspended by chains from its own sheltering roof. The tray provides room for a large amount of seed and allows moisture to drain away quickly. With minimal care this bird station should last many years and provide a great deal of bird-watching satisfaction.

CONSTRUCTION

1. Cut two pieces of 1×10 (¾'' $\times$ 9¼'') redwood stock to 16 inches. From each, rip one piece ¼ inch wide and two pieces each ¾ inch wide. Trim the rippings to 15½ inches in length and save the wider ones for use as eave boards (see step 4) and tray sides (see step 6), and the narrower ones as screen molding (also see step 6). Use the widest pieces remaining for roof boards. Trim each to 7 inches in width and bevel one edge to 22½ degrees, as shown in the exploded-view diagram.

2. Cut one piece of 1×10 redwood to 12 inches. From it, rip two pieces each ¼ inch wide for screen molding, and two pieces each ¾ inch wide for tray ends. Also, trim each of the tray ends to 11¼ inches in length.

3. Stand the roof boards together with their beveled edges flush and install a ⅜ $\times$ 1-inch corrugated fastener at each end of the ridge. Using the inverted V of the roof

23

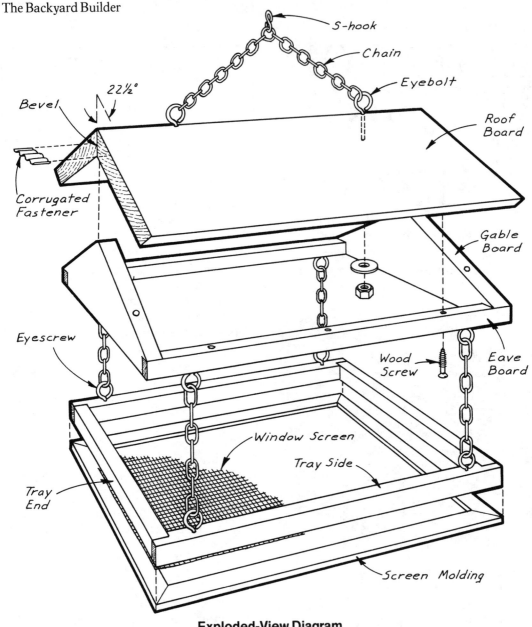

S-hook

Chain

Eyebolt

22½°

Bevel

Roof Board

Corrugated Fastener

Gable Board

Eyescrew

Wood Screw

Eave Board

Window Screen

Tray Side

Tray End

Screen Molding

Exploded-View Diagram

as a pattern, mark and cut the two gable boards to fit beneath the roof, as shown in the exploded-view diagram.

4. Cut a ¾-inch-high notch ⅜ inch deep into the ends of each gable board to receive the ends of the eave boards. Cut ¾-inch-wide rabbets ⅜ inch deep across the eave-board

ends, as shown in illustration A. Fasten the eave boards to the gable boards using 1½-inch aluminum nails.

5. Center the roof over the frame made of the gables and eaves. Fasten the frame to the roof, first by installing a pair of 2-inch #6 brass flathead wood screws through each

LUMBER CUTTING LIST

Size	Piece	Quantity
1 × 10		
¾″ × 7″ × 16″	Roof boards	2
¾″ × 3⅛″ × 12″	Gable boards	2
¾″ × ¾″ × 15½″	Eave boards	2
¾″ × ¾″ × 15½″	Tray sides	2
¾″ × ¾″ × 11¼″	Tray ends	2
¾″ × ¼″ × 15½″	Screen molding	2
¾″ × ¼″ × 12″	Screen molding	2

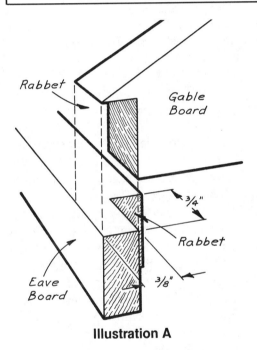

Illustration A

gable, and then by installing three 1⅝-inch #6 brass flathead wood screws through each eave. Drive all the screws into the underside of the roof.

6. Cut ¾-inch-wide rabbets ⅜ inch deep across the ends of the tray sides. Fit the tray ends between the ends of the sides and fasten them together using 1½-inch aluminum nails. Cut a piece of aluminum window screen to 11⅞ × 15⅜ inches for the bottom of the tray and fasten it to the underside of the tray frame using ⅜-inch wire staples. Miter and fasten the screen moldings in place on the underside of the tray using ¾-inch #18 wire nails.

7. Center and drill a ³⁄₁₆-inch-diameter hole 3½ inches from each end of the roof ridge for inserting eyebolts, as shown in the exploded-view diagram.

8. Cut one piece of ⅛-inch-thick brass chain to 20 inches. Open the eyes of two ³⁄₁₆ × 1½-inch brass eyebolts and slip one end of the chain inside each. Close the eyes and fasten the eyebolts to the roof using nuts and washers. Install a ⅝-inch brass S-hook in the middle link of the chain to use when hanging the bird station.

9. Insert ½-inch eyescrews in the top of the tray, 1½ inches from the ends of the tray sides. Insert eyescrews, aligned with eyescrews in the top, on the underside of the eave boards. Cut four pieces of ⅛-inch-thick brass chain to 5¾ inches each, and attach their ends to the eyescrews to suspend the tray from the roof, as shown in the exploded-view diagram.

10. Sand all wooden parts of the bird station and finish with two coats of a mixture of two parts boiled linseed oil and one part varnish.

LAWN CHAIR

This sturdy lawn chair, designed and built by the Rodale Design Group, was inspired by the Adirondack-design tradition. Our design utilizes standard widths of No. 2 pine and can be built with common tools. The chair is constructed so that its seat can be lifted out, its stringers quickly removed, and its arms and legs folded up against the back. The disassembled chair can then be tied together in a compact unit for easy transportation or winter storage.

Our chair is painted with exterior latex enamel. A durable, clear finish, such as polyurethane, could be used instead. Notice that the specifications in the instructions

SHOPPING LIST

Lumber
2 pcs. #2 pine 1 × 10 × 8'
1 pc. #2 pine 1 × 8 × 4'
3 pcs. #2 pine 1 × 4 × 8'
2 pcs. #2 pine 1 × 3 × 5'
1 pc. #2 pine 1 × 1 × 4'
Dowel
1 pc. 5/16'' × 1' hardwood
Hardware
78 flathead wood screws #8 × 1¼''
24 flathead wood screws #8 × ¾''
2 butt hinges 2½'' × 2½''
2 offset cabinet hinges 2½'' × ¾''
1 pint waterproof glue
1 quart exterior-grade enamel or
    polyurethane

call for ⅛-inch clearance in places where chair members are inserted in notches and slots, and where the seat cleats fit around the chair stringers. This allows easy assembly and disassembly of the parts. Pay attention to these clearances when building the chair, especially if it is to be painted, since multiple coats of paint will alter these dimensions somewhat, making the gaps smaller and the fits tighter. Test for ease of assembly before painting and allow the paint to dry thoroughly before assembling the finished chair.

CONSTRUCTION

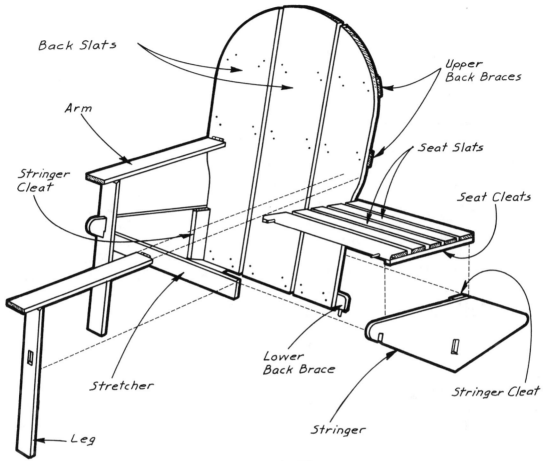

Back Slats

Upper
Back Braces

Arm

Seat Slats

Stringer
Cleat

Seat Cleats

Lower
Back Brace

Stringer Cleat

Stretcher

Stringer

Leg

Exploded-View Diagram

1. Make a pattern for the chair stringers from stiff paper or cardboard according to the dimensions provided in illustration A. Using this pattern, lay out both chair stringers on one 8-foot piece of 1 × 10 (¾″ × 9¼″) pine stock.

2. Cut out the chair stringers. Make sure the slots and notches are correctly located, angled, and dimensioned.

3. Cut two pieces of 1 × 3 (¾″ × 2½″) pine stock to 5¼ inches each for stringer cleats.

4. Cut two pieces of 1 × 3 stock to 8 inches each for additional stringer cleats.

5. Trim one end of each of the four stringer cleats to a 10-degree angle, as shown in illustration B.

6. Position one of the 5¼-inch stringer cleats so that its angled end is flush with the top of the stringer and its square end just clears the top of the slot in the side of the stringer. Line up the long side of the cleat with the inner edge of the slot, as shown

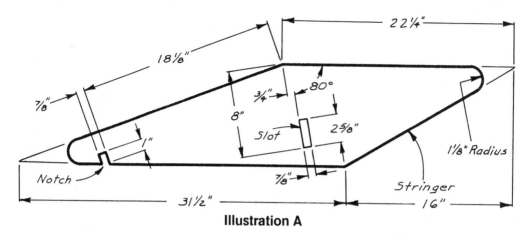

Illustration A

in illustration B. Fasten the cleat to the stringer with waterproof glue and three 1¼-inch #8 flathead wood screws. Countersink the screws.

7. Position one of the 8-inch stringer cleats so that its angled edge is flush with the top of the stringer, its bottom edge is in line with the bottom of the slot, and its long side is parallel to the long side of the cleat previously attached. Make sure there

LUMBER CUTTING LIST

Size	Piece	Quantity
1 × 10		
¾'' × 9¼'' × 47½''	Stringers (see step 1)	2
¾'' × 9¼'' × 42''	Outer back slats	2
1 × 8		
¾'' × 7¼'' × 42''	Center back slat	1
1 × 4		
¾'' × 3½'' × 26¾''	Stretcher	1
¾'' × 3½'' × 25¾''	Seat slats	5
¾'' × 3½'' × 24''	Arms	2
¾'' × 3½'' × 23''	Legs	2
1 × 3		
¾'' × 2½'' × 27''	Lower back brace	1
¾'' × 2½'' × 26¾''	Upper back braces	2
¾'' × 2½'' × 8''	Stringer cleats	2
¾'' × 2½'' × 5¼''	Stringer cleats	2
1 × 1		
¾'' × ¾'' × 19''	Seat cleats	2
Dowel		
5/16'' × 2¼''	Dowels	2

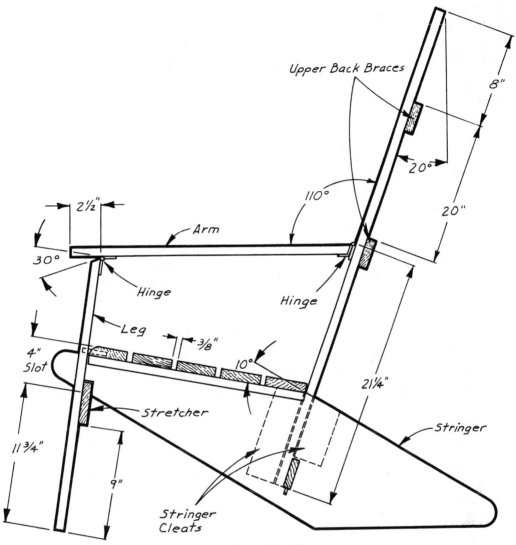

Illustration B

is a ⅞-inch gap between the two cleats. Fasten the cleat to the stringer with waterproof glue and four 1¼-inch #8 flathead wood screws. Countersink the screws.

8. Attach the remaining two stringer cleats to the second stringer. Follow the procedure given in steps 6 and 7. This time position the cleats on the face of the stringer oppo-

site the one used for the first stringer, so that a right and a left stringer are produced. When completed, with the two stringers set on edge, parallel to each other, all the cleats should be on the inside.

9. Cut five pieces of 1 × 4 (¾″ × 3½″) pine stock to 25¾ inches each for the seat slats.

10. Cut two pieces of 1 × 1 (¾″ × ¾″) pine

29

stock to 19 inches each for the seat cleats.

11. Arrange the seat slats on their faces, parallel to each other, with a ⅜-inch gap between each slat. Place a seat cleat across each end of the row of slats. Make sure that the edge of each cleat is flush with the ends of the slats and that the ends of the cleats are flush with the outside edges of the slats beneath them. Fasten the cleats to the slats with waterproof glue and two 1¼-inch #8 flathead wood screws at each end of each slat. Countersink the screws.

12. Turn the slat assembly over so it rests on the cleats, then choose the front of the seat. Drill a 5/16-inch-diameter hole centered in the edge of the front slat, 2⅜ inches from each end, as shown in illustration C. Make the holes 1¾ inches deep.

13. Round-over the top front edge of the seat, if desired, for comfort. Use a block plane or router.

14. Cut two pieces of 5/16-inch-diameter dowel to 2¼ inches each. Apply waterproof glue to one end of each dowel and insert the

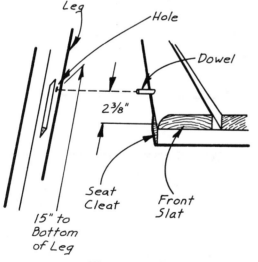

Illustration C

glued ends into the holes drilled in the front of the seat slat assembly. Leave ⅝ inch of each piece of dowel protruding from its hole.

15. Cut one piece of 1 × 8 (¾″ × 7¼″) pine stock to 42 inches for the center slat of the chair back.

16. Cut two pieces of 1 × 10 pine stock to 42 inches each for the two outer slats of the chair back.

17. Cut two pieces of 1 × 3 pine stock to 26¾ inches each for the upper braces of the chair back.

18. Place the outer slats side by side temporarily, and measuring from one end, square lines across both slats at the 8-inch and 20-inch points. These lines mark the location of the top edge of each upper back brace, as shown in illustration B.

19. Now separate the two marked slats and place the center slat between them. Arrange the three slats on their faces, parallel to one another, with a ½-inch gap between each slat. Lay one upper back brace across the three slats so that its top edge lies along the 8-inch mark, and position the other brace so its top edge lies along the 20-inch mark. Make sure the ends of the braces are flush with the outside edges of the outer slats. Fasten the two braces to the back slats with waterproof glue and 1¼-inch #8 flathead wood screws, as shown in illustration D. Be careful not to install screws where portions of the back slats will later be trimmed away.

20. Cut a 13⅜-inch radius across the top of the chair back, using a saber saw. Then, with the aid of the grid provided in illustration D, lay out and cut the curve on each side of the back's lower part. Make certain that the curve begins below the bottom edge of the brace across the middle of the back and ends 8 inches above the

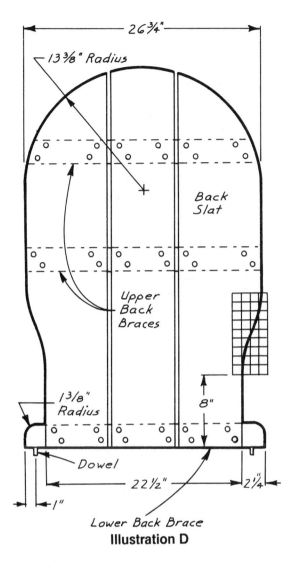

Illustration D

bottom ends of the back slats themselves. The curve should create a 2⅛-inch indentation on each side of the lower part of the seat back.

21. Cut one piece of 1 × 3 pine stock to 27 inches for the lower brace of the seat back.

22. Choose a top edge of the brace and cut a 1⅜-inch radius on each end of that edge, as shown in illustration D. Drill a 5/16-inch-

diameter hole centered in the bottom edge of the piece, 1 inch from each end. Make the holes 1½ inches deep.

23. Cut two pieces of 5/16-inch-diameter dowel to 2¼ inches each. Apply glue to one end of each piece and insert the glued ends into the holes drilled in the braces. Leave ⅞ inch of each dowel protruding.

24. Fasten the lower braces flush with the bottom ends of the back slats, using waterproof glue and 1¼-inch #8 flathead wood screws. Be sure the ends of the brace protrude equally on each side, creating a gap of 1¼ inches between the edge of each outer slat and the center of the dowel nearest it.

25. Now, cut two pieces of 1 × 4 pine stock to 23 inches each for the chair legs. Cut a 30-degree bevel on one end of each leg to form the top ends. The bevel slopes toward the front, as shown in illustration B.

26. Square a line across the rear face of each leg 15 inches from the bottom. Starting from the left edge on one leg and from the right edge on the other leg, measure ⅝ inch along the line and drill a ⅜-inch-diameter hole ⅝ inch deep as shown in illustration D.

27. Measure from the bottom end of each chair leg and square lines across each leg at 11¾ inches and 15¾ inches. Scribe vertical lines connecting these, 1 5/16 inches from each edge, to complete the layout of a ⅞ × 4-inch slot on each leg. Drill starter holes and cut out these slots with a saber saw.

28. Cut one piece of 1 × 4 pine stock to 26¾ inches for the stretcher. Position this piece across the backs of the two legs, as shown in illustration B, so that the bottom edge of the piece is 9 inches from the bottom end of the legs. Make sure the ends of the stretcher are flush with the outside edges

of both legs and that the legs are arranged so the holes in their rear faces are to the inside. Fasten the stretcher to the legs with waterproof glue and four 1¼-inch #8 flathead wood screws for each leg. Countersink the screws.

29. Cut two pieces of 1 × 4 pine stock to 24 inches each for the arms.

30. Cut a 20-degree bevel on one end of each arm to form the back ends of the arms.

31. Open the L-shaped leg of two offset hinges to 110-degree angles to fit the arms' beveled back ends, as shown in illustration B.

32. Position the top of the hinges on the outer slats of the chair back, 21¼ inches from the bottom, and ½ inch from the outer edges. The outer edges of the arms should now be in line with the outer edges of the chair back. Attach the hinges using ¾-inch #8 flathead wood screws.

33. Attach the arms to the legs with butt hinges, as shown in illustration B. Position the hinges at the tops of the legs and 2½ inches back from the ends of the arms.

Fasten with ¾-inch #8 flathead wood screws.

34. Round-over all sharp edges on the chair and sand as needed. Finish with exterior-grade enamel or polyurethane.

35. When the finish is dry, assemble the chair. To do this, first hold the back upright, with the legs folded up against it, and rock it to one side. Slip the end of the lower brace through the rectangular slot in the stringer made for that side, tilting the stringer as needed to get the protruding piece of dowel through the slot. Be sure the stringer's cleats are facing inside. Repeat this procedure to install the remaining stringer. Now lower the arms and legs. Insert the nose of each stringer through the rectangular slot cut in the leg in front of it, and hook the notched edges of the stringers over the top of the stretcher. Finally, insert the protruding dowels of the seat into the holes drilled in the backs of the legs, and drop the seat down into position.

GARDEN CHAIR

This simply constructed but elegant garden chair was created by the Rodale Design Group with outdoor use in mind. However, after a few test models had been built, particularly the double-width version pictured, we decided that this chair would make an attractive and comfortable piece of indoor furniture as well.

The smaller, outdoor chair—which is the one described in the instructions—is made inexpensively of construction-grade pine covered with two coats of exterior latex enamel. Set out on a porch, under a rose arbor or a favorite shade tree, it provides a sturdy, pleasant place to sit back and enjoy the surroundings. The indoor chair is made of mahogany, finished clear, using polyurethane. Its size is twice that of the smaller one. To build it, merely add a third rail to each pair of front and back rails, and increase the lengths of all the slats and stops.

A novel feature of the garden chair is the way in which it is assembled. No hinges, bolts, or other fasteners are used. The slatless portion of the seat rails merely slides into place between the two wooden stops attached to the back rails, until the bottom slats of both the seat and the back come together. The chair supports itself in this position, yet may be pulled apart easily for storage or transportation.

CONSTRUCTION

1. Cut two pieces of 2 × 6 (1½'' × 5½'') stock to 39½ inches each for the back rails.

2. Cut the back rails to proper shape using the grid provided in illustration A.

3. Cut two pieces of 2 × 6 stock to 35½ inches each for the seat rails.

4. Cut the seat rails to proper shape using the grid provided in illustration A.

5. Cut 20 pieces of 1 × 2 (¾'' × 1½'') stock to 23 inches each for the seat and back slats.

6. Cut two pieces of 1 × 2 to 18 inches each for the stops.

7. Cut a ¼-inch radius along all edges of the rails and slats and along the four long edges of each stop. Use a router equipped with a ¼-inch rounding-over bit.

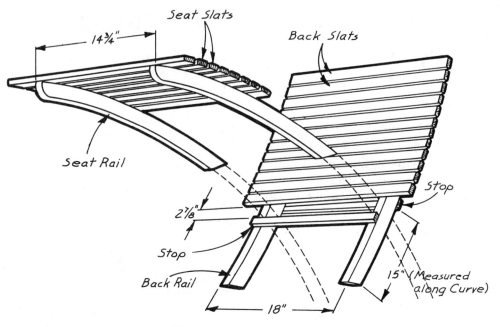

Exploded-View Diagram

8. Clamp the back rails together with their ends and edges flush. Square a line across the inside (concave) edge of both pieces every 2 inches, measuring from the top end, until you have drawn 11 lines. These lines mark the position for the back slats.

9. Unclamp and spread the back rails 18 inches apart, outside edge to outside edge, with their concave edges up. Attach 12 back slats to the rails with waterproof glue and 6d finishing nails. Center each slat so that it extends 2½ inches to the outside of each rail. Make the top edge of the first slat flush with the top ends of the back rails. Position the remaining back slats so their top edges are flush with the lines drawn across the rails.

10. Clamp the seat rails together with their ends and edges flush. Square a line across the inside (convex) edge of both pieces

LUMBER CUTTING LIST

Size	Piece	Quantity
2 × 6		
1½″ × 5½″ × 39½″	Back rails	2
1½″ × 5½″ × 35½″	Seat rails	2
1 × 2		
¾″ × 1½″ 23″	Seat and back slats	20
¾″ × 1½″ × 18″	Stops	2

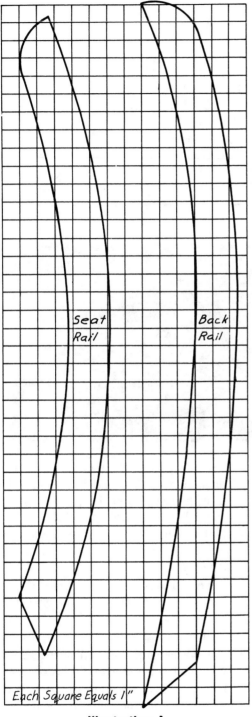

Illustration A

every 2 inches, beginning from the front end, until you have drawn seven lines. These lines mark the position for the seat slats.

11. Unclamp and spread the seat rails apart so that they measure 14¾ inches outside edge to outside edge. Fasten eight slats to the seat rails with waterproof glue and 6d finishing nails. Center each slat so that it extends 4⅛ inches to the outside of each rail. Position the first slat with its front edge flush with the front ends of the seat rails. Position the remaining slats with their front edges flush with the lines drawn across the rails.

12. Position one stop 2⅞ inches below the bottom slat of the back rail, its ends flush with the outside edges of the rails. Fasten the stop to the rails with waterproof glue and 6d finishing nails.

13. Position the other stop on the rear side of the back rails, so the ends of the stop are flush with the outside edges of the rails, and the stop's bottom edge is 15 inches from the bottom ends of the rails, measured along the curve. Fasten this stop to the rails with waterproof glue and 6d finishing nails.

14. Set all nails and fill the holes with wood filler. When the filler is dry, sand the entire chair, then finish with two coats of exterior-grade enamel or polyurethane.

PHONE-POLE GARDEN BENCH

SHOPPING LIST

Lumber
5 pcs. 2 × 4 × 8'
1 pc. telephone pole or post
    10'' diameter × 4'
Hardware
1 pc. threaded steel rod ⅜'' × 4'
6 nuts ⅜''
6 flat washers ⅜''
¼ pound galvanized common nails 10d

This small garden bench, simple to build using 2 × 4s and sections of an old telephone pole or similar large-diameter post, is versatile enough to find a home nearly anywhere in your yard. It looks particularly elegant near a garden or beneath an arbor. Fred Beucher of Hazelwood, Missouri, designed the bench shown in the photo to be 6 feet in length. This dimension is easily modified, of course, but longer lengths may require additional posts for support. Using pressure-treated lumber and painting the pieces before assembly will assure that the bench will last well into the next generation.

CONSTRUCTION

1. Cut five pieces of 2 × 4 (1½'' × 3½'') stock to 60 inches each for the seat slats, as shown on the cutting diagram. Cut two additional pieces of 2 × 4 to 13 inches each for the seat supports, and 12 additional pieces of 2 × 4 to 6 inches each for the seat spacers, also as shown.

2. Drill 1-inch-diameter holes ¾ inch deep in two of the seat slats in the locations shown in illustration A. Locate a hole 3 inches from each end and one in the center. These two pieces become the front and back slats.

3. Drill ½-inch-diameter holes through all the seat slats, including those drilled in the previous step, in the locations shown in illustration A. Be very careful to align the holes perfectly so the fastening rods (see step 10) may be easily installed.

4. Drill a ½-inch-diameter hole through the center of each spacer, also to fit the fastening rods.

5. Round off the corners on one face of each seat support, as shown in the exploded-view diagram.

6. Paint or stain all the seat pieces, as desired.

7. Cut two pieces of 10-inch-diameter post or pole to 23 inches each for the bench posts.

8. Dig two 10-inch-deep postholes spaced 48 inches apart on center in the desired location.

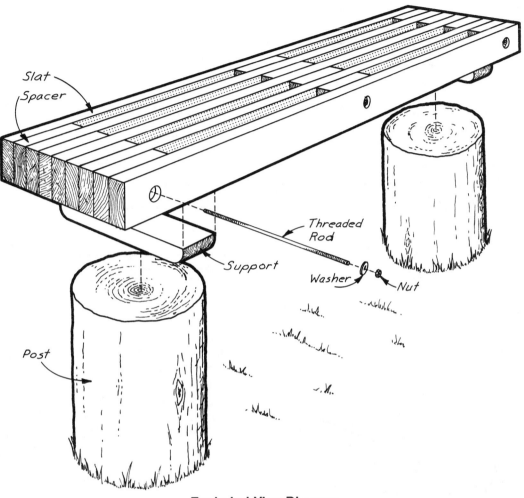

Slat

Spacer

Threaded
Rod

Washer

Nut

Support

Post

Exploded-View Diagram

LUMBER CUTTING LIST

Size	Piece	Quantity
2 × 4		
1½″ × 3½″ × 60″	Seat slats	5
1½″ × 3½″ × 13″	Seat supports	2
1½″ × 3½″ × 6″	Seat spacers	12
Post		
10″ × 23″	Posts	2

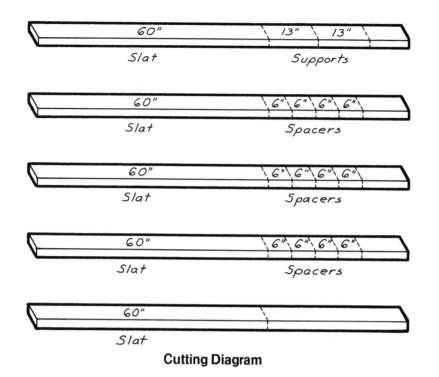

60"		13"	13"	
Slat			Supports	

60"		6"	6"	6"	6"
Slat				Spacers	

60"		6"	6"	6"	6"
Slat				Spacers	

60"		6"	6"	6"	6"
Slat				Spacers	

60"	
Slat	

Cutting Diagram

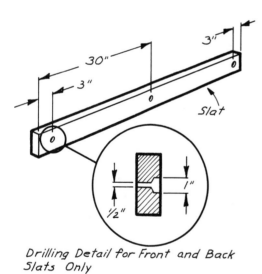

Drilling Detail for Front and Back Slats Only

Illustration A

9. Set the two posts in the holes, and adjust the height of the posts so that the tops are level with one another. Tamp earth firmly around the posts to anchor them in place.

10. Cut three pieces of ⅜-inch-diameter threaded steel rod to 15 inches each. Assemble the bench slat, as shown in the exploded-view diagram, by sandwiching the spacers and slats together with the rods installed in the predrilled holes. Be sure to locate the slats with the 1-inch holes on the outsides of the seats. To fasten the assembly together, install ⅜-inch flat washers and nuts on both ends of each rod and tighten them securely using a wrench. Trim off any excess using a hacksaw.

11. Center the seat supports across the bench seat so the supports are 48 inches apart, center-to-center. Fasten them to the slats using 10d galvanized common nails.

12. Set the completed seat bench on top of the posts, then fasten the supports to the posts with 10d galvanized common nails. To do this, start the nails holding them by hand between the slats, then drive them home using a long punch or metal rod as a nail set.

WOODEN GARDEN BENCH

This attractive wooden bench is an easy bolt-together project. Designed for outdoor use, it's as sturdy as its rugged good looks suggest. Wolmanized or other pressure-treated lumber is the best construction material to use, but with regular upkeep—such as a couple of coats of exterior enamel every few years—any type of stock will last for decades.

SHOPPING LIST

Lumber
3 pcs. $2 \times 6 \times 5'$
3 pcs. $2 \times 4 \times 6'$
Hardware
4 lag bolts $\frac{1}{4}'' \times 3\frac{1}{2}''$
28 carriage bolts $\frac{1}{4}'' \times 5\frac{1}{2}''$ with nuts
1 carriage bolt $\frac{1}{4}'' \times 5''$ with nut
2 carriage bolts $\frac{1}{4}'' \times 3\frac{1}{2}''$ with nuts
35 flat washers $\frac{1}{4}''$ I.D. $\times \frac{3}{4}''$ O.D.

CONSTRUCTION

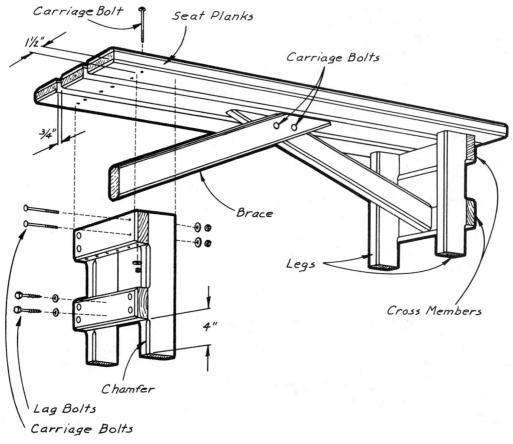

Carriage Bolt

Seat Planks

1½"

¾"

Carriage Bolts

Brace

Legs

Cross Members

4"

Chamfer

Lag Bolts

Carriage Bolts

Exploded-View Diagram

1. Cut four pieces 2×4 ($1\frac{1}{2}'' \times 3\frac{1}{2}''$) stock to $16\frac{1}{2}$ inches each for the legs of the bench. Also cut four pieces of 2×4 stock to 15 inches each for the cross members.

2. Drill $\frac{9}{32}$-inch-diameter holes through the cross members and legs to accept the carriage bolts used for assembly, as shown in the exploded-view diagram.

3. Using a router or block plane, work a $\frac{1}{4} \times \frac{1}{4}$-inch chamfer along all edges of each piece, except on the legs where the cross members overlap.

4. Bolt the leg assemblies together using $\frac{1}{4} \times 5\frac{1}{2}$-inch carriage bolts, washers, and nuts.

5. Use three pieces of 2×6 ($1\frac{1}{2}'' \times 5\frac{1}{2}''$) stock, each 60 inches in length, for the seat planks.

6. As in step 3, cut a $\frac{1}{4} \times \frac{1}{4}$-inch chamfer around all edges of each seat plank.

7. Drill $\frac{9}{32}$-inch-diameter holes through the seat planks and cross members to accept the carriage bolts used for assembly, as shown in the exploded-view diagram.

LUMBER CUTTING LIST

Size	Piece	Quantity
2×6		
$1\frac{1}{2}'' \times 5\frac{1}{2}'' \times 60''$	Seat planks	3
2×4		
$1\frac{1}{2}'' \times 3\frac{1}{2}'' \times 34\frac{1}{2}''$	Braces	2
$1\frac{1}{2}'' \times 3\frac{1}{2}'' \times 16\frac{1}{2}''$	Legs	4
$1\frac{1}{2}'' \times 3\frac{1}{2}'' \times 15''$	Cross members	4

8. Bolt the seat planks to the leg assemblies using $\frac{1}{4} \times 5\frac{1}{2}$-inch carriage bolts, washers, and nuts.

9. Cut two pieces of 2×4 stock to $34\frac{1}{2}$ inches each for the braces. Carefully lay out and cut angles at both ends of each brace where they butt against the inside of the lower cross members and underside of the center seat plank.

10. Work a $\frac{1}{4} \times \frac{1}{4}$-inch chamfer on all long edges of each brace, except on the underside of each where the braces overlap.

11. Drill $\frac{9}{32}$-inch-diameter holes through the lower cross members to accept the lag bolts.

12. Hold one of the braces in position beneath the bench, and, using the holes in the cross member as a guide, drill $\frac{3}{16}$-inch-diameter pilot holes into the end of the brace. Repeat this procedure for the other brace, using as your guide the holes in the opposite lower cross member.

13. Fasten the braces in place using $\frac{1}{4} \times 3\frac{1}{2}$-inch lag bolts and washers.

14. Now clamp the two braces together where they overlap beneath the center seat plank of the bench, and drill two $\frac{9}{32}$-inch-diameter holes through both braces. Bolt the braces together using $\frac{1}{4} \times 3\frac{1}{2}$-inch carriage bolts, washers, and nuts.

15. Holding the braces firmly to the underside of the center seat plank, drill $\frac{9}{32}$-inch-diameter holes through both the plank and one of the braces to accept a carriage bolt. Counterbore the hole $\frac{7}{8}$ inch deep and $\frac{3}{4}$ inch in diameter where it emerges from the brace. Install the $\frac{1}{4} \times 5$-inch carriage bolt, washer, and nut. Use a socket wrench to tighten, if necessary.

16. Cut all bolts off flush with their nuts, then sand the bench thoroughly and finish with exterior-grade enamel or stain, if desired.

WOODEN GARDEN BENCH WITH BACK

SHOPPING LIST

Lumber
1 pc. 2 × 6 × 10'
3 pcs. 2 × 6 × 8'
1 pc. 2 × 4 × 8'
Hardware
4 carriage bolts ¼'' × 6'' with nuts
16 carriage bolts ¼'' × 5½'' with nuts
16 carriage bolts ¼'' × 3½'' with nuts
36 flat washers ¼'' I.D. × ¾'' O.D.

This bench makes an excellent companion piece to the one featured on the previous pages. Its construction is quite similar; however, this bench features a comfortably sloping back and seat. Cross braces underneath are not necessary. As with the previous bench, Wolmanized or other pressure-treated lumber is best to use, although any construction-grade stock that has been properly protected and maintained against the elements will work just as well and last about as long. Study the exploded-view diagram carefully before beginning. Make sure you understand the angled cuts that must be made in the legs, back, and cross members to achieve a proper slope without sacrificing well-fitted, neat-appearing joints.

CONSTRUCTION

1. Cut two pieces of 2 × 6 (1½'' × 5½'') stock to 16½ inches each for the front legs. Trim one end of each piece to an angle of 87 degrees, as shown in illustration A. These angled ends form the tops of the legs.

2. Cut two pieces of 2 × 6 stock to 29 inches each for the rear legs. Lay out and cut the angled portion of each leg that forms the back of the bench.

3. Cut two pieces of 2 × 4 (1½'' × 3½'') stock to 24⅛ inches each for the top cross members. Trim both ends of each piece so they form 87-degree angles, making sure the trimmed ends of each piece are parallel with each other.

4. Cut two pieces of 2 × 4 stock to 23½ inches each for the bottom cross members.

5. Clamp or hold the cross members and legs in position and drill 9/32-inch-diameter

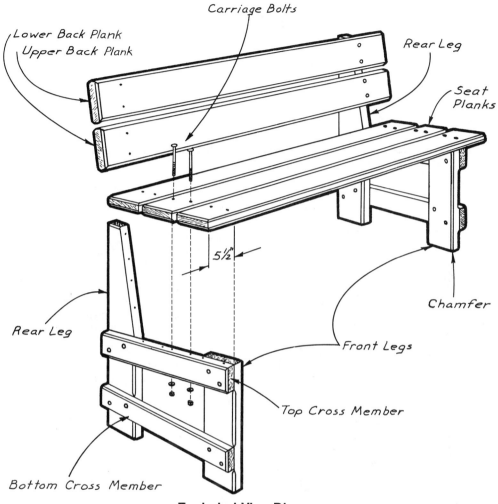

Carriage Bolts

Lower Back Plank
Upper Back Plank

Rear Leg

Seat
Planks

5½"

Chamfer

Rear Leg

Front Legs

Top Cross Member

Bottom Cross Member

Exploded-View Diagram

holes through the pieces where they over-lap, to accept the carriage bolts used in assembly.

6. Using a router or block plane, work a ¼ × ¼-inch chamfer on all edges of the legs and cross members, except where the pieces overlap, and on the angled portions of the rear legs.

7. Bolt the leg assemblies together using ¼ × 3½-inch carriage bolts, washers, and nuts.

8. Cut five pieces of 2 × 6 stock to 60 inches each for the seat and back planks. Work a ¼ × ¼-inch chamfer on all edges and ends of each piece.

9. Clamp or hold the planks in position and drill $9/32$-inch-diameter holes through both the planks and the leg-assembly pieces they overlap. Counterbore the holes ⅞ inches in diameter and ¾ inches deep at the back of the rear legs to accept the carriage bolt washers and nuts.

43

LUMBER CUTTING LIST

Size	Piece	Quantity
2 × 6		
1½″ × 5½″ × 60″	Seat and back planks	5
1½″ × 5½″ × 29″	Rear legs	2
1½″ × 5½″ × 16½″	Front legs	2
2 × 4		
1½″ × 3½″ × 24⅛″	Top cross members	2
1½″ × 3½″ × 23½″	Bottom cross members	2

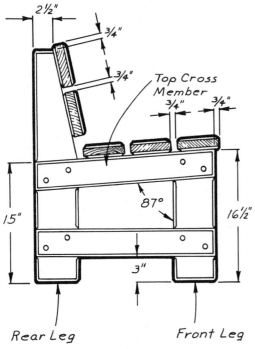

Illustration A

10. Bolt the seat and back planks to the leg assemblies using ¼ × 5½-inch carriage bolts, washers, and nuts for the seat planks and upper back plank, and ¼ × 6-inch carriage bolts, washers, and nuts for the lower back plank. Use a socket wrench, if necessary, to tighten the nuts in the counterbored holes.

11. Cut all bolts off flush with the nuts, then sand the bench thoroughly, and finish with exterior-grade enamel or stain, if desired.

GARDEN BENCH WITH WROUGHT-IRON LEGS

SHOPPING LIST

Lumber
1 pc. 2 × 12 × 4'
Mild Steel Flat Stock
2 pcs. 3/16″ × 1¼″ × 45″
2 pcs. ⅛″ × 1″ × 22″
2 pcs. ⅛″ × 1″ × 19″
2 pcs. ⅛″ × 1″ × 17″
Hardware
6 carriage bolts ¼″ × 2″ with nuts
6 flat washers ¼″ I.D. × ¾″ O.D.
rust-resistant paint
exterior-grade enamel or stain

This good-looking garden bench is designed with a wooden seat for comfort, and wrought-iron legs (actually mild steel) for sturdiness without a massive appearance. Genuine wrought iron is no longer made; it hasn't been, really, since the horse-and-buggy days. Mild steel is the modern counterpart of wrought iron, having a slightly different combination of molecules but much of the same working properties. Bending the mild steel called for in this project without heating it first is no problem. Not only are the pieces relatively thin, but they are also long enough to provide adequate leverage for producing even the

tight curves by hand. As a jig for bending the stock, position two 5/16 × 2½-inch hex- or square-head bolts vertically in a vise, as shown in illustration B, and use them as fulcrum points. Practice a bit on scrap stock before setting out to make the real thing.

The easiest and best way to join the pieces of the legs together is by welding. Bolts or rivets can be used but these inevitably loosen, and the extra effort required to drill the holes for these fasteners isn't worthwhile. If you do not know how to weld, or lack the equipment, prebend the pieces and have them joined at a welding shop. The job will probably take less than an hour and the cost will be minimal.

Preserve the metal parts of the bench by first making sure all the welds are scrubbed clean and then coating the metal thoroughly with rust-resistant paint. For a durable seat use Wolmanized or other pressure-treated lumber, or else apply several coats of exterior enamel or stain to whatever construction-grade stock you do use.

CONSTRUCTION

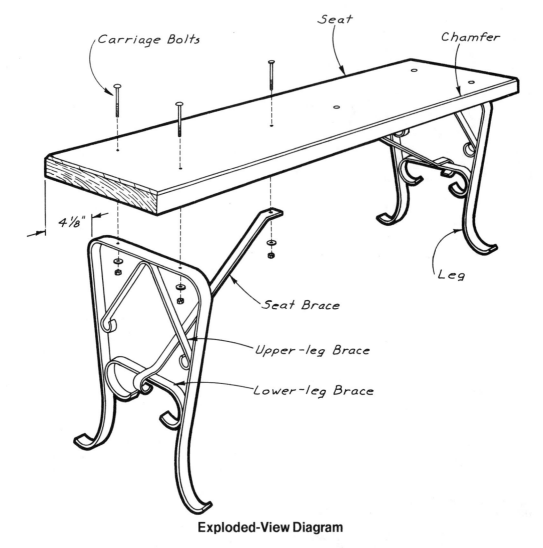

Carriage Bolts

Seat

Chamfer

4⅛"

Leg

Seat Brace

Upper-leg Brace

Lower-leg Brace

Exploded-View Diagram

1. From $\frac{3}{16} \times 1\frac{1}{4}$-inch mild steel flat stock, cut two pieces each 45 inches long for the legs.
2. From $\frac{1}{8} \times 1$-inch mild steel flat stock, cut two pieces each 22 inches long for the upper-leg braces.
3. From $\frac{1}{8} \times 1$-inch mild steel flat stock, cut the remaining metal pieces: two pieces each 19 inches long for the seat braces, and two pieces each 17 inches long for the lower-leg braces.
4. Bend the legs and braces to shape, as shown in illustration A. Use a vise with bolts held between the jaws as a bending jig, as shown in illustration B.
5. Drill $\frac{17}{64}$-inch holes in the tops of the legs

LUMBER CUTTING LIST

Size 2 × 12	Piece	Quantity
1½″ × 11¼″ × 48″	Seat	1

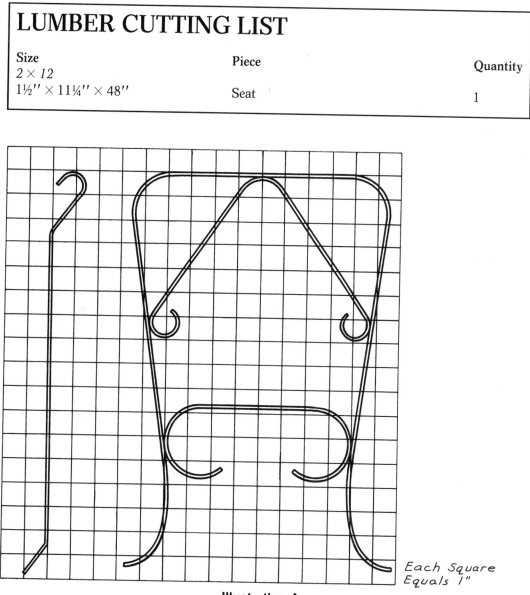

Each Square Equals 1"

Illustration A

and in one end of each seat brace to accept the carriage bolts used to fasten the seat to the legs, as shown in the exploded-view diagram.

6. Clamp and weld the legs and braces to-

gether to form the two leg assemblies, each with a seat brace attached.

7. Use one piece of 2 × 12 (1½″ × 11¼″) stock, 48 inches in length, for the seat.

8. Using a router or block plane, work a

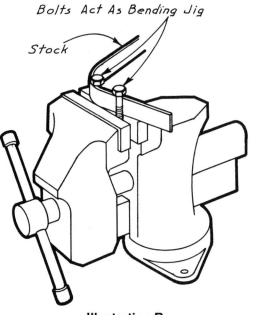

Bolts Act As Bending Jig

Stock

Illustration B

¼ × ¼-inch chamfer along the top edges and ends of the seat.

9. Drill ⁹⁄₃₂-inch-diameter holes in the seat to accept the carriage bolts used for mounting, as shown in the exploded-view diagram.

10. Before assembling the bench, clean the metal parts and finish with rust-resistant paint, and sand the seat and finish with exterior-grade enamel or stain.

11. Assemble the bench using ¼ × 2-inch carriage bolts, washers, and nuts.

GARDEN BENCH WITH WROUGHT- IRON LEGS AND ARMS

This wood and metal bench, designed with a back and armrests, is similar to the wooden garden benches featured on p. 39 and 42—one designed without a back, the other designed with one. This bench also features a gentle rearward slope for comfort.

The techniques for the construction of this bench are exactly the same as for the bench shown on p. 45. Mild steel is the metal used in place of genuine—and now unobtainable—wrought iron; welding is the principal method of joinery; and a jig made by placing two 5/16 × 2½-inch hex- or square-head bolts vertically in a vise is suitable for bending the stock to shape. Refer to p. 48 for an illustration of this jig.

Use Wolmanized or other pressure-treated lumber for the seat, or thoroughly

stain or coat with exterior enamel whatever construction-grade stock you use instead. Coat the metal parts with rust-resistant paint.

CONSTRUCTION

1. From 3/16 × 1¼-inch mild steel flat stock, cut the following: two pieces each 49 inches long for the front legs and arms, two pieces each 33 inches long for the back legs, and two pieces each 24 inches long for the seat supports.

2. From ⅛ × 1-inch mild steel flat stock, cut the remaining metal pieces: two pieces each 26 inches long for the upper-leg braces,

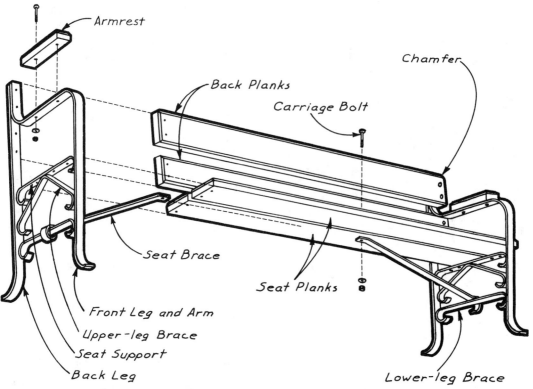

Armrest

Back Planks

Carriage Bolt

Chamfer

Seat Brace

Front Leg and Arm

Upper-leg Brace

Seat Support

Back Leg

Seat Planks

Lower-leg Brace

Exploded-View Diagram

two pieces each 24 inches long for the lower-leg braces, and two pieces also 24 inches long for the seat braces.

3. Bend the metal pieces to shape, as shown in illustration A, using the jig described on p. 45.

4. Drill $9/32$-inch-diameter holes in the seat supports, arms, back legs, and seat braces to accept the carriage bolts used for assem-

bling the bench, as shown in the exploded-view diagram. Exact spacing of the holes is not important.

5. Clamp and weld the leg, seat supports, and brace assemblies together.

6. Cut two pieces of 2×8 ($1\frac{1}{2}'' \times 7\frac{1}{4}''$) stock to 60 inches each for the seat planks.

7. Cut two pieces of 2×6 ($1\frac{1}{2}'' \times 5\frac{1}{2}''$) to 60 inches each for the back planks.

LUMBER CUTTING LIST

Size	Piece	Quantity
2×8		
$1\frac{1}{2}'' \times 7\frac{1}{4}'' \times 60''$	Seat planks	2
2×6		
$1\frac{1}{2}'' \times 5\frac{1}{2}'' \times 60''$	Back planks	2
2×3		
$1\frac{1}{2}'' \times 2\frac{1}{2}'' \times 12''$	Armrests	2

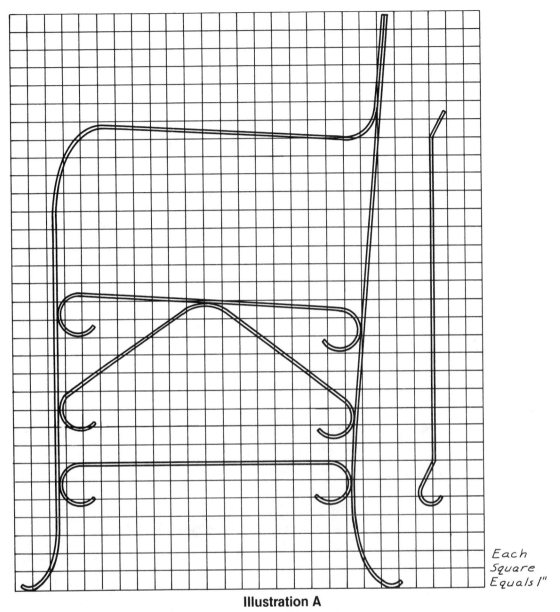

Each
Square
Equals 1"

Illustration A

8. Cut two pieces of 2 × 3 (1½″ × 2½″) to 12 inches each for the armrests.

9. Using a router or block plane, work a ¼ × ¼-inch chamfer on the upper edges and ends of all the wooden pieces.

10. Drill ⁹⁄₃₂-inch-diameter holes in the wooden pieces to accept carriage bolts. These bolts should align with those drilled in step 4.

11. Before assembling the bench, sand the wooden parts and finish with exterior-grade enamel or stain. Coat the metal parts with rust-resistant paint.

12. Assemble the bench using ¼ × 2-inch carriage bolts, washers, and nuts.

TREE BENCH

SHOPPING LIST

Lumber
1 pc. $4 \times 4 \times 6'$
2 pcs. $2 \times 6 \times 8'$
2 pcs. $2 \times 6 \times 6'$
3 pcs. $2 \times 4 \times 10'$
Hardware
48 flathead wood screws #8 $\times$ 1¼''
16 carriage bolts ¼'' $\times$ 4½'' with flat
    washers and nuts
¼ pound galvanized common nails 12d
1 pint exterior-grade stain

This simple, geometrically satisfying bench was designed by the Rodale Design Group to provide a comfortable resting place beneath a favorite shade tree. The legs of the bench are made of pressure-treated pine. Cedar is used for the seat. Redwood or cypress would also be good choices, as would ordinary construction-grade lumber, provided it was kept well-painted or coated with wood preservative.

Constructing the bench is quite easy, especially if you use a portable circular saw. The plans are also easy to alter. To accommodate most trees, allow a 3-inch gap between the trunk and the inside of the bench on all sides. (The bench shown here is intended to fit a tree whose trunk diameter measures 14 inches.) For a very young tree or for a variety that increases its trunk size rapidly, incorporate a larger gap, say up to 6 inches on all sides.

CONSTRUCTION

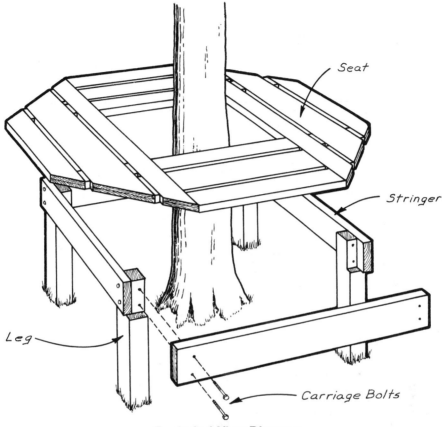

Exploded-View Diagram

1. Cut four pieces of 4 × 4 (3½″ × 3½″) stock to 16½ inches each for the legs. Cut a 5½-inch-wide rabbet 1 inch deep across two adjacent sides at the upper end of each leg to receive the stringers, as shown in illustration A.

2. Cut four pieces of 2 × 6 (1½″ × 5½″) stock to 32 inches each for the stringers. Fit them in place around the rabbeted upper sections of the four legs, as shown in the exploded-view diagram.

3. Drill two ¼-inch-diameter holes through the ends of each stringer into the legs

behind them. Stagger the holes on adjacent sides of each leg to prevent them from intersecting. Assemble the legs and stringers around a tree to make the frame, and fasten the pieces together with ¼ × 4½-inch carriage bolts, flat washers, and nuts. Adjust the ground surface beneath the legs, if necessary, to make the frame plumb and level.

4. The seat requires 12 pieces. Cut four pieces from 2 × 4 (1½″ × 3½″) stock to 49 inches each, and four additional pieces, also from 2 × 4 stock, to 28 inches each.

53

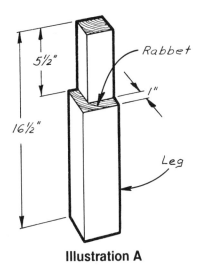

Illustration A

Cut the remaining four pieces from 2 × 6 stock to 40½ inches each.

5. Cut half-lap joints in all 12 seat pieces by following the patterns provided in illustration B. Assemble the pieces on the legs and stringers set up around the tree to form the seat.

6. Mark on the outside edges of the seat (the edges farthest from the tree) where the half-lap joints occur and connect these points by scribing diagonal lines across the four corners of the seat, as shown in illustration C.

7. Fasten the pieces of the seat together (while it is still around the tree) by installing two 1¼-inch #8 flathead wood screws at each of the 24 half-lap joints. Keep all screws inside the diagonal lines. Center the seat an equal distance from the trunk on all sides, if possible, then fasten the seat to the frame with 12d galvanized common nails. Use a saw to trim the four corners of the seat by cutting along the diagonal lines.

8. Sand the seat and round-over any rough edges. Finish the entire bench with one or two coats of exterior-grade stain.

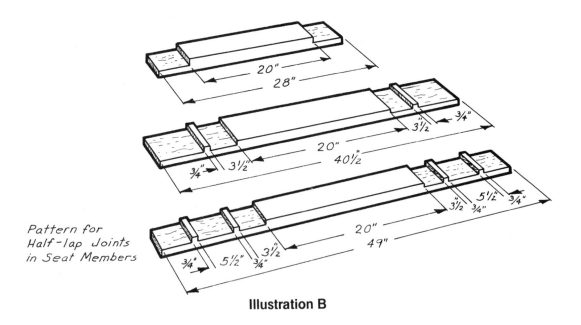

Pattern for Half-lap Joints in Seat Members

Illustration B

LUMBER CUTTING LIST

Size	Piece	Quantity
4×4		
$3\frac{1}{2}'' \times 3\frac{1}{2}'' \times 16\frac{1}{2}''$	Legs	4
2×6		
$1\frac{1}{2}'' \times 5\frac{1}{2}'' \times 40\frac{1}{2}''$	Seat members	4
$1\frac{1}{2}'' \times 5\frac{1}{2}'' \times 32''$	Stringers	4
2×4		
$1\frac{1}{2}'' \times 3\frac{1}{2}'' \times 49''$	Seat members	4
$1\frac{1}{2}'' \times 3\frac{1}{2}'' \times 28''$	Seat members	4

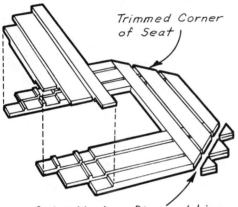

Trimmed Corner of Seat

Cut Off along Diagonal Line

Illustration C

PLANT STEPS

Plant steps—actually a miniature staircase built just like its larger cousin—are a traditional way of displaying potted flowers and other plants grown for their beauty. This version by the Rodale Design Group incorporates features that make the steps suitable for both indoor and outdoor use by employing waterproof glue and polyurethane.

SHOPPING LIST

Lumber
1 pc. $5/4 \times 10 \times 6'$
1 pc. $1 \times 8 \times 10'$
1 pc. $1 \times 3 \times 5'$
1 pc. $1 \times 2 \times 6'$
Hardware
22 flathead wood screws #8 × 2″
8 flathead wood screws #8 × 1″
½ pint waterproof glue
1 pint polyurethane

Mahogany was chosen as the building material, since not only is it very attractive when finished clear, but also strong, easily worked, and relatively inexpensive. Use the plant steps indoors in winter to show off houseplants grown inside, then move the steps outdoors in the spring and summer, where they will enhance a porch or patio.

CONSTRUCTION

1. Cut two pieces of $5/4 \times 10$ ($1\frac{1}{8}″ \times 9\frac{1}{4}″$) stock to 31½ inches each for the stringers. With a framing square lay out three steps on each stringer, each step having a rise of 8 inches and a run of 6¾ inches, as shown in illustration A. Cut out the steps, then square the ends of the stringers, also as shown.

2. Cut a 2½-inch-wide rabbet ⅜ inch deep along the inside of the back edge at the upper end of each stringer to create a recessed area for attaching the legs, as shown in the exploded-view diagram. Remember to recess the left face on one stringer and the right face on the other to create a right and left stringer.

3. Cut two pieces of 1×3 (¾″ × 2½″) stock to 24 inches each for the legs. Fit one leg into the rabbeted section of a stringer, making the top edges of each flush. Scribe a

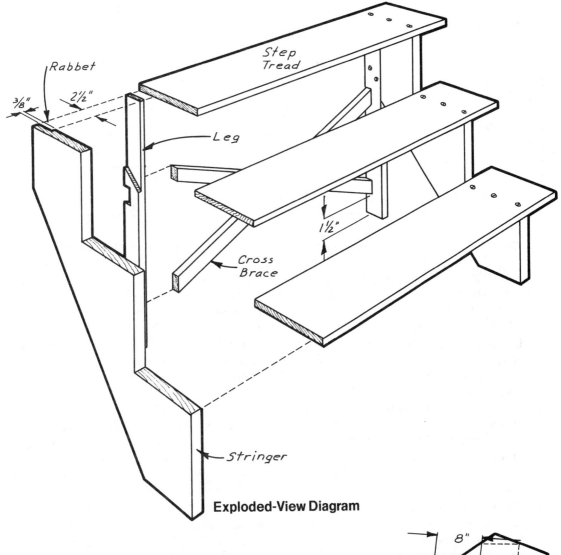

Rabbet

3/8"

2 1/2"

Step
Tread

Leg

Cross
Brace

1 1/2"

Stringer

Exploded-View Diagram

line diagonally across each leg where it touches the bottom edge of the stringer, then cut a ⅜-inch-deep rabbet above the scribed line on each leg for lapping the legs with the stringers.

4. Cut two pieces of 1 × 2 (¾″ × 1½″) stock to 33 inches each for the cross braces. Hold one end of each brace against a straight-edge while crossing them at their centers. Adjust them so their tips are spaced 15

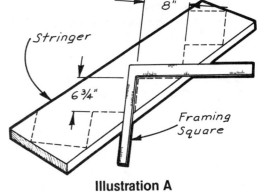

Stringer

8"

6 ¾"

Framing
Square

Illustration A

LUMBER CUTTING LIST

Size	Piece	Quantity
⁵⁄₄ × 10		
1⅛″ × 9¼″ × 31½″	Stringers	2
1 × 8		
¾″ × 7¼″ × 36″	Step treads	3
1 × 3		
¾″ × 2½″ × 24″	Legs	2
1 × 2		
¾″ × 1½″ × 33″	Cross braces	2

inches apart, outside edge to outside edge, at each end of the X. Mark the pieces where they cross and cut out those areas to a ⅜-inch depth to create a half-lap joint. Fasten the braces together with waterproof glue, clamping the joint while the glue dries.

5. Lay the cross braces across the back edges of the legs. Adjust the legs so they are parallel, spaced 30 inches apart, outside edge to outside edge, and so their lower ends extend 1½ inches below the bottom of the bracing, as shown in the exploded-view diagram. Mark the legs where the braces cross them. Also mark the ends of the braces for trimming them flush with the outside edges of the legs.

6. Cut a ¾-inch-deep notch across the back of each leg where a brace will intersect it and trim the ends of the braces. Drill and countersink a ³⁄₃₂-inch-diameter pilot hole for a #8 screw at each intersection of braces and legs, then fasten the braces to the legs using waterproof glue and 2-inch #8 flat-head wood screws.

7. Dry-fit the legs to the stringers while drilling and countersinking four pilot holes for #8 screws in the upper end of each, then fasten the legs to the stringers using waterproof glue and 1-inch #8 flathead wood screws.

8. Cut three pieces of 1 × 8 (¾″ × 7¼″) stock to 36 inches each for the step treads. Center the treads across the stringers, then drill and countersink three pilot holes for #8 screws where each tread rests on a stringer. Fasten the treads to the stringers using 2-inch #8 flathead wood screws.

9. Sand the entire project, rounding-over all sharp edges. Finish with two coats of polyurethane or other water-resistant finish.

STACKING STRAW-BERRY BOX

This strawberry box will make an attractive addition to any patio or porch. Designed by the Rodale Design Group, it is composed of six frame sections, each stacked one on top of the other. Semicircles cut into

SHOPPING LIST

Lumber
3 pcs. 1 × 4 × 8′
1 pc. 1 × 1 × 3′
Plywood
1 pc. ¼″ × 1′ × 1′ exterior grade
Hardware
¼ pound cement-coated box nails 4d
waterproof glue
copper naphthenate wood preservative
1 trash-can liner 20-gallon capacity

the frames are arranged in a pleasing, symmetrical pattern and provide growing room for 36 strawberry plants. The strawberries are planted in soil contained in a plastic bag in which holes have been punched. When the berries need replanting in fresh soil, the box unstacks easily layer by layer.

CONSTRUCTION

1. Cut 24 pieces of 1 × 4 (¾″ × 3½″) stock to 11⅞ inches each for the box frame sides. Cut a ¾-inch-wide rabbet ⅜ inch deep across one end of each piece. Then arrange all 24 pieces with their rabbeted edges on the same side and facing the same direction.

2. Arrange the box frame sides in two groups of 12 pieces. Lay out a semicircle with a 1½-inch radius midway across the upper edge of each piece in one group. On each piece of the other group, lay out two semi-circles with 1½-inch radii. Center one 2¾ inches from an end of the piece, the other 6 inches from the center of the first, along the upper edge, as shown in illustration A.

3. Cut out the semicircles on the 24 box frame sides using a saber saw or band saw, then smooth the rough surfaces with sandpaper. Set aside two pieces from each group to make the bottom frame (see step 4). Assemble the remaining pieces into five bottomless square frames, each containing a parallel

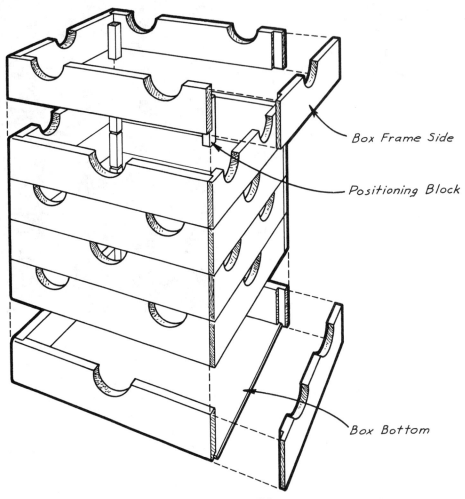

Box Frame Side

Positioning Block

Box Bottom

Exploded-View Diagram

set of pieces from each group, as shown in illustration A. Fasten each frame together using waterproof glue and 4d cement-coated box nails.

4. Cut a ¼-inch-wide rabbet ⅜ inch deep along the bottom inside edge of each of the four remaining side pieces to accept one edge of the bottom panel. Then cut a piece of ¼-inch exterior-grade plywood to 11½ × 11½ inches

for the bottom panel. Assemble the box using waterproof glue and 4d cement-coated box nails.

5. Machine a ¼-inch radius on all exposed edges of the six frames or round them over with sandpaper. Then cut 10 pieces of 1 × 1 (¾″ × ¾″) stock to 3¼ inches each for positioning blocks. Fasten two blocks in each bottomless frame using waterproof

LUMBER CUTTING LIST

Size	Piece	Quantity
1 × 4		
¾″ × 3½″ × 11⅞″	Box frame sides	24
1 × 1		
¾″ × ¾″ × 3¼″	Positioning blocks	10
Plywood		
¼″ × 11½″ × 11½″	Box bottom	1

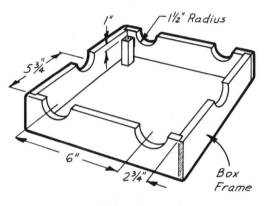

Illustration A

glue and 4d cement-coated box nails. Position the blocks in diagonally opposite corners with their lower ends extending ¾ inch below the bottom edges of the frames.

6. Sand all frames and finish them inside and out with a copper naphthenate wood preservative.

To plant strawberries in the box:

Set the bottom frame on bricks to allow air to circulate underneath. Arrange the bottomless frames one on top of the other, alternating the pattern of their semicircles, as shown in the exploded-view diagram. Line the inside of the stacked frames with a 20-gallon trash-can liner or other slightly oversize plastic bag. Tack or staple the top of the bag to the inside of the upper frame. Fill the bag with potting soil. At each semicircular opening in the stacked frame, punch through the plastic bag and insert a strawberry plant.

WOODEN WINDOW BOX

SHOPPING LIST

Lumber
1 pc. 1 × 10 × 10'
Hardware
For the sill-mounted window box:

26 brass flathead wood screws #6 × 2''
2 S-hooks 1¼''
2 eyescrews ⅜''
¼ pound galvanized finishing nails 4d
1 pc. aluminum cable or substitute (⅛''
    thickness) 5'

For the frame-mounted window box:

6 flathead wood screws #8 × 1¼''
26 brass flathead wood screws #6 × 2''
4 lag bolts ¼'' × 3''
2 flathead bolts ¼'' × ½'' with nuts
1 pc. aluminum angle ¾'' × ¾'' × 6'
2 pcs. aluminum angle ¾'' × ¾'' × 14½''

This window box, with its optional mounting arrangements, was designed by the Rodale Design Group to provide an attractive and substantial growing area for apartment or condominium dwellers. In one version the box rests directly on a windowsill and is held in place by a sturdy, yet easily removable, cable. In the other variation the box rests beneath the sill and is supported by an aluminum frame fastened to the building itself.

In our plans, the sill-mounted box is designed to fit a window opening measuring 28 inches across. The frame-mounted box is longer, measuring 32 inches in length. Naturally, you may alter the plans of either box to suit your needs. However, we recommend that you do not construct window boxes longer than 4 feet without adding considerable additional support to the windowsill or frame.

The box shown is made of cedar, chosen because of its pleasing appearance and durability. Boxes made of plastic and metal tend to overheat. Even wooden boxes, if painted a dark color, tend to absorb more heat than some plants can tolerate. If you plan to paint your window box, choose a light color that will reflect heat.

CONSTRUCTION

To build the sill-mounted window box:

1. Cut one piece of 1×10 ($\frac{3}{4}'' \times 9\frac{1}{4}''$) stock to $27\frac{7}{8}$ inches for the bottom blank. Rip a $1\frac{1}{2}$-inch-wide strip from this piece and save it for the cable-cover molding (see step 6). Rip the bottom blank again, to $7\frac{1}{4}$ inches in width, and bevel the front edge to a 14-degree angle, as shown in illustration A. Finally, trim the piece to $26\frac{5}{8}$ inches.

2. Cut one piece of 1×10 stock to $27\frac{7}{8}$ inches for the front of the box. Rip a 14-degree bevel along the bottom edge. Cut a second piece of 1×10 stock to the same length for the rear of the box, then rip it to 9 inches in width.

3. Cut one piece of 1×10 stock to 17 inches for the end blank. Rip the piece to 9 inches in width, then lay out a diagonal line across the piece, connecting a point $9\frac{1}{8}$ inches along the length of one side with a point $7\frac{1}{16}$ inches along the length of the other. Cut the blank in two along this line to create the end pieces, as shown in illustration A. Then trim the larger piece so that both are the same size.

4. Assemble the box by fitting the ends between the front and rear pieces, and inserting the bottom within all four, as shown in the exploded-view diagram and illustration A.

Drill and countersink pilot holes, then fasten the pieces together using 2-inch #6 brass flathead wood screws.

5. Drill one row of $\frac{1}{2}$-inch-diameter drainage holes in the bottom of the box. Space the holes approximately 6 inches apart.

6. Cut one piece of aluminum cable, or heavy electrical wire, plastic rope, or other rust-resistant material, to 60 inches for mounting the window box. Attach the ends to $1\frac{1}{4}$-inch S-hooks. Rout a groove to accept the cable, centered along the length of one face of the cable-cover molding cut in step 1. Then fasten the molding to the front of the box, as shown in the exploded-view diagram, using 4d galvanized finishing nails.

7. Set the box in place on the windowsill and stretch the ends of the mounting cable taut. Mark the positions where the S-hooks touch the moldings on either side of the window and install eyescrews at those points. Attach the S-hooks to the eyescrews, and then the window box is ready to fill with soil and plants.

To build the frame-mounted window box:

1. Cut two pieces of 1×10 ($\frac{3}{4}'' \times 9\frac{1}{4}''$) stock to 32 inches, one for the front of the

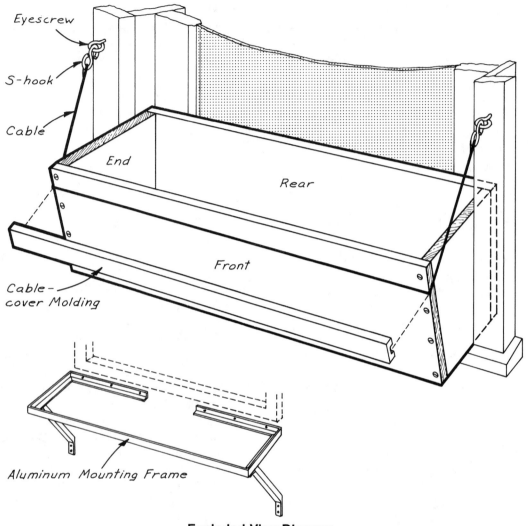

Eyescrew

S-hook

Cable

End

Rear

Front

Cable-cover Molding

Aluminum Mounting Frame

Exploded-View Diagram

box and one for the rear. Cut a 14-degree bevel along the lower edge of the front piece, and rip the rear piece to 9 inches in width. Cut a third piece to 30½ inches for the bottom. Rip the bottom to 7¼ inches in width and bevel its front edge to a 14-degree angle, as shown in illustration A.

2. Cut one piece of 1 × 10 stock to 17 inches for the end blank. Rip the piece to 9 inches

in width, then lay out a diagonal line across the piece connecting a point 9⅛ inches along the length of one side with a point 7¹/₁₆ inches along the length of the other. Cut the blank in two along this line to create the end pieces, as shown in illustration A. Then trim the larger piece so that both are the same size.

3. Assemble the box by fitting the ends between

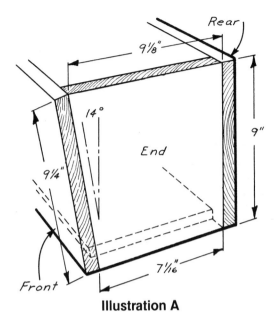

Illustration A

4. Drill one row of ½-inch-diameter drainage holes in the bottom of the box. Space the holes approximately 6 inches apart.

5. Cut one piece of ¾ × ¾-inch aluminum angle to 72 inches for the support frame. Cut 90-degree V-notches in one flange of the frame so that it can be bent to fit around the window box. Locate the notches 11¼ inches and 20 inches from each end of the piece, leaving a 32-inch segment in the middle, as shown in illustration B.

6. Center and drill three holes for #8 screws in the unnotched flanges of the end segments of the frame. Countersink the holes on the inside surface.

7. Cut two pieces of ¾ × ¾-inch aluminum angle to 14½ inches each for the frame braces. Saw away one flange on each brace, 2½ inches from the lower end and 1 inch from the upper end, as shown in illustration C. Angle each cut 45 degrees toward the center of the piece. Then center and drill one ⁹⁄₃₂-inch-diameter hole ½ inch from the upper end of each brace, and two similar holes ⁵⁄₈ inch and 2 inches respectively from the lower end, also as shown.

the front and rear pieces and inserting the bottom within all four, as shown in the exploded-view diagram and illustration A. Drill and countersink pilot holes, then fasten the pieces together using 2-inch #6 brass flathead wood screws.

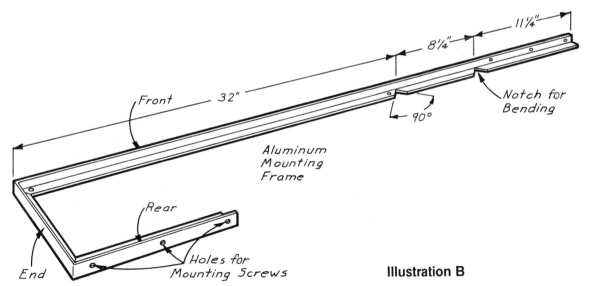

Illustration B

LUMBER CUTTING LIST

Size	Piece	Quantity
1 × 10		
For the sill-mounted window box:		
¾" × 9¼" × 27⅞"	Front	1
¾" × 9" × 27⅞"	Rear	1
¾" × 9" × 9⅛"	Box ends	2
¾" × 7¼" × 26⅜"	Bottom	1
¾" × 1½" × 27⅞"	Cable cover	1
For the frame-mounted window box:		
¾" × 9¼" × 32"	Front	1
¾" × 9" × 32"	Rear	1
¾" × 9" × 9⅛"	Box ends	2
¾" × 7¼" × 30½"	Bottom	1

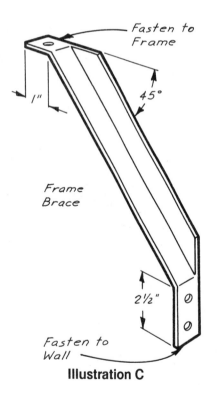

Illustration C

8. Bend the support frame to rectangular shape, then center and drill a ⁹⁄₃₂-inch hole through the notched (horizontal) flange at each end, locating the holes ¾ inch from the front edge of the frame, as shown in illustration B. Bend the cut ends of each brace to shape, as shown in the exploded-view diagram, then fasten the braces to the underside of the frame using ¼ × ½-inch flathead bolts with nuts.

9. Set the window box on the support frame and position it beneath the window. Mark the desired location of the frame, then remove the box and fasten the rear segments of the frame to the wall using 1¼-inch #8 flathead wood screws. Attach the lower ends of the braces to the wall using ¼ × 3-inch lag bolts.

10. Set the box on the support frame, fill it with soil, and you are ready to plant.

PLANTER TRELLIS

This freestanding trellis, from the Rodale Design Group, will fit a patio corner or serve as a partition for a section of yard. Heavy boxes hold the trellis erect and provide containers for its plants. If you fill the boxes with good garden soil and plant some quick-growing, climbing type of plant, soon the trellis will be alive with foliage and you will have created a beautiful little hideaway, a tiny corner of privacy in your backyard.

The framework of the planter trellis is built from construction-grade fir. The bottom panels of the planter boxes are made of

SHOPPING LIST

Lumber
1 pc. 4 × 4 × 6'
2 pcs. 2 × 12 × 8'
1 pc. 2 × 12 × 6'
2 pcs. 2 × 4 × 6'
4 pcs. 2 × 2 × 8'
2 pcs. 1 × 3 × 8'
Lattice
20 pcs. ⅛'' × 1⅛'' × 10'
Plywood
1 pc. ½'' × 3' × 3' CDX grade
Hardware
12 flathead wood screws #10 × 2½''
16 flathead wood screws #10 × 1¼''
3 carriage bolts ⅜'' × 5½''
4 carriage bolts ⅜'' × 3½''
7 hex nuts ⅜''
7 flat washers ⅜''
500 staples ½''
¾ pound finishing nails 8d
1 pint waterproof glue
1 quart exterior-grade enamel or stain

exterior-grade plywood and the seat slats and lattice are made of pine. Three posts, securely bolted to the planter boxes, provide the basic vertical structure of the trellis. Panels of lattice stock are assembled, then fastened in place with wood screws between the posts. When completed, coat the planter trellis with a good, exterior-grade enamel or stain for attractiveness and durability.

CONSTRUCTION

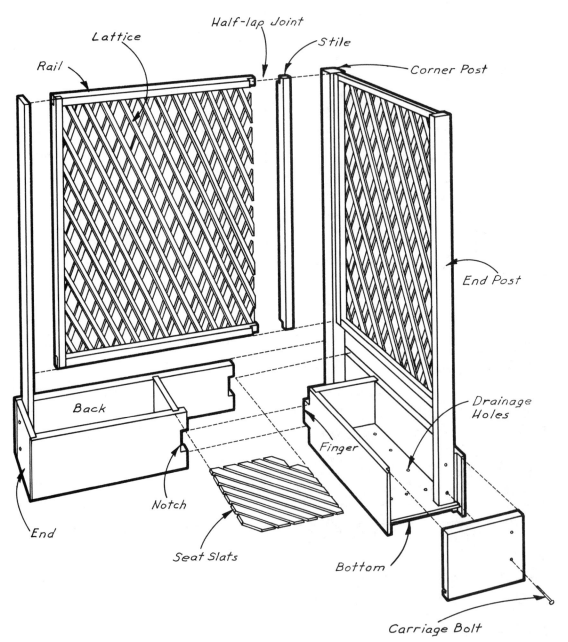

Exploded-View Diagram

1. Cut two pieces of 2×12 ($1\frac{1}{2}'' \times 11\frac{1}{4}''$) stock to $31\frac{1}{2}$ inches each for the front pieces of the planter boxes.
2. Cut two pieces of 2×12 stock to 48 inches each for the back pieces of the planter boxes.
3. Cut four pieces of 2×12 stock to $16\frac{1}{2}$ inches each for the end pieces of the planter boxes.
4. Cut finger lap joints in the front and back pieces, as shown in the exploded-view diagram and in illustrations A and B. Make the fingers $1\frac{1}{2}$ inches in length and the notches of the matching pieces $1\frac{1}{2}$ inches deep. Make both fingers and notches $3\frac{3}{4}$ inches wide and centered on the faces of their respective boards. To ensure a good fit, cut the fingers first, then use them to check the layout of the notches before cutting.
5. Cut $1\frac{1}{2}$-inch-wide rabbets $\frac{3}{4}$ inch deep across what will become the inside face of the front and back piece of each planter box, on the ends opposite those cut for the finger lap joints, as shown in illustration A.
6. Cut a $1\frac{1}{2}$-inch-wide dado $\frac{3}{4}$ inch deep across the inside face of each front and back piece, beginning $28\frac{1}{2}$ inches from the rabbeted ends of the boards, also as shown in illustration A.
7. Cut a $\frac{9}{16}$-inch-wide groove $\frac{11}{16}$ inch deep, starting $\frac{1}{2}$ inch from the bottom edge on the inside faces of all eight planter pieces, to accept the bottom panels. Cut these grooves the full length of the four end pieces, but on each front and back piece cut them only the distance between the rabbets, or the rabbets and the dadoes, as shown in illustration A.
8. Cut two pieces of $\frac{1}{2}$-inch CDX plywood

LUMBER CUTTING LIST

Size	Piece	Quantity
4×4		
$3\frac{1}{2}'' \times 3\frac{1}{2}'' \times 72''$	Corner post	1
2×12		
$1\frac{1}{2}'' \times 11\frac{1}{4}'' \times 48''$	Planter box backs	2
$1\frac{1}{2}'' \times 11\frac{1}{4}'' \times 31\frac{1}{2}''$	Planter box fronts	2
$1\frac{1}{2}'' \times 11\frac{1}{4}'' \times 16\frac{1}{2}''$	Planter box ends	4
2×4		
$1\frac{1}{2}'' \times 3\frac{1}{2}'' \times 71''$	End posts	2
2×2		
$1\frac{1}{2}'' \times 1\frac{1}{2}'' \times 55''$	Lattice panel stiles	4
$1\frac{1}{2}'' \times 1\frac{1}{2}'' \times 40''$	Lattice panel rails	4
1×3		
$\frac{3}{4}'' \times 2\frac{1}{2}'' \times 96''$	Seat slats	2
Lattice		
$\frac{1}{8}'' \times 1\frac{1}{8}'' \times 120''$	Lattice	20
Plywood		
$\frac{1}{2}'' \times 16\frac{1}{4}'' \times 28\frac{1}{4}''$	Planter box bottoms	2

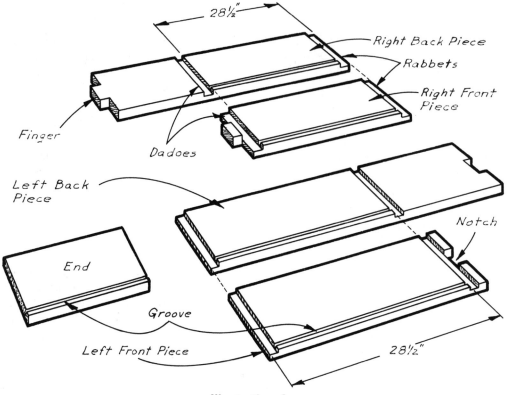

Illustration A

to 16¼ × 28¼ inches each for the bottom panels.

9. Assemble the planter boxes, as shown in the exploded-view diagram. Fasten the pieces together with waterproof glue and 8d finishing nails.

10. Drill 12 holes, each ¼-inch in diameter, in the bottom of each planter box for drainage, as shown in the exploded-view diagram.

11. Use one piece of 4 × 4 (3½″ × 3½″) stock, 72 inches in length, for the corner post.

12. Square and plumb the corner post, and fasten it to the inside back corner of the planter box assembly with three ⅜ × 5½-inch carriage bolts, washers, and nuts, as shown in illustration B. Use a ⁷/₁₆-inch bit to drill the bolt holes. Make sure the bottom of the post is flush with the bottom of the planter.

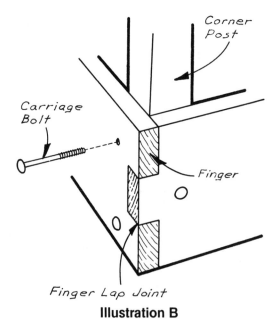

Illustration B

13. Cut two pieces of 2 × 4 (1½″ × 3½″) stock to 71 inches each for the end posts.

14. Position the end posts as shown in the exploded-view diagram. With the bottom of each post flush against the bottom panel of its planter box, square it, plumb it, then fasten it to the box end with two ⅜ × 3½-inch carriage bolts, washers, and nuts.

15. Cut four pieces of 2 × 2 (1½″ × 1½″) stock to 55 inches each for the stiles of the trellis frame.

16. Cut four pieces of 2 × 2 stock to 40 inches each for the rails of the trellis frame.

17. Cut a 1½-inch-wide rabbet ¾ inch deep across both ends of one face of each stile and rail to make half-lap joints.

18. Assemble the stiles and rails into two rectangular frames, each measuring 40 × 55 inches. Secure the frames with waterproof glue and two 1¼-inch #10 flathead wood screws in each joint.

19. Run ⅛ × 1⅛-inch lattice at 60-degree angles across the outside of each rectangular frame to create the configuration shown in the exploded-view diagram. Secure the ends of the lattice to the frames with waterproof glue and ½-inch staples. Then glue and staple each point where the lattice crisscrosses.

20. Position the lattice panels between the corner post and the end posts with the lattice turned to the outside. Fasten them in place with three 2½-inch #10 flathead wood screws inserted through each stile into the post behind it.

21. Cut two 8-foot pieces of 1 × 3 (¾″ × 2½″) stock into rough lengths for the diagonal seat slats, as shown in the exploded-view diagram. Miter one end of each piece to a 45-degree angle. Temporarily tack the short pieces in place on either side of the corner post; then, using those pieces as reference points, space the remaining pieces evenly across the square box area they will cover. Make the mitered end of each piece flush with an outside edge of the square. Then scribe a line for the remaining miter on the underside of the other ends of the pieces, using the outside edges of the box sides as a guide. Remove all pieces and cut the scribed miters. Permanently fasten all seat slats in place with waterproof glue and 8d finishing nails.

22. Finish the planter trellis with two coats of exterior-grade enamel or stain.

WINDOW TRELLIS

This trellis was designed by the Rodale Design Group to create a border around a south-facing window. Covered with a deciduous vine, the trellis will block summer sun but will still allow rays from the winter sun to penetrate the window. At the same time the trellis adds visual texture to an otherwise flat facade, giving character to the exterior of the house. It's a project that's both practical and aesthetic.

The trellis shown here was designed to fit a specific window opening, so some of

SHOPPING LIST

Lumber
2 pcs. $2 \times 4 \times 8'$
4 pcs. $2 \times 2 \times 10'$
2 pcs. $2 \times 2 \times 8'$
7 pcs. $1 \times 2 \times 8'$
Lattice
4 pcs. $\frac{1}{4}'' \times 1\frac{3}{8}'' \times 12'$
3 pcs. $\frac{1}{4}'' \times 1\frac{3}{8}'' \times 8'$
Hardware
4 pcs. steel strip $\frac{1}{8}'' \times 1\frac{1}{4}'' \times 14''$
2 carriage bolts $\frac{3}{8}'' \times 4''$
4 carriage bolts $\frac{1}{4}'' \times 3\frac{1}{2}''$
8 carriage bolts $\frac{1}{4}'' \times 2''$
6 hex nuts $\frac{3}{8}''$
12 hex nuts $\frac{1}{4}''$
6 flat washers $\frac{3}{8}''$
12 flat washers $\frac{1}{4}''$
4 eyescrews $2''$
$\frac{1}{2}$ pound common nails 6d
3-ounce box wire nails #16 $\times \frac{1}{2}''$
2 cubic feet premixed concrete
$\frac{1}{2}$ pint waterproof glue
1 pint exterior-grade enamel

its dimensions will have to be adjusted to fit other applications. In particular, the height of the posts must be correlated with the height of the window opening, and the posts should be set directly in front of the face trim of the window jambs. Since the footings sunk into the ground to support the trellis are shallow, and thus susceptible to frost heaving, a nonrigid attachment is used to tether the sides of the trellis to the window jambs. Ideally, the back posts should be set 3 inches away from the face trim of the window jambs. Any increase in this distance will necessitate adjustments of the eyescrew tethers or the use of longer rails at the top of the trellis sides.

CONSTRUCTION

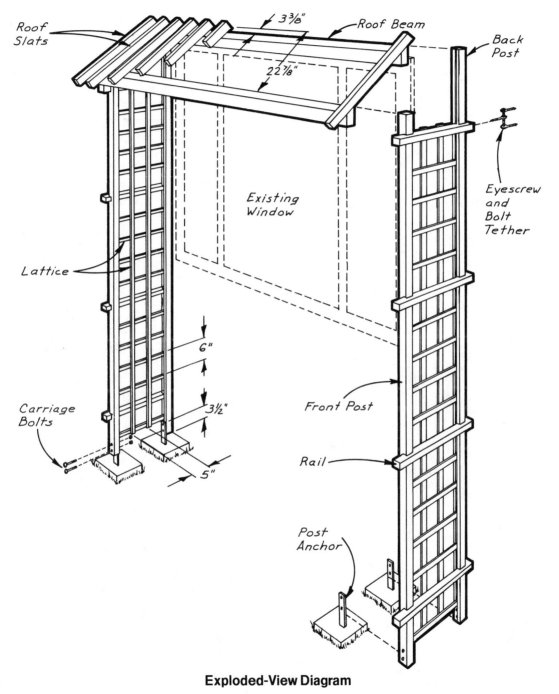

Roof
Slats

3⅜"

Roof Beam

Back
Post

22⅞"

Existing
Window

Eyescrew
and
Bolt
Tether

Lattice

6"

Carriage
Bolts

3½"

Front Post

Rail

5"

Post
Anchor

Exploded-View Diagram

73

1. Cut two pieces of 2 × 2 (1½″ × 1½″) stock to 114 inches each for the back posts, and two pieces to 104½ inches each for the front posts of the trellis. Cut a groove ⁵⁄₁₆ inch wide and ¼ inch deep the full length of one face of each post. Locate the inside edge of each groove at the center of the post to make the grooves off-center, as shown in illustration A.

2. Cut eight pieces of 2 × 2 stock to 21 inches each for rails to connect the posts in pairs on each side of the trellis. Then cut two notches each 1½ inches wide and ¾ inch deep in one face of each rail, beginning the notches 1½ inches from each end of the rails.

3. Cut four pieces of ¼ × 1⅜-inch lattice to 97½ inches each for the vertical slats of the trellis sides. Cut 26 additional pieces of the same lattice stock to 15½ inches each for the horizontal slats that will be fastened across the vertical strips.

4. Assemble the lattice into two identical networks to fit into the sides of the trellis. Space each pair of vertical slats 5 inches apart center-to-center. Measuring from the upper ends of the vertical slats, center the horizontal slats every 6 inches along their length, reserving the 1st, 6th, 11th, and 16th positions for rails, as shown in the exploded-view diagram. Fasten the horizontal slats to the vertical slats using waterproof glue and ½-inch #16 wire nails.

5. To assemble the trellis sides, lay the posts out in pairs on a flat surface with their grooves facing each other and located near the upper face of each post. Place the long post on the left side of one pair and on the right side of the other in order to create a left and right side for the trellis. Place a network of lattice with the vertical slats on the underside between each pair of posts. Fit the tips of the horizontal slats into the grooves in the posts.

6. Adjust the lattice so that the lower end of each network is 3½ inches above the lower ends of the posts that border it. Hold the post-and-lattice assemblies together by fastening the rails to the positions reserved for them on the posts using waterproof glue and 6d common nails. Then turn the trellis sides over and fasten the vertical slats to the rails using more of the same glue and ½-inch #16 wire nails.

7. Cut two pieces of 2 × 4 (1½″ × 3½″) stock to 84¾ inches each for the roof beams. Bevel what will become the upper edge of each beam to a 30-degree angle. Then cut 15 pieces of 1 × 2 (¾″ × 1½″) stock to 30 inches each for the roof slats that will be joined to the beams.

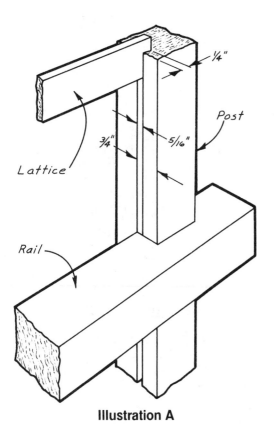

¼″

Post

¾″   ⁵⁄₁₆″

Lattice

Rail

Illustration A

LUMBER CUTTING LIST

Size	Piece	Quantity
2 × 4		
1½″ × 3½″ × 84¾″	Roof beams	2
2 × 2		
1½″ × 1½″ × 114″	Back posts	2
1½″ × 1½″ × 104½″	Front posts	2
1½″ × 1½″ × 21″	Rails	8
1 × 2		
¾″ × 1½″ × 30″	Roof slats	15
¾″ × 1½″ × 16″	Footing form long sides	8
¾″ × 1½″ × 6″	Footing form short sides	8
Lattice		
¼″ × 1⅜″ × 97½″	Vertical slats	4
¼″ × 1⅜″ × 15½″	Horizontal slats	26

8. Measuring from the upper end, draw lines across the underside of each slat at 3⅜ and 22⅞ inches, the two points where the upper tips of the beams will intersect the slats, as shown in the exploded-view diagram. Space the slats 6 inches apart center-to-center on a flat surface. Lay the beams upside down across the backs of the slats with their pointed tips touching the lines. Fasten the left end of each beam to the back of the slat at the left end of the row by first drilling a 1/16-inch pilot hole, then toenailing 6d common nails through the beams into the slat. Move on down the row, fastening beams to slats, checking the spacing of each slat before nailing it.

9. Coat the roof and the two side sections of the trellis with two coats of an exterior-grade paint of your choice. While the paint is drying, begin work on the trellis footings by laying out and digging four holes, each approximately 9 inches in diameter and 12 inches deep. Center each rear hole on the window face trim to which the trellis will be tethered and locate it as close to the house as possible. Space the front holes 16½ inches center-to-center from the rear holes. Make the grade around the four holes level.

10. Cut eight pieces of 1 × 2 stock or scrap lumber to 6 inches each for the short sides of the forms to shape the tops of the footings, and eight more pieces to approximately 16 inches each for the long sides. Fasten two short pieces between two long pieces to create four forms, each with a 6-inch square in the middle and arms extending to either side to hold the form over a hole. If the grade around the holes is not completely level, adjust the height of the forms to make them level with one another.

11. Cut four pieces of ⅛-inch-thick steel strip to 1¼ × 14 inches each for the post anchors. Bend a 2-inch hook in the end of each anchor to help secure it in concrete. Then drill a pair of 5/16-inch-diameter mounting holes through the straight end of each post anchor, centering the first of each pair ¾ inch from the end of the anchor and the second hole 2 inches from the first. Place

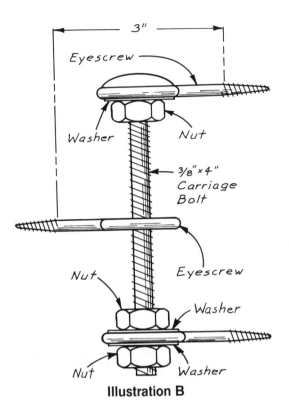

3"

Eyescrew

Washer

Nut

3/8" × 4" Carriage Bolt

Nut

Eyescrew

Washer

Nut

Washer

Illustration B

one anchor on the back side of each post so the upper tip of the anchor is aligned with the bottom edge of the lattice, and mark the posts for drilling holes to match those in the anchors.

12. Fill the holes with concrete and level it off flush with the top of each form. While the concrete is setting up, insert the hooked ends of the anchors in the holes. Make sure the anchors are plumb, square, level with

one another, and properly spaced from the house and each other. Remove the concrete forms a day later.

13. Mark the point in the center of each side section of window trim that is 97½ inches above the level of the upper mounting holes in the post anchors. Insert a 2-inch eyescrew approximately 1⅝ inches above this point on each side of the window, and another an equal distance below this point. Center another eyescrew in the back end of the top rail on each trellis side.

14. Fasten the sides of the trellis to the anchors in the footings using ¼ × 2-inch carriage bolts with nuts and washers, as shown in the exploded-view diagram. Then move the upper end of each trellis side into the position where the eyescrew attached to it is between the pair of eyescrews in the window trim behind it. Adjust the eyescrews in and out, as necessary. Then insert a ⅜ × 4-inch carriage bolt through each set of eyescrews to tether the trellis sides to the window trim. Use three ⅜-inch flat washers and three nuts to hold each bolt in place, as shown in illustration B.

15. Center the trellis roof across the top of the sides so the insides of the roof beams are flush against the outside faces of the posts, as shown in the exploded-view diagram. Drill a ¼-inch-diameter hole through each intersection of post and beam and fasten them together using ¼ × 3½-inch carriage bolts, nuts, and washers, as shown in the same diagram.

GATEWAY ARBOR

SHOPPING LIST

Lumber
4 pcs. $4 \times 4 \times 10'$ pressure-treated
11 pcs. $2 \times 4 \times 8'$ pressure-treated
Hardware
8 carriage bolts $\frac{5}{16}'' \times 4\frac{1}{2}''$
8 hex nuts $\frac{5}{16}''$
8 flat washers $\frac{5}{16}''$
¾ pound galvanized common nails 12d
1 quart exterior-grade stain

This sturdy and attractive arbor was designed by the Rodale Design Group to serve as an entrance to a garden. Its clean, rectangular shape frames the opening and invites people to walk through. The seats on either side of the arbor provide places to sit, relax, and enjoy the outdoor setting.

The trellis top of this arbor is ideal for climbing vines—grapes, roses, or honeysuckle, for example. When covered over with foliage, the arbor will provide a cool, refreshing haven in the midst of summer heat.

We have constructed our gateway arbor from pressure-treated pine to ensure its durability. The nails used to fasten the trellis cross members and seat slats to their supports are galvanized to resist rust. A good-quality stain should be used on the wood structure to give it a desired color and enhance its weatherability. With its sturdy 4×4 posts set deeply into the ground, this gateway arbor should endure and bring its owners satisfaction for many years.

CONSTRUCTION

1. Use four pieces of pressure-treated 4×4 ($3\frac{1}{2}'' \times 3\frac{1}{2}''$) stock, each 120 inches in length, for the posts.
2. Notch one face of each post to receive the top and seat supports, as shown in illustration A. Locate the notch for the top support at one end of the post. Begin the notch for the seat support 49 inches from the other end of the post. Make all notches 1 inch deep and $3\frac{1}{2} \times 3\frac{1}{2}$ inches wide.
3. Cut four pieces of pressure-treated 2×4 ($1\frac{1}{2}'' \times 3\frac{1}{2}''$) stock to $15\frac{3}{4}$ inches each for the seat supports.
4. Cut two pieces of pressure-treated 2×4 stock to 72 inches each for the top supports.
5. Cut 17 pieces of pressure-treated 2×4

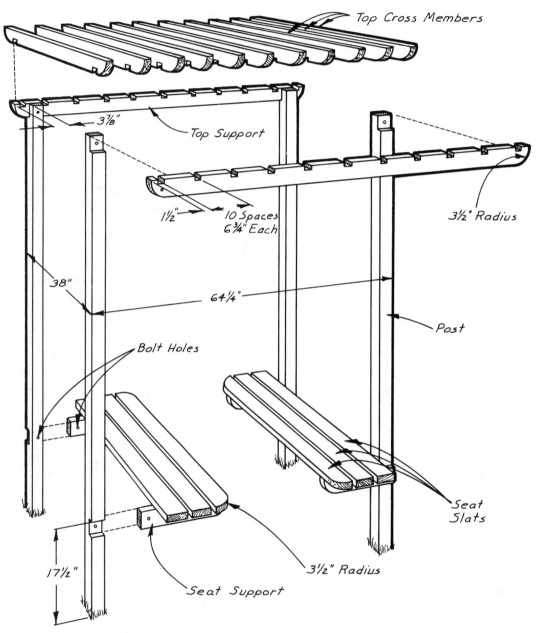

Top Cross Members

3⁷⁄₈"

Top Support

1½"

10 Spaces
6¾" Each

3½" Radius

38"

64¼"

Post

Bolt Holes

Seat
Slats

17½"

3½" Radius

Seat Support

Exploded-View Diagram

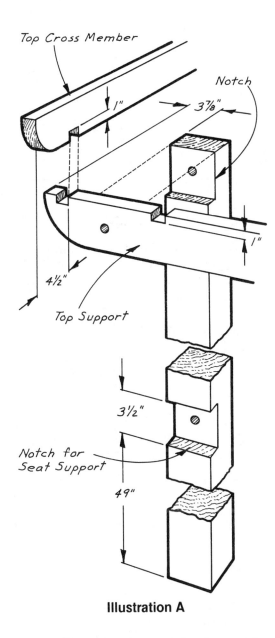

Top Cross Member

Notch

1"

3⅞"

4½"

Top Support

3½"

Notch for
Seat Support

49"

1"

Illustration A

two of the seat slats, as shown in the exploded-view diagram. Note the quarter-round pattern of these radii.

7. Cut a 3½-inch radius at one end of each seat support.

8. Cut 11 notches in each top support, on the edge opposite the one radiused, to accept the top cross members, as shown in the exploded-view diagram and illustration A. Make each notch 1 inch deep and 1½ × 1½ inches wide. Begin the first notch 1½ inches in from one end of each support. Space the notches 6¾ inches apart on center.

9. Cut a 1 × 1½-inch notch across the radiused edge of each top cross member, 4½ inches from each end, as shown in illustration A.

10. Fit the top supports in position on the posts, with each end extending outside the posts 3⅞ inches, as shown in the exploded-view diagram. Drill an ¹¹⁄₃₂-inch-diameter hole through the center of each joint formed by a post and support.

11. Fit the seat supports to the posts, as shown in the exploded-view diagram. Where post and seat support join, drill an ¹¹⁄₃₂-inch-diameter hole through the center.

12. Lay out the rectangular arrangement for the postholes. Space the holes 60¾ inches apart on center for the length and 34½ inches apart on center for the width of the rectangle. Dig each hole to a depth of 36 inches and make it wide enough to allow for squaring the posts and making them plumb.

13. Stand the posts in the holes and bolt the top supports to them. Use ⁵⁄₁₆ × 4½-inch carriage bolts, flat washers, and nuts.

14. Install a cross member at each end of the top supports to adjust the spacing of the posts. Plumb and brace the posts, then backfill and tamp the postholes.

stock to 48 inches each for the seat slats and top cross members.

6. Cut a 3½-inch radius on both ends of all top supports, top cross members, and on

79

LUMBER CUTTING LIST

Size	Piece	Quantity
4 × 4		
3½″ × 3½″ × 120″	Posts	4
2 × 4		
1½″ × 3½″ × 72″	Top supports	2
1½″ × 3½″ × 48″	Top cross members	11
1½″ × 3½″ × 48″	Seat slats	6
1½″ × 3½″ × 15¾″	Seat supports	4

15. Arrange the remaining top cross members in position on the top supports. Fasten all cross members to the supports with 12d galvanized common nails.

16. Fasten the seat supports in place with $\frac{5}{16}$ × 4½-inch carriage bolts, flat washers, and nuts.

17. Center the seat slats on the seat supports and space them evenly, as shown in the exploded-view diagram. Attach the seat slats to the supports with 12d galvanized common nails.

18. Finish the trellis with two coats of exterior-grade stain.

SUN TRELLIS

This is a sturdy trellis designed as much to provide shade as growing space. Although the posts can be sunk into the ground and the trellis located in a yard or garden setting, the intention of the project's developers — the Rodale Design Group — was that it be installed on a sun deck or open porch.

The major portion of the sun trellis is its roof. Carpenters will recognize it as a standard hip variety. Construction of the trellis roof is simple, but accuracy in laying out and cutting the pieces is important. We've included building specifications that are exact in theory. Drawn plans and actual work often differ, though, due to the accumulation of tiny construction faults caused by rough-surfaced wood, and minor measuring, sawing, and joining errors. Whenever possible, use the actual structure as a gauge for cutting rafters to size and shape, rather than relying exclusively on the dimensions presented in the instructions or cutting list. The amount of materials suggested for purchase in the shopping list, however, should be sufficient if forethought is used

SHOPPING LIST

Lumber
2 pcs. 4 × 4 × 16'
8 pcs. 4 × 4 × 10'
3 pcs. 4 × 4 × 8'
10 pcs. 2 × 4 × 10'
19 pcs. 2 × 4 × 8'
4 pcs. 1 × 6 × 12'
13 pcs. 1 × 6 × 10'
23 pcs. 1 × 6 × 8'
4 pcs. 1 × 3 × 12'
2 pcs. 1 × 3 × 8'
Hardware
14 steel mending angle brackets
    2'' × 2'' × 3'' (approx.)
2 steel mending plates ³⁄₁₆'' × 2'' × 6''
    (approx.)
56 lag bolts ¼'' × 3''
6 pounds galvanized common nails 12d
10 pounds galvanized common nails 8d
exterior-grade enamel or 2 gallons copper
    naphthenate wood preservative

in cutting individual items from large pieces of stock.

The trellis shown here is made of cedar, an attractive and durable wood (but prone to splitting), which is usually more expensive than other construction-grade stock. Pressure-treated pine is a viable alternative, especially for posts that are to be located in the ground. Cedar may be finished clear. Other lumber usually looks better painted or stained.

CONSTRUCTION

1. Cut six pieces of 4 × 4 (3½'' × 3½'') stock to 84 inches each for the trellis posts. Round-over their edges on all sides.

2. Position four of the posts to form the corners of a rectangle measuring 120 × 192 inches, as shown in the exploded-view diagram. Locate the remaining posts at the midpoint of each long side, also as shown. Toenail the posts to the deck using 12d galvanized common nails. (Use 12d galvanized common nails throughout the project, unless otherwise specified.)

3. Cut two pieces of 4 × 4 stock to 192 inches each for the side beams, and two pieces to 116 inches each for the end beams. Cut a 3½ × 3½-inch rabbet 1½ inches deep at each end of the two longer beams on what will become the inside face of each.

4. Mount the four beams on top of the six posts, fitting the end beams between the rabbeted ends of the side beams. Fasten the beams to each other and toenail them to the posts. Use only enough nails to tie the structure together until it can be plumbed and braced.

5. Cut 12 pieces of 4 × 4 stock to 30 inches each for braces between the posts and beams. Cut both ends of each brace to a 45-degree angle, as shown in the exploded-view diagram.

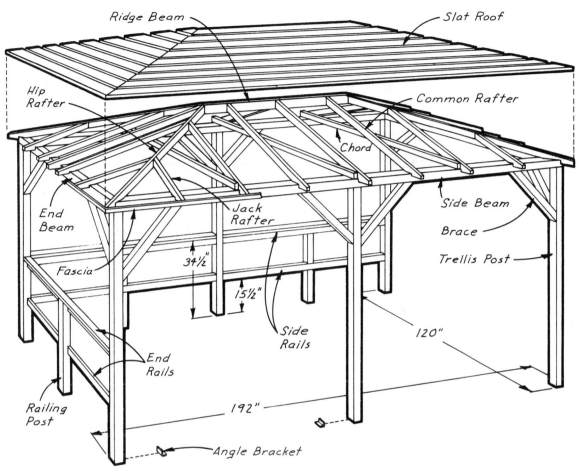

Ridge Beam · Slat Roof

Hip Rafter · Common Rafter

Chord

End Beam · Jack Rafter · Side Beam · Brace · Trellis Post

Fascia · 34½" · 15½" · Side Rails · 120"

Railing Post · End Rails · 192" · Angle Bracket

Exploded-View Diagram

6. Plumb the posts and nail two braces between each post and the beam or beams above it.

7. Fasten one steel mending angle bracket (approximately $2 \times 2 \times 3$ inches) to the deck or porch and to the inside face of the bottom of each post using $\frac{1}{4} \times 3$-inch lag bolts. Fasten two additional brackets at the upper end of each corner post, one at each intersection between the post and the beams above it. Attach the brackets to the posts and beams with $\frac{1}{4} \times 3$-inch lag bolts, as shown in illustration A.

8. Reinforce the union between the middle post on each side of the trellis and the beam above it by attaching a steel mending plate (approximately $\frac{3}{16} \times 2 \times 6$ inches) on the inside face of each using $\frac{1}{4} \times 3$-inch lag bolts.

9. Lay out the positions of the rafters on the upper surface of the four beams. Begin at one end of each beam and mark points at 23¼ inches, then every 24 inches thereafter. Make an X immediately past each mark to identify the locations for the rafters.

10. Cut three pieces of 2×4 ($1\frac{1}{2}'' \times 3\frac{1}{2}''$) stock to 120 inches each for chords to

83

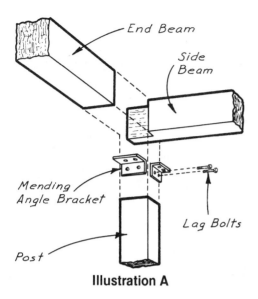

Illustration A

connect the two sides of the trellis structure. Sight down the edges of each piece to determine if there is a convex bend (called a crown) in the piece. If so, mark this edge as the upper surface and round-over the sharp edges of the underside. If desired, stop the rounding-over of the edges 3½ inches from the ends of each chord where the boards will rest on beams.

11. Lay the chords across the side beams of the trellis in the locations shown in the exploded-view diagram. Make sure the ends of each chord are flush with the outside faces of the beams beneath, and then toe-nail each chord to the beam.

12. Cut eight pieces of 2×4 stock to 66 inches each for the common rafters. On one, mark and cut the ends and bird's-mouth, as shown in illustration B. Use this rafter as a template to mark and cut the remaining seven common rafters. (The ⅞-inch plumb cut for the notch may be made in several rafters at once by holding them together with clamps.) After the rafters are all cut, round-over the edges on the underside of each, except at the notched area. Tip: After marking the plumb cut at the end of the first rafter, make a template of it with a T-bevel so that the angle may be easily reproduced on all the rafters—common, jack, and hip (see steps 16, 17, and 18).

13. Cut one piece of 2×4 stock to 73½ inches for the ridge beam. Mark the midpoint along the length of the ridge beam and nail the upper end of one common rafter to a side of the beam at that point. Make sure the top of the rafter is flush with the top of the beam.

14. With a helper, raise the ridge beam into position and nail the lower end of the attached rafter to the top of the side beam it rests against. The end of the rafter should fall over the X at the center of the beam (see step 9). Fasten a second rafter on the opposite face of the ridge beam from the first, and nail it to the upper edge of the beam on that side, also over the center X previously marked.

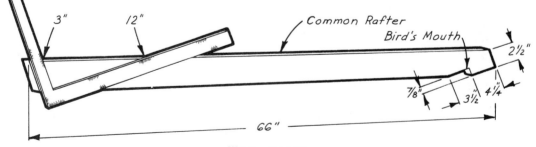

Illustration B

15. Fasten the lower end of one common rafter to the upper edge of one of the end beams, over the X marked at the center of the beam (see step 9). Fasten the upper end of the rafter to the end of the ridge beam nearest it. Do the same with a second common rafter at the other end of the ridge beam. Install the remaining four common rafters over the Xs marked on the side beams, joining them to the ridge beam on parallel 24-inch centers.

16. Lay out and cut four pieces of 2 × 4 stock to 96 inches each for the hip rafters. At one end of each, scribe the plumb-cut angle, as shown in illustration C, by using the T-bevel preset to this angle (see step 12). Set the blade of a circular saw to 45 degrees, then cut along the line to produce the compound angle also shown. Make sure you cut the angle on identical faces of two of the rafters and that you cut the faces opposite those when making the angles on the other two.

17. Position the cut end of one hip rafter against the face of the ridge beam, at one of the points shown in the exploded-view diagram. Position the lower end of the rafter directly over the corner formed where the nearest side and end beams meet. Mark the length of the overlap on the underside of the rafter and use the points to determine the dimensions of the bird's-mouth you must now

make, as shown in illustration C. To complete the notch layout, use the T-bevel to extend plumb-cut lines across one face of the rafter, then join the lines by scribing between them using a carpenter's square (held perpendicular to the lines, not the edge of the rafter), as also shown. Mark the V-shaped angle cut at the point of the notch, if desired; however, cutting the notch so precisely is not necessary.

18. Cut the bird's-mouth on the hip rafter, then cut identical notches in the other three, using the first as a template. Let the lower ends of all four rafters remain longer than necessary, for trimming later (see step 21).

19. Cut eight pieces of 2 × 4 stock to 29¼ inches each for the #1 jack rafters. Cut the lower end of each according to the dimensions shown in illustration B. Then cut the upper ends as you did the upper ends of the hip rafters; four of them beveled so.

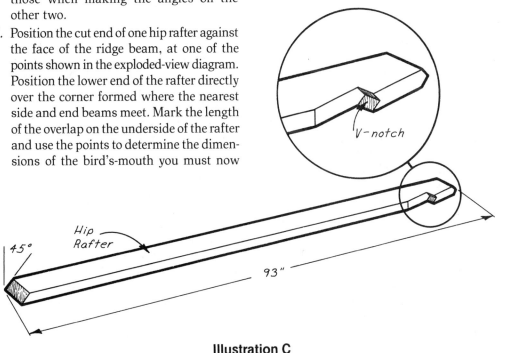

Illustration C

LUMBER CUTTING LIST

Size	Piece	Quantity
4 × 4		
3½″ × 3½″ × 192″	Side beams	2
3½″ × 3½″ × 116″	End beams	2
3½″ × 3½″ × 84″	Trellis posts	6
3½″ × 3½″ × 34½″	Railing posts	3
3½″ × 3½″ × 30″	Braces	12
2 × 4		
1½″ × 3½″ × 120″	Chords	3
1½″ × 3½″ × 113″	End railings	3
1½″ × 3½″ × 96″	Hip rafters	4
1½″ × 3½″ × 90¾″	Side railings	6
1½″ × 3½″ × 73½″	Ridge beam	1
1½″ × 3½″ × 66″	Common rafters	8
1½″ × 3½″ × 53¼″	#2 jack rafters	8
1½″ × 3½″ × 29¼″	#1 jack rafters	8
1 × 6		
¾″ × 5½″ × 144″	Roof slats	4
¾″ × 5½″ × 120″	Roof slats	13
¾″ × 5½″ × 96″	Roof slats	23
1 × 3		
¾″ × 2½″ × 144″	Fascia	4
¾″ × 2½″ × 96″	Fascia	2

they will lie in one direction, the other four beveled to lie in the direction opposite. Fasten the eight short jack rafters in place, as shown in the exploded-view diagram.

20. Cut eight pieces of 2 × 4 stock to 53¼ inches each for the #2 jack rafters. Cut the ends, bevels, and notches on these rafters the same as in the previous step. Fasten the rafters in the marked positions remaining on the side and end beams.

21. Mark and cut the end of each hip rafter in line with the ends of the jack rafters on both sides. This will produce a V-shape on the lower end of each hip rafter. Trim the undersides of these rafter ends horizontally so that they parallel the undersides of the other rafters.

22. Cut the fascia, which is applied around the perimeter of the trellis roof, from four 12-foot lengths of 1 × 3 (¾″ × 2½″) stock and two additional 8-foot lengths. If the rafters have been cut precisely, the length of the fascia along each side of the trellis should measure 202 inches, and the length across each end should measure 130 inches. When piecing boards together, remember to cut them so that they will meet over a rafter end. Miter both ends of each run of fascia boards to a 45-degree angle extending ¾ inch beyond the corner of the hip rafter

to which the fascia is attached. Nail the fascia to the ends of the rafters, as shown in the exploded-view diagram, using 8d galvanized common nails.

23. Cover the rafters on one side of the trellis roof with 1×6 ($\frac{3}{4}'' \times 5\frac{1}{2}''$) slats, as shown in the exploded-view diagram. The first course should overhang the fascia $1\frac{1}{2}$ inches. Fasten the slats to the jack and common rafters with 8d galvanized common nails. Allow the ends of the slats to extend past the middle of the hip rafters and remain unnailed for trimming.

24. Continue to apply slats along one side of the trellis roof, leaving a 2-inch gap between each course. When the side of the roof has been completely covered, snap a chalk line across the slats at both ends where they cross the middle of the hip rafters beneath them. Set the blade of a circular saw to the thickness of the slats, adjust the blade angle to obtain a plumb cut, then trim the waste from the slats along the chalked lines. Finish the nailing by fastening the ends of the slats to the rafters.

25. Nail slats across the ends of the roof next. Begin each course by cutting the end of a slat to fit against one of those attached to the side of the roof in the previous step. As before, let the untrimmed ends extend beyond the hip rafter beneath it. When both ends of the roof are covered, trim the slats off even with the centers of the hip rafters using the saw adjusted to the same settings as in the previous step.

26. Finish the roof by attaching slats to the remaining side. This time you will have to precut the ends of each slat before nailing them in place.

27. Cut three pieces of 4×4 stock to $34\frac{1}{2}$ inches each for the railing posts, as shown in the exploded-view diagram. Cut a $3\frac{1}{2}$-inch-wide dado $1\frac{1}{2}$ inches deep across one face of each post, $15\frac{1}{2}$ inches from one end, to accept the lower horizontal railing. At the other end, across the same face, cut a similar-size rabbet to accept the upper horizontal railing.

28. Center one post between two of the trellis's end posts. Position the other two posts on each side of one of the trellis's middle posts, as shown in the exploded-view diagram. Locate the dadoed faces of the posts toward the inside of the trellis and toenail them to the deck or porch.

29. Cut six pieces of 2×4 stock to $90\frac{3}{4}$ inches each for the side railings. Fit the sections together—upper as well as lower—by joining the boards of each course together end to end, where they meet at the rabbets and dadoes cut in the posts. Make sure the railings are level and their inside faces flush with the insides of the posts; then nail them in place.

30. Lay the remaining sections of railing face-down along the edge of the upper rail installed in the preceding step. Align the inside edges flush, so the two railings form a right angle, then nail them together and to the posts.

31. Cut three pieces of 2×4 stock to 113 inches each for the end railings. Install these just as you did in the preceding two steps.

32. Finish the entire trellis with exterior-grade enamel or copper naphthenate wood preservative or, if cedar was used, apply a clear finish.

DECORATIVE BLOCK MOLD

SHOPPING LIST

Lumber
1 pc. 2 × 3 × 5′
1 pc. 1 × 1 × 12′
Plywood
1 pc. ¾″ × 3′ × 4′ A-C grade
Hardware
14 flathead wood screws #6 × 1½″
4 loose pin hinges 4″ with fasteners
¼ pound finishing nails 4d
¼ pound underlayment nails 1½″
1 60-pound bag (½ cubic foot) "sand mix"
    premixed cement
½ pint waterproof glue
1 pint polyurethane

Here is a wooden mold, developed by the Rodale Design Group, for making decorative cement blocks. The blocks can be used for constructing many different projects, including the three beginning on p. 92.

After the mold has been constructed, it is simple to make a block: Mix up a 60-pound bag of "sand mix" premixed cement, pour the cement into the mold, and smooth the surface level with the top of the mold frame. The mix should be wet enough to flow freely. After 24 hours, remove one of the pins in the mold frame hinges and remove the frame. A day later, remove the mold plate itself. (You may need to give it a few taps with a hammer to loosen it.) Let the block cure for three or four more days before using.

The mold shown produces 6-inch-thick blocks that measure 14 inches high and 18 inches wide. Consider building two or more at a time. Larger or smaller blocks can be created by altering the dimensions of the mold walls and exterior frame.

CONSTRUCTION

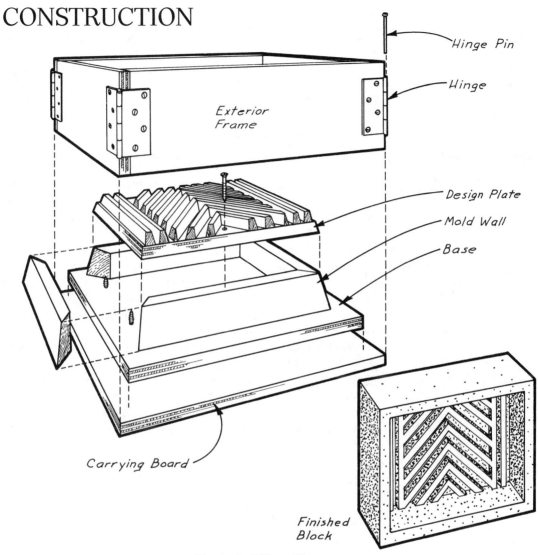

Hinge Pin

Hinge

Exterior Frame

Design Plate

Mold Wall

Base

Carrying Board

Finished Block

Exploded-View Diagram

1. For the mold wall, cut one piece of 2×3 ($1\frac{1}{2}'' \times 2\frac{1}{2}''$) stock to 60 inches. Turn the piece on edge and rip it at a 15-degree angle so that the widest edge becomes $1\frac{3}{8}$ inches in width. Then cut the piece into four sections: two each $15\frac{1}{2}$ inches long, and two each $11\frac{1}{2}$ inches long. Miter the

sections as you cut them so they will fit together in a rectangle, with their outside faces sloping, as shown in illustration A. Fasten the sections together using waterproof glue and 4d finishing nails.

2. Cut one piece of ¾-inch A-C plywood to 14×18 inches for the mold base. Center

89

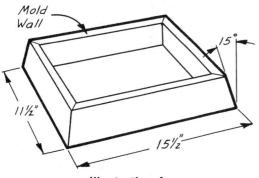

Mold Wall

11½"

15°

15½"

Illustration A

the mold wall assembly over the base and fasten the two together using waterproof glue and two 1½-inch #6 flathead wood screws per wall section. Install the screws from the underside of the base, as shown in the exploded-view diagram.

3. Cut one piece of ¾-inch plywood to 16 × 20 inches for the carrying board. Center the mold base on the carrying board and fasten it to the base using waterproof glue and 1½-inch underlayment nails.

4. Cut one piece of ¾-inch plywood (approximately 10³⁄₁₆ × 14³⁄₁₆ inches) to fit across the top of the mold wall. This is the design

plate. Bevel its upper edges to 15 degrees so it matches the outside slope of the wall.

5. With a ruler and pencil lay out the design of the block on the top surface of the design plate. Use illustration B for reference. Each wooden strip is ¾ inch wide and is spaced ⅜ inch from adjacent strips. Begin by marking the locations of the vertical strips ⅜ inch from each side edge of the plate. Then draw a line down the center of the plate to mark the point where the herringbone strips join at right angles. Lay out the top herringbone assembly first and the remaining ones in relation to it.

6. When the layout of the block design is complete, cut strips of 1 × 1 (¾″ × ¾″) stock, using knot-free pine or other wood to fit the layout. Bevel the sides and ends of all pieces to a 15-degree angle, as shown in illustration B.

7. Attach the strips to the design plate using waterproof glue and 4d finishing nails, then align the design plate on top of the mold wall. Drill pilot holes between the vertical strips, as shown in illustration B, through the plate and into the upper edge of the

LUMBER CUTTING LIST

Size	Piece	Quantity
2 × 3		
1⅜″ × 2½″ × 15½″	Mold walls	2
1⅜″ × 2½″ × 11½″	Mold walls	2
1 × 1		
¾″ × ¾″ × 144″	Strip material	1
Plywood		
¾″ × 16″ × 20″	Carrying board	1
¾″ × 14″ × 18″	Mold base	1
¾″ × 10³⁄₁₆″ × 14³⁄₁₆″	Design plate	1
¾″ × 6¾″ × 18¾″	Exterior frame	2
¾″ × 6¾″ × 14¾″	Exterior frame	2

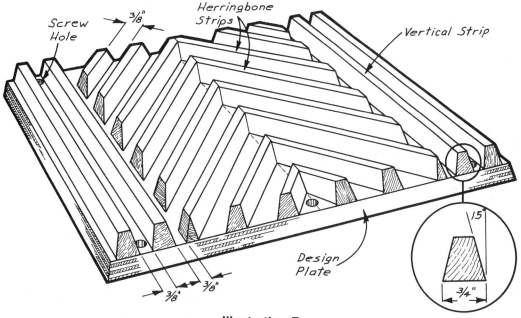

Herringbone Strips

Screw Hole

⅜"

Vertical Strip

Design Plate

15°

¾"

⅜"   ⅜"

Illustration B

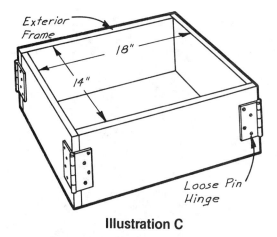

Exterior Frame

18"

14"

Loose Pin Hinge

Illustration C

mold wall. Fasten the plate to the mold wall using 1½-inch #6 flathead wood screws.

8. Cut two pieces of ¾-inch plywood to 6¾ × 18¾ inches each and two pieces to 6¾ × 14¾ inches each for the exterior frame of the mold. Fasten these pieces together with their ends lapped pinwheel-fashion, as shown in illustration C, using four 4-inch loose pin hinges. The interior dimensions of the frame should measure 14 × 18 inches.

9. Using wood putty, fill all nail and screw holes, cracks, and imperfections on any surface that will come in contact with cement when the mold is filled. Sand the entire mold and apply three layers of polyurethane to seal the wood.

10. Fit the exterior frame around the mold base, and the mold is ready to use. Coat the inside surfaces of the mold and frame with motor oil before pouring the cement. Be sure to clean and reoil the mold before each use.

WOOD AND CEMENT BLOCK PLANTER

SHOPPING LIST

Lumber
3 pcs. $1 \times 3 \times 8'$
2 pcs. $1 \times 2 \times 10'$
Plywood
1 pc. ½'' $\times 4' \times 4'$ A–C grade
Hardware
4 lag bolts 5⁄16'' $\times 2''$ with flat washers
4 lead shields 5⁄16'' $\times 1¼''$
1 box finishing nails 6d
¼ pound underlayment nails 1¼''
waterproof glue
exterior-grade enamel or stain

The Rodale Design Group created this sturdy and attractive planter to incorporate the decorative cement blocks described on p. 88. The plywood box for holding plants is 3 feet long and is decorated on each side with chamfered strips of No. 2 pine, which reflect the design of the blocks at each end.

The planter can be used either indoors or out. For indoor use, we recommend omitting the drainage holes and lining the interior of the box with plastic sheeting.

CONSTRUCTION

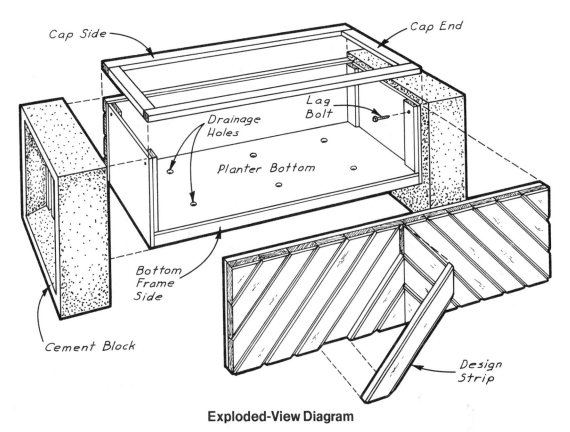

Exploded-View Diagram

1. Using the mold described on p. 88, make two decorative cement blocks, each measuring 6 inches thick, 14 inches high, and 18 inches wide. While the blocks cure, proceed with the following steps.

2. Cut two pieces of 1 × 2 (¾″ × 1½″) stock to 35 inches each for the sides of the bottom frame, and two pieces to 14 inches each for the ends. Fasten the bottom frame together with the side pieces lapped over the ends, as shown in illustration A, using waterproof glue and 1¼-inch underlayment nails. (Use waterproof glue and 1¼-inch underlayment nails throughout the project, unless otherwise specified.)

3. Cut one piece of ½-inch A-C plywood to 15½ × 35 inches for the planter box bottom. Fasten the plywood to the top of the bottom frame using glue and nails.

4. Cut two pieces of ½-inch plywood to 11¼ × 36 inches each for the box sides. Cut two additional pieces to 11¼ × 15½ inches each for the box ends. Fasten the box ends to the ends of the bottom frame so that all but the upper edges of each are aligned flush. Then fasten the box sides to the bottom frame, as shown in illustration B.

5. Cut four pieces of 1 × 2 stock to 9¼ inches each for the corner braces. Place the braces in the corners of the planter box, positioned

93

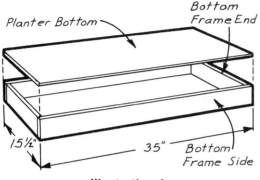

Planter Bottom

Bottom Frame End

15½"

35"

Bottom Frame Side

Illustration A

so that their wide faces are against the box ends. Fasten the braces in place by nailing them first to the box ends, then nailing into them again through the sides.

6. Chamfer the long edges on one face of 24 feet of 1×3 ($\frac{3}{4}'' \times 2\frac{1}{2}''$) stock to make the diagonal design strips for both sides of the planter box. (For a uniform edge, use a router equipped with a $\frac{3}{16}$-inch chamfering bit.) Miter two pairs of strips, fit them together along the centerline of one box side, then cut them to length, as shown in

the exploded-view diagram. Attach the strips to the box using glue and nails, then cut the remaining strips to size, using the exploded-view diagram as a reference. Chamfer the lower ends of the strips where they lie flush with the bottom of the box. (Be careful not to tear the wood when routing it across the grain.) After completing one side of the box, repeat the process on the opposite side.

7. Cut two pieces of 1×2 stock to 36 inches each for the sides of the cap, and two pieces to 15 inches each for the ends of the cap. Chamfer the bottom outside edges and corners of the two side pieces. Position the side pieces so they overlap the ends and align their outside edges flush with the strips on each side of the box. Then fasten the cap to the top of the planter box using glue and 6d finishing nails.

8. Drill 20 randomly spaced ¼-inch-diameter drainage holes through the bottom panel of the box.

9. Using wood putty, fill nail holes and other voids on the parts of the box that will be

LUMBER CUTTING LIST

Size	Piece	Quantity
1 × 3		
¾'' × 2½'' × 96''	Design strips	3
1 × 2		
¾'' × 1½'' × 36''	Cap sides	2
¾'' × 1½'' × 35''	Bottom frame sides	2
¾'' × 1½'' × 15''	Cap ends	2
¾'' × 1½'' × 14''	Bottom frame ends	2
¾'' × 1½'' × 9¼''	Corner braces	4
Plywood		
½'' × 15½'' × 35''	Box bottom	1
½'' × 11¼'' × 36''	Box sides	2
½'' × 11¼'' × 15½''	Box ends	2

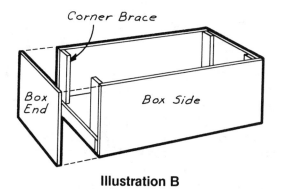

Illustration B

visible when in use. Sand the box and then apply exterior-grade enamel or stain, as desired.

10. Center and drill a $5/16$-inch-diameter hole through each corner brace $1\frac{1}{2}$ inches below the upper edge of the box. After the cement blocks have cured, position and support the box between the blocks so that all upper and side edges are flush. Transfer the locations of the holes in the braces onto the blocks, then drill $\frac{1}{2}$-inch-diameter holes into the blocks and insert $5/16 \times 1\frac{1}{4}$-inch lead shields. Use a hammer to tap the shields into the holes.

11. Attach the planter box to the blocks using $5/16 \times 2$-inch lag bolts with flat washers. Pour a shallow layer of gravel in the bottom of the box, fill with potting soil, and the box is ready to use.

WOOD AND CEMENT BLOCK PATIO BENCH

SHOPPING LIST

Lumber
4 pcs. 2 × 4 × 8'
1 pc. 1 × 8 × 4'
Hardware
32 flathead wood screws #8 × 2''
4 hex head lag bolts 5/16'' × 2'' with washers
4 lead shields 5/16'' × 1¼''
waterproof glue
1 pint exterior-grade enamel, stain,
    or other finish

This patio bench, designed by the Rodale Design Group, makes use of the decorative cement blocks described on p. 88. We chose construction-grade No. 2 pine for the seat, although for added elegance you may wish to select oak, maple, or mahogany.

The bench shown is 4 feet long. You may vary the length as you wish, provided you do not exceed 6 feet between centers without adding a third block for additional support.

CONSTRUCTION

1. Using the mold described on p. 88, make two decorative cement blocks. While the blocks cure, proceed with the following steps.
2. Cut two pieces of 1 × 8 (¾'' × 7¼'') stock to 18 inches each. Then rip the pieces to 6 inches in width for the seat base.
3. Cut eight pieces of 2 × 4 (1½'' × 3½'') stock to 47¾ inches each for the seat members.
4. Cut a 6-inch-wide rabbet ¾ inch deep across the undersides of the seat members at each end, as shown in illustration A, to accept the seat base pieces. Then cut a ⅜-inch radius on all four upper edges of each seat member, also as shown.

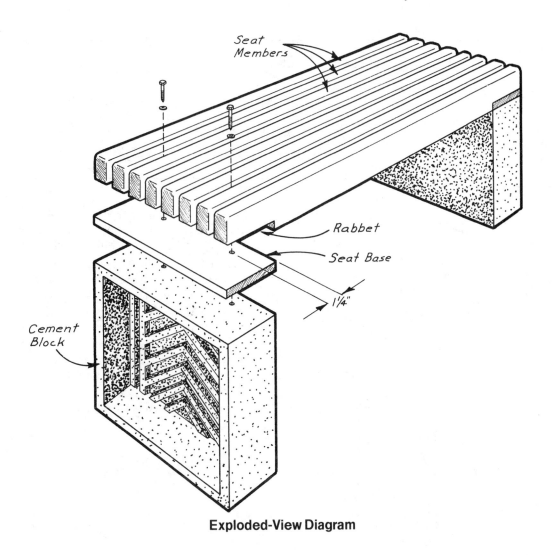

Exploded-View Diagram

5. Fit the seat bases into the rabbeted under-sides of two of the seat members. Align the ends of the bases flush with the outside edges of the seat members. Drill ⅛-inch pilot holes through the bases into the under-sides of the seat members, spacing each pair of holes 4 inches apart. Fasten the bases to the seat members using water-proof glue and 2-inch #8 flathead wood screws.

6. Position the remaining seat members evenly between the two already installed. Drill pilot holes through the bases into these seat members and fasten them in place using the same procedure described in the preceding step.

7. Drill a pair of 5/16-inch-diameter holes through each seat base for mounting the seat to the cement blocks. Center the holes 1¼ inches from the inside edges of the bases and between the second and third seat members (counting from each side),

LUMBER CUTTING LIST

Size	Piece	Quantity
2 × 4		
1½'' × 3½'' × 47¾''	Seat members	8
1 × 8		
¾'' × 6'' × 18''	Seat base	2

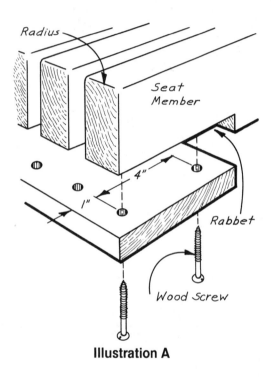

Illustration A

as shown in the exploded-view diagram.

8. Sand the seat and apply exterior-grade enamel, stain, or other finish, as desired.

9. When the blocks have cured, place the seat across their tops so the ends of the seat are aligned flush with the outside edges of the blocks. Mark the positions of the four $5/16$-inch-diameter holes onto the blocks, then remove the seat, and drill ½-inch-diameter holes into the blocks at the places marked. Using a hammer, tap lead shields into the holes, then fasten the seat in place using $5/16 × 2$-inch hex head lag bolts with washers.

CEMENT BLOCK CHARCOAL GRILL

SHOPPING LIST

Hardware
16 pcs. steel rod 5/16'' diameter × 17⅞''
4 pcs. steel angle 1¼'' × 1¼'' × 11¾''
1 stainless steel pan 2¼'' × 10½'' × 15''

This sturdy charcoal grill, designed by the Rodale Design Group, features the decorative cement blocks described on p. 88. The cooking surface is made by welding together standard steel angle and rods, both easily obtainable from most hardware stores. A stainless steel baking pan, available at hardware and department stores that sell cookware, is used to hold the charcoal.

It's easy to alter the dimensions of this grill: Just use a greater or lesser number of blocks, or arrange them in a different pattern. However, be sure to have on hand a pan that will fit the grill-rod assembly you intend to make. One final note: The grill shown here requires six blocks. To speed construc-

tion, we recommend that you make at least three cement block molds for casting.

CONSTRUCTION

1. Using the mold described on p. 88, make six decorative cement blocks, each measuring 6 inches thick, 14 inches wide, and 18 inches long.
2. Cut four pieces of 1¼ × 1¼-inch steel angle, each 11¾ inches in length, for the grill-rod support assembly. On two of the pieces, scribe a centerline along the length of one side and mark 16 points on ¾-inch centers. Note that the first and last points will be only ¼ inch from the ends of the pieces. Drill 5/16-inch-diameter holes through the pieces, centered over the points, as shown in illustration A.
3. Cut 16 pieces of 5/16-inch-diameter steel rod to 17⅞ inches each for the grill rods. Weld the rods into the holes drilled in the grill-rod supports. Take care to keep the supports properly aligned. When assembled, the supports should be parallel, and the

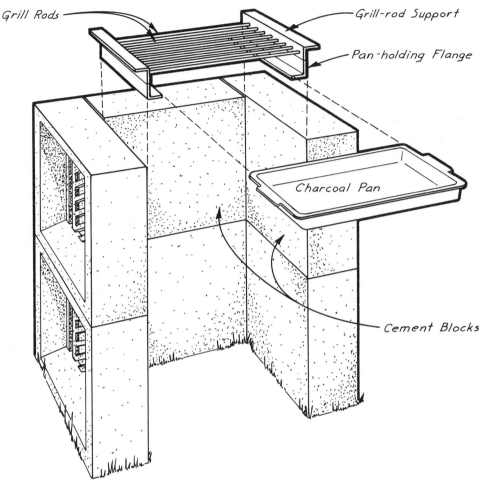

Grill Rods

Grill-rod Support

Pan-holding Flange

Charcoal Pan

Cement Blocks

Exploded-View Diagram

rods should be at right angles between them.

4. Butt the two remaining pieces of steel angle against the rod supports, as shown in illustration A, and weld them together to create the pan-holding flange.

5. When the cement blocks have cured, stack them, as shown in the exploded-view diagram, to form the back and sides of the grill. If you wish, pour a U-shaped concrete foundation beforehand for the blocks to sit on, and bond the blocks to each other or to the foundation by spreading a ½-inch layer of mortar between each piece.

6. Set the grill-rod assembly on the cement blocks, as shown in the exploded-view diagram. Slide a 2¼ × 10½ × 15-inch stainless steel pan onto the pan-holding flange. The grill is now ready to use; however, before cooking on it the first time, build a hot fire in the pan and allow any oil or plating on the rods to burn off.

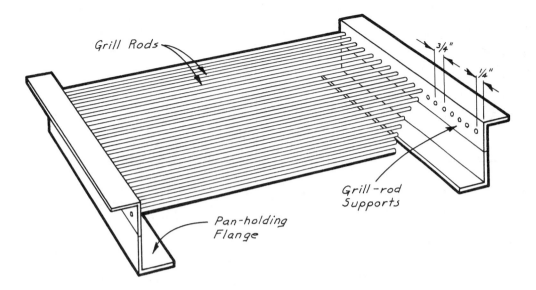

Grill Rods

3/4"

1/4"

Grill-rod
Supports

Pan-holding
Flange

Illustration A

OUTDOOR COOKING CENTER

This outdoor cooking center works as well as any commercially available gas-fired grill, yet has the added feature of a Chinese wok for the grilling surface. It has been dubbed the "Wok on Wheels" by the Rodale Design Group. The wok will add variety to any patio meal by allowing you to prepare

SHOPPING LIST

Lumber
2 pcs. $1 \times 2 \times 10'$
2 pcs. $1 \times 2 \times 8'$
Dowel
1 pc. $\frac{3}{8}'' \times 3'$ hardwood
Mild Steel Flat Stock
2 pcs. $\frac{3}{16}'' \times 1\frac{1}{4}'' \times 19\frac{1}{2}''$
4 pcs. $\frac{3}{16}'' \times 1\frac{1}{4}'' \times 17''$
2 pcs. $\frac{3}{16}'' \times 1\frac{1}{4}'' \times 16\frac{13}{16}''$
2 pcs. $\frac{3}{16}'' \times 1\frac{1}{4}'' \times 8''$
3 pcs. $\frac{3}{16}'' \times 1\frac{1}{4}'' \times 7\frac{1}{2}''$
Mild Steel Rod
2 pcs. $\frac{1}{2}'' \times 36\frac{1}{4}''$
2 pcs. $\frac{1}{2}'' \times 34''$
2 pcs. $\frac{1}{2}'' \times 2\frac{1}{4}''$
Connections
1 LP gas tank 20 pound
1 LP gas burner 6'' (see p. 103)
1 LP gas regulator with $\frac{3}{8}''$ MPT connectors
1 LP gas air mixer $\frac{3}{8}'' \times 1''$
1 LP gas valve $\frac{1}{8}''$
1 LP gas hose $\frac{3}{8}'' \times 24''$
1 pipe nipple $1'' \times 3\frac{1}{2}''$
1 close pipe nipple $1''$
1 bushing $\frac{1}{8}'' \times \frac{3}{8}''$
1 90-degree elbow $1''$
1 90-degree street elbow $\frac{1}{8}''$
Hardware
2 wheels 6'' diameter $\times \frac{1}{2}''$ hub
2 axle snap caps $\frac{1}{2}''$
4 hex head bolts $\frac{1}{4}'' \times 1''$
4 tee nuts $\frac{1}{4}''$
2 fender washers $1\frac{1}{2}''$
4 spring pin catches $\frac{3}{8}'' \times 3\frac{1}{2}''$
$\frac{1}{4}$ pound finishing nails 2d
1 burner shroud $4\frac{1}{2}'' \times 30''$
1 shroud seam lock $1\frac{1}{2}'' \times 4\frac{1}{2}''$
$\frac{1}{2}$ pint waterproof glue
rust-resistant paint
polyurethane

stir-fried vegetables and meats. Of course, a standard griddle is easily used instead, so traditional patio meals can also be served.

Welding is required to build this project. The frame is simple to build of mild steel bar and round stock, but if you do not have the equipment, take the plans to a welding shop and let them do the job for you. The mild steel, obtainable at any metal supply shop, can be brazed with an oxyacetylene outfit (instead of welded), if this is more convenient.

The wok is available through many commercial outlets. The liquid propane (LP) gas tank is also available through a variety of stores, and the connections are available from most plumbing or hardware suppliers. The gas burner, the "Buzzer Burner," model number 106, is available from Charles A. Hones, 607 Albany Avenue, Box 518, North Amityville, New York, NY 11701. The phone number is (516) 842-8886. Other suitable burners may be available in your area.

CONSTRUCTION

1. Cut four pieces of steel to $3/16 \times 1\frac{1}{4} \times 17$ inches each for the base pieces.
2. Cut two pieces of steel to $3/16 \times 1\frac{1}{4} \times 16^{13}/_{16}$ inches each for the base cross members.
3. Cut two pieces of steel to $3/16 \times 1\frac{1}{4} \times 8$ inches each for the intermediate cross members.
4. Cut two pieces of steel to $3/16 \times 1\frac{1}{4} \times 19\frac{1}{2}$ inches each for the tray supports.
5. Cut three pieces of steel to $3/16 \times 1\frac{1}{4} \times 7\frac{1}{2}$ inches each for the burner support and two upper cross members.
6. Cut two pieces of $\frac{1}{2}$-inch-diameter steel rod to $36\frac{1}{4}$ inches each for the longer legs, and two pieces to 34 inches each for the shorter legs. The shorter legs are for the axle side of the base, and the longer legs rest on the ground after assembly.
7. Cut two pieces of $\frac{1}{2}$-inch-diameter steel rod to $2\frac{1}{4}$ inches each for the axles.
8. Clean and file all the pieces in preparation for welding or brazing. Arrange a clean, flat work area since the base pieces must be square and level during assembly.
9. Arrange the base pieces, as shown in illustration A, and weld or braze the corners.

Be sure that the pieces are of equal length, and that the base is square.

10. Weld or braze the base cross members and the intermediate cross members to the base pieces.
11. Weld or braze the tray support pieces, the upper cross members and the gas burner support, as shown in illustration A.
12. Heat and bend the steel-rod legs to shape, as shown in illustration B.
13. Weld or braze the legs to the inside corner of the base and to the tray support pieces. This requires careful workmanship. First, be sure the pieces are level and square, then tack-weld the pieces together, test to check the squareness, and finally, join the corners securely.
14. Weld or braze a $1\frac{1}{2}$-inch fender washer to the bottom of each of the longer legs.
15. Weld or braze a $1 \times 3\frac{1}{2}$-inch pipe nipple to the gas burner support so that $1\frac{1}{4}$ inches of nipple extend above the support.
16. Drill $\frac{1}{2}$-inch-diameter axle holes through the base pieces in the positions shown in illustration A.
17. Insert the axles into the drilled holes and

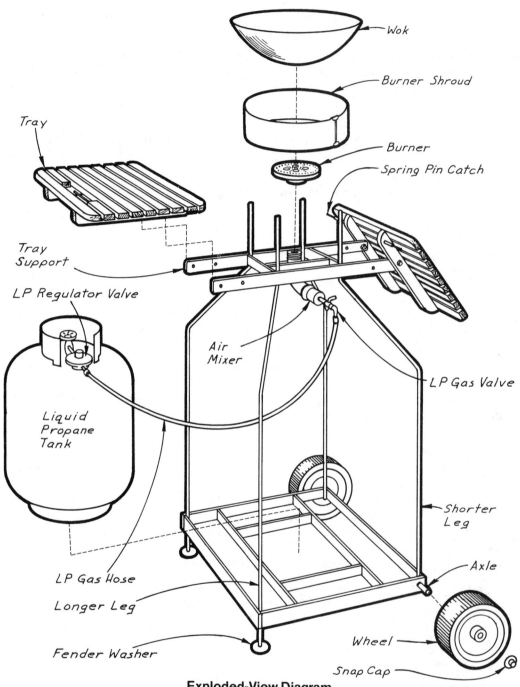

Wok

Burner Shroud

Tray

Burner

Spring Pin Catch

Tray Support

LP Regulator Valve

Air Mixer

LP Gas Valve

Liquid Propane Tank

Shorter Leg

Axle

LP Gas Hose

Longer Leg

Wheel

Fender Washer

Snap Cap

Exploded-View Diagram

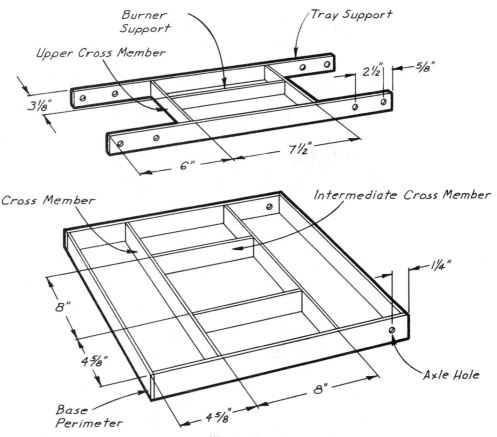

Illustration A

weld the axles to the base pieces.

18. Drill $9/32$-inch-diameter holes in the tray supports, in the positions shown in illustration A, so they can accept the $1/4 \times 1$-inch hex head bolts and spring pin catches.

19. Grind away any slag on the metal parts. If the parts have been brazed, be sure to scrub them free of flux residue. Sand the pieces, clean them with paint thinner, then paint them with rust-resistant paint. Now the framework is complete, and you can move on to the wood pieces.

20. Cut four pieces of 1×2 ($3/4'' \times 1\frac{1}{2}''$) stock to $15\frac{1}{2}$ inches each for the tray support rails.

21. Cut 17 pieces of 1×2 stock $19\frac{1}{2}$ inches each for the tray tops.

22. Cut two pieces of 1×2 stock to $5\frac{1}{4}$ inches each for the seasoning rack end pieces.

23. Cut three pieces of $3/8$-inch-diameter wood dowel to $8\frac{1}{4}$ inches each for the seasoning rack bottom pieces.

24. Cut two pieces of dowel to 3 inches each for support pins.

25. Cut a $1\frac{1}{2}$-inch-diameter radius on the ends of the support rails, and also on the ends of the four tray top pieces.

26. Hold the support rails to the steel tray supports of the frame, and mark the positions of the tray pivot holes and spring pin

105

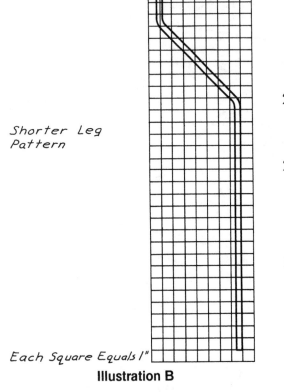

Top of Leg

Shorter Leg Pattern

Each Square Equals 1"

Illustration B

catch holes. Drill $\frac{9}{32}$-inch-diameter holes through the support rails on the marks.

27. Drill a $\frac{3}{8}$-inch-diameter × $\frac{3}{8}$-inch-deep hole centered 1 inch from each end on the edge of one radiused top tray piece and, also in one plain top tray piece, to accept the support pins, as shown in illustration C. Drill holes through the two short tray top pieces to match the positions of the support pin holes.

28. Drill three $\frac{3}{8}$-inch-diameter holes in two of the tray support rails in the positions shown in illustration C, to accept the seasoning tray dowels.

29. Sand the tray pieces in preparation for finishing. If you wish, use a router to cut a $\frac{1}{4}$-inch radius on all the edges of the tray pieces, except the top edges of the support rails. Do not apply a finish at this time (see step 31).

30. Assemble the seasoning rack pieces and the support pins as a unit. Maintain a $\frac{1}{4}$-inch gap between the pieces with a $\frac{1}{4}$-inch-wide piece of scrap wood. Install the seasoning rack flush to the end of one set of tray support rails, using waterproof glue and 2d finishing nails. Install the remainder of the tray top pieces in the same way, then assemble the second set of tray pieces.

LUMBER CUTTING LIST

Size	Piece	Quantity
1 × 2		
$\frac{3}{4}'' × 1\frac{1}{2}'' × 19\frac{1}{2}''$	Tray tops	17
$\frac{3}{4}'' × 1\frac{1}{2}'' × 15\frac{1}{2}''$	Tray support rails	4
$\frac{3}{4}'' × 1\frac{1}{2}'' × 5\frac{1}{4}''$	Seasoning rack end pieces	2
Dowel		
$\frac{3}{8}'' × 8\frac{1}{4}''$	Seasoning rack bottom pieces	3
$\frac{3}{8}'' × 3''$	Support pins	2

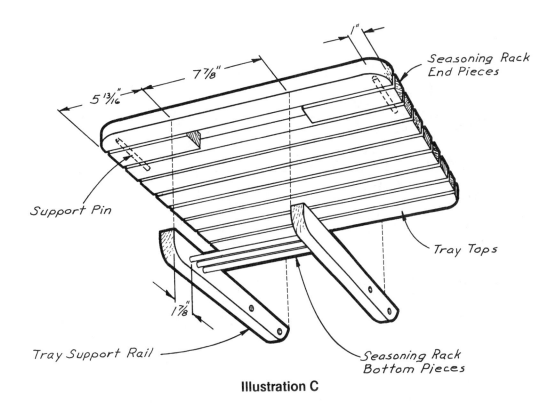

Illustration C

31. Sink the nail heads, fill the nail holes, and apply polyurethane to the tray pieces.

32. Enlarge the ¼-inch-diameter holes to ⅜-inch diameter and install a ¼-inch tee nut into each of the pivot holes in the tray support rails, and install a ⅜ × 3½-inch spring pin catch in each of the support rails.

33. Assemble the 20-pound LP gas tank connections, as shown in illustration D, with an LP gas regulator and 24 inches of LP gas hose fitted with ⅜-inch male pipe thread (MPT) connectors. Add a ⅛ × ⅜-inch bushing and a 90-degree ⅛-inch street elbow. Fit a ⅛-inch LP gas valve to the street elbow on one side and a ⅜ × 1-inch LP air mixer on the other side of the valve. Connect the air mixer to a 1-inch 90-degree elbow through a 1-inch close pipe nipple, and the elbow to the 1 × 3½-inch pipe

nipple that was welded to the burner support. Add the burner to the 1 × 3½-inch pipe nipple. Now the gas connections are complete.

34. Cut one piece of aluminum flashing to 4½ × 30 inches for the burner shroud, and a second piece 1½ × 4½ inches for the seam lock strip, as shown in illustration E.

35. Trim the shroud piece corners to 45-degree angles, and bend the long edges of the shroud flashing to form closed ¼-inch hems. Bend the short edges to form partially closed hems.

36. Bend the long edges of the seam lock strip to form partially closed ¼-inch hems. Fit the seam lock strip over the hems of the shroud, with the hems of the shroud on the inside of the circle, and hammer the hems of both pieces closed. Bend the remaining

107

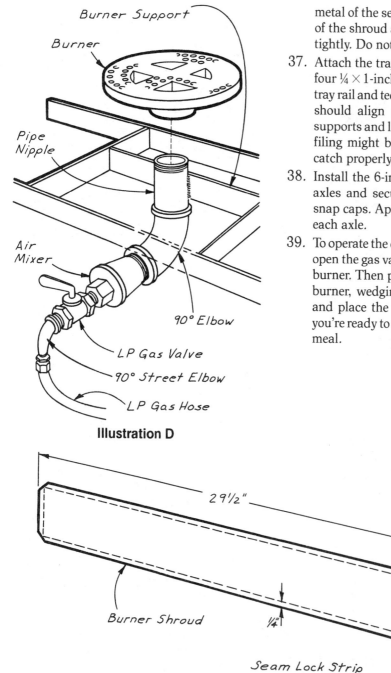

Burner Support

Burner

Pipe Nipple

Air Mixer

90° Elbow

LP Gas Valve

90° Street Elbow

LP Gas Hose

Illustration D

metal of the seam lock strip over the edges of the shroud and hammer the ends down tightly. Do not paint the shroud.

37. Attach the trays to the tray supports with four $\frac{1}{4} \times 1$-inch hex head bolts, one in each tray rail and tee nut. The spring pin catches should align with the holes in the tray supports and lock the trays securely. Some filing might be required so that the pins catch properly in the tray support holes.

38. Install the 6-inch-diameter wheels on the axles and secure them with $\frac{1}{2}$-inch axle snap caps. Apply a small amount of oil to each axle.

39. To operate the outdoor cooking center, first open the gas valve and ignite the gas at the burner. Then place the shroud around the burner, wedging it between the leg tops, and place the wok on the leg tops. Now you're ready to prepare your stir-fried patio meal.

29½"

1"

Burner Shroud

¼"

4"

4½"

Seam Lock Strip

Illustration E

PROJECTS FOR THE GARDEN

SOIL MIXER

This device is the invention of James Garber of Lowpoint, Illinois. With it, you can mix the components of planting soil easily and quickly, merely by rotating the canister in the frame by means of the hand crank. Garber employs his mixer to blend the soil he used in his greenhouse bedding plant business.

The soil mixer is not difficult to construct, but it must be sturdily built. Lap joints are suggested for the frame pieces, lag and carriage bolts are specified as fasteners. You may alter the joining methods, if you wish, but consider adding extra bracing where necessary. You may also wish to add wheels to the mixer to make it more portable.

Though the photograph of Garber's

mixer shows a canister that is six-sided—an elongated hexagon—we've chosen to redesign the shape to one that has five sides. This pentagonal canister is easier to rotate, yet, like Garber's hexagonal one, is also shaped so that soil does not stick in the inside corners.

CONSTRUCTION

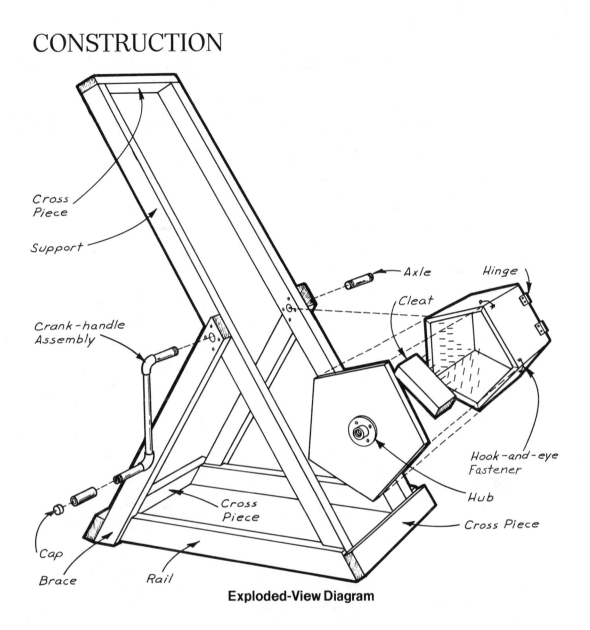

Cross
Piece

Support

Crank-handle
Assembly

Cap

Brace

Rail

Cross
Piece

Axle

Cleat

Hinge

Hook-and-eye
Fastener

Hub

Cross Piece

Exploded-View Diagram

1. Cut two pieces of 2×4 ($1\frac{1}{2}'' \times 3\frac{1}{2}''$) stock to 72 inches each for the stand supports. Cut one end of each to a 60-degree angle, as shown on the cutting diagram. Cut four pieces of 2×4 stock to 38 inches each for the braces and rails. Trim the ends

of each piece to 60-degree angles, also as shown on the cutting diagram.

2. Cut the angled half-lap joints on the rails, as shown in illustration A. Make certain to cut on the correct sides of the pieces.

3. Cut three pieces of 2×4 stock, one to 20

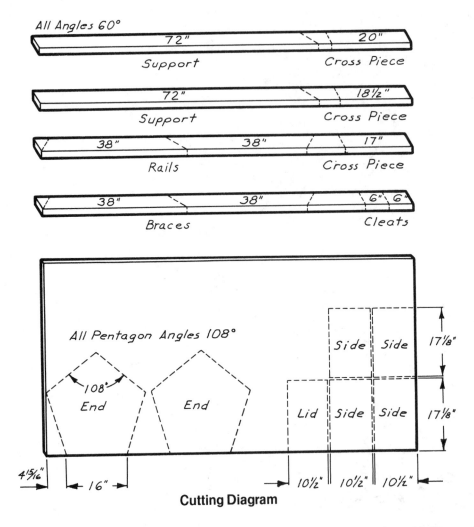

Cutting Diagram

inches, one to 18½ inches, and one to 17 inches, for the cross pieces.

4. Lay the stand supports flat on the floor, then lay a rail on top and align the angles. Drill ³⁄₁₆-inch-diameter pilot holes and fasten the front joints using two ¼ × 2¼-inch lag bolts, fitted with washers, per joint.

5. Fasten the braces to the supports and rails using lag bolts for the lower rear joint, but use four ¼ × 3½-inch carriage bolts for each of the upper joints. Drill ⁵⁄₁₆-inch-diameter pilot holes for the carriage bolts,

and install them together with flat washers and nuts. (Don't place a carriage bolt in the center of the joint, since the axles go there; see step 7.)

6. Set the two sides of the stand upright, then fasten the lower front cross piece using ¼ × 2¼-inch lag bolts. Fasten the lower rear cross piece the same way. Fasten the top cross piece by tipping the assembly over onto the supports so it is easier to reach.

7. Drill a 1-inch-diameter hole through the

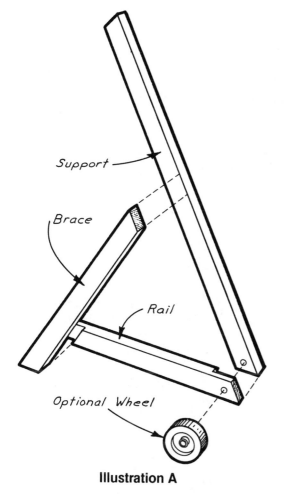

Illustration A

9. Cut two pieces of 2×4 stock to 6 inches each for the cleats. Drive scrap nails in the sides and along three edges of these pieces for teeth to break up the soil. Then hold the cleats on edge and center them on the inside faces of the end panels. Drill $3/32$-inch-diameter pilot holes, and fasten the cleats onto the panels, as shown in the exploded-view diagram, using four $1\frac{1}{2}$-inch #8 flathead wood screws.

10. Drive scrap nails into the inside faces of the end panels and side pieces at intervals of approximately 2 inches, for additional soil-breaking teeth.

11. Set the five side pieces on edge, on a strong, level workbench or on the floor. Position them with their beveled edges touching so they form a pentagon. Place one of the end panels on top of the side pieces. Align the edges while keeping the joints of the side pieces together, then tack the end panel on the side pieces using 4d finishing nails. Do

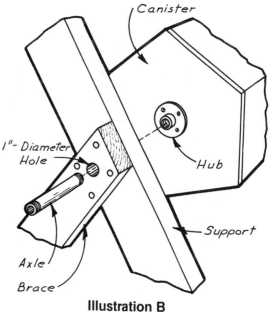

Illustration B

supports and braces, as shown in illustration B, so that the axles (made of $\frac{1}{2}$-inch galvanized pipe; see step 17) will fit through the frame.

8. Now build the canister. Start by cutting the end panels from $\frac{3}{4}$-inch exterior-grade plywood, as shown in the cutting diagram, then cut the side pieces, also as shown. Bevel the angles on the ends of the five pieces to 54 degrees each, so when assembled, the pieces will form a perfect pentagon. Label one of the pieces the lid.

115

LUMBER CUTTING LIST

Size	Piece	Quantity
2 × 4		
$1\frac{1}{2}'' \times 3\frac{1}{2}'' \times 72''$	Supports	2
$1\frac{1}{2}'' \times 3\frac{1}{2}'' \times 38''$	Braces	2
$1\frac{1}{2}'' \times 3\frac{1}{2}'' \times 38''$	Rails	2
$1\frac{1}{2}'' \times 3\frac{1}{2}'' \times 20''$	Rear bottom cross piece	1
$1\frac{1}{2}'' \times 3\frac{1}{2}'' \times 18\frac{1}{2}''$	Front bottom cross piece	1
$1\frac{1}{2}'' \times 3\frac{1}{2}'' \times 17''$	Top cross piece	1
$1\frac{1}{2}'' \times 3\frac{1}{2}'' \times 6''$	Cleats	2
Plywood		
$\frac{3}{4}'' \times 27'' \times 27''$	Canister ends	2
$\frac{3}{4}'' \times 10\frac{1}{2}'' \times 16''$	Canister sides	4
$\frac{3}{4}'' \times 10\frac{1}{2}'' \times 16''$	Canister lid	1

not nail the end panel to the lid. Turn the pentagon over and tack the other end panel in place. (Again, avoid nailing the panel to the lid.)

12. Use screws to fasten the canister together permanently. First drill and countersink eight pairs of pilot holes through the end panels and into the edges of each side piece except the lid. Then drive in 1½-inch #8 flathead wood screws.

13. Pry the lid from the finished canister. Trim one long edge of the lid so it fits easily back in place. (Removing about ⅛ inch should do.) Then set the lid back in the canister.

14. Install two 1½ × 2-inch hinges and two hook-and-eye fasteners, as shown in the exploded-view diagram, to hold the lid in place. Bend the hook shanks so they fit the 72-degree pentagon angles.

15. Locate the center of each canister end panel, then fasten a ½-inch pipe flange in place on each panel using eight ¾-inch #8 flathead wood screws for the canister hub.

16. Paint the exterior of the canister, if desired.

17. Use two ½ × 5-inch pipe nipples for axles. With help from an assistant, install the canister between the supports of the frame by inserting the axles through the holes at the tops of the supports and then screwing them into the pipe flanges on the canister end panels.

18. Assemble the crank handle by tightening a ½-inch pipe elbow onto one axle and then installing a 12-inch pipe nipple onto the elbow. Add a second elbow and a 5-inch pipe nipple, as shown in the exploded-view diagram. Slide a 1 × 4-inch length of pipe over the handle, then install a ½-inch pipe cap at the end to keep the tubing in place. Tighten a second pipe cap onto the other axle.

19. Wheels are optional. To install them, drill ⅝-inch-diameter holes through the rails and support joints in the positions shown in illustration A. Slide a ⅝ × 22½-inch steel rod through the holes to serve as an axle. Install two 5-inch flat washers over each end of the axles, then attach the wheels and lock them in place with snap hubs.

EASY-DUMPING SOIL SIFTER

SHOPPING LIST

Lumber
1 pc. 2 × 4 × 12'
1 pc. 2 × 4 × 10'
2 pcs. 2 × 4 × 8'
1 pc. 1 × 6 × 3'
1 pc. 1 × 4 × 8'
1 pc. 1 × 2 × 8'
Hardware
2 lawn-mower wheels 6''
46 flathead wood screws #6 × 2''
22 flathead wood screws #6 × 1¼''
2 carriage bolts ½'' × 4½'', each with
    three washers, one locknut, one
    ordinary nut
1 box wire staples ⅜''
2 butt hinges 3½''
2 eyescrews ½''
1 pc. sash chain 4'
1 pc. ½-inch mesh hardware cloth 33'' × 3'
¼ pint waterproof glue

Gardeners working with rocky soil or with manure and compost piles will find this sifter very useful. Built by the Rodale Design Group with an eye toward saving labor, the bottom frame is constructed so

that a wheelbarrow may be rolled beneath the sifting screen. The screen box is also hinged, simplifying the process of emptying debris onto the ground or into a cart after each load is sifted. Finally, the unit is mounted on wheels to provide easy movement to and from the locations where it is to be used.

We constructed our sifter out of construction-grade lumber. Since this tool will likely be left outdoors to endure all types of weather, we fastened the joints with waterproof glue and wood screws. If merely nailed together, these joints will inevitably twist, turn, and pull apart. We coated our sifter with an exterior-grade stain and chose ½-inch mesh hardware cloth as the best material for general-purpose soil screening.

117

CONSTRUCTION

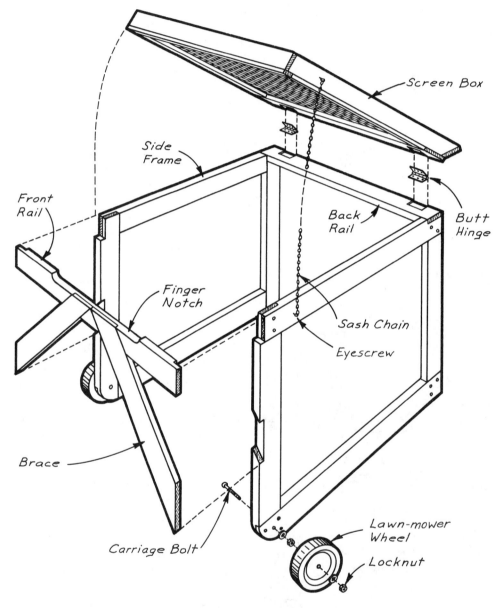

Screen Box

Side Frame

Front Rail

Back Rail

Butt Hinge

Finger Notch

Sash Chain

Eyescrew

Brace

Carriage Bolt

Lawn-mower Wheel

Locknut

Exploded-View Diagram

1. Cut four pieces of 2×4 ($1\frac{1}{2}'' \times 3\frac{1}{2}''$) stock to 28 inches each for the upright members of the side frames, and an additional four pieces to 36 inches each for the cross members. Cut half-lap joints on the ends of all pieces for joining them into two identical rectangular frames. Dry-fit the frames together and label one the left side, the other the right.

2. Fasten the side frames together using waterproof glue and $1\frac{1}{4}$-inch #6 flathead wood screws. Insert three screws into each lower joint, following the pattern shown in illustration A, to allow for a radius and a wheel bolt hole to be added later to each lower front corner. Insert two screws into each upper joint, as shown in the same illustration, avoiding areas that will later be notched.

3. Center and drill a $\frac{1}{2}$-inch-diameter hole through the front corner of each side frame, 3 inches above the bottom edge, for at-

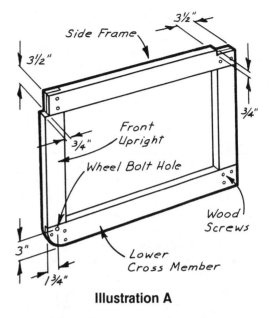

Illustration A

taching wheels, as shown in illustration A. Also cut a $3\frac{1}{2}$-inch radius on each of these corners.

LUMBER CUTTING LIST

Size	Piece	Quantity
2×4		
$1\frac{1}{2}'' \times 3\frac{1}{2}'' \times 37\frac{1}{2}''$	Screen box sides	2
$1\frac{1}{2}'' \times 3\frac{1}{2}'' \times 36''$	Side frame cross members	4
$1\frac{1}{2}'' \times 3\frac{1}{2}'' \times 33''$	Side frame connecting rails	2
$1\frac{1}{2}'' \times 3\frac{1}{2}'' \times 33''$	Screen box front end	1
$1\frac{1}{2}'' \times 3\frac{1}{2}'' \times 28''$	Side frame uprights	4
1×6		
$\frac{3}{4}'' \times 5\frac{1}{2}'' \times 33''$	Screen box slanted end	1
1×4		
$\frac{3}{4}'' \times 3\frac{1}{2}'' \times 33''$	Screen box batten	1
$\frac{3}{4}'' \times 3\frac{1}{2}'' \times 23\frac{3}{8}''$	Braces	2
1×2		
$\frac{3}{4}'' \times 1\frac{1}{2}'' \times 33''$	Screen box batten	1
$\frac{3}{4}'' \times 1\frac{1}{2}'' \times 30\frac{7}{8}''$	Screen box battens	2

4. Cut two pieces of 2 × 4 stock to 33 inches each for rails to connect the two side frames. Cut a 1½-inch rabbet ¾ inch deep across both ends on one face of each rail. Then cut a 1½ × 3½-inch notch ¾ inch deep into the edge at the upper front corner of each side frame for attaching one rail in a vertical position there. Also cut notches to these same dimensions on top of the upper rear corners for attaching the other rail in a horizontal position, as shown in illustration A.

5. Cut a finger notch 15 inches long and 1 inch deep into the upper edge of the front rail to provide space for gripping the underside of the screen box, as shown in the exploded-view diagram. Then cut two pieces of 1 × 4 (¾″ × 3½″) stock to 23⅜ inches each for braces. Cut both ends of each brace to a 45-degree angle for fitting the braces diagonally between the front rail and the side frames, as shown in the exploded-view diagram.

6. Notch the outside face of the front rail and the front edge of the side frames ¾ inch deep, where needed to accept the ends of the braces. Then fasten the rails and braces to the side frames using waterproof glue and 2-inch #6 flathead wood screws. Insert two screws into each joint, preferably avoiding end grain.

7. Cut two pieces of 2 × 4 stock to 37½ inches each for the sides of the screen box, then cut one end of each piece to a 45-degree angle to receive the angled end piece, as shown in illustration B. Cut another piece of 2 × 4 stock to 33 inches for the front end of the box, then cut 1½-inch-wide rabbets ¾ inch deep across the ends of the piece for receiving the front ends of the side pieces.

8. Cut one piece of 1 × 6 (¾″ × 5½″) stock to 33 inches for the slanted end of the screen box. Simultaneously rip the piece to 4¾ inches in width while beveling the ripped edge to a 45-degree angle. Fasten the screen box frame together using waterproof glue and 2-inch #6 flathead wood screws, except near the upper edges of the slanted end where 1¼-inch #6 flathead wood screws should be used.

9. Cut a piece of ½-inch mesh hardware cloth to 33 × 36 inches and fasten it to the bottom of the screen box frame using ⅜-inch wire staples. Also cut one piece of 1 × 4 and one piece of 1 × 2 stock, each 33 inches in length, for battens to secure the edges of the hardware cloth. Fasten the wider batten across the underside of the slanted end of the screen box using 2-inch #6 flathead wood screws. Drill pilot holes first, at the angle appropriate for inserting screws into the slanted end.

10. Fasten the remaining batten (cut in step 9) across the underside of the front end of the screen box using 2-inch #6 flathead wood screws. Then cut two pieces of 1 × 2 stock to 30⅞ inches each and fasten them

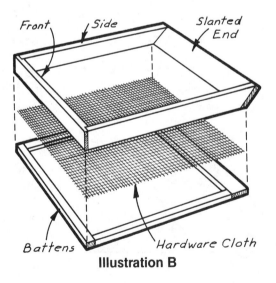

Illustration B

as battens on the bottom of the two sides of the screen box using the same-dimension fasteners.

11. Fasten the screen box to the back rail of the bottom frame using a pair of 3½-inch butt hinges. Mortise the hinges into the top of the rail and into the bottom of the wide batten on the screen box so the box will sit flush on the bottom frame.

12. Round-over all sharp edges on the soil sifter and apply a coat of exterior-grade stain or other finish, if desired. Then cut one piece of sash chain to 48 inches. Attach a ½-inch eyescrew to the center of one upper cross member on the bottom frame, approximately 6 inches from the front edge, and another eyescrew in the same position on the frame of the box screen above it. Attach one end of the sash chain to one eyescrew, the other end of the chain to the other eyescrew, to create a stop when lifting and dumping the screen box.

13. Fasten a pair of 6-inch lawn-mower wheels to the lower front corners of the sifter bottom frame using ½ × 4½-inch carriage bolts with two nuts and three washers for each. Use one washer and nut to secure each bolt in the wooden frame. Then add the wheel with a washer on either side, and a locknut to hold the wheel and washers on the bolt.

HANGING SOIL SIFTER

SHOPPING LIST

Lumber
1 pc. 1 × 4 × 10'
1 pc. ¾'' × ¾'' × 4' (baluster stock)
Hardware
12 flathead wood screws #8 × 1½''
wire staples ⅝''
3 screw hooks #10 × 1½''
1 pc. nylon rope ⅜'' × 16'
1 pc. ½-inch mesh hardware cloth 2' × 3'

Here is a soil sifter that hangs from rafters or an improvised stand, and makes the chore of sifting garden soil an easy one indeed. Not only does it free you from having to bear the weight of the sifter and soil it contains, but it also allows you to sift larger quantities of soil at one time as well, because the frame can hold more soil than one that must be shaken only by hand. This hanging soil sifter is the product of Dr. Lee Reich of New Paltz, New York. Dr. Reich is a research botanist and fre-

quently uses the sifter in his work.

The hanging sifter is easy to build. It's nothing more than a wooden frame with ½-inch mesh hardware cloth stretched and fastened across one side. Ropes, suspended between screw hooks installed at the corners of the frame and in rafters directly above, are used for hanging. To operate the sifter, merely shovel in soil and rapidly shake the frame back and forth.

Changing the size of sifted particles is easy too. Merely insert a piece of smaller-size mesh on top of the ½-inch size permanently attached, then fill and shake as before. You might want to cut several different pieces of mesh to size and use each in succession when a particularly fine-sifted soil is desired.

To get rid of the debris left in the frame after sifting, just detach the frame from the ropes and dump the contents out. For storage, lift the sifter up to the rafters and hook it to its own fasteners.

CONSTRUCTION

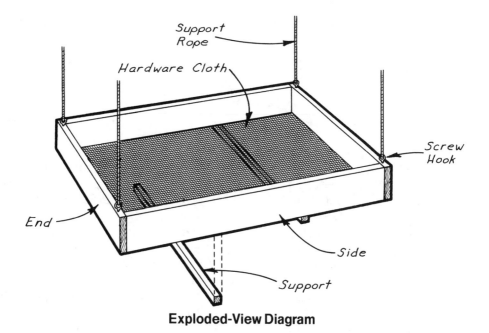

Exploded-View Diagram

1. Cut two pieces of 1 × 4 (¾″ × 3½″) stock to 34½ inches each for the sides, and two pieces of the same stock to 24 inches each for the ends, as shown in the cutting diagram.

2. Assemble the sides and ends together to form the sifter frame, using simple butt joints fastened with wood screws. Attach the ends across the sides, as shown in the exploded-view diagram, so the dimensions of the sifter measure 24 × 36 inches. Drill and countersink ⁵⁄₆₄-inch-diameter pilot holes, then install two 1½-inch #8 flat-head wood screws at each corner.

3. Cut one piece of ½-inch mesh hardware cloth to 24 × 36 inches and fasten it across the underside of the frame pieces using ⅝-inch wire staples. Trim away any excess mesh.

4. Cut two pieces of baluster stock (¾″ × ¾″) to 24 inches each. Place them across the mesh-covered underside of the frame, 12

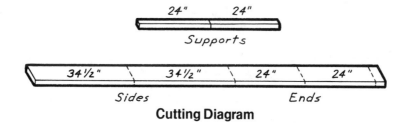

Cutting Diagram

123

LUMBER CUTTING LIST

Size	Piece	Quantity
1 × 4		
¾″ × 3½″ × 34½″	Frame sides	2
¾″ × 3½″ × 24″	Frame ends	2
Baluster Stock		
¾″ × ¾″ × 24″	Hardware cloth supports	2

inches from the ends, then drill and countersink ⁵⁄₆₄-inch-diameter pilot holes ⅜ inch from the ends of the pieces. Fasten the pieces to the frame with 1½-inch #8 flathead wood screws.

5. Drill ⅛-inch-diameter pilot holes in the top edge of each end piece 1 inch from the corners of the frame, and install four 1½-inch #10 screw hooks to hold the support ropes (see step 7).

6. Install screw hooks into the rafters above the work area. First drill ⅛-inch-diameter pilot holes 22 inches apart along one rafter to match the screw-hook spacing on the sifter frame. Then install the two screw hooks. Next, position and install the other set of hooks on a parallel rafter. If the rafters are 24 inches on center, skip one rafter so that the screw hooks are 36 inches apart. If the rafters are on 16-inch centers, or oddly spaced, try to make the spacing as close to 36 inches as possible; otherwise, the ropes will hang at an angle and may make the sifter difficult to shake. An alternative is to drive the screw hooks into two boards at the proper 36-inch spacing, then attach the boards across the rafters with large screws so the hooks on each side are 22 inches apart.

7. Cut four pieces of ⅜-inch-diameter nylon rope to lengths that will hang the sifter at a comfortable working height. Tie loops in both ends of each piece and hang the frame from the screw hooks. Adjust the loops, if necessary, so that the sifter hangs level.

WHEEL-BARROW FLAT CARRIER/ SOIL SIFTER

SHOPPING LIST

For the basic bed:
Lumber
1 pc. 2 × 4 × 6'
1 pc. 1 × 4 × 12'
Plywood
1 pc. ¾'' × 4' × 4' A-C grade
Hardware
28 flathead wood screws #8 × 1½''
2 carriage bolts ¼'' × 6'' with nuts
2 carriage bolts ¼'' × 2½'' with nuts
4 flat washers ⅜''

For the soil sifter:
Lumber
1 pc. 1 × 10 × 6'
1 pc. 1 × 6 × 12'
Plywood
1 pc. ¾'' × 2' × 2' exterior grade
Dowels
2 pcs. ¾'' × 3' hardwood
Hardware
48 flathead wood screws #8 × 1½''
¼ pound wire staples ½''
1 pc. wire mesh 1' × 16''

Eleanor Pugh of Wolf Creek, Oregon, found her ordinary wheelbarrow awkward for hauling certain loads, so she converted it to the specialized carrier pictured here. By discarding the original pan and replacing it with a wide, shallow bed whose weight is centered low and forward over the front wheel, she is able to carry large garden flats, firewood, and other unwieldy items easily and with little risk of tipping them over. Ms. Pugh also constructed the three-part soil sifter pictured, which nests comfortably within the carrier. The top unit of the sifter—the sifting screen—moves easily

back and forth on rollers made from dowels.

Almost any wheelbarrow can be fitted with the type of bed Ms. Pugh has designed. Since the new bed's mounting bolts are installed in the factory-drilled holes for the originals, no drilling or modifying of the wheelbarrow frame is necessary. The dimensions of the project presented here approximate the specifications submitted by Ms. Pugh and naturally reflect her needs and the constraints of the wheelbarrow frame with which she was working. Alter the plans to suit your needs and existing wheelbarrow frame as well. Use pressure-

125

treated or preservative-coated lumber, if possible, for durability and long life of both the bed and the soil sifter. Ms. Pugh also points out that replacing a solid plastic wheel—if your wheelbarrow is so equipped —with a pneumatic (air-filled) rubber one will produce additional load-handling capability, especially over rough terrain.

CONSTRUCTION

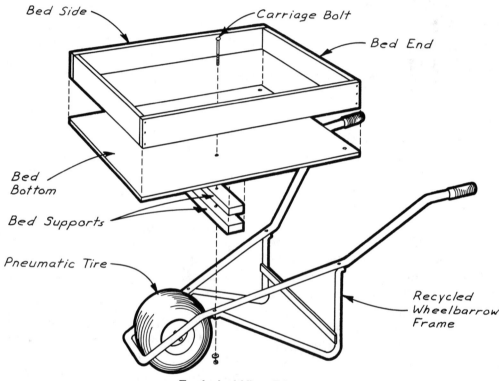

Exploded-View Diagram

To build the basic bed:

1. After removing the original pan and mounting bolts from the wheelbarrow frame, cut two pieces of 1 × 4 (¾″ × 3½″) stock to 36 inches each for the sides of the new bed, and two additional pieces to 24 inches each for the ends.
2. Assemble the sides and ends, as shown in illustration A, so that the rectangular frame produced measures 36 × 25½ inches. Check for squareness by measuring between diagonal corners (both measurements should be the same), then drill ³⁄₃₂-inch-diameter pilot holes, and fasten the pieces together with 1½-inch #8 flathead wood screws.

126

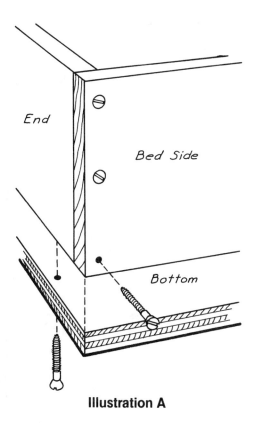

Illustration A

3. Cut a piece of ¾-inch A-C grade plywood to measure 25½ × 36 inches for the bottom of the bed. Set it on top of the frame constructed in the previous steps and, after aligning it so that all edges are flush with the frame's sides and ends, fasten the bottom to the frame using 1½-inch #8 flathead wood screws as in step 2.

4. Cut two pieces of 2 × 4 (1½″ × 3½″) stock to 25½ inches each for the bed supports. As shown in the exploded-view diagram, these are mounted across the wheelbarrow's original tubular frame and serve to keep the new bed level when the wheelbarrow is at rest. Depending upon the design of your own wheelbarrow frame, you may need additional supports to mount the bed level.

5. Position the bed and supports on the wheelbarrow frame. Center the bed so it overlaps the frame members equally on each side, then slide the bed forward so that its weight (and the weight of its future contents) lies directly over the front wheel. Reach underneath the wheelbarrow and, using an awl or sharp nail, mark the location of the wheelbarrow frame's holes onto the supports, and the position of the supports onto the underside of the bed.

6. Remove the bed and supports from the frame. Drill ⅜-inch-diameter holes in the supports at the locations marked for the wheelbarrow frame holes, then replace the supports in position on the underside of the bed. Using the drilled holes as guides, drill similar-size holes through the bed to accommodate the mounting bolts.

7. Replace the supports and bed in position on the wheelbarrow frame, then fasten the pieces together with two ¼ × 2½-inch, and two ¼ × 6-inch carriage bolts, ⅜-inch flat washers, and nuts. Paint the wheelbarrow if desired, and it is ready for use. If you wish, construct the optional soil sifter arrangement that follows.

To make the soil sifter:

1. Make the sifter frame—the middle component of the three-unit arrangement—first. Begin by cutting two pieces of 1 × 10 (¾″ × 9¼″) stock to 20 inches each for the sides, and two additional pieces to 14½ inches each for the ends.

2. Cut two notches, each ½ inch deep by approximately 2 inches long, in one edge of each side piece, as shown in illustration B. Each notch should begin 4 inches from one end of the piece.

3. Assemble the sides and ends of the frame, as shown in illustration B (the ends fit between the sides), then drill ³⁄₃₂-inch-

127

LUMBER CUTTING LIST

Size	Piece	Quantity
For the basic bed:		
2 × 4		
1½'' × 3½'' × 25½''	Bed supports	2
1 × 4		
¾'' × 3½'' × 36''	Bed sides	2
¾'' × 3½'' × 24''	Bed ends	2
Plywood		
¾'' × 25½'' × 36''	Bed bottom	1
For the soil sifter:		
1 × 10		
¾'' × 9¼'' × 20''	Sifter frame sides	2
¾'' × 9¼'' × 14½''	Sifter frame ends	2
1 × 6		
¾'' × 5½'' × 19½''	Flat sides	2
¾'' × 5½'' × 16''	Sifting screen sides	2
¾'' × 5½'' × 12½''	Flat ends	2
¾'' × 5½'' × 12''	Sifting screen ends	2
Plywood		
¾'' × 14'' × 19½''	Flat bottom	1
Dowels		
¾'' × 20''	Rollers	2

diameter pilot holes, and fasten the pieces together with 1½-inch #8 flathead wood screws.

4. Build the flat that collects the sifted soil next. Begin by cutting two pieces of 1 × 6 to 19½ inches each for the sides of the flat, and two additional pieces to 12½ inches each for the ends.

5. Assemble the sides and ends of the flat, as shown in illustration B. Drill ³⁄₃₂-inch-diameter pilot holes, then fasten the pieces together using 1½-inch #8 flathead wood screws.

6. Cut a piece of ¾-inch exterior-grade plywood to measure 14 × 19½ inches for the bottom of the flat. Fasten it to the frame, as

shown in illustration B, using 1½-inch #8 flathead wood screws. Make sure the pieces of the frame remain square to each other during fastening, and that the edges of the bottom are flush with the outside surfaces of the frame's ends and sides.

7. Finally, make the sifting screen. Begin by cutting two pieces of 1 × 6 to 16 inches each for the sides, and two additional pieces to 12 inches each for the ends. Assemble the pieces, as shown in illustration B, using 1½-inch #8 flathead wood screws.

8. Cut a section of mesh screening—the size of the mesh openings is optional—to 12 × 16 inches and fasten it to the bottom of the

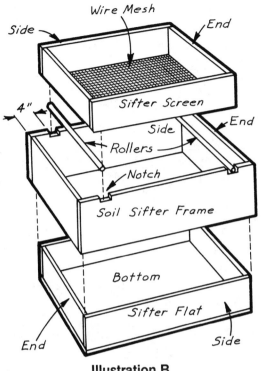

Wire Mesh

Side

End

Sifter Screen

4"

Rollers

Side

End

Notch

Soil Sifter Frame

Bottom

Sifter Flat

End

Side

Illustration B

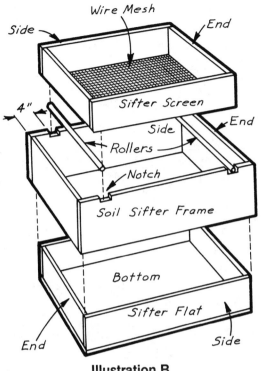

frame made in the previous step. Use ½-inch wire staples spaced about 2 inches apart. (Fine mesh requires closer spacing of staples than coarse mesh.)

9. Cut two pieces of ¾-inch dowel to 20 inches each for the rollers. Assemble the soil sifter in the wheelbarrow, as shown in the photograph. Then place the rollers in the notches cut into the upper edges of the sifter frame so that the sifting screen may be easily rocked back and forth during operation.

INSULATED PROPAGA-TION BOX

SHOPPING LIST

Lumber
2 pcs. 1 × 2 × 8'
Plywood
1 sheet ½" × 4' × 8' exterior grade
Hardware
30 flathead wood screws #6 × 1½"
staples ⅝"
1 pc. 6-mil polyethylene 3' × 61"
1 sheet rigid-foam insulation 1" × 4' × 8'
1 heating cable 30'
exterior-grade nontoxic enamel

Canadian Peter Weis of Fulford Harbour, British Columbia, developed this insulated propagation box to avoid the costs of keeping his greenhouse warm. A heating cable in the bottom of the box supplies warmth to the roots of the plants, thereby decreasing the need for warming the surrounding air as well. By using several boxes of this type in his greenhouse, Weis reduced his heating bill 90 percent!

The box is also insulated to retain the output of the heating cable, which is maintained at 70°F. Weis suggests that any water used on the plants be prewarmed to 70°F as well, adding that very little water is necessary because of the plastic cover that fits over the box to complete its assembly.

You will need one 4 × 8-foot sheet of exterior-grade plywood per box, and a similar-sized piece of foam insulation. We recommend using rigid-foam insulation, normally colored blue, rather than the less-effective and coarser variety, usually colored white.

CONSTRUCTION

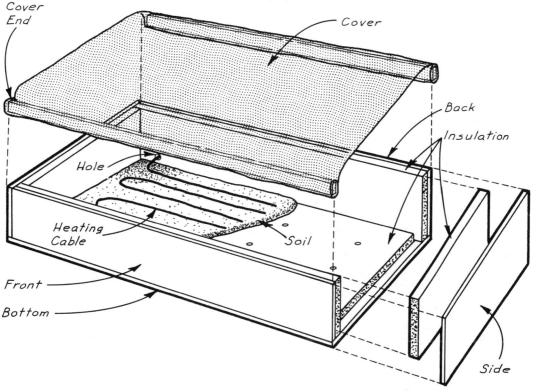

Cover End

Cover

Back

Insulation

Hole

Heating Cable

Soil

Front

Bottom

Side

Exploded-View Diagram

1. Refer to the cutting diagram, then cut the pieces for the propagation box from a 4 × 8-foot sheet of ½-inch exterior-grade plywood. The pieces should measure as follows: 27 × 61 inches for the bottom panel; 9 × 60 inches for the front panel; 11¾ × 60 inches for the back panel; and for the side panels, two 27-inch-long pieces that taper from 9 inches to 11¾ inches, all as shown.

2. Fasten the side panels so they overlap the ends of the front and back panels. Drill three ¹⁄₁₆-inch-diameter pilot holes with ⅛-inch-diameter shank holes per corner joint, then install 1½-inch #6 flathead wood screws to fasten the pieces together.

The assembled box should measure 27 × 61 inches.

3. Flip the box over and fasten the bottom panel to the side, front, and back panels. Use 1½-inch #6 flathead wood screws, after first drilling pilot and shank holes as in the previous step.

4. Paint the box inside and out with exterior-grade nontoxic enamel.

5. From a 4 × 8-foot sheet of 1-inch-thick rigid-foam insulation, cut panels, as shown in the cutting diagram, to insulate the box. Start by cutting the back panel to 11¾ × 60 inches. Press the panel into place. No glue or fasteners are needed. Cut the front panel

131

LUMBER CUTTING LIST

Size	Piece	Quantity
1 × 2		
¾'' × 1½'' × 61''	Cover ends	2
Plywood		
½'' × 27'' × 61''	Bottom panel	1
½'' × 11¾'' × 60''	Back panel	1
½'' × 9'' × 60''	Front panel	1
½'' × 11¾'' × 27''	Side panels	2

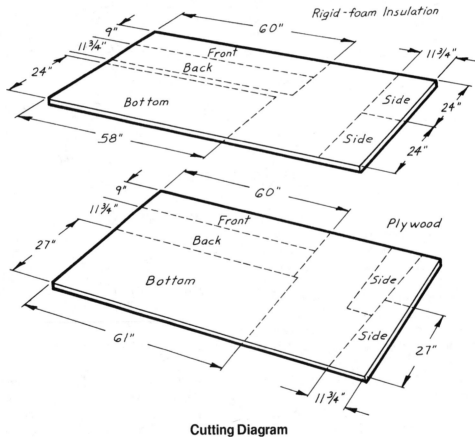

Cutting Diagram

to 9 × 60 inches and push it into place. Then cut the two side panels to 11¾ × 25½ inches each and push them into the box. Trim the top edge of each side panel flush with the box sides. Finally, cut the bottom panel to 25 × 58 inches and push it into place as well.

6. Flip the box over and drill ¼-inch-diameter drainage holes through the plywood bottom and foam panels. A dozen holes, evenly spaced, should be sufficient.

7. Set the propagation box in its permanent location, then spread a 1-inch layer of sand or fine gravel on the bottom of the box. Drill a 1-inch-diameter hole through the back of the box for the heating cable, as shown in the exploded-view diagram, positioning the hole just slightly above the top of the sand. Lay the heating cable on top of the sand, looping it back and forth within the box. Do not cross the cable over itself at any point. Spread potting soil over the cable to a depth of 3 inches.

8. Now build a cover for the box, using 6-mil polyethylene sheeting and two pieces of 1 × 2 (¾″ × 1½″) lumber. First, cut two pieces of 1 × 2 stock to 61 inches each for the ends. Cut the polyethylene to 36 × 61 inches. Then, roll the ends in the plastic and staple the assembly so it won't unroll. To use, lay the cover on top of the box, as shown in the exploded-view diagram, so that the ends hold the cover in place over the top of the box. Now you're ready to plant. Don't forget to plug in the heating cable!

PROPAGA- TION TRAY

Terry Luft of Didsbury, Alberta, Canada, considers raising seedlings to be the most important step in becoming a happy and successful gardener. His sturdy propagation tray is easy to build and will start a lot of seedlings.

The tray is built of ordinary 2 × 4 lumber and contains a heating cable to keep the soil warm. Heating the soil is one of the best ways to promote healthy, fast-growing plant roots. A translucent polyethylene cover over the ample 2 × 8-foot tray keeps water loss at a minimum and adds a greenhouse effect if the tray is located in a sunny area. Luft suggests that the propagation tray be made to operate automatically by adding a thermostat to control the heating cable and by installing a timer-controlled grow light.

SHOPPING LIST

Lumber
2 pcs. 2 × 4 × 10'
2 pcs. 1 × 2 × 8'
Plywood
1 pc. ⅜'' × 2' × 8' CDX
Hardware
4 flathead wood screws #8 × 1¼''
staples ⅝''
¼ pound galvanized common nails 12d
¼ pound galvanized common nails 4d
1 pc. 4-mil polyethylene 4' × 12'
4 pcs. garden hose ½'' I.D. × 42''
1 heating cable 30'
exterior-grade nontoxic enamel

CONSTRUCTION

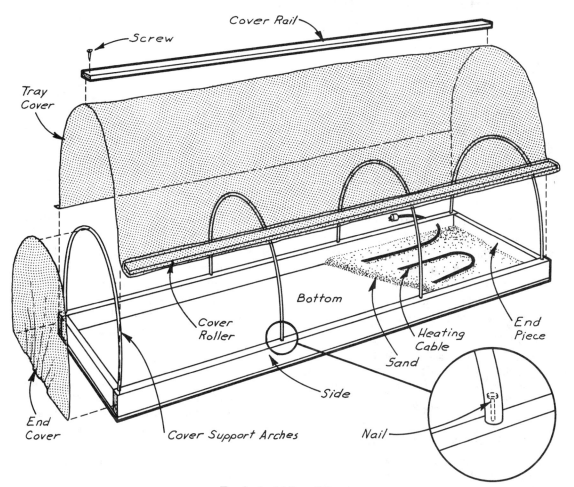

Cover Rail

Screw

Tray Cover

Cover Roller

Bottom

Heating Cable

End Piece

Sand

Side

End Cover

Cover Support Arches

Nail

Exploded-View Diagram

1. Cut two pieces of 2 × 4 (1½″ × 3½″) stock to 96 inches each for the side pieces of the tray. (Cut one piece from each of two 10-foot 2 × 4s if using the lumber lengths specified in the shopping list.) Then, cut two pieces of 2 × 4 stock to 21 inches each for the end pieces.

2. Fasten the ends and sides together to make the 2 × 8-foot rectangular tray frame, as

shown in the exploded-view diagram. Use 12d galvanized common nails.

3. Cut one piece of ⅜-inch CDX plywood to 24 × 96 inches for the bottom panel. Fasten the panel to the tray frame with 4d galvanized common nails. Align the edges of the panel so they are flush with the outer faces of the tray frame.

4. Drive eight 12d galvanized common nails

135

LUMBER CUTTING LIST

Size	Piece	Quantity
2 × 4		
1½″ × 3½″ × 96″	Side pieces	2
1½″ × 3½″ × 21″	End pieces	2
1 × 2		
¾″ × 1½″ × 96″	Cover rail	1
¾″ × 1½″ × 96″	Cover weight	1
Plywood		
⅜″ × 24″ × 96″	Bottom panel	1

into the top edges of the frame's side pieces, leaving 2 inches of each nail exposed. Space the nails 24 inches apart, and place them so each nail has a partner directly across the tray, as shown in the exploded-view diagram. The nails hold the cover support arches (see step 5).

5. Cut four pieces of ½-inch-I.D. garden hose to 42 inches each for the cover support arches. Attach them to the frame by pushing the ends of each hose over a pair of nails.

6. Cut one piece of 4-mil polyethylene sheet to 48 × 96 inches for the tray cover.

7. Use a 96-inch length of 1 × 2 (¾″ × 1½″) stock for the cover weight. Roll it up in one of the long edges of the cover one or two turns, then fasten the 1 × 2 to the polyethylene using ⅝-inch staples. This rolled edge is now the front of the cover.

8. Drape the cover over the support arches and center it end-to-end. Position the rolled-edge strip against the front side piece of the frame, and pull the polyethylene tight over the support arches toward the rear. Staple the loose, long edge of the poly-ethylene to the rear side piece of the tray

frame, being sure to keep the rolled front edge aligned with the front of the tray.

9. Cut two pieces of polyethylene to 42 × 48 inches each for the end covers. To fasten them in place, first roll the main cover back and remove the support arch at each end of the tray frame. Roll one 42-inch edge of each end cover around one piece of hose, then staple the polyethylene to the hoses to keep it in place.

10. Push the ends of the support arches back onto the nails. Pull the bottom edge of the polyethylene out from the frame, fold and gather the excess so that it conforms to the curvature of the tray supports, then staple the bottom edges to the frame. Trim away any excess polyethylene.

11. Use a full 96-inch length of 1 × 2 stock for the cover rail. Hold the 1 × 2 centered on top of the support arches and polyethylene cover, then drill ⅛-inch-diameter pilot holes through the rail and into the support arches. Remove the rail from the support arches, enlarge the holes in the rail to ⁵⁄₁₆-inch-diameter, then countersink them with a ½-inch-diameter bit. Return the rail to the support arches and fasten it in place using 1¼-inch #8 flathead wood screws.

12. Drill a 1-inch-diameter hole through the rear side piece of the tray frame to accept a plug from a heating cable (see step 4). Also drill several evenly spaced ½-inch-diameter holes through the bottom panel to promote drainage. Then paint the tray frame with exterior-grade nontoxic enamel to prevent moisture damage to the wooden parts.

13. When the paint has dried thoroughly, spread a layer of sand in the tray to a depth of about 1 inch.

14. Obtain a 30-foot heating cable and push the plug through the hole in the rear side piece of the frame. Loop the cable back and forth inside the tray on top of the sand, then cover with 2½ inches of potting soil.

15. If you wish to install any optional auxiliary equipment, such as a grow light, a timer for the light, or a thermostat for the heating cable, do this now. Follow the directions supplied with each appliance. Afterward, you are ready to plant.

RAISED-BED GARDEN-ING SYSTEM

SHOPPING LIST

Lumber
1 pc. 2 × 10 × 8′
2 pcs. 1 × 10 × 8′
2 pcs. 1 × 2 × 8′
Hardware
12 hex head lag bolts ⁵⁄₁₆″ × 3″
12 flat washers ⁵⁄₁₆″
½ pound cement-coated or galvanized
    common nails 6d

Together with the four projects that follow (see p. 142-157), here is an entire raised-bed gardening system developed by the Rodale Design Group. It makes intensive-style cultivation, especially in limited spaces, even more efficient and easy than it already is. The system is based on the simple-to-build wooden gardening frames shown here, each of which encloses 16 square feet of growing space. The 4 × 4-foot

138

frame size allows you to easily reach the center of the growing bed from any side. As a result, groups of frames may be

arranged in any pattern with no loss of convenience. This size also permits easy purchasing of lumber and reduces the amount of extra materials in the form of bracing that would be required if the various add-on accessories that make up the rest of the system were larger.

These accessories are a cold frame, sunshade, trellis, and fence panels. The cold frame and sunshade allow you to garden virtually anywhere, anytime. By using them, you can extend your growing season throughout all but the most severe months. The trellis lets you cultivate bountiful yields of vine crops by growing them vertically. Several trellis units can be attached to each frame. Installing the fence panels converts

139

any frame into a compost bin of 30-cubic-foot capacity.

The frames may be placed on tilled or untilled ground, or even on concrete if the plants you decide to grow require only shallow soil. You then fill each frame with compost- and fertilizer-enriched soil of your own making. Use pressure-treated lumber, if possible, for the frames and accessories. Otherwise, treat the wood yourself with copper naphthenate wood preservative. This chemical is not harmful to plants and will not contaminate them for use as food. Also use cement-coated, galvanized, or aluminum nails, and plated or brass hardware to protect against rust. For the cold frame, the flexible fiberglass glazing specified lasts the longest. Less durable, clear or translucent plastic sheeting may be substituted, however, and will work just as well.

CONSTRUCTION

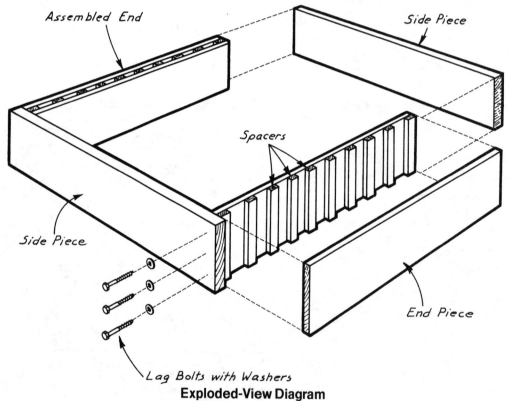

Exploded-View Diagram

To make one raised-bed gardening frame:

1. Cut two pieces of 2 × 10 (1½″ × 9¼″) stock to 48 inches each for the side pieces.
2. Cut four pieces of 1 × 10 (¾″ × 9¼″) stock to 45 inches each for the end pieces.
3. Cut 20 pieces of 1 × 2 (¾″ × 1½″) stock to 9¼ inches each for the spacers.
4. If pressure-treated stock is not used, apply copper naphthenate wood preservative to each piece.

5. Nail pairs of end boards together, sandwiching spacers in between, as shown in illustration A. The strength of the end-piece assemblies depends on their being nailed together from both sides. To do this, first mark the locations of the spacers on the end pieces so that if the spacers move during nailing they can be easily repositioned. Next, arrange the spacers between a pair of end boards and drive 6d cement-coated or galvanized common nails through the entire assembly from one side only. Then turn the assembly over and nail from that side. Repeat this procedure to con-

struct the remaining end piece.

6. Set the side pieces against the ends positioned for assembly. Do this on a flat surface and be sure that the boards meet squarely. Clamp the boards together or have someone hold them in place while you drill three $\frac{3}{8}$-inch-diameter pilot holes through the ends of each side piece, as shown in the exploded-view diagram, and into the outer spacers of the end pieces as well.

7. To complete the gardening frame, install $\frac{5}{16} \times 3$-inch hex head lag bolts and washers into the drilled holes and tighten them securely.

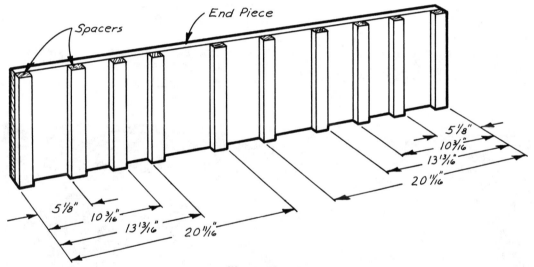

Illustration A

LUMBER CUTTING LIST

Size	Piece	Quantity
2 × 10		
1½″ × 9¼″ × 48″	Side pieces	2
1 × 10		
¾″ × 9¼″ × 45″	End pieces	4
1 × 2		
¾″ × 1½″ × 9¼″	Spacers	20

COLD FRAME FOR RAISED-BED GARDEN-ING SYSTEM

SHOPPING LIST

Lumber
1 pc. $1 \times 4 \times 5'$
2 pcs. $1 \times 2 \times 8'$
Lattice
1 pc. $\frac{1}{4}'' \times 1'' \times 8'$
Plywood
1 pc. $\frac{3}{4}'' \times 2' \times 4'$ exterior grade
Hardware
32 flathead wood screws #8 $\times 1\frac{1}{4}''$
10 flathead wood screws #6 $\times \frac{3}{4}''$
2 finishing washers #6
6 screen-door hooks 2''
4 eyescrews 2''
2 storm-window fasteners (hook-and-hanger type)
2 turn-buttons 2''
1 pc. fiberglass-reinforced plastic glazing $4' \times 54\frac{1}{2}''$

This easy-to-build cold frame is a versatile accessory to the Rodale-designed raised-bed gardening system described on p. 138. The cold frame stacks on top of the gardening frame, which is the basic unit of the system, and is held in place by posts that slip between the spacers in the gardening frame's doubled end pieces.

The cold frame is made up of two curved plywood ends, each with a removable panel to allow ventilation, when needed, covered with a flexible glazing of fiberglass-reinforced translucent plastic. The glazing can be fastened securely to the frame to seal out the harsh air of early or late growing-season weather, or rolled and fastened back to let in warmer air when plants are hardening off. Clear or translucent plastic sheeting will work as well as fiberglass but won't last as long. Be sure to use exterior-grade plywood and treat it beforehand with copper naphthenate wood preservative. It's also a good idea to paint or otherwise seal the ends of the plywood to prevent the gradual deterioration of the glue binding the laminations. Use pressure-treated or preservative-coated lumber as well for the smaller pieces, and use plated or brass hardware.

CONSTRUCTION

1. Cut two pieces of ¾-inch plywood to 12 × 46½ inches each for the two cold frame ends.

2. Lay the pieces on a flat surface. Then, using a cord with a pencil attached, scribe the 29-inch radius of the top edges and the 27-inch radius of the removable panels onto the pieces, as shown in illustration A. Also mark a line 2 inches from the lower edge of each piece to locate the panel's bottom edge. Finally, round off the panel corners by joining the layout lines for the top and bottom with curved lines, each having a 2-inch radius.

3. Cut out the cold frame ends and the panels within them. Start by making a plunge cut using a circular saw, then switch to a saber saw. Cut the panels carefully. Excess trimming and smoothing will cause them to fit poorly into their openings.

4. Cut four pieces of 1 × 2 (¾″ × 1½″) stock to 11 inches each for the stops, which hold the panels in place in the cold frame ends.

5. Fasten the stops on the inside of the cold frame across the panel openings, as shown in the exploded-view diagram. Use 1¼-inch #8 flathead wood screws. Trim the ends of the stops to match the curvature of the cold frame ends.

6. Cut two pieces of 1 × 4 (¾″ × 3½″) stock to 3½ inches each for the cross member supports that are fastened to the top inside edges of the cold frame ends. In each support, cut a notch ¾ inches wide × 1½ inches deep, as shown in illustration B.

7. Center and fasten the cross member supports to the top inside edges of the cold frame ends. Use two 1¼-inch #8 flathead wood screws for each support.

8. Cut four pieces of 1 × 4 stock to 12 inches each for the support posts, which join the cold frame to the gardening frame.

9. Slip the support posts between the end spacers of the gardening frame. Set the cold frame ends on the top edge of the gardening frame, outside the posts, and mark the position of the posts on the ends so that, when attached, the end pieces will align properly on top of the gardening frame with the posts in place. Then remove the posts and ends from the gardening frame

143

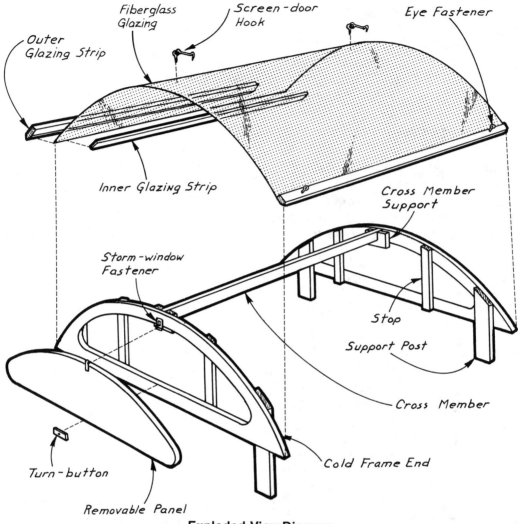

Outer Glazing Strip

Fiberglass Glazing

Screen-door Hook

Eye Fastener

Inner Glazing Strip

Cross Member Support

Storm-window Fastener

Stop

Support Post

Cross Member

Turn-button

Cold Frame End

Removable Panel

Exploded-View Diagram

and fasten the posts to the ends with 1¼-inch #8 flathead wood screws.

10. Cut one piece of 1 × 2 stock to 46½ inches for the cross member that supports the glazing.

11. Cut two pieces of 1 × 2 stock to 48 inches each for the outer glazing strips. Bevel the edges of the outer strips, as shown in illustration C, so that they will shed water.

12. Cut two pieces of lattice (¼″ × 1″) to 46½ inches each for the inner strips.

13. If pressure-treated stock is not used, apply copper naphthenate wood preservative to all parts of the cold frame.

14. Install the hook portion of a storm-window fastener on each cold frame end, centered above the panel opening, as shown in illustration A. Then fit each panel in place,

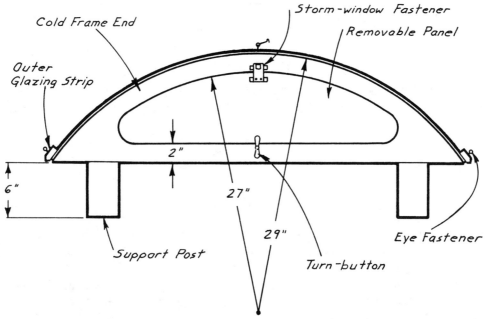

Cold Frame End

Storm-window Fastener

Removable Panel

Outer Glazing Strip

2"

6"

27"

29"

Support Post

Turn-button

Eye Fastener

Illustration A

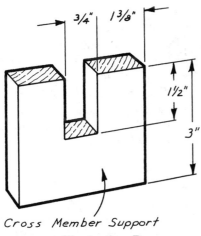

3/4" 1 3/8"

1 1/2"

3"

Cross Member Support

Illustration B

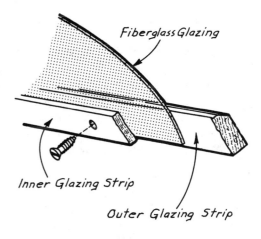

Fiberglass Glazing

Inner Glazing Strip

Outer Glazing Strip

Illustration C

and mark and install the slotted portion of each fastener on the panels themselves.

15. Hang the panels from the hook portions of the fasteners and press the panels into

place. Then install a turn-button on each cold frame end, centered beneath each fitted panel, to hold the panels in place.

16. Cut one piece of fiberglass-reinforced

145

LUMBER CUTTING LIST

Size	Piece	Quantity
1 × 4		
¾″ × 3½″ × 12″	Support posts	4
¾″ × 3½″ × 3½″	Cross member supports	2
1 × 2		
¾″ × 1½″ × 48″	Outer glazing strips	2
¾″ × 1½″ × 46½″	Cross member	1
¾″ × 1½″ × 11″	Stops	4
Lattice		
¼″ × 1″ × 46½″	Inner glazing strips	2
Plywood		
¾″ × 12″ × 46½″	Cold frame ends	2

plastic glazing to 48 × 54½ inches.

17. Fasten the cross-member across the width of the glazing at its midpoint. Use two 2-inch screen-door hooks as fasteners, fitted with #6 finishing washers where the hooks penetrate the glazing on the outside, as shown in illustration A. This will allow the glazing to be opened partway on the cold frame, yet still be fastened securely.

18. Attach the inner and outer glazing strips to the front and rear edges of the glazing, sandwiching the glazing in between, as shown in illustration C. Fasten with ¾-inch #6 flathead wood screws.

19. Install eyescrews at both ends of each outer glazing strip to align with the hooks installed in the cross member.

20. Install the completed cold frame ends on top of the gardening frame, then install the glazing by fitting the cross member between the ends and into the notched cross member supports.

21. Finally, install screen-door hooks in the upper corners of the gardening frame itself, to align with the eyescrews attached to the ends of the outer glazing strips. Use the hooks to secure the glazing when you wish to completely cover the area within the gardening frame.

SUNSHADE FOR RAISED-BED GARDEN-ING SYSTEM

SHOPPING LIST

Lumber
1 pc. 1 × 4 × 10'
5 pcs. 1 × 2 × 8'
Lattice
13 pcs. ¼" × 2" × 8'
Dowel
1 pc. ⁵⁄₁₆ × 1' hardwood
Hardware
24 flathead wood screws #6 × ¾"
4 loose pin hinges 2" × 3"
½ pound finishing nails 6d
¼ pound aluminum nails 1"
exterior-grade enamel

This slatted sunshade is also part of the Rodale-designed raised-bed gardening system described on p. 138. The shade allows you to grow crops, such as lettuce, chard, spinach, and other low-to-the-ground plants that do not like direct sunlight or high heat, right through the summer months in most areas. The overlapping rows of slats that make up each shade filter the direct rays of the sun, and the box construction encloses a layer of semidead air that helps to keep temperatures cool inside the gardening frame. Like the other accessories to the gardening system, this one also attaches to the gardening frame by means of posts that slip between the spacers in the gardening frame's ends.

Make the sunshade of pressure-treated lumber, or use stock you treat yourself with copper naphthenate wood preservative. A coat or two of white exterior-grade paint

will also extend the life of the shade and furnish extra cooling as well, by reflecting rather than absorbing sunlight. As with any outdoor project, all hardware and fasteners should be rustproof or at least rust-resistant.

CONSTRUCTION

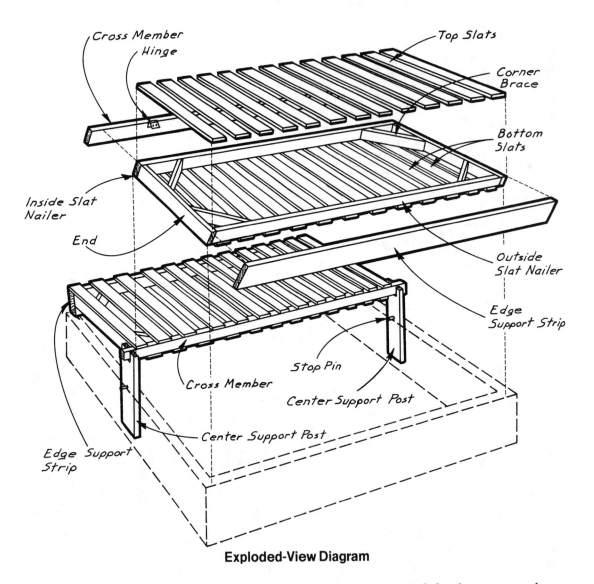

Cross Member
Hinge

Top Slats

Corner
Brace

Bottom
Slats

Inside Slat
Nailer

End

Outside
Slat Nailer

Edge
Support Strip

Stop Pin

Cross Member

Center Support Post

Center Support Post

Edge Support
Strip

Exploded-View Diagram

1. Cut two pieces of 1×4 ($\frac{3}{4}'' \times 3\frac{1}{2}''$) stock to $44\frac{3}{8}$ inches each, one for the edge support strip of each shade half. Also cut two pieces of 1×4 stock to 12 inches each for the shade's center support posts.

2. Cut two pieces of 1×2 ($\frac{3}{4}'' \times 1\frac{1}{2}''$) stock

to 48 inches each for the cross members. These rest in notches cut in the support posts and are fastened with hinges to the shade half-frames. Also cut two pieces of 1×2 stock to $44\frac{3}{8}$ inches, one for the inside slat nailer of each half-frame, to which

LUMBER CUTTING LIST

Size	Piece	Quantity
1 × 4		
¾″ × 3½″ × 44⅜″	Edge support strips	2
¾″ × 3½″ × 12″	Center support posts	2
1 × 2		
¾″ × 1½″ × 48″	Cross members	2
¾″ × 1½″ × 44⅜″	Inside slat nailers	2
¾″ × 1½″ × 42⅞″	Outside slat nailers	2
¾″ × 1½″ × 21½″	Ends	4
¾″ × 1½″ × 6″	Corner braces	8
Lattice		
¼″ × 2″ × 23″	Top slats	26
¼″ × 2″ × 22¼″	Bottom slats	24
Dowel		
⁵⁄₁₆″ × 2½″	Stop pins	2

the hinged cross members are attached.

3. For the shade half-frames themselves, cut two pieces of 1 × 2 stock to 42⅞ inches each for the outside slat nailers (to which the edge support strips will also be attached; see step 7), four pieces to 21½ inches each for the ends, and eight pieces to 6 inches each for the corner braces. Miter the ends of each corner brace to a 45-degree angle so they will fit tightly against the inside edges of the frames, when assembled.

4. Cut 26 pieces of ¼ × 2-inch lattice stock to 23 inches each for the top slats, whose ends project over the edges of both the slat nailer and the front side, and 24 pieces of lattice stock to 22¼ inches each for the bottom slats, whose ends butt flush against the inner face of each outside piece.

5. Finally, cut two pieces of ⁵⁄₁₆-inch-diameter dowel to 2½ inches each for the stop pins. These are inserted through holes drilled in the support posts to regulate the height of

the sunshade above the center of the growing frame (see step 12).

6. If pressure-treated stock is not used, apply copper naphthenate wood preservative to all parts of the sunshade.

7. Assemble the shade half-frames. To make one frame, first fasten together the outside slat nailer and the edge support strip, then attach the ends, inside slat nailer (1½ inches longer than the outside slat nailer), and corner braces. Use 6d finishing nails throughout. Repeat the procedure to assemble the other frame.

8. Cut a notch 1⅝ inches wide by 1⅝ inches deep in one end of each center support post. Center the notch so both halves fall equally on each side of each post's centerline.

9. Paint all parts of the sunshade, including the slats, before assembly. Use two coats of exterior-grade enamel. White is recommended.

10. After the paint is dry, attach the top and bottom slats to each frame. Overlap the

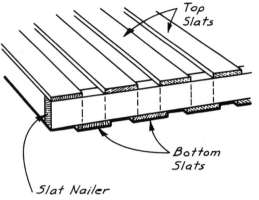

Illustration A

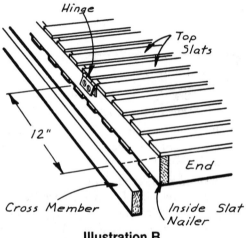

Illustration B

slats so they act as baffles to break up direct sunlight, as shown in illustration A. Use two 1-inch aluminum nails per slat.

11. Attach two pairs of 2 × 3-inch loose pin hinges between the hinge side of each half-frame and its accompanying cross member. You will need four hinges in all. Use ¾-inch #6 flathead wood screws as fasteners. Locate the hinges approximately 12 inches from the ends of each half-frame. Be sure to attach the hinges at the top of each frame so that when the half-frame is in place on the gardening frame, it will open upward, as shown in illustration B.

12. Drill a 5/16-inch-diameter hole along the centerline of each support post, 6 inches from the ends. Insert the short lengths of dowel, cut in step 5, through each hole. Glue is not necessary.

13. Finally, assemble the sunshade by first inserting the support posts between the center spacers at each end of the gardening frame, so that the edge of the frame contacts the stop pin in each post. Then install the half-frames in place by setting the ends of the cross members in the support-post notches and letting the dropped front portion of each front side piece rest on the top edge of the gardening frame.

TRELLIS FOR RAISED-BED GARDEN-ING SYSTEM

This simple trellis attachment fits the Rodale-designed raised-bed gardening system described on p. 138. The trellis is a cinch to build and is easy to disassemble for storage. No metal fasteners are used. As many as four trellises can be installed on a single gardening frame, with comfortable spacing in between, for raising crops such as peas, beans, and cucumbers. For squash, melons, tomatoes, or other vine crops, using only two or three trellises works better. Pea netting, hung from brass cup hooks, lets plants climb easily and is strong enough to support all but the heaviest melons or squash. Use pressure-treated lumber, if possible; otherwise, preserve untreated stock yourself with copper naphthenate wood preservative.

CONSTRUCTION

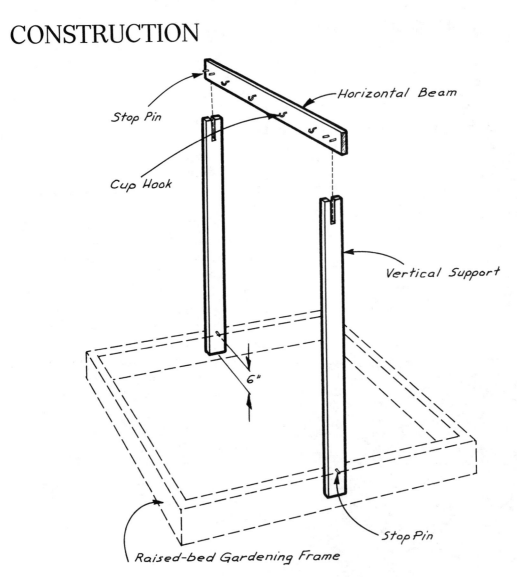

Horizontal Beam

Stop Pin

Cup Hook

Vertical Support

6"

Stop Pin

Raised-bed Gardening Frame

Exploded-View Diagram

1. Cut two pieces of 1 × 4 (¾″ × 3½″) stock to 48 inches each for the vertical supports, and one piece of 1 × 4 stock to 48 inches for the horizontal beam.

2. Cut six pieces of 5/16-inch-diameter dowel to 2½ inches each for the stop pins.

3. If pressure-treated stock is not used, apply

copper naphthenate wood preservative to all the wood pieces and allow them to dry thoroughly.

4. Cut a deep notch ¾ inch wide × 3½ inches deep, centered in the top of each vertical support.

5. Drill one 5/16-inch-diameter hole in each

LUMBER CUTTING LIST

Size	Piece	Quantity
1 × 4		
¾'' × 3½'' × 48''	Vertical supports	2
¾'' × 3½'' × 48''	Horizontal beam	1
Dowel		
⁵⁄₁₆'' × 2½''	Stop pins	6

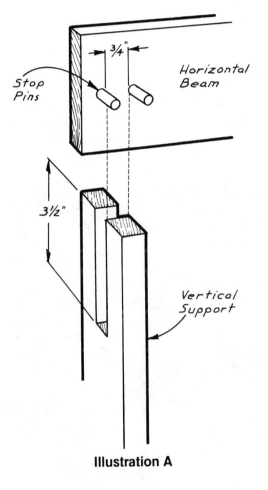

Illustration A

vertical support, centered 6 inches from the bottom end.

6. Drill two ⁵⁄₁₆-inch-diameter holes through each end of the horizontal beam, as shown in illustration A. The distance between each hole in a pair should equal ¾ inch (the thickness of the stock used for the vertical supports).

7. Install six ¾-inch brass cup hooks at evenly spaced intervals along one face of the horizontal beam. From these hooks, hang pea netting or other trellis material upon which plants may climb.

8. Insert the stop pins through the holes near the bottoms of the vertical supports and at the ends of the horizontal beam (glue is not necessary).

9. Insert the vertical supports in the raised-bed gardening frame, then slip the horizontal beam into the notches in the tops of the supports. The top of each support should slide between a pair of stop pins. Trim the netting or trellis material off close to the surface of the soil within the gardening frame.

FENCE PANELS FOR RAISED-BED GARDEN-ING SYSTEM COMPOST BIN

SHOPPING LIST

Lumber
11 pcs. 1 × 4 × 8'
4 pcs. 1 × 2 × 8'
Dowel
1 pc. 5⁄16'' × 2'
Hardware
160 flathead wood screws #8 × 1¼''
48 flathead wood screws #6 × ¾''
8 strap hinges 3''

This assembly of fence panels completes the Rodale-designed raised-bed gardening system described on p. 138. Installed on top of a gardening frame, these panels extend its height by about 2 feet, transforming the frame into a conveniently sized compost bin with a capacity of 30 cubic feet. Panels that fit over the ends of the gardening frame are made with vertical posts long enough to slip down into place between the spacers in the frame's ends, just like the other components of the system. Panels that fit over the front and back of the frame are fastened to the end units with sturdy strap hinges so they will fold flat for storage. In addition, one of the end panels is actually made in three sections.

The middle section lifts out for easy loading and removal of material.

Pressure-treated lumber and plated steel fasteners are best for making these panels. If you cannot find pressure-treated lumber, coat untreated stock yourself with copper naphthenate wood preservative.

154

CONSTRUCTION

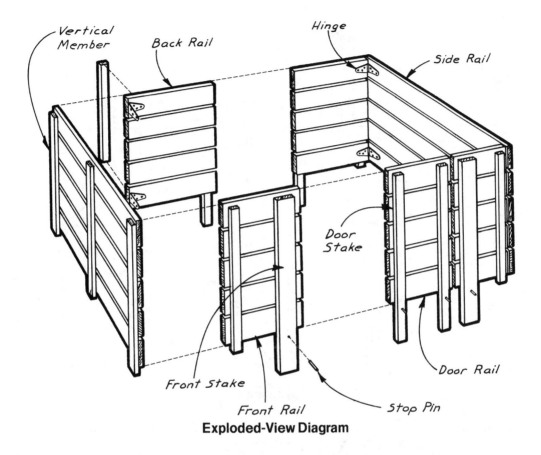

Vertical Member

Back Rail

Hinge

Side Rail

Door Stake

Front Stake

Front Rail

Stop Pin

Door Rail

Exploded-View Diagram

1. Cut and label the following pieces of 1 × 4 (¾″ × 3½″) stock: 10 pieces to 45 inches each for the side rails; 10 pieces to 22½ inches each for the back rails; 10 pieces to 14¼ inches each for the front rails; 2 pieces to 29½ inches each for the front stakes; and 5 pieces to 15½ inches each for the door rails.

2. Cut and label the following pieces of 1 × 2 (¾″ × 1½″) stock: 10 pieces to 22½ inches each for the vertical members; 2 pieces to 29½ inches each for the back stakes; and 2 pieces to 29½ inches each for the door stakes.

3. Cut six pieces of ⁵⁄₁₆-inch-diameter dowel to 2½ inches each for the stop pins.

4. If pressure-treated stock is not used, apply copper naphthenate wood preservative to all the pieces of lumber and allow them to dry thoroughly.

5. Drill one ⁵⁄₁₆-inch-diameter hole centered 6 inches from the bottom of each door stake, front stake, and back stake to accept the stop pins.

6. Insert the stop pins into the holes (glue is not necessary), then insert the stakes between the spacers in the ends of the garden frame, as shown in illustration A. Now position each door rail, side rail, and back rail one at a time in its respective location, and mark each piece so that it can be

155

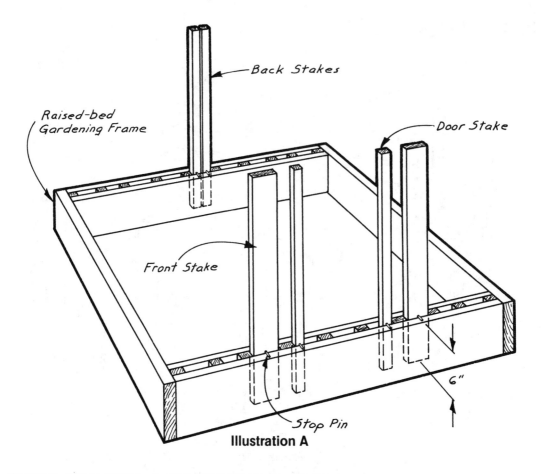

Back Stakes

Raised-bed
Gardening Frame

Door Stake

Front Stake

Stop Pin

6"

Illustration A

LUMBER CUTTING LIST

Size	Piece	Quantity
1 × 4		
¾″ × 3½″ × 45″	Side rails	10
¾″ × 3½″ × 29½″	Front stakes	2
¾″ × 3½″ × 22½″	Back rails	10
¾″ × 3½″ × 15½″	Door rails	5
¾″ × 3½″ × 14¼″	Front rails	10
1 × 2		
¾″ × 1½″ × 29½″	Back stakes	2
¾″ × 1½″ × 29½″	Door stakes	2
¾″ × 1½″ × 22½″	Vertical members	10
Dowel		
5/16″ × 2½″	Stop pins	6

joined accurately to the stakes when they are removed and laid flat on a work surface.

7. Remove the stakes from the frame. Also remove the stop pins from the stakes, if desired, to make working easier. Lay out each panel—stakes and rails—in their respective positions. Then fasten the rails to the stakes with 1¼-inch #8 flathead wood screws. Use two screws per joint. Make sure all rails are square to all stakes and that the rails align squarely end-to-end where the panels form corners.

8. Fasten 3-inch strap hinges to the inside of the top and bottom rail at the ends of each panel which joins the bin's four corners, as shown in the exploded-view diagram. You will need only eight hinges in all. Use ¾-inch #6 flathead wood screws as fasteners. Be sure the edges of the rails in each panel remain aligned.

9. Install each hinged-together unit on the raised-bed gardening frame. In the opening at one end, between the two narrow panels, install the small center section to complete the bin.

BIG BOX GARDEN

SHOPPING LIST

Lumber
9 pcs. 2 × 8 × 8' pressure-treated
Hardware
4 pcs. steel reinforcing rod (rebar) ½"
    diameter × 30"
16 wood screws #10 × 1"
8 straps for ½" pipe

You can obtain all the advantages of a double-dug garden and then some with this large, three-tiered garden box designed by the Rodale Design Group. The box rises nearly 2 feet above ground level and has a capacity of 58 cubic feet. You can fill it with your own mix of gardening soil, pre-loosened and enriched with a hearty supply of organic matter. The "big box," as we call it, is also just the thing for growing items with specific needs (such as melons),

or for establishing a growing area where drainage is difficult. It goes without saying that the big box is a boon to gardeners who have difficulty stooping.

The big box garden is constructed of pressure-treated pine to maximize its durability. Notches cut in the ends of the lum-

ber allow easy assembly and disassembly. Steel reinforcing rods (called rebar in the building-construction trades), strapped to the outside of the lapped ends of the box, give the joints stability. The height of the box may be easily altered by adding or removing courses of lumber, or by building it using boards of different widths. Naturally, the overall dimensions of the box may be altered as well, to suit individual needs, merely by using lumber of different dimensions than that which we've specified for ours.

CONSTRUCTION

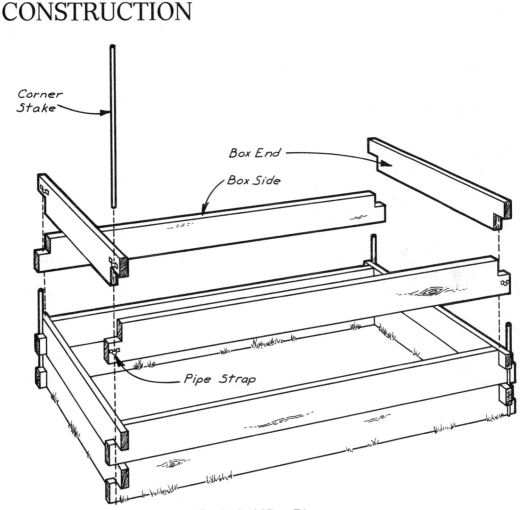

Exploded-View Diagram

1. Use six pieces of pressure-treated 2 × 8 (1½″ × 7¼″) stock, each 96 inches in length, for the box sides.
2. Cut six pieces of pressure-treated 2 × 8 stock to 48 inches each for the box ends.
3. Cut a 3-inch-wide notch 3⅝ inches long at both ends of all 12 boards, as shown in illustration A.
4. Cut four pieces of ½-inch-reinforcing rod to 30 inches each for the corner stakes.
5. Form a rectangle with the bottom course of boards, lapping their notched ends, as shown in the exploded-view diagram. Level the ground beneath the boards, if necessary. Then place the remaining two courses on top of the first one.
6. Drive a stake into the ground at each corner to hold the sides of the box together securely. Keep the stakes themselves in place by fastening two pipe straps around each one and anchoring the straps to alternating sides and ends of the box at the corners. Use 1-inch #10 wood screws.
7. Fill the box with prepared garden soil.

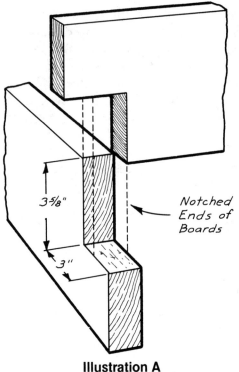

Illustration A

LUMBER CUTTING LIST

Size	Piece	Quantity
2 × 8		
1½″ × 7¼″ × 96″	Box sides	6
1½″ × 7¼″ × 48″	Box ends	6

CABIN-JOINTED PLANTER

SHOPPING LIST

Lumber
4 pcs. $2 \times 4 \times 8'$
Hardware
¼ pound fence staples
1 pc. plastic sheet $2' \times 10'$
20 pounds gravel

This sturdy, outdoor box for containing plants, shrubs, or dwarf trees is ruggedly beautiful in its simplicity. No fasteners need be used in its construction: The pieces interlock at the corners like the notched logs of a log cabin, hence the planter's name. As an added bonus, the planter may be easily disassembled for moving, merely by lifting the pieces off one another. The planter shown in the photo and plans belongs to its builder, Fred Beucher, of Hazelwood, Missouri.

All the pieces of the cabin-jointed planter should be pressure-treated to prevent decay. In addition, attaching a sheet of plastic to the inside of the box will keep the soil from contacting the wood directly and also prevent soil from seeping out the bottom. A layer of gravel added to the planter before filling it with soil will promote effective drainage.

CONSTRUCTION

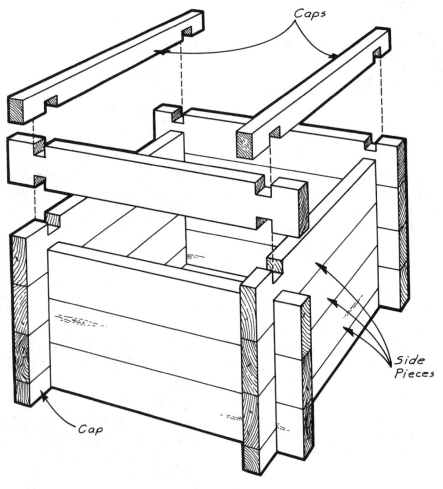

Caps

Side Pieces

Cap

Exploded-View Diagram

1. Cut 14 pieces of 2×4 ($1\frac{1}{2}'' \times 3\frac{1}{2}''$) stock to 24 inches each to make the sides of the box.

2. Rip two of the pieces cut in step 1 to measure approximately $1\frac{1}{2}'' \times 1\frac{1}{2}''$ for the four caps.

3. Lay out and cut notches measuring $\frac{7}{8}$ inch deep $\times$ $1\frac{1}{2}$ inches wide in each piece (not including the caps), 2 inches from each

end, as shown in illustration A. An efficient way to do this is first to clamp all 14 pieces together face-to-face, making sure their ends are flush, then scribe across their top edges using the $1\frac{1}{2}$-inch-wide tongue of a framing square. Use a portable circular saw to cut the notches, setting the blade for a $\frac{7}{8}$-inch depth of cut and making repeated passes between the scribed lines. After you have cut the notches on

LUMBER CUTTING LIST

Size	Piece	Quantity
2 × 4		
1½″ × 3½″ × 24″	Side pieces	14
2 × 2		
1½″ × 1½″ × 24″	Caps	4

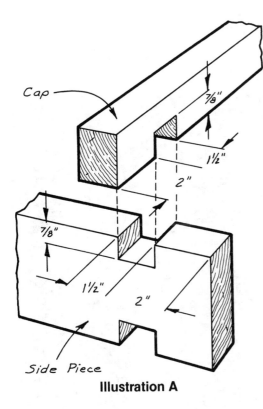

Illustration A

the upper halves of the pieces, flip the stack over and repeat.

4. Clamp the four caps together and follow the procedure in the previous step to cut ⅞ × 1½-inch notches in their upper halves only, as shown in illustration A.

5. Assemble the planter by stacking the interlocking pieces, as shown in the exploded-view diagram, then placing the caps on top, notches downward. If you wish to make the assembly permanent, drive 8d galvanized common nails through each overlapping section as the pieces are set in place.

6. To prevent decay and loss of soil, line the assembled planter with a sheet of plastic, using fence staples to attach it to the inside walls. Now it's ready to use. Add a few inches of gravel first to allow good drainage, then add the soil.

PATIO PLANTER

H. R. Hebbe of St. Paul, Minnesota, designed this attractive system of boxes with trellises to raise tomatoes and vine crops on his patio. Plant production has been startling: an average of 38 cucumbers from two plants raised in one box alone, and 99 tomatoes, also from two plants raised in one box! The secret? Hebbe says it's because he waters from the bottom up instead of from the top down. The planters rest on a bed of gravel within a sturdy metal pan, also part of the project. At watering time Hebbe fills the pan, not the boxes, and lets the plants soak up moisture on their own. For frost protection, the entire trellis frame can be covered with a large plastic trash bag without interfering with normal watering.

SHOPPING LIST

Lumber
12 pcs. 1 × 4 × 8′
Hardware
12 flathead wood screws #8 × 1½″
1 pound galvanized common nails 8d
1 pound galvanized common nails 3d
1 pc. nylon cord ⅛″ × 25′
1 pc. tin 2′ × 56″
6 cubic feet gravel
1 gallon nontoxic exterior-grade enamel
    or stain

CONSTRUCTION

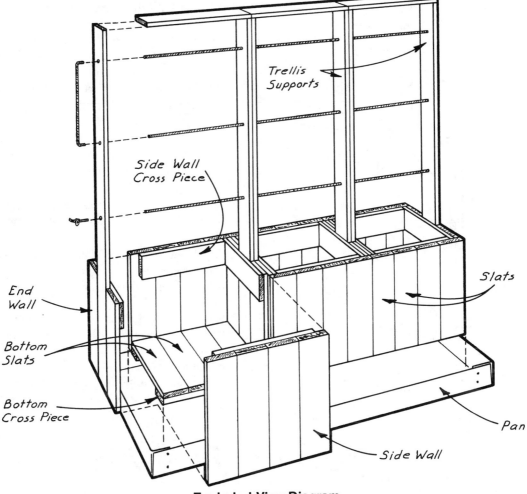

Trellis
Supports

Side Wall
Cross Piece

End
Wall

Bottom
Slats

Bottom
Cross Piece

Slats

Pan

Side Wall

Exploded-View Diagram

1. Cut the following pieces of 1 × 4 (¾″ × 3½″) stock: 6 pieces to 48 inches each for the trellis supports; 36 pieces to 12 inches each for the slats; 6 pieces to 11 inches each for the side wall cross pieces; and 6 pieces to 10½ inches each for the end wall cross pieces.
2. Arrange two slat pieces, one trellis sup-

port, and one end wall cross piece to build one end wall, as shown in illustration A. Place the support between the slats so that the ends of each piece are flush, then place the cross piece flush with the ends of the slats. Fasten the pieces together using 3d galvanized common nails. Clinch the nails over if they protrude. Repeat the

165

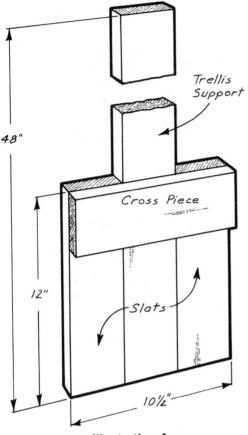

Illustration A

process to build a total of six end walls.

3. Arrange four slats and one side wall cross piece to build one side wall. Place the slats together with their ends flush, center the cross piece across one end of the slats, as shown in the exploded-view diagram, then fasten the pieces together using 3d galvanized common nails. Repeat the process to build a total of six side walls.

4. Attach the side walls to the end walls to make three boxes. (The end walls fit between the sides, as shown in the exploded-view diagram.) Fasten the pieces together using 8d galvanized common nails.

5. Cut six pieces of 1 × 4 stock to 12½ inches each for the bottom cross pieces, and 12 pieces to 10½ inches each for the bottom slats.

6. Arrange four bottom slats so that their ends are flush, then position two cross pieces on top of the slats. Fasten the pieces together using 3d galvanized common nails to make one bottom panel. Trim the bottom panel to approximately 10½ × 12½ inches so it fits inside one of the boxes. Then repeat the previous steps to construct two additional bottom panels and trim them to fit the other two boxes. Drill a dozen

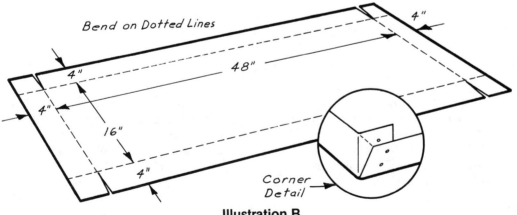

Illustration B

LUMBER CUTTING LIST

Size	Piece	Quantity
1 × 4		
¾″ × 3½″ × 48″	Trellis supports	6
¾″ × 3½″ × 14″	Trellis cross pieces	3
¾″ × 3½″ × 12½″	Bottom cross pieces	6
¾″ × 3½″ × 12″	Slats	36
¾″ × 3½″ × 11″	Side wall cross pieces	6
¾″ × 3½″ × 10½″	Bottom slats	12
¾″ × 3½″ × 10½″	End wall cross pieces	6

or so evenly spaced ½-inch-diameter holes through each bottom panel to allow water to reach the plant roots.

7. Fasten the bottom panels inside the boxes using 8d common galvanized nails. Fasten the slats to the panels on all four sides so there are no loose slats.

8. Cut three pieces of 1 × 4 stock to 14 inches for the trellis cross pieces. Drill and countersink ⅛-inch-diameter pilot holes, then fasten these pieces to the top of the supports using two 1½-inch #8 flat-head wood screws per joint.

9. Obtain a sheet of tin measuring 24 × 56 inches for the bottom pan. Cut the corners of the sheet as shown in illustration B.

Fold the sheet to form the pan, then solder the corners or drill ⅛-inch-diameter holes and fasten them using ⅛ × ½-inch pop rivets.

10. Apply a coat of exterior-grade, nontoxic enamel or stain to the boxes and bottom pan.

11. Spread gravel in the bottom of the pan to a depth of about 1 inch. Set the boxes in the pan and fill them with garden soil.

12. Drill ¼-inch-diameter holes through the trellis supports, spacing the holes at 12-inch intervals along the centerline. Thread 25 feet of ⅛-inch-diameter nylon cord through the holes in the supports, as shown in the exploded-view diagram. Now the patio planter is ready for use.

MEASUR-ING WHEEL

Homer Habersham of Columbus, Ohio, put together this measuring wheel that he uses to quickly and accurately measure the length of garden rows, property lines, and other distances. The 7⅝-inch-diameter wheel (salvaged from a lawn mower) has a circumference very close to 24 inches and is marked with a stripe painted across the tire tread. Each time the wheel is rolled along the ground one revolution—from stripe to stripe—Homer counts one 24-inch interval. A plastic clicker mounted on the wheel makes a sound each time the wheel goes around as well.

SHOPPING LIST

Dowel
1 pc. 1″ × 5′ hardwood or broom handle
Hardware
1 wheel 7⅝″ diameter × ½″ hub
2 panhead sheet-metal screws #6 × ½″
1 hex head machine bolt ½″ × 4″
2 nuts ⅝″
3 flat washers ⅝″
1 plastic angle (from milk jug) 2″ × 3″

LUMBER CUTTING LIST

Size	Piece	Quantity
Dowel		
1″ × 60″	Handle	1

168

CONSTRUCTION

1. Obtain a standard 1-inch-diameter dowel or broom handle approximately 60 inches in length. Drill a ½-inch-diameter hole 2 inches from the bottom to receive the axle bolt.

2. Fit a 7⅝-inch-diameter lawn-mower wheel onto a ½ × 4-inch hex head machine bolt, then install a ⅝-inch flat washer followed by a ⅝-inch nut, as shown in the exploded-view diagram.

3. Fit an additional ⅝-inch flat washer on the bolt, then push the bolt through the hole in the handle. Add another washer and nut to secure the wheel and axle to the handle.

4. Cut one corner section from a plastic milk jug to make a 2 × 3-inch angle for the clicker. Position the clicker on the inside of the wheel and drill two ¹⁄₁₆-inch-diameter pilot holes through the clicker into the wheel tread. Fasten the clicker in place using two ½-inch #6 panhead sheet metal screws.

5. Rotate the wheel a few times to make sure the clicker strikes the handle with each revolution. Adjust, if necessary.

6. Paint a bright stripe across the tire tread in line with the clicker. Now the measuring wheel is complete.

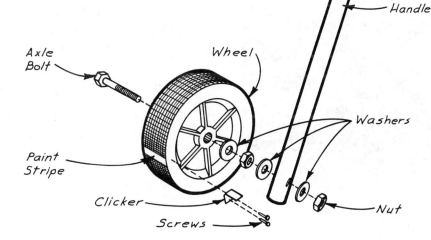

Exploded-View Diagram

ROW MARKER

Here's a garden row marker that is more than just two sticks and some twine. Its smooth styling is the product of Herman Kashmarek of Corcoran, Minnesota.

Kashmarek turned the spool of the row marker on a lathe from a block of maple. To make things simpler, our plans show how to make a suitable spool from plywood disks instead. Naturally, either way works. Use the method for which you have the tools. The handle and spikes of the marker are shaped from scraps.

To use the row marker, push the short

SHOPPING LIST

Lumber
1 pc. 1 × 6 × 1'
1 pc. 1 × 1 × 3'
Plywood
1 pc. ¾'' × 1' × 1' exterior grade
1 pc. ¼'' × 1' × 1' exterior grade
Dowel
⅜'' × 3½'' hardwood
Hardware
1 pc. sheet metal 6'' × 6''
2 flathead wood screws #8 × 1½''
6 roundhead wood screws #6 × ⅝''
1 roundhead wood screw #6 × ½''
1 hex head machine bolt ¼'' × 2½''
2 machine bolt nuts ¼''
3 flat washers 5/16''
1 flat washer 3/16''
1 eyescrew #8 × 1½''
100' nylon cord ⅛''

spike into the ground at the end of a row, then walk, holding the marker itself, to the opposite end of the row, unwinding the cord as you go. When you're in position, lock the spool with the locking dowel, pull the cord tight, and push the spike end of the marker into the earth. You now have a taut, straight line along which to plant your seeds. By the way, the spikes, when not used as row guides, make fine dibble sticks for planting.

CONSTRUCTION

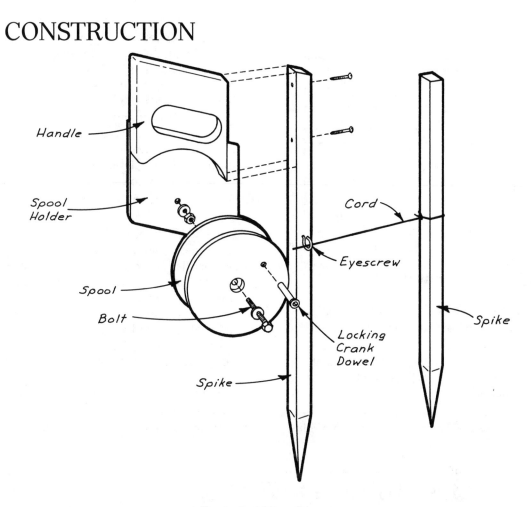

Handle

Spool Holder

Spool

Bolt

Spike

Cord

Eyescrew

Locking Crank Dowel

Spike

Exploded-View Diagram

1. Cut two pieces of 1 × 1 (¾" × ¾") stock for the spikes, the first to 19 inches, and the second to 15 inches. Trim one end of each spike to a point, beginning about 3 inches from the end.

2. Cut one piece of 1 × 6 (¾" × 5½") stock to 6 inches long, then shape it to make the handle, as shown in illustration A.

3. Drill and countersink two 3/16-inch-diameter pilot holes, then, fasten the handle to the longer spike using carpenter's wood glue and two 1½-inch #8 flathead wood screws,

as shown in the exploded-view diagram.

4. Cut two disks from ¾-inch exterior-grade plywood, each 2¾ inches in diameter, for the spool core pieces.

5. Cut two more disks from ¼-inch exterior-grade plywood, each 4½ inches in diameter, for the spool sides.

6. Apply wood glue and stack the disks to make the spool, keeping it as symmetrical as possible.

7. When the glue has set, drill a ¾-inch-diameter hole ¼ inch deep in the center

171

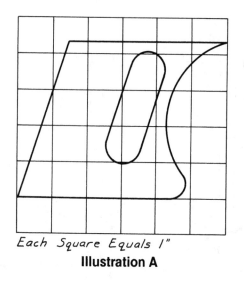

Each Square Equals 1"

Illustration A

of one side of the spool, then drill a ¼-inch-diameter hole through the center of the spool.

8. Drill a ⅜-inch-diameter hole through the spool for the locking crank dowel, 1¼ inches off-center.

9. Cut one 6 × 6-inch piece of sheet metal to the spool-holder shape shown in illus-

tration B. (If you wish, substitute ¼-inch exterior-grade plywood for the sheet metal.) Then, drill the ¼-inch-diameter hole in the position also shown. Fasten the spool holder to the handle by drilling ³⁄₁₆-inch-diameter holes through the sheet metal, and ¹⁄₁₆-inch-diameter pilot holes in the handle, as shown in the exploded-view diagram. Fasten the holder with ⅝-inch #6 roundhead wood screws.

10. Sand the spool and handle. Apply exterior-grade enamel of your choice.

11. Attach the spool to the handle with a ¼ × 2½-inch hex head machine bolt, three ⁵⁄₁₆-inch flat washers, and two nuts. Fit one washer on the bolt, then slip the bolt through the spool so the bolt head and washer seat in the countersunk center hole. Fit a second washer and a nut on the bolt, push the bolt through the hole in the spool holder, then fit another washer and nut on the bolt. Tighten the nuts so the bolt is snug, but be sure the spool still turns easily.

12. Cut one piece of ⅜-inch-diameter hard-

LUMBER CUTTING LIST

Size	Piece	Quantity
1 × 6		
¾″ × 5½″ × 6″	Handle	1
¾″ × 5½″ × 4¾″	Spool holder	1
1 × 1		
¾″ × ¾″ × 19″	Spike	1
¾″ × ¾″ × 15″	Spike	1
¾″ Plywood		
¾″ × 2¾″ diameter	Spool cores	2
¼″ Plywood		
¼″ × 4½″ diameter	Spool sides	2
Dowel		
⅜″ × 3½″	Locking crank dowel	1

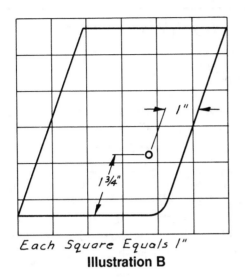

1"

1¾"

Each Square Equals 1"

Illustration B

wood dowel to 3½ inches for the locking crank dowel. Drill a 1/16-inch-diameter pilot hole into the end of the dowel, then fasten a 3/16-inch flat washer to the end with a ½-inch #6 roundhead wood screw. Push the other end of the dowel into the off-center hole in the spool.

13. Drill a 3/32-inch-diameter pilot hole in the handle spike, and install a 1½-inch #8 eyescrew to hold the cord.

14. Thread the end of a ⅛-inch-diameter nylon cord, 100 feet long, through the eyescrew, then tie it onto the spool. Pull the crank dowel out of the spool enough to turn the spool, then wind the cord onto the spool. When the line is on, tie the free end to the short spike. Now the row marker is complete.

PLANTING GUIDE

SHOPPING LIST

Lumber
1 pc. 1 × 2 × 5′
Hardware
8 galvanized nails 6d
1 pc. wire ⅛″ × 8′

This small planting guide uses guide wires that can be moved to space seeds 3, 4, 6, or 12 inches apart. The inventor is James Luckinbill of Grass Valley, California.

Luckinbill's garden plots measure 2 × 8 feet, which correspond nicely to the size of his planting guide. To use the guide, he places it over the garden bed and sows seed at each point where two guide wires cross, as well as where each wire meets a side of the frame. With his 2-foot-wide plots, Luckinbill can move down both sides while planting and cover up one-half of the garden bed with each pass.

174

CONSTRUCTION

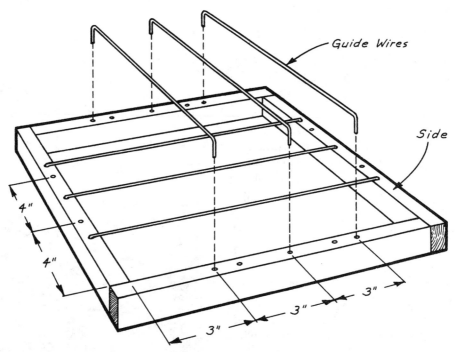

Exploded-View Diagram

1. Cut four pieces of 1×2 ($\frac{3}{4}'' \times 1\frac{1}{2}''$) stock to $12\frac{3}{4}$ inches each for the sides.

2. Assemble the side pieces pinwheel fashion, as shown in the exploded-view diagram, so that the resulting frame measures $13\frac{1}{2}$ inches on each side. Use 6d galvanized common nails.

3. Cut six pieces of $\frac{1}{8}$-inch-diameter wire to $14\frac{1}{2}$ inches each for the guide wires. Make 90-degree bends in each guide wire, $\frac{3}{4}$ inch from each end, to form pins.

4. Drill $\frac{1}{8}$-inch-diameter holes, in the positions shown in the exploded-view diagram, to fit the guide wires.

5. Insert the guide wires into the holes in the frame using either the 3-, 4-, or 6-inch spacing, depending upon your planting needs.

LUMBER CUTTING LIST

Size	Piece	Quantity
1×2		
$\frac{3}{4}'' \times 1\frac{1}{2}'' \times 12\frac{3}{4}''$	Sides	4

GARDEN-ER'S SEED PLANTER

SHOPPING LIST

Lumber
1 pc. 1 × 3 × 8'
Dowels
1 pc. ¾'' × 1' hardwood
1 pc. ¼'' × 3' hardwood
Hardware
1 self-tapping screw (for sheet-metal use)
    ¼'' × ¼''
1 slotted-head setscrew ¼'' × ¼''

Anyone who plants a garden from seed knows not only how important it is to sow each seed at a specified depth and at a specified distance from its neighbor, but also how tedious and time-consuming this task can be. Walter Souders of Ambler, Pennsylvania, has developed this gardener's seed planter that makes planting row crops easy, quick, and accurate.

The planter is simple to make. Essentially, it is a long board with holes drilled through it at 1-inch intervals. You align the board with the planting row, push a pointed dowel through the outermost hole at each end into the ground to keep the board in place, then drop seeds in the holes along the board at whatever intervals the directions call for. When all the seeds have been dropped in the holes, a special setting tool—a dowel with a setscrew device attached—is used to push each seed into the earth a specified amount. After all the seeds have been sown and set to their proper depth, you remove the planter board and cover the entire row with fine, sifted soil. Because the seeds you plant are set to uniform depth, all the seeds of a given variety will sprout at the same time. Also, since seeds are planted only one at a time and at calculated intervals, little thinning, if any, should be needed later. Finally, using

the gardener's seed planter, you can achieve straight, picture-postcard-looking garden rows. These will not only make your garden neat and attractive, but also will ease the tasks of weeding, tilling, and side dressing as well.

CONSTRUCTION

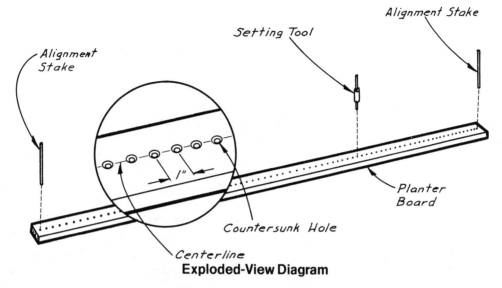

Exploded-View Diagram

1. Use one piece of 1 × 3 (¾″ × 2½″) stock 96 inches in length for the planter board.
2. Scribe the board's centerline along one face, running the entire length of the board.
3. Mark the centerline at 1-inch intervals, then drill ⁵⁄₁₆-inch-diameter holes through the board at each of these points, as shown in the exploded-view diagram.
4. To complete the planter board, countersink the top of each hole, using a ½-inch-diameter countersink bit, or use sandpaper to bevel the holes.
5. Now cut two pieces of ¼-inch-diameter dowel to 10 inches each for the planter board alignment stakes. Bevel one end of each to a point so that it will easily penetrate the soil. Set the finished stakes aside.
6. Cut one length of ¼-inch-diameter dowel to 7½ inches for the setting tool shaft.
7. Cut one length of ¾-inch-diameter dowel to 4 inches for the setting tool handle.
8. Drill a ¼-inch-diameter hole lengthwise

through the center of the handle to accept the shaft, as shown in illustration A. An accurate way to do this is to drill a hole from each end so they meet in the center. Ream the hole or sand the shaft so the handle slides easily with the shaft installed (see step 11).

9. For the setscrew, drill a ³⁄₁₆-inch-diameter hole in the handle, 2 inches from one end, at right angles to the shaft hole.
10. Install a ¼ × ¼-inch self-tapping screw (used for joining sheet metal; available at hardware stores) into the setscrew hole. The self-tapping screw will cut threads in the hole as it enters. Remove the screw when the threads are complete. Then, in its place install a ¼ × ¼-inch slotted-head setscrew for permanent use, as shown in illustration A.
11. Slide the handle onto the shaft of the setting tool. To adjust the tool, extend one end of the shaft beyond the handle by the amount specified in the seed-planting

LUMBER CUTTING LIST

Size	Piece	Quantity
1 × 3		
¾'' × 2½'' × 96''	Planter board	1
Dowels		
¾'' × 4''	Setting tool handle	1
¼'' × 10''	Planter board alignment stakes	2
¼'' × 7½''	Setting tool shaft	1

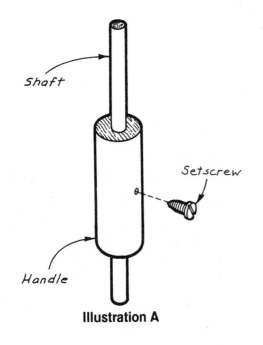

Illustration A

instructions, then add ¾ inch to compensate for the thickness of the planter board. Tighten the setscrew to hold the shaft snugly in the handle; do not overtighten.

12. Apply a finish to the planter board and alignment stakes, if you desire. Alternating colors surrounding the holes in the planter board will make it easier to use as a seed spacing guide. Do not apply a finish to the setting tool, since most types of finish will prevent the handle from sliding easily on the shaft.

PARALLEL-OGRAM PLANTING GUIDE

SHOPPING LIST

Lumber
1 pc. 1 × 6 × 4'
1 pc. 1 × 2 × 2'
Hardware
5 roundhead brass screws #4 × 1''
1 carriage bolt ¼'' × 1½'' with flat washer
    and wing nut
aluminum carpet tacks ⅜''
copper carpet tacks ⅜''

This handy planting guide was created by the Rodale Design Group to simplify spacing and sowing at planting time. Gardeners who plant intensively rather than in conventional rows will find it especially useful. By extending the guide's three row markers apart a distance equal to the spacing you wish the plants to have, accurate sowing at any interval of spacing becomes merely a matter of locking the markers in place with a wing nut, setting the guide on the garden, and pressing the seeds into the soil at locations identified by notches in each marker.

179

The notches are coded: Some are unmarked; others are identified with carpet tacks of different varieties. By sowing seeds at notches lacking tacks, when the row markers are set 4 inches apart, you will produce a grid of plants 4 inches from each other on all sides. Sowing at notches identified by aluminum tacks, when the markers are spread 8 inches apart, produces a pattern of plants on 8-inch centers. Sowing plants at notches bearing copper tacks, when the markers are set 12 inches apart, creates a grid of crops each 12 inches from its neighbor. Other spacing intervals are possible, of course. Just spread the markers apart the desired distance, then note which notches on each marker lie that same distance from each other. Plant seeds at these locations.

Our planting guide is made of cedar, finished clear so it looks nice and doesn't cause splinters.

CONSTRUCTION

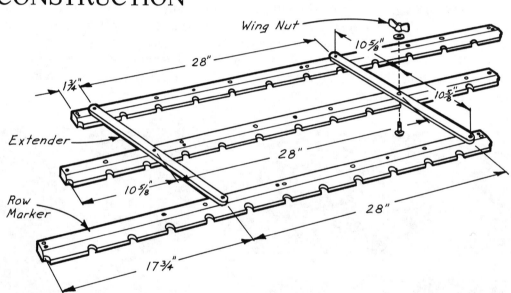

Exploded-View Diagram

1. Cut one piece of 1 × 6 (¾″ × 5½″) stock to 48 inches, then rip it into three pieces, each 1¾ inches in width, for the row markers.

2. Drill ⅝-inch-diameter half-circles on 4-inch centers along one edge of each marker for seed planting notches, as shown in the exploded-view diagram. To drill the half-circles, clamp each marker firmly against a stationary piece of scrap lumber the same thickness as the marker, then center an ordinary bit where the pieces meet, and drill a complete hole through both. If you wish, saw or chisel V-notches on each marker instead.

3. Rip a 30-degree bevel (or something approximate) along the notched edge of each marker. Leave the edge about ¼ inch thick.

LUMBER CUTTING LIST

Size	Piece	Quantity
1 × 6		
¾″ × 1¾″ × 48″	Row markers	3
1 × 2		
⅜″ × ¾″ × 22″	Extenders	2

4. Drive ⅜-inch aluminum carpet tacks beside the end notches and beside alternate notches along the length of each marker to designate 8-inch planting intervals. Drive ⅜-inch copper carpet tacks at the end notches also, and at every third notch along each marker, to designate 12-inch intervals. (Notches with no tack beside them indicate 4-inch intervals; see step 8.)

5. Rip a piece of 1 × 2 (¾″ × 1½″) stock or scrap lumber into two pieces, each measuring ⅜ × ¾ × 22 inches, for extenders. Sand or file a radius on the ends of each, if desired.

6. Center and drill a ⅛-inch-diameter hole ⅜ inch from each end of both extenders to accept pivot screws. Drill a similar hole centered midway along the length of one extender, and drill a ¼-inch-diameter hole centered midway along the other. The larger hole is for the lock bolt.

7. Scribe the locations for the lock bolt and pivot screws on the three markers, as shown in the exploded-view diagram. Drill a ¼-inch-diameter hole through the middle marker at the location for the lock bolt, then insert a ¼ × 1½-inch carriage bolt through the hole from the nonbeveled side. Hammer the head of the bolt slightly into the wood. Install the extenders using 1-inch #4 roundhead brass screws at all locations where a ⅛-inch hole was drilled. On the end of the lock bolt, install a flat washer and wing nut.

8. Spread the markers (they should always remain parallel) until the notches without tacks are 4 inches apart when measured across adjacent markers. Scribe a line along the edge of one extender (the one held in place by the lock bolt) where it crosses the middle marker. Label the line "4," to designate this planting guide setting. Spread the markers farther until the notches marked with aluminum tacks are 8 inches apart when measured across. Scribe this setting also with a line along the extender where it crosses the middle marker, and label it "8." Drive an aluminum tack at the spot as well. Finally, spread the markers so that notches marked with copper tacks are 12 inches apart, and mark that setting as you did the others; however, install a copper tack instead of an aluminum one.

9. Close the guide completely so that all three markers meet. Drill a ⅜-inch-diameter hole in the middle marker near one end so the guide may be hung on a nail when not in use.

10. Sand and finish the guide, if desired.

GARDEN STAKES

SHOPPING LIST

Lumber
1 pc. 1 × 10 × 5'
Hardware
9 pcs. aluminum rod ³/₁₆'' diameter × 9''
epoxy glue
exterior-grade enamel

These colorful garden stakes will liven up any garden during the long wait between seed time and harvest. Though intended by the Rodale Design Group (who came up with the patterns) partly to fulfill the traditional functions of locating seed rows and identifying their contents, their other purpose is to add an eye-catching touch of the unusual to the garden environment. Children will love them. Our designers made patterns for nine different fruits and vegetables, which they then cut out of pieces of No. 2 pine, painted with bright-colored enamel, and fastened to lengths of aluminum rod.

The instructions tell how to make one copy of each of our garden stakes. Probably you will want to make more than one of some vegetables, omit some you do not plan to grow, and develop additional patterns for fruits and vegetables that are missing from our collection. Use your imagination and whatever materials you already have at hand to create your own colorful set of garden stakes. If you like, glue all your patterns to one long board rather than cutting individual pieces as suggested in the steps that follow.

CONSTRUCTION

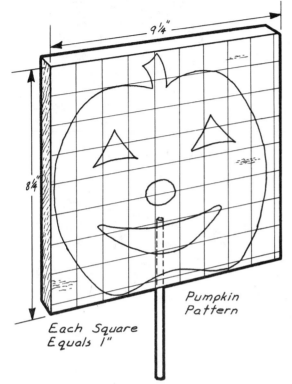

Pumpkin
Pattern

Each Square
Equals 1"

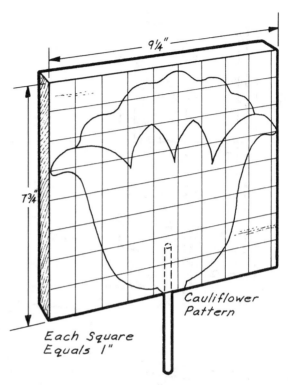

Cauliflower
Pattern

Each Square
Equals 1"

1. Using the grids provided on the cutting diagrams as guides, lay out the shapes of the nine fruits and vegetables on pieces of paper. Cut them out to create your patterns.

2. Cut one piece of 1 × 10 (¾″ × 9¼″) stock to 8¼ inches, and another piece to 7¾ inches. Glue the pumpkin pattern to the first piece and the cauliflower pattern to the second. Cut out both vegetable shapes.

3. Cut one piece of 1 × 10 stock to 9 inches. Rip it into two pieces, one 4 inches in width, leaving the other approximately 5⅛ inches in width. Glue the butternut squash pattern to the first, the corn pattern to the second, then cut out both vegetable shapes.

4. Cut one piece of 1 × 10 stock to 8 inches, then rip it down the middle. Glue the carrot pattern to one piece, the onion pattern to the other. Cut out both vegetable shapes.

5. Cut one piece of 1 × 10 stock to 6¾ inches, then rip it into two pieces. Make one piece 5 inches in width, leaving the other approximately 4⅛ inches wide. Glue the beet pattern to the first, the cucumber pattern to the second. Cut out both shapes.

6. Cut one piece of 1 × 10 stock to 11¼ inches. Rip off a 3¼-inch-wide strip and glue the watermelon pattern to it. Cut out the shape.

7. Drill a 3/16-inch-diameter hole several inches into each vegetable and fruit shape to receive a support stake, as shown on the respective cutting diagram. Also, cut nine pieces of 3/16-inch-diameter aluminum rod, each 9 inches in length, for the stakes themselves. Round-over the ends of all pieces, then fasten one stake in each fruit

183

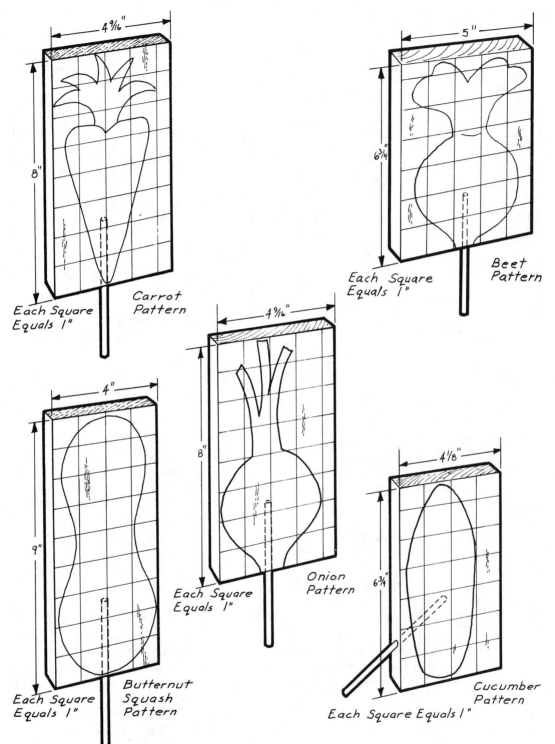

4 9/16"

8"

Each Square
Equals 1"

Carrot
Pattern

5"

6 3/4"

Each Square
Equals 1"

Beet
Pattern

4 9/16"

8"

Each Square
Equals 1"

Onion
Pattern

4"

9"

Each Square
Equals 1"

Butternut
Squash
Pattern

4 1/8"

6 3/4"

Cucumber
Pattern

Each Square Equals 1"

184

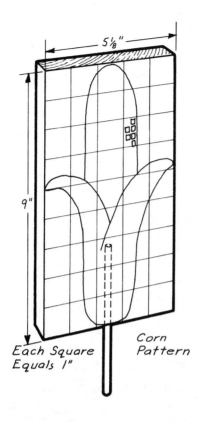

Corn
Pattern

Each Square
Equals 1"

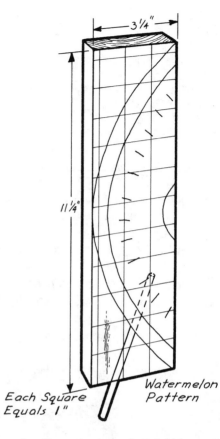

Each Square
Equals 1"

Watermelon
Pattern

and vegetable shape using epoxy glue.

8. Sand the wooden parts of the garden stakes and round-over all edges, except where crisp lines are desired. Paint the various parts of each fruit and vegetable the appropriate color.

LUMBER CUTTING LIST

Size	Piece	Quantity
1 × 10		
¾″ × 9¼″ × 8¼″	Pumpkin	1
¾″ × 9¼″ × 7¾″	Cauliflower	1
¾″ × 5⅛″ × 9″	Corn	1
¾″ × 5″ × 6¾″	Beet	1
¾″ × 4⁹⁄₁₆″ × 8″	Carrot	1
¾″ × 4⁹⁄₁₆″ × 8″	Onion	1
¾″ × 4⅛″ × 6¾″	Cucumber	1
¾″ × 4″ × 9″	Butternut squash	1
¾″ × 3¼″ × 11¼″	Watermelon	1

MODULAR TUNNEL CLOCHE

SHOPPING LIST

Lumber
2 pcs. $1 \times 3 \times 10'$
3 pcs. $1 \times 3 \times 8'$
Lattice
6 pcs. $\frac{1}{4}'' \times 1\frac{5}{8}'' \times 10'$
3 pcs. $\frac{1}{4}'' \times 1\frac{5}{8}'' \times 8'$
Hardware
8 pcs. 20-gauge sheet metal $1\frac{5}{8}'' \times 3''$
44 roundhead machine screws #8 $\times$ 1''
    with nuts
12 carriage bolts $\frac{1}{4}'' \times 2''$ with wing nuts
1 box staples $\frac{1}{4}''$
3 cup hooks
1 pc. 6-mil polyethylene $7' \times 17'$
3 pcs. 6-mil polyethylene $32'' \times 32''$
3 pcs. elastic banding $\frac{1}{2}'' \times 2'$
1 pint copper naphthenate wood preservative

This modular cloche system, created by the Rodale Design Group, is more elaborate than the plastic milk jugs so commonly used by many gardeners to warm the soil around early- and late-season plants. The system consists of 4×4-foot sections of wooden framework that can be joined together to form a tunnel of any length down a garden row or over a raised bed. Each section of the tunnel has a square

base and bowed top framework, and also has a door opening to allow access to the area within. The tunnel itself is made of polyethylene. For the purpose of this project, the tunnel cloche we built consists of three modules. The total dimensions are 4 feet wide and 12 feet long. The materials listed for purchasing and cutting are for a tunnel system this size. Should you wish to add or subtract modules, according to individual needs, merely alter the materials list. The construction of all modules is the same.

CONSTRUCTION

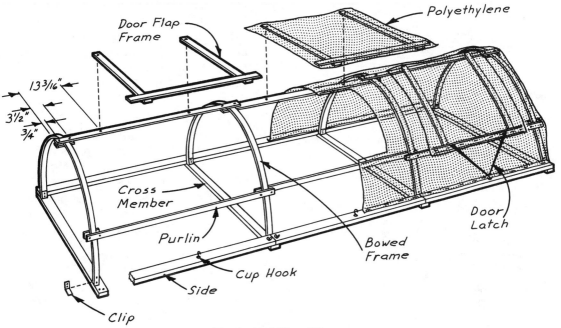

Exploded-View Diagram

1. Cut six pieces of 1×3 ($\frac{3}{4}'' \times 2\frac{1}{2}''$) stock to 48 inches each for the sides of the base. Drill a $\frac{5}{16}$-inch-diameter hole centered $\frac{5}{8}$ inch from the ends of each of these pieces to accept bolts for connecting them with cross members.

2. Cut four pieces of 1×3 stock to 53 inches each for the cross members. Drill a $\frac{5}{16}$-inch-diameter hole $\frac{5}{8}$ inch from each side and $1\frac{1}{4}$ inches from the ends of each cross member to accept bolts for connecting the sides and cross members, as shown in illustration A. Note that only one of each pair of holes will be used in the cross members positioned at the ends of the assembled cloche.

3. Cut four pieces of $\frac{1}{4} \times 1\frac{5}{8}$-inch lattice to 72 inches each for the bowed frame of the tunnel, and eight pieces of 20-gauge sheet metal to $1\frac{5}{8} \times 3$ inches each for clips that attach to the ends of the bowed frame pieces. Bend the clips to an angle of approximately 60 degrees, then drill a pair of $\frac{3}{16}$-inch-diameter holes through one end of each clip, as well as matching holes through one end of each frame piece.

187

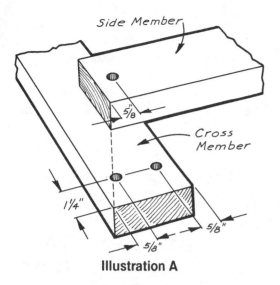

Illustration A

Fasten the clips to the underside of the frame pieces using 1-inch #8 roundhead machine screws with nuts, as shown in illustration B.

4. Cut six pieces of ¼ × 1⅝-inch lattice to 52 inches each for purlins to connect the upper parts of the bowed frame pieces. Also cut four pieces of lattice to 4¼ inches each for clips to hold purlins on the bowed frame pieces that will form the ends of the tunnel.

5. Drill a pair of ³/₁₆-inch-diameter holes centered 2¾ inches apart through each of the four short lattice pieces and through each end of the six long lattice pieces. Center the first hole of each pair ¾ inch from the ends of the pieces, as shown in the exploded-view diagram. Also drill a ³/₁₆-inch-diameter hole centered 13³/₁₆ inches from the ends of three of the long pieces for attaching the door flap framework.

6. Cut six pieces of ¼ × 1⅝-inch lattice to 26 inches each for the side pieces of the door flap frames. Also cut three pieces of lattice to 32 inches each for the bottom members of the frames. Center and drill

a ³/₁₆-inch-diameter hole 1³/₁₆ inch from the ends of each side piece, and a similar hole 3³/₁₆ inches from the ends of each bottom piece to receive fasteners.

7. Finish all wooden frame parts of the tunnel with copper naphthenate wood preservative (or something with similar, nontoxic properties), then begin assembling the frame. Fasten the sides of the base to the upper face of the cross members using ¼ × 2-inch carriage bolts with wing nuts, as shown in illustration B. Loosen the wing nuts enough to slip the end clips attached to the bowed frame members between the side and cross members of the base, then tighten the nuts to hold the bowed frame in place, as shown in illustration B.

8. Position the three purlins drilled to hold the ends of the door flap frames across the center of the bowed frame and fasten them, as shown in the exploded-view diagram. Use 1-inch #8 roundhead machine screws with nuts. The short pieces of lattice are used at both ends of the tunnel

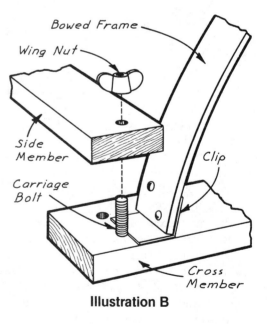

Illustration B

LUMBER CUTTING LIST

Size	Piece	Quantity
1 × 3		
¾″ × 2½″ × 53″	Base cross members	4
¾″ × 2½″ × 48″	Base side members	6
Lattice		
¼″ × 1⅝″ × 72″	Bowed frame pieces	4
¼″ × 1⅝″ × 52″	Purlins	6
¼″ × 1⅝″ × 32″	Door flap frame bottoms	3
¼″ × 1⅝″ × 26″	Door flap frame sides	6
¼″ × 1⅝″ × 4¼″	End wall clips	4

frame to clip the ends of the purlins to the frame. The middle purlins run beneath the bowed frame to allow the same method of fastening.

9. Fasten the remaining purlins and end wall clips to the bowed frame members approximately 11 inches above ground level on one side of the tunnel to create the framework for the bottom of the door openings. Follow the same method of fastening used in the preceding step.

10. Cut one piece of 6-mil polyethylene to 84 × 204 inches. Cover the tunnel frame, fastening the polyethylene to the frame members with ¼-inch staples. Cut a 24-inch-wide opening at the center of each cloche module between the upper and lower purlins to form doors into the tunnel.

11. Fasten two side pieces to each bottom piece of door flap framework using 1-inch #8 roundhead machine screws with nuts, then fasten one flap frame assembly to the upper purlin of each module, as shown in the exploded-view diagram. Cut three pieces of 6-mil polyethylene, each 32 × 32 inches, for door flaps. Fasten one flap to each frame using ¼-inch staples.

12. Cut three pieces of ½-inch-wide elastic banding to 24 inches each for door latches. Staple the ends of each band about 24 inches apart on a bottom member of a door flap frame. Then fasten a cup hook to the center of each side piece of the base below the door opening so the door flaps can be latched, as shown in the exploded-view diagram.

TRIAN-GULAR CLOCHE

SHOPPING LIST

Lumber
4 pcs. 1 × 2 × 8'
Dowels
2 pcs. ⅜" × 3' hardwood
Hardware
staples ¼"
3 butt hinges and mounting screws
    1½" × 2"
¼ pound common nails 18 gauge × ⅝"
1 pc. 4-mil polyethylene 3' × 10'
1 pint copper naphthenate wood preservative

A cloche is like a portable cold frame. The triangular type shown here is designed for row planting and may be used to start crops early in the spring or to extend production into late fall or even winter. This cloche design is lightweight, easy to build, and inexpensive. Since it folds easily, it is also a cinch to store and carry. Alter the dimensions given if you wish to build cloches of different lengths, widths, or heights. Plants that have already developed, for instance, may need a cloche with more growing room inside than the one shown.

CONSTRUCTION

1. Use four pieces of 1 × 2 (¾" × 1½") stock, 96 inches in length, for the horizontal members of the cloche.

2. Drill three evenly spaced ⅜-inch-diameter holes, each ¾ inch deep, in one edge of each horizontal member. Holes drilled in pairs of horizontal members should line up.

3. Cut six pieces of ⅜-inch-diameter dowels to 12 inches each for the vertical members. These should fit into the holes drilled in step 2.

4. Assemble the two halves of the cloche frame using three vertical members and two horizontal members for each half. Nail

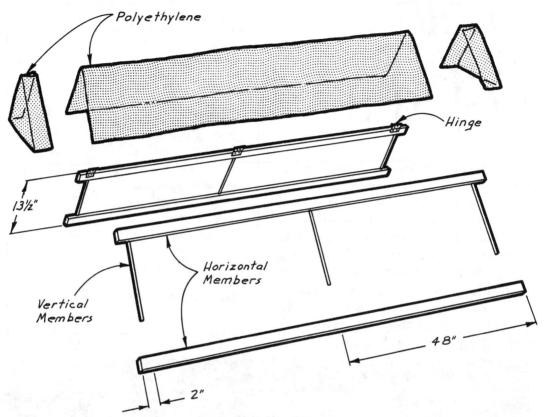

Exploded-View Diagram

the pieces together using 18-gauge × ⅝-inch common nails.

5. Coat the frame halves with copper naphthenate wood preservative.

6. Fasten the halves together with three 1½ × 2-inch butt hinges.

7. Staple polyethylene over the frame so that when the frame is open it forms a triangle.

Allow enough polyethylene so the frame folds flat. Cover the ends of the cloche with polyethylene as well, at least during the coldest growing periods. At other times you will want to leave the ends open for proper ventilation (and to keep the air inside from becoming too warm!).

LUMBER CUTTING LIST

Size	Piece	Quantity
1 × 2		
¾″ × 1½″ × 96″	Horizontal members	4
Dowels		
⅜″ × 12″	Vertical members	6

CUBICAL PLANT COVERS

These plant covers are designed to fit over individual plants and protect them from both early- and late-season frost. They are easy and inexpensive to make and light-weight to carry. Although you may wish to make your plant covers all the same size, the three shown here are made to nest together for economical storage. Naturally, you may alter the dimensions to suit your needs. Large covers may need to be staked down during windy weather.

SHOPPING LIST

Lumber
2 pcs. 1 × 2 × 10'
1 pc. 1 × 2 × 8'
Dowels
6 pcs. ⅜'' × 3' hardwood
Hardware
staples ¼''
common nails 18 gauge × ⅝''
¼ pound cement-coated box nails 4d
1 pc. 4-mil polyethylene 14'' × 5'
    (for 12-inch cube)
1 pc. 4-mil polyethylene 16'' × 80''
    (for 14-inch cube)
1 pc. 4-mil polyethylene 18'' × 8'
    (for 16-inch cube)
1 quart copper naphthenate wood
    preservative

CONSTRUCTION

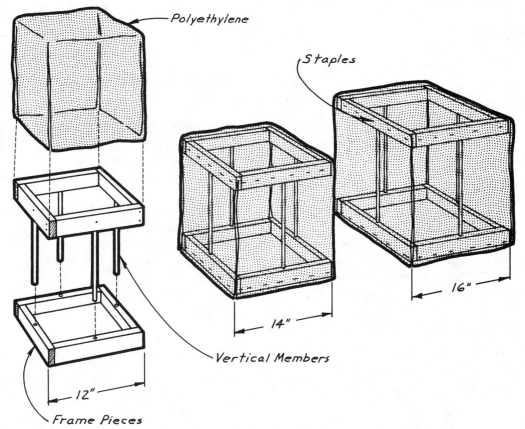

Exploded-View Diagram

1. Cut eight pieces of 1×2 ($\frac{3}{4}'' \times 1\frac{1}{2}''$) stock to $11\frac{1}{4}$ inches each for the frame pieces of the 12-inch cube.

2. Cut eight pieces of 1×2 stock to $13\frac{1}{4}$ inches each for the frame pieces of the 14-inch cube.

3. Cut eight pieces of 1×2 stock to $15\frac{1}{4}$ inches each for the frame pieces of the 16-inch cube.

4. Nail the frame members of each size together to form two identical squares for each cube. Use the 4d cement-coated box nails.

5. Drill $\frac{3}{8}$-inch-diameter holes $\frac{3}{4}$ inch deep in one edge of each square (one hole in the middle of each frame piece, as shown in the exploded-view diagram). Holes drilled in identical squares should line up.

6. Cut four pieces of $\frac{3}{8}$-inch-diameter dowel to 12 inches each for the vertical members of the 12-inch cube.

7. Cut four pieces of $\frac{3}{8}$-inch-diameter dowel to 14 inches each for the vertical members of the 14-inch cube.

8. Cut four pieces of $\frac{3}{8}$-inch-diameter dowel to 16 inches each for the vertical members of the 16-inch cube.

9. Assemble the cubes by combining the ap-

193

LUMBER CUTTING LIST

Size	Piece	Quantity
1 × 2		
¾" × 1½" × 15¼"	Frame pieces for 16-inch cube	8
¾" × 1½" × 13¼"	Frame pieces for 14-inch cube	8
¾" × 1½" × 11¼"	Frame pieces for 12-inch cube	8
Dowels		
⅜" × 16"	Vertical members for 16-inch cube	4
⅜" × 14"	Vertical members for 14-inch cube	4
⅜" × 12"	Vertical members for 12-inch cube	4

propriate vertical members with pairs of identical squares. Fasten the verticals in place in the holes drilled for them using the 18-gauge × ⅝-inch common nails.

10. Coat each cube with copper naphthenate wood preservative.

11. Staple polyethylene around all four sides and across the top of each cube.

CLOCHE AND TRELLIS SYSTEM

Here's a versatile gardening system developed by the Rodale Design Group, based on concrete anchors that are buried in the ground at 4-foot intervals. The anchors may be used at the beginning and end of each season to position cloches made from PVC tubing and polyethylene; then, during the main part of the growing season, the cloches may be dismantled and the anchors used to support a trellis framework that can be covered with netting or string. Both the cloche and the trellis are described in the step-by-step instructions, along with the anchors. Since the anchors we made are intended to be arranged in a square, we cast a radius on one upper corner of each to minimize the chances of snagging a garden hose. This rounding of corners may either be eliminated or added to other corners, according to the intended location and uses of the anchors.

By the way, the anchors need not be limited to garden applications. They may also be used to support such things as clothesline poles, fences, and poles for backyard games like badminton.

SHOPPING LIST

Lumber
2 pcs. $2 \times 2 \times 10'$
1 pc. $1 \times 3 \times 4'$
4 pcs. $1 \times 2 \times 8'$
Plywood
1 pc. $\frac{1}{2}'' \times 2' \times 2'$ A–C grade
Hardware
8 sheet-metal screws #8 $\times \frac{3}{4}''$
8 eyebolts $\frac{5}{16}'' \times 5''$
4 carriage bolts $\frac{1}{4}'' \times 2\frac{1}{2}''$ with washers and nuts
4 carriage bolts $\frac{1}{4}'' \times 1\frac{1}{4}''$ with washers and nuts
8 wing nuts $\frac{5}{16}''$
1 box staples $\frac{5}{8}''$
4 corner brackets $1\frac{1}{2}'' \times 1\frac{1}{2}''$
$\frac{1}{4}$ pound finishing nails 4d
4 pcs. PVC pipe $2''$ I.D. $\times 1'$
2 pcs. PVC tubing $\frac{3}{4}''$ I.D. $\times 8'$
12 pcs. polyethylene pipe $\frac{3}{4}''$ diameter $\times 4''$
1 pc. 4-mil polyethylene $5' \times 7'$
2 pcs. 4-mil polyethylene $30'' \times 5'$
4 20-pound bags "sand mix" premixed cement
polyurethane
1 quart motor oil (new or used)

CONSTRUCTION

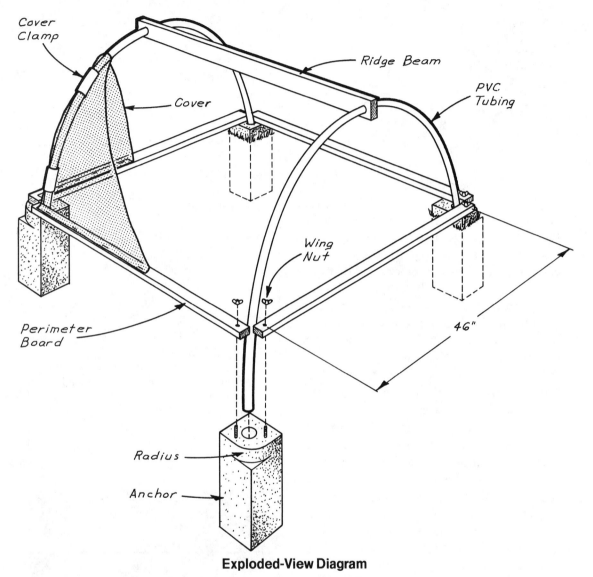

Exploded-View Diagram

To make the anchors:

1. Cut four pieces of ½-inch A-C-grade plywood to 6 × 12 inches each for the sides of the mold. Fasten the pieces together at right angles into two half-molds, as shown in illustration A, using carpenter's wood glue and 4d finishing nails.

2. Cut one piece of ½-inch plywood to 2¾ × 2¾ inches, then cut it in half diagonally. Glue one piece to the top of the other to make a 1-inch-thick right triangle. Cut a concave radius on the long side of the piece, then fasten it to the upper inside corner of one

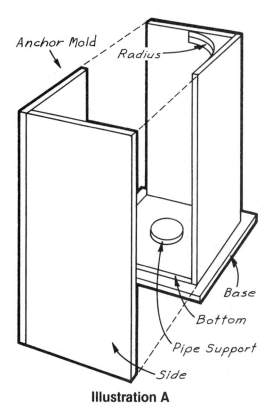

Illustration A

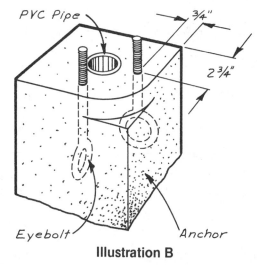

Illustration B

half-mold, as shown in illustration A, using wood glue and 4d finishing nails.

3. Cut one piece of ½-inch plywood to 8 × 8 inches for the base of the mold. Cut an additional piece of ½-inch plywood to 5½ × 5½ inches for the bottom of the mold, and fasten it to the center of the base using wood glue and 4d finishing nails. Then cut a 2-inch-diameter plywood circle and fasten it to the center of the mold bottom to form a pipe support.

4. Sand the inside of the mold until smooth and finish it with polyurethane. Before using the mold, wipe the inner surfaces with motor oil to prevent the concrete from adhering to it.

5. Form a square with the half-molds around the mold bottom and hold them together with a strap clamp. Cut a piece of 2-inch-I.D. PVC pipe to 12 inches in length and mount it on the support in the bottom center of the mold. Combine a 20-pound bag of "sand mix" cement with water and pour it into the mold. Insert a $5/16 \times 5$-inch eyebolt, head down, into the center of the concrete on each partly radiused side of the anchor, as shown in illustration B. Leave approximately 2 inches of thread on each bolt exposed above the concrete.

6. Allow the concrete to set up overnight, then unclamp the sides of the mold and remove the anchor. Reoil the mold and use it again to make as many anchors as desired.

To build the cloche:

1. Cut two pieces of ¾-inch-I.D. PVC tubing, to 8 feet each for the bowed part of the cloche frame. Also cut one piece of 1 × 3 (¾″ × 2½″) stock to 48 inches for the ridge beam. Center and drill a 1-inch-diameter hole 1 inch from each end of the beam and run the PVC tubes through the holes until the beam is at their centers.

2. Bury the cloche anchors in the ground so they form a 46-inch square at the centers of their tubes and their radii are at the four outside corners, as shown in the

197

LUMBER CUTTING LIST

Size	Piece	Quantity
2 × 2		
1½″ × 1½″ × 60″	Trellis corner posts	4
1 × 3		
¾″ × 2½″ × 48″	Cloche ridge beam	1
1 × 2		
¾″ × 1½″ × 48″	Cloche perimeter boards	4
¾″ × 1½″ × 48″	Trellis headers	2
¾″ × 1½″ × 43″	Trellis cross members	2
Plywood		
½″ × 8″ × 8″	Anchor mold base	1
½″ × 6″ × 12″	Anchor mold sides	4
½″ × 5½″ × 5½″	Anchor mold bottom	1
½″ × 2¾″ × 2¾″	Anchor mold radius blank	1
½″ × 2″ diameter	Anchor mold pipe support	1

exploded-view diagram.

3. Cut four pieces of 1 × 2 (¾″ × 1½″) stock to 48 inches each for perimeter boards to fit between the anchors. Drill ⅜-inch-diameter holes through the ends of these boards where necessary to fit them over the bolts embedded in the anchors, as shown in the exploded-view diagram. Fasten the perimeter boards to the anchor bolts using wing nuts.

4. Insert the ends of the PVC tubing into the pieces of pipe embedded in the anchors to form two parallel arches with the ridge beam at their peak. Cut one piece of clear polyethylene to 60 × 84 inches to cover the top of the cloche, and two pieces each to 30 × 60 inches to cover the sides.

5. Cut 12 pieces of ¾-inch polyethylene pipe to 4 inches each, then split them lengthwise to form cover clamps. Spread the precut polyethylene sheets over the cloche frame and fasten them to the PVC tubing with the cover clamps, as shown in the exploded-view diagram. Staple the bottom edges of the corners to the perimeter boards using ⅝-inch staples.

To build the trellis:

1. Cut four pieces of 2 × 2 (1½″ × 1½″) stock to 60 inches each for the corner posts. Drill a ¼-inch-diameter hole through each post, centered ¾ inch from the upper end. Insert the posts into the pipes embedded in the anchors.

2. Cut two pieces of 1 × 2 stock to 48 inches each for headers to fit between the upper ends of the posts. Drill ⁵⁄₁₆-inch-diameter holes centered 1 inch from the ends of the headers, then fasten the headers to the inside faces of the posts using ¼ × 2½-inch carriage bolts with washers and nuts, as shown in illustration C.

3. Fasten a pair of 1½ × 1½-inch corner brackets to the inside face of each header using ¾-inch #8 sheet-metal screws. Locate the brackets where they will hold a pair

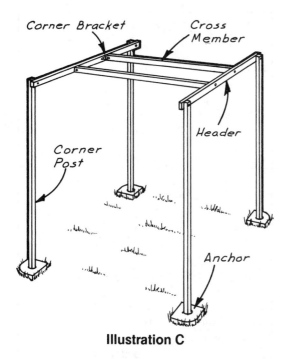

Corner Bracket
Cross Member
Header
Corner Post
Anchor

Illustration C

of cross members 16 inches apart and centered between the posts, as shown in illustration C.

4. Cut two pieces of 1×2 stock to 43 inches each for the cross members. Drill $5/16$-inch-diameter holes through the ends of the cross members in line with the outer holes in the corner brackets. Fasten the cross members to the corner brackets using $1/4 \times 1 1/4$-inch carriage bolts with washers and nuts.

5. Complete the trellis by wrapping the wooden framework with grow netting or string.

TRIED AND TRUE COLD FRAME

SHOPPING LIST

Lumber
1 pc. $1 \times 4 \times 10'$
1 pc. $1 \times 2 \times 5'$
Plywood
1 sheet $\frac{1}{2}'' \times 4' \times 8'$ A-C grade
Dowels
2 pcs. $\frac{5}{8}'' \times 3'$ hardwood
Hardware
1 wooden frame storm window
    $32\frac{1}{4}'' \times 62\frac{3}{8}''$
10 flathead wood screws #8 $\times$ $1\frac{1}{2}''$
2 carriage bolts $\frac{5}{16}'' \times 2''$ with flat washers
    and wing nuts
3 tee hinges 3'' with fasteners
4 eyescrews $1\frac{1}{2}''$
1 dozen finishing nails 4d
1 box aluminum nails $1\frac{1}{4}''$
$\frac{1}{2}$ pint waterproof glue
1 quart exterior-grade primer/sealer
1 quart exterior-grade enamel
1 quart copper naphthenate wood
    preservative

This simply designed cold frame is easy and inexpensive to build. An interesting feature is its dual window-positioning system. Rods attached to both sides of the cold frame can be raised to any of three positions to hold the glazing wide open when full ventilation is desired or while tending the plants inside. When only a small amount of ventilation is needed, wooden cams attached to the front of the frame adjust to hold the glazing open just 1 to 3 inches.

The front, rear, and side panels of the cold frame all may be taken from a single sheet of plywood. An old wooden storm window serves as the glazing. The window shown here measures $32\frac{1}{4} \times 62\frac{3}{8}$ inches. If your window measurements are different, change the width of the frame's sloping top to 1 inch less than the width of your window, and make the length of the frame $1\frac{1}{8}$ inches less than the window's length. Retain the height of the front and rear pieces used in our design, but allow the slope of the window and the width of the box to change as necessary.

The cold frame can be easily dismantled for storage. The only maintenance it should need is periodic repainting and caulking.

CONSTRUCTION

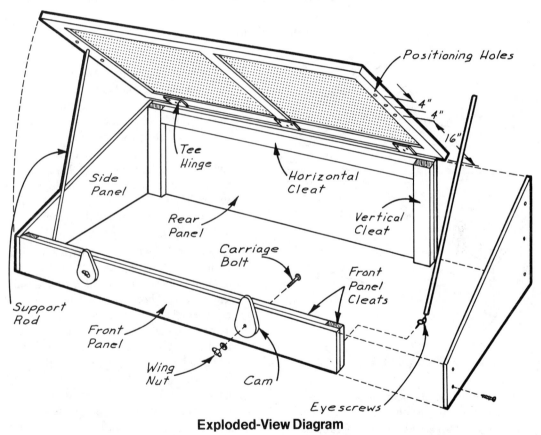

Exploded-View Diagram

1. Lay out the front, rear, and side panels on a sheet of $\frac{1}{2}$-inch A-C-grade plywood, as shown on the cutting diagram. Cut out all four pieces. The rear panel will be $\frac{1}{2}$ inch wider than its final size, making it easier to bevel its upper edge (see step 4).

2. Cut two pieces of 1×2 ($\frac{3}{4}'' \times 1\frac{1}{2}''$) stock to $18\frac{1}{2}$ inches each for the vertical cleats

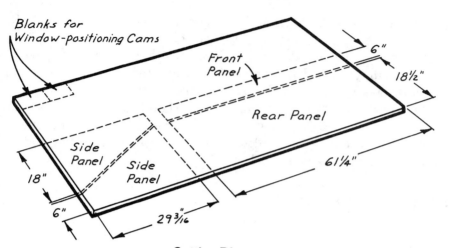

Cutting Diagram

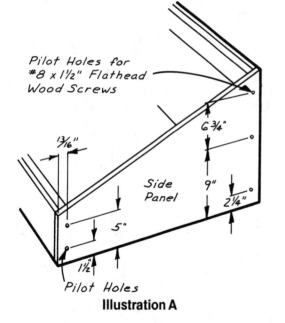

Illustration A

that attach to the rear panel. Fasten the cleats across the ends of the panel, as shown in the exploded-view diagram, using waterproof glue and 1¼-inch aluminum nails. Avoid nailing at the three points on each end where screws will be inserted to hold the side panels in place (see step 7), as shown in illustration A.

3. Measure the distance between the two vertical cleats, then cut one piece of 1×4 (¾″ × 3½″) stock to that length (approximately 58¼ inches) for a horizontal cleat. Fasten this cleat to the upper edge of the rear panel, between the two vertical cleats, using waterproof glue and 1¼-inch aluminum nails. Avoid putting nails in areas where hinges will be attached (see step 9) or near the upper edge of the panel, which will be trimmed away (see step 4).

4. Lay the rear panel down with the cleats facing up. Position one of the side panels against it, overlapping the edge and making sure the bottom and back edges of each panel are aligned flush. Scribe a line across the edge of the rear panel and vertical cleat where they are crossed by the upper edge of the side panel. Do the same using the other side panel at the opposite edge. Now connect the two slanted lines by scribing each face of the rear panel along its entire length, from edge to edge. Using a table saw or portable circular saw, rip and bevel the top edge of the rear panel.

5. Cut two pieces of 1×2 stock to 6 inches each for the front panel vertical cleats. Fasten the cleats to the panel using water-

proof glue and 1¼-inch aluminum nails. Avoid nailing where screws will be inserted from the side (see step 7), as shown in illustration A.

6. Measure the distance between the two front panel cleats, then cut one piece of 1 × 4 stock to that length (approximately 58¼ inches) and fasten this cleat horizontally between them, flush with the upper edge of the panel, using waterproof glue and 1¼-inch aluminum nails.

7. Temporarily fasten the side panels to the rear and front panels using 4d finishing nails or small brads. Drive the nails only partway into the wood for easy removal later. Drill a pair of 3/32-inch-diameter pilot holes centered 13/16 inch from the front edge of each side panel, as shown in illustration A. Drill the first hole 1½ inches above the base of the panel and the second 5 inches above. Center and drill three pilot

holes of the same diameter through the back edge of each side panel, also as shown. Install 1½-inch #8 flathead wood screws in the holes, then remove all temporary fasteners.

8. Cut the two window-positioning cams out of ½-inch plywood by following the pattern shown in illustration B. Drill a 5/16-inch-diameter hole through each cam at the point shown in the illustration. Center and drill two 5/16-inch-diameter holes each 4¼ inches above the bottom edge of the front panel and 15 inches from the ends to accept the bolts for fastening the cams. Attach the cams to the outside of the front panel using 5/16 × 2-inch carriage bolts with flat washers and wing nuts. Install the bolts from inside the panel, as shown in the exploded-view diagram.

9. Position the window on top of the cold frame so the rear edges of each are flush. Make sure both ends of the window hang slightly over the outer edges of the cold frame sides. Fasten the window to the cold frame using three 3-inch tee hinges. Locate one hinge 4 inches from each end of the window's rear edge and one in the center. Check to make sure the window opens and shuts properly.

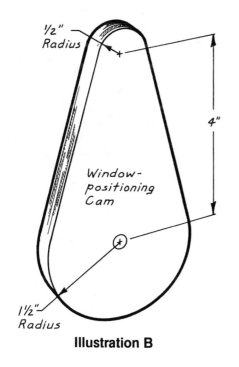

½"
Radius

4"

Window-positioning Cam

1½"
Radius

Illustration B

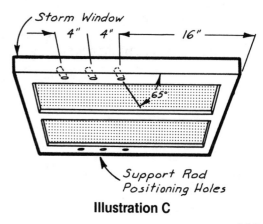

Storm Window
4" 4" 16"

65°

Support Rod
Positioning Holes

Illustration C

LUMBER CUTTING LIST

Size	Piece	Quantity
1 × 4		
¾'' × 3½'' × 58¼''	Front and rear horizontal cleats	2
1 × 2		
¾'' × 1½'' × 18½''	Rear vertical cleats	2
¾'' × 1½'' × 6''	Front vertical cleats	2
Plywood		
½'' × 24⅛'' × 29³⁄₁₆''	Side panel blanks	2
½'' × 18½'' × 61¼''	Rear panel blank	1
½'' × 6'' × 61¼''	Front panel	1
½'' × 3'' × 6''	Positioning cam blanks	2
Dowels		
⅝'' × 36''	Window support rods	2

10. Fasten four 1½'' eyescrews together to make two linked pairs. Install one end of each pair into a front panel vertical cleat, 4¼ inches above the base of the cold frame. Then obtain two ⅝ × 36-inch dowels for the window support rods and drill a ⅛-inch-diameter pilot hole into one end of each. Install the rods on the remaining eyescrews to fasten them to the frame.

11. Center and drill three ¹¹⁄₁₆-inch-diameter holes at each end of the window frame, into the underside about halfway through the thickness of the wood. Locate one hole in each group 16 inches from the rear edge of the window and the others on 4-inch centers toward the front, as shown in illustration C. Drill the holes at an angle (approximately 65 degrees) to receive the support rods when the window is in the open position, also as shown.

12. Dismantle the cold frame to prepare it for painting. Sand all sharp edges and coat all bare wood surfaces with copper naphthenate wood preservative. After allowing the preservative to dry completely, paint the entire frame and, if necessary, the window with an exterior-grade primer/sealer.

13. Reglaze the window if its glazing is loose. Fill in any cracks or holes in the window or frame with caulk. Paint the wooden parts of the cold frame with two coats of quality exterior-grade enamel. Reassemble the cold frame when you are ready to use it.

WINDOW-SASH COLD FRAME

Alan and Marilyn Elliott of Bethlehem, Pennsylvania, built this cold frame using ideas gathered partly from Nancy Bubel's *Seed-Starter's Handbook* (Rodale Press, 1978). Salvaged materials were used throughout. The cold frame is sunk into the ground 12 inches below grade, to help temper outside conditions, and is insulated throughout with rigid-foam panels. The dimensions of the frame allow easy access to plants while at the same time providing them with ample room to grow. Although the unit is designed to be freestanding, the Elliotts erected theirs against the south-facing wall of a utility shed.

The Elliotts determined the height and depth of their cold frame primarily to provide comfortable working conditions—an easy arm's reach to the back of the frame, for instance, as well as an easy reach to the bottom. The cold frame's length is based on the size of the windows they obtained, which measure 29¼ × 36 inches. You should have on hand the windows you will use for your cold frame before you

SHOPPING LIST

Lumber
1 pc. 2 × 10 × 8'
1 pc. 2 × 6 × 8'
12 pcs. 2 × 4 × 8'
Plywood
2 sheets ⅝'' × 4' × 8' exterior grade
1 pc. ⅝'' × 4' × 4' exterior grade
Sheathing and Insulation
2 sheets ½'' × 4' × 8' water-resistant
    cellulose insulation board
3 sheets rigid-foam insulation ¾'' × 4' × 8'
Hardware
3 window sashes 29¼'' × 3' (approx.)
36 flathead wood screws #8 × 1''
6 flathead wood screws #6 × ¾''
6 strap hinges 6''
3 utility handles 4''
1 pound galvanized common nails 16d
1 pound galvanized common nails 6d
2 concrete blocks 8'' × 8'' × 16''
8' tubular vinyl weather stripping
15' closed-cell foam weather stripping
    ⅛'' × ½''
¼ ton gravel
2 tubes latex caulk

begin to build. We've designed the instructions so you should have no trouble adjusting the plans to suit. (For reference, we've included the full specifications of the Elliotts' cold frame. Chances are, for yours only the height and depth will be similar.)

You must sheathe the inside of the cold frame to protect the insulation from the soil. In the cold frame shown here, inexpensive, moisture-resistant cellulose sheathing, often called insulation board, is used. This is the same type of material home builders use to sheathe buildings before adding siding. Instead of this, however, you may line the inside of the cold frame with stone or brick, after the cold frame has been set in position. This will have some thermal effect, since the lining will absorb heat during the day and then give it off during the night, warming the plants. Night insulation may also be made, to ensure even further that plants survive in cold temperatures. Merely cut additional slabs of rigid foam from the pieces used to insulate the inside of the cold frame, and place these over the windows on the outside. Weight the slabs down with bricks or stones.

Since the Elliotts' cold frame is against a wall, hook-and-eye fasteners were installed so that the windows of the cold frame could be fastened upright when it was necessary to work inside the frame or to ventilate the frame during warm weather. You should do this too if your cold frame is similarly located. If it is freestanding, though, the hinges should allow the windows to merely fold flat against the top board.

CONSTRUCTION

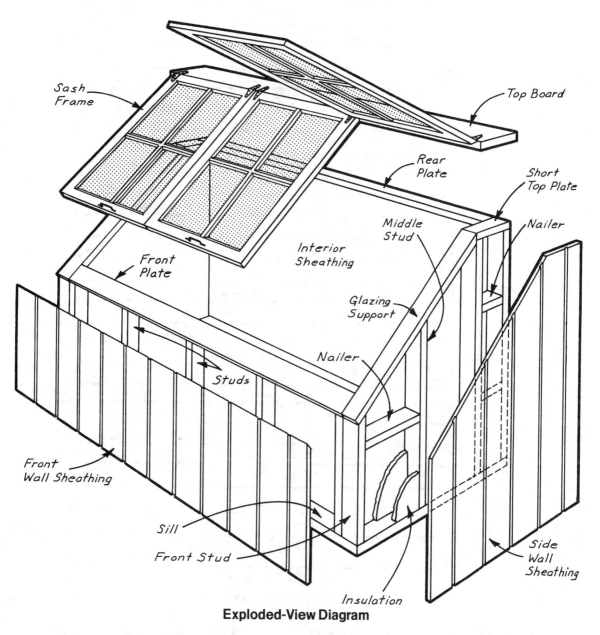

Sash Frame

Top Board

Rear Plate

Short Top Plate

Nailer

Middle Stud

Interior Sheathing

Front Plate

Glazing Support

Nailer

Studs

Front Wall Sheathing

Sill

Front Stud

Insulation

Side Wall Sheathing

Exploded-View Diagram

1. Calculate the overall width of your cold frame by laying the window sashes you've obtained in a straight line, as shown in illustration A, leaving a gap of ⅛ inch between sashes, just as they will be positioned in the finished cold frame. Measure

207

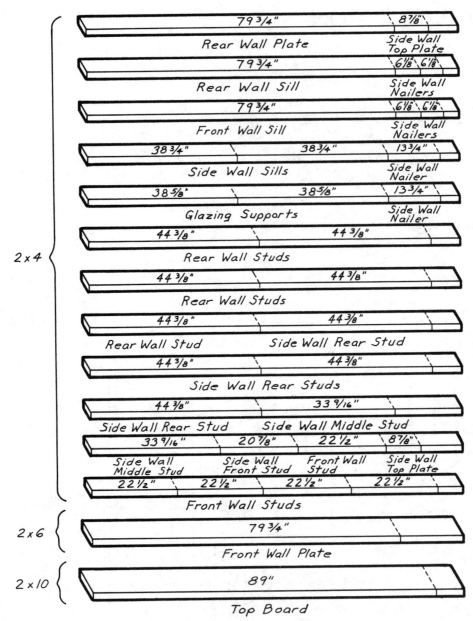

79 3/4"　8 7/8"

Rear Wall Plate　Side Wall Top Plate

79 3/4"　6 1/8"　6 1/8"

Rear Wall Sill　Side Wall Nailers

79 3/4"　6 1/8"　6 1/8"

Front Wall Sill　Side Wall Nailers

38 3/4"　38 3/4"　13 3/4"

Side Wall Sills　Side Wall Nailer

38 5/8"　38 5/8"　13 3/4"

Glazing Supports　Side Wall Nailer

2 x 4

44 3/8"　44 3/8"

Rear Wall Studs

44 3/8"　44 3/8"

Rear Wall Studs

44 3/8"　44 3/8"

Rear Wall Stud　Side Wall Rear Stud

44 3/8"　44 3/8"

Side Wall Rear Studs

44 3/8"　33 9/16"

Side Wall Rear Stud　Side Wall Middle Stud

33 9/16"　20 7/8"　22 1/2"　8 7/8"

Side Wall Middle Stud　Side Wall Front Stud　Front Wall Stud　Side Wall Top Plate

22 1/2"　22 1/2"　22 1/2"　22 1/2"

Front Wall Studs

2 x 6

79 3/4"

Front Wall Plate

2 x 10

89"

Top Board

Lumber Cutting Diagram

the overall width of the sashes across the top and bottom. Be sure both measurements are the same. Use this figure as the overall width of your cold frame. It cor-

responds to the 88-inch overall width of the cold frame shown in these plans.

2. Cut three pieces of 2 × 4 (1½″ × 3½″) stock, and one piece of 2 × 6 (1½″ × 5½″)

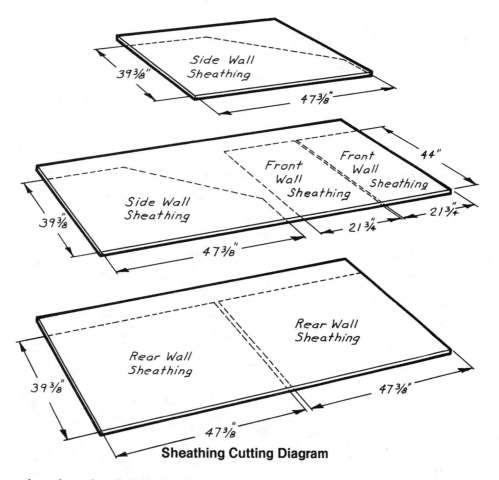

Sheathing Cutting Diagram

stock, each to a length 8¼ inches less than the overall width measurement calculated in the previous step (79¾ inches in the plans). Use the 2 × 4s for the rear plate and the front and rear sills. Use the 2 × 6 for the front plate.

3. Cut pieces of 2 × 4 stock to 44⅜ inches each for the rear wall studs. Five studs are shown in the plans. You should cut as many studs as you will need to fit across the rear wall area, spaced on 16-inch centers.

4. Construct the rear wall, as shown in illustration B, by placing the rear plate and sill parallel to each other and on edge,

then nailing the studs — also placed on edge — between them at 16-inch intervals on center, using 16d galvanized common nails.

5. Cut as many front studs as you did rear studs (see step 3). Use 2 × 4 stock and cut each stud to 22½ inches in length. Miter one end of each stud to a 40-degree angle, as shown in illustration C.

6. Construct the front wall, as shown in illustration B, using the same procedures as for the rear (see step 4).

7. Cut two pieces of 2 × 4 stock to 38¾ inches each for the side wall sills. Cut four pieces of 2 × 4 stock to 44⅜ inches each for the rear studs of each wall. Cut two

LUMBER CUTTING LIST

Size	Piece	Quantity
2 × 10		
1½″ × 9¼″ × 89″	Top board	1
2 × 6		
1½″ × 5½″ × 79¾″	Front wall plate	1
2 × 4		
1½″ × 3½″ × 79¾″	Rear wall plate	1
1½″ × 3½″ × 79¾″	Rear wall sill	1
1½″ × 3½″ × 79¾″	Front wall sill	1
1½″ × 3½″ × 38¾″	Side wall sills	2
1½″ × 3½″ × 44⅜″	Rear wall studs	5
1½″ × 3½″ × 44⅜″	Side wall rear studs	4
1½″ × 3½″ × 38⅝″	Glazing supports	2
1½″ × 3½″ × 33⁹⁄₁₆″	Side wall middle studs	2
1½″ × 3½″ × 22½″	Front wall studs	5
1½″ × 3½″ × 20⅞″	Side wall front studs	2
1½″ × 3½″ × 13¾″	Side wall nailers	2
1½″ × 3½″ × 8⅞″	Side wall top plates	2
1½″ × 3½″ × 6⅛″	Side wall nailers	4
Plywood		
⅝″ × 39⅜″ × 47⅜″	Rear wall sheathing	2
⅝″ × 39⅜″ × 47⅜″	Side wall sheathing	2
⅝″ × 44″ × 21¾″	Front wall sheathing	2
Sheathing		
½″ × 79¾″ × 47⅜″	Rear wall interior sheathing	1
½″ × 79¾″ × 22½″	Front wall interior sheathing	1
½″ × 30¾″ × 47⅜″	Side wall interior sheathing	2

short pieces of 2 × 4 stock to 8⅞ inches each for the short horizontal top plates located at the rear of each wall, as shown in the exploded-view diagram. Finally, cut two pieces of 2 × 4 stock to 20⅞ inches each for the front stud of each wall. Miter one end of each stud across a face to a 40-degree angle, as shown in illustration C.

8. Assemble the partial side walls by nailing the two rear studs of each between the sill and plate, as shown in the exploded-view diagram, using 16d galvanized common nails. Then attach each front stud, also as shown.

9. Assemble the rear wall, front wall, and both partial side walls together on a level spot by nailing each unit to the other at the corners, as shown in the exploded-view diagram. Use 16d galvanized common nails. Brace the corners with scrap strips of lumber, if necessary, to keep them square while nailing.

10. Cut two pieces of 2 × 4 stock to 38⅝ inches each for the glazing supports. Posi-

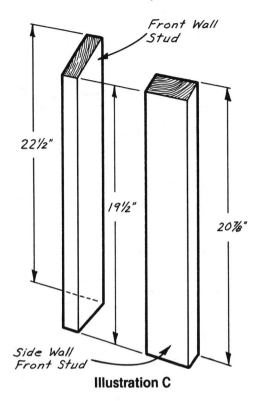

Illustration A

88"

⅛" Gap

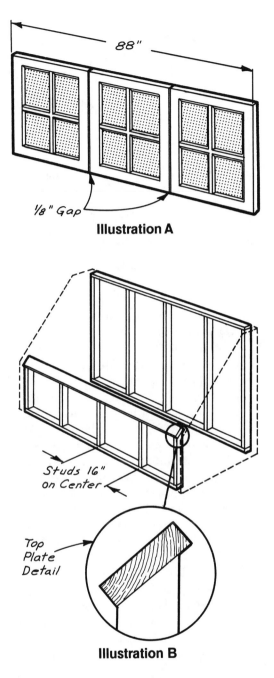

Illustration B

Studs 16" on Center

Top Plate Detail

22½"

19½"

20⅞"

Front Wall Stud

Side Wall Front Stud

Illustration C

angle necessary for the supports to meet flush with the ends of the plates, as shown in illustration D, then trim the supports to this angle, and fasten them in place using 16d galvanized common nails.

11. Complete the side walls by installing the middle studs and nailers in each. Cut two pieces of 2×4 stock to $33\frac{9}{16}$ inches each for the studs, and miter each across the face at one end so they fit beneath the sloping glazing supports. Fasten the studs in place between the sills and the supports, using 16d galvanized common nails. Cut two pieces of 2×4 stock to $13\frac{3}{4}$ inches each for the horizontal nailers at the front of each wall, and cut four pieces of 2×4 stock to $6\frac{1}{8}$ inches each for the pairs of nailers at the rear. Install the nailers, as shown in the exploded-view diagram, evenly spaced between the sills and the

tion each, as shown in the exploded-view diagram, on top of the mitered front studs of the side walls and against the ends of the short horizontal top plates. Scribe the

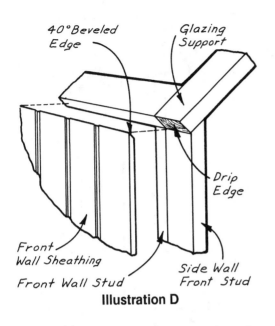

Illustration D

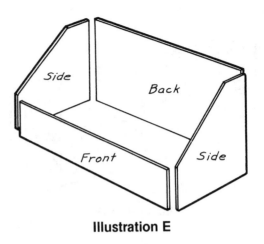

Illustration E

top plates or glazing supports, also using 16d galvanized common nails.

12. The sheathing comes next. To begin, cut two pieces of ⅝-inch exterior-grade plywood to 39⅜ × 47⅜ inches each to fit the rear wall (86¾″ × 47⅜″ in the plans), and fasten them in place flush with the sides, top, and bottom of the assembled framework using 6d galvanized common nails.

13. Next, cut two pieces of ⅝-inch plywood to the exact dimension of the side walls, but add ⅝ inch to the length of each (39⅜″ × 47⅜″ in the plans) so the rear edges of the sides will cover the end grain of the sheathing on the rear wall. Fasten the side wall sheathing in place using 6d galvanized common nails.

14. Finally, cut two pieces of ⅝-inch plywood each equal to one-half the width of the front wall plus ⅝ inch (44 inches in the plans) by 21¾ inches high. Cut a 40-degree bevel along the top edge of each panel so the sheathing will butt against the lower edge of the front wall's sloping plate. The

surface of the plate then forms a drip edge, as shown in illustration D. Fasten the front sheathing in place so it covers the end grain of the side panels, using 6d galvanized common nails.

15. Cut one piece of 2 × 10 (1½″ × 9¼″) stock for the top board. Its length should equal the overall width of the cold frame, including the sheathing on both side walls, plus 1 inch (89 inches in the plans). This will allow the board to overhang the sides slightly and afford some protection against rain. Align the board evenly with the front ends of the plates on the side walls. Check that the cold frame is square and that the overhang of the board is equal on both sides, then fasten the top board to the cold frame sides and rear wall using 16d galvanized common nails.

16. Insulate the wall cavities with 1-inch-thick slabs of rigid-foam insulation, cut to fit, as shown in illustration E. For the best effect, use two thicknesses in each cavity. Press the first against the inside of the sheathing, but insert the second only until it is flush with the visible edges of the studs, thus creating an airspace between the two slabs. Insulation in the walls requires no fasteners. When finished, how-

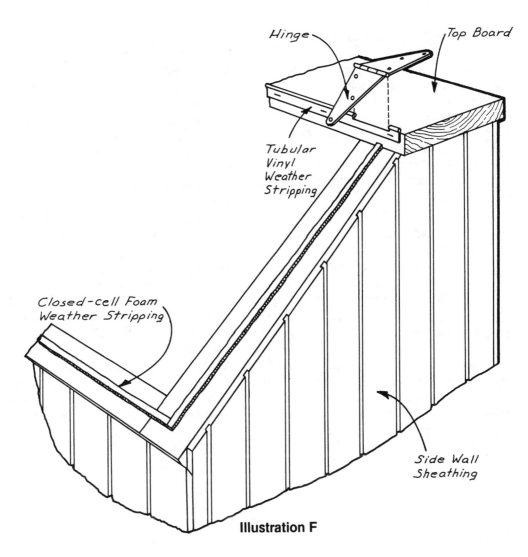

Hinge

Top Board

Tubular
Vinyl
Weather
Stripping

Closed-cell Foam
Weather Stripping

Side Wall
Sheathing

Illustration F

ever, insulate the underside of the top board with a single thickness of foam, fastened with 6d galvanized common nails.

17. To line the inside of the cold frame, cut panels of ½-inch water-resistant cellulose sheathing to fit, and fasten the panels in place using 6d galvanized common nails driven through the sheathing into the cold frame studs and nailers. (In the plans, the sizes of these panels are as follows: 79¾ × 47⅜ inches for the rear wall panel,

fastened in place first; 79¾ × 22½ inches for the front wall, installed next; and 30¾ × 47⅜ inches for each of the sides, installed last and trimmed to fit along the sloping top edge.)

18. Caulk the seams of the cold frame, and paint or stain the outside, if you wish. Afterward, install closed-cell foam weather stripping to the top edges of the glazing supports and front wall top board where the window sashes will rest, as shown

213

in illustration F. Nail a strip of tubular vinyl weather stripping to the top edges of the glazing supports and front wall top board where the window sashes will rest, as shown in illustration F. Nail a strip of tubular vinyl weather stripping across the front edge of the top board, also as shown. The tube portion of the weather stripping should project above the level of the board. Trim it later when installing the hinges (see step 20).

19. Position the window sashes across the front of the cold frame, flush with the sides and outside face of the front wall sheathing. Scribe, then bevel the top edge of each sash so it fits closely against the top board. Paint the sashes.

20. Place the finished sashes in position on the cold frame, then lay 6-inch strap hinges along the top board for fastening to each window's vertical rails. Carefully center the knuckle of each hinge over the seam between the windows and the top board, trimming away sections of the tubular weather stripping where necessary. Finally, drill ⅛-inch-diameter pilot holes in the cold frame and window sashes for the mounting screws, using the hinges themselves as templates, then fasten the hinges in place using 1-inch #8 flathead wood screws.

21. Position a lift handle on the front edge of each sash, and fasten them using ¾-inch #6 flathead wood screws.

22. Now prepare a location for the finished cold frame by digging a pit about 14 inches deep, 8 feet long, and 4 feet wide. Spread 2 inches of gravel on the floor of the pit.

23. With help from at least one assistant, set the cold frame in the pit, leveling it if necessary. Then pile additional gravel around the perimeter of the cold frame to a depth of 10 inches. On top of the gravel, pile soil to grade level, then cover the surface of the area with mulch, more gravel, or a planting of grass.

24. Fill the cold frame to a depth of at least 13 inches with a mix of compost, peat, sand, and topsoil. Place two concrete blocks inside the cold frame for stepping stones. Plant whenever conditions in your area are right.

FRENCH DOUBLE COLD FRAME

SHOPPING LIST

Lumber
1 pc. 2 × 6 × 8'
1 pc. 2 × 3 × 4'
4 pcs. 1 × 2 × 8'
1 pc. 1 × 2 × 6'
Plywood
1 pc. ¾'' × 3' × 4' A–C grade
Hardware
16 flathead wood screws #8 × 2''
24 flathead wood screws #8 × 1½''
24 flathead wood screws #6 × ¾''
16 hex head sheet-metal screws #6 × ½''
2 lag bolts ¼'' × 3''
2 flat washers ¼''
16 nylon washers #6
4 strap hinges 3''
2 screen hangers
4 turn-buttons 2''
4 pcs. acrylic safety glazing
　　⅛'' × 21¼'' × 23¾''
1 cartridge silicone sealant
1 pint waterproof glue
1 quart copper naphthenate wood
　　preservative

The design of this cold frame, originally built by David Miskell of Shelburne, Vermont, then modified by the Rodale Design Group, is adapted from a type used by French market gardeners. It is essentially a modular system, made up of a variable number of sections, each consisting of two 2 × 2-foot window sashes tied together with strap hinges, supported by a ridge beam and a pair of vented end walls. The construction steps given here are for a cold frame containing two sections plus the end

walls. The number of sections may be varied from one to as many as you wish. To modify the plans, all you need do is alter the length of the beam to correspond with the number of sections you decide to make. Short vertical posts set in the ground at 8- or 10-foot intervals may be used to support a series of ridge beams if a long row of sections is desired. Remember that your growing beds must be the same width (or at least no wider) than that of the frame: 4 feet.

The French double cold frame is designed to be placed over permanent growing beds but is meant to be removed when not needed. Cover the beds with the frame

215

to get plants started early in the year. Prop the sections open as the weather gets warmer, then remove the sections during the main part of the growing season. Replace the sections in the fall to extend the growing season late into the year. The panels in the end walls may be removed or left in place, as needed, to provide cross ventilation when the frame sections are closed, or to restrict heat loss during very cool weather.

We chose to glaze these frames with acrylic plastic rather than glass. Though acrylic costs more than glass, it is durable and safer to use since it does not readily shatter. Also, acrylic is easier to install than glass. We merely put a bead of silicone sealant in the glazing grooves cut around the top of each sash frame and then attached the sheets of acrylic directly to the frame, using two sheet-metal screws inserted through the top and two through the bottom of each sheet. To finish the frame, we coated all wooden parts with copper naphthenate wood preservative.

CONSTRUCTION

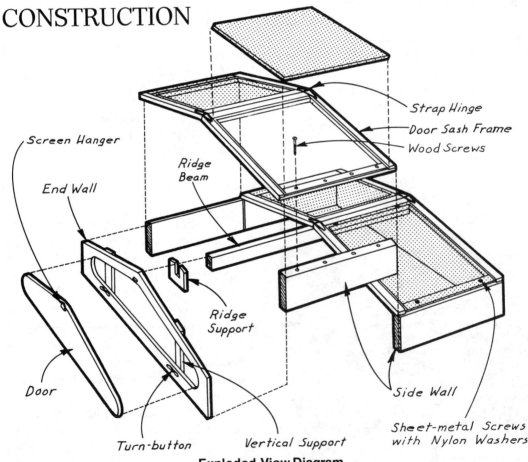

Exploded-View Diagram

1. Cut two pieces of ¾-inch A–C-grade plywood to 12 × 45 inches each for the end walls of the cold frame.

2. Cut gables on each end wall that reduce its height from 12 inches in the center to 5½ inches at either end, as shown in illustration A.

3. Lay out a door opening on each end wall, as shown in illustration A. Note that the bottom of the door is 1⅝ inches above the bottom of the panel and that the door is 7 inches high at its 3½-inch-wide center. The door extends 18½ inches to either side of the center of the panel and has a 1⅞-inch radius at either end. Once the shape of the doors is traced out on the end walls, cut out the doors carefully and save the pieces. To cut the doors, begin by making a plunge cut using a circular saw. Finish the job using a saber or keyhole saw.

4. Cut two pieces of ¾-inch plywood to 3½ × 3½ inches each for the end wall ridge supports.

5. Cut a 1½-inch-wide and 2½-inch-deep notch in the top center of each ridge support to form a U-shape.

6. Center the ridge supports on the inside face of the end wall pieces with the bottom of their notches 2½ inches below the ridge of the end walls. Fasten the supports to the end walls with waterproof glue and 1½-inch #8 flathead wood screws. Trim the tops of the supports flush with the sloping tops of the end walls.

7. Cut four pieces of 1 × 2 (¾″ × 1½″) stock to 9 inches each for the vertical supports.

8. Position one vertical support 10½ inches in from each side of each end wall piece, as shown in illustration A. Fasten two vertical supports to each end wall with waterproof glue and 1½-inch #8 flathead wood screws. Trim the tops of the vertical supports flush with the slope of the end walls.

9. Fasten each door to the end wall from which it was cut using one screen hanger

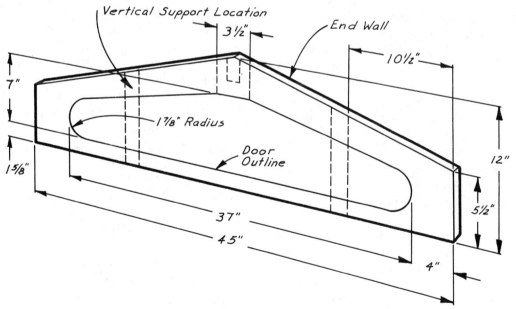

Illustration A

LUMBER CUTTING LIST

Size	Piece	Quantity
2 × 6		
1½'' × 5½'' × 23¾''	Side walls	4
2 × 3		
1½'' × 2½'' × 46''	Ridge beam	1
1 × 2		
¾'' × 1½'' × 25¼''	Sash frame sides	8
¾'' × 1½'' × 23¾''	Sash frame tops	4
¾'' × 1½'' × 23¾''	Sash frame bottoms	4
¾'' × 1½'' × 9''	Vertical supports	4
Plywood		
¾'' × 12'' × 45''	End walls	2
¾'' × 3½'' × 3½''	Ridge supports	2

and two turn-buttons. Position the screen hangers on the opposite sides of the walls from the ridge supports and the turn-buttons opposite the vertical supports, as shown in the exploded-view diagram.

10. Cut one piece of 2 × 3 (1½'' × 2½'') stock to 46 inches for the ridge beam of the cold frame. Rip a 16-degree double-slope on the top edge of the ridge beam to make it conform with the peak of the end walls.

11. Cut eight pieces of 1 × 2 stock to 23¾ inches each for the top and bottom pieces of the door sash frames.

12. Cut eight pieces of 1 × 2 stock to 25¼ inches each for the side pieces of the door sash frames.

13. Cut a ⅜-inch-deep rabbet, 1½ inches in width, across each end of one face of each door sash frame piece to make end-lap joints.

14. Select a bottom piece for each door sash frame and rip or plane 3/16 inch off the face of each piece that previously received rabbets, as shown in illustration B. The glazing will later cover this surface.

15. Join the ends of the door frame pieces together to form four rectangular glazing frames. Secure each half-lap joint with waterproof glue and clamp it until the glue dries.

16. Rip parallel 16-degree angles along the top and bottom edges of each assembled door sash frame, as shown in illustration B.

17. Rout a 3/16-inch-deep rabbet, 5/16 inch in width, on the upper inside edges of the top and side pieces of each door sash frame to receive the glazing.

18. Cut four pieces of 2 × 6 (1½'' × 5½'') stock to 23¾ inches each for the side walls of the cold frame.

19. Rip a 16-degree angle along the top edge of each side piece to make it conform to the slope of the end walls.

20. Fasten the side walls to the bottoms of the door sash frames with waterproof glue and four 2-inch #8 flathead wood screws per frame.

21. Break all sharp edges and sand all parts of the cold frame, then coat them with copper naphthenate wood preservative.

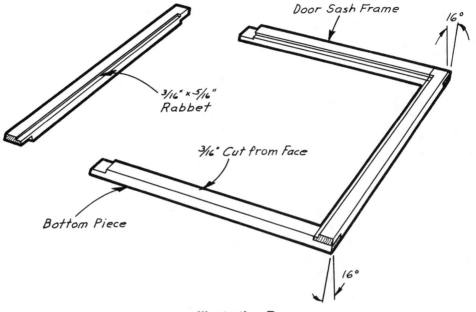

Illustration B

22. Cut or purchase four pieces of ⅛-inch-thick acrylic safety glazing, each 21¼ × 23¾ inches.

23. Fasten the pieces of acrylic to the door sash frames with silicone sealant, and four ½-inch #6 hex head sheet-metal screws and nylon washers per frame.

24. To assemble the cold frame, suspend the ridge beam on the ridge supports in the two end walls. Fasten the end walls to the ridge beam with ¼ × 3-inch lag bolts and ¼-inch flat washers.

25. Lay out the door sashes in pairs, straddling the ridge beam of the cold frame, and fasten the pairs together with 3-inch strap hinges. Use ¾-inch #6 flathead wood screws to attach the hinges to the sash.

INDOOR-OUTDOOR GREEN-HOUSE

Dick Adler of Greenwood, Wisconsin, built this portable greenhouse, which resembles a cabinet, using wood frames covered with clear plastic. He specifies using greenhouse plastic in particular, since it is more durable than standard polyethylene and does not deteriorate as rapidly when

exposed to sunlight. The base of the greenhouse is merely a plywood platform on short legs. The entire unit disassembles easily so the greenhouse can be moved indoors or out depending on the season. Because of its clear sides and top, when indoors the greenhouse may be placed in front of a window yet still transmit full sunlight into the rest of the room.

SHOPPING LIST

Lumber
3 pcs. $2 \times 4 \times 8'$
17 pcs. $2 \times 2 \times 10'$
1 pc. $1 \times 12 \times 12'$
Plywood
1 sheet $\frac{3}{4}'' \times 4' \times 8'$ exterior grade
Hardware
8 flathead wood screws #8 $\times$ 3''
10 flathead wood screws #8 $\times$ 2''
120 flathead wood screws #6 $\times$ 1¼''
12 hanger bolts ¼'' $\times$ 3''
12 cap nuts ¼''
12 flat washers ¼''
staples 5/16''
10 butt hinges 3'' $\times$ 3''
4 hook-and-eye fasteners 1''
4 eyescrews ¼'' $\times$ 1''
¼ pound galvanized common nails 16d
2 turnbuckles 2''
4 pcs. wire 2'
1 pc. clear 6-mil greenhouse plastic 12' $\times$ 40'
1 pint waterproof glue
exterior-grade enamel or stain

CONSTRUCTION

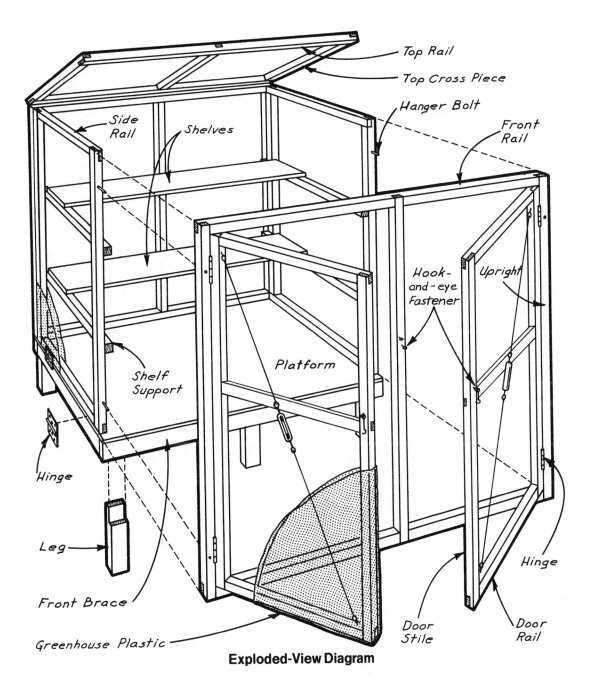

Exploded-View Diagram

221

1. Cut 10 pieces of 2 × 2 (1½″ × 1½″) stock to 60 inches each for the uprights. Across the ends of each piece, cut a 1½ × 1½-inch notch, ¾ inch deep, for half-lap joints, as shown in illustration A.

2. Cut four pieces of 2 × 2 stock to 72 inches each for the rails of the front and back panels. Cut notches for half-lap joints across each end, as described in the previous step, and also in the center of each piece, to accept the uprights.

3. Fasten the front uprights to the front rails with waterproof glue. Then drill two 1/16-inch-diameter pilot holes through each joint, followed by ⅛-inch-diameter shank holes. Countersink the tops of the shank holes, then install 1¼-inch #6 flathead wood screws in the pilot holes.

4. Cut four pieces of 2 × 2 stock to 48 inches each for the rails of the two side panels. Cut half-lap notches in the ends of each piece to accept the uprights.

5. Fasten the side panel uprights to the side panel rails using the same methods and fasteners described in step 3. Be sure the frames are square before setting them aside to allow the glue to dry.

6. Cut two pieces of 2 × 2 stock to 72 inches each for the top panel rails, and three pieces to 48 inches each for the top panel cross pieces. Cut half-lap notches in the ends of each piece, and notches in the centers of the rails.

7. Fasten the top panel frame pieces together using waterproof glue and 1¼-inch #6 flathead wood screws. Follow the same procedure described in step 3.

8. Cut six pieces of 2 × 2 stock to 33½ inches each for the door rails, and four pieces to 56½ inches each for the door stiles. Cut half-lap notches in the ends of all the pieces, and in the center of each of the stiles. Fasten the rails and stiles together with waterproof glue and 1¼-inch #6 flathead wood screws to make two door frames.

9. Cut one sheet of ¾-inch plywood to 48 × 60 inches for the platform.

10. Cut two pieces of 2 × 4 (1½″ × 3½″) stock to 60 inches each for the platform front and back braces, and two pieces to 45 inches each for the braces on the sides.

11. Fasten the front and back braces to the side braces using 16d galvanized common nails, as shown in illustration B.

12. Cut six pieces of 2 × 4 stock to 8 inches each for the platform legs. Cut 3½ × 3½-inch half-lap notches, ¾ inch deep, across the top of each leg, as shown in illustration B.

13. Position legs at each end and in the center of the front and back braces. Drill and countersink ⅛-inch-diameter pilot holes and fasten the legs to the braces using 2-inch #8 flathead wood screws, two per joint.

14. Paint all parts of the greenhouse using

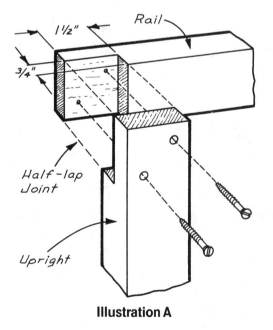

Illustration A

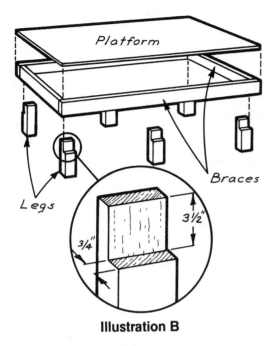

Illustration B

exterior-grade enamel or stain.

15. Lay out a 12×40-foot sheet of 6-mil greenhouse plastic, or a sheet large enough to accommodate all the panels twice. Cut the following: two pieces $12\frac{1}{2} \times 6\frac{1}{2}$ feet each for the front and back panels; two pieces $8\frac{1}{2} \times 5\frac{1}{2}$ feet each for the side panels; and two pieces $4 \times 5\frac{1}{2}$ feet each for the door panels.

16. When the paint has dried on the frames, wrap each frame in the sheet cut to fit it. To do this, center one edge of each sheet on a frame upright. Fasten that edge of the plastic to the upright using $\frac{5}{16}$-inch staples. Then wrap the rest of the sheet around the frame and staple it while pulling the entire panel taut and wrinkle-free. Fold the top and bottom edges of the sheet, trimming excess plastic, where necessary, and staple them neatly to the frame edges.

17. Attach the door panels to the front frame using four 3×3-inch butt hinges fastened with $1\frac{1}{4}$-inch #6 flathead wood screws. Install the hinges so that only the knuckles are exposed. Also install two 1-inch hook-and-eye catches on the door stiles and center upright.

18. Cut four pieces of 2×2 stock to 48 inches each for the shelf supports. Fasten these to the side panels, centered 20 and 40 inches from the top, as shown in illustration C. Drill $\frac{1}{8}$-inch-diameter pilot holes and $\frac{3}{16}$-inch-diameter countersunk shank holes, then use 3-inch #8 flathead wood screws to fasten the shelf supports to the side panel frames.

19. Fasten the back panel to the side panels. Do this by aligning the panels and drilling four $\frac{3}{16}$-inch-diameter holes through the back panel uprights and into the uprights in the side panels. Enlarge the holes in the back panel to $\frac{1}{4}$-inch-diameter; then install $\frac{1}{4} \times 3$-inch hanger bolts, followed by $\frac{1}{4}$-inch flat washers and $\frac{1}{4}$-inch cap nuts.

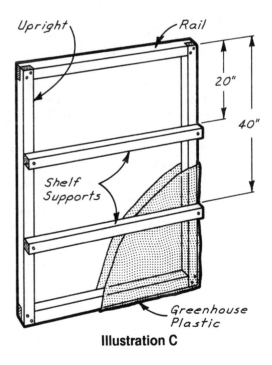

Illustration C

LUMBER CUTTING LIST

Size	Piece	Quantity
2 × 4		
1½″ × 3½″ × 60″	Platform front and back braces	2
1½″ × 3½″ × 45″	Platform side braces	2
1½″ × 3½″ × 8″	Platform legs	6
2 × 2		
1½″ × 1½″ × 72″	Front and back rails	4
1½″ × 1½″ × 72″	Top panel rails	2
1½″ × 1½″ × 60″	Uprights	10
1½″ × 1½″ × 56½″	Door stiles	4
1½″ × 1½″ × 48″	Side panel rails	4
1½″ × 1½″ × 48″	Shelf supports	4
1½″ × 1½″ × 48″	Top panel cross pieces	3
1½″ × 1½″ × 33½″	Door rails	6
1 × 12		
¾″ × 11¼″ × 69″	Shelves	2
Plywood		
¾″ × 48″ × 60″	Platform	1

20. Cut two pieces of 1 × 12 (¾″ × 11¼″) stock to 69 inches each for the shelves. Slide these onto the shelf supports.

21. Position the front panel against the side panels and fasten it in place with four anchor screws, flat washers, and cap nuts, following the procedure described in step 19.

22. Set the top panel in place so it rests on the upper edges of the panels previously installed, then fasten it to the back panel using two 3 × 3-inch butt hinges. Use 1¼-inch #6 flathead wood screws. Install two 1-inch hook-and-eye fasteners to hold the top panel closed.

23. Set the cabinet on the base and fasten it using four 3 × 3-inch butt hinges and hanger bolts, as shown in the exploded-view diagram. Fasten the hinges to the base first using 1¼-inch #6 flathead wood screws, then position the hanger bolts using the hinges as guides. Install flat washers and cap nuts.

24. Obtain two 2-inch turnbuckles, four ¼-inch eyescrews, and four pieces of wire each 24 inches in length. Install the eyescrews on the inside faces of the door stiles and rails, as shown in the exploded-view diagram. Attach the wires to the turnbuckles and then install each assembly, also as shown. Adjust the turnbuckles so the doors swing freely in the frames.

TOMATO-FRAME GREEN-HOUSE

Growing plenty of big, red, juicy tomatoes in Kettle Falls, Washington, where the growing season is short, is not an easy thing to do. Neither is coming up with money for an expensive greenhouse. Patti and Mike Lyman, however, found a solution to both problems in their tomato frame greenhouse shown here, which they designed and built themselves, mostly from salvaged materials and good old American ingenuity.

The tomato frame greenhouse is well thought-out, and incorporates many solar design features. The greenhouse wall, which

SHOPPING LIST

Lumber
9 pcs. $2 \times 10 \times 10'$
3 pcs. $2 \times 10 \times 8'$
4 pcs. $2 \times 4 \times 10'$
3 pcs. $2 \times 4 \times 8'$
9 pcs. $2 \times 2 \times 10'$
8 pcs. $2 \times 2 \times 8'$
5 pcs. $2 \times 2 \times 6'$
90 pcs. $1 \times 6 \times 6'$
3 pcs. $1 \times 2 \times 10'$
5 pcs. $1 \times 2 \times 8'$
4 pcs. $1 \times 2 \times 6'$
6 pcs. cedar posts 6'' diameter $\times$ 10'
6 pcs. cedar posts 6'' diameter $\times$ 6'
Hardware
5 inner tubes (truck size)
½ pound fence staples ⅝''
4 hook-and-eye fasteners 3''
15 patches Velcro fabric $2'' \times 2''$
2 pounds galvanized common nails 12d
1 pound galvanized common nails 6d
1 pc. wire mesh (4'' $\times$ 4'' squares) $6' \times 30'$
1 pc. tent canvas $30'' \times 30'$
1 pc. 10-mil woven greenhouse plastic
    $12' \times 35'$
1 pc. 10-mil woven greenhouse plastic
    $10' \times 16'$
5 gallons exterior-grade white enamel

faces south and is painted white to reflect sunlight, is 8 feet high and 30 feet long, supported by 6-inch-diameter cedar posts sunk 2 feet into the ground. A trellis made of heavy wire mesh slants down in front of the wall and is used for growing the Lymans' luscious tomato crop. At the base of the trellis is a compost-filled raised bed measuring 4×30 feet, in which Patti and Mike grow other prize vegetables.

The entire growing area can be covered, totally or partially, by a wide sheet of woven greenhouse plastic. (This was the Lymans' only expense. Originally, they chose inexpensive 4-mil polyethylene, but when this wore out after only a few seasons, they replaced it with the longer-lasting 10-mil product.) The plastic is attached to the top of the wall, where it may be rolled up and stored out of the way under a canvas cover during the summer months, and slants down across the growing area where it drapes over a railing in front of the raised bed. To facilitate the handling of the plastic during storage and unrolling, a walkway built of sturdy planks is located on the wall, halfway up on the back side, running its full length. Pivoting doors also made of plastic sheeting close off the ends of the structure, but they may be swung open when cross ventilation is desired.

The back (north-facing) side of the wall must be insulated to prevent wind and cold temperatures from penetrating it. The Lymans made do with strips of scrap carpeting, but we recommend bales of straw or slabs of standard polystyrene rigid-foam insulation. To the base in front of the wall (on the south side), the Lymans attached a row of water-filled, truck inner tubes to absorb and radiate heat during the early part of the growing season, before the rising plants obscure them from the sun. Small openings at the ends of the tubes are left open so that Patti and Mike can fill them using a garden hose.

The tomato frame greenhouse makes use of a lot of materials, especially wood. It can be quite expensive to build unless salvaged lumber is available. We suggest that you build the raised bed first—siting it carefully along an east-west axis to take full advantage of the sun—and even plant it if the season is appropriate. Gradually set about gathering materials until you have what you need; then build the greenhouse around the existing bed.

CONSTRUCTION

1. Cut three pieces of 2 × 10 (1½″ × 9½″) stock, each 96 inches in length, into six pieces, each 45 inches in length, for the ends of the three raised beds.

2. Use six pieces of 2 × 10 stock, each 120 inches in length, for the sides of the beds.

3. Fasten the ends of the beds between the sides to create three 48-inch-wide beds each 120 inches long. Use 12d galvanized common nails.

4. Arrange the beds end-to-end in a single row, 30 feet long, just in front of (to the south of) where you intend to build the greenhouse wall. Ideally, the row of beds should lie along an east-west axis, as described in the introduction. The beds may be filled with soil and planted immediately, if desired, or this may be done later, after the greenhouse has been completed.

5. Dig six postholes, each 24 inches deep, at 6-foot intervals along the north side of the row of raised beds. Leave a 12-inch gap between the holes and the sides of the beds.

6. Set six cedar posts, each 6 inches in diameter and 120 inches in length, in the holes. Plumb and level the posts, making sure all are aligned parallel to the sides of the raised

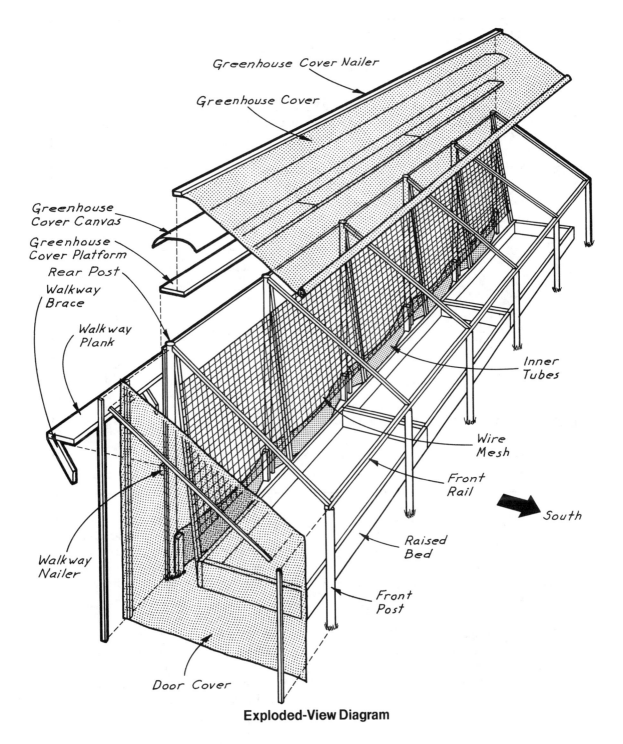

Greenhouse Cover Nailer

Greenhouse Cover

Greenhouse Cover Canvas

Greenhouse Cover Platform

Rear Post

Walkway Brace

Walkway Plank

Inner Tubes

Wire Mesh

Front Rail

South

Walkway Nailer

Raised Bed

Front Post

Door Cover

Exploded-View Diagram

LUMBER CUTTING LIST

Size	Piece	Quantity
2 × 10		
1½″ × 9½″ × 120″	Raised bed sides	6
1½″ × 9½″ × 120″	Walkway planks	3
1½″ × 9½″ × 45″	Raised bed ends	6
2 × 4		
1½″ × 3½″ × 120″	Walkway nailers	3
1½″ × 3½″ × 24″	Walkway braces	9
1½″ × 3½″ × 18″	Inner-tube nailers	10
2 × 2		
1½″ × 1½″ × 120″	Trellis supports	6
1½″ × 1½″ × 120″	Greenhouse cover poles	3
1½″ × 1½″ × 96″	Greenhouse cover supports	6
1½″ × 1½″ × 96″	Door pivot poles	2
1½″ × 1½″ × 72″	Front rails	5
1 × 6		
¾″ × 5½″ × 120″	Greenhouse cover platform	3
¾″ × 5½″ × 72″	Wall sheathing	87
1 × 2		
¾″ × 1½″ × 120″	Greenhouse cover nailers	3
¾″ × 1½″ × 96″	Pivot pole nailers	2
¾″ × 1½″ × 96″	Door plastic nailers	3
¾″ × 1½″ × 72″	Pole-splicing strips	4
Cedar Posts		
6″ × 120″	Wall posts	6
6″ × 72″	Front posts	6

beds, then tamp them in place.

7. Fasten 6-foot lengths of 1 × 6 (¾″ × 5½″) stock, or other lumber if you are using scrap, across the posts, to build the greenhouse wall. Attach this sheathing to the north side of the row of posts, using 12d galvanized common nails.

8. Nail three pieces of 2 × 4 (1½″ × 3½″) stock, each 120 inches in length, end-to-end against the north side of the wall at a height of about 48 inches, for the walkway nailers. Fasten the nailers in place with their narrow edges facing up, using 12d galvanized common nails spaced at 8-inch intervals. When finished, go around to the south side of the wall and hammer over the nails protruding from the sheathing to further clinch the nailers to the wall.

9. Next, position three pieces of 2 × 10 stock, each 120 inches in length, end-to-end on top of the nailers, for the walkway planks. Lay the planks flat, butted against the wall with their ends flush with the ends of the wall sheathing. Fasten the planks to the walkway nailers using 12d galvanized common nails spaced at 10-inch intervals.

Install the bracing (see next step) before walking on the planks.

10. Finally, to complete the walkway, cut nine pieces of 2 × 4 stock to 24 inches each for the diagonal braces that support the walkway planks. The ends of each brace must be mitered to fit flat against both the wall and the underside of the planks. To accomplish this, scribe one length of 2 × 4 and use it as a template for the others. Hold the 2 × 4 on edge against one end of the wall so the corners of the 2 × 4 overlap the end of the plank

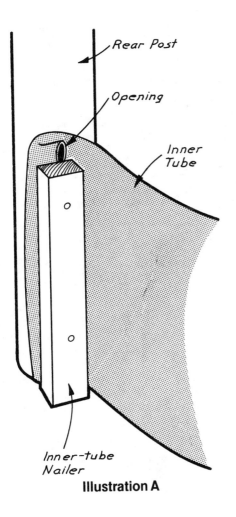

Rear Post

Opening

Inner Tube

Inner-tube Nailer

Illustration A

and the ends of the sheathing boards. Scribe the wide face of the 2 × 4 where it meets the other boards and label which angle is which (the two are not the same). Cut all the braces to shape, then fasten them, three to a plank—one below each end and one in the middle—against the wall, using 12d galvanized common nails.

11. Now paint the south side of the wall, including the posts, with white exterior-grade enamel to reflect sunlight onto the raised beds. Painting the north side of the wall and the walkway is not necessary.

12. Insulate the wall's north side, either by stacking bales of straw against it or by attaching slabs of standard polystyrene rigid-foam insulation.

13. For heat storage at the base of the wall's south side, cut five truck inner tubes in such a way that each can be unrolled from its normal doughnut shape into a single long tube, as shown in illustration A.

14. Cut 10 pieces of 2 × 4 stock to 18 inches each for inner-tube nailers.

15. Stretch the inner tubes across the posts (on the south side of the wall), and fold the ends of each tube under, against the posts, as shown in illustration A. Position the nailers against the tubes, also as shown, so a small opening is left at the top of each tube. Then fasten the nailers to the posts so that the tubes are sandwiched between the two using 12d galvanized common nails. When you are ready to put the greenhouse into action, use the small openings at the tops of the tubes to fill the tubes with water from a garden hose. The water-filled tubes will absorb and radiate heat early in the season, until garden foliage obscures them from direct sunlight.

16. Now set six pieces of 2 × 2 (1½″ × 1½″) stock, each 120 inches in length, a few inches into the ground against the rear of

the growing beds, opposite each of the cedar posts supporting the greenhouse wall. Set the 2 × 2s at one angle so that each meets the top of the post with which it is aligned. Then fasten the 2 × 2s to the posts using 12d galvanized common nails.

17. Cut one section of 4 × 4-inch wire mesh to 6 × 30 feet for the trellis. Fasten the mesh to the slanted 2 × 2 poles using ⅝-inch fence staples. Keep the lower edge of the mesh off the ground a few inches to avoid rust.

18. For the front of the greenhouse, set six cedar posts, each 6 inches in diameter and 72 inches in length, in holes dug 24 inches deep on the south side of the raised beds. Locate the front posts in line with the rear posts that support the wall, and install them as in steps 5 and 6. Leave a 12-inch gap between the posts and the sides of the raised beds.

19. Fasten five pieces of 2 × 2 stock, each 72 inches in length, end-to-end across the tops of the front posts to form the front rail. Use 12d galvanized common nails. This front rail should be parallel with the rear wall, as shown in the exploded-view diagram.

20. Fasten six pieces of 2 × 2 stock, each 96 inches in length, between the tops of the rear posts and the tops of the front posts, using 12d galvanized common nails. Trim one end of these slanting poles, which form the supports for the plastic greenhouse, at an angle so they fit flush against the tops of the rear posts. Fasten the other end of each pole across the top of the front rail, then trim off any overlap.

21. Attach three pieces of 1 × 6 stock, each 120 inches in length, end-to-end across the tops of the wall posts so they form a wide platform upon which the rolled-up greenhouse cover can be stored when not in use

(see step 24). Fasten the boards to the posts with 12d galvanized common nails.

22. Unless pressure-treated lumber has been used, paint the 2 × 2 greenhouse framework and the 1 × 6 cover platform, or coat the wood with copper naphthenate wood preservative.

23. To protect the greenhouse cover in storage, obtain a piece of tent canvas 30 inches wide by 30 feet long. Center the canvas over the 1 × 6 platform on top of the wall posts so that equal amounts hang over the front and rear edge, and fasten the material in place using ⅝-inch fence staples.

24. Glue 2 × 2-inch squares of Velcro fasten-

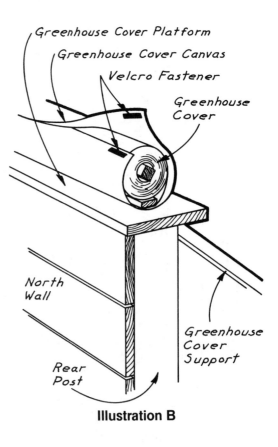

Greenhouse Cover Platform

Greenhouse Cover Canvas

Velcro Fastener

Greenhouse Cover

North Wall

Rear Post

Greenhouse Cover Support

Illustration B

ing material to the mounted canvas at 2-foot intervals. Fasten one row of squares to the underside of the canvas that hangs over the north side of the wall, and the other row to the top surface of the canvas that hangs over the wall's south side. This way, the cover can be overlapped and easily fastened, as shown in illustration B.

25. Drape a section of 10-mil woven greenhouse plastic measuring 12 × 35 feet, over the slanting cover supports and canvas-covered platform. Be sure the plastic is straight, then roll the upper edge over three strips of 1 × 2 (¾" × 1½") stock, each 120 inches in length, laid end-to-end along the top of the platform. Nail the strips to the platform, using 6d galvanized common nails, to anchor the plastic in place across the top of the greenhouse wall.

26. Splice together three pieces of 2 × 2 stock, each 120 inches in length, end-to-end using four 72-inch-long pieces of 1 × 2 strips, as shown in illustration C. Nail the pieces together using 6d galvanized common nails.

27. Roll the bottom edge of the greenhouse plastic two or three times over the pole made in the previous step, then fasten the plastic to the pole using ⅝-inch fence staples. The cover is complete now and should extend from the top of the greenhouse, over the slanting supports, and down over the front rail. The bottom edge of the plastic, with the pole wrapped inside, should barely touch the ground in

front of the greenhouse. To store the cover out of the way, simply roll it up and set it on top of the platform, then wrap the canvas around it, securing the canvas with the Velcro squares.

28. To close the ends of the greenhouse, make swing-away doors that pivot from the top, as shown in illustration D. Begin by obtaining two pieces of 2 × 2 stock, each 96 inches in length, for the pivoting poles that attach to the end posts of the wall.

29. Next, cut two pieces of 10-mil woven greenhouse plastic to the size of the greenhouse's end openings, but add a margin of a few inches on each side for fastening purposes. Extra plastic can be trimmed off later.

30. To make each door, fasten the longest edge of the plastic to the 96-inch pivot pole by sandwiching the plastic between the pole and 96-inch lengths of 1 × 2. Attach the 1 × 2s to the pole with 6d galvanized common nails.

31. Fasten the slanted top edge of each door piece of plastic to the cover support nearest each end of the greenhouse, also using 96-inch strips of 1 × 2 and 6d galvanized common nails, as in the previous step.

32. Attach the front (shortest) edge of the door plastic to the end posts at the front of the greenhouse.

33. Mount two hook-and-eye fasteners on the

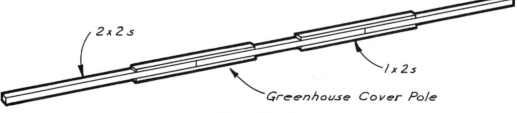

2 x 2 s

1 x 2 s

Greenhouse Cover Pole

Illustration C

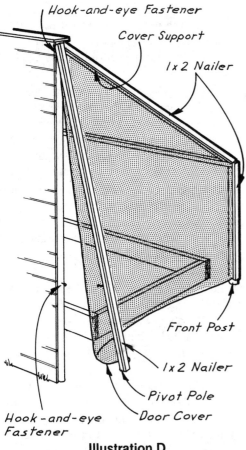

Hook-and-eye Fastener

Cover Support

1 x 2 Nailer

Front Post

1 x 2 Nailer

Pivot Pole

Hook-and-eye
Fastener

Door Cover

Illustration D

end posts of the greenhouse wall and on the pivot poles of the doors. Screw the eye portion of each fastener into the posts, one at the top, the other about 3 feet from the bottom. Mount the other half of each fastener on the pivot poles, then attach them to the eyes to hold the doors closed.

34. Crimp the upper hook on each pole so that it will not slip from the eye. To open each door, merely unlatch the lower hook-and-eye fastener, then pivot the pole upward and toward the front of the greenhouse.

CANTA-LOUPE FENCE

Victor Frang, of Akron, Ohio, designed and built this clever fence to add vertical space to his garden. Designed to hold cantaloupes, the fence also works well for cucumbers and other vine crops. Innovative hanging supports hold the individual fruits. These supports are easy to construct and can be made as the fruit develops. Although both the fence and the supports are shown here, you may wish to build just the supports alone and hang them from an existing fence.

Frang developed two types of melon supports. One style makes use of an empty 12-ounce tin can, plus a short length of 1×4 lumber and a few nails. The second style is simply a small shelf with hangers. The advantage of the tin-can support is that large, round melons cannot roll off easily. If

SHOPPING LIST

Lumber
2 pcs. $2 \times 4 \times 8'$ pressure-treated
1 pc. $1 \times 6 \times 3'$
1 pc. $1 \times 4 \times 5''$ support
2 pcs. $1 \times 1 \times 8'$ (baluster stock)
Hardware
common nails 2d
finishing nails 8d
finishing nails 4d
2 pcs. vinyl-coated mesh ($3'' \times 3''$
    squares) $3' \times 66''$
1 12-ounce tin can

you are growing only small melons or squash or cucumbers, however, the shelf-type supports work just as well.

Use ordinary scrap lumber — untreated with preservative or lead-based paint — for the supports. Using treated lumber might permit a transfer of toxic chemicals to the fruit. When selecting materials for the fence, however, use pressure-treated lumber for the posts. These do not come into contact with the fruit and will last many times longer than posts of untreated stock. Use vinyl-coated mesh for the fencing. Coated mesh lasts longer than the uncoated variety; in addition, it looks more attractive in your garden.

The wire mesh is held in place without fasteners on the posts. It is easily removed in winter for cleaning and storage. To remove the mesh, pull the bottom cross piece away from the lower notches on the posts and lift the upper cross piece out of the notches in the tops of the posts.

Frang notes that his fence becomes so

thick with vine foliage that you can't see through it. In one season he harvested 29 cantaloupes from a 5 × 6-foot section. Fruit will bear on both sides of the fence if you let the vines grow freely. By pinching off wild shoots, vines can be contained to any area you wish.

CONSTRUCTION

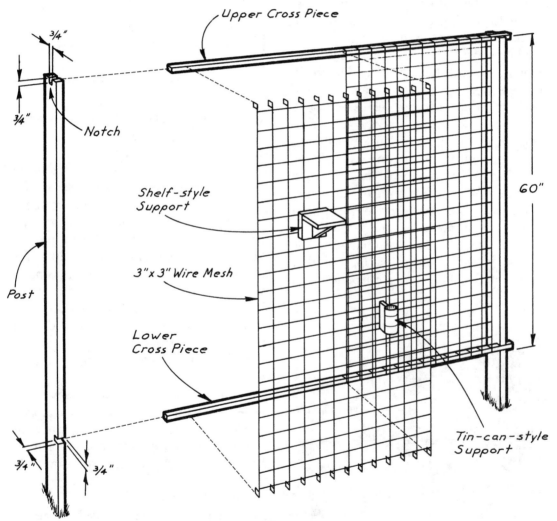

Exploded-View Diagram

To build the fence:

1. Cut two pieces of 1 × 1 (¾'' × ¾'') stock to 78 inches each for the upper and lower fence cross pieces.

2. Use two 2 × 4s (1½'' × 3½'') each 96 inches long for the fence posts. Cut a ¾-inch-wide notch, ¾ inch deep by 1½ inches long, in each post, centered across one end, as shown in the exploded-view diagram. These notches hold the upper fence cross piece.

3. Cut ¾-inch-wide notches, ¾ inch deep by 1½ inches long, across the front faces of the posts—at right angles to the notches in the tops—60 inches from the top of the notched ends, to hold the lower fence cross piece, as shown in the exploded-view diagram.

4. Set the posts in 24-inch-deep holes approximately 6 feet apart. Set the first post, plumb it with a long level or plumb bob to make sure the post is vertical, then set the second post. Use the fence cross pieces as guides to determine the exact distance between the posts. The ends of each cross piece should extend beyond the posts on either side approximately 1½ inches. Hold the cross pieces level, adjusting the height of the second post, if necessary, then plumb the second post as you did the first. Pack soil firmly around both posts to seat them permanently.

5. Now cut two pieces of vinyl-coated 3 × 3-inch mesh fencing to 36 × 66 inches each. Although the actual height of the mesh needed is just short of 60 inches (see step 7), allow an extra 6 inches for the tails, the wire that is wrapped around the upper and lower cross pieces.

6. Fit the upper cross piece in place in the notches at the tops of the posts, then position one section of the wire mesh against the cross piece so that one side butts against a post and the top tails extend slightly above the cross piece. Wrap the tails around the top cross piece, as shown in illustration A. Fasten the second section of mesh beside the first, in the same way.

7. Fasten the tails at the bottom of each section of mesh to the lower cross piece. Perform this step carefully so that the bottom edge of the cross piece hangs approximately ¼ inch above the bottom of the lower-post

LUMBER CUTTING LIST

Size	Piece	Quantity
2 × 4		
1½'' × 3½'' × 96''	Posts	2
1 × 6		
¾'' × 5½'' × 5½''	Shelf back	1
¾'' × 5½'' × 5½''	Shelf	1
¾'' × 5½'' × 4¾'' × 7¼''	Triangular shelf brace	1
1 × 4		
¾'' × 3½'' × 5''	Tin-can bracket	1
Baluster Stock		
¾'' × ¾'' × 78''	Fence cross pieces	2

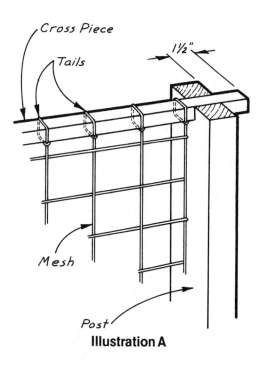

Illustration A

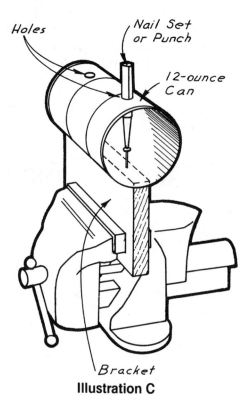

Illustration B

Illustration C

notches. When all the tails have been attached, fit the cross piece in the notches by pressing downward and in, forcing it into place.

To build the melon supports:

1. To make one support of the tin-can variety, first remove the bottom from an empty 12-ounce tin can. Also remove any labels, then paint the can, if desired, with lead-free, nontoxic paint.

2. Cut a length of 1×4 ($\frac{3}{4}'' \times 3\frac{1}{2}''$) to 5 inches for the bracket.

3. One inch from each end of the bracket, drive an 8d finishing nail into the edge, as shown in illustration B, then bend the nails over to form hooks. (Space the hooks as required to fit your fence if the mesh size is other than 3×3 inch.)

4. Now clamp the bracket in a vise and attach the tin can to the edge of the bracket oppo-

236

site the hooks with two 2d common nails. Position the can so its top rim extends ⅛ inch beyond the top edge of the bracket. If necessary, drill holes through the sides of the can and use a nail set or punch to drive the nails into the bracket, as shown in illustration C.

5. To make a shelf-type melon support, cut two pieces of 1 × 6 (¾″ × 5½″) to 5½ inches each for the shelf and back, and one piece of 1 × 6 to 4¾ inches for the shelf braces.

6. Cut the 4¾-inch piece diagonally from corner-to-corner to make two shelf braces. Use one brace only, per shelf.

7. Using 4d finishing nails, fasten the shelf and back together at right angles, then fasten the brace between them, as shown in illustration D. Drill ¹⁄₁₆-inch-diameter pilot holes in each piece to avoid splitting the wood.

8. Drive two 8d finishing nails into the back, ⅜ inch below the top edge and 1 inch from each side edge, and bend the nails to form hooks. The bracket is now complete, unless you wish to apply nontoxic paint or other finish.

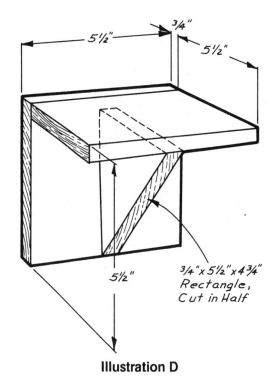

Illustration D

SNOW-FENCE TRELLIS

Here is a project so simple it almost builds itself. Called a snow-fence trellis by its designer, Joanne Smith of Southampton, New York, the only materials needed for its construction are a section of new or used snow fence, four stakes, and a few short lengths of soft steel wire.

Joanne's trellis covers an area 4 feet square. On it she raises cucumbers and cantaloupes. A larger trellis is just as easy to build using a longer or wider section of fence. Additional stakes are necessary, however, to provide the extra support needed.

SHOPPING LIST

Lumber
1 pc. 2 × 2 × 10'
Hardware
1 pc. snow fence 4' × 7'
4 pcs. soft steel wire 8''

LUMBER CUTTING LIST

Size	Piece	Quantity
2 × 2		
1½'' × 1½'' × 30''	Stakes	4

CONSTRUCTION

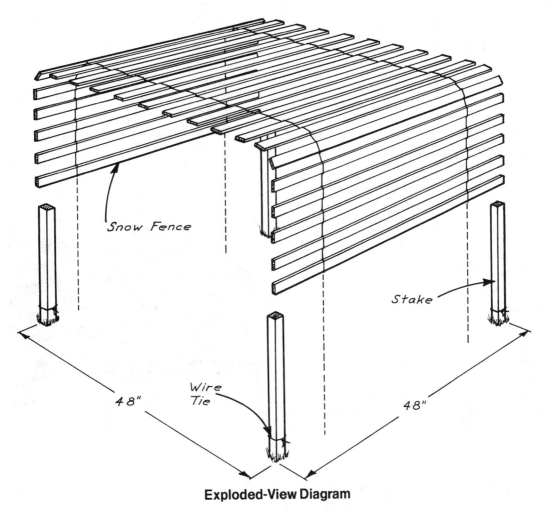

Snow Fence

Stake

Wire Tie

48"

48"

Exploded-View Diagram

1. To make a trellis that is 48 inches wide and 18 inches tall, begin by obtaining an 84-inch length of 48-inch-wide snow fence.

2. Cut four pieces of 2 × 2 (1½″ × 1½″) stock to approximately 30 inches each for the stakes. Sharpen an end of each stake so it can be easily driven into the ground.

3. Position the stakes to form the corners of a square measuring 48 inches on each side. Drive the stakes into the ground until only 18 inches of each is exposed.

4. Bend the snow fence 18 inches from each end to form a three-sided enclosure, as shown in the exploded-view diagram. Fit the enclosure over the stakes, then use lengths of wire to fasten the 18-inch sections to them. Loop each wire first around a stave, then around a stake. Twist the wire tight to fasten the fence securely.

CUCUMBER TRELLIS

This very large, practical, and easy-to-build trellis for cucumbers or general vine crops is producing bumper crops in the garden of Theodore Brooks in Pinehurst, North Carolina. Brooks designed and built the trellis with commonly available materials — 1 × 4s, wire mesh fencing, plus a few nails, bolts, and staples. Besides keeping cucumbers and melons off the ground, the trellis creates a vine-shaded, tent-shaped area between the two side frames that stays cool enough to raise lettuce throughout the summer.

The trellis disassembles for winter storage, but you can let it remain in the garden year-round if you construct it of pressure-treated lumber. The wire mesh fencing, too, is durable and will survive outdoors for several seasons before needing replacement.

SHOPPING LIST

Lumber
6 pcs. 1 × 4 × 8'
4 pcs. 1 × 4 × 6'
Hardware
2 hex head galvanized bolts ⅜" × 2" with nuts
4 flat washers ½"
fence staples ½"
galvanized common nails 8d
4 pcs. wire mesh (2" × 3" squares) 3' × 8'

CONSTRUCTION

1. Use six pieces of 1 × 4 (¾" × 3½") stock, each 96 inches in length, for the horizontal members of the trellis.

2. Use four pieces of 1 × 4 stock, each 72 inches in length, for the end members of the trellis.

3. Position three of the 96-inch 1 × 4s across the ends and centers of two of the 72-inch 1 × 4s, as shown in the exploded-view diagram, to make each of the trellis frames. Fasten the boards

of each frame together with 8d galvanized common nails, making sure to keep the horizontal members of each frame square with and flush to the end members. Make two frames.

4. Cut four pieces of wire mesh (2 × 3-inch squares) to 36 × 96 inches each.

5. Fasten two pieces of mesh to each frame with ½-inch fence staples, as shown in the exploded-view diagram. Keep the mesh square with the frame members.

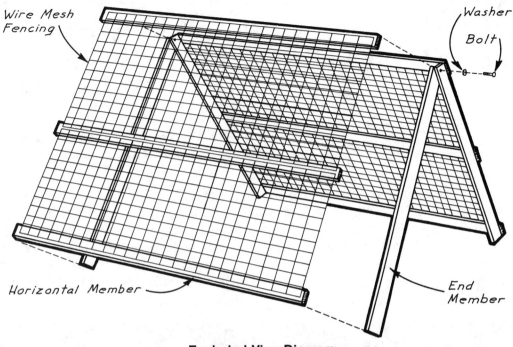

Exploded-View Diagram

Cut off any loose wires that protrude beyond the outside edges of the frames.

6. Stand the two frames together at an angle, overlapped at the top and approximately 5 feet apart at the base. (Adjust this measurement to suit your garden area.)

7. Drill a ½-inch-diameter hole through the ends where the frames overlap, then insert a ⅜ × 2-inch hex head bolt fitted with a ½-inch flat washer in each hole. Note: Do not stand on the side frames to drill the holes. Secure each bolt with a second washer, plus a nut.

LUMBER CUTTING LIST

Size	Piece	Quantity
1 × 4		
¾″ × 3½″ × 96″	Horizontal frame members	6
¾″ × 3½″ × 72″	End members	4

BEAN TRELLIS

This bean trellis was featured in Rodale's *Organic Gardening* magazine in May 1980. To us it seemed that the builder, Harold Frisch of New Milford, New Jersey, had such a good idea that it deserved to be shown again here. This trellis is simple and inexpensive to build—strong and very lightweight. It will support a bumper crop of beans and can be easily moved from spot to spot in the garden, or to and from a storage area in the winter.

By the way, Frisch points out that if the trellis is to be left bare and out in the open, it is a good idea to tie white ribbons to it as a warning to flying birds of the nearly invisible danger presented by the mesh.

242

CONSTRUCTION

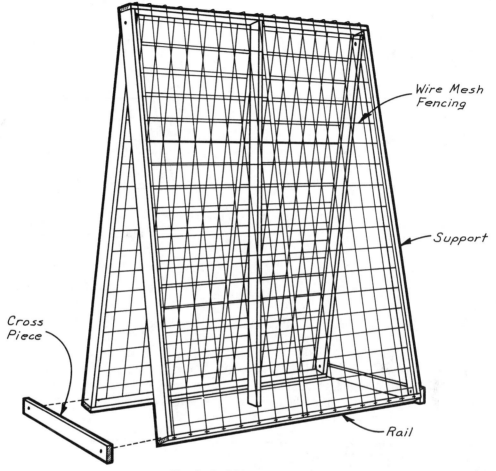

Wire Mesh Fencing

Support

Cross Piece

Rail

Exploded-View Diagram

1. Cut three pieces of 1×4 ($\frac{3}{4}'' \times 3\frac{1}{2}''$) stock to 72 inches each for the rails. Retain the 24-inch cutoffs to be used for the cross pieces.

2. Use five pieces of 1×4 stock, each 96 inches in length, for the supports. Fasten one rail to two of the supports, as shown in illustration A. To do this, bolt the ends of the support against the side of each rail, drill and countersink $\frac{1}{8}$-inch-diameter pilot holes through the rails and into the end grain of the supports, then fasten the pieces using $1\frac{1}{2}$-inch #8 flathead wood screws.

3. Build a second support and rail assembly, except leave off one rail to form the top ends of the supports, as shown in the

243

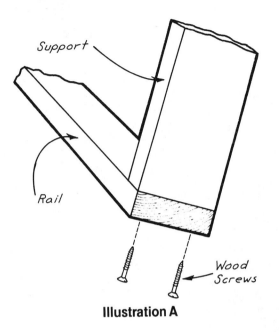

Illustration A

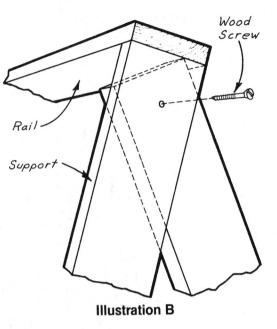

Illustration B

exploded-view diagram.

4. Fasten the two support assemblies at their tops, as shown in illustration B, using a single 1½-inch #8 flathead wood screw at each end.

5. Using two of the cut-off cross pieces from step 1, fasten the supports together at the bottom. Drill pilot holes through the cross pieces into the supports, then use

1½-inch #8 flathead wood screws.

6. Drape two sections of wire mesh, 3 × 16 feet each, over the support frames. Fasten the mesh to the frames using ⅝-inch fence staples.

7. Place the bean trellis in the garden, then prop the middle support under the top rail to strengthen the rack in the center. Now it's ready for planting.

LUMBER CUTTING LIST

Size	Piece	Quantity
1 × 4		
¾″ × 3½″ × 96″	Supports	5
¾″ × 3½″ × 72″	Rails	3
¾″ × 3½″ × 24″	Cross pieces	2

SUPER TRELLIS

SHOPPING LIST

Hardware
3 pcs. steel pipe 1½'' diameter × 8'
6 pcs. steel pipe 1'' diameter × 10'
3 tee fittings 1½''
3 pipe couplers 1''
450' biodegradable binder twine ⅛''

This may be the sturdiest trellis you'll ever see. It's also one which forever ends the winter storage problems associated with wooden varieties. The materials used in building this trellis are steel pipe and disposable binder twine. The pipe remains in the garden year-round, and the twine becomes compost at season's end. Wilbur Hargreaves of Hopewell, Ohio, designed and built the trellis shown here, using salvaged pipe.

To use the trellis, plant crops below each vine support twine. When the plants emerge, train them onto the supports, where they will form a tentlike canopy over the trellis. If you plant beans, Hargreaves suggests that you not immediately harvest the hard-to-reach upper ones. Rather, let them dry on the vine for use as seeds for next year's crop. To harvest the dried beans, merely cut the twine at the top rail of the trellis. After picking off the pods, lay the vines and twine together in the garden rows to decompose over the winter.

CONSTRUCTION

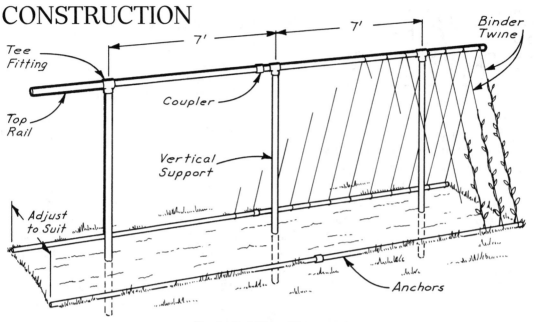

Exploded-View Diagram

1. Cut three pieces of 1½-inch-diameter steel pipe to 96 inches each for the vertical supports. Thread one end of each piece to accept a standard tee connection.

2. Obtain three 1½-inch tee fittings and tighten them on the ends of the vertical supports.

3. Dig three 18-inch-deep holes where the trellis is to stand. Locate the holes in a straight line, spaced as shown in the exploded-view diagram. (For 20-foot garden rows, as shown, center the middle support and locate the other two supports 7 feet from it.)

4. Set the vertical supports in the holes and tamp the earth firmly around them. Align the three tee fittings so that the top rail will slide through them.

5. Obtain six 10-foot sections of 1-inch-diameter pipe for the top rail and the two anchors. Thread one end of each piece to accept the couplers (see next step).

6. Fasten the 10-foot sections of pipe together in pairs, using 1-inch pipe couplers, to make the top rail and two anchors, each 20 feet long. (Rail and anchor lengths can be made up using any combination of salvaged pipe sections.)

7. Slide the top rail through the tee fittings, and center it end to end. If necessary, disconnect unions or couplers that interfere with sliding the pipe through, then reconnect them after the rail is in place.

8. Prepare the area around the trellis for planting.

9. Lay the two anchor sections on the ground alongside the vertical supports about 36 inches from each side of the posts.

10. Cut 24 pieces of biodegradable binder twine to 18 feet each for the vine supports. Tie each piece to one anchor at 10-inch intervals, then lead them up to the top rail. Wrap each strand once around the top rail, then lead them down and tie them off to the anchor on the opposite side.

REDWOOD TOMATO TRELLIS

SHOPPING LIST

Lumber
6 pcs. redwood ¼″ × 1½″ × 8′
Hardware
1 pc. baling wire 1/16″ × 100″

This very attractive tomato trellis was designed by George Ibarreta of Antioch, California. Made of redwood for good looks as well as durability, the trellis is deceptively simple to construct and will give any garden a finished, well-cared-for appearance.

The trellis is also remarkably sturdy and, in the size shown here, provides ample space and support for most tomato plants. Naturally, you may alter the plans to suit your own needs. Cedar, instead of redwood, may also be used to obtain the same durable and attractive results.

CONSTRUCTION

1. Cut four pieces of ¼″ × 1½″ redwood lath to 48 inches each for the legs. Trim one end of each piece to a point, as shown in the exploded-view diagram. Cut eight pieces of lath to 17 inches each for the cross pieces, and two pieces to 20 inches each for the diagonal braces.

2. Attach the cross pieces to the legs using 5-inch lengths of baling wire. First lay the cross pieces one at a time over the legs, spacing the cross pieces at 10-inch intervals beginning from the top. Square the pieces, then drill two ⅛-inch-diameter holes through them, spaced diagonally 1 inch apart.

LUMBER CUTTING LIST

Size	Piece	Quantity
Lath		
¼″ × 1½″ × 48″	Legs	4
¼″ × 1½″ × 20″	Diagonal braces	2
¼″ × 1½″ × 17″	Cross pieces	16

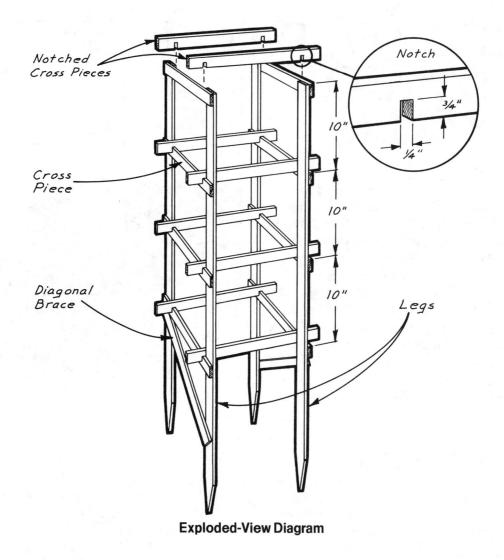

Exploded-View Diagram

Thread a wire through each pair of holes, then twist the ends together to fasten them. Clip off any surplus wire and flatten the ends against the legs.

3. Fasten the diagonal braces across the legs, as shown in the exploded-view diagram, using the twisted wire method described in the previous step. Trim the ends of the braces flush with the legs.

4. Cut eight pieces of ¼'' × 1½'' lath to 17 inches each for the notched cross pieces. Cut ¼-inch-wide notches ¾ inch deep, 2¾ inches from the ends of the cross pieces, as shown in the exploded-view diagram.

5. Assemble the trellis by inserting the pointed ends of the leg assemblies into the ground beside your tomato plants, then attaching the notched cross pieces between them.

PVC TRELLIS

Joseph R. Lyman of Sheridan, Wyoming, built this trellis to hold beans, peas, and cucumbers. It is made of PVC pipe and is held in place by concrete-filled cans, with sections of pipe embedded in them, buried in the ground. The webbing on which the plants grow is made of nylon cord.

The PVC trellis is virtually indestructible, yet is lightweight and easily portable. The concrete ballast can be dug up and moved without trouble to facilitate tilling or changes in garden design, or, if desired, the trellis frame can merely be lifted free of the ballast pipes that support it. Exceptionally strong winds may occasionally topple the trellis, particularly if it is supporting full-grown foliage. In most cases, though, the framework remains firm, bending and flexing in the wind rather than breaking as might be the case if similarly sized wooden pieces were used. If you live in an unusually windy locale, cut the ballast pipes to longer lengths and bury the containers deeper. Or use larger ones, such as one-gallon paint cans.

PVC pipe is not difficult to work with. Use a saw and miter box to cut the lengths squarely, and bevel the ends slightly with a sharp pocketknife so the cement will form a proper bond. The only real trick is to make sure the parts are perfectly aligned before cementing them. This is done by assembling the parts dry beforehand and then marking them carefully for reassembly. PVC cement sets permanently within seconds, so there

is very little time to correct mistakes. Once bonded, joints cannot be taken apart.

PVC solvent and cement are also hazardous, in the same league with paint thinners. Note precautions listed on containers and follow the manufacturer's instructions regarding safe application and use.

CONSTRUCTION

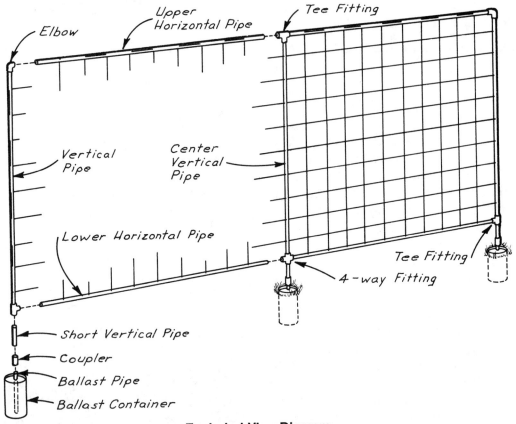

Upper Horizontal Pipe

Tee Fitting

Elbow

Vertical Pipe

Center Vertical Pipe

Lower Horizontal Pipe

Tee Fitting

4-way Fitting

Short Vertical Pipe

Coupler

Ballast Pipe

Ballast Container

Exploded-View Diagram

1. Cut three pieces of ¾-inch PVC pipe to 8¼ inches each for the ballast pipes. Cut the pipe off squarely and slightly bevel the ends. (Do this also on all sections of pipe cut in the steps that follow.)

2. Obtain three 2-pound coffee cans for ballast containers. Mix approximately 20 pounds of concrete, pour it equally into all three cans, then insert one ballast pipe in the center of each. Make sure the pipes are well-seated in the cans and standing exactly vertical; then set the cans aside until the concrete cures (approximately 36 hours).

3. Cut four pieces of pipe to 46⅝ inches each for the upper and lower horizontal pieces.

4. Cut three pieces of pipe to 40½ inches each for the vertical pieces.

5. Cut three pieces of pipe to 4½ inches each for the short sections that fit below the tee and four-way fittings at the base of the trellis, as shown in the exploded-view diagram.

6. Assemble the trellis pieces without cement and mark the joints for proper realignment during final assembly. Use the exploded-view diagram as a guide. Begin by joining

the upper horizontal to a tee fitting, then install an elbow fitting at each end. Install the three vertical pipes next, and adjust the fittings until the verticals and horizontals are exactly perpendicular. Place a tee fitting on the lower end of each outside vertical and a four-way fitting on the middle vertical, then add the lower horizontal pieces between them. Install the short verticals, then slip coupler fittings over their lower ends. Check that all joints are square. With a sharp pencil, draw a line across each fitting and onto the horizontal or vertical pieces attached to it. When reassembling the parts with cement, align the pencil marks on each piece to achieve the correct fit.

7. Now disassemble and cement the trellis joints one at a time. Clean the ends of each piece and the insides of each fitting with PVC solvent cleaner (be careful not to eradicate the alignment marks scribed in the previous step), apply PVC cement, then reassemble the joint so the alignment marks line up properly. Use gloves when joining pipe to avoid contact with solvent and cement. Also avoid breathing fumes. PVC cement dries completely within 30 seconds, so be sure pipe joints are accurately fitted from the beginning. Disassemble, clean, and cement each joint until the trellis is completely reassembled and all joints are cemented tight.

8. Drill ¼-inch-diameter holes in the horizontal and vertical pieces for installing the trellis webbing, as shown in illustration A. Drill the holes at 4-inch intervals, beginning 3 inches from the fittings on the horizontal pieces and 4 inches from the fittings on the verticals. Drill all the way through each pipe. Holes at top and bottom, and on sides, should be parallel to give the webbing a neat appearance.

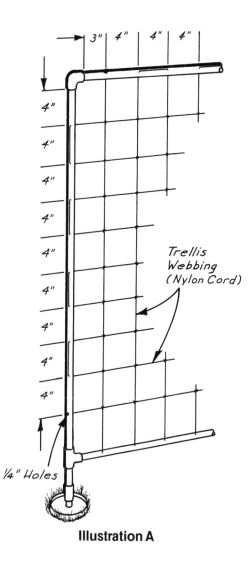

Illustration A

9. Install the horizontal webbing. Use 85 feet of ⅛-inch-diameter nylon cord. Begin by threading an end of the cord through the top hole in one of the outside verticals and tying a knot to secure it. Then pass the cord through the highest hole in the middle vertical, and on through the corresponding hole in the remaining outside vertical. Thread the cord along successively lower

251

rows as shown in illustration A. When finished, pull the webbing tight (but not so tight as to distort the shape of the trellis frame), tie the end off, and sever the remaining cord by burning through it with a match or cigarette lighter to melt the ends and prevent fraying.

10. Using a 75-foot length of ⅛-inch-diameter nylon cord, weave the vertical webbing as you did the horizontal in the previous step. However, at each point where a vertical and horizontal cross, tie the two together

as shown in illustration A.

11. To assemble the finished trellis, first set the concrete-filled ballast containers at 48-inch intervals and bury them to within a few inches of the tops of the ballast pipes. Then install the trellis itself by slipping the couplers at the lower end of each vertical pipe over the ends of the corresponding ballast pipes. Do not cement the couplers to the ballast pipes. When finished, tamp earth firmly around the ballast containers to embed them in the ground.

TOP-HAT TRELLIS SYSTEM

This is a trellising arrangement for the serious gardener. Built of 2×2 stock and ¾-inch plywood, the top-hat trellis system actually resembles a swing set more

than a gardening aid. It is exceptionally strong and stable, perfect for use in high-wind areas, and excellent for raising prize-winning vine crops, especially melons.

The towers of each trellis are made up of legs connected to a junction piece that resembles a top hat. Additional leg pieces connected between towers function as support members from which twine or garden netting can be hung for plants to climb. All trellis pieces are interchangeable, so not only is the construction of the towers and support members easy, but also the assembly and disassembly. Rearranging the trellis-system pattern from year to year, or even in midseason, is no problem either. The tower legs merely slip into place. No fasteners are used. The horizontal support members are held only by a single bolt at each end.

Two trellis towers linked together and hung with twine or garden netting provide 36 square feet of vertical garden space. Using this modular approach can simplify your garden planning. Additional growing space can be gained by training plants to climb the legs of each tower and by hanging twine from the eyebolt beneath the lower disks of each junction piece. You might wish to schedule building a few pairs of trellis towers and support members each year for a period of several years. That way you can gradually accumulate a large system over time without seeming to spend a great deal of effort in construction.

The top-hat trellis system will last a long, long time if built of sound materials and maintained regularly. Use pressure-treated lumber or apply copper naphthenate wood preservative to untreated stock. In addition, exterior-quality paint (lead-free, of course) may be applied every few years for further protection.

The list of materials needed shows what you must obtain in order to build two trellis towers with horizontal support members between, as shown in the exploded-view diagram.

CONSTRUCTION

To make two trellis towers and two horizontal support members:

1. Cut one piece of ¾-inch exterior-grade plywood to a 12-inch-diameter circle for the bottom disk.

2. Cut two pieces of ¾-inch plywood to 8-inch-diameter circles for the top disk, which is made double thick (see step 7).

3. Cut one piece of 2 × 2 (1½″ × 1½″) stock to 3¾ inches for the disk spacer.

4. Lay out the four rectangular cutouts on the bottom disk, as shown in illustration A, then cut them out. Begin by first drilling ½-inch-diameter holes in the corners of each area, then remove the waste, using a saber saw or keyhole saw, and trim with a chisel or wood rasp.

5. Drill one ⅜-inch-diameter hole centered in the bottom disk (to accept the eyebolt), and four additional ⅜-inch-diameter holes for the horizontal support members, as shown in illustration A.

6. Now lay out the four rectangular cutouts on one of the pair of top disks. Make these

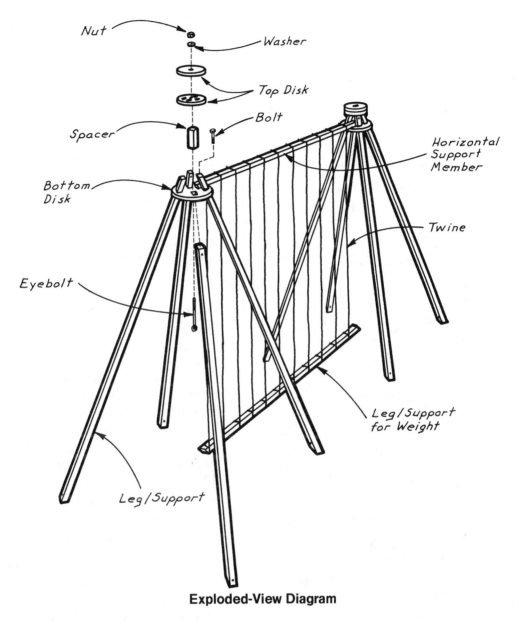

Nut

Washer

Top Disk

Spacer

Bolt

Horizontal
Support
Member

Bottom
Disk

Twine

Eyebolt

Leg/Support
for Weight

Leg/Support

Exploded-View Diagram

cutouts by following the same procedure described in step 4.

7. Fasten the two top disks together with carpenter's wood glue and 4d cement-coated box nails.

8. Drill a ⅜-inch-diameter hole through the center of the glued-up, double-thick top disk, as shown in illustration A.

9. Drill a ⅜-inch-diameter hole centered through the length of the disk spacer. To

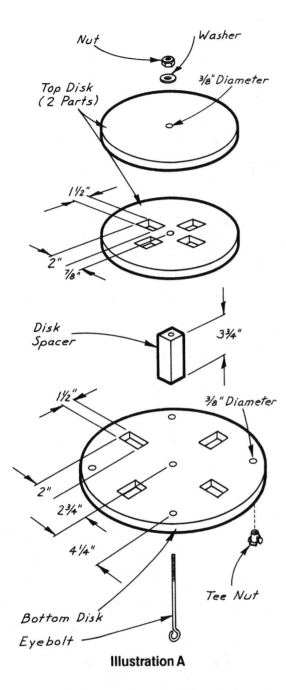

Nut

Washer

Top Disk
(2 Parts)

3/8" Diameter

1½"

2"

7/8"

Disk
Spacer

3¾"

1½"

3/8" Diameter

2"

2¾"

4¼"

Tee Nut

Bottom Disk

Eyebolt

Illustration A

make this long hole, drill from both ends of the spacer, toward the middle, so that the finished hole will be centered properly.

10. Cut four pieces of 2×2 stock to 79¼ inches each for the interchangeable tower leg/horizontal support members. Cut the ends of each piece to a 20-degree angle, with the angles parallel to each other, as shown in illustration B. Cut a fifth support to the same dimensions for use in stringing the trellis netting (see step 18).

11. Drill a 5/16-inch-diameter hole through both ends of each leg/ support. Center the holes across the width of each piece, 2 inches from each end.

12. Sand all the pieces, and, if necessary, apply copper naphthenate wood preservative and exterior-grade enamel.

13. When the pieces are dry, hammer 5/16-inch tee nuts into each of the holes in the bottom disk, except the center hole.

14. To assemble the junction piece, insert a $\frac{3}{8} \times 6\frac{1}{2}$-inch eyebolt into the center hole of the bottom disk, then attach the disk spacer and top disk. Add a washer and nut, then tighten the bolt, keeping the rectangular holes in the bottom and top disks aligned.

15. To assemble the trellis tower, insert four leg/support members through the rectangular holes in the bottom disk, wedging them into the hole in the top disk.

16. Follow steps 1 through 15 to construct a second tower.

17. To join two trellis towers together, install a single leg/support member between the top and bottom disks of two junction pieces. Attach the member to the bottom disk at each end by inserting 5/16 × 2½-inch machine bolts through the holes and screwing them into the tee nuts.

18. Use an additional leg/support member, as shown in the exploded-view diagram and photograph, to act as a weight when stringing netting or twine down from the support member joining the towers.

LUMBER CUTTING LIST

Size	Piece	Quantity
2 × 2		
1½'' × 1½'' × 79¼''	Tower legs/support members	10
1½'' × 1½'' × 3¾''	Disk spacers	2
Plywood		
¾'' × 12'' diameter	Bottom disks	2
¾'' × 8'' diameter	Top disks	4

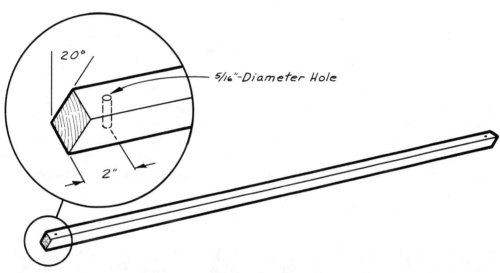

20°

5/16''-Diameter Hole

2''

Illustration B

GARDEN-ROW BIRD SCREEN

SHOPPING LIST

Lumber
3 pcs. 2 × 2 × 8'
Hardware
1 box staples ⅝''
¼ pound galvanized common nails 16d
4 pcs. welded-steel reinforcing mesh
    (6'' × 6'' squares) 6'
1 pc. nylon netting 6' × 12'

Here is a simple-to-build bird screen that is cleverly designed and lightweight as well. James Marble of Phoenix, Arizona, devised it to protect young plants from "air raids," and he reports great success since he has been using it.

Construction of the frame is with common 2 × 2 stock, which is available at any lumberyard. The arches are made by cutting and bending strips of welded-steel reinforcing mesh, the type used in concrete-block work to strengthen the joints. This material is available at home-building supply stores. Its great strength makes it sturdy and durable, yet the mesh is not difficult to bend by hand to the arched shape required. Nylon netting is used as the screening material. Garden supply centers usually carry it or something similar.

Almost any size screen can be made. The simple design allows for easy modifications in height, length, or width. The screen shown here—Marble's own—covers a 4 × 8-foot garden area, and the netting is raised approximately 14 inches off the ground.

258

CONSTRUCTION

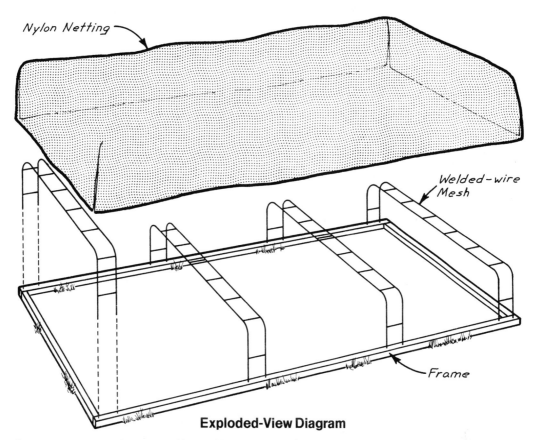

Nylon Netting

Welded-wire Mesh

Frame

Exploded-View Diagram

1. Use two pieces of 2×2 ($1\frac{1}{2}'' \times 1\frac{1}{2}''$) stock, each 96 inches in length, for the sides of the frame. Cut two additional pieces of 2×2 stock to 45 inches each for the ends.

2. Nail the sides and ends together, as shown in the exploded-view diagram. Use 16d galvanized common nails. The assembled frame should measure 48×96 inches.

3. Cut four sections of 6×6-inch welded-steel reinforcing mesh to 72 inches each for the arches. Use bolt cutters or a hacksaw to cut the mesh: It's too hard for lightweight snips. Leave tails on the ends of each arch, as shown in the exploded-view diagram, to insert in the frame.

4. Mark the positions for the arches on the frame. The first marks should be 1 inch from each end of the frame, and the arches themselves should be evenly spaced about 20 inches apart on center.

5. Drill $\frac{1}{4}$-inch-diameter holes, centered on each marked location, to accept the tails of the arches. Drill each hole 1 inch deep. Be careful to avoid striking the nails at each end of the frame.

6. Bend the mesh sections into similarly curved arches, and insert the tails of each into the holes in the sides of the frame.

7. Drop the netting over the arches. Staple the netting to one side of the frame, then

LUMBER CUTTING LIST

Size	Piece	Quantity
2 × 2		
1½″ × 1½″ × 96″	Frame sides	2
1½″ × 1½″ × 45″	Frame ends	2

stretch the material (not too tightly) across the arches and staple it to the other side. Staple the ends of the netting to the ends of the frame, if you wish, or leave them loose provided they touch the ground.

8. To use the completed bird screen, merely place it over the growing bed or garden row. Lift the screen off when you wish access to the plants.

REMOV-ABLE GARDEN FENCE

SHOPPING LIST

Lumber
2 pcs. $4 \times 4 \times 5'$
3 pcs. $1 \times 4 \times 8'$
10 pcs. $1 \times 4 \times 6'$
Hardware
104 drywall screws $1\frac{1}{4}''$
1 quart exterior-grade enamel

This fence, built by the Rodale Design Group, easily lifts free from its posts to provide access to a garden for plowing or tilling by heavy equipment, or to a section of lawn for mowing or trimming. The section of fence described here is long enough to allow a pickup truck to pass between its posts when the fence is removed. The key feature of this design is the use of U-blocks attached to the posts. The fence rails slip in and out of the notches in these blocks instead of being permanently fastened to the posts with nails or screws.

The design of this removable fence is readily adaptable to different situations. Where a fence is already in place, a single section may be cut free from its supports and modified to fit into U-blocks appropriately positioned on the existing posts. If a new fence is desired, the size and shape of posts, rails, and slats may be altered from those we have designed. In either case, a single section of the fence may be made removable while the remainder is permanently attached to its posts, or, if you like, the entire fence may be made removable except for the posts.

We built our fence from construction-grade pine. Other materials are also suitable. Just be sure to select a durable wood for the posts. Cedar, redwood, or pressure-treated pine are the best choices. Paint your fence

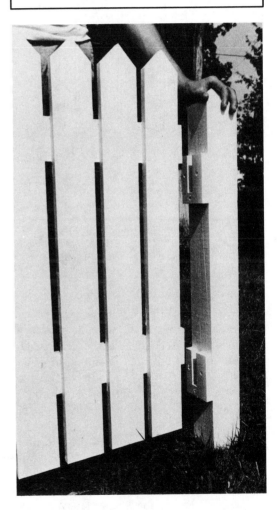

as we have, or finish it with a copper naphthenate wood preservative and stain for a more natural look.

CONSTRUCTION

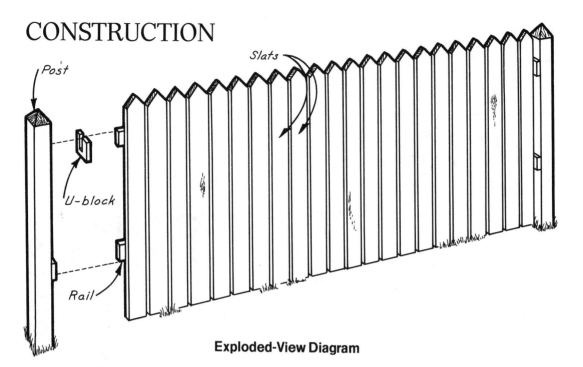

Post

Slats

U-block

Rail

Exploded-View Diagram

1. Cut 22 pieces of 1 × 4 (¾'' × 3½'') stock to 35 inches each for the vertical slats.

2. Beginning at the center of one end of each slat, cut a 45-degree angle toward each side to form a point, as shown in illustration A.

3. Use two pieces of 1 × 4 stock, each 96 inches in length, for the fence rails.

4. Attach the rails to the slats, as shown in illustration A. Attach the first slat on each rail ¾ inch from one end so that the rails will rest in the U-blocks attached to the posts (see step 9). Maintain a ¾-inch space among all slats. Position the upper edge of the top rail 4½ inches below where the slats begin to angle toward a point, and position the upper edge of the bottom rail 15½ inches below the lower edge of the top rail. Insert two 1¼-inch drywall screws where the rails and slats overlap. When all slats are in place, trim off the remaining ends of the rails, leaving a ¾-inch extension on each to rest in the U-blocks.

5. Cut four pieces of 1 × 4 stock to 4½ inches each for the U-blocks.

6. Notch the four U-blocks, as shown in illustration B. Note that the notch is not centered on the block. It begins 1 inch from the rear edge of the block but is 1⅝ inches from the block's front edge. The notch itself is ⅞ inch wide and 3½ inches deep.

7. Use two pieces of 4 × 4 (3½'' × 3½'') stock, each 60 inches in length, for fence posts.

8. Cut one end of each post at a 45-degree angle on all four faces to create the four-sided point, as shown in the exploded-view diagram.

9. Attach one pair of U-blocks to the inside of each post. Set the wider portion of the blocks toward the fronts of the posts so that when the fence is installed, the seam between the slats and rails will be in line with the centers of the posts, as shown in the exploded-view diagram. The upper edge

LUMBER CUTTING LIST

Size	Piece	Quantity
4 × 4		
3½″ × 3½″ × 60″	Fence posts	2
1 × 4		
¾″ × 3½″ × 96″	Rails	2
¾″ × 3½″ × 35″	Slats	22
¾″ × 3½″ × 4½″	U-blocks	4

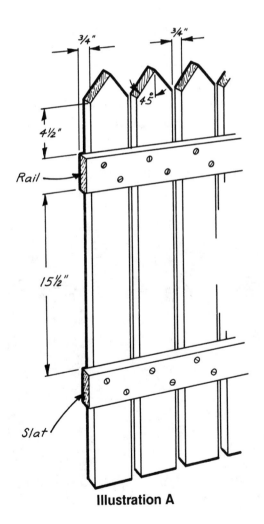

Illustration A

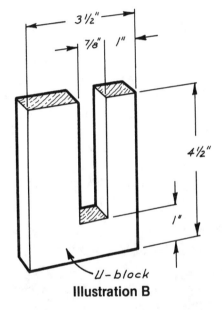

Illustration B

of the top U-block should be placed 4½ inches below the point where the faces of the post begin to angle inward. The upper edge of the bottom U-block should be 14½ inches below the lower edge of the top U-block. Predrill four holes in each U-block to prevent splitting and attach it to its post with 1¼-inch drywall screws.

10. Install the posts 2 feet deep in the ground, at the right distance apart for the rails to fit between them.

11. Paint the fence as desired.

263

SECTIONAL GARDEN FENCE

SHOPPING LIST

Lumber
1 pc. 4 × 4 × 8'
1 pc. 2 × 2 × 8'
5 pcs. 1 × 2 × 8'
Mild Steel Flat Stock
2 pcs. 16 gauge 2'' × 1'
1 pc. 16 gauge 2'' × 13''
2 pcs. 16 gauge ¾'' × 10''
Hardware
4 lag bolts ¼'' × 2''
¼ pound fence staples ½''
¼ pound galvanized common nails 4d
1 pc. galvanized chicken-wire fencing
   2' × 8'

This efficient and very attractive sectional fence was designed and built by Jack R. Schackleton of Menasha, Wisconsin. It is made up of lightweight panels each consisting of a pair of two-piece wooden rails with chicken-wire fencing sandwiched in between. The panels are removable for easy tilling, planting, or harvesting, merely by lifting them out of their metal sockets, which are attached to heavy base pieces resting on the ground. The sockets are made of mild steel strips easily bent to shape with the aid of a vise. The entire fence can be disassembled and stored under cover during the winter.

Pressure-treated lumber is suggested for this project, along with galvanized chicken wire and fasteners. If pressure-treated 1 × 2 stock is not available in your area, treat it yourself by applying two coats of copper naphthenate wood preservative.

CONSTRUCTION

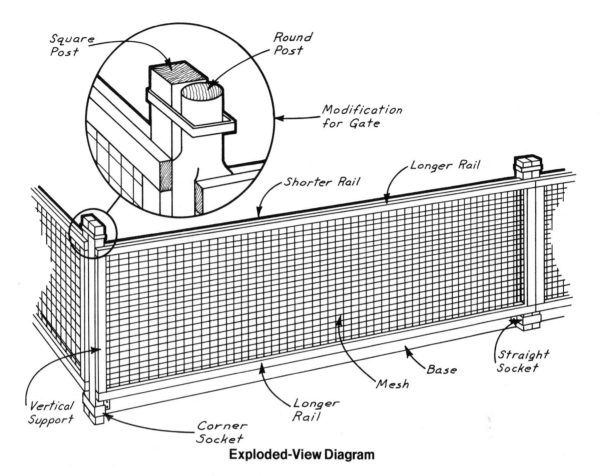

Exploded-View Diagram

To make one fence panel:

1. Choose two straight 8-foot lengths of 1×2 ($\frac{3}{4}'' \times 1\frac{1}{2}''$) stock for the longer rails, which are shown in the exploded-view diagram. Trim the pieces to exactly 96 inches each, if necessary.

2. Cut two pieces of 1×2 to 93 inches each for the shorter rails, and two additional pieces to 23 inches each for the vertical supports.

3. Cut two pieces of 2×2 ($1\frac{1}{2}'' \times 1\frac{1}{2}''$) stock to $32\frac{1}{2}$ inches each for the posts.

4. If pressure-treated stock is not used, apply copper naphthenate wood preservative to the pieces cut in steps 1 through 3. If you wish, paint the pieces after the preservative has thoroughly dried. (Painting the pieces after assembly is tedious, and certain parts will be impossible to reach.)

5. Position the two longer rails parallel to each other and 24 inches apart, on a level spot such as a garage floor.

6. Cut a piece of 24-inch-wide galvanized chicken-wire fencing to 96 inches. Align the rails with the edges of the fencing and fasten them with $\frac{1}{2}$-inch fence staples. Be

LUMBER CUTTING LIST

Size	Piece	Quantity
4 × 4		
3½'' × 3½'' × 96''	Base section	1
2 × 2		
1½'' × 1½'' × 32½''	Posts	2
1 × 2		
¾'' × 1½'' × 96''	Longer rails	2
¾'' × 1½'' × 93''	Shorter rails	2
¾'' × 1½'' × 23''	Vertical supports	2

sure the rails remain parallel. Drive the heads of the staples in until they are flush with the surface of the wood.

7. Fasten the shorter rails on top of the longer rails (sandwiching the chicken-wire fencing in between) so that 1½ inches of the longer rails is exposed at each end. Trim the shorter rails to obtain this dimension, if necessary. Then fasten the rails together using 4d galvanized common nails. (Drive the nails in at a slight angle so the points won't protrude.)

8. Flip the fence section over so that the longer rails face up. Place the posts under the ends of the longer rails, one at each end, and align them so that 3½ inches of each post extends past one pair of longer and shorter rails. Fasten the posts to the protruding ends of the longer rail using 4d galvanized common nails.

9. Mark a point on each post 3½ inches from the other end. Position the remaining rail assembly at the 3½-inch mark, then fasten it to the posts with 4d galvanized common nails as in the previous step.

10. Position one vertical support against each post and mark its length so that, when cut, the support will fit tightly between the rails. Cut both supports to length, apply preservative or paint to the cut ends, and nail the supports to the posts with 4d

galvanized common nails, as shown in the exploded-view diagram.

11. For each straight post socket (two are required for each fence section), cut one piece of 2-inch-wide, 16-gauge mild steel flat stock to 12 inches, and bend it to the shape shown in illustration A. To do this, first mark a point 2 inches from one end of the strip, then place the strip in a strong vise. At the mark, bend the strip 90 degrees to make the first 2-inch tab. Next measure 1⅝ inches from the inside corner of the first bend, then bend the strip 90 degrees at that mark. Measure 3½ inches from the inside corner of the second bend and make the third bend, measure 1⅝ inches from the third bend to make the fourth bend, then finally measure 2 inches from the fourth bend to allow for the second tab. Cut off and discard the waste metal beyond that point. Drill two ¼-inch-diameter holes in each tab (four holes per socket) for fastening later.

12. For each corner socket (only one is needed per fence corner) cut one piece of 2-inch-wide, 16-gauge mild steel flat stock to 13 inches. Make consecutive bends in the stock with the aid of the vise, as described in the previous step, using illustration B as a guide. Cut off and discard the waste metal to leave the final tab end of

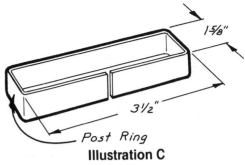

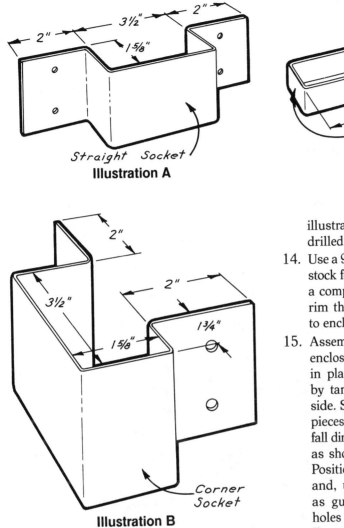

illustration C as a guide. No holes need be drilled in the post rings.

14. Use a 96-inch length of 4×4 ($3\frac{1}{2}'' \times 3\frac{1}{2}''$) stock for the base piece of the section. (For a complete fence you will need enough to rim the perimeter of the space you wish to enclose.)

15. Assemble all the fence components at the enclosure site. First lay all the base pieces in place, level them, and stabilize them by tamping earth against them on each side. Set the fence sections along the base pieces, positioning the posts so they don't fall directly against joints in the base pieces, as shown in the exploded-view diagram. Position the post sockets over the posts and, using the holes in the socket tabs as guides, drill $3/16$-inch-diameter pilot holes into the base pieces of the fence. Fasten the sockets to the base pieces with $\frac{1}{4} \times 2$-inch lag bolts. Install the post rings to fasten pairs of posts together at their tops.

16. To open a section of fence, merely remove the post rings and lift the section posts free of their sockets. However, if you wish to make a gate, such as the one shown in the exploded-view diagram, round the exposed top and bottom portions of one of the posts in a section. It is not necessary to modify either the ring or post socket.

the socket 2 inches long. Drill two $\frac{1}{4}$-inch-diameter holes in each tab to accept fasteners.

13. Cut 10-inch-long strips of $\frac{3}{4}$-inch-wide, 16-gauge mild steel flat stock for post rings (two are needed per fence section). Bend them as in the previous steps, using

267

MODULAR GARDEN FENCE

SHOPPING LIST

Lumber
6 pcs. $1 \times 3 \times 8'$
5 pcs. $1 \times 2 \times 8'$
Hardware
¼ pound fence staples ⅝''
1 pound galvanized common nails 8d
1 pc. poultry netting $1'' \times 30'' \times 8'$

Jerry Stone of Hackettstown, New Jersey, designed this lightweight, sectional fence to protect his garden each summer. In winter he stores the entire fence in his garage.

Each section—or module—of the fence is a uniform size so that all the panels are interchangeable. A series of end, middle, and corner connectors are used to link the panels in whatever arrangement is desired. Stone's fence panels measure 30×96 inches. Naturally, you may design panels to whatever dimensions suit your individual needs. Stone does point out that panels longer than 96 inches are awkward to handle.

Pressure-treated lumber is recommended. However, for a durable substitute brush wood preservative such as copper naphthenate onto ordinary lumber, then apply exterior-grade paint or stain.

CONSTRUCTION

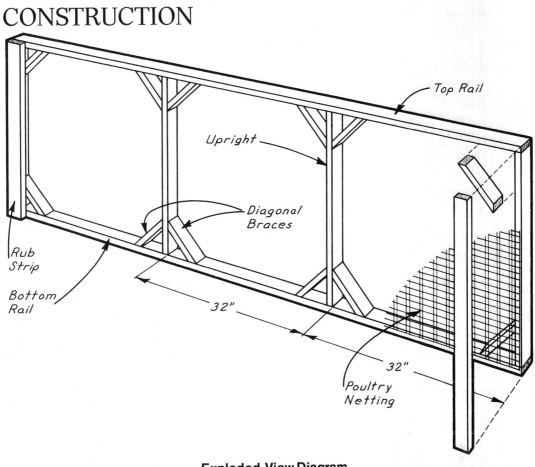

Top Rail

Upright

Diagonal
Braces

Rub
Strip

Bottom
Rail

32"

32"

Poultry
Netting

Exploded-View Diagram

1. Cut the following pieces of 1×2 ($\frac{3}{4}'' \times 1\frac{1}{2}''$) furring strip stock to build one 8-foot section of fence: two pieces to 96 inches each for the top and bottom rails, four pieces to 30 inches each for the uprights, two pieces also to 30 inches each for the rub strips, and 12 pieces to 8 inches each for the diagonal braces. Miter the ends of the braces to 45-degree angles as you cut them.

2. Fasten the uprights to the rails on 32-inch centers, as shown in the exploded-view diagram. Then fasten the braces at the corners and where the inner uprights join the rails, also as shown. Use 8d galvanized common nails. Clinch the nails over if they

protrude from the rails or uprights.

3. Fasten a 30×96-inch section of 1-inch mesh poultry netting to one edge of the fence using $\frac{5}{8}$-inch fence staples, spaced at 12-inch intervals. Stretch the netting taut as you staple it.

4. Fasten the rub strips to the ends of the fence, over the poultry netting, as shown in the exploded-view diagram. Use 8d galvanized common nails.

5. To make an end cap, cut three pieces of 1×3 ($\frac{3}{4}'' \times 2\frac{1}{2}''$) furring strip stock to $31\frac{1}{2}$ inches each. Fasten the pieces together as shown in illustration A, using 8d galvanized common nails.

269

LUMBER CUTTING LIST

Size	Piece	Quantity
1 × 3		
¾″ × 2½″ × 31½″	End caps	3
¾″ × 2½″ × 31½″	Center connectors	6
¾″ × 2½″ × 31½″	Corner connectors	6
¾″ × 2½″ × 24″	Stakes	3
1 × 2		
¾″ × 1½″ × 96″	Rails	2
¾″ × 1½″ × 30″	Uprights	4
¾″ × 1½″ × 30″	Rub strips	2
¾″ × 1½″ × 8″	Diagonal braces	12

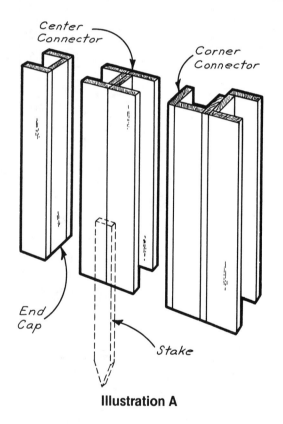

Illustration A

6. To make a center connector to join two panels end to end, cut six pieces of 1 × 3 furring to 31½ inches each. Fasten the

pieces together as shown in illustration A, using 8d galvanized common nails.

7. To make a corner connector, cut six pieces of 1 × 3 furring to 31½ inches each. Fasten the pieces together as shown in illustration A, using 8d galvanized common nails.

8. Cut three pieces of 1 × 3 to 24 inches each for stakes. Trim one end of each to a point, as shown in illustration A.

9. To construct a gate (not shown), assemble a 48-inch-long section of fence and install it between two regular 8-foot sections, each fitted with an end cap. Hang the gate by means of two 1½-inch butt hinges.

10. If pressure-treated stock is not used, apply copper naphthenate wood preservative to each piece. Then paint or stain, if desired.

11. To erect the fence, stand the sections upright and join them with the appropriate connectors, or install end caps as necessary. Drive stakes into the ground beside each connector and end cap so that about 8 inches of each stake protrudes aboveground, then nail the stakes to the connectors using 8d galvanized common nails. Be sure the nails penetrate only the connectors and not the fence sections themselves; otherwise, the sections cannot be removed.

TOTAL GARDEN-ENCLOSING SYSTEM

SHOPPING LIST

Lumber
46 pcs. $1 \times 4 \times 8'$
Hardware
1 pc. flat mild steel $\frac{3}{16}'' \times 1'' \times 8'$
96 flathead wood screws #8 $\times 2\frac{1}{2}''$
8 flathead wood screws #8 $\times \frac{3}{4}''$
30 hex head bolts $\frac{1}{4}'' \times 2''$
30 wing nuts $\frac{1}{4}''$
30 fender washers $\frac{3}{8}''$
1 box fence staples $\frac{5}{8}''$
2 strap hinges $3'' \times 3''$ with screws
2 eyescrews $1''$
1 hook-and-eye fastener $2''$
1 turnbuckle $3''$
galvanized common nails 8d
1 roll poultry netting $1'' \times 8' \times 70'$
1 pc. baling wire $8'$

Enclosing your entire garden in wire mesh might be a radical approach to fighting garden pests, but it is effective. Malcolm Smith of Waterford, Connecticut, built this modular, garden-enclosing system to protect his blueberry patch. Since the walls are individually framed units, the entire structure can be easily dismantled and rearranged to protect other crops as well.

Each unit of the enclosure, including the roof panels, is identical. Mr. Smith built eight units, including two roof panels, to enclose his 8×16-foot plot. The system can be enlarged merely by adding more units. However, if the enclosure is to be wider than 8 feet, vertical posts must be added between the walls to support the roof panels.

271

CONSTRUCTION

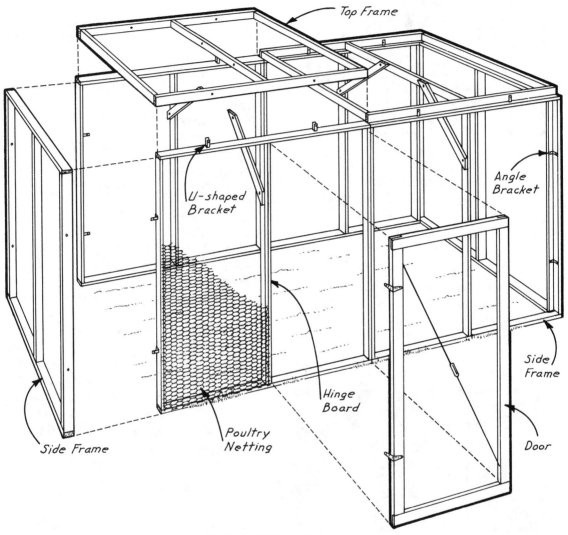

Top Frame

Angle Bracket

U-shaped Bracket

Side Frame

Poultry Netting

Hinge Board

Door

Side Frame

Exploded-View Diagram

1. Use 16 pieces of 1×4 (¾″ × 3½″) stock, each 96 inches in length, for the rails. Cut 24 pieces of 1×4 stock to 94½ inches each for the cross pieces.

2. Drill ⅜-inch-diameter holes in the rails and cross pieces for the fastening bolts. Position the holes in the rails 24 inches from each end, and in the cross pieces 23¼ inches from each end.

3. In the rails only, cut 1-inch-wide clearance notches ½ inch deep in one edge of each piece. Center the notches 24 inches from the ends, aligned with the bolt holes, as shown in illustration A.

LUMBER CUTTING LIST

Size	Piece	Quantity
1 × 4		
¾″ × 3½″ × 96″	Rails	16
¾″ × 3½″ × 94½″	Cross pieces	24
¾″ × 3½″ × 94½″	Hinge board	1
¾″ × 3½″ × 94″	Door rails	2
¾″ × 3½″ × 45¾″	Door cross pieces	2
¾″ × 3½″ × 24″	Diagonal braces	4

4. Position two rails and three cross pieces, as shown in illustration A, to make up one 8 × 8-foot frame. The notches in the rails must be facing the same direction. Drill and countersink ⅛-inch-diameter pilot holes through the rails and into the cross pieces, then fasten the pieces together with 2½-inch #8 flathead wood screws. Set the frame on a level surface and square the corners.

5. Obtain a 96-inch-wide roll of 1-inch mesh poultry netting. Fasten the free end of the netting to one edge of the frame using ⅝-inch fence staples, spaced every 12 inches. Then unroll the netting across the frame to the other side. Fasten the netting to the other members of the frame, then cut the remainder of the roll free.

6. Assemble the remaining seven frames and cover them with poultry netting, as described in the previous steps.

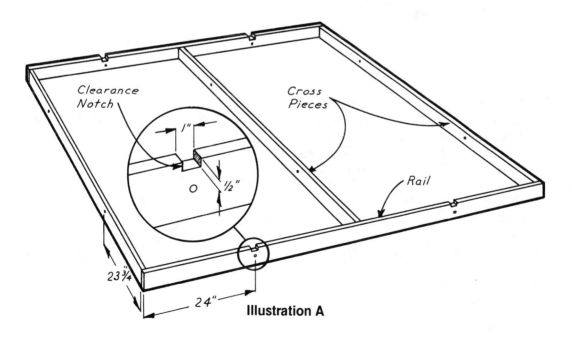

Illustration A

273

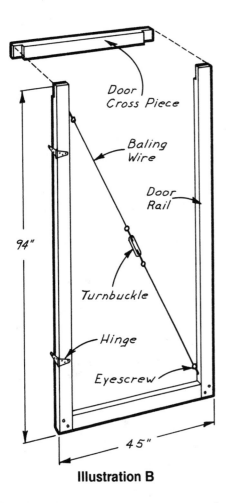

Illustration B

of the rails, square the assembly, and mark both the rails and cross pieces for half-lap joints. Cut the joints, then assemble the door using carpenter's wood glue and six ¾-inch #8 flathead wood screws.

9. Install the door in the panel using two 3 × 3-inch strap hinges. Then attach poultry netting to the rails and cross pieces, as described in step 5.

10. Obtain a 3-inch turnbuckle, two 1-inch eyescrews, and two 48-inch lengths of baling wire. Twist the wire to secure it to the turnbuckle and eyescrews, as shown in illustration B. Then install this assembly on the door. To hold the completed door closed, install a hook-and-eye fastener.

11. Cut 16 pieces of ³⁄₁₆ × 1-inch-wide mild steel flat stock to 5½ inches each for the U-shaped brackets and angle brackets. Bend 8 of each to the shapes shown in illustration C, then drill two ⅜-inch-diameter holes in each angle bracket, and a single hole in each U-shaped bracket, also as shown.

12. Level the perimeter of your garden area

7. To build a door into one or more of the panels, first cut one piece of 1 × 4 stock to 94½ inches for the hinge board, as shown in the exploded-view diagram. Cut away half of the netting from the panel in which the door will be located, and fasten the hinge board flat against the panel's center cross piece using 8d galvanized common nails.

8. For the door itself, shown in illustration B, cut two pieces of 1 × 4 stock to 94 inches each for the rails, and two pieces of 1 × 4 stock to 45¾ inches each for the cross pieces. Lay the cross pieces flat on top of the ends

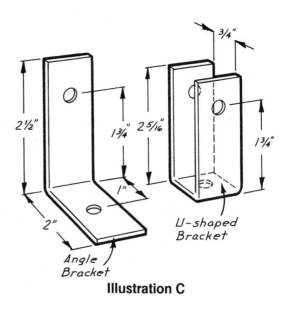

Illustration C

and set the first two wall panels in place, with the rails horizontal, using temporary braces to hold them upright. Fasten the frames together by installing ¼ × 2-inch hex head bolts, fitted with fender washers and nuts, through the bolt holes drilled in step 2.

13. Arrange and fasten the remaining three walls pinwheel-fashion, as shown in the exploded-view diagram, using ¼ × 2-inch hex head bolts, fender washers, and angle brackets. The end walls should measure 8 feet, 3½ inches; the side walls 16 feet, 3½ inches.

14. Square the enclosure by measuring across diagonally opposite corners and adjusting the four walls until the two measurements are equal.

15. With help from an assistant, lift the two roof panels onto the top of the wall units and fasten the panels together using ¼ × 2-inch hex head bolts fitted with fender washers and nuts. Then attach the panels to the walls using four U-shaped brackets and ¼ × 2-inch hex head bolts fitted with fender washers and nuts. (Fasten the brackets and bolts through the holes drilled in the frame members in step 2.)

16. Cut four pieces of 1 × 4 stock to 24 inches each for diagonal braces. Miter each end to a 45-degree angle.

17. Enter the enclosure, then fasten the braces between the center cross pieces in the walls and the adjacent cross pieces in the roof, as shown in the exploded-view diagram. To do this, first hold the braces in position and drill ⅜-inch-diameter holes through their ends using the predrilled holes in the cross pieces as guides. Then install ¼ × 2-inch hex head bolts fitted with fender washers and nuts to attach the braces to the cross pieces.

FOUR GARDEN GATES

Here is a selection of garden gates, designed by the Rodale Design Group to pleasantly and functionally complement typical fences or hedgerows many people have surrounding their yards or gardens. None is too difficult to build, although the pipe-frame model requires threading and welding.

These examples are working models. While they do function and have actually been constructed, they are meant more to spur interest in individual designs than to be copied exactly. Picket fences, especially, lend themselves to flights of fancy and are fun to build. During the last century scores of patterns evolved.

Rounding the tops of pickets or tapering

them to a point has more than just aesthetic value. The sloping surfaces allow the pickets to shed water, extending their useful life. The same principle is even more important when applied to fence and gateposts because of their thicker dimensions. Cut their tops on an angle or shape them to a point as well, so they too will shed moisture and be slower to succumb to the effects of water.

SHOPPING LIST

For the pipe-frame gate:
Hardware
2 butt hinges 2½'' × 2½''
1 exterior gate latch
1 pc. turkey wire 31'' × 34''
40' 18-gauge wire lacing
1 pc. steel pipe ¾'' I.D. × 33½''
2 pcs. steel pipe ¾'' I.D. × 31½''
2 pcs. steel pipe ¾'' I.D. × 16¼''
4 pipe elbows ¾'' × 90 degrees
1 pipe union ¾''
1 pint rust-resistant enamel

For the plywood-panel gate:
Lumber
1 pc. 1 × 4 × 12'
1 pc. 1 × 2 × 12'
Plywood
1 pc. ⅝'' × 3' × 3' T1-11
Hardware
2 strap-type, exterior gate hinges
1 exterior gate latch
¼ pound aluminum nails 1¼''
1 pint exterior-grade enamel or stain

For the tension-brace gate:
Lumber
1 pc. 2 × 4 × 10'
1 pc. 2 × 4 × 8'
3 pcs. 1 × 3 × 10'
1 pc. 1 × 3 × 4'
Hardware
10 carriage bolts ¼'' × 1¾'' with washers and nuts
2 strap-type, exterior gate hinges
1 exterior gate latch
¼ pound galvanized common nails 4d
1 pint exterior-grade enamel or stain

For the compression-brace gate:
Lumber
1 pc. 2 × 4 × 10'
1 pc. 2 × 4 × 8'
1 pc. 1 × 3 × 12'
1 pc. 1 × 3 × 10'
1 pc. 1 × 3 × 8'
Hardware
8 carriage bolts ¼'' × 1¾'' with washers and nuts
2 strap-type, exterior gate hinges
1 exterior gate latch
¼ pound galvanized common nails 4d
1 pint exterior-grade enamel or stain

CONSTRUCTION

To build the pipe-frame gate:

1. Cut two pieces of ¾-inch-diameter steel pipe, each 31½ inches in length, for the vertical members of the frame. Also cut one piece of ¾-inch-diameter steel pipe, 33½ inches in length, for the top horizontal

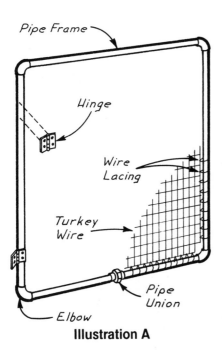

Illustration A

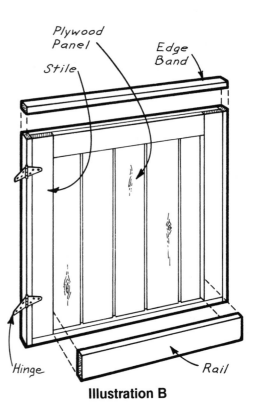

Illustration B

member, and two pieces, each 16¼ inches in length, for the bottom horizontal members. Thread both ends of all pieces.

2. Assemble the five pieces of pipe into a rectangular frame using 90-degree elbows at the corners and a pipe union between the short bottom pieces, as shown in illustration A. Then weld a pair of 2½-inch butt hinges to one of the vertical frame members, spacing the hinges 22½ inches apart on center, also as shown.

3. Cut a piece of turkey wire, 31 × 34 inches, for the gate panel. Fold the loose ends of the wire back over the last cross wire. Lace the wire panel to the pipe frame using 18-gauge wire.

4. Paint the gate with rust-resistant enamel and mount it on the gatepost. Fasten a latch to the side of the gate opposite the hinges.

To make the plywood-panel gate:

1. Cut one piece of ⅝-inch T1-11 plywood to

34½ × 34½ inches for the gate panel. Also cut two pieces of 1 × 4 (¾″ × 3½″) stock to 34½ inches each for the stiles, and two pieces to 27½ inches each for the rails.

2. Fasten the frame to the front of the plywood panel with the rails between the stiles, as shown in illustration B. Use 1¼-inch aluminum nails.

3. Cut one piece of 1 × 2 (¾″ × 1½″) stock to 36 inches for the top edge band, another piece to 34½ inches for the bottom edge band, and two pieces to 35¼ inches each for the side edge bands. Center these pieces on the frame and panel edges, lapping them in the manner shown in illustration B. Fasten the edge bands to the frame and panel using 1¼-inch aluminum nails.

4. Finish the gate with exterior-grade enamel or stain. Hang the gate on a post using a

LUMBER CUTTING LIST

Size	Piece	Quantity
For the plywood-panel gate:		
1 × 4		
¾″ × 3½″ × 34½″	Stiles	2
¾″ × 3½″ × 27½″	Rails	2
1 × 2		
¾″ × 1½″ × 36″	Top edge band	1
¾″ × 1½″ × 35¼″	Side edge bands	2
¾″ × 1½″ × 34½″	Bottom edge band	1
Plywood		
⅝″ × 34½″ × 34½″	Gate panel	1
For the tension-brace gate:		
2 × 4		
1½″ × 3½″ × 44⅝″	Diagonal tension brace	1
1½″ × 3½″ × 36″	Rails	2
1½″ × 3½″ × 34″	Stiles	2
1 × 3		
¾″ × 2½″ × 39″	Pickets	10
For the compression-brace gate:		
2 × 4		
1½″ × 3½″ × 39¾″	Diagonal compression brace	1
1½″ × 3½″ × 36″	Rails	2
1½″ × 3½″ × 34″	Stiles	2
1 × 3		
¾″ × 2½″ × 39″	Pickets	2
¾″ × 2½″ × 37″	Pickets	2
¾″ × 2½″ × 35″	Pickets	2
¾″ × 2½″ × 33″	Pickets	2
¾″ × 2½″ × 31″	Pickets	2

pair of strap-type, exterior gate hinges, then install a gate latch.

To make the tension-brace gate:

1. Cut two pieces of 2 × 4 (1½″ × 3½″) stock to 36 inches each for the rails, and two pieces to 34 inches each for the stiles of the gate frame. Cut half-lap joints on the ends of all pieces so they may be joined into a rectangular frame, as shown in illustration C. Fit the pieces together without fastening them.

2. Cut one piece of 2 × 4 stock to 44⅝ inches for the diagonal tension brace. Lay the brace across the frame from the top corner of the hinge side to the bottom corner of the opposite side. Mark the ends of the brace for cutting on an angle to fit the inside edges of the stiles, as shown in illustration C. Also scribe the bottom rail along the lower edge of the brace, and the

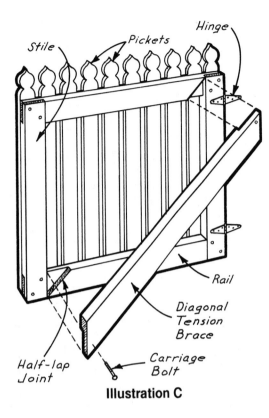

Illustration C

upper end of each picket as shown in Illustration C, or to whatever shape desired; then space them evenly across the front of the gate with their lower ends flush with the bottom edge of the frame. Fasten the pickets to the gate frame using 4d galvanized common nails.

5. Finish the gate with exterior-grade enamel or stain. Then fasten it to a gatepost using a pair of exterior gate hinges. Attach a latch to the other side.

To make the compression-brace gate:

1. Cut two pieces of 2×4 ($1\frac{1}{2}'' \times 3\frac{1}{2}''$) stock to 36 inches each for the rails of the gate frame, and two pieces to 34 inches each for the stiles. Cut half-lap joints on the ends of all pieces so they will fit together into a rectangle. Drill and countersink pilot holes, then fasten the frame together using

top rail along the upper edge of the brace, to mark the inside edges for extending two of the half-lap joints to create room for the brace. Finally, mark the underside of the ends of the brace, where needed, to cut half-lap joints to fit the rails.

3. Cut the ends of the brace at the angles marked, then cut half-lap joints on them. Extend one half-lap joint on each rail, as marked, to receive the ends of the brace. Fit the five pieces of the gate frame together, then drill and countersink $\frac{1}{4}$-inch-diameter pilot holes for 10 bolts, positioned as shown in illustration C. Fasten the frame and brace together using $\frac{1}{4} \times 1\frac{3}{4}$-inch carriage bolts with washers and nuts.

4. Cut 10 pieces of 1×3 ($\frac{3}{4}'' \times 2\frac{1}{2}''$) stock to 39 inches each for the pickets. Cut the

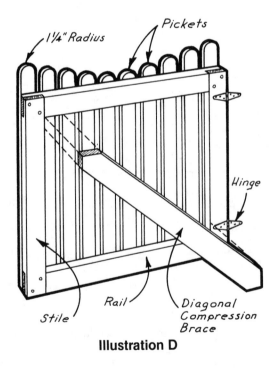

Illustration D

two ¼ × 1¾-inch carriage bolts with washers and nuts for each joint, as shown in illustration D. Make sure the gate frame is square when bolted together.

2. Cut one piece of 2 × 4 stock to 39¾ inches for the diagonal compression brace. Lay the brace across the gate so it runs from the bottom corner of the hinge side to the top corner of the opposite side. Mark and cut the ends of the brace to fit inside the frame, as shown in illustration D.

3. Cut 10 pieces of 1 × 3 (¾″ × 2½″) stock for pickets. Make the 2 longest pieces 39 inches each and each succeeding pair 2 inches shorter than the pair before. Then cut a 1¼-inch radius on the upper end of each picket.

4. Place the gate frame on a flat surface and fit the brace in position. Space the pickets evenly across the front of the frame, aligning their lower ends flush with the bottom edge of the frame. The upper ends of the pickets should form a concave curve across the top of the gate. Fasten the pickets to the brace and frame using 4d galvanized common nails.

5. Finish the gate with exterior-grade enamel or stain and mount it on a gatepost using a pair of strap-type, exterior gate hinges. Install your choice of latch.

FENCE-FRAME COMPOST BINS

Bill Leonard of Lewisville, North Carolina, built these attached compost bins from angle iron, 2 × 4 lumber, and 48-inch widths of 2 × 4-inch welded wire-mesh fencing. The open center bin and large enclosed bin on the right are used for mixing and turning fresh material. The smaller enclosed bin on the left holds the finished product.

About two weeks' time is required in Leonard's region for composting with this unit. After first piling the fresh material

SHOPPING LIST

Lumber
2 pcs. 2 × 4 × 14'
1 pc. 2 × 4 × 10'
11 pcs. 2 × 4 × 8'
Hardware
48 flathead wood screws #8 × 1½''
12 lag bolts ⅜'' × 4''
12 lag bolts ⅜'' × 1½''
24 flat washers ⅜''
200 fence staples ⅝''
1 pc. nylon rope ⅜'' × 16'
1 pc. welded wire mesh (2'' × 4'' squares) 4' × 14'
1 pc. welded wire mesh (2'' × 4'' squares) 4' × 5'
5 pcs. welded wire mesh (2'' × 4'' squares) 4' × 4'
6 pcs. angle iron ¾'' × ¾'' × 6'

into one of the two turning bins, Bill then transfers the contents back and forth from one bin to another about five times during the interval. At the same time, he also switches the front panel of the larger bin (held in place only by short lengths of rope) to enclose the area filled with composting material. The final transfer is made directly into the holding bin. Its front panel is also removable for easy access.

Each turning bin has a capacity of 80 cubic feet. The holding bin has a capacity of 64 cubic feet, since the fresh material reduces in bulk during the composting process. Pressure-treated lumber is best to use, since it resists decay. Plated fasteners should also be used to delay the onset of rust.

Shown here is a complete compost bin, including a 14-foot fence section. Use a fence already standing, if available, as Leonard did.

CONSTRUCTION

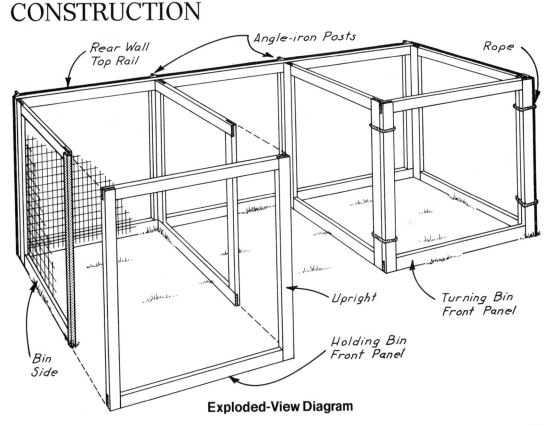

Exploded-View Diagram

1. Use two pieces of 2 × 4 (1½″ × 3½″) stock, each 168 inches in length, for the rear wall rails. Cut four pieces of 2 × 4 stock to 48 inches each for the rear wall uprights.

2. Cut one section of 48-inch-wide welded wire mesh (2 × 4-inch mesh size) to 168 inches.

3. Lay the two rear wall rails face down and parallel to each other, 48 inches apart.

283

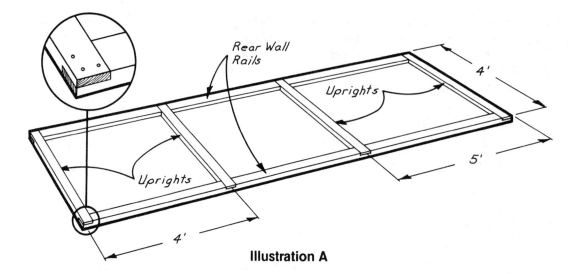

Illustration A

Carefully lay the uprights on top of the rails, keeping their ends flush to the edges. Space the uprights as shown in illustration A. Mark the pieces for half-lap joints, then cut half-lap joints in the rear rail and on the ends of the uprights. Attach the rear wall uprights to the rear rails, also as shown, using three 1½-inch #8 flathead wood screws per joint.

4. Fasten the 48-inch-wide mesh fencing to the rear wall using ⅝-inch fence staples driven at intervals of approximately 10 inches.

5. Move the completed rear wall to its intended location. Stand the wall vertically and temporarily brace it with scrap lumber. Against the outside of the wall, in line with the uprights, drive four 72-inch lengths of ¾ × ¾-inch angle iron 24 inches into the ground until their ends are flush with the upper edge of the wall's top rail. Drill ⁹⁄₁₆-inch-diameter holes through the angle iron into the top and bottom rails. Stop when the bit touches wood, then switch to a ³⁄₁₆-inch bit and continue drilling into the wood, approximately 1 inch. Fasten the angle-iron posts to the rear wall rails using

LUMBER CUTTING LIST

Size	Piece	Quantity
2 × 4		
1½″ × 3½″ × 168″	Rear wall rails	2
1½″ × 3½″ × 60″	Front panel rails	2
1½″ × 3½″ × 48″	Turning and holding bins	22
1½″ × 3½″ × 48″	Uprights	12
1½″ × 3½″ × 48″	Side panel rails	8
1½″ × 3½″ × 48″	Front panel rails	2

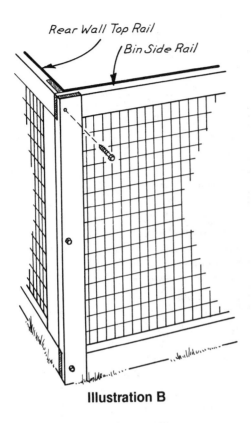

Rear Wall Top Rail

Bin Side Rail

Illustration B

⅜ × 1½-inch lag bolts and washers.

6. Next make the turning and holding bins. Begin by cutting 22 pieces of 2 × 4 stock to 48 inches each, then cut two pieces of 2 × 4 stock to 60 inches each. Also cut five sections of 48-inch-wide mesh fencing (the same as used for the rear wall) to 48 inches each, and an additional piece to 60 inches.

7. Assemble five panels, each measuring 48 × 48 inches, and one panel measuring 48 × 60 inches for the bin sides and fronts, as shown in the exploded-view diagram. Construct each panel using half-lap joints, following the procedures described for building the rear wall (see step 3).

8. Join four of the equal-sided panels to the rear wall, as shown in illustration B, to form the bin sides. To fasten the sides, first butt an upright of each panel against an upright of the rear wall. Drill three ¼-inch-diameter pilot holes from the outside of the rear wall into each upright, then enlarge the holes in the rear wall to ⅜ inch. Install ⅜ × 4-inch lag bolts fitted with washers.

9. Adjust the bin sides so they are perpendicular to the rear wall, then drive 72-inch lengths of angle iron into the ground for posts, just as you did for the rear wall in step 5. Position each angle iron so it covers the leading edge of each upright. Drill ⅜-inch and 3/16-inch pilot holes, also as described in step 4, and fasten the supports to the uprights using ⅜ × 1½-inch lag bolts and washers.

10. Use the two remaining panels for the front of each bin. The longer panel is for the turning bin, and the shorter one is for the holding bin. Fasten the panels to the bin sides with 24-inch lengths of nylon rope, singed at each end with a match or lighter to prevent fraying.

COMPOST DRUM

This very practical composting drum was designed in 1979 by Oscar Nesterick of Erie, Pennsylvania, and he still uses it to produce fine compost for his 14×40-foot garden. Merely by rotating the drum twice each day he is able to compost grass clippings and other vegetable matter in only one week.

A stand built of 2×4 lumber supports the composting barrel, which is nothing more than a recycled 55-gallon drum with a few lengths of angle iron mounted inside which serve as paddles to churn the contents. A sheet-metal door allows loading and unloading, and a 2×4, fastened to one end of the drum, is used for cranking it over. According to Nesterick, the barrel revolves surprisingly easily even when fully loaded. To dispense the compost, you merely park your wheelbarrow on the ramp at the base of the stand, rotate the barrel, and open the door. (By the way, when planning to build the stand, make sure your wheelbarrow will fit beneath the drum. You may

SHOPPING LIST

Lumber
1 pc. $2 \times 8 \times 10'$
1 pc. $2 \times 4 \times 10'$
4 pcs. $2 \times 4 \times 8'$
Plywood
1 pc. $\frac{3}{4}'' \times 18'' \times 20''$ exterior grade
Hardware
1 55-gallon steel drum
1 pc. 16-gauge sheet steel or aluminum $8\frac{1}{2}'' \times 16''$
8 sheet-metal screws $\frac{3}{16}'' \times \frac{1}{2}''$
9 machine screws $\frac{3}{8}'' \times \frac{3}{4}''$ with nuts
8 machine screws $\frac{3}{16}'' \times \frac{1}{2}''$ with lockwashers and nuts
12 lag bolts $\frac{3}{8}'' \times 3''$
20 carriage bolts $\frac{3}{8}'' \times 3\frac{1}{2}''$ with nuts
37 flat washers $\frac{3}{8}''$
2 butt hinges $1\frac{1}{2}'' \times 1\frac{1}{2}''$
1 utility hasp lock
$\frac{1}{2}$ pound galvanized common nails 10d
3 pcs. angle iron $1\frac{1}{2}'' \times 1\frac{1}{2}'' \times 30''$
copper naphthenate wood preservative or latex-base enamel

have to make the legs of the stand longer than specified.)

All the materials for the compost drum should be treated against rot and decay, either by painting — use latex-base paint — or by using copper naphthenate wood preservative, which is safe for the garden area. Pressure-treated lumber may also be used. In addition, be sure that residue from what was originally stored inside the recycled drum will not be harmful. Cleaned drums are available through certain distributors. (Check your phone book or call a chemical supply company.) If you intend to clean a drum yourself, look for one that was used to store vegetable oil or some other food product.

CONSTRUCTION

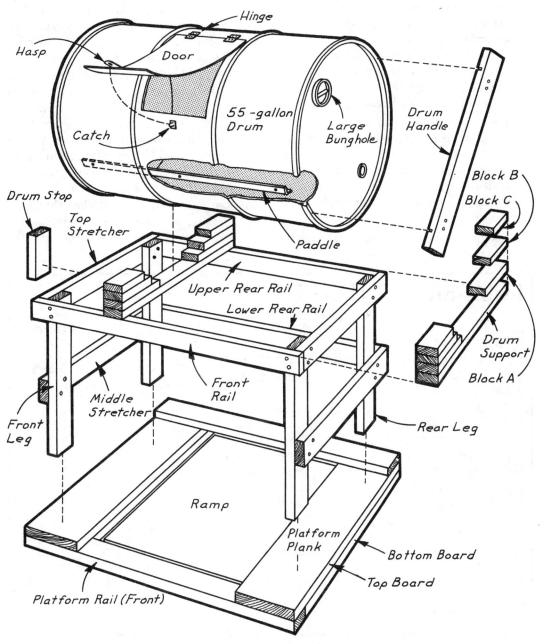

Exploded-View Diagram

1. Mark and remove an 8 × 12-inch area between the two ribs of a standard 55-gallon drum for the door opening. To cut the opening, first drill a ⅜-inch-diameter starter hole inside the marked rectangle, but close to the line, then use a saber saw fitted with a metal cutting blade. Do not use a cutting torch, since fumes inside the drum may cause it to explode. Be very careful of the sharp edges left by the saw. When finished, smooth them with a large file.

2. Thoroughly clean the interior of the drum using the door opening for access. Taking the drum to a coin-operated car wash and using the high-pressure, hot-water hose with detergent is probably the easiest method, but washing the drum out by hand is also satisfactory.

3. Cut three pieces of ⅛ × 1½ × 1½-inch angle iron to 30 inches each for paddles. Smooth any sharp edges with a file.

4. Drill three holes, each ⅜ inch in diameter, through one side of each piece of angle iron, as shown in illustration A. One hole should be centered along the length of the angle iron, the other two should be drilled 3 inches from each end.

5. Hold each drilled piece against the *outside* of the drum (for easy layout), and mark the locations of the holes onto the drum sides so that, when drilled, the holes will be in the positions shown in illustration A. Label the pieces and drum sides to correspond so that you can easily reposition the pieces inside the drum during assembly.

6. Remove the plug from the large bunghole and slide the three paddles inside the drum through the hole. Fasten the three paddles

LUMBER CUTTING LIST

Size	Piece	Quantity
2 × 8		
1½″ × 7½″ × 28″	Top platform planks	2
1½″ × 7½″ × 24½″	Bottom platform planks	2
2 × 4		
1½″ × 3½″ × 34″	Platform rails	2
1½″ × 3½″ × 34″	Drum handle	1
1½″ × 3½″ × 31″	Front rail	1
1½″ × 3½″ × 28″	Upper and lower rear rails	2
1½″ × 3½″ × 26″	Drum supports	2
1½″ × 3½″ × 24½″	Middle stretchers	2
1½″ × 3½″ × 24½″	Top stretchers	2
1½″ × 3½″ × 18″	Legs	4
1½″ × 3½″ × 9″	Drum stop	1
1½″ × 3½″ × 7½″	Blocks A	4
1½″ × 3½″ × 5½″	Blocks B	4
1½″ × 3½″ × 4″	Blocks C	4
Plywood		
¾″ × 18″ × 20″	Ramp	1

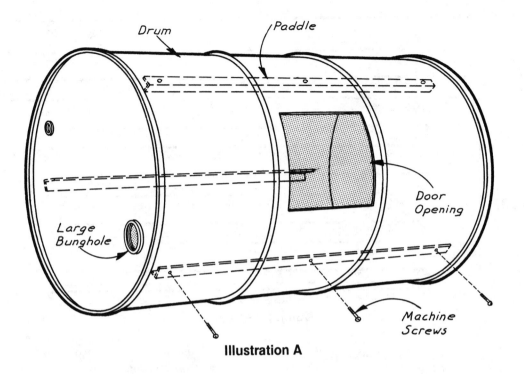

Drum

Paddle

Door
Opening

Large
Bunghole

Machine
Screws

Illustration A

inside the drum using nine ⅜ × ¾-inch machine screws fitted with washers and nuts.

7. Cut one piece of 16-gauge sheet metal to 8½ × 16 inches for the door.

8. Hold the door centered over the drum's door opening, then position two 1½ × 1½-inch butt hinges at the top and mark the locations for the mounting-screw holes in both the door and the drum, as shown in the exploded-view diagram. Remove the door and hinges, drill ¼-inch-diameter holes at the marked locations, then install the door and hinges using ³⁄₁₆ × ½-inch machine screws, lockwashers, and nuts.

9. Hold a hasp lock and catch in position on the door. Mark the positions of the mounting screws and drill ¼-inch-diameter holes on the marks as in the previous step. Fasten the hasp lock and catch to the lid and drum with ³⁄₁₆ × ½-inch sheet-metal screws.

10. Cut two pieces of 2 × 8 (1½″ × 7½″) stock to 28 inches each for the tops of the platform, and two additional pieces to 24½ inches each for the bottoms of the platform. Nail the boards together in pairs (one short board plus one long board) to make two planks, each 3 inches thick, as shown in the exploded-view diagram. Use 10d galvanized common nails. For this and the next several steps, you may wish to refer to the cutting diagram as a guide for efficient use of stock.

11. Cut two pieces of 2 × 4 (1½″ × 3½″) stock to 34 inches each for the platform rails. Fasten these with 10d galvanized common nails across the ends of the planks, as shown in the exploded-view diagram, to form the sides of the base. Fasten the rails flush with the ends and edges of the planks, as shown, with one rail on top of the platform in the rear, and the other rail on the bottom in the front.

289

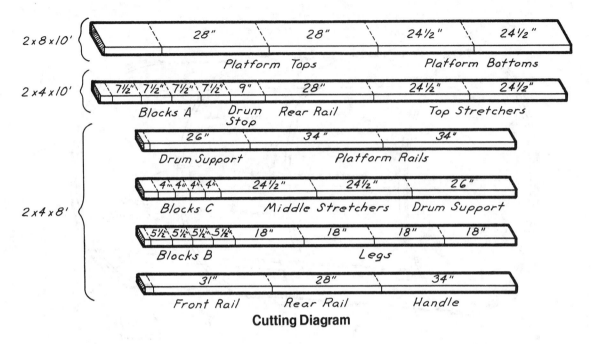

Cutting Diagram

12. Cut four pieces of 2 × 4 stock to 18 inches each for the legs.

13. Cut four pieces of 2 × 4 stock to 24½ inches each for the two middle and two top stretchers.

14. Align the top stretchers flush with the tops of the legs, so that each stretcher projects 1½ inches beyond the outside edge of the rear leg it rests against. Drill two holes, each ⁷⁄₁₆ inch in diameter, through the stretchers and legs, and fit ⅜ × 3½-inch carriage bolts through the holes, as shown in illustration B. Secure the bolts with washers and nuts.

15. Position the middle stretchers flush with the front edges of the front legs and 10 inches from the upper surface of the platform planks, as shown in illustration B. In this step, the stretchers should project 1½ inches beyond the outside edges of the rear legs. Make certain the stretchers are square to the legs, then drill ⁷⁄₁₆-inch-diameter holes, as before, through the pieces and secure

the joints with ⅜ × 3½-inch carriage bolts, washers, and nuts.

16. Cut one piece of 2 × 4 stock to 31 inches for the front rail.

17. Cut two pieces of 2 × 4 stock to 28 inches each for the upper and lower rear rails.

18. Lay the two end assemblies on their rear edges and position the front rail. Drill two ¼-inch-diameter pilot holes through each end of the rail and into the legs. Fasten the front rail to the side assemblies with ⅜ × 3-inch lag bolts fitted with washers.

19. Turn the assembly onto the front edges to fasten the rear rails in place. Align the lower rail between the ends of the middle stretchers and drill two ¼-inch-diameter pilot holes through each end of the rail and into the legs. Insert and tighten four ⅜ × 3-inch lag bolts fitted with washers. Hold the upper rail in place between the ends of the top stretchers, drill ¼-inch-diameter pilot holes, and secure it to the legs also using four ⅜ × 3-inch lag bolts

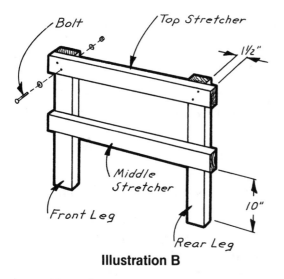

Illustration B

with washers.

20. Cut one piece of 2×4 to measure $3\frac{1}{2} \times 9$ inches for the drum stop. Position the stop vertically, centered along one top stretcher, as shown in the exploded-view diagram, so the stop extends about 6 inches above the stretcher's top edge. Drill $\frac{1}{4}$-inch-diameter pilot holes and fasten the stop with two $\frac{3}{8} \times 3$-inch lag bolts fitted with washers.

21. Cut two pieces of 2×4 stock to 26 inches each for the drum supports.

22. Position the drum supports across the stand, spaced so that when the project is assembled the ribs of the drum will lie just inside the supports. Use the drum itself as a guide. Nail the drum supports to the front and upper rear rail with 10d galvanized common nails.

23. Cut four pieces of 2×4 stock to $7\frac{1}{2}$ inches each for blocks A, another four pieces to $5\frac{1}{2}$ inches each for blocks B, and finally four pieces to 4 inches each for blocks C, as shown in the exploded-view diagram,

24. Nail the blocks on top of each other, as shown, so that their outer ends are flush with the ends of the drum supports and their inner ends are stepped to cradle the drum. When finished, check the fit of the drum in the cradles and trim away any high corners of the blocks with a hand plane. Minor high places will wear away with use.

25. Cut one piece of $\frac{3}{4}$-inch exterior-grade plywood to 18×20 inches for the ramp. Sand the edges, if desired.

26. Cut one piece of 2×4 stock to 34 inches for the drum handle. Round the ends and sand off any sharp edges.

27. Center the handle on one end of the drum and mark where the rim of the drum touches the handle at both ends. Notch the handle, using the marks as a guide, so that the handle will lie flush against the drum top, as shown in the exploded-view diagram.

28. Now apply copper naphthenate wood preservative or latex-base enamel to the entire drum stand, including the ramp and drum handle.

29. To assemble the compost drum and stand, first attach the drum handle. Drill two $\frac{7}{16}$-inch-diameter holes 7 and 9 inches from each end of the handle. Center the handle across the top of the drum, mark the hole positions, then drill $\frac{7}{16}$-inch-diameter holes in the drum top. Install the drum handle with $\frac{3}{8} \times 3\frac{1}{2}$-inch carriage bolts, washers, and nuts.

30. Set the ramp in position under the drum stand, and the project is complete.

MANURE-TEA BREWER

SHOPPING LIST

Hardware
1 55-gallon steel drum
2 wire-mesh or plastic milk-bottle carriers
8 machine screws ¼″ × 1½″ with nuts (for plastic carriers only)
20 sheet-metal screws #6 × ½″
8 flat washers ⁵⁄₁₆″ (for plastic carriers only)
4 pcs. aluminum mesh 13″ × 3′
1 pc. aluminum mesh 30″ × 3′ (optional)
2 pcs. angle iron 1″ × 1″ × 4′
4 pcs. steel pipe 2½″ O.D. × 44″
1 pc. steel pipe 2½″ O.D. × 21¾″
1 pipe nipple ¾″ × 3″
2 pcs. garden hose ½″ × 27″
2 pcs. garden hose ½″ × 15½″
1 hose bib faucet ¾″
1 pint rust-resistant enamel

Manure tea is a polite name for liquid fertilizer made from fresh manure and water. Joe Horvath of Interlochen, Michigan, concocts his in this manure-tea brewer that he designed and built himself, using a 55-gallon drum and 2½-inch steel pipe. He devised a brewing basket also, made from discarded milk-bottle carriers, joined to two lengths of angle iron. The basket fits inside the drum. When filled with manure, its function is the same as an ordinary tea bag in a pot. A spigot at the bottom of the drum is used to drain the finished brew. Horvath uses a garden hose, connected directly to

the spigot, to apply the tea, which makes the process just as clean and simple as watering the garden.

The brewer must be elevated higher than the level of your garden for the hose to work by gravity. This usually means you'll have to build some kind of stand. You could use cement blocks or stones for this, or even make a wooden stand similar to the one described for use with the compost drum (see p. 286). The stand Joe Horvath built, however, requires only medium-level welding skills and is quite strong as well as inexpensive. It will last forever if kept from rusting.

A note about cutting open the barrel: Even though it's noisy using a saber saw for this, it's safer than using a cutting torch. Use a torch only if you're absolutely sure that what was originally in the drum did not leave fumes behind that might explode. Even then, filling the drum with water and cutting it while full is cheap insurance against an accident.

The manure-tea brewer will make two batches before it needs to be recharged. After the second batch has brewed, remove the spent manure and use it to build compost.

CONSTRUCTION

To make the brewing basket and drum:

1. Cut two pieces of 1 × 1-inch angle iron to 48 inches each for the handles of the brewing basket.

2. Obtain two milk-bottle carriers (wire-mesh or plastic) for the basket compartments.

3. Arrange the carriers side by side on a level work surface. Lay the handles over the long top edges formed by the carriers, as shown in the exploded-view diagram. Center the carriers along the length of the handles. If you are using wire-mesh carriers, weld the handles in place in at least four places per side. If the carriers are of plastic mesh, mark places where bolts with washers can be installed, then drill 5/32-inch-diameter holes through the sides of the angle iron, and fasten the handles to the carriers using 1/4 × 1 1/2-inch machine screws, washers, and nuts. Use the washers between the mesh and the nuts.

4. Cut four pieces of aluminum mesh to 13 × 36 inches each. Two pieces of mesh are used to line each carrier and act as filters. Fold the pieces as shown in the exploded-view diagram and insert them in the carriers.

5. Measure the length and width of the combined carriers, which form the brewing basket, then add 1 inch to each figure to calculate the size of the opening that must be cut in the drum. Lay out the opening on a 55-gallon drum, being careful to center the opening along the drum's length and to locate the opening in line with the bungholes, as shown in the exploded-view diagram. The larger bunghole must be at the top so that the smaller hole directly below may be fitted with a faucet (see step 9).

6. Drill a 3/8-inch-diameter hole at each of the four corners of the marked-out drum opening, then use a saber saw to remove the waste section of metal. File the edges smooth, then rinse the drum thoroughly with soap and water.

7. Cut sections of 1/2-inch garden hose, two pieces equal to the length of the opening, and two equal to the width. Add some extra to the latter to allow for the curvature of the drum. Slit the sections lengthwise and slip them over the sawn edges of the opening. Drill 1/8-inch-diameter holes through the base and into the drum at 6-inch intervals. Fasten the hose sections to the drum using 1/2-inch #6 sheet-metal screws.

8. Remove the threaded plug from the small bunghole. Usually this can be done with a wrench. If the plug is concave, tap it around using an old screwdriver, or cold chisel, and a hammer.

9. Install a 3/4 × 3-inch pipe nipple in the small bunghole. To the nipple, attach a 3/4-inch hose bib faucet, as shown in the exploded-view diagram.

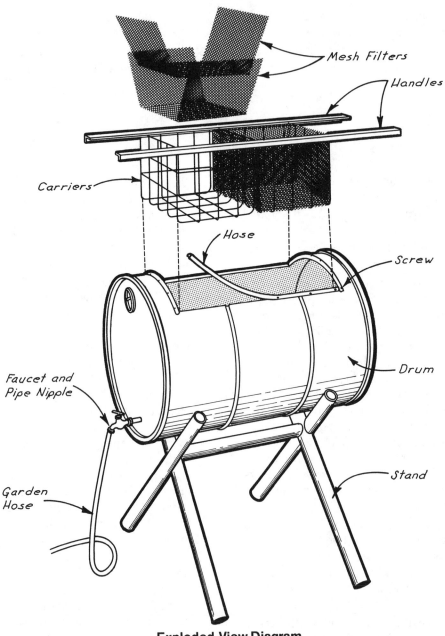

Mesh Filters

Handles

Carriers

Hose

Screw

Faucet and
Pipe Nipple

Drum

Garden
Hose

Stand

Exploded-View Diagram

To make the stand:

1. Cut four pieces of 2½-inch-O.D. steel pipe to 44 inches each for the legs. Use a hacksaw (you'll need plenty of blades), torch, or plumber's pipe cutter.

2. Cut one piece of 2½-inch-O.D. steel pipe to 21¾ inches for the cross piece. If you use a torch for cutting, you can make the formed

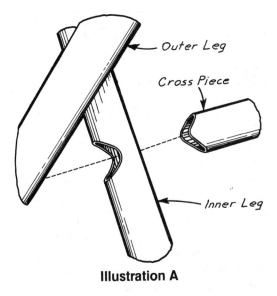

Outer Leg

Cross Piece

Inner Leg

Illustration A

ends of the cross piece, as shown in illustration A, without trouble. If you're using a hacksaw, you'll find it easier merely to cut V-shaped notches in the pipe ends instead.

3. Cut notches in two of the legs, also as shown in illustration A. Use a torch, or cut V-notches with a hacksaw and radius them with a half-round file. The notches should be centered along the length of the pieces and measure 2½ inches long by 1¼ inches deep.

4. Fit the notched legs over the unnotched ones to form two crisscrossed pairs. Support each pair on a level work surface. Make sure that each leg of a pair crosses the other at right angles, then weld the members of each pair together.

5. With one of the leg assemblies still lying flat from the previous step, hold the cross piece so that it is vertical while fitting one of its notched ends over the center of the crisscrossed legs, opposite the joint that holds the legs together. Tack-weld the cross piece in position. Now right the partially assembled stand, brace the other end of the cross piece against the remaining pair of legs, and tack-weld this joint also. Check that the legs are square to the cross piece, and that the cross piece is horizontal. Adjust the pieces, if necessary, then complete the cross-piece welds.

6. Paint the stand and drum with rust-resistant enamel.

To use the manure-tea brewer, place the drum in the stand so the opening faces up. Fill the brewing basket (lined with the aluminum-mesh filters) with fresh manure, then place it into the opening, suspended by the handles. Fill the drum with water. Wait at least 24 hours for complete brewing, then open the faucet to distribute the contents. The drum can be filled and emptied twice before a new charge of manure is required. If you find it necessary, keep a section of fine aluminum mesh over the drum opening to prevent mosquitoes from breeding in the water.

FEEDI-GATOR

Robert Howard of New Braunfels, Texas, calls this device a feedigator. He coined the term by combining the two words, feeder and irrigator. As the term implies, the feedigator does both. It's a trickle-hose irrigator that brews rich manure-tea fertilizer at the same time.

All you need are a 30-gallon trash can, the upper half of a 55-gallon drum, a long length of garden hose, some gravel, and a small piece of screen. There is no welding required. There are no plumbing connections to make and no moving parts to assemble. After putting it together, merely set it on a level spot, supported off the ground so it

SHOPPING LIST

Hardware
1 55-gallon steel drum
1 30-gallon plastic trash can
12 sheet-metal screws #8 × ½''
1 pc. wire mesh ⅜'' × 1' × 1'
10 pounds gravel
1 pc. garden hose ⅝''

will be higher than the garden you plan to irrigate, then fill the inner container with manure and the outer container with water. As the mixture drains out (which takes about an hour), direct the hose around the base of the plants to give them water plus a vigorous nutritional boost.

When locating materials for the feedigator, if possible, choose a drum that has been used to store vegetable oil or some other harmless, nonflammable material. In any case, use a saber saw to cut the drum in two, rather than a torch. Fumes inside the drum could touch off an explosion. (If you must use a torch in spite of this warning, fill the drum with water first, and cut the drum while the water drains out.) Also, do not use the hose you attach to the feedigator for any other purpose. Since it carries raw manure, it can never be cleaned thoroughly enough not to contaminate any other water put through it. Remove the female connection from the hose end. That way, no extension section can be attached which might later be removed itself and put to some accidentally hazardous use.

CONSTRUCTION

1. Begin by cutting the drum in half. The top section—with the bungholes—is the one you need. Scribe completely around the drum's circumference, taking care to keep the line parallel to the rims of the drum so that the edge of the cut section will be

level. Next, turn the drum on its side, drill a ⅜-inch-diameter starter hole on the waste side of the line, then use a saber saw, fitted with a metal-cutting blade, to saw the drum in two along the scribed line.

2. Cover the cut edge of the drum's top section with a 72-inch length of garden hose, slit lengthwise. If you are using a single length of hose for the entire project, cut this length from the end with the female connector.

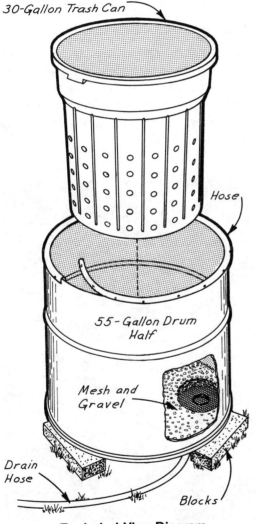

30-Gallon Trash Can

Hose

55-Gallon Drum Half

Mesh and Gravel

Drain Hose

Blocks

Exploded-View Diagram

Remove and discard the connector. After slipping the hose over the rim of the drum, drill 3/32-inch pilot holes through the hose and metal every 6 inches, then fasten the hose to the rim with ½-inch #8 sheet-metal screws.

3. Turn the drum section onto its cut edge so that the drain hose can be installed in the ¾-inch bunghole. Unscrew the plug, then screw in the male end of a length of garden hose long enough to fulfill your watering needs. The threads of the hose connector will not be a perfect match, but since the system is not under much pressure, the connection will hold. Tighten with pliers.

4. Place supports, such as three concrete blocks, on a level spot close to your garden. Gravel, sand, or mulch may be spread over the spot beforehand to help keep weeds down. Place the drum section on the supports so that the hose may be directed toward the garden. Fill the drum section with water and check that it drains correctly.

5. Now prepare a 30-gallon, plastic trash can for use as the manure holder. Drill holes in the bottom and sides of the can using a large-diameter drill bit. Although the size is not critical, the larger the hole, the quicker the drainage will be. A ⅝- or ¾-inch spade bit works well. Drill the holes 3 inches apart over all surfaces of the trash can.

6. Assemble the feedigator by first placing a section of wire mesh over the drain hole in the bottom of the drum to prevent the garden hose from blocking. Three-eighths-inch mesh works well. Then pour approximately 10 pounds of gravel over the screen and bottom of the drum to further filter out solid material. Place the manure holder in the center of the drum on top of the gravel base. Now load the trash can with manure. Don't worry if you accidentally spill some into the drum. Fill the drum with water when you are ready to nourish your garden.

SLATTED COMPOST-TEA SIEVE

SHOPPING LIST

Lumber
2 pcs. $4 \times 4 \times 12'$
4 pcs. $2 \times 2 \times 8'$
13 pcs. $1 \times 6 \times 8'$
Hardware
1 2-gallon bucket or watering can
1 pound galvanized common nails 8d
1 pc. tin $4' \times 5'$

The simple, clean design of this sieve for making compost tea allows it to fit well with any garden, whether it is a truck patch or an elegant planting of herbs. Jerry Shadomy of Corvallis, Oregon, is the builder.

For sturdiness and good looks, the sieve should be built of cedar, redwood, or other rot-resistant lumber. The slatted design allows air to infiltrate throughout the compost, accelerating decomposition. To produce the fertilizing tea, the sieve may be watered regularly or merely allowed to collect rainwater. Either way, the results are the same. A funnel made from sheet metal attached below the bin collects the finished product, channeling it into a bucket or watering can placed on the ground to catch the runoff.

CONSTRUCTION

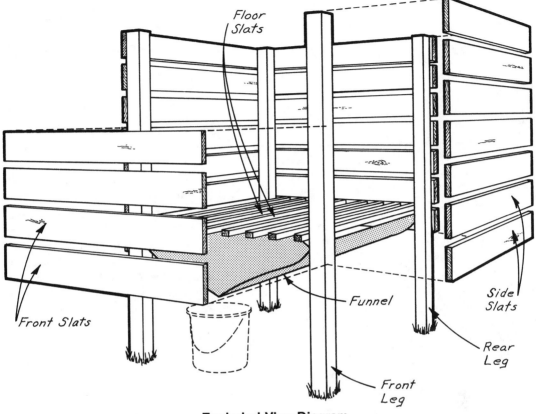

Floor Slats

Front Slats

Funnel

Side Slats

Rear Leg

Front Leg

Exploded-View Diagram

1. Cut four pieces of 4 × 4 (3½″ × 3½″) stock to 72 inches each for the legs.

2. Cut 11 pieces of 1 × 6 (¾″ × 5½″) stock to 49½ inches each for the front and back slats, and 14 pieces to 46½ inches each for the side slats.

3. Assemble the sides of the sieve first. Arrange the legs in two pairs, and position seven side slats on each pair. Position the first two slats of each side flush with the ends of the legs, and place the remaining slats 1½ inches apart. The ends of the slats should be flush with the edges of the legs.

Fasten the slats to the legs using 8d galvanized common nails.

4. Stand the two sides upright, opposite each other, 48 inches apart, then fasten the seven back slats to the legs so that they cover the ends of the side slats. Use 8d galvanized common nails.

5. Obtain a 48 × 60-inch sheet of tin for the funnel. Bend the tin in half across the 60-inch width, then reopen it to form a crease along which the liquid can run.

6. Fasten the funnel to the inner sides of the legs, just below the slats, so that the crease

299

LUMBER CUTTING LIST

Size	Piece	Quantity
4 × 4		
3½″ × 3½″ × 72″	Legs	4
2 × 2		
1½″ × 1½″ × 48″	Floor slats	8
1 × 6		
¾″ × 5½″ × 49½″	Front and back slats	11
¾″ × 5½″ × 46½″	Side slats	14

slants downward about 2 inches from back to front. Nail through the tin using 8d galvanized common nails.

7. Fasten the remaining four slats to the front of the legs, aligned with the bottom four side slats. This low front makes filling the sieve easier.

8. Cut eight pieces of 2 × 2 (1½″ × 1½″) stock to 48 inches each for the floor slats. Push them through the sieve so that they rest on the lowest front and back slats and are spaced about 6 inches apart.

9. Place a bucket or watering can under the funnel in front of the sieve. Fill the sieve with compost, beginning with larger stalks and graduating to finer materials, such as grass and leaves. Add water to the compost from the top (or wait for rain) and collect the tea in the bucket.

TRICKLE-HOSE TAKE-UP REEL

SHOPPING LIST

Lumber
1 pc. $1 \times 10 \times 20''$
3 pcs. $1 \times 4 \times 10'$
Hardware
6 flathead wood screws $\#10 \times 2\frac{1}{2}''$
24 flathead wood screws $\#8 \times 1\frac{1}{2}''$
1 pc. galvanized pipe $\frac{1}{2}''$ I.D. $\times 3'$
1 quart exterior-grade enamel

For Dana and Mary Bahr of Ottertail, Minnesota, gathering up and storing drip-irrigation hose for the winter is more than just an average, year-end gardening chore. The amount of hose spread out over their 10-acre melon patch measures some 2,000 feet (more than a third of a mile)! Your garden may not be this vast, but you may be able to benefit nonetheless from the hose take-up reel designed by the Bahrs for their enormous task. Strong and sturdy this reel is easy to build and holds a lot of hose neatly. The large handles provide plenty of

leverage for hauling in hose at season's end and provide an assistant with the means to easily help you haul the hose out again come spring.

Salvaged lumber is quite suitable for making the trickle-hose take-up reel. Our instructions, however, show how to cut all the wooden pieces from only three 10-foot lengths of standard 1×4 lumber plus one 20-inch length of standard 1×10, with very little waste. Besides a handful of screws, the only other materials needed are a 36-inch length of galvanized pipe for the reel's shaft, and some paint for finishing.

The Bahrs require three reels to store their quantity of hose. More than likely, only one reel will be adequate for most gardeners. If you wish, the size of the reel may be made even smaller merely by shortening the lengths of the six wooden reel stretchers, and by shortening the shaft to correspond.

CONSTRUCTION

1. From one 10-foot 1×4 ($\frac{3}{4}'' \times 3\frac{1}{2}''$), cut two pieces of stock to 24 inches each for the base pieces of the stand. Also cut two pieces of stock to 16 inches each for the stand's uprights, and one piece of stock to

   34 inches for the cross piece. For accuracy, lay out and cut each piece one at a time, and label the pieces as they are cut.

2. From a second 10-foot 1×4, cut three pieces of stock to 30 inches each for three

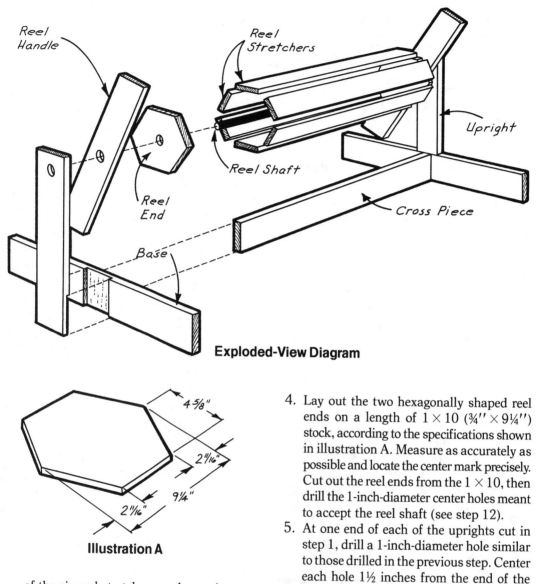

Exploded-View Diagram

Illustration A

of the six reel stretchers, and one piece to 20 inches for one reel handle. Again, lay out and cut each piece individually.

3. From a third 10-foot 1 × 4, cut another three pieces of stock to 30 inches each for the remaining three reel stretchers. Also cut one piece of stock to 20 inches for the other reel handle.

4. Lay out the two hexagonally shaped reel ends on a length of 1 × 10 (¾″ × 9¼″) stock, according to the specifications shown in illustration A. Measure as accurately as possible and locate the center mark precisely. Cut out the reel ends from the 1 × 10, then drill the 1-inch-diameter center holes meant to accept the reel shaft (see step 12).

5. At one end of each of the uprights cut in step 1, drill a 1-inch-diameter hole similar to those drilled in the previous step. Center each hole 1½ inches from the end of the upright.

6. Lay the other end of each upright across the inside face of each of the base pieces to scribe the half-lap joints shown in illustration B. Make sure the uprights overlap the base pieces at precise right angles and are centered exactly halfway between the ends of each base. Scribe the width of each piece onto

LUMBER CUTTING LIST

Size	Piece	Quantity
1 × 10		
¾'' × 9¼'' × 10'	Reel ends	2
1 × 4		
¾'' × 3½'' × 34''	Cross piece	1
¾'' × 3½'' × 30''	Reel stretchers	6
¾'' × 3½'' × 24''	Base pieces	2
¾'' × 3½'' × 20''	Reel handles	2
¾'' × 3½'' × 16''	Uprights	2

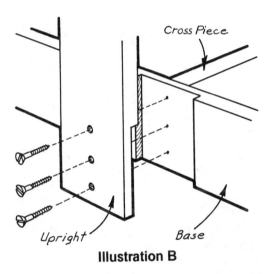

Illustration B

base/upright units, as shown in both the exploded-view diagram and illustration B, to complete the stand. Using the pilot holes drilled in the previous step as guides, drill corresponding 3/16-inch-diameter pilot holes into the ends of the cross piece while holding it in place, then fasten each unit to the cross piece using 2½-inch #10 flathead wood screws.

9. Now assemble the reel. First, mount the reel handles to the reel ends by centering the handles across the ends, as shown in the exploded-view diagram, and fastening them using four 1½-inch #8 flathead wood screws for each assembly. Drill 3/32-inch-diameter pilot holes; be careful not to locate any mounting screws near the centers of the reel ends.

10. Using the holes drilled through the reel ends as guides, drill 1-inch-diameter holes through the reel handles as well. Avoid splitting the outside faces of the handles by drilling the holes from the inside, just until the bit begins to protrude. Then turn the pieces over and drill from the outside to remove the remaining waste.

11. Now position the reel ends, with their handles parallel to each other and facing outward, about 30 inches apart. Place

the one it overlaps, then carefully cut or chisel away half the thickness of each piece within the scribed lines so the pieces look as pictured in the illustration. After test-fitting, glue each pair of cutaway pieces together, making sure they remain at right angles to each other during clamping.

7. After the glued pieces have dried, remove the clamps, then drill three 3/16-inch-diameter pilot holes in each base/upright unit, in the locations shown in illustration B.

8. Position the cross piece between the two

one of the six reel stretchers across parallel edges of the reel ends, as shown in the exploded-view diagram, and adjust the distance between them until the ends of the stretcher are flush with their outside faces. At each end of the stretcher, drill two $\frac{3}{32}$-inch-diameter pilot holes through the stretcher and into the edge of the reel end, then fasten the pieces together using $1\frac{1}{2}$-inch #8 flathead wood screws. Repeat the procedure to fasten the remaining five stretchers.

12. Mount the completed reel by holding it in position between the uprights and inserting a 36-inch length of $\frac{1}{2}$-inch I.D. galvanized pipe through the holes in the reel ends and uprights. The reel should turn freely in the stand. If it does not, enlarge the holes in the uprights slightly.

13. Finally, paint the stand to protect it from decay and moisture. (Remove the shaft before painting, however, so that it won't stick in the holes.)

DOUBLE DIGGER FOR RAISED-BED GARDENING

SHOPPING LIST

Steel Stock
2 pcs. square steel tubing 1¼″ × 8′
2 pcs. bar stock ³⁄₁₆″ × 1½″ × 5″
6 pcs. hay-rake tines ⁵⁄₁₆″ × 18″
1 quart rust-resistant enamel

Ron Thuma is the mayor of Hartford, Kansas, and an avid raised-bed gardening enthusiast. This U-bar-style digger he has designed lets him prepare and maintain his double-dug beds easily and quickly throughout the gardening season, and makes the yearly task of redigging practically effortless.

The double digger is made of square-section steel tubing braced with flat steel bar stock and welded together. It is fitted with tines from a tractor-drawn hay rake, which are tempered and made of very strong steel, and are therefore able to withstand the stresses encountered by being used to pry up and sift through settled earth. The tines must be straight, however, or nearly straight sections cut from longer curved tines, in order for the tool to be used comfortably. To use the double digger, you merely plunge it into the ground like a spading fork, then rock the handlebars backward to lever up the soil. By working backward down the length of a gardening bed, you leave in your wake a raised mound of fluffy, aerated soil just right for planting. The double digger is intended for bed main-

305

tenance only, not for digging new beds in hard, unspaded ground.

Welding, drilling, and grinding steel are the processes required to build the double digger. If you cut the tubing yourself, a welding shop or even a local garage should be able to make quick work of joining the pieces by following the cutting diagram shown on p. 307. The digger also makes an excellent project for beginning welders.

Naturally, the size of the double digger may be altered to suit your needs or the materials you have on hand. However, according to Thuma, a width of 28 inches seems to be the practical limit before the tool becomes awkward to use.

CONSTRUCTION

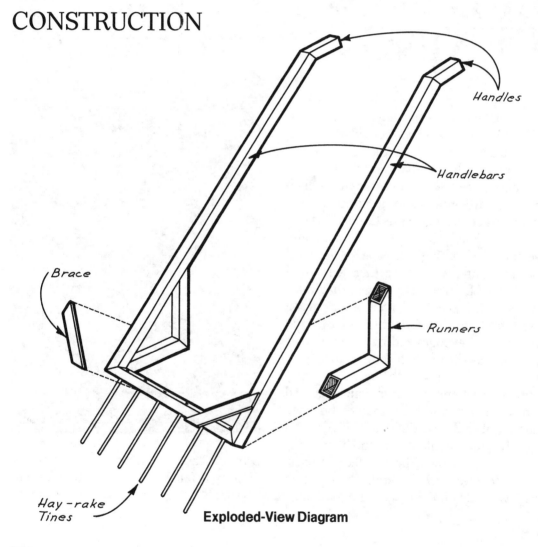

Brace

Handles

Handlebars

Runners

Hay-rake Tines

Exploded-View Diagram

1. Cut two pieces of 1¼-inch-square steel tubing to 60 inches each, for the digger's handlebars. Cut each length from one section of 8-foot tubing, as shown in the cutting diagram. Note that the cuts are made at 45-degree angles.

2. Mark the 8-inch-long segments on the handlebars for the handles, then scribe the 15-degree cut line as shown, perpendicular to the angled cut made in the previous step. Cut the handles from the handlebar tubing.

3. Cut the 24-inch-long front bar from one of the remaining 3-foot lengths of tubing. Make the cut at a 45-degree angle, as shown in the cutting diagram.

4. Cut the remaining pieces of tubing into 12-inch pieces to make the runners. All the cuts should be at 45-degree angles, as shown in the cutting diagram. When finished, clean all the pieces cut in steps 1, 2, and 3, to prepare them for welding.

5. Drill holes through the front bar at 4-inch

intervals to hold the hay-rake tines, as shown in the exploded-view diagram. The size of the holes depends on the size of the tines you intend to install. Thuma used 5/16-inch-diameter tines and drill holes that were 11/32 inch in diameter.

6. Position the handlebars against the ends of the front bar, in preparation for welding. If possible, assembly should be done on a welding table. In any case, the work surface used should be level so that the parts of the digger will be aligned properly. Use a square to bring the pieces together along their mitered edges, then clamp the pieces to the bench so they won't move. Tack-weld both handlebars in place. After rechecking to make sure each handlebar is square to the front bar, finish the welds by running a continuous bead over each seam until the miters are fully closed. Afterward, grind the welds smooth on one side of the handlebars so that the runners will seat flat against them, as shown in the exploded-

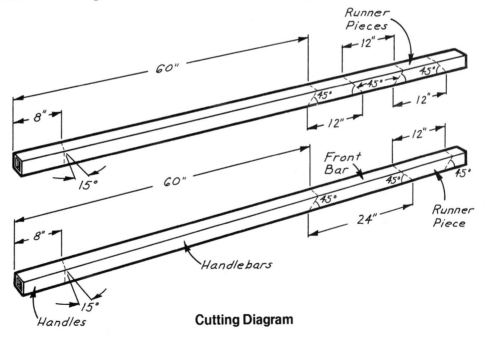

Cutting Diagram

view diagram. The remaining portions of the welds need not be ground.

7. Cut two 5-inch pieces of bar stock to make the braces. Miter the ends to 45-degree angles now if you wish, or do so after welding the pieces to the handlebars and front bar. Weld the pieces in place across the unground side of the handlebars, as shown in the exploded-view diagram.

8. Assemble the runners cut in step 4 by welding pairs of them together along their mitered edges. Tack-weld each pair first, then hold them in place against the smooth sides of the handlebars so that one end is flush with the leading edge of the front bar and the opposite end rests on the handlebars, as shown in the exploded-view diagram. Adjust the sides of each runner, if necessary, for a good fit. Tack-weld the runners to the handlebars and front bar, then finish all the welds by running continuous beads around the seams. Check your work by trying to pull the design

apart from all directions. It should be very sturdy at all points.

9. Weld the handles to the handlebars in the position shown in the exploded-view diagram. As before, tack-weld them first, then finish with continuous welds. Grind all sides of the finished welds so that the handles are smooth.

10. Finally, insert six hay-rake tines, each 18 inches long, in the holes drilled in the front bar. Weld the tops of the tines only where they show through the holes in the top of the front bar, in order not to damage (draw) the temper of the prongs. As an extra precaution, wrap a wet cloth around the tines during welding to act as a heat sink.

11. Grind off any welding slag from the digger that might make digging difficult. Be certain that the handles are smooth, and remove any sharp welds on top of the front bar. Apply several coats of rust-resistant good-quality enamel.

BICYCLE HOE CULTI-VATOR

┌─────────────────────────────────┐

SHOPPING LIST

Hardware
1 discarded bicycle
1 cultivator head
1 hex head machine bolt ⅝″ × 4″
1 hex head machine bolt ⅝″ × 2″
3 hex nuts ⅝″
1 pc. schedule-40 seamless steel pipe
     1″ diameter × 12′
1 pc. schedule-40 seamless steel pipe
     1″ diameter × 6″
rust-resistant enamel

└─────────────────────────────────┘

You may not recognize this large-wheeled hoe cultivator as having once been a bicycle, but that's what Morris Dunnuck of Ossian, Indiana, began with. First, he removed parts of the frame (and in the process relocated the front wheel to the rear), and then made adjustable handlebars from lightweight steel pipe. Finally, he mounted a cultivator head found at a garage sale. Total cost for the whole project: just a

few dollars and a few hours time. The hardest part of the job was deciding to cut up the bicycle frame.

Almost any conventional bicycle frame will work, but the sturdier models do best. Dunnuck chose a woman's bike, but only because one was available. The handlebars and small cross piece between them (part of the adjusting mechanism), are made from schedule-40 seamless steel pipe. Don't use electrical conduit, even if you're tempted. Conduit has a plating that gives off harmful fumes when welded or brazed. Besides, the schedule-40 pipe is stronger.

Do not use the bicycle cultivator to break new ground. All hoe cultivators, this one included, are meant only to control weeds and make hills along garden rows for crops such as potatoes and corn. There are different varieties of cultivator heads made, and you may wish to obtain several in order to perform specialized tasks. Garage sales and farm auctions are the best places to look for cultivator heads. Garden supply stores often carry them also, and there are several mail-order suppliers that offer them as well.

CONSTRUCTION

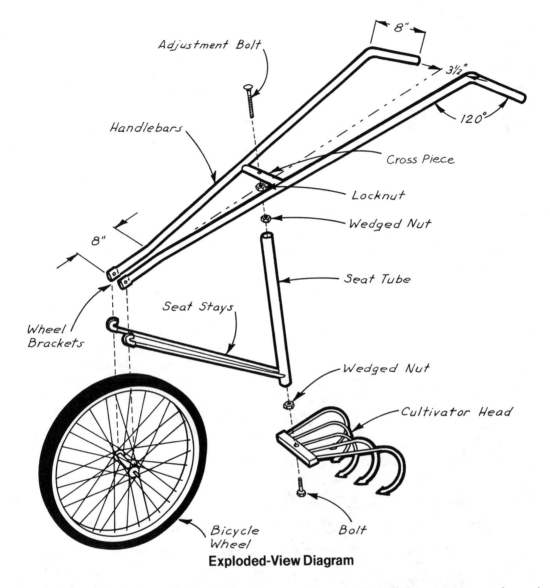

Adjustment Bolt

Handlebars

Cross Piece

8"

3½"

120°

Locknut

Wedged Nut

Seat Tube

Seat Stays

Wheel
Brackets

8"

Wedged Nut

Cultivator Head

Bicycle
Wheel

Bolt

Exploded-View Diagram

1. Strip the bicycle frame of all moving parts, including the wheels, handlebars, fork, and seat. Save the front wheel (you may need to recondition it), for relocation to the rear dropout (see step 8).
2. Using a hacksaw fitted with a new blade,

cut the bicycle frame apart, as shown in illustration A. Make the first cut through the top tube, where it joins the top of the seat tube, and the second cut across both wheel stays, where they join the rear dropout. Make the third cut through the lower end

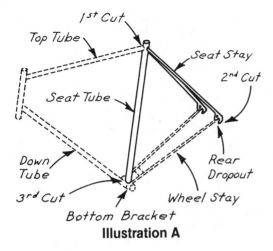

Illustration A

of the seat tube itself, just above the bottom bracket. After removing the entire front portion of the bicycle frame plus the rear wheel stays, you should be left with only the rear portion, which includes the seat tube (minus the bottom bracket) and the seat stays. File the cut edges of the frame tubing smooth.

3. Cut two pieces of 1-inch-diameter schedule-40 seamless steel pipe to 72 inches each for the handlebars. Bend the tubing, as shown in the exploded-view diagram, to form the handle grips. Bending can be done either by using a tubing bender (most rental stores carry them), or, by packing the tubing with sand, then bending it around a post or some other curved surface. Remove the sand after the bends have been made.

4. Lay the bent tubing on a flat surface, and hammer the tube ends opposite the handle grips flat to make the wheel brackets. The flattened areas must be in line with the curve of the hand grips, as shown in the exploded-view diagram, and be about 2 inches long. Next, bend the tubing at right angles to the curve of the hand grips so the handlebars will flare outward when they

are attached to the wheel. Locate the bend 8 inches from the flattened end of each handlebar, and make each bend so the handle-grip end flares 3½ inches from the line of the flattened end, as shown in the exploded-view diagram.

5. To house the axle, drill one hole in each piece of tubing, 5/16 inch in diameter, centered in the flattened end. Test-fit each hole on the axle of the salvaged front wheel. The fit should be snug but the pieces should still slide easily.

6. Cut one piece of 1-inch-diameter schedule-40 pipe to 6 inches for the cross piece.

7. Shape the ends of the cross piece so the cross piece fits between the handlebars, as shown in illustration B. Use a round file, testing the pieces often, until a reasonably tight fit is achieved.

8. Now fit the salvaged front wheel into the slots in the rear dropout, then slide the handlebars onto the axle ends and tighten the axle nuts. Hold the cross piece between the handlebars, and pivot the bars so the

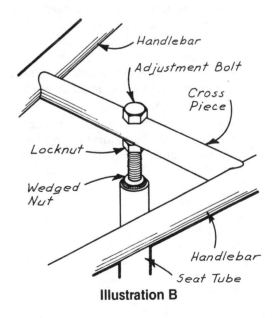

Illustration B

311

cross piece, when in place, rests directly on the seat tube where it was cut from the bottom bracket. Adjust the fit of the cross piece again, if necessary using a file, so that the fit is tight, then clamp the cross piece in place between the handlebars, by drawing the open ends of the handlebars together with a clamp.

9. Braze or weld the cross piece in place between the handlebars. If welding, use a very light touch since the tubing will melt quickly. Brazing, using a brass rod, is easier and much less likely to ruin the metal. Place wet rags between the cross piece and the wheel to protect the hub. When finished, remove the clamp and clean the weld by grinding. Brazed joints must be scrubbed free of flux as well.

10. Reposition the handlebars so the cross piece again rests on top of the bicycle frame seat tube. Sighting down from above, use a center punch to make an indentation on top of the cross piece directly over the center of the seat tube. Then drill a single hole, $1/16$ inch in diameter, vertically through the cross piece, centered on the punched mark. Insert a $5/8 \times 4$-inch hex head machine bolt into the hole. Check to see that the bolt slides freely in and out and extends into the seat tube without touching the sides. If necessary, ream the hole in the cross piece slightly to achieve a vertical fit.

11. Pivot the handlebars up and away from the seat tube. Rest the bottom (seat-post end) of the seat tube on a block of wood, then with a second block and a mallet, wedge a $5/8$-inch nut into the upper end of the seat tube, level with the top, as shown in illustration B. Grind the nut slightly if it does not go in evenly or easily after a few taps. When finished, bring the handlebars back into position and check to see that the bolt in the cross piece will thread onto the wedged nut. If it does not, either adjust the position of the nut or loosen the fit of the bolt in the cross piece by reaming the hole a bit more.

12. Remove the bolt from the wedged nut, then thread on a second $5/8$-inch nut to act as a locknut. To adjust the handlebars, loosen the locknut and turn the bolt in the wedged nut until the desired height is reached. Then tighten the locknut firmly against the underside of the cross piece.

13. Next, fasten the cultivator head to the bottom of the seat tube. Using the same procedure as in step 11, wedge a $5/8$-inch nut into the end of the seat tube. Then, drill a hole $11/16$ inch in diameter into the cultivator head and fasten the head to the seat tube with a $5/8 \times 2$-inch hex head machine bolt. (As an alternative, you may weld the cultivator head to the salvaged bicycle seat post, and install it using the original seat post bolt and nut located on the seat tube. However, you will need additional seat posts if you choose to obtain a variety of heads for your cultivator.)

14. Paint the completed cultivator with rust-resistant enamel.

GARDEN CULTIVATOR

Cultivators like this one usually cost more than $100 new, and finding a good second-hand model can be a problem as well. Build one, though, as did Gregg Delp of Shelbyville, Indiana, and you'll save yourself both time and money. Delp purchased the handles and a cultivator head from a farm supply store, salvaged a 24-inch-diameter balloon-type bicycle wheel and tire, and put together the frame using 1-inch-wide flat steel stock.

The cultivator adjusts for shallow or deep cultivation. Adjustments are made by raising or lowering the vertical members attached to the cultivator head, which changes its height by about 2 inches.

As with all cultivators, this one is designed only for use in loose ground, for turning under weeds growing between garden rows. It should not be considered a plow or a tiller. Use it for its intended purpose and it should last several lifetimes.

SHOPPING LIST

Dowel
1 pc. ¾″ × 16″ hardwood
Mild Steel Flat Stock
2 pcs. ⅛″ × 1″ × 30″
2 pcs. ⅛″ × 1″ × 24¾″
2 pcs. ⅛″ × 1″ × 5″
2 pcs. ⅛″ × 1″ × 4″
Hardware
1 cultivator head
1 set cultivator handlebars 4′
1 bicycle wheel 24″ diameter
1 machine bolt ½″ × 2″ with nut
2 machine bolts ⅜″ × 1″
4 machine bolts ⅜″ × ½″
4 carriage bolts ⅜″ × 1¼″
2 nuts ½″
10 nuts ⅜″
8 lockwashers ⅜″
4 flat washers ⅜″
1 lockwasher ½″
1 flat washer ½″
1 turnbuckle 2″
2 pcs. 12-gauge wire 28″

CONSTRUCTION

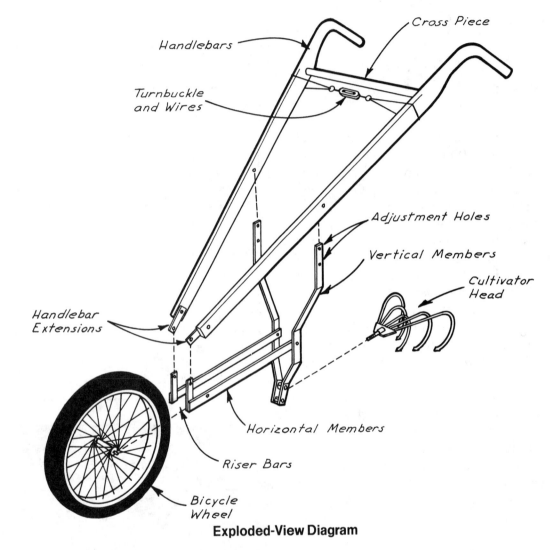

Exploded-View Diagram

1. Obtain two 30-inch pieces of ⅛″ × 1″ mild steel flat stock for the vertical members of the frame. Drill ⅜-inch-diameter holes through the pieces, where indicated in illustration A, to accommodate the fastening bolts. Use the first and second holes from the top end as adjustment holes for the cultivator head.

2. Bend the vertical members to match the measurements shown in illustration A, at 7, 14½, 21, and 26 inches, starting from the top end.

3. Cut two pieces of flat steel to 24¾ inches each for the horizontal members. Drill ⅜-inch-diameter holes ½ inch from one end of each piece to accommodate the

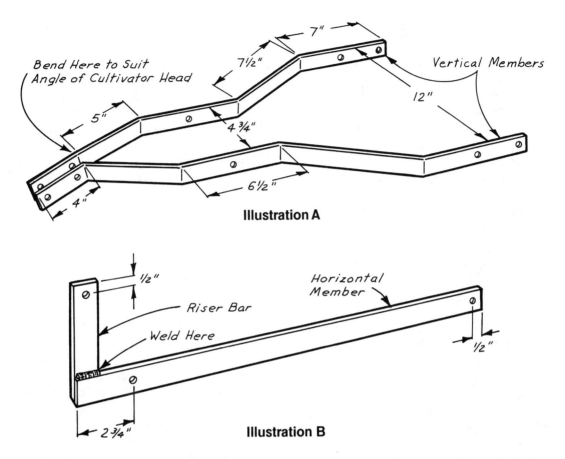

Illustration A

Illustration B

fastening bolts, and 2¾ inches from the other end of each piece to accommodate the wheel axles.

4. Cut two pieces of flat steel to 4 inches each for the riser bars. Drill 13/32-inch-diameter holes ½ inch from one end of each piece to accommodate the fastening bolts.

5. Cut two pieces of flat steel to 5 inches each

for the handlebar extensions. Drill 13/32-inch-diameter holes in each piece, ½ inch from one end and 1 inch from the opposite end, to accommodate the fastening bolts.

6. Weld the riser bars to the ends of the horizontal members at 90-degree angles, as shown in illustration B.

7. Obtain a pair of 48-inch-long cultivator

LUMBER CUTTING LIST		
Size	**Piece**	**Quantity**
Dowel		
¾'' × 16''	Cross piece	1

handlebars. (Make sure you've got both a right-hand and a left-hand bar.) Drill 13/32-inch-diameter holes through both handlebars, in the locations shown in the exploded-view diagram, to accommodate the fastening bolts.

8. Fasten the vertical members to the inside faces of the handlebars using 3/8 × 1 1/4-inch carriage bolts fitted with 3/8-inch flat washers and nuts. Install the bolts in the second holes from the top end.

9. Fasten the horizontal members to the vertical members using 3/8 × 1/2-inch machine bolts fitted with lockwashers and nuts.

10. Fasten the handlebar extensions to the ends of the handlebars using 3/8 × 1 1/4-inch carriage bolts fitted with lockwashers and nuts.

11. Fasten the handlebar extensions to the tops of the riser bars using 3/8 × 1/2-inch machine bolts fitted with lockwashers and nuts.

12. Obtain one 24-inch-diameter bicycle wheel and fasten it to the horizontal members using the axle nuts and flat washers.

13. Cut one piece of 3/4-inch-diameter dowel to 16 inches for the handlebar cross piece. Drill 3/4-inch-diameter holes 1/4 inch deep into the inside faces of the handlebars, in

the locations shown in the exploded-view diagram, to accept the cross piece.

14. Obtain two 28-inch-long pieces of 12-gauge wire and loop them over the handlebars, as shown in the exploded-view diagram, just below the cross piece. Fasten a 2-inch turnbuckle to the wires and tighten it until the cross piece is securely in place.

15. Use two 1/2-inch machine nuts for spacers at the bottom end of the vertical members. Fasten the spacers in place using two 3/8 × 1-inch machine bolts, fitted with lockwashers and nuts, to make the cultivator-head bracket, as shown in the exploded-view diagram.

16. Obtain a cultivator head like the one pictured, and fasten it to the bracket made in step 15 using a 1/2 × 2-inch machine bolt fitted with flat washer, lockwasher, and nut.

17. Adjust the vertical members so that the cultivator head is parallel to the ground. To do this, cut a V-shaped section from the vertical members at the bottom bend, just above the bottom bracket. Bend the vertical members to the required angle, then weld the pieces in that position.

18. Apply a durable finish to the handlebars and paint the metal parts.

GARDEN-ER'S ROLLING CRICKET

SHOPPING LIST

Plywood
1 pc. ¾″ × 4′ × 4′ B-C grade
1 pc. ⅜″ × 2′ × 4′ B-C grade
Dowel
1 pc. 1¼″ × 3′ hardwood
Hardware
12 flathead wood screws #8 × 1½″
¼ pound galvanized common nails 3d

This ingenious rolling seat eliminates a lot of the kneeling, bending, and stooping of gardening. It was designed by L. Austin Strauch of Argyle, Texas, who uses it to propel himself along garden rows when thinning plants, cultivating, or harvesting. The wide, rollerlike wheels travel easily over tilled garden soil or harder packed earth between rows. A gentle push with the legs directs the cricket in a straight line. Gently twisting the body at the same time swivels the cricket in whatever direction you wish to turn.

Although this project is easy to build, there are 68 narrow strips to cut for the wheels. Strauch did the work on a band saw, first resawing ¾-inch solid stock into two ⅜-inch thicknesses. Our plans call for ⅜-inch plywood, which is already the correct

thickness and may easily be cut into strips using any saw.

CONSTRUCTION

1. Cut four 10-inch-diameter circles from ¾-inch B-C grade plywood for the wheels. Drill a 1⅜-inch-diameter hole in the center of each piece to accept the dowels for the axles (see step 10).

2. Rip a sheet of ⅜-inch plywood 24 inches long × 48 inches wide into 68 strips, each 1 inch wide × 12 inches long, for the treads. The grain of the outer plies of each tread must run parallel to the 12-inch sides. To make the treads easily and accurately, crosscut the sheet first into two halves,

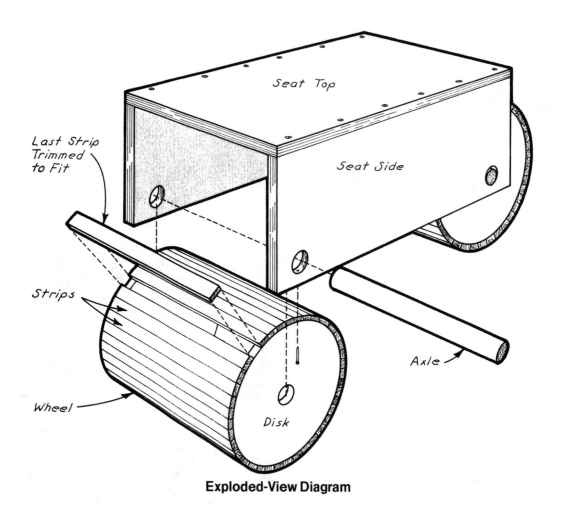

Exploded-View Diagram

each 12 inches wide, then rip each section into 1-inch widths.

3. If you wish to paint the inside of the wheels and treads, do so now, since they cannot be reached after the wheels are assembled.

4. Assemble each wheel by aligning the ends of the treads with the outside edges of the wheels, as shown in the exploded-view diagram, then nailing them in place using 3d galvanized common nails. Be sure each tread is square to the edge of the wheel and that the treads fit tightly against one another.

Trim the last tread, if necessary, or cut a new tread slightly wider than 1 inch, to finish the job. Afterward, paint the outside of the wheels and treads, if desired.

5. Cut two pieces of ¾-inch plywood to 8 × 24 inches each for the sides of the seat, and one piece to 14½ × 24 inches for the top.

6. Drill two 1½-inch-diameter holes in each side piece to accept the axles, as shown in the exploded-view diagram. Locate each pair of holes 1 inch from a long edge of the piece, and 2¼ inches from the short edges.

LUMBER CUTTING LIST

Size	Piece	Quantity
¾'' *Plywood*		
¾'' × 14½'' × 24''	Seat	1
¾'' × 8'' × 24''	Sides	2
¾'' × 10'' diameter	Wheel disks	4
⅜'' *Plywood*		
⅜'' × 1'' × 12''	Wheel strips	68
Dowel		
1¼'' × 14½''	Axles	2

Check the fit of the dowel (see step 10) in the holes. It should slip easily in and out and rotate freely.

7. Scribe the long sides of the top with a line ⅜ inch from the edge, then mark off points every 4 inches along the line to locate screw positions. Also mark points 1 inch from the ends of each line.

8. Position the top across the upper edges of the side pieces (farthest from the axle holes) to form an open-ended, three-sided box. Drill and countersink pilot holes on the marks scribed in the top to accept 1½-inch #8 flathead wood screws. Disassemble the pieces, apply carpenter's wood glue to the upper edges of the sides, then reassemble the pieces and fasten them together with screws.

9. If desired, paint the seat before proceeding since its underside is inaccessible after the wheels are added.

10. Cut two pieces of 1¼-inch-diameter dowel to 14½ inches each for the axles. Position the wheels between the side pieces, then thread each axle through the holes in the sides and wheels. Make sure the ends of the axles are flush with the outside face of each side, then drive a 3d galvanized common nail through the lower edge of the sides at each hole and into the axle to lock it in place. (If you anticipate removing the wheels again, use screws instead of nails to lock the axles.)

THE BAKSAVER

F. B. Johns of Charlotte, North Carolina, developed this rolling stool as a way to avoid stooping and bending while gar-

SHOPPING LIST

Plywood
1 pc. ¾'' × 20'' × 20'' A-C grade
1 pc. ⅜'' × 4' × 4' A-C grade
Hardware
12 pcs. flat mild steel ⅛'' × 1 × 2½''
2 pcs. steel rod ½'' diameter × 15''
6 flathead wood screws #8 × 1''
24 flathead wood screws #8 × ⅝''
4 flathead washers ⅝''
4 cotter pins ⅛'' × 1''
¼ pound common nails 2d

dening. He calls it the Baksaver. Although he built the original to serve his own needs, the device became so popular among those who saw it that Mr. Johns built nearly 100 of them! The wide wheels of the Baksaver make it ideal for use in the garden or in any situation where you must work close to the ground.

CONSTRUCTION

1. Cut eight 9-inch-diameter disks from ¾-inch A-C grade plywood for the two-piece wheels. Drill a ½-inch-diameter hole through the center of each disk to fit the axle (see step 3).

2. From a piece of ⅜-inch A-C grade plywood, cut 72 pieces to 1¼ × 3 inches each for the wheel strips. Refer to the cutting diagram to lay out the pieces. Cut the first strip to use as a guide, then cut each additional strip in succession to allow for the saw kerf.

3. Obtain two 15-inch lengths of ½-inch-diameter steel rod for the axles. Arrange the wheel disks in pairs, with the good side of each disk facing out. Slide one pair of disks onto the end of each axle, then separate each disk 3 inches from its partner.

4. Place a wheel strip across a pair of disks, at right angles to the faces of the disks, and fasten it in place with 2d common nails (one nail at each end of the strip). Fasten the remaining strips, using a piece of ⅜-inch-thick scrap plywood to position each

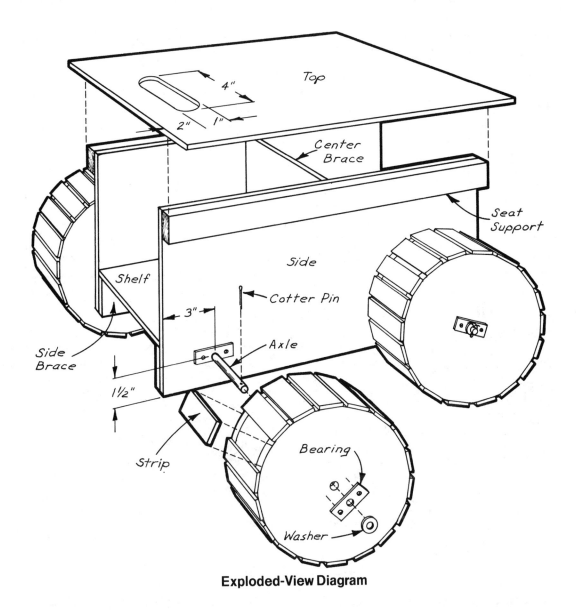

4"

2" 1"

Top

Center
Brace

Seat
Support

Side

Shelf

Cotter Pin

3"

Axle

Side
Brace

1½"

Strip

Bearing

Washer

Exploded-View Diagram

strip ⅜ inch from its neighbor. Repeat the procedure for the remaining three wheels.

5. Refer to the cutting diagram and cut the following pieces out of ⅜-inch plywood: one piece to 13 × 21 inches for the seat top; two pieces to 8½ × 21 inches each for the sides; one piece to 7 × 21 inches for the

shelf; two pieces to 2½ × 21 inches each for the side braces; and one piece to 7 × 5⅝ inches for the center brace.

6. Cut two pieces of ¾-inch plywood to 1½ × 21 inches each for the seat supports.

7. Place the two side pieces good side down. Position the side braces flush with one

LUMBER CUTTING LIST

Size	Piece	Quantity
¾'' Plywood		
¾'' × 1½'' × 21''	Supports	2
¾'' × 9'' diameter	Wheel disks	8
⅜'' Plywood		
⅜'' × 13'' × 21''	Top	1
⅜'' × 8½'' × 21''	Sides	2
⅜'' × 7'' × 21''	Shelf	1
⅜'' × 7'' × 5⅝''	Center brace	1
⅜'' × 2½'' × 21''	Side braces	2
⅜'' × 1¼'' × 3''	Wheel strips	72

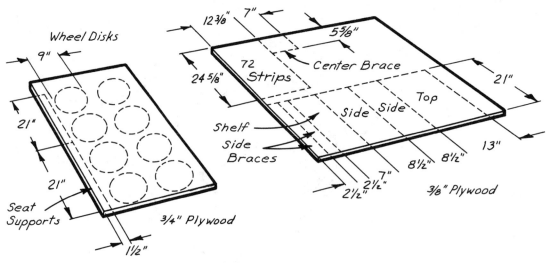

Cutting Diagram

long edge of each side piece, and fasten the braces to the side pieces using carpenter's wood glue and three 1-inch #8 flathead wood screws per brace. Drill and countersink ⅛-inch pilot holes for the screws.

8. Turn the side pieces over and fasten the seat supports flush with the top of the side pieces using wood glue and 2d common nails.

9. Fasten the shelf, good side up, to the top edges of the side braces. Apply wood glue to the edges of the braces, position the shelf, then nail through the shelf into the braces.

10. Apply wood glue to three edges of the center brace. Position the brace, centered front-to-back across the shelf and butted vertically, its ends touching the side pieces. Fasten

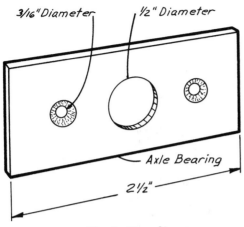

3/16" Diameter   1/2" Diameter

Axle Bearing

2 1/2"

Illustration A

the brace by nailing through the side pieces and into the ends of the brace.

11. Apply wood glue to the top edges of the side pieces and center brace, then center the seat top on them. Fasten the seat top to the supports with 2d common nails.

12. Position and drill four ½-inch-diameter axle holes through the side panels, as shown in the exploded-view diagram. Center the holes 1½ inches from the bottom edge, and 3 inches from each end of the side pieces.

13. Cut the hole for the seat top handle grip, if desired, as shown in the exploded-view diagram.

14. Make 12 axle bearings from pieces of ⅛-inch flat mild steel, each 1 × 2½ inches, as shown

in illustration A. Drill a ½-inch-diameter hole centered in each piece, then drill and countersink two ³⁄₁₆-inch-diameter holes in the locations shown for the mounting screws.

15. Center four axle bearings over the axle holes on the outside of the side panels. Drill ⅛-inch-diameter pilot holes and fasten the bearings to the side panels with ⅝-inch #8 flathead wood screws.

16. Position and fasten axle bearings over the axle hole in each wheel disk, so the sides of each wheel have a bearing. Use ⅝-inch #8 flathead wood screws as fasteners.

17. Drill ⅛-inch-diameter pilot holes through the axle shafts, ¼ inch from each end, to fit ⅛-inch-diameter cotter pins (see step 19).

18. Paint the wheels and seat as you desire. Paint the wheels by rolling them through a pan of paint so the paint covers the inside of the treads. Brush off the excess paint, and allow the pieces to thoroughly dry before proceeding.

19. Install a cotter pin through one hole in each of the axles and lock the pin by bending the shank. Slide a ⅝-inch washer and one wheel on each axle, then slide the axles through the axle holes in the seat sides. Fit the other wheel on each axle, then install another set of washers and the remaining cotter pins. Lock them by bending the shanks.

GARDEN SINK

With a garden sink you can clean freshly picked vegetables without bringing dirt into the kitchen. It's a handy place to prepare vegetables also. The cuttings can be thrown directly onto the compost pile, saving you the extra trip out to the garden from indoors.

This garden sink consists of a rot-resistant 4 × 4 post, anchored in the ground

SHOPPING LIST

Lumber
1 pc. 4 × 4 × 7'
1 pc. 1 × 4 × 6'
1 pc. 1 × 2 × 8'
Plywood
1 sheet ¾'' × 4' × 8' exterior grade
Hardware
1 2-gallon bucket
1 plastic basin 6'' × 12'' × 14''
6 flathead wood screws #12 × 2''
12 flathead wood screws #6 × ⅝''
2 cabinet hinges 2''
¼ pound galvanized common nails 12d
¼ pound finishing nails 6d
¼ pound coated box nails 6d
80 pounds premixed concrete
1 pc. pipe ½'' I.D. × 30''
2 pipe nipples ½'' × 6''
2 pipe elbows ½'' × 90 degrees
2 pipe clips ½''
1 hose bib faucet ½''
1 drainpipe 1¼'' × 14''
100 pounds gravel
1 hose coupling adaptor ½''
1 basket strainer 1¼''
waterproof glue
exterior-grade enamel or stain

with concrete, supporting a sink cabinet that holds a basin made from a plastic tub. A faucet and feed line connected to a garden hose supply water. Used water may either be caught in a bucket placed underneath the basin or allowed to run into a gravel-filled pit around the base of the cabinet. The cabinet itself is a great place to store small garden tools, gloves, extra hose, and seeds. If you wish, you can direct the used water right into the garden by attaching an elbow to the drainpipe beneath the basin, and attaching to that a hose or drainpipe extension.

In warm climates an underground water supply line could be installed instead of a garden hose. Where freezing occurs in winter, though, it's best to use the setup shown and to disconnect the hose when the weather turns cold.

The garden sink is inexpensive to build. To reduce the cost still further, use discarded items and materials, where possible. Purchase pressure-treated lumber, especially for the main post, or treat the lumber before applying the final finish. The choice of plumbing pipe and faucet is yours: any type of pipe, including PVC, ABS, polybutylene, galvanized iron, or copper will do.

CONSTRUCTION

1. Cut one piece of 4×4 ($3\frac{1}{2}'' \times 3\frac{1}{2}''$) stock to 60 inches for the main post, and one piece to 24 inches for the cross piece.

2. Cut a half-lap joint in the top of the main post and the center of the cross piece to form a T-shaped post when assembled, as shown in illustration A. Fasten the two pieces together with waterproof glue and 12d galvanized common nails.

3. Cut one piece of ¾-inch exterior-grade plywood to 16×24 inches for the cabinet back panel, one piece to 16×24 inches for the front panel, one piece to 20×24 inches for the top panel, one piece to 15×24 inches for the bottom panel, and two pieces to $15 \times 15\frac{1}{4}$ inches each for the side panels. Label the pieces as they are cut to avoid confusion during assembly.

LUMBER CUTTING LIST

Size	Piece	Quantity
4 × 4		
$3\frac{1}{2}'' \times 3\frac{1}{2}'' \times 60''$	Main post	1
$3\frac{1}{2}'' \times 3\frac{1}{2}'' \times 24''$	Cross piece	1
1 × 4		
$\frac{3}{4}'' \times 3\frac{1}{2}'' \times 14''$	Splashboards	4
1 × 2		
$\frac{3}{4}'' \times 1\frac{1}{2}'' \times 25\frac{1}{2}''$	Edge trim	2
$\frac{3}{4}'' \times 1\frac{1}{2}'' \times 20''$	Edge trim	2
Plywood		
$\frac{3}{4}'' \times 20'' \times 24''$	Cabinet top panel	1
$\frac{3}{4}'' \times 16'' \times 24''$	Cabinet back panel	1
$\frac{3}{4}'' \times 16'' \times 24''$	Cabinet front panel	1
$\frac{3}{4}'' \times 15'' \times 24''$	Cabinet bottom panel	1
$\frac{3}{4}'' \times 15'' \times 15\frac{1}{4}''$	Cabinet side panels	2

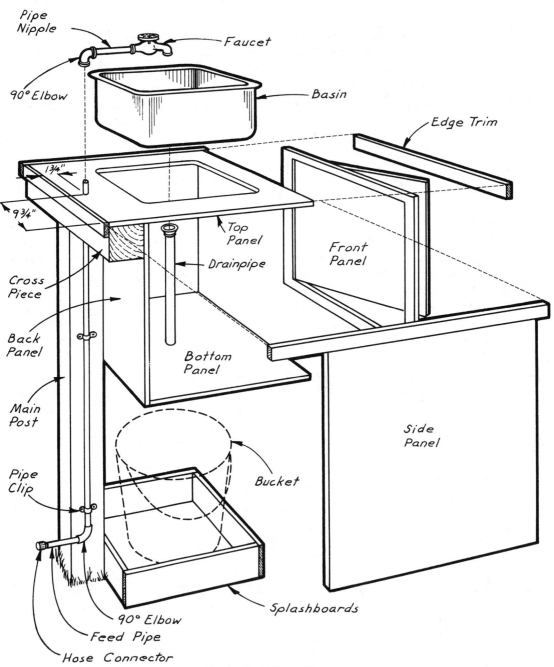

Pipe
Nipple

Faucet

90° Elbow

Basin

Edge Trim

1¾"

9¾"

Top
Panel

Front
Panel

Cross
Piece

Drainpipe

Back
Panel

Bottom
Panel

Side
Panel

Main
Post

Pipe
Clip

Bucket

90° Elbow
Feed Pipe
Hose Connector

Splashboards

Exploded-View Diagram

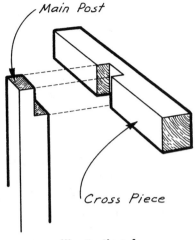

Illustration A

4. Mark the perimeter of the door, a 13 × 20-inch rectangle, centered on the front panel. Carefully cut the door from the panel and save both pieces of plywood.

5. Assemble the top, front, bottom, and back panels, as shown in the exploded-view diagram, with waterproof glue and 6d coated box nails. Do not install the side panels at this time. Instead, nail a temporary diagonal brace to the top and back panels to hold the cabinet rigid.

6. On the top panel, scribe the perimeter of the 12 × 14-inch plastic tub to be used as the basin. The dimensions of the cutout you will make should allow the basin to be supported only by its rim when fitted into the hole. Cut the hole in the top panel.

7. Cut a 3¾-inch-diameter hole in the bottom of the basin for the fitting. Locate the hole toward the rear, but in a section that is also flat. Avoid raised lettering, rib strengtheners, or other obstacles that will cause the fitting to leak.

8. Fit the basin in place in the top panel, then stand the 1¼-inch-diameter × 14-inch drainpipe in the drain hole, and mark the bottom panel by scribing around the pipe.

Remove both the basin and the drainpipe. Cut a hole in the bottom panel to accept the drainpipe.

9. Fasten the side panels to the cabinet with waterproof glue and 6d coated box nails. Make sure the cabinet is square before fastening the side panels.

10. Center the cabinet on the cross piece and main post, then drill and countersink four ⅛-inch-diameter pilot holes evenly spaced across the back panel. Drill from inside the cabinet into the cross piece. Drill two additional holes through the back panel and into the main post. Insert six 2-inch #12 flathead wood screws in the holes and secure the cabinet.

11. Drill a ⅞-inch-diameter hole through the top panel and cross piece, 1¾ inches from the back edge of the top and 9¾ inches from an end of the cross piece, to accept a ½-inch-I.D. feed pipe.

12. Cut two pieces of 1 × 2 (¾″ × 1½″) stock to 20 inches each and two pieces to 25½ inches each for edge trim. Fasten the edge trim to the edges of the top panel with waterproof glue and 6d finishing nails.

13. Cut four pieces of 1 × 4 (¾″ × 3½″) stock to 14 inches each for the splashboards. Assemble them with waterproof glue and 6d coated box nails to form the frame, as shown in the exploded-view diagram.

14. Now dig a pit for the French drain in the location where the sink will be installed. Dig the pit approximately 12 inches deep, 24 inches wide, and 18 inches front to back, as shown in illustration B. Also dig a 6-inch-diameter posthole, centered along the rear edge of the pit, for the main post.

15. Install the main post, with the cabinet attached, in the posthole. Adjust the height of the cabinet by altering the depth of the hole. Plumb the main post by using temporary braces nailed to the cabinet and

327

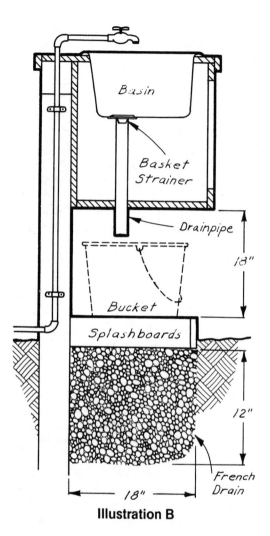

Illustration B

16. Install the cabinet door using 2-inch cabinet hinges and wood screws.

17. Seal all imperfections in the plywood cabinet with wood filler, then finish the cabinet panels, door, cross pieces, main post, and splashboards with an exterior-grade enamel or stain.

18. To make the feed pipe, first attach a ½-inch hose bib faucet to a ½ × 6-inch pipe nipple. Then attach the nipple to a ½-inch × 90-degree elbow, and the elbow to a ½-inch × 30-inch section of plumbing pipe.

19. Slide the feed pipe through the ⅞-inch-diameter hole in the top of the cabinet. Attach a ½-inch × 90-degree elbow to the bottom end of the feed pipe, and add a second ½-inch × 6-inch pipe nipple to the elbow.

20. Attach a ½-inch hose coupling adaptor to the pipe nipple. Secure the feed pipe to the main post with two ½-inch pipe clips. Fasten the pipe clips with 6d coated box nails.

21. Install a 1¼-inch basket strainer in the basin and attach the drainpipe. Reinstall the basin in the top of the cabinet, with the drainpipe extending through the hole in the bottom panel.

22. Place the splashboards under the sink and fasten them to the main post with 12d galvanized common nails. Place a two-gallon bucket under the sink drainpipe. Connect the feed pipe to your garden hose, and test the water supply line and drain connections. Your garden sink is now ready to use.

angled to the ground. Mix 80 pounds of concrete and pour it around the base of the post. Fill the French-drain pit with gravel, tamping it as the pit is filled, to contain the concrete. Allow the concrete to cure.

ORCHARD LADDER

SHOPPING LIST

Lumber
5 pcs. select mahogany 5/4 × 4 × 8′
Dowels
2 pcs. 1¼″ × 6′ hardwood
Hardware
2 pcs. steel rod ⅜″ diameter × 3½″
    (optional)
24 flathead wood screws #6 × 1″
1 broom spring-clip
½ pound galvanized common nails 10d
4 pcs. aluminum sheet ⅛″ × 3⅛″ × 8″
1 pc. steel pipe ¾″ I.D. × 19¼″
2 tee fittings ¾″
1 pipe coupling ¾″ (optional)

Whether you are the owner of a large orchard or only have a couple of fruit trees planted near your house, this Rodale-designed orchard ladder will come in handy when you need to prune and thin your trees and pick their fruit. The ladder is in two sections. Combine them and you can reach the upper levels of large fruit trees. Use the top section alone for working in small trees or in the lower levels of large trees.

The top section of the ladder is tapered to a narrow point. This enables the ladder to fit into the crotch of a tree, giving it greater stability. This section also has a pivoting leg intended to supplement support from a tree branch. (The upper section of the ladder is not designed to serve as a conventional stepladder.)

A metal rung made of pipe, threaded at each end to accept an ordinary tee fitting or homemade nut, serves to clamp both halves of the ladder together. The metal rung is located in the lower portion of the ladder's top section and fits into reinforced slots cut in the upper portion of the ladder's bottom section. The homemade nut requires welding, but it is less bulky than a tee fitting and less apt to hamper maneuvering the ladder among dense foliage.

The materials used to make the ladder are readily available from a lumberyard and hardware store. The side rails and support leg are made from 5/4 stock. The ladder pictured is built of a common, construction-grade mahogany that is strong, free of knots, and relatively inexpensive. Any strong wood would be acceptable, except perhaps oak,

which would make the ladder heavy to carry. Fir and yellow pine would also work well, but avoid white pine because of its lack of structural strength. Standard hardwood dowels are used for all the rungs except the clamping rung, which is made of ordinary galvanized pipe. The ends of the ladder are reinforced with ⅛-inch-thick aluminum plates where they overlap the rungs. As for finishing, wooden ladders should never be painted, because paint can hide cracks that may develop. Instead, treat the wood with copper naphthenate wood preservative, if desired, or simply leave the ladder unfinished.

CONSTRUCTION

To make the bottom section:

1. Cut two pieces of 5/4 × 4 (1⅛″ × 3½″) select mahogany to 73¾ inches each for the rails of the ladder.

2. Clamp the two rails together and lay out the position of the rungs, as shown in illustration A. Note that the center of the first rung is 11⅜ inches from the bottom ends of the rails, but that all five rungs are spaced every 12 inches on center.

3. With the rails still clamped together, drill a 1¼-inch-diameter hole through both rails at each rung location. Drill these holes as straight as possible to ensure a good fit for the rungs.

4. Drill a 1⅛-inch-diameter hole at a point 2⅜ inches from the top end of the rails. Now unclamp the rails and, using a saw, extend each top hole to the end of the rail to create a 1⅛-inch-wide slot, as shown in illustration A.

5. Round-over all edges of the rails with sandpaper, a wood rasp, or a router equipped

with a ¼-inch rounding-over bit.

6. Cut two pieces of ⅛-inch-thick aluminum sheet to 3⅛ × 8 inches each for reinforcing plates.

7. Drill a 1⅛-inch-diameter hole positioned 2³⁄₁₆ inches on center from one end of each aluminum plate. Using a saw, extend each hole to the end of the piece to create the 1⅛-inch-wide slot pictured in illustration A, which should also be identical to the slots cut in each rail in step 4.

8. Drill and countersink six ⁵⁄₃₂-inch screw holes in each plate.

9. Check to see that the pipe to be used as a rung in the top half of the ladder is able to slide in and out of the slots cut in the aluminum plates and the rails. Widen the slots, if necessary, then position the aluminum plates on the rails so the slots in each coincide. Note that ³⁄₁₆ inch of the rail should be visible on either side of the plates and above the ends.

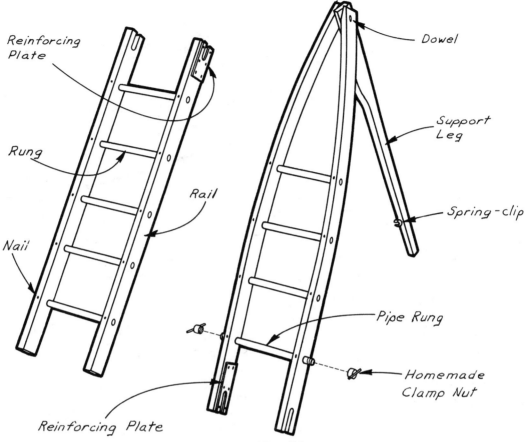

Exploded-View Diagram

LUMBER CUTTING LIST

Size	Piece	Quantity
5/4 × 4		
1″ × 3½″ × 83″	Rails for top section	2
1″ × 3½″ × 83″	Support leg	1
1″ × 3½″ × 73¾″	Rails for bottom section	2
Dowels		
1¼″ × 18″	Rungs for bottom section	5
1¼″ × 16½″	Rungs for top section	2
1¼″ × 14½″	Top rung for top section	1
1¼″ × 3½″	Pivot dowel	1

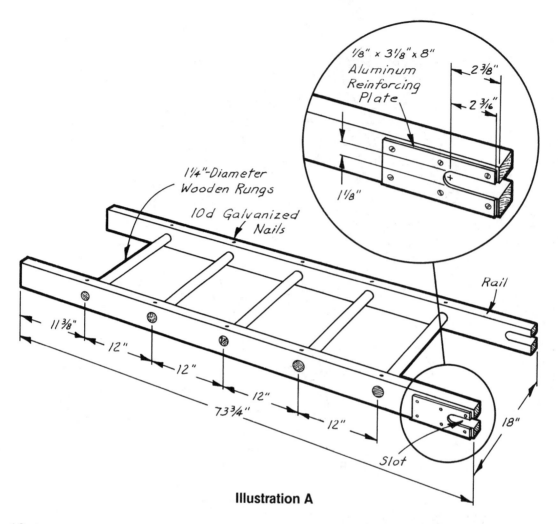

Illustration A

10. With the aluminum plates in position, drill ¹⁄₁₆-inch pilot holes in the rails and fasten the plates to the rails with 1-inch #6 flat-head wood screws.

11. Cut five pieces of 1¼-inch dowel to 18 inches each for rungs.

12. Assemble the bottom section of the ladder by inserting the rungs in the rails. Make sure the ladder is consistently 18 inches in width, outside edge to outside edge, and that the rails are turned so their aluminum plates face out, as shown in illustration A.

All rungs should be flush with the rails.

13. Drill a ⁹⁄₆₄-inch pilot hole through one edge of each rail at each point where a rung enters the rail. Extend the pilot holes through the rungs but not all the way through the rails. Secure the rungs with 10d galvanized common nails.

To make the top section:

1. Cut two pieces of 5/4 × 4 mahogany to 83 inches each for the rails.

2. Clamp the rails together to mark the posi-

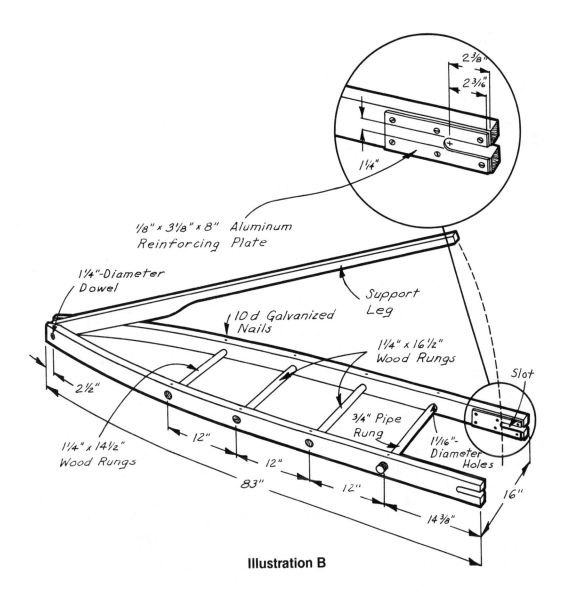

Illustration B

tion of the rungs. Begin by marking the position for a hole 2⅜ inches on center from the bottom. This hole will form part of a slot, as shown in illustration B. From that point measure and mark the position of the four rungs, one every 12 inches on center.

3. With the rails still clamped together, drill

a 1¼-inch-diameter hole through the two pieces at the points marked for the slot and for the second, third, and fourth rungs. For the first rung, which is made of pipe, drill a 1 1/16-inch-diameter hole through both pieces.

4. Unclamp the rails and with a saw cut out a 1¼-inch-wide slot between the first hole

333

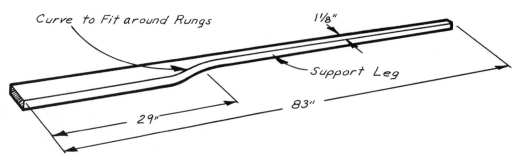

Illustration C

and the bottom end of each rail, as shown in illustration B.

5. Cut one piece of 5/4 × 4 mahogany to 83 inches for the support leg. Cut the leg to the shape pictured in illustration C so that after assembly it can be clamped to the rungs of the ladder (see step 22).

6. Round-over all edges of the rails and support leg with sandpaper, a wood rasp, or a router equipped with a ¼-inch rounding-over bit.

7. Cut two pieces of ⅛-inch-thick aluminum sheet to 3⅛ × 8 inches each for reinforcing plates.

8. Drill a 1¼-inch-diameter hole through each plate, centered 2³⁄₁₆ inches from one end. Cut out the area from the hole to the end to form a 1¼-inch-wide slot in each piece, as shown in illustration B. These slots should be identical to those cut in the ends of the rails in step 4.

9. Drill and countersink six ⁵⁄₃₂-inch screw holes in each reinforcing plate.

10. Check the slots in the plates and rails to make sure the top rung of the ladder's lower section slides easily in and out. Widen the slots, if necessary.

11. Now position the plates on the rails and drill ¹⁄₁₆-inch pilot holes in the rails, using the holes in the plates as guides. Fasten the plates to the rails with 1-inch #6 flathead wood screws.

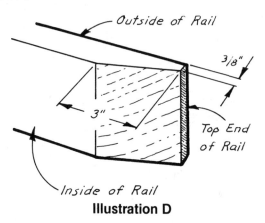

Illustration D

12. Cut the top ends of the rails to the angle shown in illustration D. Before measuring and cutting, note that the insides of the rails are those to which the aluminum plates are attached. Lay out the angles to be cut so they run from a point ⅜ inch from the outside edge of the rail end to a point 3 inches along the inside of the rail from the end.

13. Clamp the top ends of the rails in position on either side of the support leg. The diagonal edges of the rails should lie flush against the sides of the leg. Drill a 1¼-inch-diameter hole through all three pieces, centered 2½ inches from their clamped ends.

14. Cut one piece of 1¼-inch dowel to 3½ inches in length. Insert the dowel through the holes drilled in the previous step. Then

drill a 9/64-inch pilot hole in one edge of each rail. Extend these holes through the dowel, but not all the way through the remainder of the rails. Secure the dowel with 10d galvanized common nails. Do not drive a nail into the support leg. Leave it free to pivot on the dowel.

15. Cut one piece of 1¼-inch dowel to 14½ inches for the top rung. Pull the rails together so that the outside width of the ladder at the lower edge of the top rung is 14 inches. Ream the holes for the rung with drill or rasp, if necessary, to accommodate the bend in the rails at that point, and fit the rung in place. After the rung is in place, drill a 9/64-inch pilot hole from the top edge of each rail down through each end of the dowel, and secure the rung with 10d galvanized common nails.

16. Cut two pieces of 1¼-inch dowel to 16½ inches each for the second and third rungs. Fit these rungs into place with the rails pulled together so that at the point of the yet-to-be-installed bottom rung, the ladder measures 16 inches in width from outside edge to outside edge. Secure the second and third rungs with 10d galvanized common nails as in the previous step.

17. Saw, chisel, and sand smooth any protruding ends of dowels to make them flush with the sides of the ladder.

18. Cut one piece of ¾-inch-I.D. pipe to 19¼ inches for the bottom rung. Thread each end approximately 1½ inches. (Take the pipe to a plumber for threading if you can't get this done where you purchase it.)

19. Place the pipe rung in position on the ladder and drill 9/64-inch pilot holes through both the rails and the rung. Then remove the pipe and widen the pilot holes in it to 5/32 inch. Finally, reinsert the pipe in the ladder, line up the pilot holes, and secure the rung with 10d galvanized common nails.

20. Ordinary tee fittings may be used as clamping nuts. If you wish to make homemade nuts, begin by sawing a ¾-inch pipe coupling in half. Use one section for each nut.

21. Cut two pieces of ⅜-inch steel rod to 3½ inches each for the clamp handles. Weld (do not braze) one piece of rod to the sawn edge of each piece of coupling. Screw the clamps on the ends of the threaded pipe.

22. Attach a broom spring-clip to the inside of the support leg so that the leg can be clipped to the pipe rung when not in use, as shown in the exploded-view diagram.

23. Treat the wooden parts of the ladder with a copper naphthenate wood preservative, if desired.

24. To assemble the bottom section of the ladder to the top, fit the slotted ends of the top over the upper rung of the bottom section, inside the rails. The slots in the ends of the bottom section should slide over the protruding ends of the pipe rung in the top section. Tighten the tee fittings or clamping nuts to secure the sections together.

APPLE PICKER

SHOPPING LIST

Lumber
1 pc. bamboo 8'
Hardware
heavy cloth for tube 2' × 10'
heavy cloth to cover hooks 1' × 1'
heavy thread or cord, as needed
1 pc. 9-gauge wire 3'
duct tape 2'

Perhaps you are familiar with the type of apple picker that has a basket at the top of a long pole and a hook to pull the apples loose from the tree. Pete Bologna of Brethren, Michigan, submitted this version of that apple picker, but his device gives the apples an easy ride to the gathering basket through a cloth tube. This breaks the fall and keeps the apples from being bruised.

Pete uses a pole made of bamboo, but PVC pipe or 2 × 2 lumber would work as well. Use heavy 9-gauge wire to form the hoop and hooks. Wire of smaller diameter will bend or break. For the cloth tube, use muslin, lightweight canvas, or whatever strong cloth you may have, even a string of old trouser legs sewn together. Keep in mind the working conditions—branches, moisture, heavy apples—and stitch the cloth together with waxed thread, fishing line, or some other strong, waterproof material.

CONSTRUCTION

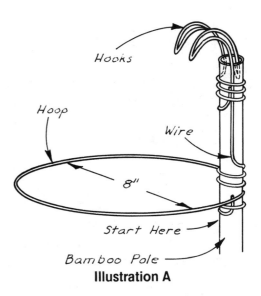

Illustration A

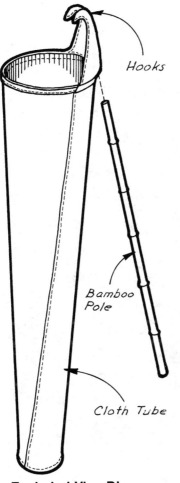

Exploded-View Diagram

1. Begin by wrapping 36 inches of 9-gauge wire around an 8-foot bamboo pole to form the hoop and hooks, as shown in illustration A. Then secure the wire to the pole with a few additional wraps of strong duct tape.

2. Cut or patch together cloth for the tube. To surround the hoop, one end of the cloth must be about 24 inches wide. The tube itself should be about 10 feet long and may taper to about 5 inches at the bottom.

3. Cover the hooks above the hoop with a separate piece of cloth, about 1 foot square. Drape the piece over the hoop and hooks, slit the cloth between the hooks in order to cover each one separately, then stitch the cut edges together and stitch the cloth to the tube, as shown in the exploded-view diagram.

4. Now test the picker. Bend the hooks closer together, if necessary, to harvest small apples, and reshape the hoop if plucked apples fail to drop straight in.

HERB DRYING RACK

SHOPPING LIST

Lumber
1 pc. 1 × 3 × 3'
Dowels
3 pcs. ¾'' × 3' hardwood
Hardware
1 pc. mild steel rod ¼'' diameter × 13''
4 flathead wood screws #6 × 1½''
½ pint brushing lacquer
Miscellaneous
8 wooden balls ⅞'' with 5/16'' holes

This compact herb drying rack, designed and built by the Rodale Design Group, is simple to make and is attractive as well. It may be mounted on a kitchen or attic wall, or wherever you wish to dry herbs. The back and end caps of the rack are made of ordinary pine; however, any good-looking wood may be used. For strength and durability, the drying arms, which pivot on a short length of steel rod, should be cut from ¾-inch hardwood dowels. The dowels and steel rod can be purchased at most hardware stores. Wooden balls separate the drying arms. These balls are available at most craft shops.

Spread the arms of the rack apart when using them, and fold them flat against the wall when they are not being used. If their number and length do not suit your needs, alter the plans accordingly. These herb drying racks make great gifts. Consider making several at one time and presenting them to friends or relatives at holiday time.

CONSTRUCTION

1. Cut one piece of 1 × 3 (¾'' × 2½'') stock to 18¾ inches for the back of the herb drying rack. Cut a 1¼-inch radius on each end of this piece. Drill a 3/16-inch-diameter hole at the center of each radius for a mounting hole, as shown in the exploded-view diagram.

2. Cut one piece of 1 × 3 stock to 8 inches for the end cap blank. Cut a 1¼-inch radius on each end of this blank. Then cut a

2¾-inch-long piece from each end of the blank to create the two end caps. Drill a ¹⁷⁄₆₄-inch-diameter hole ⅜ inch deep into the center of the radius on each end cap to accept the pivot rod.

3. Cut a ¾-inch-wide dado ⅜ inch deep across the front face of the back piece, 2½ inches in from each end, to accept the end caps. Drill two ³⁄₁₆-inch-diameter pilot holes through the back of each dado for screws to hold the end caps in place.

4. Cut seven pieces of ¾-inch dowel for drying arms. Cut the first piece to 8 inches and make each subsequent piece 2 inches longer than the previous one. The seventh piece will thus be 20 inches in length.

5. Drill a ¹⁷⁄₆₄-inch-diameter hole through one end of each drying arm. Center each hole ⅞ inch from one end. Round-over the sharp edges on both ends of all the arms.

6. Break all sharp edges on the back piece and end caps. Finish all wooden parts, including the drying arms and spacer balls, with two coats of brushing lacquer.

7. Cut one piece of ¼-inch steel rod to 13 inches for the pivot rod.

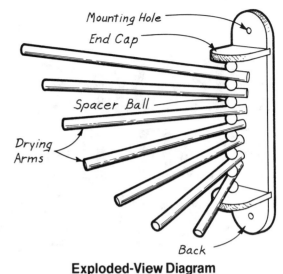

Exploded-View Diagram

8. Assemble the rack as shown in the exploded-view diagram, arranging the drying arms in descending order of length, starting with the longest arm at the top. Place a spacer ball above and below each arm. Fit the end caps into the dadoes and secure them with 1½-inch #6 flathead wood screws.

LUMBER CUTTING LIST

Size	Piece	Quantity
1 × 3		
¾″ × 2½″ × 18¾″	Back	1
¾″ × 2½″ × 8″	End cap blank	1
Dowels		
¾″ × 20″	Drying arm	1
¾″ × 18″	Drying arm	1
¾″ × 16″	Drying arm	1
¾″ × 14″	Drying arm	1
¾″ × 12″	Drying arm	1
¾″ × 10″	Drying arm	1
¾″ × 8″	Drying arm	1

PROJECTS FOR INDOOR GARDENERS

PROPAGA-TION BED

SHOPPING LIST

Lumber
1 pc. 1 × 4 × 12′
Hardware
wire staples 5/16″
box nails 6d
1 pc. 4-mil plastic 3′ × 5′

The Rodale Design Group created this simple polyethylene-covered frame to fit over a pair of 2½ × 20 × 24-inch wood flats, converting them into a plant propagation bed. When set in a sunny location or under a fluorescent grow lamp, this bed will give seedlings and cuttings the warmth and humidity they need to develop quickly. However, if water droplets form and run down the inside of the plastic cover, the humidity level inside the bed is too high. At such times, temporarily remove the cover to allow the planting medium to dry out a bit.

CONSTRUCTION

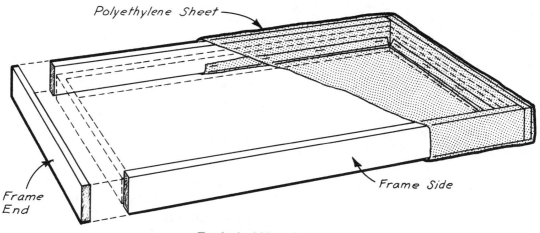

Polyethylene Sheet

Frame Side

Frame End

Exploded-View Diagram

1. Cut two pieces of 1×4 (¾″ × 3½″) stock to 42 inches each for the frame sides, and two pieces to 24⅜ inches each for the frame ends. Lap the side pieces over the end pieces and fasten them together into a rectangular frame using 6d box nails.

2. Cut one piece of plastic sheet to 36×60 inches. Stretch the plastic over the top, down the sides, and around the bottom of the frame. Fasten the edges of the plastic to the inside of the frame using 5/16-inch wire staples.

LUMBER CUTTING LIST

Size	Piece	Quantity
1 × 4		
¾″ × 3½″ × 42″	Frame sides	2
¾″ × 3½″ × 24⅜″	Frame ends	2

PLASTIC-ENCLOSED FLAT

SHOPPING LIST

Hardware
1 wooden flat 2½'' × 20'' × 2'
wire staples ⁵⁄₁₆''
1 pc. 4-mil plastic 4' × 5'
4 pcs. coat-hanger wire (straightened,
    41'' each) or 13' brazing rod
    (⅛'' thickness)

Here is a tall, enclosed flat that serves well as a propagation bed for rooting large cuttings. Devised by the Rodale Design Group, the project consists of an ordinary garden flat to which a simple framework covered with plastic sheeting is attached. The flat shown here uses ordinary coat-hanger wire for the framework. However, since brazing is one method suggested for fastening the project together anyway, ⅛-inch brazing rod for the framework will work just as well. The plastic covering is clear polyethylene vapor barrier. Kitchen-quality plastic wrap is an adequate substitute.

CONSTRUCTION

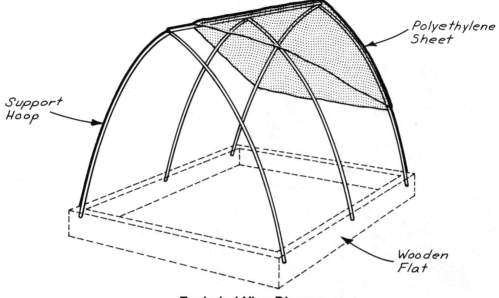

Polyethylene
Sheet

Support
Hoop

Wooden
Flat

Exploded-View Diagram

1. Drill three pairs of parallel holes, each ⅛ inch in diameter and approximately 1 inch deep, into the upper edges of a 2½ × 20 × 24-inch wooden flat. Locate the holes in the sides of the flat, one pair at the center and the others near the ends.

2. Cut three pieces of coat-hanger wire or ⅛-inch brazing rod to 41 inches each for support hoops. Bend the hoops and insert their ends into the holes in the flats, as shown in the exploded-view diagram.

3. Cut an additional piece of wire or rod to 22½ inches for the top brace. Braze the brace to the tops of the hoops, or fasten it in place by wrapping it with lightweight wire or by using epoxy glue.

4. Cover the frame with a 48 × 60-inch piece of clear plastic. Staple the plastic to the rear and sides of the flat, leaving one end free to open and close.

345

PLANT CARRIER

SHOPPING LIST

Lumber
1 pc. 1 × 6 × 3'
1 pc. 1 × 2 × 3'
Plywood
1 pc. ½'' × 2' × 3' A-C grade
Hardware
1 box finishing nails 4d
exterior-grade paint or varnish

Plant carriers are useful for transporting potted plants from one location to another and for holding pots steady while repotting. The model shown here was designed by the Rodale Design Group. Made of exterior plywood and No. 2 pine, then finished with exterior-quality paint, this carrier has space for eight flowerpots: two each of four different sizes.

CONSTRUCTION

1. Cut one piece of ½-inch A-C grade plywood to 14¼ × 28¼ inches for the tray. On it, lay out four pairs of circles — with diameters of 3 inches, 3½ inches, 4 inches, and 4½ inches — arranged as shown in the exploded-view diagram. To cut them out, first drill a starter hole in each circle, then remove the rest of the waste wood using a saw. Smooth the rough edges with sandpaper.

2. Cut two pieces of 1 × 6 (¾'' × 5½'') stock to 14¼ inches each for the carrier's ends. Along the length of each, cut a ½-inch-wide dado ⅜ inch deep, as shown in illustration A, to house the ends of the tray.

3. Cut handle holes on the upper part of each carrier end. To do this, drill a pair of 1¼-inch-diameter holes approximately 4 inches apart, equally spaced from the midpoint of the piece, above the dado cut in

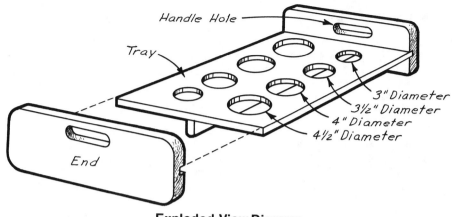

Exploded-View Diagram

the previous step. Remove the waste wood between the holes using a saw, then smooth the inner edges. If desired, also cut a 1-inch radius on the corners of the end pieces, as shown in illustration A. Finally, round-over all exposed edges.

4. Cut one piece of 1 × 2 (¾″ × 1½″) stock to 27½ inches for the tray support.

5. Assemble the carrier using carpenter's wood glue and 4d finishing nails. Set the nail heads below the surface and fill the holes with wood putty. Sand the carrier smooth, then finish with exterior-grade paint or varnish.

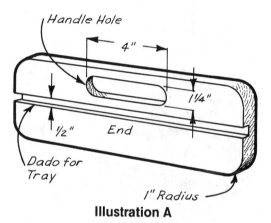

Illustration A

LUMBER CUTTING LIST

Size	Piece	Quantity
1 × 6		
¾″ × 5½″ × 14¼″	Tray ends	2
1 × 2		
¾″ × 1½″ × 27½″	Tray support	1
Plywood		
½″ × 14¼″ × 28¼″	Tray	1

WINDOW-MOUNTED SEED STARTER

This large-size seed-starting unit, designed by the Rodale Design Group, makes it possible to start a sizable portion of your garden well in advance of planting time to

gain full use of even the shortest growing season. The shelves are removable to facilitate the propagation of tall seedlings or indoor plants and to permit easy disassembly and storage.

Two drawers, located beneath the bottom shelf, have been incorporated into the project to hold tools, potting soil, and other seed-starting materials. The drawer unit rests on a windowsill for support. The seed starter shown here is designed to fit a window that measures 36×57 inches including the top and side trim.

Brazing is required to construct the metal support frames that attach the project to the wall.

CONSTRUCTION

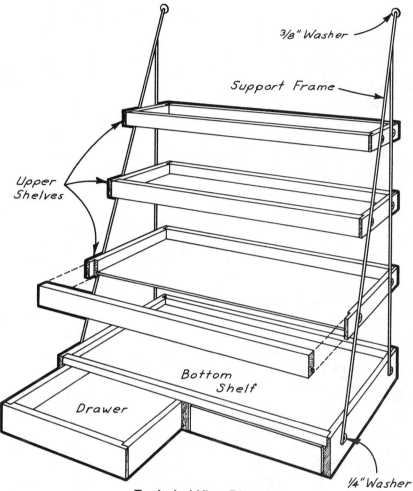

3/8" Washer

Support Frame

Upper Shelves

Bottom Shelf

Drawer

1/4" Washer

Exploded-View Diagram

1. Cut one piece of 1×6 (¾" $\times$ 5½") stock to 35¼ inches for the rear piece of the drawer unit. Cut a ½-inch-wide groove ⅜ inch deep along the inside face of the piece, 1 inch below the upper edge, as shown in illustration A.

2. Cut two pieces of 1×6 stock to 18 inches each for the sides of the drawer unit. Cut a groove along the length of each piece to the same dimensions as in the previous step. Label one piece left, the other right, then cut a ¾-inch-wide rabbet ⅜ inch deep across the rear end of each piece, and a stopped rabbet of the same dimensions partially across the front, all as shown in illustration A. The stopped rabbets should extend

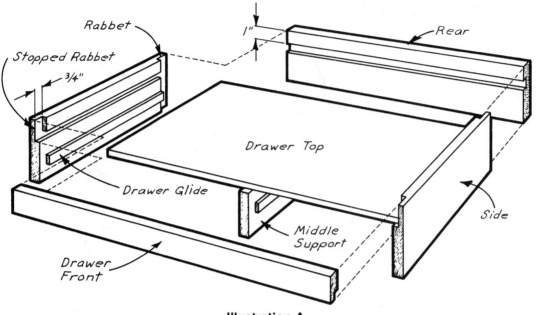

Illustration A

from the upper edge of each side piece only down to the lower surface of the lengthwise groove.

3. Cut one piece of 1×2 ($\frac{3}{4}'' \times 1\frac{1}{2}''$) stock to 35¼ inches for the front of the drawer unit. Cut a ½-inch-wide rabbet ⅜ inch deep along the lower inside edge of the piece, as shown in illustration A.

4. Cut six pieces of 1×6 stock to 16⅞ inches each for the drawer fronts and sides. Rip a ⅜-inch-wide strip from four of the pieces to use as drawer glides, then rip all six pieces each to 4 inches in width. Cut an additional piece of 1×6 stock to 17¼ inches

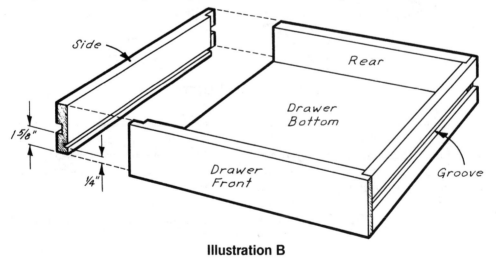

Illustration B

LUMBER CUTTING LIST

Size	Piece	Quantity
1 × 6		
¾″ × 5½″ × 35¼″	Drawer unit rear	1
¾″ × 5½″ × 18″	Drawer unit sides	2
¾″ × 4″ × 17¼″	Middle support	1
¾″ × 4″ × 16⅞″	Drawer fronts	2
¾″ × 4″ × 16⅞″	Drawer sides	4
¾″ × ⅜″ × 16⅞″	Drawer glides	4
1 × 4		
¾″ × 3½″ × 16⅛″	Drawer backs	2
1 × 2		
¾″ × 1½″ × 35¼″	Shelf fronts	3
¾″ × 1½″ × 35¼″	Shelf backs	3
¾″ × 1½″ × 35¼″	Drawer unit front	1
¾″ × 1½″ × 14″	Shelf sides	2
¾″ × 1½″ × 10½″	Shelf sides	2
¾″ × 1½″ × 7″	Shelf sides	2
½″ Plywood		
½″ × 17¼″ × 35¼″	Drawer unit panel	1
¼″ Plywood		
¼″ × 16⅛″ × 16½″	Drawer bottoms	2
¼″ × 13¼″ × 35¼″	Shelf panel	1
¼″ × 9¾″ × 35¼″	Shelf panel	1
¼″ × 6¼″ × 35¼″	Shelf panel	1

and rip it to 4 inches in width for the middle support.

5. Cut a ¾-inch-wide rabbet ⅜ inch deep across the inside face at both ends of the drawer front, and across the rear end of each side piece, as shown in illustration B. Along the inside face of all three pieces, cut a ¼-inch-wide groove ⅜ inch deep, ¼ inch above the lower edge, also as shown. Centered along the outside faces of the side pieces, cut a ¾-inch-wide groove ⅜ inch deep, again as shown in illustration B.

6. Cut two pieces of ¼-inch exterior-grade plywood to 16⅛ × 16½ inches each for the drawer bottoms. Cut two pieces of 1 × 4

(¾″ × 3½″) stock to 16⅛ inches each for the drawer backs. Assemble the two drawers, as shown in the exploded-view diagram, using carpenter's wood glue and 5d finishing nails.

7. Cut one piece of ½-inch A-C grade plywood to 17¼ × 35¼ inches for the bottom shelf, which forms the top of the drawer unit. Assemble the drawer unit, as shown in the exploded-view diagram, using wood glue and 5d finishing nails.

8. Set the drawers in the drawer openings and mark the proper locations for the drawer glides on the middle support and drawer-unit sides. Position the rear ends of the

glides flush with the back of the unit, then fasten the glides in place using wood glue and 1-inch #16 brads.

9. Cut six pieces of 1×2 stock to 35¼ inches each for the front and rear pieces of the three remaining shelves. Cut additional pieces of 1×2 stock for the side pieces, two each to 14 inches, 10½ inches, and 7 inches. On the side pieces only, cut a ¾-inch-wide rabbet ⅜ inch deep across the ends of the inside faces. On all the pieces, cut a ¼-inch-wide groove ⅜ inch deep ¼ inch above the lower edge.

10. From ¼-inch plywood cut the bottom panels for the three upper shelves. Make them all 35¼ inches in length and cut one each to widths of 13¼ inches, 9¾ inches, and 6¼ inches. Assemble the three shelves using wood glue and 5d finishing nails.

11. If desired, round-over the exposed edges of the shelves and drawers using sandpaper or a router equipped with a ¼-inch rounding-over bit. Then sand all surfaces and apply two coats of polyurethane. Seal the inside joints of the shelves with clear silicone caulk to protect them from moisture.

12. On a work surface suitable for brazing, lay out a right triangle whose base (horizontal line) measures 14 inches and whose height (vertical line) measures 49½ inches. Measure and scribe a horizontal line 2¾ inches from the base to mark the height of the drawer unit, then select desired heights for the remaining three shelves and scribe horizontal lines across the triangle to mark their positions as well.

13. Cut two pieces of ¼-inch-diameter steel rod to 60½ inches each and two pieces to 49½ inches each for the support frames. Place one of the shorter rods along the height and one of the longer rods along the hypotenuse (slanted side) of the triangle drawn on the work surface in the previous step. Align the lower ends of the rods flush with the base of the triangle, allowing the upper end of the longer rod to extend above the triangle. Braze the rods together where they meet.

14. Braze a ¼-inch-I.D. flat washer to the lower end of each rod, as shown in the exploded-view diagram. Braze additional pairs of ¼-inch washers to the rods at the three other shelf positions.

15. Lay out a second triangle, which is a mirror image of the first, so that the two triangles now represent the left and right support frames. Measure and scribe identical drawer-unit and shelf position lines, then braze ¼-inch washers to the rods at those points, as in the previous step. Finally, braze a ⅜-inch-I.D. flat washer to the upper end of each long rod in a position that will allow the rods to rest flush against the wall when the frames are in place.

16. File the brazed areas free of scale, then clean each support frame using steel wool. Finally, apply rust-resistant enamel to the frames.

17. Place the drawer unit in position on the windowsill so the rear piece of the unit rests flush against the window trim. Temporarily support the unit, then hold the support frames in position with their washers flush against the sides of the unit and the rear of each frame flush against the wall. Mark locations for fasteners, then remove the unit and frames and fasten the lower ends of the frames to the unit using ¾-inch #12 roundhead wood screws.

18. Attach the remaining shelves to the frames, also using ¾-inch #12 roundhead wood screws. Position the shelves so they leave ½-inch clearance between them and the window trim when installed. Finally, set the entire project in place and fasten the upper ends of the support frames to the wall using 2½-inch #14 roundhead wood screws or other appropriate fasteners.

HANGING LOG BASKET

SHOPPING LIST

Lattice
1 pc. ¼″ × 1½″ × 3′
Dowels
4 pcs. ¾″ × 3′ hardwood
1 pc. ¼″ × 3′ hardwood
Hardware
1 leather thong 8′
boiled linseed oil
turpentine

This decorative hanging basket will hold one flowerpot placed in a saucer measuring up to 6 inches in diameter. Ordinary dowel stock was used for the logs, but for a rustic effect, try using carefully chosen small branches collected outdoors. Small-diameter dowels glued in place hold the basket together. A leather thong suspends the basket from a ceiling hook. Containers of different sizes can be made merely by using longer or shorter logs. The finish is an old-fashioned, homemade variety: boiled linseed oil and turpentine. (Do not boil linseed oil yourself. Instead purchase boiled linseed oil from a paint or hardware store.)

CONSTRUCTION

1. Cut 16 pieces of ¾-inch dowel to 8⅞ inches each for the sides of the basket. In each log, center and drill a ¼-inch-diameter hole ¾ inch from each end, being careful to make each pair of holes parallel.

2. On two logs, cut a ¼-inch-wide groove ¼ inch deep and 7 inches long along one side to receive the ends of the bottom slats, as shown in the exploded-view diagram. Center each groove along the length of the log, perpendicular to the holes previously drilled.

3. Cut four pieces of ¼ × 1½-inch lattice stock to 7⅛ inches each for the bottom slats. (If this material is unavailable, substitute ¼-inch-wide rippings from 2 × 4 stock.) Space the slats an equal distance apart, then install them between the grooves in the bottom logs using carpenter's wood glue.

4. Cut four pieces of ¼-inch dowel to 6 inches each for the corner posts. Insert the posts into the holes drilled in the 2 bottom logs, then stack the remaining 14 logs in parallel pairs, alternating the direction of each pair as shown in the exploded-view diagram. Glue each piece in place as you install it.

LUMBER CUTTING LIST

Size	Piece	Quantity
Lattice		
¼'' × 1½'' × 7⅛''	Bottom slats	4
Dowels		
¾'' × 8⅞''	Sides	16
¼'' × 6''	Corner posts	4

5. Apply a finish of equal parts of boiled linseed oil and turpentine to the assembled basket. Two coats should be sufficient.

6. Tie together the two ends of an 8-foot leather thong, then double it to create four smaller loops of equal size. Slip each loop under the top log at one corner of the basket and hook it around the end of the log below, as shown in the exploded-view diagram. Then tie the upper ends of the four loops together, also as shown, to create an additional loop for suspending the basket from a ceiling hook.

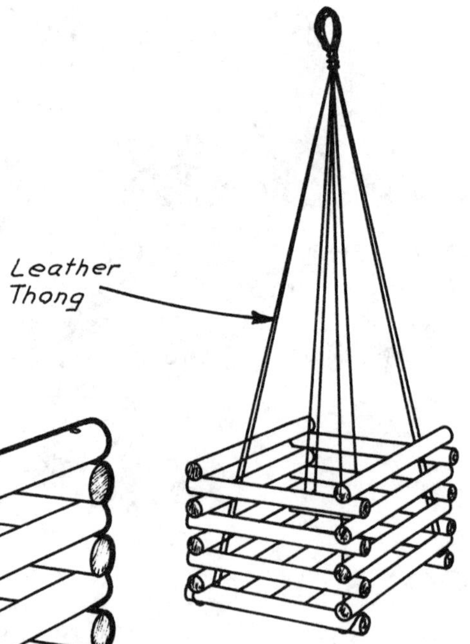

Leather Thong

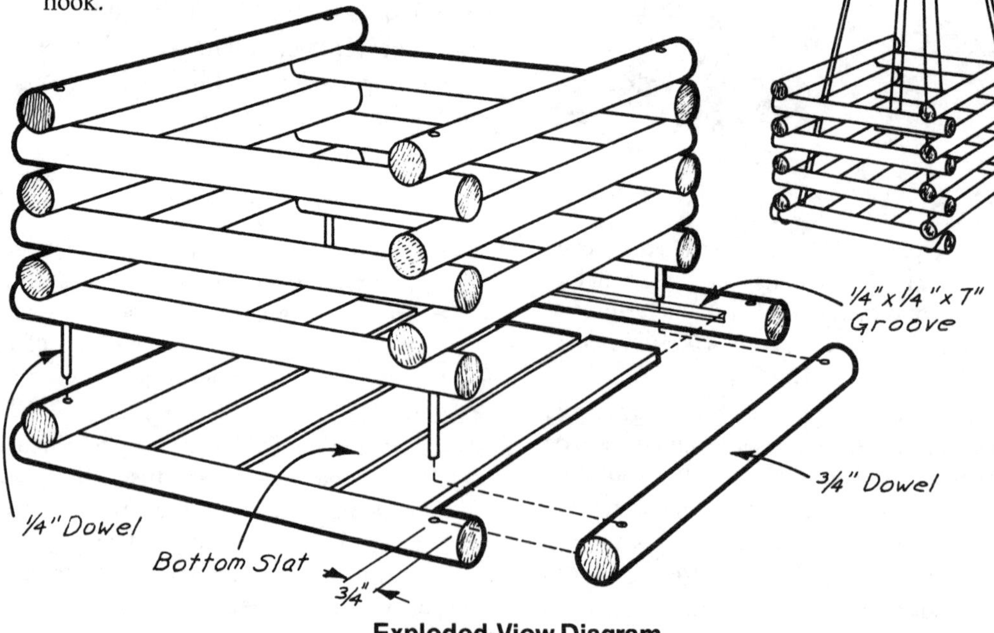

¼"x ¼ "x 7" Groove

¾" Dowel

¼" Dowel

Bottom Slat

¾"

Exploded-View Diagram

HANGING WOOD AND COPPER PLANTER

SHOPPING LIST

Lumber
1 pc. 5/4 × 5/4 × 6'
1 pc. 1 × 6 × 6''
Hardware
1 clay saucer 12'' diameter
4 pcs. brazing rod ⅛'' × 23''
2 pcs. brazing rod ⅛'' × 2''
1 pc. brazing rod 1/16'' × 10''
4 pcs. brazing rod 1/16'' × 9½''
1 copper pipe coupling 4'' diameter
epoxy glue
polyurethane

This intriguing planter was designed by the Rodale Design Group to hold a standard 12-inch-diameter clay saucer at the lower level and a 4-inch-diameter pot made from a copper pipe coupling at the upper level. The wooden framework for the saucer is suspended from lengths of brazing rod joined together at the top. The platform for the smaller pot is suspended from thinner rod, hooked to a central ring, and can be easily detached. Brazing is suggested for joining the rods together. However, very careful wrapping of the rods with wire and then coating the wrappings with epoxy glue is an adequate substitute.

CONSTRUCTION

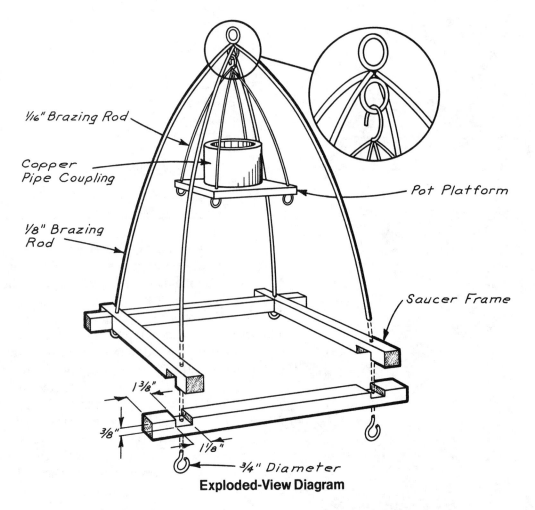

1/16" Brazing Rod

Copper
Pipe Coupling

1/8" Brazing
Rod

Pot Platform

Saucer Frame

1 3/8"

3/8"

1 1/8"

3/4" Diameter

Exploded-View Diagram

1. Cut four pieces of 5/4 × 5/4 (1⅛″ × 1⅛″) stock to 16 inches each for the saucer frame. Notch the pieces so they will interlock when assembled, as shown in the exploded-view diagram.

2. Cut one piece of 1 × 6 (¾″ × 5½″) stock to 5½ inches for the pot platform. For the pot, obtain a 4-inch-diameter copper pipe coupling (about 2 inches high). The pot may be joined directly to the platform (see

step 6). However, if desired, center the coupling on the platform, mark its outer and inner circumference, then use a fly cutter mounted in a drill press to cut a ¼-inch-deep groove between the lines to create a recessed fitting.

3. Assemble the saucer frame, then drill a ⅛-inch-diameter hole through the center of each joint where the pieces overlap. Drill a 1/16-inch-diameter hole through each cor-

LUMBER CUTTING LIST

Size	Piece	Quantity
5/4 × 5/4		
1⅛″ × 1⅛″ × 16″	Saucer frame pieces	4
1 × 6		
¾″ × 5½″ × 5½″	Pot platform	1

ner of the pot platform. Round-over the outside edges of all the pieces, sand, then finish with two coats of polyurethane.

4. Cut four pieces of ⅛-inch brazing rod to 23 inches each for suspending the saucer frame. Bend the lower end of each rod to form a ¾-inch-diameter circle. Thread the pieces up through the holes in the corners of the frame and braze them together at the top. Form two rings from additional ⅛-inch brazing rod, then braze them one above the other, sandwiching the joined ends of the longer rods between them, as shown in the exploded-view diagram.

5. Cut four pieces of 1/16-inch brazing rod to 9½ inches each. Bend a ½-inch-diameter circle in the lower end of each and thread the rods up through the holes in the corners of the pot platform. Form a hook using additional 1/16-inch rod, then braze the rod ends and the hook together at the top, so that the entire assembly will hang from the lower ring attached to the saucer frame.

6. Join the pipe coupling to the platform with a generous amount of epoxy glue. When dry, fill the pot with water to check for leaks. Add more epoxy, if necessary, or seal the joint around the inside with a bead of silicone caulk. Suspend the pot platform (with pot attached) from its ring, then attach the entire planter to a sturdy hook installed overhead.

HANGING PLANTER FOR THREE PLANTS

SHOPPING LIST

Lumber
1 pc. 1 × 6 × 5′
Dowel
1 pc. ³⁄₁₆″ × 3′ hardwood
Hardware
4 brass cup hooks ½″
2 pcs. brass-plated chain (cut to fit)
polyurethane

This wooden plant hanger is designed to hold three 5-inch-diameter plant pots with matching saucers. We recommend that you purchase the pots and saucers first, then alter the dimensions of the planter to fit them, if necessary.

CONSTRUCTION

1. Cut two pieces of 1 × 6 (¾″ × 5½″) stock to 19 inches each, then rip a 1-inch-wide strip from each. Round-over the long edges of the strips, using sandpaper or a router equipped with a ¼-inch rounding-over bit, then cut them into four pieces, each 5⅜ inches in length. Use these for end spacers, as shown in illustration A. Trim each original piece to 4 inches in width for the planter sides.

2. Cut one piece of 1 × 6 stock to 11 inches in length, then rip it in two so that one piece measures 1½ inches wide and the second piece measures 2¼ inches wide. Round-over the long edges of these pieces, then cut each into two 5⅝-inch lengths. Use the wide pieces for bottom spacers and the narrow pieces for top spacers, as shown in illustration A.

3. Lay out the openings in each side piece, as shown in illustration A. To make the openings, drill pairs of 1½-inch-diameter holes, as shown (use a brace and expandable bit, or a hole saw mounted in a drill press). Then remove the remaining waste wood with a saber or coping saw. Use the saw also to cut a 1-inch radius on the corners of each side piece, then round-over all the edges, including those inside the openings.

4. Center the two bottom spacers between

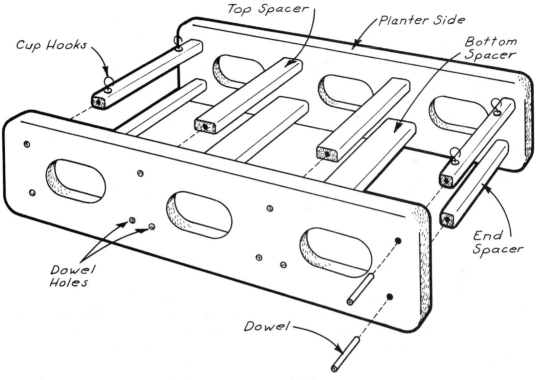

Exploded-View Diagram

the openings in the side pieces, aligning the upper faces of the spacers flush with the bottoms of the openings, as shown in illustration A. Center the two top spacers also between the holes, but align their lower faces with the top of the holes, also as shown. Fasten the spacers to the sides using carpenter's wood glue.

5. Position the end spacers between the sides, as shown in illustration A, $7/16$ inch from

LUMBER CUTTING LIST

Size	Piece	Quantity
1×6		
$\frac{3}{4}'' \times 4'' \times 19''$	Planter sides	2
$\frac{3}{4}'' \times 2\frac{1}{4}'' \times 5\frac{3}{8}''$	Bottom spacers	2
$\frac{3}{4}'' \times 1\frac{1}{2}'' \times 5\frac{3}{8}''$	Top spacers	2
$\frac{3}{4}'' \times 1'' \times 5\frac{3}{8}''$	End spacers	4
Dowel		
$\frac{3}{16}'' \times 1\frac{1}{2}''$	Dowels	20

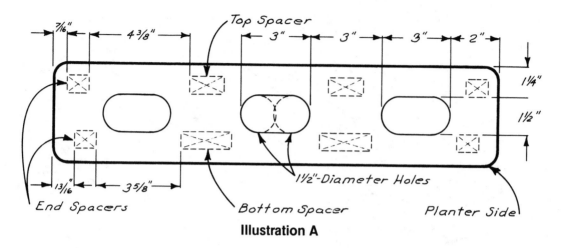

Illustration A

the ends at the top of the planter and ¹³⁄₁₆ inch from the ends at the bottom. Fasten them in place using wood glue.

6. Drill ³⁄₁₆-inch-diameter holes through the planter sides into the ends of each spacer to receive dowels. Drill a pair of holes into the ends of the two bottom spacers and single holes into each of the others, as shown in the exploded-view diagram. Install a ³⁄₁₆ × 1½-inch hardwood dowel into each hole using wood glue.

7. Trim the dowel ends flush with the planter sides. Sand the planter and apply polyurethane.

8. Cut two pieces of brass-plated chain to the length needed to hang the planter at the desired height. Install a pair of brass cup hooks on each end spacer at the top of the planter, then bend the hooks around the ends of the chains. To hang the planter, install ceiling hooks, then loop the center links of the chains over the hooks.

THREE-TIERED HANGING PLANT SHELF

SHOPPING LIST

Lumber
2 pcs. $1 \times 2 \times 10'$
1 pc. $1 \times 2 \times 8'$
Plywood
1 pc. $\frac{1}{4}'' \times 3' \times 4'$ exterior grade
Hardware
2 S-hooks $2''$
6 eyescrews $\frac{3}{4}''$
4 pcs. twist-link brass machine chain
    $\frac{3}{4}'' \times 55''$
2 pcs. twist-link brass machine chain
    $\frac{3}{4}'' \times 22''$
8 copper-clad sash-chain clips $\frac{5}{8}''$ diameter
finishing nails 4d
polyurethane

This sturdy, yet lightweight, hanging planter, built by the Rodale Design Group, contains three shelves made of luan plywood and 1×2 select pine. The shelves are suspended from twist-link brass chain and are adjustable in height. Their number and size may be varied to fit the location and the type of plants being displayed. The planter is finished with several coats of polyurethane for an attractive appearance and for protection against water damage.

CONSTRUCTION

1. Cut four pieces of 1×2 ($\frac{3}{4}'' \times 1\frac{1}{2}''$) stock to 48 inches each for the side rails of the upper and lower shelves, and two pieces to 30 inches each for the side rails of the middle shelf. Also, cut six pieces of 1×2 stock to $9\frac{1}{4}$ inches each for the end rails of all three shelves.

2. Cut two pieces of $\frac{1}{4}$-inch exterior-grade plywood to $9\frac{1}{4} \times 47\frac{1}{4}$ inches each for the bottom panels of the upper and lower shelves, and one piece to $9\frac{1}{4} \times 29\frac{1}{4}$ inches for the bottom panel of the middle shelf. Drill $\frac{1}{2}$-inch-diameter holes through the four corners of the upper and middle panels to provide space for the chains. Center the holes $\frac{5}{8}$ inch from the sides of the panels and $1\frac{1}{8}$ inches from the ends. In the upper panel, also center and drill two holes $19\frac{1}{8}$ inches from one end and $\frac{5}{8}$ inch from each side.

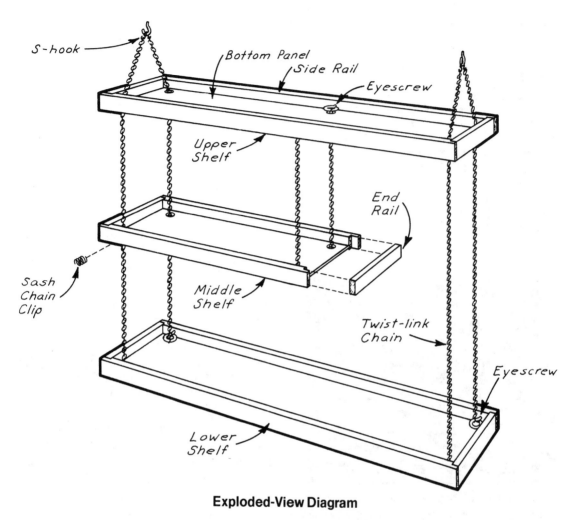

Exploded-View Diagram

3. Cut a ¼-inch-wide groove ⅜ inch deep along the inside face of all 12 rails, beginning ¼ inch above the bottom edge, to house the edges of the bottom panels, as shown in illustration A. Then cut a ¾-inch-wide rabbet ⅜ inch deep across the inside face of the ends of the side rails to accept the end rails.

4. Assemble the shelves using carpenter's wood glue and 4d finishing nails. Fit the bottom panels into the grooves in the rails, then nail the side rails to the end rails.

5. Round-over all exposed edges of each shelf, using sandpaper or a router equipped with a ¼-inch rounding-over bit. Then sand the shelves and finish them with two or more coats of polyurethane.

6. Cut two pieces of twist-link brass chain to 22 inches each. Pry open a pair of ¾-inch eyescrews and attach them through the top link of each chain. Reclose the eyes. Install the eyes (with chains attached) in the side rails of the top shelf immediately above the middle holes in the shelf's bottom panel.

LUMBER CUTTING LIST

Size	Piece	Quantity
1 × 2		
¾″ × 1½″ × 48″	Upper shelf side rails	2
¾″ × 1½″ × 48″	Lower shelf side rails	2
¾″ × 1½″ × 30″	Middle shelf side rails	2
¾″ × 1½″ × 9¼″	End rails	6
Plywood		
¼″ × 9¼″ × 47¼″	Upper shelf bottom panel	1
¼″ × 9¼″ × 47¼″	Lower shelf bottom panel	1
¼″ × 9¼″ × 29¼″	Middle shelf bottom panel	1

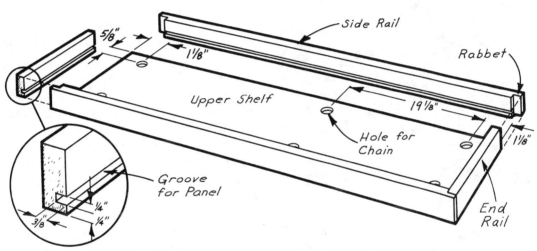

Illustration A

7. Cut four pieces of chain to 55 inches each. Attach a ¾-inch eyescrew through the bottom link of each chain, as in the previous step, then install these eyescrews into the side rails of the lower shelf, centered across the width of the shelf and 1½ inches from each end.

8. Thread the shelves onto the chains, as shown in the exploded-view diagram. Adjust the height of the middle shelf and hold it at the desired position by fastening sash-chain clips to the links immediately beneath the shelf.

9. Fasten additional clips to the chains beneath the ends of the upper shelf to hold it at the proper height. Join the upper ends of the long chains with S-hooks, as shown in the exploded-view diagram, then use those hooks to hang the planter at the desired location from eyescrews or ceiling hooks installed overhead.

HANGING PLANT WINDOW EXTENDER

SHOPPING LIST

Lumber
1 pc. $1 \times 2 \times 8'$
Dowels
2 pcs. $\frac{5}{8}'' \times 3'$ hardwood
Hardware
2 screw hooks $\frac{3}{8}''$
4 eyescrews $\frac{3}{8}''$
4 pcs. chain $\frac{1}{4}''$ (cut to fit)
brushing lacquer

This window extender resembles a horizontal ladder suspended across the top of a window frame. It allows you to hang a number of plants in front of a window to receive the light they need. Not only does this extender provide space for a large number of plants, but using it can be a beautiful and efficient way to display them as well.

The rails of the extender shown here are made of mahogany and sized to fit a 40⅝-inch-wide window. The rungs are hardwood dowels. The entire project was finished first with stain and then with two coats of clear lacquer. The extender is suspended from short chains connected to screw hooks fastened above the top of the window.

LUMBER CUTTING LIST

Size	Piece	Quantity
1 × 2		
$\frac{3}{4}'' \times 1\frac{1}{2}'' \times 40\frac{5}{8}''$	Rails	2
Dowels		
$\frac{5}{8}'' \times 8\frac{7}{8}''$	Rungs	5

CONSTRUCTION

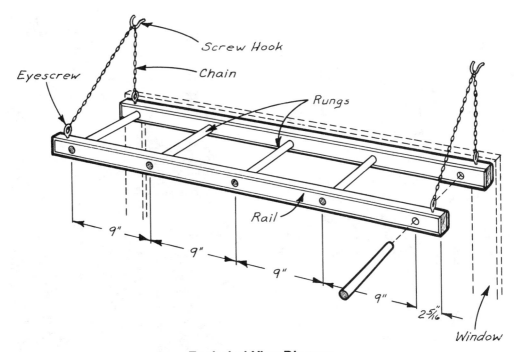

Exploded-View Diagram

1. Cut two pieces of 1×2 ($\frac{3}{4}'' \times 1\frac{1}{2}''$) stock to $40\frac{5}{8}$ inches each for the rails. Also cut five pieces of $\frac{5}{8}$-inch-diameter dowel to $8\frac{7}{8}$ inches each for the rungs.

2. Center and drill $\frac{5}{8}$-inch-diameter holes through the rails $2\frac{5}{16}$ inches from each end. Center and drill additional holes on 9-inch centers between the holes at the ends, as shown in the exploded-view diagram.

3. Rout or plane a $\frac{3}{16} \times \frac{3}{16}$-inch chamfer on all edges of the rails. Fasten the rungs into the holes in the rails using carpenter's wood glue.

4. Sand the window extender, stain it, if desired, then finish it with two coats of brushing lacquer.

5. Install two screw hooks into studs in the wall above the window. Insert $\frac{3}{8}$-inch eyescrews near the four corners of the ladder's upper surface, spaced to match the hooks. Cut four pieces of $\frac{1}{4}$-inch chain to lengths sufficient to hang the ladder the desired height above the window.

365

SLAT-STYLE WINDOW EXTENDER

If you have more sun-loving indoor plants than window space available for them, what you need is a window extender. The one shown here—created by the Rodale Design Group—not only increases the width of a windowsill but also provides a shelf as well, and rails for hanging plants from the top.

Our extender is made of mahogany and finished with clear lacquer. Though the design is simple, the appearance of the finished product is distinctive yet would be compatible with any interior decor. The plans shown are for a window measuring $34\frac{1}{2} \times 57$ inches including trim. To modify these specifications for your own use, merely alter the lengths of the pieces.

SHOPPING LIST

Lumber
2 pcs. $1 \times 2 \times 12'$
6 pcs. $1 \times 2 \times 8'$
Hardware
3 flathead wood screws #6 × 3''
40 flathead wood screws #6 × 1¼''
1 pint brushing lacquer

CONSTRUCTION

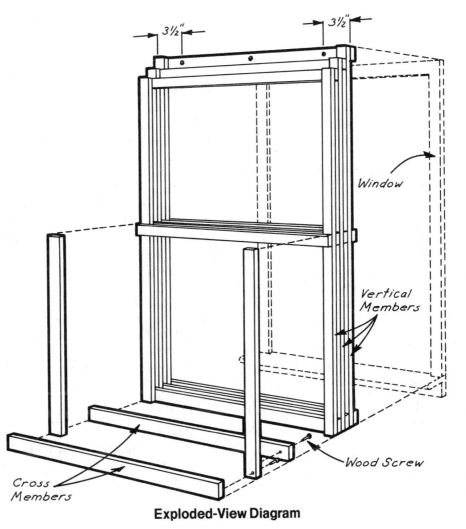

Exploded-View Diagram

1. Cut 12 pieces of 1 × 2 (¾″ × 1½″) stock to 34½ inches each for the cross members. Then cut 8 pieces of the same stock for vertical members. For these, cut 2 pieces to 57 inches each, 2 to 55½ inches each, 2 to 54 inches each, and 2 to 28⅜ inches each.

2. Rout or plane a ³⁄₁₆ × ³⁄₁₆-inch chamfer on the edges of all pieces, or round them over using a router equipped with a ¼-inch rounding-over bit. Sand the pieces smooth. Assemble the window extender one layer at a time, inserting all fasteners from the window side to minimize their visibility.

3. Start the first layer of the structure by fastening the lower ends of the two shortest

367

LUMBER CUTTING LIST

Size	Piece	Quantity
1 × 2		
¾″ × 1½″ × 57″	Vertical members	2
¾″ × 1½″ × 55½″	Vertical members	2
¾″ × 1½″ × 54″	Vertical members	2
¾″ × 1½″ × 34½″	Cross members	12
¾″ × 1½″ × 28⅜″	Vertical members	2

vertical members to the ends of a cross member. Align the ends of the cross member with the outer edges of the vertical members, and the lower ends of the vertical members with the bottom edge of the cross members, as shown in the exploded-view diagram. Drill $\frac{1}{16}$-inch pilot holes, then fasten the vertical members to the cross member using carpenter's wood glue and 1¼-inch #6 flathead wood screws. Place the screws off-center to leave room for screws in the next layer.

4. Begin the second bottom layer of the extender by fastening a cross member to the lower ends of the vertical members, offsetting the screws to avoid hitting those previously installed. Align the second cross member with the first and fasten using wood glue and 1¼-inch #6 flathead wood screws. Fasten a cross member to the upper ends of these vertical members following the same procedure.

5. Continue assembly by alternately fastening vertical members to cross members, then cross members to vertical members. Align the cross members horizontally with one another at the bottom and the middle of the structure. At the top, align the cross members with the upper ends of the vertical members, as shown in the exploded-view diagram.

6. When assembly is complete, drill and countersink three holes in the upper cross member that will fit against the head of the window. Center one hole midway along the length of the cross member and center the other two holes 3½ inches from the ends.

7. Finish the window extender with two coats of brushing lacquer, then install it in the window using 3-inch #6 flathead wood screws.

WINDOW EXTENDER WITH GLASS SHELVES

This window extender combines the beauty of natural wood with glass to create an attractive set of shelves for window plants. The shelves are removable for easy cleaning and for reaching the window. If you like, one or more of the shelves may be left out to provide room for tall plants. Hanging plants may be attached to the cross ties at the top of the extender.

The wood used in this project, which was designed by the Rodale Design Group, is mahogany. We took the shelves, made

from a piece of recycled plate glass, to a glass shop for cutting and to have the edges polished, a difficult job without sophisticated power equipment. The wooden parts of the extender are finished with an oil stain and two coats of brushing lacquer to accentuate the contrast between their grain and the glass. The plans shown here are for a window extender to fit a window measuring $34\frac{1}{2} \times 57$ inches.

SHOPPING LIST

Lumber
2 pcs. $1 \times 2 \times 12'$
Dowels
5 pcs. $\frac{5}{8}'' \times 3'$ hardwood
2 pcs. $\frac{1}{2}'' \times 3'$ hardwood
Hardware
4 pcs. glass ($\frac{1}{4}''$ thickness) $7\frac{7}{8}'' \times 34\frac{1}{2}''$
2 L-hooks $3''$ with fasteners
16 plastic shelf stops $\frac{1}{4}'' \times \frac{1}{4}''$
epoxy glue
brushing lacquer

CONSTRUCTION

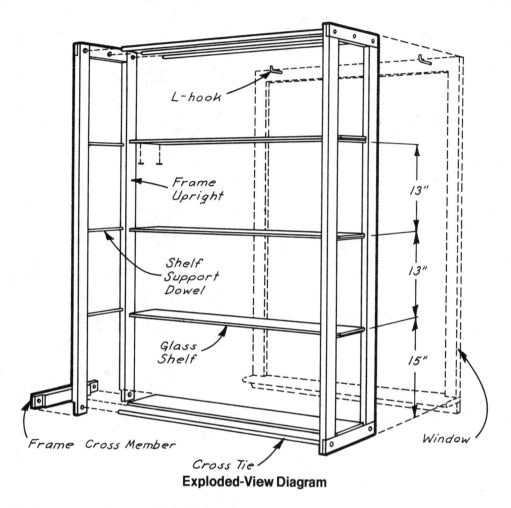

L-hook

Frame Upright

Shelf Support Dowel

Glass Shelf

Frame Cross Member

Cross Tie

13"

13"

15"

Window

Exploded-View Diagram

1. Cut four pieces of 1 × 2 (¾″ × 1½″) stock to 57 inches each for the frame uprights and four pieces to 11 inches each for the frame cross members. Cut half-lap joints on the ends of all pieces so they can be fastened together into two rectangular frame sections.

2. Drill ½-inch-diameter holes ¾ inch deep into the inside edges of the frame uprights to receive shelf support dowels. On each upright, center one hole 15 inches from the lower end and two additional holes on 13-inch centers above it, as shown in the exploded-view diagram. Chamfer the inside edges of the uprights in the areas around the holes. Complete the chamfers after the frame is assembled (see step 4).

3. Cut six pieces of ½-inch-diameter dowel to 9½ inches each for the shelf supports. Fasten the frames together using carpenter's wood glue in the half-lap and dowel joints. Clamp the frames while the glue sets.

LUMBER CUTTING LIST

Size	Piece	Quantity
1 × 2		
¾″ × 1½″ × 57″	Frame uprights	4
¾″ × 1½″ × 11″	Frame cross members	4
Dowels		
½″ × 9½″	Shelf supports	6
⅝″ × 34½″	Cross ties	5

4. Drill a ⅝-inch-diameter hole through the center of each corner of both frame sections to receive the ends of the cross ties. Center and drill an additional hole through the middle of the upper cross member on each frame section, as shown in the exploded-view diagram. Complete the chamfers on the inside edges of the frames. Chamfer the outside edges as well.

5. Cut five pieces of ⅝-inch-diameter dowel to 34½ inches each for the cross ties. Glue the ends of the cross ties into the holes drilled in the frames. Hold the completed frame square while the glue sets.

6. Sand the window extender frame, stain it, if desired, then finish it with two coats of brushing lacquer.

7. Cut or purchase four pieces of ¼-inch-thick glass, each 7⅞ × 34½ inches, for the shelves. Have the edges ground smooth. Using epoxy glue, fasten a pair of ¼ × ¼-inch plastic shelf stops on the undersides of the shelves at each end, so that they fit against the inside edges of the shelf supports and keep the shelves centered.

8. Set the window extender in position on the windowsill. Mark the top trim of the window in two places, then install 3-inch L-hooks on which to hang the extender. Fasten the extender in place, as shown in the exploded-view diagram.

FREE-STANDING WINDOW BOX AND SHELVES

SHOPPING LIST

Lumber
1 pc. $1 \times 10 \times 10'$
1 pc. $1 \times 10 \times 8'$
1 pc. $1 \times 6 \times 8'$
Plywood
1 pc. $\frac{1}{4}'' \times 4' \times 4'$ exterior grade
Hardware
finishing nails 6d
silicone caulk
polyurethane

This window box and storage unit allows you to grow house plants near a window without having to set them on a narrow sill. The shelves beneath offer space for books and other items, or for potted plants that need less direct light. Since the unit is freestanding, it is easy to relocate and need not be attached to wall or window trim.

The window box and shelves shown here were designed by the Rodale Design Group to fit a window 38 inches wide positioned 40 inches above the floor. To permit the unit to stand flush against the wall in spite of a baseboard heating element at floor level, the lower rear portion of each side piece was cut away. Before buying and cutting material to our plans, take your own measurements and adjust the specifications to fit your needs.

CONSTRUCTION

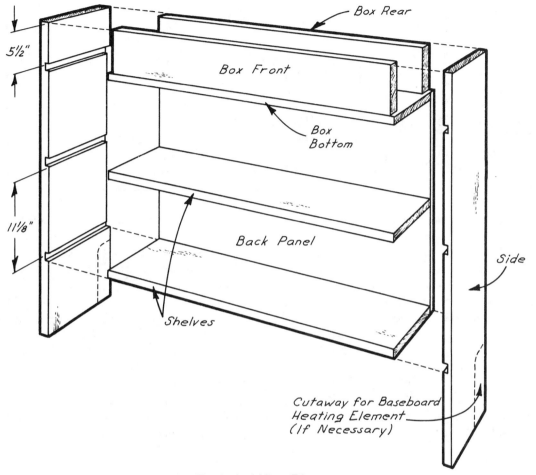

Box Rear

5½"

Box Front

Box Bottom

11⅛"

Back Panel

Side

Shelves

Cutaway for Baseboard
Heating Element
(If Necessary)

Exploded-View Diagram

1. Cut two pieces of 1×10 (¾″ × 9¼″) stock to 39¾ inches each for the sides. If necessary, cut away the lower rear portion of each piece, as shown in the exploded-view diagram, to clear floor-level obstructions such as a baseboard heating element.

2. Cut ¾-inch-wide dadoes ⅜ inch deep across the inside face of each side piece, to receive the ends of the box bottom and the two

shelves below it. Cut the first dado 5½ inches from the top of the piece, then cut the others to leave a space of 11⅛ inches between each, as shown in the exploded-view diagram. Remember to make both a right and a left piece.

3. Cut three pieces of 1×10 stock to 37¼ inches each for the box bottom and the two shelves. Trim each of the pieces to 9 inches

373

LUMBER CUTTING LIST

Size	Piece	Quantity
1 × 10		
¾″ × 9¼″ × 39¾″	Sides	2
¾″ × 9″ × 37¼″	Shelves	2
¾″ × 9″ × 37¼″	Box bottom	1
1 × 6		
¾″ × 5½″ × 36½″	Box front	1
¾″ × 5½″ × 36½″	Box rear	1
Plywood		
¼″ × 37¼″ × 30″	Back panel	1

in width. Also, cut two pieces of 1 × 6 (¾″ × 5½″) stock to 36½ inches each for the box front and rear.

4. Rabbet the rear edges of each side piece between the uppermost dado and the cutaway rear portion, to receive the back panel. Make the rabbets ¼ inch wide and ⅜ inch deep. Measure the length of the rabbets, then cut one piece of ¼-inch exterior-grade plywood to that measurement (for the model pictured here: 30 inches for the length and 37¼ inches for the width).

5. Assemble the complete unit using carpenter's wood glue and 6d finishing nails. First install the box bottom and shelves so their front edges are flush with the front of the side pieces, then install the box front and rear pieces between the sides. Finally, install the back panel.

6. Round-over all exposed edges, if desired, using sandpaper or a router equipped with a ¼-inch rounding-over bit. Fill any nail holes, then sand the entire project, and stain, if desired. Then apply three coats of polyurethane.

7. After the finish is completely dry, seal the inside edges of the window box with clear silicone caulk.

PLANT DISPLAY CART

SHOPPING LIST

Lumber
1 pc. $2 \times 2 \times 2'$
2 pcs. $1 \times 10 \times 8'$
3 pcs. $1 \times 6 \times 10'$
4 pcs. $1 \times 3 \times 10'$
Plywood
2 sheets $\frac{1}{2}'' \times 4' \times 8'$ A-C grade
Hardware
4 fluorescent light fixtures 3' or 4' with $\frac{5}{8}''$ fasteners
48 flathead wood screws #10 $\times$ $1\frac{1}{4}''$
4 stem-type casters $2\frac{1}{4}''$ with $\frac{3}{8}''$-diameter sockets
finishing nails 4d
box nails 5d
silicone caulk
polyurethane

This pine and plywood cart was built by the Rodale Design Group primarily for displaying plants; however, the fluorescent fixtures mounted beneath the upper and middle shelves do more than just add highlights—they encourage growth as well. Casters attached to the corners of the cart allow it to be easily wheeled about.

CONSTRUCTION

1. Cut four pieces of 1×6 ($\frac{3}{4}'' \times 5\frac{1}{2}''$) stock to $49\frac{1}{4}$ inches each for the upper and lower rails, and another four pieces to $24\frac{5}{8}$ inches each for the upper and lower ends.

2. Cut two pieces of 1×10 ($\frac{3}{4}'' \times 9\frac{1}{4}''$) stock to $49\frac{1}{4}$ inches each for the middle rails, and another two pieces to $24\frac{5}{8}$ inches each for the middle ends.

3. Cut a $\frac{3}{4}$-inch-wide rabbet $\frac{3}{8}$ inch deep across the inside face of both ends of each end piece to receive the ends of the rails.

4. Cut a $\frac{1}{2}$-inch-wide rabbet $\frac{3}{8}$ inch deep along one inside edge of the upper and lower rails and end pieces. Cut a groove of the same dimensions on the inside face of the middle rails and end pieces, 4 inches from

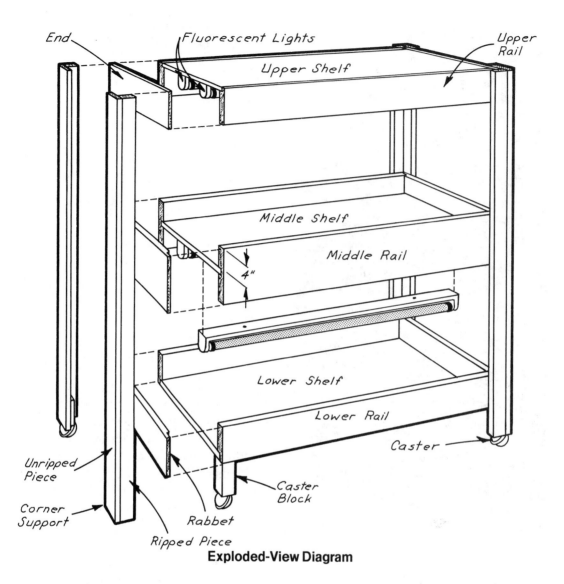

End · Fluorescent Lights · Upper Rail

Upper Shelf

Middle Shelf

Middle Rail

4"

Lower Shelf

Lower Rail

Caster

Unripped Piece

Corner Support

Caster Block

Rabbet

Ripped Piece

Exploded-View Diagram

one edge, as shown in the exploded-view diagram.

5. Cut three pieces of ½-inch A-C grade plywood to 23⅞ × 49¼ inches. Use one for the upper shelf of the cart, one for the middle shelf, and one for the lower shelf.

6. Group the rails, ends, and shelves together in three assemblies, as shown in the exploded-view diagram. Fasten the pieces

using carpenter's wood glue in all the joints, and drive 5d box nails through the end pieces into the rails.

7. If desired, round-over the edges of each assembly using sandpaper or a router equipped with a ¼-inch rounding-over bit.

8. Cut eight pieces of 1 × 3 (¾" × 2½") stock to 54 inches in length for corner supports. Rip four of the pieces to 1¾ inches

LUMBER CUTTING LIST

Size	Piece	Quantity
2 × 2		
1½″ × 1½″ × 4″	Caster blocks	4
1 × 10		
¾″ × 9¼″ × 49¼″	Middle rails	2
¾″ × 9¼″ × 24⅝″	Middle ends	2
1 × 6		
¾″ × 5½″ × 49¼″	Upper rails	2
¾″ × 5½″ × 49¼″	Lower rails	2
¾″ × 5½″ × 24⅝″	Upper ends	2
¾″ × 5½″ × 24⅝″	Lower ends	2
1 × 3		
¾″ × 2½″ × 54″	Corner support pieces	4
¾″ × 1¾″ × 54″	Corner support pieces	4
Plywood		
½″ × 23⅞″ × 49¼″	Shelves	3

in width. Fasten pairs of ripped and un-ripped pieces together, using wood glue and 4d finishing nails, to form four 2½ × 2½-inch L-shaped supports, as shown in the exploded-view diagram.

9. Cut four pieces of 2 × 2 (1½″ × 1½″) stock to 4 inches each for caster blocks. Center and drill a ⅜-inch-diameter hole 1½ inches deep into the lower end of each.

10. Round-over the edges of the four corner supports, if desired, using sandpaper or a router as in step 7. Then fasten a caster block at one end of each piece using wood glue and 4d finishing nails. Be sure to align the blocks flush with the bottom edges of the supports.

11. Set the lower shelf assembly between the corner supports, resting each corner of the unit on a caster block. Drill ⅛-inch pilot holes through the rails and ends and into the corner supports, then fasten the shelf in place using 1¼-inch #10 flathead wood screws. Next, install the upper shelf assembly in the same manner. Be sure the shelf itself is flush with the tops of the corner supports. Finally, install the middle shelf assembly as you did the other two. Locate it where desired between the upper and lower shelves, but position it so that its deeper portion is toward the bottom of the cart.

12. Sand all surfaces and apply three coats of polyurethane. When dry, seal the inside of the middle and lower shelf assemblies with silicone caulk.

13. Mount pairs of 36- or 48-inch fluorescent light fixtures beneath the upper and middle shelves using ⅝-inch sheet-metal screws as fasteners. Arrange the fixtures so that all electrical cords are at the same end of the cart.

14. Insert ⅜-inch-diameter caster sockets into the holes drilled in the caster blocks, then install 2¼-inch stem-type casters.

MOBILE HERB PLANTER

The Rodale Design Group created this mobile herb planter to make herb growing possible in all climates year-round. Consisting of three planting boxes suspended from a frame that rides on casters, this planter is equally at home in a living room

or on a patio. The planting boxes are held on the frame by a simple method that makes their removal quick and easy. Each box has notches cut in the front edge of its bottom piece and is mounted on the frame at a slightly forward tilt so that it will drain into the box immediately below it. The lowest box drains into a small aluminum pan that sits on the front cross member of the frame.

We built our mobile herb planter out of redwood, both for appearance and durability. However, while working on the project, we discovered that some of our redwood "one-by" stock was thinner than the standard ¾-inch stock. This forced us to modify some dimensions called for in our design although the plans still reflect the use of stock exactly ¾ inch thick, when specified. We recommend that you check the actual dimensions of your material before purchase and be prepared to alter the width of rabbets and mortises called for in this design if necessary to compensate for undersize stock.

Before filling your planting boxes with potting soil, line the bottom of each with approximately 1 inch of gravel to help drainage. Both your herbs and your planting boxes will be the better for it.

CONSTRUCTION

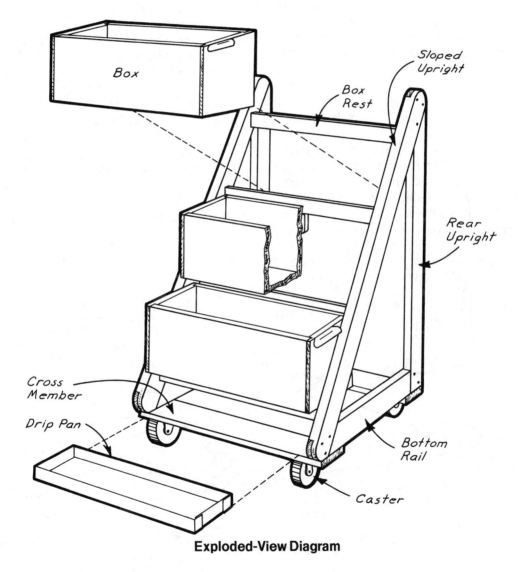

Exploded-View Diagram

1. Cut two pieces of 2 × 4 (1½″ × 3½″) stock to 58½ inches each for the sloped uprights of the planter frame. Also cut two pieces of the same material to 50¾ inches each for the rear uprights, and two pieces to 29¼ inches each for the bottom rails of the frame. Arrange the frame pieces into two triangles, one facing left and the other facing right, as in illustration A, to make a right and a left side of the frame. Lap the ends of the pieces so that the lower end of the rear upright and both ends of the sloped upright are on top in both triangles. Mark the pieces for cutting half-lap joints where they intersect.

2. Mark the center points for mortises, which will be cut later, on the inside faces of the sloped uprights, at the four locations shown in illustration A. Then cut half-lap joints on the six frame pieces and fasten them together using waterproof glue and 1¼-inch #8 aluminum flathead wood screws. Insert the screws following the pattern shown in the illustration, avoiding areas that will be trimmed away. When the glue is dry, cut a 1¾-inch radius on the tips of the two acute (less than 90 degrees) angles of each triangle, as shown in the same illustration.

3. Working from the reference points marked in the preceding step, lay out four rectangles, each ¾ × 2½ inches and tilted approximately 2 degrees forward, on the inside faces of the sloped uprights. Mortise out the area inside each rectangle to a depth of ¾ inch to receive the ends of the box rests. Then round-over the inside and outside edges of both triangular frames using a sanding block or a router equipped with a ¼-inch rounding-over bit.

4. Cut two pieces of 1 × 6 (¾″ × 5½″) stock to 26¾ inches each for cross members to connect the bottom rails of the frame. Cut two more pieces of 1 × 6 stock to 25¾ inches each, then rip them into four pieces, each 2½ inches in width, for box rests. Assemble the planter frame by inserting the ends of the box rests in the mortises cut in the sloped uprights and attaching the cross members to the undersides of the rails at the locations shown in the exploded-view diagram. Apply waterproof glue to all joints.

5. Insert a pair of 1¼-inch #8 aluminum

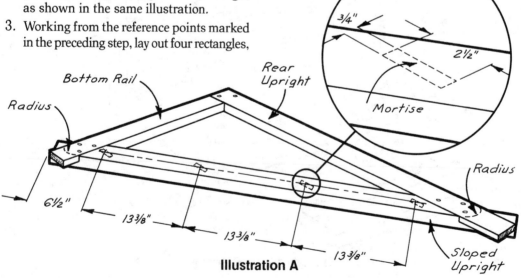

Illustration A

LUMBER CUTTING LIST

Size	Piece	Quantity
2 × 4		
1½″ × 3½″ × 58½″	Sloped uprights	2
1½″ × 3½″ × 50¾″	Rear uprights	2
1½″ × 3½″ × 29¼″	Bottom rails	2
1 × 12		
¾″ × 11¼″ × 9¼″	Box end blanks	6
¾″ × 10¼″ × 23⅜″	Box backs	3
¾″ × 1½″ × 5½″	Handles	6
1 × 10		
¾″ × 8⅝″ × 23⅜″	Box fronts	3
¾″ × 8″ × 23⅜″	Box bottoms	3
¾″ × ½″ × 23⅜″	Stops	3
¾″ × ¾″ × 3½″	Hold-in latches	3
1 × 6		
¾″ × 5½″ × 26¾″	Cross members	2
¾″ × 2½″ × 25¾″	Box rests	4

flathead wood screws into the ends of each cross member to hold them in place on the rails while the glue sets. Similarly, secure each joint of the box rest and frame by angling a pair of 1½-inch #6 aluminum flathead wood screws through the rear face of the box rest into the frame. After the frame has been assembled, mount two fixed and two swivel casters on the undersides of the cross members, as shown in the exploded-view diagram.

6. Cut three pieces of 1 × 12 (¾″ × 11¼″) stock to 23⅜ inches each for the box backs, and six pieces to 9¼ inches each for the box ends. Rip each of the back pieces to 10¼ inches in width, saving the rippings for later use. Cut each end piece to the shape and dimensions shown in illustration B. Then cut a ¾-inch-wide rabbet ⅜ inch deep along the front, back, and bottom inside edges of all the end pieces, remembering to make half of them left-end pieces and the other half right-end pieces.

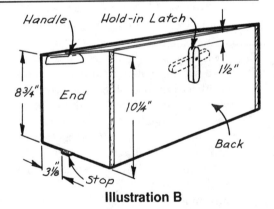

Illustration B

7. Cut six pieces of 1 × 10 (¾″ × 9¼″) stock to 23⅜ inches each for the box fronts and bottoms. Rip a ½-inch-wide strip off of three of the pieces and save for use in step 9 as stops for the bottom of the boxes. Use the 8⅝-inch-wide pieces for the box fronts. Rip the remaining three pieces to 8 inches each for use as the box bottoms.

8. Cut four notches in the front edge of each bottom piece for drainage, as shown in illustration C. Then assemble the boxes by

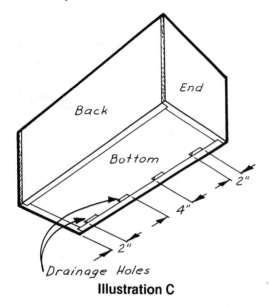

Illustration C

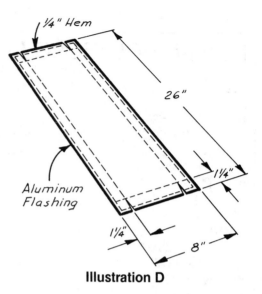

Illustration D

fitting the front, back, and bottom pieces into the rabbets cut in the end pieces. For a neat appearance, put the ripped edges of the pieces on the bottom where possible. Fasten the boxes together using waterproof glue and 5d aluminum finishing nails.

9. Cut the remaining 1 × 12 stock into six pieces, each 1½ × 5½ inches, for handles. Round-over all sharp edges on the handles and otherwise shape them for gripping. Fasten the handles just beneath the upper edges on the ends of the boxes, as shown in illustration B, using waterproof glue and 3d aluminum finishing nails. Fasten one stop (cut in step 7) to the underside of each box 3⅛ inches behind the front edge, as shown in illustration B, using waterproof glue and 3d aluminum finishing nails.

10. From other rippings cut three pieces of stock, each ¾ inch square and 3½ inches long, for the box hold-in latches. Cut a radius on both ends of all the hold-ins, then center and drill an ¹¹⁄₆₄-inch-diameter hole 1 inch from one end of each piece to accept the shank of a #8 screw. Also center and drill a ³⁄₆₄-inch-diameter pilot hole 2½ inches below the upper edge on the back of each box for attaching a hold-in latch. Fasten

the hold-ins to the boxes using 1¼-inch #8 aluminum flathead wood screws. Make each latch snug enough against its box so that it cannot move on its own, but still loose enough to be turned when necessary.

11. Round-over all sharp edges on the boxes and mount them in the frame. Hook the stop on the underside of each box behind a rest, then turn the hold-in latch to the side to allow the upper part of the box to drop flush against the front of the next rest above, as shown in the exploded-view diagram. Return the latch to the vertical position to hold the box in place.

12. Cut a piece of aluminum flashing to 8 × 26½ inches for the drip pan. Make 1¼-inch cuts 1¼ inches from each side at both ends of the flashing, as shown in illustration D. Fold a ¼-inch hem along both side edges, then bend up the sides along the line of the cuts to a 90-degree angle. Bend the tips of the sides in at a 90-degree angle and the ends up behind them. Fold a ¼-inch hem in the ends over the tips of the sides. Crimp the hems firmly flat and seal the four corners to the pan with a water-resistant sealant. Set the pan on the front cross member of the planter.

ADJUST-ABLE PLANT POLE

SHOPPING LIST

Lumber
4 pcs. 5/4 × 5/4 × 8'
1 pc. 1 × 8 × 4'
1 pc. 1 × 3 × 10'
Dowel
1 pc. ¼" × 3' hardwood
Hardware
12 flathead wood screws #6 × 1¼"
1 carriage bolt ⅜" × 4" with hex nut
1 tee nut ⅜"
6 cup hooks ⅝"
finishing nails 6d
polyurethane

This plant pole incorporates supports for both hanging and stationary potted plants into an attractive vertical column of flowers and greenery. The Rodale Design Group built the unit—which is made of No. 2 pine—to fit an 8-foot ceiling, although an adjustment screw at the bottom allows it to fit a slightly lower or higher ceiling as well. The adjustment mechanism is merely a carriage bolt inserted into a tee nut on the underside of the column. To prevent marring the floor or permanently denting a carpet, use a furniture coaster or small hollowed-out block of wood or plywood to place between the bolt head and the floor. Or, use a doubled-over scrap of carpeting.

CONSTRUCTION

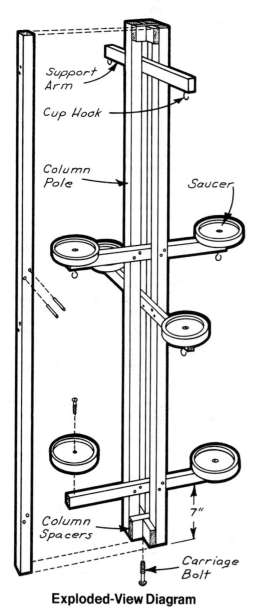

Exploded-View Diagram

1. Cut four pieces of 5/4 × 5/4 (1⅛″ × 1⅛″) stock to 94 inches each for the column poles.

2. Cut four pieces of 1 × 3 (¾″ × 2½″) stock to 27 inches each for the support arms. Rip the leftover piece into two lengths, each 1⅛ inches in width. From them cut four pieces, each 4 inches in length, for column spacers.

3. On a 48-inch length of 1 × 8 (¾″ × 7¼″) stock, lay out six circles, each 6 inches in diameter, positioned close together to save material. Cut out the circles with a band saw or saber saw. From the leftover stock, cut two blocks for column spacers, each 3 inches wide and 4 inches long.

4. Fasten the column poles together into two pairs, separating the upper and lower ends of the pieces that form each pair by a 1⅛-inch-wide spacer, as shown in the exploded-view diagram. Use carpenter's wood glue and 6d finishing nails. Then, also using glue and nails, fasten the two pairs together into a single column. Install a 3-inch-wide spacer at each end to separate the pairs, also as shown.

5. Cut 16 pieces of ¼-inch dowel to 2-inch lengths. Center the support arms between poles in the assembled column, alternating the directions of the arms, as shown in the exploded-view diagram. Locate the top and bottom arms 7 inches from each end of the column and the other arms where desired. Fasten the arms in place by drilling ¼-inch-diameter holes through the column into the arms and inserting the glue-coated dowels. Use four dowels to secure each arm.

6. Using a router, recess the centers of the circles cut in step 3 to a ¼-inch depth, leaving a ½-inch-wide rim, to form pot saucers. Center the saucers 1 inch from the ends of the lower three support arms, then fasten the saucers to the arms using wood glue and pairs of 1¼-inch #6 flathead wood screws.

7. Install ⅝-inch cup hooks into the undersides

LUMBER CUTTING LIST

Size	Piece	Quantity
5/4 × 5/4		
1⅛″ × 1⅛″ × 94″	Column poles	4
1 × 8		
¾″ × 3″ × 4″	Column spacers	2
¾″ × 6″ diameter	Pot saucers	6
1 × 3		
¾″ × 2½″ × 27″	Support arms	4
¾″ × 1⅛″ × 4″	Column spacers	4
Dowel		
¼″ × 2″	Dowels	16

of the upper three support arms—1 inch from the end of each arm—to provide hooks for hanging plants.

8. Into the underside of the wide spacer at the bottom of the column, drill a ½-inch-diameter hole 3½ inches deep. Using a hammer, install a ⅜-inch tee nut into the hole.

9. Trim any protruding dowel ends flush with the surface of the column. Sand the project smooth and, if desired, round-over all exposed edges. Finally, apply two coats of polyurethane.

10. Install a ⅜-inch hex nut onto a ⅜ × 4-inch carriage bolt, then thread the bolt into the tee nut at the base of the plant-pole column. Raise the pole vertically between the floor and ceiling, then adjust the carriage bolt, as needed, to secure the pole. Tighten the hex nut against the tee nut to lock the bolt in position.

WOOD-HEATING ACCESSORIES

AX
RACK

Finally, here is a safe, convenient, and wonderfully simple place to store axes out of harm's way. This wooden ax rack, designed by Beryl Stringer of Blodgett, Oregon, will

SHOPPING LIST
Lumber
1 pc. 2 × 4 × 8'
1 pc. 1 × 1 × 18''
Plywood
1 pc. ¾'' × 1' × 2' exterior grade
Hardware
finishing nails 8d
exterior-grade enamel (optional)
copper naphthenate wood preservative

save you hours you might otherwise spend resharpening nicked or dull ax blades and, more importantly, may even save you or someone else from serious injury.

The rack is really a series of compartments, each designed to house one ax. The sides of each compartment act as dividers, separating the blades of axes stored side by side. Beryl built the rack pictured here to store three axes. It is a simple matter to revise the design so the rack holds more, or fewer. You might want to add an extra compartment or two to hold accessories as well, such as sharpening stones or gloves. Any lumber can be used. Beryl chose common construction-grade 2 × 4s and a base of ¾-inch plywood. Sealing the wood with preservative after the project is finished is a good idea. Better yet, paint the rack with bright red enamel or some other highly visible color.

CONSTRUCTION

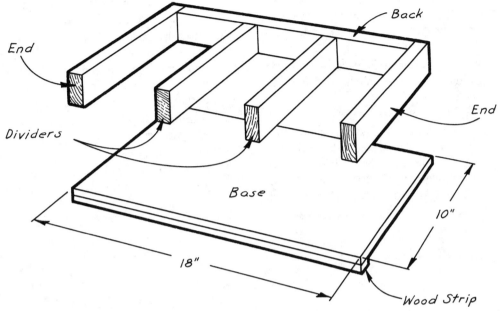

Exploded-View Diagram

1. Cut two pieces of 2×4 ($1\frac{1}{2}'' \times 3\frac{1}{2}''$) stock to 10 inches each for the ends of the rack. Also cut two pieces of 2×4 stock to $8\frac{1}{2}$ inches each for the dividers, and one piece of 2×4 stock to 15 inches for the back.

2. Cut one piece of $\frac{3}{4}$-inch exterior-grade plywood to 10×18 inches for the base.

3. Cut one piece of 1×1 ($\frac{3}{4}'' \times \frac{3}{4}''$) stock to 18 inches for the strip of wood, attached underneath the front of the rack, which tilts the rack toward the rear, as shown in the photo.

4. Nail the two ends to the back using 8d finishing nails.

LUMBER CUTTING LIST

Size	Piece	Quantity
2 × 4		
$1\frac{1}{2}'' \times 3\frac{1}{2}'' \times 15''$	Back	1
$1\frac{1}{2}'' \times 3\frac{1}{2}'' \times 10''$	Ends	2
$1\frac{1}{2}'' \times 3\frac{1}{2}'' \times 8\frac{1}{2}''$	Dividers	2
1 × 1		
$\frac{3}{4}'' \times \frac{3}{4}'' \times 18''$	Wood strip	1
Plywood		
$\frac{3}{4}'' \times 10'' \times 18''$	Base	1

5. Place the ends and back on the plywood base and nail them in place with 8d nails. Sink the nail heads into the plywood so they won't come in contact with the ax blades later on.

6. Nail the wood strip in place with 8d nails, again sinking the nail heads below the wood.

7. Now choose three axes and position them on the rack. Set the first ax against one of the ends so the blade faces the back of the rack. Position a divider against the blade, perpendicular to the back, and mark the position of the divider. Then remove the ax, turn the rack over, and nail the divider in place by driving the nails through the base, upward into the divider.

8. Turn the rack right side up again, and place the second ax in place. Set another divider against the second blade and mark its position, then turn the rack over again to nail the second divider in place.

9. A third ax should slip easily into the third compartment.

10. Apply copper naphthenate wood preservative or exterior-grade enamel to the ax rack to complete the project.

WOOD-CUTTER'S TOTE

This tote makes it easy for you to carry all the little odds and ends you need while cutting and splitting firewood: small tools, gasoline, bar oil, and extra chain for your saw; and wedges and a maul for splitting. Your maul—slipped through a hole at each end of the tote—serves as the tote's handle. The maul's head fits securely in the built-in compartment, outboard of the tote's tray.

The tote is designed with perforated hardboard and dowels forming its base, to keep chips and sawdust from collecting on the bottom. It's a good idea to paint the finished product with several coats of durable, brightly colored enamel to keep it from hiding itself in the brush.

This project is not meant to be of a fixed size. You'll find it more satisfactory if you first arrange all the items you'll need to put in it—particularly the maul—and then cut the pieces to produce a tote that suits your individual needs. Refer to the lumber cutting list for the dimensions of the tote shown here.

SHOPPING LIST

Lumber
1 pc. $1 \times 6 \times 6'$
Plywood
1 pc. $\frac{3}{4}'' \times 2' \times 4'$ exterior grade
Perforated Hardboard
1 pc. $\frac{1}{4}'' \times 2' \times 2'$
Dowels
2 pcs. $\frac{1}{2}'' \times 3'$ hardwood
Hardware
galvanized common nails 5d
waterproof glue
exterior-grade enamel

CONSTRUCTION

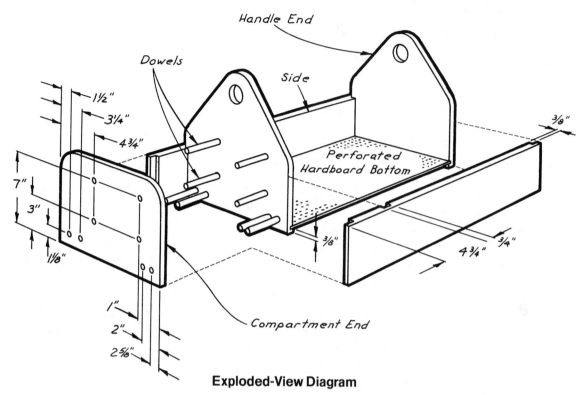

Handle End

Dowels

Side

Perforated
Hardboard Bottom

1½"

3¼"

4¾"

7"

3"

1⅛"

⅜"

⅜"

¾"

4¾"

1"

2"

2⅝"

Compartment End

Exploded-View Diagram

1. Lay out and cut two pieces of ¾-inch exterior-grade plywood for the handle ends, as shown in the cutting diagram. Note: Depending on the size of the maul you will use for the handle, the height of the handle ends may need to be greater than that shown.

2. Cut one piece of ¾-inch plywood to 12¾ × 8¾ inches for the compartment end. Round off the top corners of the piece to suit, or to a 2½-inch radius, as shown in the cutting diagram.

3. Clamp the compartment end face-to-face with one of the handle ends so the bottom edges of each are flush. Then drill eight holes, each ½ inch in diameter, through both pieces to accept the dowels that form the compartment bottom and partitions,

as shown in the exploded-view diagram.

4. Now clamp the handle ends together and drill a hole through both pieces to accept the maul handle you will use to carry the tote. Depending on the diameter of your maul handle, you may have to make the hole larger than that shown. If you lack a drill bit that is large enough, drill two holes side by side, then remove the waste between them with a saber saw, and smooth the opening with a rasp and file.

5. Cut two pieces of 1 × 6 (¾" × 5½") stock to 26¾ inches each for the sides of the tote.

6. Rabbet the ends of each side piece ⅜ inch deep and ¾ inch wide to accept one of the handle ends and the compartment end.

LUMBER CUTTING LIST

Size	Piece	Quantity
1 × 6		
¾'' × 5½'' × 26¾''	Sides	2
Plywood		
¾'' × 12¾'' × 14'' (approx.)	Handle ends	2
¾'' × 12¾'' × 8¾''	Compartment end	1
Perforated Hardboard		
¼'' × 12¾'' × 21¼''	Bottom	1
Dowels		
½'' × 5½''	Dividers	8

7. Cut a dado ⅜ inch deep and ¾ inch wide in each side piece, 4¾ inches from one end, to accept the remaining handle end.

8. Cut a dado ⅜ inch deep and ¼ inch wide along the bottom of each handle end to accept the bottom. Set the dado in ⅜ inch from the bottom edge of each piece.

9. Cut one piece of ¼-inch perforated hardboard to 12¾ × 21¼ inches for the bottom.

10. Assemble the tote—except for the dowels—using waterproof glue and 5d galvanized common nails.

11. Cut eight pieces of ½-inch-diameter dowel to 5½ inches each for the compartment bottom and dividers.

12. Install the dowels and glue them in place.

13. Sand the tote thoroughly, then paint with a bright color of exterior-grade enamel.

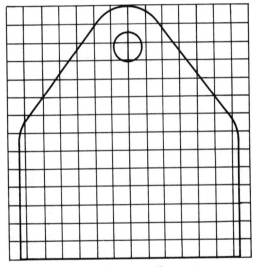

Each Square Equals 1''
Cutting Diagram

WOOD HARVES- TER

SHOPPING LIST

Lumber
2 pcs. $2 \times 4 \times 10'$
7 pcs. $2 \times 3 \times 8'$
4 pcs. $2 \times 2 \times 10'$
1 pc. $1 \times 6 \times 8'$
Plywood
2 sheets $\frac{3}{8}'' \times 4' \times 8'$ exterior grade
Hardware
20 lag bolts $\frac{3}{8}'' \times 4''$
2 lag bolts $\frac{3}{8}'' \times 3''$
22 flat washers $\frac{3}{8}''$
1 pound galvanized common nails 12d
1 pound galvanized common nails 6d

With Don Campbell's firewood harvester—actually just a well-thought-out sawing jig mounted on a pair of sturdy skids—it's a simple task to cut small-diameter logs and tree trimmings into usable firewood of uniform length. Campbell, who lives in Wentworth, New Hampshire, uses the harvester primarily on his woodlot, but it might just as well be situated near a woodpile, behind an outbuilding, or in a corner of the yard.

Campbell built the harvester pictured in the photograph from rough-sawn lumber that he milled himself from logs. Ordinary lumberyard stock works just as well of course, and since it is readily available, its use is specified in the construction steps that follow. After the photograph was taken, Campbell added plywood safety shields to the side of the jig where the operator stands. The shields keep small logs and fragments caught by the chain saw from flying out. Safety shields for the harvester are shown in the exploded-view diagram and illustrations, and construction details are also given.

To design your own harvester, first determine the length to which you wish to cut the logs. Campbell uses 22-inch lengths. Place the uprights of the jig, which not only hold the stack of uncut wood in place but also act as cutting guides, across the skids according to this predetermined interval.

Also measure the length of your chain-saw bar. Make the overall width of the harvester 2 inches less than this figure. (Since Campbell's bar measures 20 inches, his harvester is 18 inches wide.)

Using the harvester is easy. Merely fill the jig with wood, piling it so the ends are flush with the tips of the skids at one end. Stop when the pile nears the top of the jig. Fire up your chain saw, then insert the blade successively in each gap between an upright and a safety shield, and slice straight down through the pile to produce the logs.

CONSTRUCTION

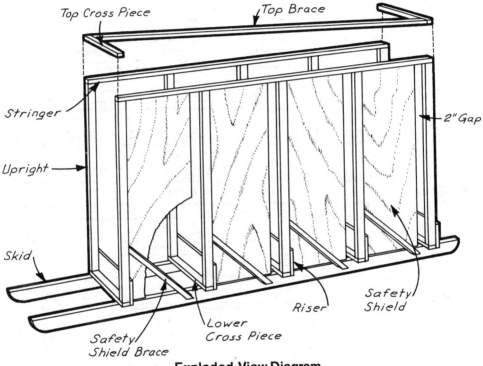

Exploded-View Diagram

1. Cut 10 pieces of 2×3 ($1\frac{1}{2}'' \times 2\frac{1}{2}''$) to 45 inches each for the uprights. Cut 5 additional pieces to 18 inches each (or the length of your chain saw minus 2 inches) for the lower cross pieces. Follow the cutting diagram to get the most from the lumber specified in the shopping list.

2. Build five U-shaped assemblies using the cross pieces and uprights, as shown in the exploded-view diagram. To make each assembly, butt a cross piece across the ends of two uprights, keeping their ends and edges flush. Drill a ¼-inch-diameter pilot hole through each end of the cross

395

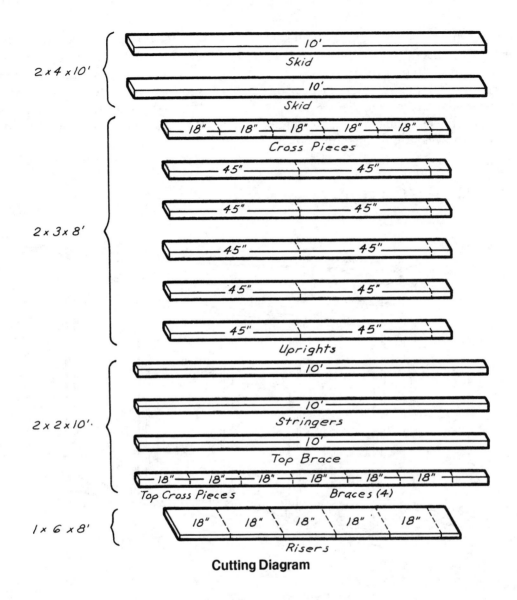

2 x 4 x 10' { 10'
Skid

10'
Skid

2 x 3 x 8' { 18" 18" 18" 18" 18"
Cross Pieces

45" 45"

45" 45"

45" 45"

45" 45"

45" 45"
Uprights

2 x 2 x 10' { 10'

10'
Stringers

10'
Top Brace

18" 18" 18" 18" 18" 18"
Top Cross Pieces   Braces (4)

1 x 6 x 8' { 18" 18" 18" 18" 18"
Risers

Cutting Diagram

piece into the end grain of the mating upright, then fasten the pieces using ⅜ × 4-inch lag bolts fitted with washers.

3. Use two pieces of 2 × 4 (1½″ × 3½″) stock, each 120 inches in length, for the skids. Round the bottom edges of each skid to a gentle lengthwise curve about 8 inches long so they will pull easily across the ground.

4. Place the skids together face-to-face and mark their top edges at intervals according to the lengths into which you wish to cut logs placed in the harvester.

5. Set the skids approximately 15 inches apart, then position an upright assembly across them so the ends of the cross piece overlap the skids evenly on each side, and so the

LUMBER CUTTING LIST

Size	Piece	Quantity
2 × 4		
1½″ × 3½″ × 120″	Skids	2
2 × 3		
1½″ × 2½″ × 45″	Uprights	10
1½″ × 2½″ × 18″ (or to suit; see step 1)	Lower cross pieces	5
2 × 2		
1½″ × 1½″ × 120″ (or to suit; see step 6)	Stringers	2
1½″ × 1½″ × 120″	Diagonal brace	1
1½″ × 1½″ × 18″ (or to suit; see step 7)	Top cross pieces	2
1½″ × 1½″ × 18″	Safety shield braces	4
1 × 6		
¾″ × 5¼″ × 18″ (or to suit; see step 9)	Risers	5
Plywood		
⅜″ × 23″ × 48″ (or to suit; see step 10)	Safety shields	4

outside face of each skid is in line with the inside face of each upright, as shown in illustration A. Locate the uprights just to the right of the marks on the top edges of the skids. Drill a ¼-inch pilot hole through each end of the cross piece into the skid below and fasten the pieces with ⅜ × 4-inch lag bolts fitted with washers. Repeat the procedure to fasten the remaining upright assemblies.

6. Cut two pieces of 2 × 2 (1½″ × 1½″) stock to a length that equals the distance between and including the upright assemblies farthest apart, as shown in the exploded-view diagram. Nail the stringers across the ends of the uprights, making sure the uprights remain square to the skids. Use 12d galvanized common nails.

7. Cut two pieces of 2 × 2 stock, each to the same length as the lower cross pieces cut in step 1, for the top cross pieces. Fasten these, as shown in the exploded-view diagram, directly above the two outside upright assemblies, at right angles to the stringers.

8. Fit a 120-inch length of 2 × 2 stock diagonally across the top stringers to serve as the top brace. To fit the brace, lay it across the stringers, scribe the ends to meet the top cross pieces and/or to lie flush with the outside edges of the stringers. Then trim the ends to the scribed lines. Drill a ¼-inch-diameter pilot hole at each end of the brace into the stringer below, then fasten the brace in place using ⅜ × 3-inch lag bolts fitted with washers.

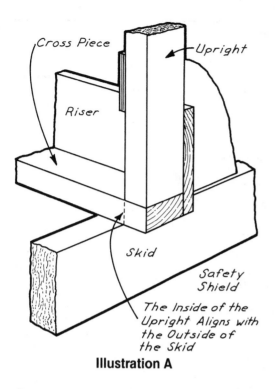

Illustration A

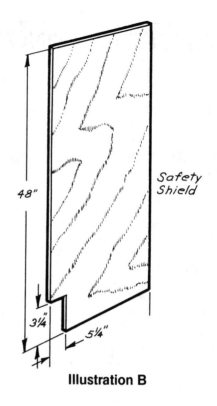

Illustration B

9. Cut five pieces of 1 × 6 (¾″ × 5¼″) stock each to the width of the cross pieces, for the risers. Place these on edge across the tops of the skids, flush against the uprights and cross pieces, as shown in the exploded-view diagram. Fasten the risers in place using 6d galvanized common nails.

10. Cut four panels of ⅜-inch exterior-grade plywood for safety shields. Each panel should be 48 inches in length and as wide as the log-length interval marked on the skids (see step 4) minus 3 inches. Notch one corner of each panel, as shown in illustration B, so that when the panels are in place, they will fit over the risers.

11. Attach the safety shields along one side of the harvester framework. Slide them into

place against the inside faces of the uprights— flush with the left edge of each— and against the stringer even with the top. Between panels there should be a 2-inch-wide vertical gap immediately to the left of each upright. Fasten the panels in place using 6d galvanized common nails.

12. Cut four pieces of 2 × 2 stock to 18 inches each for the safety shield braces. Miter the ends of each brace to a 45-degree angle, then fasten them in place against the riser-side edges of the uprights and the top of the skid. Use 12d galvanized common nails. Nail the lower portions of the shields to the braces using 6d nails.

FIVE-BAY SAWBUCK

Here is a nice-looking and very sturdy jig for cutting small-diameter branches into uniform stove-wood lengths. Its unusual name derives from the five spaces between the pairs of upright cutting guides that make up the jig's major assembly. The entire device was designed and built by Charles Con-

SHOPPING LIST

Lumber
1 pc. 2 × 10 × 8′
2 pcs. 2 × 6 × 10′
5 pcs. 2 × 4 × 8′
Hardware
20 lag bolts ¼″ × 3½″
40 carriage bolts ¼″ × 3″
40 nuts ¼″
60 flat washers ¼″

stantinides of Hornby Island, British Columbia, Canada.

Constantinides chose intervals of 16½ inches for the bays, because this was an appropriate length for wood to fit his stove. Intervals of any length can be achieved merely by altering the positions of the cutting guides along the rail. Constantinides also points out that the width of the cutting guides should not exceed the length of your chain-saw bar.

The sawbuck may be mounted on sawhorses or on commercially available adjustable-leg supports, as shown in the photograph. To use the sawbuck, gather branches and stack them between the uprights of the guides. Saw through the pile, directing the saw down between each closely spaced pair of guides and also at each end of the jig itself. Then tie each uniform stack of stove-wood pieces together with twine for easy carrying.

CONSTRUCTION

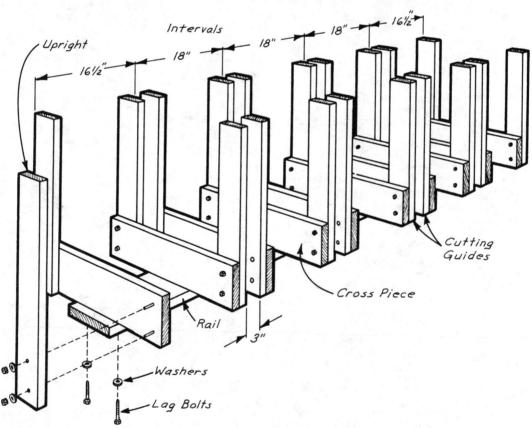

Exploded-View Diagram

1. Cut 10 pieces of 2 × 6 (1½″ × 5½″) stock to 21 inches each for the guide cross pieces.

2. Cut 20 pieces of 2 × 4 (1½″ × 3½″) stock to 22 inches each for the guide uprights.

3. Drill two 1-inch-diameter holes ¾ inch deep in the ends of the uprights, as shown in illustration A. Then drill ¼-inch-diameter holes through their centers to produce counterbored holes that will accept the fastening bolts (see step 4).

4. To assemble the guides, position the uprights square to and flush with the ends of the cross pieces, as shown in the exploded-view-diagram. Drill ¼-inch-diameter holes through the cross pieces using the holes in the uprights as guides. Insert and tighten ¼ × 3-inch carriage bolts fitted with ¼-inch flat washers and nuts in the holes, so the heads of the bolts are recessed in the counterbored holes.

5. Cut one piece of 2 × 10 (1½″ × 9¼″) stock to 87 inches for the rail.

6. Mark off interval positions on the rail, as shown in the exploded-view diagram, to position the guides.

7. Fasten the 10 guides to the rail as follows: Center the guides across the rail on the interval marks, making certain the cross pieces face correctly. Drill two 3/16-inch-diameter holes through the rail and into each cross piece. Separate the pieces, then

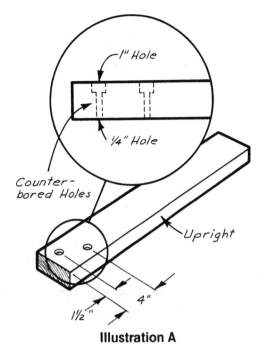

Illustration A

using the started holes as guides, deepen the holes in the cross pieces. Redrill the holes in the rail, enlarging them to ¼-inch diameter. Finally, realign the pieces and install ¼ × 3½-inch lag bolts fitted with ¼-inch flat washers into the holes to fasten the guides to the rail.

8. Fasten the completed sawbuck to a set of sturdy sawhorses using large C-clamps, or to an adjustable-leg assembly using lag bolts.

LUMBER CUTTING LIST

Size	Piece	Quantity
2 × 10		
1½″ × 9¼″ × 87″	Rail	1
2 × 6		
1½″ × 5½″ × 21″	Cross pieces	10
2 × 4		
1½″ × 3½″ × 22″	Uprights	20

FIREWOOD CUTTING JIG

SHOPPING LIST

Lumber
1 pc. 2 × 6 × 8'
2 pcs. 2 × 4 × 8'
1 pc. 1 × 4 × 10'
1 pc. 1 × 4 × 8'
Hardware
12 flathead wood screws #8 × 1½''
6 lag bolts ¼'' × 3''
8 lag bolts ¼'' × 2''
14 flat washers ¼''
2 loose pin hinges 3'' × 3''
1 pound galvanized common nails 8d

This firewood cutting jig, designed by Paul Poresky of Myrtle Point, Oregon, is easy and inexpensive to build and makes short work of bucking small-diameter logs and tree branches into usable lengths just right for the stove. Basically two log rails connected by cross pieces, with a few added uprights, the jig sets up across two sawhorses and functions like a carpenter's miter box.

The logs are held in place against the uprights while the cross pieces act as guides for the saw blade. The cross pieces are spaced at

equal intervals to produce logs of uniform length. Poresky's jig cuts logs into 18-inch segments. You can easily alter the plans to make a jig that suits your individual requirements.

A feature of this jig is that the base is hinged, allowing you to quickly dump freshly cut logs onto the ground in front of the sawhorses. This lets you load the jig, cut, and reload again all in a matter of seconds. Poresky sets the jig next to a pile of uncut logs and works until he has accumulated a pile of cut logs in front of him that nearly equals the height of the jig. Then he moves

the jig around to another side of the pile of uncut logs and builds a second jig-high pile, and so on. When finished, Poresky lets the cut logs dry in the loose heaps where they fell. He says they dry faster and that when it comes time to stack them, they weigh less than when freshly cut.

You may build the jig from scrap or slab lumber, or purchase low-grade construction stock. When the jig becomes worn and nicked from the chain saw, remove the lag bolts and hinges and build a new one. Convert the old jig to firewood.

CONSTRUCTION

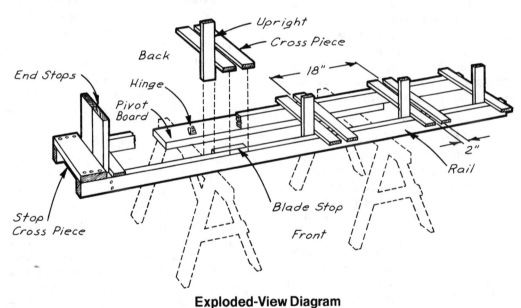

Exploded-View Diagram

1. Cut two pieces of 2×4 ($1\frac{1}{2}'' \times 3\frac{1}{2}''$) stock to 80 inches each for the rails of the jig. Hold these pieces together face-to-face with their ends flush, then mark across their edges the positions of the stop cross piece and end stops, as shown in the exploded-view diagram. Divide the remaining length of the rails into 18-inch intervals, also as shown. (The last mark should fall 1 inch short of the ends opposite those from which

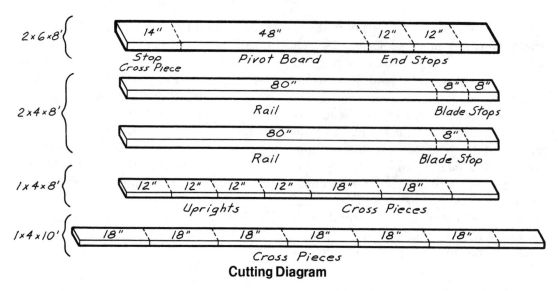

Cutting Diagram

you began measuring.)

2. Cut one piece of 2×6 ($1\frac{1}{2}'' \times 5\frac{1}{2}''$) stock to 14 inches for the stop cross piece. Separate the rails and place the cross piece in position across their edges at the ends marked for them. Be sure the edges and ends of all pieces are flush, then fasten the cross pieces to the rails using 8d galvanized common nails.

3. Cut two pieces of 2×6 to 12 inches each for the end stops. Position them against the inside edge of the stop cross piece, as shown in the exploded-view diagram, then drill two $\frac{3}{16}$-inch-diameter pilot holes through each stop and into the cross piece. Fasten the end stops to the cross piece using $\frac{1}{4} \times 3$-inch lag bolts fitted with $\frac{3}{8}$-inch washers. When finished, drill one additional pilot hole through the outer face of each rail and into the edge of the end stop nearest it. Install a third $\frac{1}{4} \times 3$-inch lag bolt and washer into each end stop to prevent further movement.

4. Cut eight pieces of 1×4 ($\frac{3}{4}'' \times 3\frac{1}{2}''$) stock to 18 inches each for the cross pieces. Since these serve as cutting guides for the saw,

position them across the rails in pairs, centered along each 18-inch interval mark. Separate the cross pieces so each lies 1 inch from a mark. Align their ends so they overlap each rail by 2 inches, then fasten them in place using 8d galvanized common nails. Locate the nails away from the 2-inch space between the boards to minimize the chances of their being struck by a saw blade.

5. Next, cut four pieces of 1×4 to 12 inches each for the uprights. These keep the logs from rolling off the jig while being cut. Position the uprights as shown in the exploded-view diagram (against the front rail and to the left of each pair of cross pieces when the end stops are also to the left), and hold each in place with its lower end flush with the rail's bottom inside edge. Drill two $\frac{3}{16}$-inch pilot holes through each upright and into the rail, locating the holes as shown in illustration A, then fasten the upright to the rail using $\frac{1}{4} \times 2$-inch lag bolts fitted with $\frac{3}{8}$-inch washers.

6. Cut three pieces of 2×4 to 8 inches each for the blade stops, which are attached to the front rail under the cross pieces. (Use

LUMBER CUTTING LIST

Size	Piece	Quantity
2 × 6		
1½″ × 5½″ × 48″	Pivot board	1
1½″ × 5½″ × 14″	Stop cross piece	1
1½″ × 5½″ × 12″	End stops	2
2 × 4		
1½″ × 3½″ × 80″	Rails	2
1½″ × 3½″ × 8″	Blade stops	3
1 × 4		
¾″ × 3½″ × 18″	Cross pieces	8
¾″ × 3½″ × 12″	Uprights	4

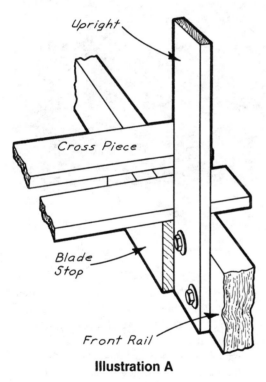

Illustration A

face of the front rail, then position the blade stops along the inside edge so they will lie underneath the cross pieces, as shown in illustration A. Nail the stops to the rail using 8d galvanized common nails. Locate the nails away from the opening between the members of each pair of cross pieces to keep them out of the path of the saw blade.

7. Cut one piece of 2 × 6 to approximately 48 inches for the pivot board. (Use the remaining 2 × 6 stock for this piece.) Center the board along the rear rail of the jig, slipping it underneath so the rail rests on the pivot board, flush with the board's inside edge. Fasten the pivot board to the rail using two 3-inch loose pin hinges and 1½-inch #8 flathead wood screws. (Drill 3/32-inch-diameter pilot holes for the screws.)

8. The jig is now ready for use. Clamp or nail it across a pair of sturdy sawhorses. Place a log against the uprights and slide it so that one end contacts the end stops. Stand by the front rail and saw through the log at 18-inch intervals, using the cross pieces as your guide, then lift the entire jig up and away from you to dump the sections onto the ground.

the remaining 2 × 4 stock for these pieces.) These extend the life of the jig by preventing the front rail from being quickly sawn through. Tip the jig so it rests on the outside

405

WOOD VAULT STAIRS

SHOPPING LIST

Lumber
6 pcs. $2 \times 10 \times 8'$
Hardware
lag bolts $\frac{1}{4}'' \times 6''$ (4 per tread)
flat washers $\frac{1}{4}''$ (4 per tread)
exterior-grade enamel

Robert Martin of Bayport, New York, heats his home with a basement wood furnace. For convenience, he stores firewood in the outside basement entrance, greatly enlarging its capacity by using the removable stairs shown here. With the stairs out, the vaultlike storage area holds more than a cord of wood. When the heating season ends, he returns the entrance to normal use by putting the stairs back in position.

You will have to measure the dimensions of your basement entrance in order to determine the lumber sizes and specifications necessary to build this project. Use the dimensions shown on these plans as a guide only.

CONSTRUCTION

1. Cut two pieces of 2×10 ($1\frac{1}{2}'' \times 9\frac{1}{4}''$) stock to $90\frac{1}{2}$ inches each for the stair carriages. Lay out and cut the angles on the ends of the carriages so that they will fit inside the vault, as shown in illustration A.
2. Lay out the locations of the treads, as shown in illustration A. Cut $1\frac{1}{2}$-inch-wide dadoes $\frac{3}{4}$ inch deep in the carriages to accept the treads.
3. Cut six pieces of 2×10 stock to 40 inches each for the treads.

4. Set one of the two carriages on edge. Position a tread in the first dado. Drill two $\frac{3}{16}$-inch-diameter holes through the carriage and into the end of the tread, then enlarge the holes in the carriage to $\frac{1}{4}$-inch diameter. Install $\frac{1}{4} \times 6$-inch lag bolts fitted with $\frac{1}{4}$-inch flat washers in the holes to secure the tread to the carriage. Fasten the remaining treads to the carriage following the same procedure.

5. Fasten the second carriage to the ends of the treads using $\frac{1}{4} \times 6$-inch lag bolts fitted

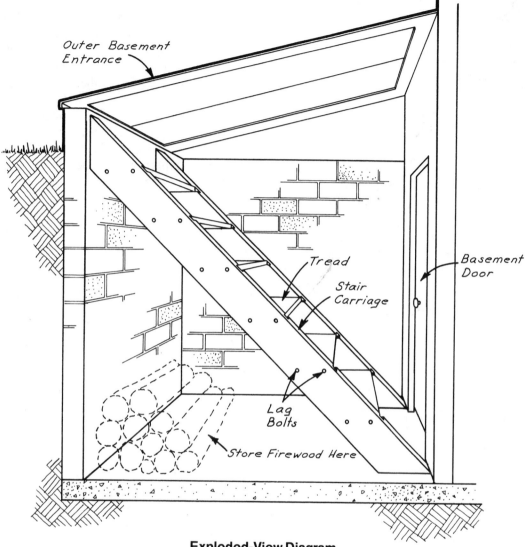

Exploded-View Diagram

LUMBER CUTTING LIST

Size	Piece	Quantity
2 × 10		
1½″ × 9¼″ × 90½″	Stair carriages	2
1½″ × 9¼″ × 40″	Treads	6

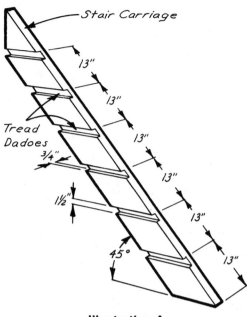

Stair Carriage

13"

13"

13"

Tread
Dadoes

3/4"

13"

1½"

13"

45°

13"

Illustration A

with ¼-inch flat washers. Follow the same procedures described in the previous step.

6. Install the steps in the basement entrance so that the bottom of the carriages rests squarely on the vault floor. Make adjustments, if necessary, so that the carriages do not protrude above the walls.

7. Remove the steps from the vault and paint them. If the lumber is not already pressure-treated, you might want to treat it with copper naphthenate wood preservative before painting.

FIREWOOD CHUTE

This firewood chute is an efficient and simple solution to getting firewood into the basement easily. Pam and Dick Driscoll of Danville, Pennsylvania, developed it to aid arthritis patients (Pam is a nurse). Actually the chute is a great work-saver for anyone, since the chute greatly reduces the amount of lifting and walking usually associated with burning wood.

The firewood chute is supposed to fit into an existing basement window. Though the plans here show a 4×18-inch chute, you'll need to size the unit you build to fit your window. Some modifications to the window itself — such as removing a grill or fixed windowpane — may also be necessary. When finished, installing a lock on the inside of the sliding door will restore security to the basement.

SHOPPING LIST

Lumber
1 pc. $2 \times 2 \times 8'$
2 pcs. $1 \times 2 \times 8'$
Plywood
1 pc. $\frac{3}{4}'' \times 2' \times 8'$ exterior grade
Hardware
1 pc. sheet metal $18'' \times 61\frac{1}{2}''$
18 flathead wood screws #8 $\times 1\frac{1}{2}''$
2 carriage bolts $\frac{3}{8}'' \times 2\frac{1}{2}''$ with nuts
2 flat washers $\frac{3}{8}''$
1 hook-and-eye fastener $2''$
7 masonry anchors $\frac{3}{8}''$
$\frac{1}{4}$ pound cement-coated nails 6d

CONSTRUCTION

1. Cut two pieces of $\frac{3}{4}$-inch exterior-grade plywood to 4×60 inches each for the sides of the chute. Cut one additional piece to 18×60 inches for the bottom. (Most likely you will have to modify the bottom further to fit the width of your window. To do this, trim the bottom 2 inches narrower than the window width.)

2. Fasten the side pieces to the edges of the bottom panel with 6d cement-coated nails.
3. Cut two pieces of 2×2 ($1\frac{1}{2}'' \times 1\frac{1}{2}''$) stock to 36 inches each for the support legs. Drill $\frac{3}{8}$-inch-diameter holes through the support legs, centered 2 inches from one end, then drill holes through the side pieces 4 inches from one end and 2 inches from each edge.

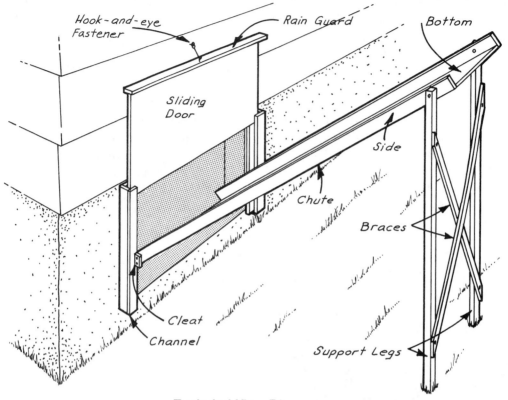

Hook-and-eye Fastener

Rain Guard

Bottom

Sliding Door

Side

Chute

Braces

Cleat

Channel

Support Legs

Exploded-View Diagram

4. Fasten each support leg to the chute with one ⅜ × 2½-inch carriage bolt fitted with a washer and nut.

5. Cut two pieces of 1 × 2 (¾″ × 1½″) stock to 30 inches each for diagonal braces. Fasten these crisscross fashion on the support legs, as shown in the exploded-view diagram, using 1½-inch #8 flathead wood screws. To do this, drill ⅛-inch-diameter pilot holes in the support legs and ¼-inch-diameter shank holes in the braces, then install the screws. Push the second brace against the support legs, bending it slightly over the first brace to get it in place. Trim the ends flush with the support legs.

6. Cut six pieces of 1 × 2 stock to 14 inches each for the channel backs, sides, and fronts.

7. Fasten two of the pieces cut in step 6 vertically alongside the basement window. To do this, first drill three ¼-inch-diameter holes evenly spaced through the pieces. Position the pieces vertically alongside the basement window, mark the hole locations on the foundation, and pull the pieces away. Drill ⅜-inch-diameter holes on the marks, and push in ⅜-inch masonry anchors. Then fasten the 1 × 2s to the foundation with 1½-inch #8 flathead wood screws. These 1 × 2s are the back pieces in the exploded-view diagram.

LUMBER CUTTING LIST

Size	Piece	Quantity
2 × 2		
1½″ × 1½″ × 36″	Support legs	2
1 × 2		
¾″ × 1½″ × 30″	Diagonal braces	2
¾″ × 1½″ × 24″	Rain guard	1
¾″ × 1½″ × 14″	Channel backs	2
¾″ × 1½″ × 14″	Channel sides	2
¾″ × 1½″ × 14″	Channel fronts	2
¾″ × 1½″ × 3½″	Cleats	2
Plywood		
¾″ × 18″ × 60″	Chute bottom	1
¾″ × 4″ × 60″	Chute sides	2
¾″ × 14″ × 22¾″	Sliding door	1

8. Fasten 1 × 2 side pieces (also cut in step 6) to the back pieces already installed. Use 6d cement-coated nails. Then fasten the fronts (the remaining 1 × 2s) to the side pieces with 6d cement-coated nails.

9. Cut one piece of ¾-inch plywood to 14 × 22¾ inches for the sliding door that fits inside the channels already assembled.

10. Cut one piece of 1 × 2 stock to 24 inches for the sliding door rain guard. Fasten the rain guard to one long edge of the sliding door using four 1½-inch #8 flathead wood screws.

11. Drill a ⅛-inch-diameter pilot hole in the center of the top face of the rain guard and install a 2-inch hook-and-eye fastener. Slide the door into the channels, then raise it as far as possible without the door coming free. Locate and install the eye part of the hook-and-eye fastener on the wall at this point. Use a masonry anchor, if appropriate.

12. Remove the sliding door from the channels, and push the chute into the window. Stop when the edge of the chute is just over the inside of the window ledge.

13. Cut two pieces of 1 × 2 stock to 3½ inches each for the cleats. Fasten these to the sides of the chute with 1½-inch #8 flathead wood screws so that the cleats butt against the channels.

14. Pull the chute from the window. Paint the chute and sliding door, if desired.

15. Cut a piece of light-gauge sheet metal to 18 × 61½ inches for the lining. Fasten this to the chute by laying it on top of the chute bottom, then bending a ¾-inch edge over the ends of the bottom using a hammer. Drill ⅛-inch-diameter holes through the metal and fasten the lining to the edges of the chute bottom with 6d cement-coated nails.

16. Return the sliding door to the channels and lower it all the way. From inside your house, install locks on the sliding door and window ledge, if desired.

ATTACHED WOODBOX

Carl Walker built the wood storage box pictured here and attached it to his frame house in Puyallup, Washington. The box holds a three-day supply of wood, but its major feature is the opening in the rear of the box that connects it directly with the inside of the house. Firewood may be brought in anytime. There is no need to brave the great outdoors except to fill the box when supplies are low. A small, insulated door mounted on the interior wall of the house closes off the opening when not in use. In the Walkers' home, the door is located close to the wood stove and is made of the materials saved during construction of the opening. Not only is this home-attached woodbox a labor and space saver, it saves heat too, because doors to the outside don't have to be opened to bring in fuel.

SHOPPING LIST

Lumber
6 pcs. #2 pine $2 \times 4 \times 8'$ (pressure-treated, if desired)
Plywood Siding
1 sheet $\frac{5}{8}'' \times 4' \times 8'$
Plywood
1 pc. $\frac{1}{2}'' \times 2' \times 6'$ exterior grade
Roofing Material
approximately 12 square feet (to match house)
Hardware
flathead wood screws #8 $\times \frac{5}{8}''$
4 hex head lag bolts $\frac{1}{4}'' \times 3''$
3 steel strap hinges $8''$ with screws
1 pound galvanized common nails 10d
1 pound galvanized common nails 6d

The woodbox is made from 2×4 framing lumber. Our plans differ somewhat from the photograph by calling for weather-resistant plywood siding. The paint and roofing materials match the home's exterior. An unusual feature of the box is its V-shaped floor, which causes the wood to slide automatically from the sides of the box toward the center so that only a small access door inside the house is necessary. A lid on the box makes loading easy and keeps the wood dry.

Our instructions include only the materials and steps needed to build the box itself. The exploded-view diagram also shows a typical exterior wall; however, you'll need to cut and frame out the door opening and make the door on your own. Do insulate and weather-strip the door to keep out the cold. Try to position the box so that framing the opening requires removing only a minimum number of studs.

412

CONSTRUCTION

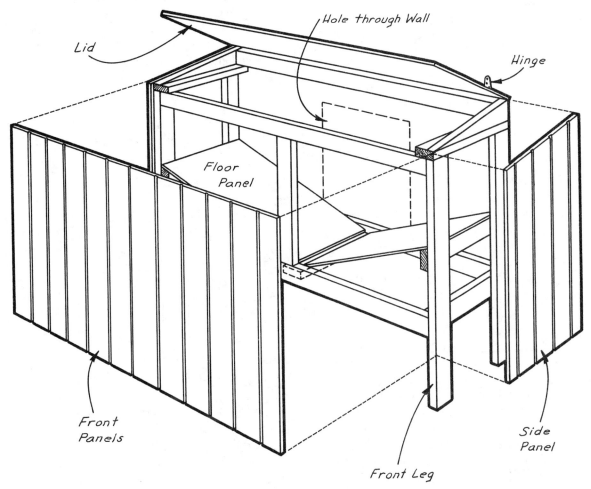

Lid

Hole through Wall

Hinge

Floor Panel

Front Panels

Side Panel

Front Leg

Exploded-View Diagram

1. Cut four pieces of 2×4 ($1\frac{1}{2}'' \times 3\frac{1}{2}''$) stock, each 8 feet in length, into pairs so that one portion of each 2×4 measures 39 inches in length, and the other portion measures 56 inches in length. Use the four shorter boards as legs for the box and the remaining four boards as cross members.

2. From a single piece of 2×4 stock at least 3 feet long (for ease of cutting), make two diagonally sawn pieces each 20 inches long, as shown in illustration A, for lid supports.

3. Cut four additional pieces of 2×4 stock to 20 inches each for the upper and middle stringers.

4. Cut three pieces of 2×4 stock to 17 inches each. Use two of the pieces for the lower stringers and the third piece for the floor support.

413

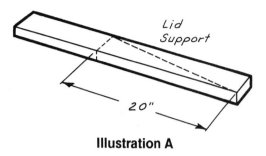

Lid
Support

20"

Illustration A

5. Now lay two legs on edge for the front of the box frame, then place two cross members on the ground between them, face down, so that, when nailed together and raised upright, the outer surface of the cross members will be flush with the edges of the legs. Position the front cross members as shown in illustration B, then nail the legs to the cross members using 10d galvanized common nails. (Refer to illustration B when following all the steps related

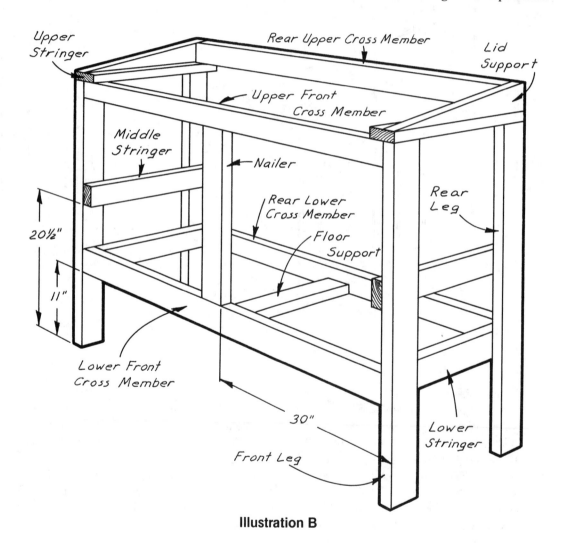

Upper
Stringer

Rear Upper Cross Member

Lid
Support

Upper Front
Cross Member

Middle
Stringer

Nailer

Rear
Leg

Rear Lower
Cross Member

Floor
Support

20½"

11"

Lower Front
Cross Member

30"

Lower
Stringer

Front Leg

Illustration B

LUMBER CUTTING LIST

Size	Piece	Quantity
2 × 4		
1½'' × 3½'' × 56''	Cross members	4
1½'' × 3½'' × 39''	Legs	4
1½'' × 3½'' × 20½''	Nailer	1
1½'' × 3½'' × 20''	Upper and middle stringers	4
1½'' × 3½'' × 20''	Lid supports (2)	1
1½'' × 3½'' × 17''	Lower stringers	2
1½'' × 3½'' × 17''	Floor support	1
Plywood Siding		
⅝'' × 30'' × 30''	Front panels	2
⅝'' × 20⅝'' × 33½''	Side panels	2
⅝'' × 17⅞'' × 30''	Floor panels	2
Plywood		
½'' × 21'' × 61¼''	Lid	1

to making the box frame. Also, use 10d galvanized common nails when fastening all 2 × 4 frame members.)

6. Lay the remaining two legs on edge for the rear of the frame and nail one rear cross member between them, positioned as shown in illustration B.

7. Join both pairs of legs together by nailing the two upper stringers flat across the tops of the legs, front to rear.

8. Fasten the lower stringers between the front and rear pairs of legs, positioning them 11 inches from the lower ends of the legs.

9. Join the two middle stringers across the inside faces of the legs, 20½ inches from the legs' lower ends.

10. Fasten the floor support between the lower front and rear cross members. Center the support 30 inches from the outer surface of each pair of legs, and position it so its lower surface is flush with the lower edges of both cross members.

11. Cut a single piece of 2 × 4 stock so that it fits tightly between the upper and lower cross members at the front of the frame—as shown in illustration B—to serve as the nailer for the box siding (see step 16) and as additional support for the frame. The nailer's approximate length should be 20½ inches. Fasten it in place by toenailing it into the cross members.

12. Nail the lid supports to the tops of the upper stringers, flush with the stringers' ends and outside edges. Both lid supports should slope downward toward the front of the box frame.

13. Fasten the rear upper cross member in place between the lid supports at the rear of the frame. Use a hand plane to bevel the upper surface of the cross member so it matches the slope of the lid supports. Now the box frame is complete.

14. Cut a single sheet of ⅝-inch exterior-grade plywood siding into pieces for the front, side, and floor panels, according to the cutting diagram. Measure the frame before cutting the pieces in case minor discrep-

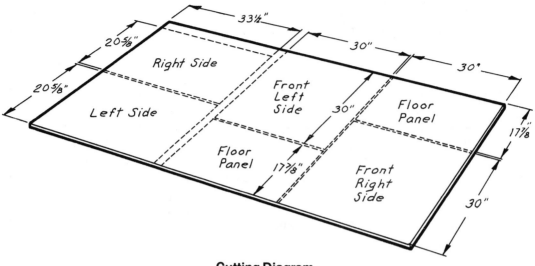

Cutting Diagram

ancies during construction require slight changes in the dimensions specified in the diagram. Be sure to label each piece as it is cut from the sheet. Do not cut the angled tops of the side panels at this time.

15. Fasten the two sloping floor panels (each measuring 17⅞″ × 30″) in place between the upper surfaces of the middle stringers and the upper surface of the floor support, as shown in the exploded-view diagram. Position the panels so their rear edges are flush with the rear of the box frame. Use 6d galvanized common nails. (Use 6d nails for all steps where plywood is fastened to the frame.) Before nailing, bevel the upper inside edge of each middle stringer to suit the slope of the floor panels, if desired.

16. Nail the front panels (each measuring 30″ × 30″) in place so they overlap vertically in the center, over the nailer. The side edges of the panels should be flush with the outer surfaces of the frame's front legs, and the panels' lower edges should extend 2 inches below the bottom edge of the lower cross member.

17. Temporarily attach the side panels (each measuring 20⅝″ × 33½″) in place. Their front edges should overlap the edges of the front panels, and the bottom edges of all four panels should be even and level. Scribe the upper portion of each side panel to match the angles of the sloping lid supports. Remove the side panels, cut them to size, then reattach them permanently.

18. Cut one piece of ½-inch exterior-grade plywood to 21 × 61¼ inches for the lid of the box.

19. Hold the lid on top of the box, centered on the lid supports and with the rear edge flush with the outer surface of the rear upper cross member. Position three 8-inch steel strap hinges evenly across the rear edge of the lid, then mark the locations of the holes. Remove the lid from the box, drill pilot holes for ⅝-inch #8 flathead wood screws, then fasten one side of each of the hinges to the lid by installing the screws.

20. Now move the box to its location against the outside wall where the access hole is to be cut. Reach inside the box and scribe an opening measuring 18 inches high and 24

inches wide on the outside wall. The lower edge of the opening should be even with the upper edge of the rear lower cross member of the box, and the opening itself should be centered on both sides of the floor support, as shown in the exploded-view diagram. Move the box away, then cut and frame the opening in the wall. You will also have to construct a door inside the house to close off the opening into the box. You may do this now or after the box has been attached to the house and finished.

21. After the opening is complete, move the box back into its location against the side of the house. Drill four ¼-inch-diameter pilot holes through the rear upper and lower cross members, then change bits and drill ⅛-inch-diameter pilot holes into the house siding. Fasten the box securely to the house using ¼ × 3-inch hex head lag bolts. Masonry walls will require masonry bolts with sleeve anchors instead of lag bolts.

22. Position the lid on the box once again, then drill pilot holes into the siding for the remaining hinge mounting screws. Fasten the hinges to the siding with ⅝-inch #8 flathead wood screws, or masonry bolts if necessary.

23. Caulk the seam along the wall if the house siding is the flush variety. If you have aluminum or clapboard siding, make a wooden molding strip for each side of the box, notched to fit the siding laps. Fasten these strips in place using 6d galvanized common nails.

24. Nail roofing felt and roof shingles or cedar shakes to the lid. For a neat appearance, match the materials on the house roof, if possible.

25. If pressure-treated lumber has not been used, apply copper naphthenate wood preservative to all parts of the box. Paint the exterior of the box, preferably to match the color of your house.

FIREWOOD RACK

SHOPPING LIST

Lumber
3 pcs. $1 \times 4 \times 10'$ (or to suit dimensions of
    rack base; see steps 6 and 8)
2 pcs. $1 \times 4 \times 8'$
Hardware
1 freight skid
32 flathead wood screws #8 $\times$ ¾″
12 hex head lag bolts ⅜″ $\times$ 1½″
32 hex head lag bolts ⅜″ $\times$ 1¼″
44 flat washers ¼″
6 steel angle brackets 3″ $\times$ 3″ $\times$ 3½″

Here is a sturdy firewood rack that costs very little in materials and can be built in only a few hours. Christopher Kirchberg of Salem, Massachusetts, designed the rack, and he reports that it fits nicely on his enclosed patio.

The base of the rack is a salvaged freight skid. Skids are of heavier construction than freight pallets and are distinguishable by having only two lengthwise runners (called skids, naturally enough) supporting a single layer of cross pieces called the deck. A pallet usually has three lengthwise timbers sandwiched between cross pieces attached both top and bottom. Pallets are normally built of cheap softwood.

Skids, on the other hand, are frequently made of oak.

The actual size of your firewood rack will depend on the size of the base you obtain. Also, the height of the uprights can vary depending on how much wood you have to stack and how high you want to stack it. The uprights Kirchberg chose are 30 inches high. His rack holds a supply of wood adequate for five days' heating in his Massachusetts home.

Kirchberg's rack is also without finish, because it is not exposed to weather. If you plan to use your rack outdoors, we recommend that you apply copper naphthenate wood preservative to it, and drape a tarpaulin over the top to keep rain and snow off the firewood. Leave the sides exposed for air circulation.

CONSTRUCTION

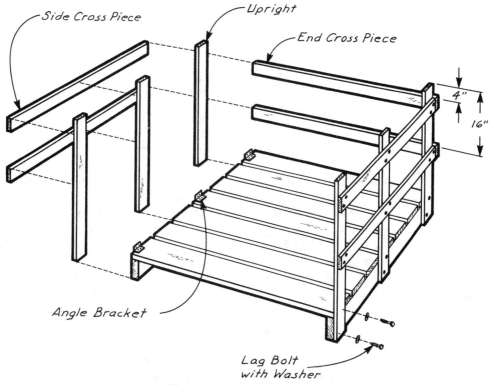

Side Cross Piece

Upright

End Cross Piece

4"

16"

Angle Bracket

Lag Bolt
with Washer

Exploded-View Diagram

1. First, check that the corners of the skid you are using for the rack base are square. To do this, measure across diagonal corners. Both measurements should be equal. If they are not, bring the corners square using clamps, and refasten them, where necessary, with 8d galvanized common nails. If the skid is built of hardwood, drill ⅛-inch-diameter pilot holes first, before you nail.

2. Cut six pieces of 1 × 4 (¾″ × 3½″) to 30 inches each for the uprights.

3. Turn the rack base onto one side. Consult the exploded-view diagram for the locations of the uprights, then clamp one upright in position against the upper side of the

base, square with the deck and perpendicular to the skid so that the upright will be vertical when the base is set down flat.

4. Drill two ⅛-inch-diameter pilot holes through the clamped upright a short distance into the skid board. Drill the holes diagonally apart from each other for strength and to avoid splitting the wood grain of either piece. Now fasten the upright permanently using two ⅜ × 1½-inch hex head lag bolts fitted with ¼-inch flat washers, then remove the clamp. Using the same procedure, fasten two more uprights to that side of the base, then flip the base onto the other side and attach the remaining three uprights.

419

LUMBER CUTTING LIST

Size	Piece	Quantity
1 × 4		
¾'' × 3½'' × 30''	Uprights	6
¾'' × 3½'' × length of rack base (see step 6)	Side cross pieces	4
¾'' × 3½'' × width of rack base plus 3'' (see step 8)	End cross pieces	2

5. Return the base with the uprights attached to its normal position — resting on the skid — and attach 3 × 3 × 3½-inch steel angle brackets to the uprights and deck boards where they meet, as shown in the exploded-view diagram. Drill ⅛-inch-diameter pilot holes first, holding each bracket in place as a guide, then fasten the brackets with ¾-inch #8 flathead wood screws.

6. Now cut four pieces of 1 × 4 to the length of the rack base, for the side cross pieces.

7. Fasten the side cross pieces to the outside of the uprights, as shown in the exploded-view diagram. Attach each cross piece as you did the uprights in steps 3 and 4, by first clamping them in position and drilling two diagonally spaced ⅛-inch-diameter pilot holes through the cross pieces and into the uprights at each joint. For fasteners,

use ⅜ × 1¼-inch hex head lag bolts with ¼-inch flat washers.

8. Measure across the width of the base, including the thickness of the joined cross piece and upright at each corner. Assuming 1 × 4s are used, as specified, the total measurement should be 3 inches greater than the width of the skid itself. Cut two pieces of 1 × 4 to this length for the end cross pieces.

9. Attach the end cross pieces across the back of the rack base at the same height as the side cross pieces, as shown in the exploded-view diagram. Fasten the cross pieces to the uprights as in step 7, using the same fasteners.

10. If you wish, apply a finish or copper naphthenate wood preservative to the log rack to protect it against weathering.

SWING-SET WOOD RACK

SHOPPING LIST

Recycled Material
2 discarded swing sets or 1 double swing set
Hardware
1 pc. 1″-O.D. schedule-40 steel tubing 11′
13 hex head bolts ¼″ × 6″ with nuts
6 hex head bolts ¼″ × 4″ with nuts
4 hex head bolts ¼″ × 3″ with nuts
2 hex head bolts ¼″ × 2½″ with nuts
50 flat washers ⅜″
rust-resistant enamel

Jason Javaras of Fredericksburg, Virginia, recycled the family swing set to build this sturdy firewood rack. It's lightweight yet strong, just like the swing set was, and holds a one-week supply of wood (about one-fifth of a cord). During the heating season the rack sits on the front porch. In spring, Jason moves it back to the woodpile for storage. To obtain all the necessary parts, Javaras used a large, deluxe-model swing set, the type with a slide and a glider as well as swings. If one of these larger sets cannot be found, two smaller sets can be used instead.

The swing-set wood rack requires no welding. All parts bolt together. Where possible, cut the tubing to include ends with holes already drilled. Even though you'll have to drill some holes yourself anyway, this will save you some time and a little wear and tear on your tools. Also, the factory-made holes will be precisely drilled. Using them as often as possible will make it easier to align parts during assembly. The tubing on most swing sets measures approximately 2½ inches in diameter. For the wood rack, some additional 1-inch-diameter tubing is also necessary to make the braces. Larger swing sets usually use 1-inch-diameter tubing on accessory items such as the slide or glider. If you find you must purchase new tubing for bracing, select 1-inch-O.D. schedule-40 steel tubing.

Disassemble the swing set completely before you start the wood rack, so that you can clean all the pieces and coat them with rust-resistant paint. When cutting the tubing to size, use a hacksaw and a miter box. Don't forget to apply paint to the freshly cut edges to prevent rust. For drilling holes, you'll find a commercial drill guide—the

421

kind that attaches to a standard portable electric drill and automatically guides the bit to the exact center on round stock—very useful. An accurate job can also be done using a center punch to locate the holes. In all cases, drill ⅜-inch-diameter holes and use ¼-inch-diameter bolts. This will allow a little play between pieces when aligning them. Install a washer on both ends of each bolt to avoid flattening the tubing.

CONSTRUCTION

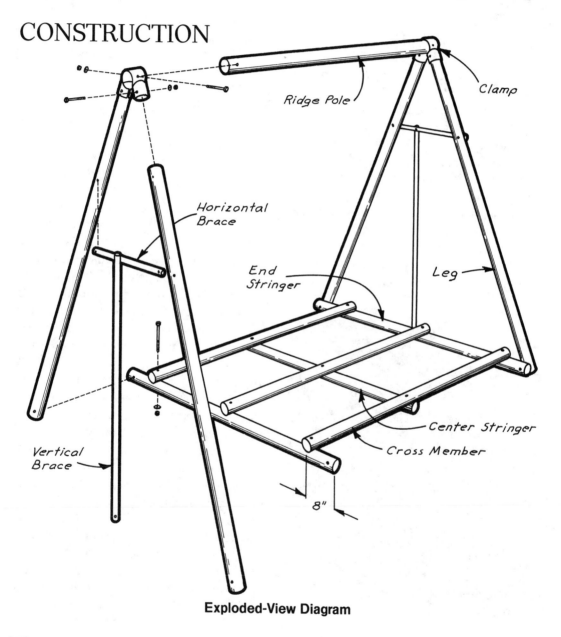

Exploded-View Diagram

1. After disassembling the swing set, shorten the ridge pole to a length of 46 inches to make the ridge pole for the wood rack.

2. Trim off the bottoms of the four swing-set legs to 69½ inches each to make the legs of the rack.

3. Assemble the legs to the ridge pole using the leg clamps from the swing set. Reattach the clamps using the factory-made holes in the ridge pole and legs, where possible. Drill new ⅜-inch-diameter holes, where necessary. Fasten all parts using ¼ × 3-inch hex head bolts (each fitted with a washer at each end) and nuts. When assembled, the wood rack frame should stand freely and resemble a shortened version of the original swing set. Move the assembled frame to a level spot before tightening the bolts permanently.

4. Now make the base of the wood rack from lengths of 2½-inch tubing left over from steps 1 and 2. To begin, cut two pieces of tubing to 52 inches each for the end stringers, and one piece to 38 inches for the center stringer. Set the two end stringers in place against the legs, as shown in the exploded-view diagram. With the ends of the stringers flush to the outside of the legs, drill ⅜-inch-diameter holes through the legs and stringers. Attach the legs to the stringers with ¼ × 6-inch hex head bolts, washers, and nuts.

5. Cut three pieces of 2½-inch-diameter tubing to 60 inches each for the cross members. Place the two outer cross members each 8 inches from the ends of the stringers, as shown in the exploded-view diagram, then drill ⅜-inch-diameter holes through the pieces and attach the cross members to the stringers with ¼ × 6-inch hex head bolts,

washers, and nuts. Center the middle cross member between the two outer cross members and attach it to the stringers in the same manner.

6. Mount the center stringer beneath the three cross members, as shown in the exploded-view diagram, using ¼ × 6-inch hex head bolts, washers, and nuts.

7. Cut two pieces of 1-inch-O.D. tubing to 48 inches each for vertical bracing, and two pieces to 18 inches each for horizontal bracing. Install the horizontal bracing by holding each piece against the legs of the wood rack frame, as shown in the exploded-view diagram, 48 inches above ground level. Mark the braces and legs for drilling, then make a ⅜-inch-diameter hole through the ends of each brace and through the legs. Fasten the horizontal braces to the legs with ¼ × 4-inch hex head bolts, washers, and nuts.

8. Hold an end of one vertical brace against one of the end stringers (where the stringer and middle cross member overlap) and hold the other end against the horizontal brace. Mark the pieces for drilling so that, when fastened, the vertical and horizontal braces will be at right angles, as shown in the exploded-view diagram. Drill ⅜-inch-diameter holes through the vertical and horizontal braces and the end stringer, then fasten the brace using one ¼ × 2½-inch hex head bolt and one ¼ × 4-inch hex head bolt, both with washers and nuts. Repeat the procedure to attach the remaining vertical brace.

9. Tighten all loose bolts, then trim off excess threads using a hacksaw. Paint the finished wood rack with rust-resistant enamel.

HOOP-STYLE FIREWOOD RACK

SHOPPING LIST

Hardware
3 pcs. electrical conduit ½'' diameter × 10'
3 pcs. steel rod ½'' diameter × 6''
5 roundhead machine bolts ¼'' × 2½'' with
   lockwashers and nuts
4 roundhead machine bolts ¼'' × 1'' with
   lockwashers and nuts
rust-resistant enamel

The shape of this wood rack follows a classic design often seen in catalogs and magazines. Gary Helmic of Mason, Michigan, devised it in a way that requires no welding and very little expense. Even after five years and storing over 50 cords of wood, the rack shows little sign of wear.

Helmic formed the large hoops and base of the rack—all made from ordinary ½-inch-diameter electrical conduit—by bending them around large cylinders, specifically an outdoor propane tank and a tree stump. You'll have to find similar forms for the hoops, but you can use a conduit-bending tool for the base. Instead of welding, the sections of tubing are joined together

using inserts made from short lengths of steel rod, locked in place with bolts, lockwashers, and nuts.

CONSTRUCTION

1. Use two 10-foot lengths of ½-inch-diameter electrical conduit for the hoops. Bend the tubing, either freehand or around a large cylinder, to form the two large hoops, each approximately 3 feet in diameter.

2. Cut two pieces of ½-inch-diameter steel rod to 6 inches each for the hoop connectors. Using a hammer, drive a connector into one end of each piece of tubing until 3 inches remain protruding. Drill a 9/32-inch-diameter hole through each assembly and lock the connectors in place by installing ¼ × 1-inch roundhead machine bolts, lockwashers, and nuts. Trim off the excess threads on each bolt.

3. Bring the ends of each hoop together and push them over the protruding connectors until the tubing meets. Drill 9/32-inch-diameter holes through the tubing and connectors, as in the previous step, then

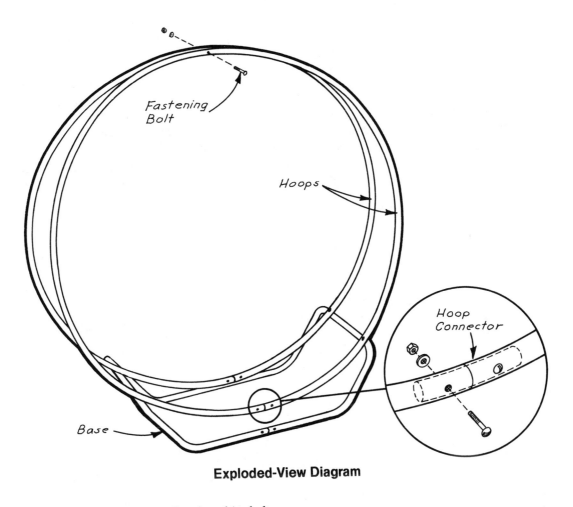

Fastening Bolt

Hoops

Hoop Connector

Base

Exploded-View Diagram

install ¼ × 1-inch roundhead machine bolts, lockwashers, and nuts (also as before), to fasten the tubing permanently to shape.

4. Lay the two hoops on top of each other with the connectors touching. Find the point directly opposite the connectors and drill ⁹⁄₃₂-inch-diameter holes through both hoops at that point. Fasten the two hoops together using a ¼ × 2½-inch roundhead machine bolt, lockwasher, and nut.

5. Use a third 10-foot section of ½-inch-diameter electrical conduit for the base.

6. Following the bending pattern shown in illustration A, bend the base piece to shape

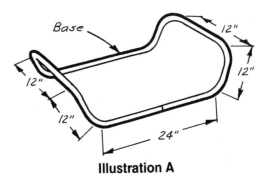

Base

12"

12"

12"

12"

24"

Illustration A

using a conduit-bending tool, or by bending the conduit freehand around a cylinder.

7. Cut one piece of ½-inch-diameter steel rod to 6 inches to connect the ends of the base. Bring the tubing ends together and insert the rod as you did with the hoops, then drill ¼-inch-diameter holes and fasten the ends of the tubing to the connector using ¼ × 1-inch roundhead machine bolts, lockwashers, and nuts. Cut off the excess threads from each bolt.

8. Set the base upright and support the two connected hoops vertically in the base so the hoop connectors are located on the bottom. Spread the hoops until they are 12 inches apart, then drill ⁹⁄₃₂-inch-diameter holes through both the hoops and the base where they touch. Fasten the hoops to the base using ¼-inch × 2½-inch machine bolts, lockwashers, and nuts.

9. Finally, sand all the pieces lightly, then paint the rack with rust-resistant enamel.

FIREWOOD PLATFORM

SHOPPING LIST

Lumber
1 pc. $2 \times 4 \times 8'$
2 pcs. $1 \times 8 \times 8'$
Hardware
8 flathead wood screws #12 × 3½″
¼ pound common nails 6d

The slanting sides of this firewood platform, designed by David Bramhill of Norwich, Connecticut, direct the weight of logs placed on it inward toward the center. The result: a fuel storage rack of surprisingly large capacity.

Bramhill used rough-sawn lumber direct from a mill to build the platform pictured here. Ordinary-dimension stock from a lumberyard may be easier for many readers to obtain, so that's what we've specified in the instructions. The cutting diagram shows how to use single lengths of purchased stock most efficiently.

CONSTRUCTION

1. Cut the supports for the floor and sides from a single 8-foot length of 2×4 (1½″ × 3½″) stock. Follow the cutting diagram. Lay out and cut each piece in succession so that the lengths of the pieces are not reduced by the saw kerf. When finished, you should have two floor supports, each 27 inches long, both ends of which should be cut at 45-degree angles; and four side supports, each 10 inches long, one end of which should be square and the other end cut at a 45-degree angle.

2. Assemble the side supports to the floor supports to make two U-shaped frames, as shown in the exploded-view diagram. To fasten the pieces of each frame, first clamp the floor supports to a workbench. Hold the angled ends of the side supports tightly in place against the ends of the floor supports, then drill and countersink ⅛-inch-diameter pilot holes for #12 screws at angles through the floor supports and into the side supports, as shown in illustration A. Apply carpenter's wood glue and fasten the pieces with 3½-inch #12 flathead wood screws.

3. Unclamp the frames from the bench, turn them upside down so they rest on the ends of the side supports, then drill two more ⅛-inch pilot holes at each corner, this time

427

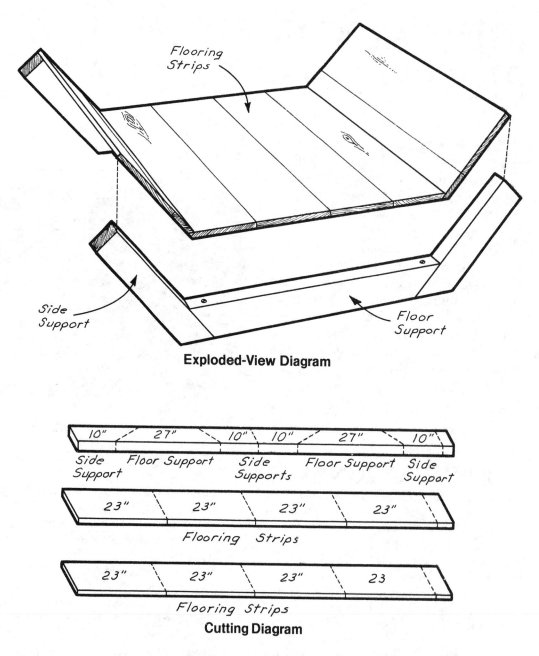

Exploded-View Diagram

10" | 27" | 10" | 10" | 27" | 10"

Side Support | Floor Support | Side Supports | Floor Support | Side Support

23" | 23" | 23" | 23"

Flooring Strips

23" | 23" | 23" | 23

Flooring Strips

Cutting Diagram

through the side supports and into the floor supports. Install 3½-inch #12 flathead wood screws.

4. Cut two 8-foot lengths of 1 × 8 (¾″ × 7¼″)

stock into eight pieces, each 23 inches long, for the flooring strips. Bevel a long edge on two strips to a 45-degree angle.

5. Arrange the frames parallel to each other,

LUMBER CUTTING LIST

Size	Piece	Quantity
2 × 4		
1½'' × 3½'' × 27''	Floor supports	2
1½'' × 3½'' × 10''	Side supports	4
1 × 8		
¾'' × 7¼'' × 23''	Flooring strips	8

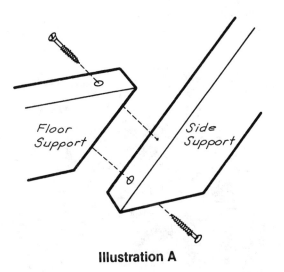

Illustration A

with the ends of the side supports pointing up, and fit a beveled flooring strip in place at one corner of the frames, bevel-side down.

Adjust the frames flush with the ends of the strip, then fasten the strip to the frames using 6d common nails.

6. Attach two unbeveled flooring strips next to the first strip, fastening each to the frames using 6d common nails.

7. Rip or plane the final beveled strip to fit, then install it bevel-side down against the remaining corner of the frames.

8. Bevel both edges of one 23-inch strip to 45-degree angles, then rip the piece in half lengthwise. Fasten the pieces bevel-side down to the floorboards at the corners of the frame, as shown in the exploded-view diagram. Use 6d common nails.

9. Attach the remaining strips of flooring to the side supports, using 6d common nails. Rip the final piece on each side so that it fits flush with the ends of the supports.

10. Paint the finished platform, if desired.

FUEL-STORAGE BIN

SHOPPING LIST

Lumber
1 pc. $1 \times 6 \times 12'$
2 pcs. $1 \times 4 \times 10'$
1 pc. $1 \times 2 \times 6'$
Plywood
2 sheets ¾'' $\times 4' \times 8'$ A-C grade
Hardware
½ pound finishing nails 6d
¼ pound underlayment nails 1¼''

This large wood- or coal-storage bin solves the problem of foot-soiled carpets and wandering wood chips. Not only are the bin's compartments large enough to hold several days' supply of kindling, firewood, or coal, there is also room for a coal or ash bucket, newspapers, and other fireplace accessories. The wood-storage portion is located in the upper portion of the bin to eliminate stooping to pick up heavy logs.

The bin itself is assembled with simple butt joints and shelf cleat construction. The facing attached to the front of the bin to cover the shelf joints is half-lapped, but is easy to make if the measurements are carefully made. The bin shown here incorporates a plinth, or base section, which makes the unit stationary and gives it a finished appearance. The plinth also keeps debris from getting underneath the bin and raises the compartments a few inches off the floor. Casters could be added instead of the plinth if you foresee the need to move the bin frequently. With the bin mounted on wheels you could roll it to your door, load it, and move it back to the fireplace area without

tracking in snow and dirt. Although the bin shown here is without doors, these too can be added. Make or purchase them to match your present furniture and mount them in any conventional way.

CONSTRUCTION

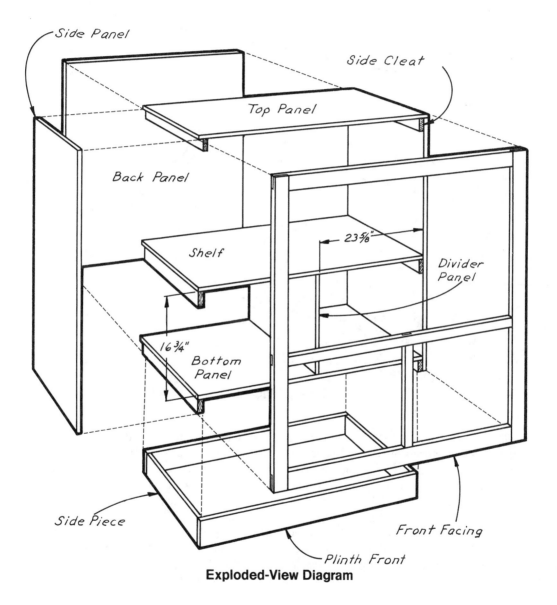

Exploded-View Diagram

Side Panel

Side Cleat

Top Panel

Back Panel

Shelf

23⅝"

Divider
Panel

16¾"

Bottom
Panel

Side Piece

Front Facing

Plinth Front

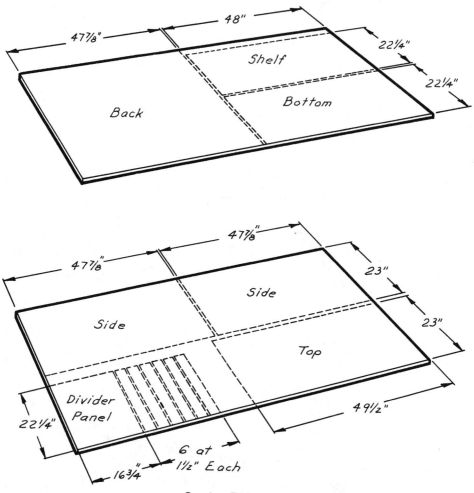

Cutting Diagram

1. All the basic cabinet pieces are cut from two 4 × 8-foot sheets of ¾-inch A-C grade plywood. The facing and plinth are cut from dimensional lumber. Start by laying out the cabinet pieces and side cleats on the plywood sheets, as shown in the cutting diagram. Mark separate cutting lines for each piece, leaving room between them for the saw kerf. Cut out the pieces to their finished sizes.

2. Glue and nail the side cleats to the inside faces of the side panels using carpenter's wood glue and 1¼-inch underlayment nails. Sink the nail heads. Be sure to align the cleats in matching pairs on each side panel, so the horizontal cabinet pieces will be level when installed. The ends of the cleats should be ¾ inch from the back edges of the side panels so that the cabinet back will fit flush in the recess.

LUMBER CUTTING LIST

Size	Piece	Quantity
1 × 6		
¾″ × 5½″ × 46½″	Plinth front	1
¾″ × 5½″ × 46½″	Plinth back	1
¾″ × 5½″ × 20″	Plinth sides	2
1 × 4		
¾″ × 3½″ × 49½″	Top facing	1
¾″ × 3½″ × 49½″	Bottom facing	1
¾″ × 3½″ × 48⅝″	Side facing	2
1 × 2		
¾″ × 1½″ × 49½″	Shelf facing	1
¾″ × 1½″ × 20″	Divider facing	1
Plywood		
¾″ × 47⅞″ × 48″	Back	1
¾″ × 23″ × 49½″	Top	1
¾″ × 23″ × 47⅞″	Sides	2
¾″ × 22¼″ × 48″	Shelf	1
¾″ × 22¼″ × 48″	Bottom	1
¾″ × 16¾″ × 22¼″	Divider	1
¾″ × 1½″ × 22¼″	Side cleats	6

3. After the cleats are dry, glue and nail the bottom panel, shelf, and top panel to them using wood glue and 6d finishing nails, sinking the heads. Check the cabinet for squareness. Next, position the vertical divider panel close to or at the center of the cabinet and glue and nail it in place, also with 6d finishing nails, sinking the heads. Be sure the panel is vertical. Now glue and nail the back panel in place after first marking where it will contact the cleats and shelf so you can hit there with the nails. Use 6d finishing nails as with the other pieces, and sink the heads.

4. Construct the plinth. Its height may vary to suit your taste. We found that 5½ inches, or the width of ordinary 1 × 6 (¾″ × 5½″) lumber, was easy to use. Cut two pieces of 1 × 6 to 20 inches each for the sides, and also two pieces 46½ inches each for the back and front. Nail these together with 6d finishing nails and sink the nail heads. The side pieces should butt against the ends of the front and back pieces to hide their end grain. Fill the nail holes with wood putty or plastic wood and finish sand the plinth.

5. Center the cabinet on the plinth and fasten the two units together with 6d finishing nails driven through the bottom panel from inside the cabinet. Sink the nail heads.

6. Now cut and assemble the face, as shown in illustration A. This can be done in two ways, either by putting the entire facing together as a unit and then attaching it to the cabinet, or by fitting each piece to the

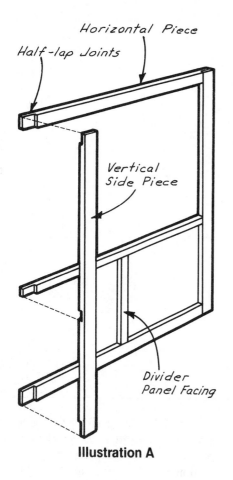

Horizontal Piece

Half-lap Joints

Vertical
Side Piece

Divider
Panel Facing

Illustration A

cabinet individually. Either way works well, but building the face pieces as a unit requires very careful measuring and cutting. If you decide to fit the pieces individually, attach the divider panel facing first, then the horizontal pieces and finally the two vertical side pieces. Cut the half-lap joints so that the upper edge of the horizontal facing pieces is flush with the upper surfaces of the shelf, bottom, and top panels. Fasten the facing to the cabinet with 6d finishing nails and sink the nail heads.

7. Fill all nail holes in the cabinet and finish sand the entire unit. Apply paint or another finish, as desired.

TRA-DITIONAL FIREWOOD BOX

SHOPPING LIST

Lumber
4 pcs. $2 \times 12 \times 12'$
26 pcs. wood plugs $\frac{1}{2}'' \times \frac{3}{4}''$
Hardware
1 continuous hinge $1\frac{1}{2}'' \times 1\frac{1}{2}'' \times 3'$
26 flathead wood screws #12 $\times 3\frac{1}{2}''$
18 flathead wood screws #6 $\times 1\frac{1}{2}''$

George Getty of Johnstown, Pennsylvania, built this traditional firewood-storage box that holds one day's supply of wood. He obtained the rugged, knotty-pine look by using framing lumber, specifically, a few leftover 2×12 floor joists.

You must joint (plane) the edges of the 2×12s to make them square before using them for cabinet lumber. If a jointer is not available and you have to pay to have the boards jointed, consider purchasing 5/4-inch-thick ($1\frac{1}{8}$-inch actual thickness) cabinet lumber instead. Getty also surface-planed the $1\frac{1}{2}$-inch-thick lumber down to $1\frac{1}{4}$ inches, but full-thickness lumber can be used with the same results.

This firewood box is heavy. You might want to add casters to make it more mobile. Then you can wheel it to the door, load it, and wheel it back to its home near the wood stove.

CONSTRUCTION

1. Cut six pieces of 2×12 ($1\frac{1}{2}'' \times 11\frac{1}{4}''$) stock to 37 inches each for the front and rear panels (see the cutting diagram). Use the three best boards for the front panel, and the three remaining boards for the rear panels.

2. Place the three boards for the front panel in long bar clamps. Apply carpenter's wood glue sparingly to the edges to be joined and tighten the clamps. Be sure the ends of the boards remain flush. When the glue has set, repeat the clamping procedure to make up the rear panel.

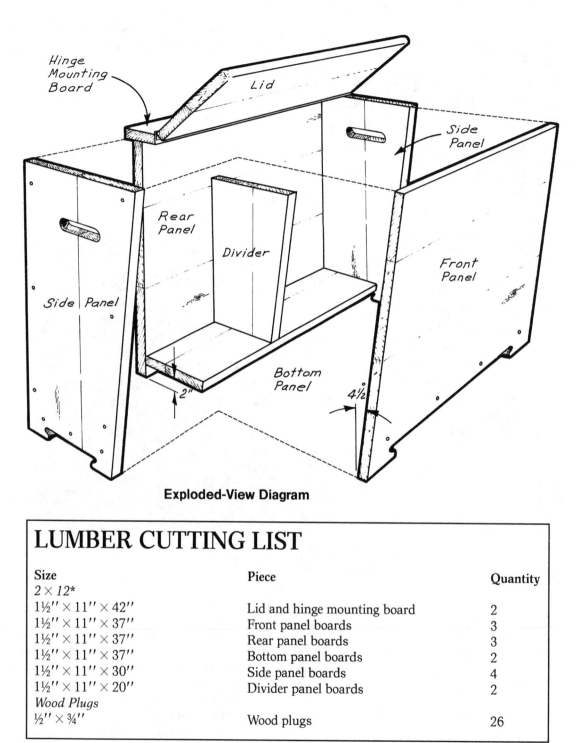

Exploded-View Diagram

LUMBER CUTTING LIST

Size	Piece	Quantity
2 × 12		
1½″ × 11″ × 42″	Lid and hinge mounting board	2
1½″ × 11″ × 37″	Front panel boards	3
1½″ × 11″ × 37″	Rear panel boards	3
1½″ × 11″ × 37″	Bottom panel boards	2
1½″ × 11″ × 30″	Side panel boards	4
1½″ × 11″ × 20″	Divider panel boards	2
Wood Plugs		
½″ × ¾″	Wood plugs	26

*Width of boards is 11″, measured after edge-jointing.

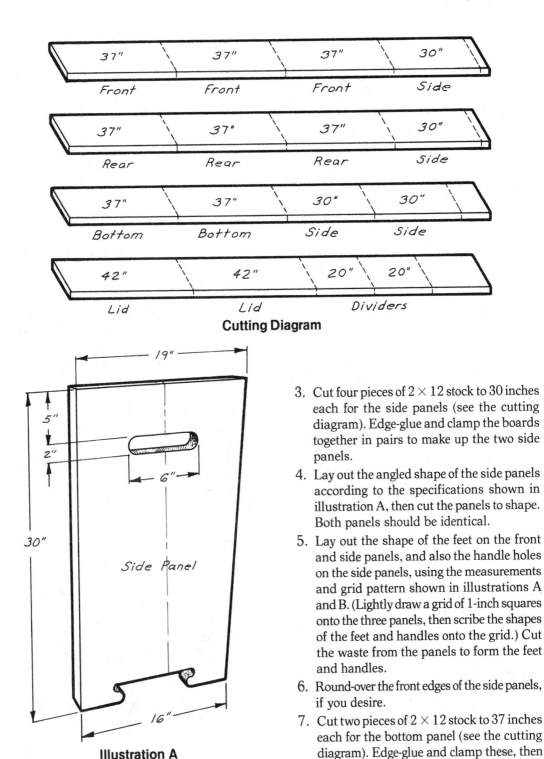

Cutting Diagram

| 37" | 37" | 37" | 30" |
| Front | Front | Front | Side |

| 37" | 37" | 37" | 30" |
| Rear | Rear | Rear | Side |

| 37" | 37" | 30" | 30" |
| Bottom | Bottom | Side | Side |

| 42" | 42" | 20" | 20" |
| Lid | Lid | Dividers | |

Illustration A

19"
5"
2"
6"
30"
16"
Side Panel

3. Cut four pieces of 2×12 stock to 30 inches each for the side panels (see the cutting diagram). Edge-glue and clamp the boards together in pairs to make up the two side panels.

4. Lay out the angled shape of the side panels according to the specifications shown in illustration A, then cut the panels to shape. Both panels should be identical.

5. Lay out the shape of the feet on the front and side panels, and also the handle holes on the side panels, using the measurements and grid pattern shown in illustrations A and B. (Lightly draw a grid of 1-inch squares onto the three panels, then scribe the shapes of the feet and handles onto the grid.) Cut the waste from the panels to form the feet and handles.

6. Round-over the front edges of the side panels, if you desire.

7. Cut two pieces of 2×12 stock to 37 inches each for the bottom panel (see the cutting diagram). Edge-glue and clamp these, then

437

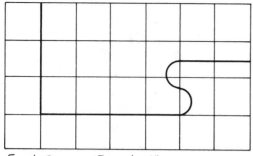
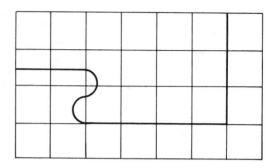

Each Square Equals 1"

Illustration B

set the saw to cut at a 4½-degree angle and rip the panel to a width of 12¾ inches, measured across the wide face. The beveled long edge matches the outward slope of the front and side panels.

8. Begin assembly by fastening the bottom panel to the rear panel, as shown in illustration C. Clamp the bottom panel in place and drill and countersink four holes, first ¼-inch-diameter shank holes through the rear panel and then ⅛-inch-diameter pilot holes into the bottom panel. Then, drill ½-inch-diameter plug holes ½ inch deep into the ¼-inch-diameter shank holes. All the holes for this project, except those for the hinge, are like those just described. Apply wood glue to the edge of the bottom

panel and fasten the panels with 3½-inch #12 flathead wood screws. When tightened fully, the heads of the wood screws should lie ½ inch below the surface of the wood.

9. Next, fasten the side panels to the bottom and rear panels. Placement of the screws is critical since plugs, used later to cover the screw holes (see step 15), will show. Position the panels, one at a time, and drill and countersink three screw holes, the first centered and the others 4 inches to each side of center, across the bottom of the panels. Apply wood glue and fasten the side panels with 3½-inch #12 flathead wood screws. Then drill three more holes in each panel, in the positions shown in the exploded-view diagram, and fasten the side panels to the rear panel.

10. Fasten the front panel next. Apply wood glue and align the front panel so an equal amount of lip is exposed along the side panels. Drill and countersink holes through the side panels into the edges of the front panel and fasten the panel with 3½-inch #12 flathead wood screws.

11. Cut two pieces of 2 × 12 lumber to make up the 14⅜ × 20-inch divider panel (see the cutting diagram). Glue the pieces, then cut the panel to 12¾ inches across the bottom edge, and 14⅜ inches across the top edge. Test-fit the panel and trim it, if nec-

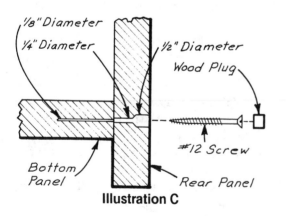

⅛" Diameter

¼" Diameter

½" Diameter

Wood Plug

#12 Screw

Bottom Panel

Rear Panel

Illustration C

essary, so it fits tightly inside the box. Install the divider without glue or fasteners, if you wish, so it is adjustable, or glue it in place to make it a permanent fixture.

12. Cut two pieces of 2 × 12 stock to 42 inches each to make the lid (see the cutting diagram). Edge-glue the pieces, then rip a 4-inch-wide strip from one long edge of the panel for the hinge mounting board. Trim the remaining panel to 16 inches wide. Round-over the front and side edges, if desired.

13. Fasten the lid and hinge mounting board together with a 36-inch length of continuous hinge. To do this, clamp the pieces together face-to-face with the edges and ends flush. Center the hinge on the edges of the pieces, then drill 1/16-inch-diameter pilot holes, and fasten the hinge with 1½-inch #6 flathead wood screws.

14. Center the lid and hinge mounting board on top of the box. Then bring the rear edge of the mounting board flush against the outside face of the rear panel. Drill and countersink holes through the mounting board and into the edge of the rear and side panels. Fasten the hinge mounting board to the box with 3½-inch #12 flathead wood screws. No glue is necessary.

15. Plug all the screw holes with ½-inch-diameter wood plugs. Apply wood glue and push the plugs into the holes, then cut them flush with the panel surfaces using a fine-toothed saw. (Place masking tape or thin cardboard on the wood surrounding each plug to avoid marring the surface with the saw.)

16. Sand the cabinet panels smooth, then apply the finish of your choice.

FIREWOOD CART

The Rodale Design Group designed this firewood cart to transport stove-length wood from the woodlot or woodpile to the house. Support legs attached to the uprights fold out to allow the cart to be placed in a horizontal position for loading. Wood stacked on the cart can be held in place by a heavy

SHOPPING LIST

Lumber
2 pcs. $2 \times 3 \times 8'$
Plywood
1 pc. $\frac{1}{4}'' \times 2' \times 4'$ exterior grade
Dowels
1 pc. $1'' \times 3'$
2 pcs. $\frac{5}{8}'' \times 3'$
Hardware
2 rubber tires $8''$ diameter
1 pc. cold-rolled steel rod $\frac{1}{2}''$ diameter $\times 18''$
2 acorn nuts $\frac{1}{2}$-13NC (or cotter pins)
4 flat washers $\frac{1}{2}''$
$\frac{1}{4}$ pound finishing nails 4d
1 box underlayment nails $1\frac{1}{4}''$
$\frac{1}{2}$ pint waterproof glue
1 pint exterior-grade paint or stain

rubber shock cord. The width of the cart is narrow enough to fit easily through a doorway. When not needed for hauling wood, the firewood cart doubles as a light hand truck for moving boxes, trash cans, and other items.

CONSTRUCTION

1. Cut two pieces of 2×3 ($1\frac{1}{2}'' \times 2\frac{1}{2}''$) stock to 48 inches each for the uprights. On each piece, cut a $1\frac{1}{4}$-inch radius on the upper end, and a $2\frac{1}{2}$-inch-wide rabbet $\frac{3}{4}$ inch deep on the lower end, across the outside face, as shown in illustration A.

2. Drill a 1-inch-diameter hole through each upright, centered $1\frac{1}{4}$ inches from the upper end, to receive the frame dowel that will serve as the cart handle (see step 6). Also, center and drill one $\frac{5}{8}$-inch-diameter hole

11 inches below the upper end of each upright to receive the leg pivot dowel (see step 11), and a second hole $\frac{7}{8}$ inch from the rear edge and $9\frac{1}{4}$ inches below the upper end of each upright to receive the leg stop dowel (see step 6), all as shown in illustration A.

3. Cut two pieces of 2×3 stock to 30 inches each for the bottom rails. Beginning $20\frac{1}{4}$ inches from the front end, cut a $2\frac{1}{2}$-inch-wide dado $\frac{3}{4}$ inch deep across the inside

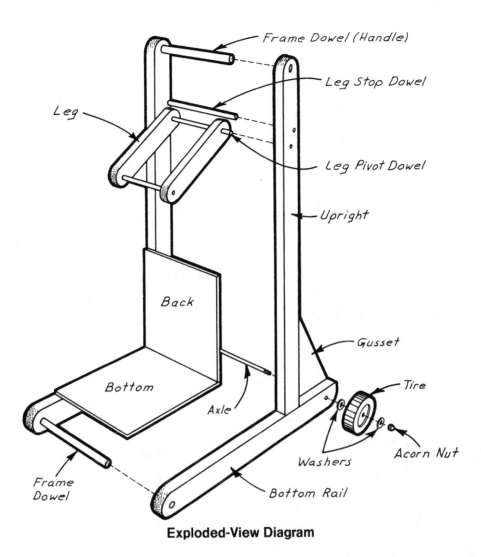

Frame Dowel (Handle)

Leg Stop Dowel

Leg

Leg Pivot Dowel

Upright

Back

Gusset

Tire

Bottom

Axle

Acorn Nut

Washers

Frame
Dowel

Bottom Rail

Exploded-View Diagram

face of each rail to accept the rabbeted ends of the uprights (see step 5). Be sure to make a left and a right rail.

4. On each bottom rail, cut a 1¼-inch radius on the front end and the lower corner of the rear end. Then drill a 1-inch-diameter hole centered 1¼ inches from the front end and a ½-inch-diameter hole centered 3 inches from the rear end. The first hole is for a frame dowel (see step 6), the second hole for the cart axle (see step 13).

5. Fit the rabbeted ends of the uprights into the dadoes cut into the bottom rails and secure the joints with waterproof glue and 1¼-inch underlayment nails installed from the inside so they will not be visible on the finished cart.

6. Cut two pieces of 1-inch-diameter dowel to 14 inches each for frame dowels. Install them, as shown in the exploded-view diagram, in the holes drilled in steps 2 and 4 using waterproof glue. Drive a 4d finishing

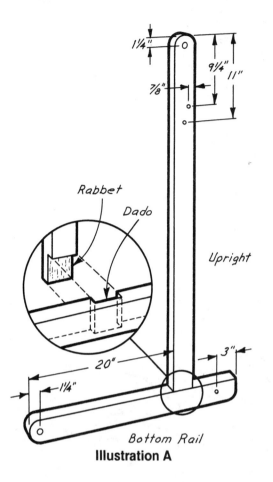

Illustration A

to the front of the uprights in a similar manner. Its bottom edge should rest on the first plywood piece.

8. Cut two pieces of ¼-inch plywood, each 9¾ inches wide and 16¾ inches high, for gussets to fit between the uprights and bottom rails, against the back of the square plywood piece installed in the previous step. Using illustration B and the exploded-view diagram as a guide, drill a ½-inch-diameter hole for the axle and further cut each gusset to final shape. Then fasten the gussets in place using waterproof glue and 1¼-inch underlayment nails.

9. Cut two pieces of 2 × 3 stock to 14 inches each for the legs. Cut a 1¼-inch radius on both ends of each leg, then center and drill a ⅝-inch-diameter hole 1¼ inches from the ends.

10. Cut one piece of ⅝-inch dowel to 10⅞ inches for a leg brace. Fasten it between the lower ends of the legs using waterproof glue and 4d finishing nails. Make sure the ends of

nail into each joint for extra strength. Also cut one piece of ⅝-inch-diameter dowel to 14 inches for the leg stop. Fasten it in place, using waterproof glue, in the hole drilled for it in step 2.

7. Cut one piece of ¼-inch exterior-grade plywood to 14 × 18 inches for the bottom, and fasten it to the upper edges of the bottom rails using waterproof glue and 1¼-inch underlayment nails. Make sure the rear edge of the plywood is flush against the uprights, and the side edges are flush with the outside edges of the bottom rails. Cut a second piece of ¼-inch plywood to 14 × 14 inches for the back, and fasten it

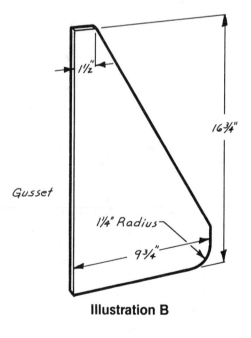

Illustration B

LUMBER CUTTING LIST

Size	Piece	Quantity
2 × 3		
1½″ × 2½″ × 48″	Uprights	2
1½″ × 2½″ × 30″	Bottom rails	2
1½″ × 2½″ × 14″	Legs	2
Plywood		
¼″ × 14″ × 18″	Bottom piece	1
¼″ × 14″ × 14″	Back piece	1
¼″ × 9¾″ × 16¾″	Gussets	2
Dowels		
1″ × 14″	Frame dowels	2
⅝″ × 14″	Leg stop	1
⅝″ × 14″	Leg pivot	1
⅝″ × 10⅞″	Leg brace	1

the dowel are flush with the outsides of the legs and that the legs are parallel.

11. Cut one piece of ⅝-inch-diameter dowel to 14 inches for the leg pivot rod. Thread the rod through the holes in the uprights and the upper ends of the legs, as shown in the exploded-view diagram. Drive 4d finishing nails through the legs and into the rod, but do not fasten the rod to the uprights, since it must remain free to pivot.

12. Sand the cart and eliminate any sharp edges. Finish it with exterior-grade stain or enamel.

13. Cut one piece of ½-inch-diameter cold-rolled steel rod to 18 inches for the axle. Cut threads on the final ½ inch of each end to accept nuts, or drill holes for cotter pins. Paint the axle, if desired, then insert it into the cart frame. Place a ½-inch flat washer over each axle end, then mount 8-inch-diameter rubber tires. Add a second washer after each tire, then secure the tires on the axle with acorn nuts or cotter pins.

DUSTLESS ASH CONTAINER

SHOPPING LIST

Lumber
1 pc. 5/4 × 3 × 1'
Hardware
1 pc. 24-gauge galvanized steel sheet
    20¼'' × 28''
2 panhead screws #8 × 1¼''
7 oval head mild steel rivets or steel pop rivets
    ⅛'' × ¼''
heat-resistant paint (optional)

This device is designed to be used with the ash hoe, described on p. 447, and offers an easy, dust-free method of removing ashes from your wood stove. The container's backless design allows it to be placed against the mouth of the stove, where the stove's natural draft draws the dust away as the ashes are being scraped into it, as shown in the photograph.

A product of the Rodale Design Group, the dustless ash container is made of lightweight sheet metal, easily formed by clamping between two square-edged pieces of hardwood and using a light ball-pein or tinsmith's hammer to turn the seams or hem them (fold them over) flat. The container pictured was designed to fit a particular stove. Before you build your container, measure the opening of your own stove and

alter our dimensions accordingly, so that your container fits tightly into the opening.

CONSTRUCTION

1. Cut one piece of 24-gauge galvanized steel sheet to 20¼ × 28 inches. Trace the layout of the ash container on it, as shown in illustration A, using a straightedge and a scratch awl or nail. Cut out the pattern using metal-cutting shears. Drill holes for #8 screws, where indicated on the cutting diagram, in what will become the top of the container.

2. Hem (fold over and flatten) the edges marked with Xs in illustration A. Along all other seams, except the flap that extends from the back of the bottom, bend the metal to 90-degree angles. Be sure to turn all seams in the same direction so that all the hems will be located on the inside of the container.

3. Bend the flap that extends from the back of the container bottom in three places to

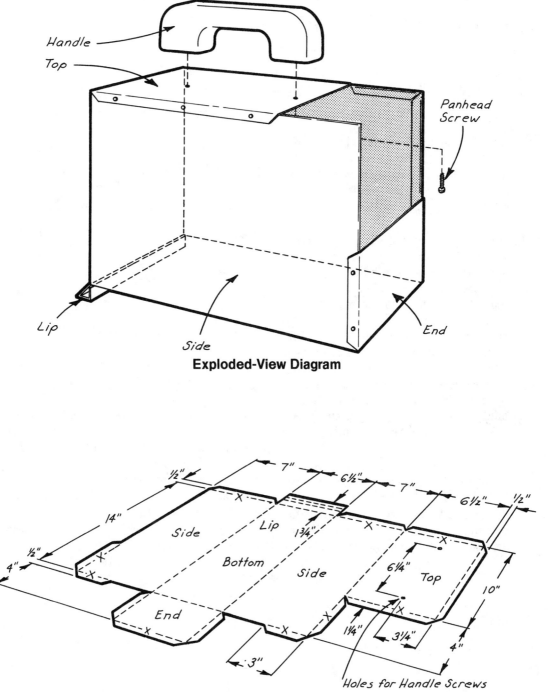

Exploded-View Diagram

Illustration A

445

LUMBER CUTTING LIST

Size	Piece	Quantity
5/4 × 3		
1⅛″ × 2½″ × 8½″	Handle	1

create a triangular lip that will fit over the bottom edge of the stove-door opening. This will hold the ash container in place against the stove and provide a small ramp for raking ashes up into the body of the container.

4. Drill a pair of rivet holes in each seam tab located at the front end of the box. Drill three ⅛-inch rivet holes in the single seam tab that folds from the box top over the edge of one side. Fold the seam tabs in place. Then, using the holes as guides, mark the locations of aligning holes in the sides using a center punch. Drill holes in those locations as well to permit riveting the parts together. Fasten the seam tabs to the box sides using ⅛ × ¼-inch oval head mild steel rivets or steel pop rivets in each hole. Remove any sharp corners with a file.

5. Lay out the shape of a handle, approximately 8½ inches in length, on a piece of 5/4 × 3 (1⅛″ × 2½″) stock, as shown in illustration B. Cut out the inside of the handle; then, using a router, file, or sandpaper, radius both the outer and inner

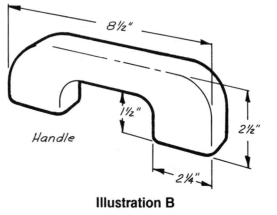

Illustration B

edges of the handle, as shown in the same illustration.

6. Center the handle over the holes in the top of the ash container and mark the screw-hole locations. Remove the handle and drill ⅛-inch pilot holes to receive #8 screws, then fasten the handle to the box using a pair of 1¼-inch #8 panhead screws, installed from underneath.

7. Paint the container and handle with heat-resistant paint, if desired.

ASH HOE

This handy, easy-to-make tool for raking ashes out of a wood stove was designed to be used with the dustless ash container featured on p. 444. Like the container, the ash hoe is a product of the Rodale Design Group, and the hoe pictured here was sized to fit a particular stove. The length of the hoe was determined by the depth of that stove plus the length of the ash container made to fit it. If your requirements vary significantly, simply modify the dimensions shown in our plans. The curved hoe blade was cut to a 3-inch radius to make it useful for scraping creosote from the inside of a 6-inch-diameter stovepipe. You will have to alter this dimension if your stovepipe is a different diameter.

SHOPPING LIST

Hardware
1 pc. 16-gauge mild steel sheet 2½″ × 5¾″
1 pc. mild steel rod ⁵⁄₁₆″ diameter × 38″
2 mild steel rivets ⅛″ × ¼″
heat-resistant paint (optional)

CONSTRUCTION

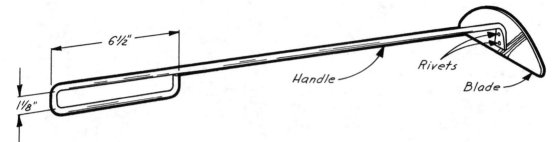

Exploded-View Diagram

1. Cut one piece of 5/16-inch-diameter mild steel rod to approximately 38 inches in length for the hoe handle. Bend the handle to the shape shown in the exploded-view diagram. When forming the loop at the end, be sure to leave adequate room for inserting gloved fingers.

2. Flatten about 1 inch of the straight end of the hoe handle to a 1/8-inch thickness and bend this section down at a 90-degree angle, as shown in the exploded-view diagram.

3. Cut a piece of 16-gauge mild steel sheet to 2½ × 5¾ inches for the blade. Cut a curve with a 3-inch radius across the top of the blade and round the sharp points, as shown in illustration A.

4. Drill a pair of 1/8-inch-diameter holes through

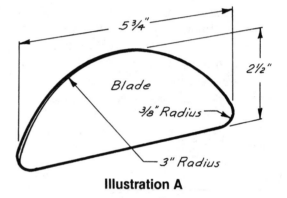

Illustration A

both the blade and the flattened part of the handle. Fasten the blade to the handle using a pair of 1/8 × 1/4-inch mild steel rivets.

5. Coat the ash hoe with heat-resistant paint, or finish as desired.

STORAGE, SHEDS, AND OUTBUILDINGS

ROOT-CELLAR STORAGE BOXES

SHOPPING LIST

Lumber
1 pc. 1 × 12 × 8'
3 pcs. 1 × 8 × 8'
Plywood
1 pc. ¼'' × 3' × 4' exterior grade
Hardware
4 casters 1¾''
1 pound finishing nails 6d
1 pound finishing nails 3d
1 box wire nails 18 gauge × ¾''
polyurethane

This system of interlocking boxes was designed by the Rodale Design Group as a root-cellar storage unit for fruits and vegetables. The boxes stack on top of one another and are kept from shifting about by means of simple cleats, which project from each upper box into the box below. The bottom box is equipped with casters so that the unit can be easily moved. The boxes shown here are constructed of No. 2 pine and plywood and finished with polyurethane.

CONSTRUCTION

1. Cut two pieces of 1 × 12 (¾'' × 11¼'') stock to 24 inches each for the sides of the bottom box, and two pieces to 14½ inches each for the ends. Save the leftover material for use in step 5.

2. Cut six pieces of 1 × 8 (¾'' × 7¼'') stock to 24 inches each for the sides of the upper three boxes, and six pieces to 14½ inches each for the ends. Save the leftover material for use in step 6.

3. Cut a 1½-inch-deep notch along the upper edge of each box side, stopping 3½ inches

from each end, as shown in the exploded-view diagram.

4. Center and cut a 1-inch-wide slot 8 inches long in each box end, 1 inch below the upper edge, as shown in the exploded-view diagram. Using a file, or a router equipped with a ⅜-inch rounding-over bit, radius the edges of the slots to provide a comfortable grip.

5. Cut the piece of 1 × 12 stock left over from step 1 to 14½ inches in length. Then rip it into two pieces, each ½ inch wide, for the

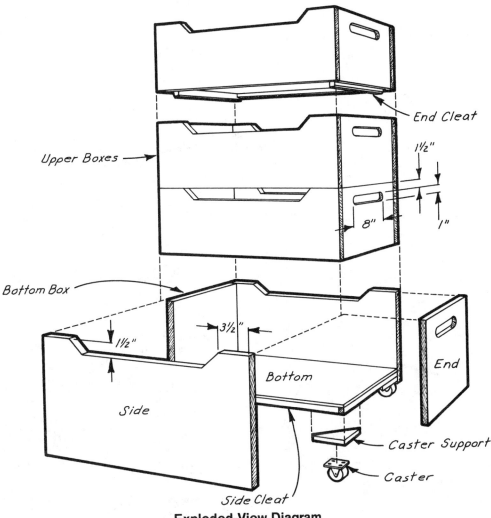

Exploded-View Diagram

end cleats of the bottom box, and six pieces, each 1 inch wide, for the end cleats of the upper boxes. Using a block plane, chamfer one long edge of each upper box cleat, as shown in illustration A.

6. Cut the piece of 1 × 8 stock left over from step 2 to 21 inches in length, then rip it into eight pieces, each ½ inch wide, for the side cleats of the four boxes.

7. If desired, round-over the outside edges of

all box sides and ends using sandpaper or a router equipped with a ⅜-inch rounding-over bit. Then assemble the boxes by fastening the sides to the ends using carpenter's wood glue and 6d finishing nails.

8. Fasten the end cleats to the lower inside edges of the three upper boxes using wood glue and 3d finishing nails. Position the cleats so that they project ½ inch below the bottom edges of each box and their

453

LUMBER CUTTING LIST

Size	Piece	Quantity
1 × 12		
¾″ × 11¼″ × 24″	Bottom box sides	2
¾″ × 11¼″ × 14½″	Bottom box ends	2
¾″ × 1″ × 14½″	Upper box end cleats	6
¾″ × ½″ × 14½″	Bottom box end cleats	2
1 × 8		
¾″ × 7¼″ × 24″	Upper box sides	6
¾″ × 7¼″ × 14½″	Upper box ends	6
¾″ × 4″ × 4″	Caster support blanks	2
¾″ × ½″ × 21″	Side cleats	8
Plywood		
¼″ × 14½″ × 22½″	Box bottoms	4

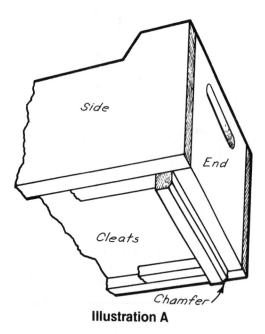

Illustration A

chamfered edges face outward, as shown in illustration A. Position the side cleats between them, also as shown, turned so their lower faces are flush with the bottom edges of the box sides, and their upper edges are flush with the upper edges of the end cleats. Fasten the side cleats, also using wood glue and 3d finishing nails.

9. To the underside of the bottom box, fasten the remaining cleats, all positioned the same way, so that their upper edges are 2 inches above the bottom of the box and their lower edges are flush with each other. Use wood glue and 3d finishing nails.

10. Cut four pieces of ¼-inch exterior-grade plywood to 14½ × 22½ inches each for box bottoms. Fasten these to the upper surfaces of the cleats in each box, using wood glue and ¾-inch × 18-gauge wire nails.

11. Cut two 4 × 4-inch squares of 1 × 8 stock in half diagonally to produce four triangular pieces for caster supports. Fasten these in the lower corners of the bottom box—to the undersides of the cleats—using wood glue and 3d finishing nails.

12. Sand the boxes and coat them with polyurethane. Fasten 1¾-inch casters to the caster supports.

VEGETABLE BIN

This old-fashioned vegetable bin looks right at home in a country kitchen. Designed and built by the Rodale Design Group primarily to store root vegetables, the unit contains four sturdy, individual bins that pivot to open and close. Each bin also lifts out completely for easy loading and cleaning. The perforated patterns on the bin fronts provide ventilation as well as decoration.

The vegetable bin is made of No. 2 pine, plywood, and tempered hardboard. The exterior wooden parts were stained and

shellacked. Then the entire piece, including the insides of the individual bins, received two coats of brushing lacquer to allow easy cleaning with soap and water.

CONSTRUCTION

To build the cabinet:

1. Cut two pieces of 1×10 ($\frac{3}{4}'' \times 9\frac{1}{4}''$) stock to $35\frac{1}{4}$ inches each for the sides. Lay out the pattern of the feet at the lower end of each piece, as shown in illustration A. Cut out the feet on both side pieces, then label one side left and the other side right.

2. Cut one piece of 1×10 stock to $40\frac{1}{2}$ inches for the bottom.

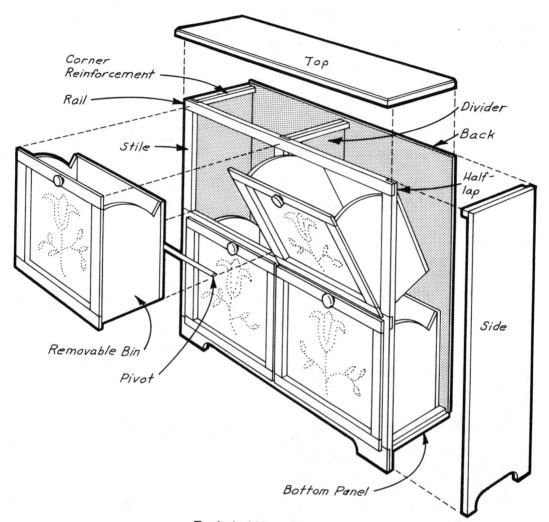

Exploded-View Diagram

3. Cut one piece of 1×12 ($\frac{3}{4}'' \times 11\frac{1}{4}''$) stock to 44 inches and trim it to 11 inches in width for the top. Cut a $\frac{1}{4} \times \frac{1}{4}$-inch chamfer along the upper edge of both ends and along one of the long sides to give the top a finished appearance.

4. Cut a $\frac{1}{4}$-inch-wide rabbet $\frac{3}{8}$ inch deep along the rear inside edges of both side pieces as well as in the top and bottom pieces to receive the plywood back, as shown in the exploded-view diagram.

5. Cut two pieces of 1×4 ($\frac{3}{4}'' \times 3\frac{1}{2}''$) stock to 9 inches each. Out of these rip five pieces, each $\frac{3}{4}$ inch wide, for corner reinforcements. Drill three evenly spaced screw holes, each $\frac{3}{16}$ inch in diameter, in each reinforcement, to be used when attaching them to the underside of the cabinet top and bottom.

6. Cut one piece of 1×10 stock to $31\frac{3}{4}$ inches, then rip it to 9 inches in width, for the middle divider. Position a reinforcement to

LUMBER CUTTING LIST

Size	Piece	Quantity
1 × 12		
¾″ × 11″ × 44″	Cabinet top	1
1 × 10		
¾″ × 9¼″ × 40½″	Cabinet bottom	1
¾″ × 9¼″ × 35¼″	Cabinet sides	2
¾″ × 9″ × 31¾″	Cabinet middle divider	1
1 × 4		
¾″ × 3½″ × 42″	Lower cabinet rail	1
¾″ × ¾″ × 9″	Reinforcement blocks	5
¾″ × ⅜″ × 18⅝″	Cleats	4
1 × 2		
¾″ × 1½″ × 42″	Top and middle cabinet rails	2
¾″ × 1½″ × 35¼″	Cabinet stiles	3
¾″ × 1½″ × 19⅜″	Bin rails	8
¾″ × 1½″ × 14⅝″	Bin stiles	8
½″ Plywood		
½″ × 9¼″ × 17⅝″	Bin bottoms	4
½″ × 9¼″ × 13⅞″	Bin sides	8
¼″ Plywood		
¼″ × 32½″ × 41¼″	Cabinet back	1
¼″ × 11¾″ × 18⅝″	Bin backs	4
Tempered Hardboard		
⅛″ × 13⅜″ × 17⅝″	Bin front panels	4
Molding		
¾″ × 18¾″	Pivots	4

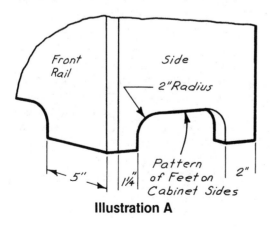

Illustration A

one side of the divider at its upper end, as shown in the exploded-view diagram, so that the top and ends of the block are flush with the divider's upper edges and the screw holes are vertical. Attach the block to the divider with carpenter's wood glue and 3d finishing nails. Position two reinforcements on the inside face of each cabinet side, one block flush with the upper edge of each side, the other block raised 2 inches above each side's lower end, even with the top of the cutout forming the legs. Locate the front end of each block flush with the front

457

edges of the cabinet sides, so that space is left behind the blocks to fit the cabinet back. Turn the blocks so the screw holes are vertical and attach them to the sides with wood glue and 3d finishing nails.

7. Cut one piece of ¼-inch exterior-grade plywood to 32½ × 41¼ inches for the back.

8. Assemble the cabinet frame. To do this, rest the bottom piece on the lower reinforcement blocks attached to the sides, so the front and rear edges of the bottom are flush with those of the sides. Locate the rear edge of the top flush with the rear edges of the sides and further position the top so its ends extend 1 inch beyond the sides in each direction. Fasten the top and bottom to the reinforcement blocks using wood glue and 1¼-inch #6 flathead wood screws.

9. Position the middle divider between the center of the top and the bottom, keeping the front edges of all three pieces flush. Attach the divider to the top with wood glue and by installing 1¼-inch #6 flathead wood screws through the holes in the reinforcement block. Drive 6d finishing nails through the bottom into the lower end of the divider. Fasten the back panel in place using wood glue and ⅞-inch × 18-gauge wire nails.

10. Cut three pieces of 1 × 2 (¾″ × 1½″) stock to 35¼ inches each for the stiles (vertical members) of the front frame, and two pieces to 42 inches each for the frame's top and middle rails (horizontal members). Then cut one piece of 1 × 4 stock to 42 inches for the frame's lower rail.

11. Arrange the frame pieces as shown in the exploded-view diagram. Mark each piece where it intersects another, then cut all the pieces so that half-lap joints are formed at these intersections. Cut on the front faces

of the stiles and the back faces of the rails so that only the rails will be visible at the joints.

12. Lay out the pattern of the legs on the bottom rail of the cabinet frame, as shown in the exploded-view diagram. The legs are each 5 inches in width, but the radius of their curve is the same as that of the side pieces. Cut out the legs, then glue and clamp the entire front frame together, making sure its sides are square. After the glue has set, fasten the frame to the body of the cabinet with wood glue and 6d finishing nails.

13. Cut four pieces of ¾-inch-diameter halfround to 18¾ inches each for pivots. Fasten the pivots to the front frame at the lower part of each bin opening, as shown in the exploded-view diagram, using wood glue and 3d finishing nails.

To build the bins:

1. Cut eight pieces of 1 × 2 stock to 14⅝ inches each for the stiles of the bin frames, and another eight pieces to 19⅜ inches each for the rails. Cut half-lap joints in all pieces, so the rails are visible on the outside, as shown in illustration B. Fasten the four bin frames together with wood glue.

2. Cut a ⅜ × ⅜-inch rabbet along the top inside edge of each bin frame. Cut a ⅞-inch-wide rabbet also ⅜ inch deep along the other three inside edges of each frame.

3. Cut eight pieces of ½-inch A-C grade plywood to 9¼ × 13⅞ inches each for bin sides. Shape the upper end of each side according to the pattern shown in illustration C. Then cut four additional pieces of ½-inch plywood to 9¼ × 17⅝ inches each for the bin bottoms.

4. Cut four pieces of ¼-inch plywood to 11¾ × 18⅝ inches each for the backs of the bins.

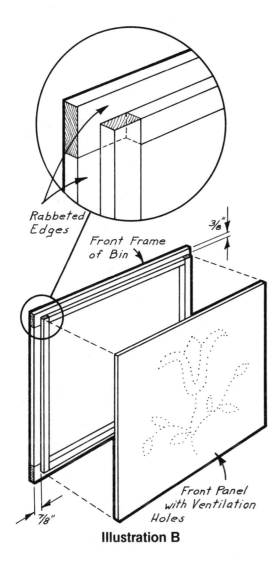

Illustration B

place using wood glue and $\frac{7}{8}$-inch × 18-gauge wire nails.

6. Cut one piece of 1 × 4 stock to 18⅝ inches, then rip it into four pieces, each ⅜ inch in width, for cleats. Fasten one cleat to the underside of each bin with wood glue and ¾-inch × 18-gauge wire nails, leaving a ¾-inch space between each cleat and the front frame of the bin to which it is attached.

7. Cut four pieces of ⅛-inch tempered hardboard to 13⅜ × 17⅝ inches each for the bin front panels. Trace a design on the front of each panel and imprint it on the panel by drilling a series of small ventilation holes, as shown in illustration B.

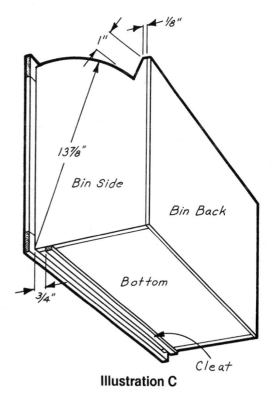

Illustration C

5. Assemble the bins by fastening the side and bottom pieces into the rabbets on the sides and bottoms of the frames, as shown in illustration C, using wood glue and 4d cement-coated box nails. Note that the bottom fits between the side pieces and that the back covers the rear edges of both the bottom and the sides. Fasten the back in

To finish the cabinet and bins:

1. Drive all nails on the outside of the cabinet frame below the surface, using a nail set. Putty the holes.

2. Sand all exposed wooden parts of cabinet and bins and round-over all sharp edges. Stain to the desired color, then seal the stained wood with shellac.

3. Fasten the drilled hardboard panels to the insides of the front frames of the bins using wood glue and ¾-inch × 18-gauge wire nails. Attach a 1-inch-diameter wooden drawer pull in the center of each frame's upper rail.

4. Finish the entire cabinet and bins, inside and out, with two coats of brushing lacquer to enhance its appearance and to allow cleaning with soap and water. Blow lacquer out of the holes in the bin panels if clogging occurs.

JELLY CUPBOARD

Here is a fine place to store those special harvest treats, your jams, jellies, and preserves. Designed by the Rodale Design Group, this Shaker-style jelly cupboard is attractive, functional, and easy as well as inexpensive to build. We used No. 2 pine throughout (except for the door and back panels, which are of mahogany-faced plywood), but any attractive wood, hard or soft, will do. The half-lap joints used in the frame and panel door are easy to cut compared to traditional mortise-and-tenon joints (though their strength and finished look are much the same), and even the curved feet at the base of the cupboard should pose no problem. A router is needed to groove the pieces of the door frame (unless you have access to a table saw), but except for that, the entire project is easy to build using only hand tools.

The shelves of our cupboard are spaced so that the top two will hold pints, and the remaining four will hold quarts. Of course, it is quite simple to alter the number and spacing of the shelves to match your own storage needs. Traditional cupboards, such as this one, were usually painted, and you may wish to paint yours. We finished ours clear, using two coats of brushing lacquer.

SHOPPING LIST

Lumber
1 pc. 5/4 × 8 × 6'
1 pc. 1 × 12 × 10'
2 pcs. 1 × 12 × 8'
3 pcs. 1 × 4 × 8'
1 pc. 1 × 4 × 5'
Plywood
1 sheet ¼'' × 4' × 8' exterior grade
Hardware
1 surface-mounted door lock
2 butt hinges 1½'' × 1½''
1 porcelain pull 1¼''
½ pound finishing nails 6d
¼ pound wire nails 18 gauge × ⅞''
1 pint brushing lacquer

CONSTRUCTION

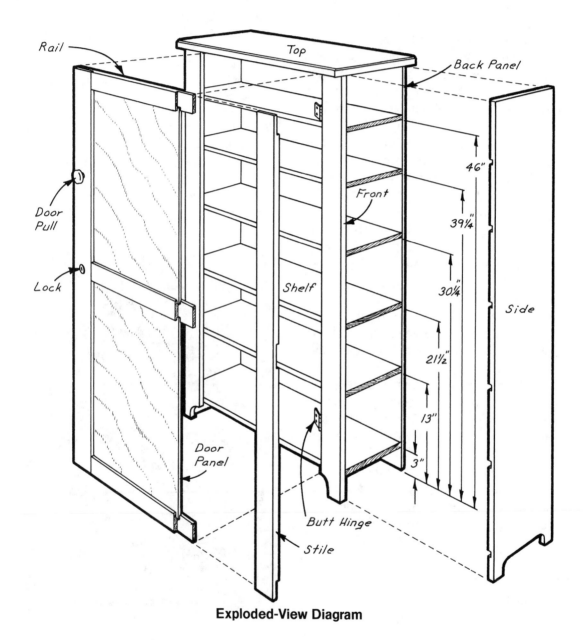

Exploded-View Diagram

LUMBER CUTTING LIST

Size	Piece	Quantity
5/4 × 8		
1⅛″ × 7¼″ × 36″	Cupboard top	2
1 × 12		
¾″ × 11¼″ × 52⅞″	Cupboard sides	2
¾″ × 11¼″ × 29¼″	Bottom shelf	1
¾″ × 11″ × 29¼″	Shelves	5
1 × 4		
¾″ × 3½″ × 52⅞″	Cupboard front pieces	2
¾″ × 3½″ × 50¼″	Door stiles	2
¾″ × 3½″ × 22¹³⁄₁₆″	Door rails	3
Plywood		
¼″ × 29¼″ × 49⅞″	Cupboard back panel	1
¼″ × 16⁹⁄₁₆″ × 20⅝″	Door panels	2

1. Cut two pieces of 5/4 × 8 (1⅛″ × 7¼″) stock to 36 inches each. Edge-glue the pieces together to make a blank for the top of the cupboard. After the glue has set, trim the blank to 32 inches in length and 13 inches in width. Then cut a ¼-inch chamfer along the upper edge of both ends and the front.

2. Cut two pieces of 1 × 12 (¾″ × 11¼″) stock to 52⅞ inches each for the cupboard sides. Lay out the pattern for the feet at the bottom of each side, as shown in illustration A. Label one piece as the cupboard's left side and the other as the cupboard's right.

3. Cut two pieces of 1 × 4 (¾″ × 3½″) stock to 52⅞ inches each for the front pieces of the cupboard. Label a left and a right piece, then cut the lower end of each to form a foot, as shown in the exploded-view diagram. Make the curve of these feet the same as that of the feet on the side pieces.

4. Cut one piece of 1 × 12 stock to 29¼ inches for the bottom shelf.

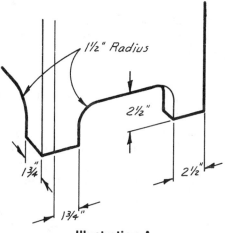

Illustration A

5. Cut one piece of ¼-inch exterior-grade plywood to 29¼ × 49⅞ inches for the back panel of the cupboard.

6. Cut a ¼-inch-wide rabbet ⅜ inch deep along the inside rear edge of the two cupboard sides and along the bottom shelf, to accept the back panel. Cut an identical groove on the lower rear edge of the top, but stop this

groove 1 inch short of the ends of the piece if you do not wish it to show on the finished project.

7. Cut five pieces of 1 × 12 stock to 29¼ inches each for the shelves. Trim each shelf to 11 inches in width.

8. Cut six dadoes, each ¾ inch wide and ⅜ inch deep, on the inside face of each cupboard side piece, to receive the shelves, as shown in the exploded-view diagram. To locate these dadoes, measure from the lower end of each side piece and mark points at 3, 13, 21½, 30¼, 39¼, and 46 inches. These points mark the lower edges of the six dadoes.

9. Spread a thin bead of carpenter's wood glue inside each dado and on the ends of each shelf. Fit the shelves into the dadoes and use clamps to pull all the pieces firmly into place. Make sure the front edges of all the shelves and sides are flush, leaving a ¼-inch space behind the shelves for the cupboard back. Check all angles to make sure each measures 90 degrees. For extra strength, drive 6d finishing nails at angles through the cupboard sides and into the ends of the shelves.

10. Fit the back panel into the rabbeted side pieces and against the shelves, then fasten the panel with wood glue and ⅞-inch × 18-gauge wire nails. Next, turn the cupboard over and attach the two front pieces in place so their outer edges are flush with the outside edges of the cupboard sides. Fasten the front pieces to the sides and shelf edges using wood glue and 6d finishing nails.

11. Stand the cupboard upright. Center the top piece lengthwise over the sides and fit its grooved edge against the projecting upper edge of the back. Fasten the top in place with wood glue and 6d finishing nails driven down through the top into the front and side pieces.

12. Cut two pieces of 1 × 4 stock to 50¼ inches each for the door stiles, and three pieces to 22¹³⁄₁₆ inches each for the rails. Cut half-lap joints on the ends of the three rails, as well as on the ends and at the center of the two stiles, as shown in the exploded-view diagram. Cut all the pieces so that the rails will overlap the inside face of each stile.

13. Cut a ¼-inch-wide groove ⅜ inch deep along the inside edge of each rail and stile to accept the door panels. Locate the grooves ¼ inch from the outside face on each board. Stop the grooves short of the ends of the stiles so they will not be visible on the assembled door. Note that the center rail must be grooved on both edges.

14. Cut two pieces of ¼-inch plywood to 16⁹⁄₁₆ × 20⅝ inches each for the door panels. Assemble the doors by gluing and clamping the rails and stiles together with the panels fitted (without glue) into the grooves.

15. Fit the assembled door to the front of the cupboard and make any necessary adjustments to achieve a good fit. Hang the door using a pair of 1½ × 1½-inch butt hinges, positioned as shown in the exploded-view diagram.

16. Install a surface-mounted door lock and a 1¼-inch porcelain pull on the door, also as shown in the exploded-view diagram.

17. Set all nails below the surface of the wood, putty the nail holes, then sand the outside of the cupboard. Finish with two coats of brushing lacquer.

UNDER-STAIR STORAGE SHELVES

Space found beneath a stairway is often wasted. This is especially true of the bottom flight of a series of stairs, such as the run leading to a basement. This set of storage shelves designed and built (for a specific house) by the Rodale Design Group can remedy this situation by providing a lot of usable space where there previously was none. Since the framing underneath the main floor of the house was exposed, as were the stair carriages, we felt justified in using rough lumber for the project. The open construction also simplified mounting the shelves, since they could be easily nailed to exposed joists and to the underside of the stairs themselves.

Since our shelves were made to fit a particular location, the dimensions given in the diagrams and step-by-step instructions should be used for reference only.

CONSTRUCTION

1. Cut two pieces of 2×4 ($1\frac{1}{2}'' \times 3\frac{1}{2}''$) stock to the length needed to fit them between the basement floor and ceiling, as vertical supports for shelves (89 inches each in our sample project). Use 12d common nails as fasteners for these and the remaining 2×4 framing members to be cut in subsequent steps.

2. Fasten the vertical supports to the nearest floor joist behind the stair header, as shown in the exploded-view diagram. Locate and space the vertical supports (21 inches apart outside to outside in our sample project) in such a way that one end of each shelf support can be attached to the outside edge of a vertical support with its other end attached to a stair carriage, as shown in illustration A.

3. Cut two pieces of 2×4 stock for bottom shelf supports. Make each the length needed

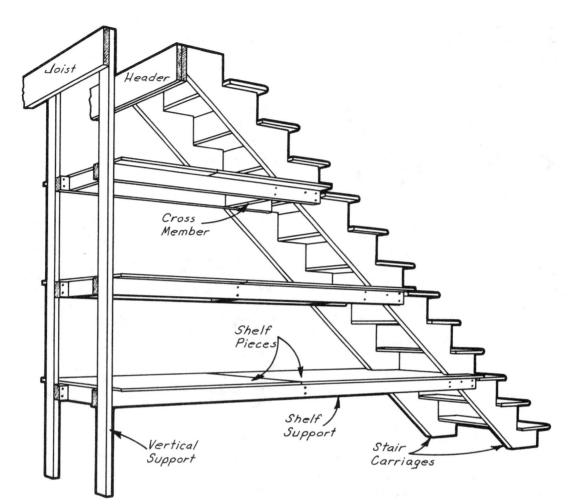

Exploded-View Diagram

to stretch from the side of a vertical support to a point ½ inch behind the third step of the stairway (96 inches in our sample project, as shown in the exploded-view diagram). Fasten these two shelf supports in place making sure they are both parallel and level.

4. Cut two pieces of 2 × 4 stock for middle shelf supports. Make each the length needed to reach from the side of a vertical support to a point ½ inch behind the sixth step of the stairway (79½ inches in our sample project). Fasten these two shelf supports in

place making certain they are both parallel and level.

5. Cut two pieces of 2 × 4 stock for top shelf supports. Make each the length needed to extend from the side of a vertical support to a point ½ inch behind the ninth step of the stairway (53½ inches in our sample project). Fasten these two shelf supports in place, making certain they are both parallel and level.

6. Cut eight pieces of 2 × 4 stock, each to the length needed to serve as cross members between parallel shelf supports (18 inches

LUMBER CUTTING LIST

Size	Piece	Quantity
2 × 4		
1½″ × 3½″ × 96″	Bottom shelf supports	2
1½″ × 3½″ × 89″	Vertical supports	2
1½″ × 3½″ × 79½″	Middle shelf supports	2
1½″ × 3½″ × 53½″	Top shelf supports	2
1½″ × 3½″ × 18″	Shelf support cross members	8
Plywood		
¾″ × 32″ × 48″	Bottom shelf pieces	2
¾″ × 32″ × 48″	Middle shelf piece	1
¾″ × 32″ × 31″	Top shelf piece	1
¾″ × 32″ × 22¼″	Middle shelf piece	1
¾″ × 32″ × 22″	Top shelf piece	1

in our sample project). Nail one cross member between each pair of shelf supports just inside the vertical supports and another as near as possible to the back edges of the stair carriage, as shown in the exploded-view diagram. Before fastening center cross members in place for the middle and bottom shelves, determine the dimensions of the plywood sheathing to be used for these shelves. Fasten the center cross members where they can serve as nailers for ends of adjoining pieces of sheathing, as shown in the exploded-view diagram.

7. Before cutting the plywood sheathing into shelf pieces, calculate the most economical way to utilize the material. In our sample project, all shelves were made a fraction under 32 inches in width, as shown in the cutting diagram, so that each sheet of plywood could be cut into three pieces (across

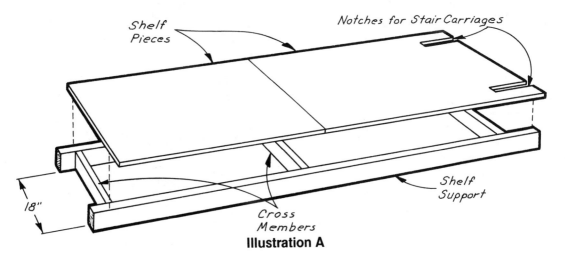

Illustration A

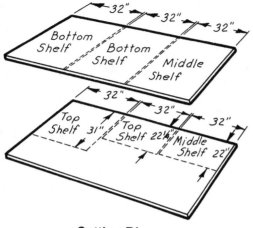

Cutting Diagram

the grain of the outer plies).

8. Cut two pieces of ¾-inch A-D grade plywood for the bottom shelf pieces (each measured 32 × 48 inches in our sample project). Notch one end of the back piece to fit around the stair carriage. Fasten these shelving pieces to their supports using 6d box nails.

9. Cut two pieces of ¾-inch plywood for the middle shelf pieces (in our sample project, one was 48 inches in length, the other 22¼ inches). Notch the back piece to fit around the stair carriage and fasten both pieces in place as in the previous step.

10. Cut two pieces of ¾-inch plywood for the top shelf pieces (one piece was 31 inches, the other 22 inches in length in our sample project). Notch the back piece to fit around the stair carriage and fasten both in position as in the previous two steps.

CLOSET CUPBOARD

This mighty storage unit, from the Rodale Design Group, has lots of applications as a built-in and will suit a variety of locations. Installed in the kitchen, the closet cupboard can serve as a pantry. In the basement or garage it can store tools or painting supplies. The closet cupboard can even be put to use in a bedroom or hallway to serve as a wardrobe or linen closet.

The model pictured and described here was custom-built to suit a particular location, a recess in the kitchen of a specific house.

SHOPPING LIST

Lumber
8 pcs. $1 \times 2 \times 8'$
2 pcs. $1 \times 2 \times 6'$
1 pc. $1 \times 1 \times 6'$
Plywood
2 sheets $\frac{3}{4}'' \times 4' \times 8'$ A-C grade
1 pc. $\frac{3}{4}'' \times 4' \times 4'$ A-C grade
1 sheet $\frac{1}{4}'' \times 4' \times 8'$ exterior grade
Paneling
1 sheet $\frac{1}{4}'' \times 4' \times 8'$
Hardware
12 strap hinges 5'' with screws
4 friction catches
4 cabinet door handles
$\frac{1}{4}$ pound finishing nails 6d
1 box wire nails 18 gauge $\times \frac{5}{8}''$
1 pound cement-coated box nails 6d
$\frac{1}{4}$ pound cement-coated box nails 3d
1 gallon latex enamel

When in place, the design of the cupboard is such that the doors lie flush with the existing adjacent wall. The doors are mounted with hinges to posts in the wall, rather than to the closet sides, and the recessed area where the cupboard is installed is raised slightly above floor level so that clearance for the lower doors is automatically provided. Keep these two considerations in mind as you design your own closet cupboard. If you choose to hinge the doors directly to the closet sides, stiffen the structure by installing a fixed shelf across the center of the closet where the top and bottom doors meet. If the bottom doors require clearance beneath them to open freely, construct a low base on which to mount the cabinet. You might choose to install the closet cupboard in an open area, so it functions as a room divider. In that case, try framing the unit with vertical posts anchored

469

to the floor and ceiling.

The dimensions given in the instructions are, obviously, for a specific cupboard.

They're easy to alter, however, once you've studied the plans and adapted them to suit your own needs.

CONSTRUCTION

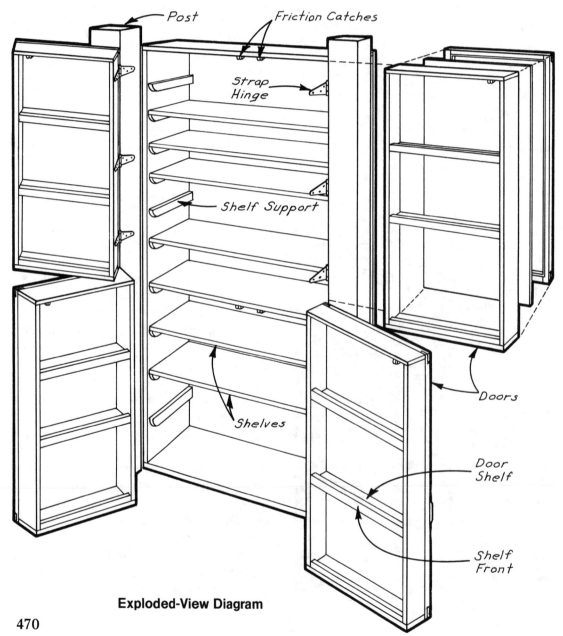

Exploded-View Diagram

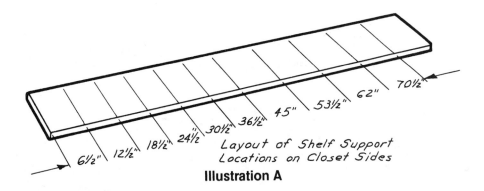

6½"   12½"   18½"   24½"   30½"   36½"   45"   53½"   62"   70½"

*Layout of Shelf Support
Locations on Closet Sides*

Illustration A

1. Cut two pieces of ¾-inch A-C grade plywood to 12 × 78¾ inches each for the closet sides. Use the cutting diagram as a guide for cutting these and all other pieces of plywood. Lay out the locations for the shelf supports on one of the pieces, along one edge. To do this, first identify the left end as the top of the closet side, then stretch a tape from left to right and make the first mark at 6½ inches, as shown in illustration A. Make an additional mark every 6 inches along the edge of the piece until six

LUMBER CUTTING LIST

Size	Piece	Quantity
1 × 2		
¾″ × 1½″ × 40″	Door panel frame sides	8
¾″ × 1½″ × 20⅛″	Door panel frame tops and bottoms	8
¾″ × 1½″ × 17¾″	Shelf fronts	8
¾″ × 1½″ × 11⅞″	Shelf supports	20
1 × 1		
¾″ × ¾″ × 17¾″	Fronts for door bottoms	4
¾″ Plywood		
¾″ × 12″ × 78¾″	Closet sides	2
¾″ × 12″ × 40½″	Closet top and bottom	2
¾″ × 11⅞″ × 38⅞″	Closet shelves	7
¾″ × 5″ × 38½″	Door sides	4
¾″ × 4¾″ × 38½″	Door sides	4
¾″ × 4¾″ × 20⅛″	Door tops and bottoms	8
¾″ × 4″ × 18⅝″	Door shelves	8
¼″ Plywood		
¼″ × 40½″ × 80¼″	Closet back	1
Paneling		
¼″ × 17⅞″ × 37¾″	Door panels	4

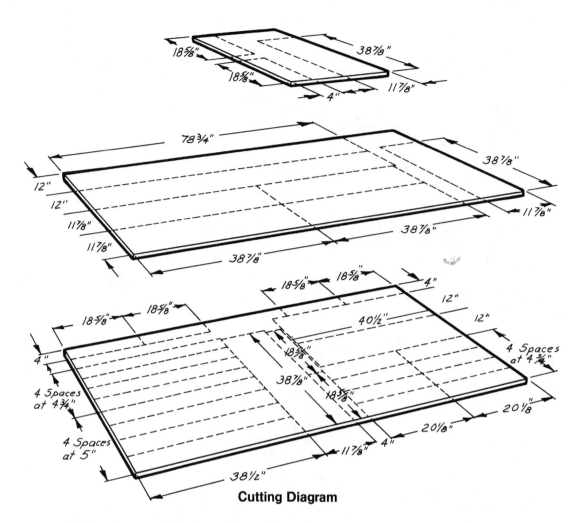

Cutting Diagram

points have been marked, then scribe an X immediately to the right of each mark to indicate the places for the supports. Continue measuring and marking four more positions, spacing each 8½ inches from the one before.

2. Place the other side piece face-to-face against the marked one and square a line across the edges of both boards at the 10 points. Open the boards and lay them edge to edge, then continue the lines across the inside face of each piece. Now cut 20 pieces of 1 × 2 (¾″ × 1½″) stock to 11⅞ inches

each for the shelf supports. Cut a 1-inch radius on the exposed front corner of each support, if desired. Position the supports so their upper edges lie along the marked lines, and align the rear edges of the supports flush with the rear edges of the side pieces. Fasten the supports in place with carpenter's wood glue and 3d cement-coated box nails.

3. Cut two pieces of ¾-inch plywood to 12 × 40½ inches each for the top and bottom of the closet. Also cut one piece of ¼-inch exterior-grade plywood to 40½ × 80¼

inches for the back of the closet. Fasten the top and bottom pieces to the closet sides, as shown in the exploded-view diagram, using wood glue and 6d cement-coated box nails. Fasten the back to the sides using wood glue and ⅝-inch × 18-gauge wire nails.

4. Cut seven pieces of ¾-inch plywood, or more if desired, to 11⅞ × 38⅞ inches each for shelves.

5. Cut four pieces of ¾-inch plywood to 4¾ × 38½ inches each, and four pieces to 5 × 38½ inches each for the sides of the doors. Bevel the long edges on the four wider pieces to 12 degrees, keeping the edges parallel to each other, as shown in illustration B.

6. Cut eight additional pieces of ¾-inch plywood to 4¾ × 20⅛ inches each for the tops and bottoms of the doors. Trim one end of each piece to a 12-degree angle. Fasten the top and bottom pieces across the ends of the door sides with wood glue and 6d cement-coated box nails to form four frames, each having one angled side, as shown in illustration B. The finished doors will be mounted with their angled sides meeting at the center of the cabinet.

7. Cut eight pieces of 1 × 2 stock to 40 inches each for the sides of the door panel frames, and eight pieces to 20⅛ inches each for the tops and bottoms. Rabbet the ends of all the pieces so they can be fastened together in half-lap joints. Then assemble the pieces to form four rectangular frames using wood glue. When the glue has set, use a router to cut a continuous rabbet, ⅜ inch wide and ¼ inch deep, around the inside edge of each frame to receive a panel.

8. Cut four pieces of ¼-inch-thick paneling to 17⅞ × 37¾ inches each for door panels. Set the panels in the rabbeted door frames and fasten them in place with wood glue and ⅝-inch × 18-gauge wire nails. Fasten one panel/frame assembly to the wider side of each door frame using wood glue and 6d finishing nails.

9. Cut eight pieces of ¾-inch plywood to 4 × 18⅝ inches each for door shelves. Cut a 12-degree angle across one end of each shelf, as shown in illustration B, so that it will fit inside the door frame. Identify the top and bottom of each door, remembering to make two right-hand and two left-hand doors. Position two shelves inside each door, where desired, and fasten them in place using wood glue and 6d cement-coated box nails driven through the frame from the outside.

10. Cut eight pieces of 1 × 2 stock to 17¾

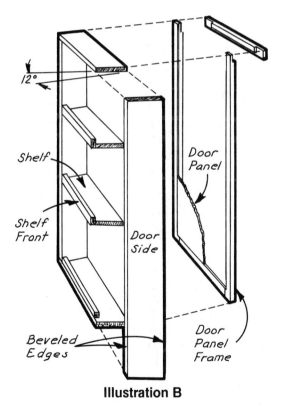

Illustration B

Labels on illustration: 12°, Shelf, Shelf Front, Beveled Edges, Door Panel, Door Side, Door Panel Frame

inches each for shelf fronts. Cut one end of each piece to a 12-degree angle. Fasten the shelf fronts to the edges of the door shelves so that the bottom edges of each pair of pieces are flush, using wood glue and 6d cement-coated box nails.

11. Cut four pieces of 1×1 (¾'' × ¾'') stock to 17¾ inches each for fronts to fit the bottoms of the doors, as shown in illustration B. Cut one end of each piece to a 12-degree angle. Position these pieces on top of the front edge of the door bottoms so the face of each front is flush with the edge of each door bottom. Fasten these pieces to the door sides and bottoms with wood glue and box nails.

12. Finish the closet and doors with paint or other coating, as desired. Then fasten three 5-inch strap hinges to the side of each door. Recess the hinges so their outer faces are flush with those of the door sides.

13. Make any necessary adjustments to the floor height in the location chosen for the closet cupboard, then install and anchor the closet in place. Mount the doors on adjacent posts, walls, or on the closet sides. Insert the shelves. Attach a handle to each door, and mount friction catches to both the closet frame and the inside of each door.

ADJUST-ABLE STORAGE SHELVES

SHOPPING LIST

Lumber
6 pcs. $2 \times 4 \times 10'$
1 pc. $2 \times 4 \times 8'$
Plywood
2 sheets $\frac{5}{8}'' \times 4' \times 8'$ A-C grade
Dowels
6 pcs. $\frac{3}{4}'' \times 6'$ hardwood or broom handles
Hardware
1 pound common nails 10d

These dowel-supported shelves, easily adjustable to any height, are a full 24 inches deep and can be made any length you wish. Rich Weinhold, the designer, of Salem, Oregon, uses the shelves to store home-canned foods in his garage. The plans shown here are for one 8-foot-long unit with four shelves, adjustable in 4-inch increments. Naturally, you may modify any of the specifications to suit your own requirements.

The large dowels that support the shelves double as hangers. Weinhold found that broom handles do wonderfully for this purpose. He also used discarded 24-inch-wide doors for a few of the shelves, in place of plywood, which is more expensive.

CONSTRUCTION

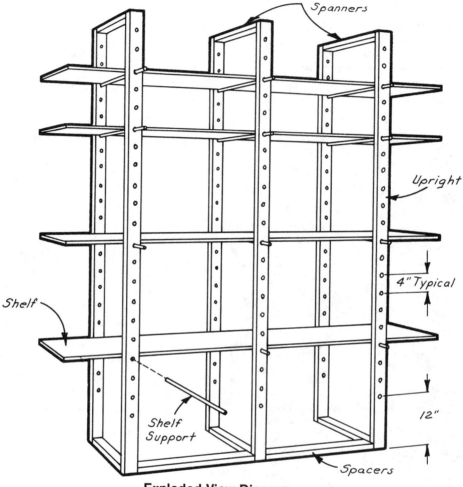

Exploded-View Diagram

1. Cut six pieces of 2×4 ($1\frac{1}{2}'' \times 3\frac{1}{2}''$) stock to 96 inches each for the uprights. If using 10-foot 2×4s, as specified in the shopping list, save the 24-inch cutoffs for the spanners (see step 3).

2. Drill 1-inch-diameter holes through the uprights to hold the shelf supports (see step 7). Position the holes at 4-inch inter-vals beginning 12 inches from one end of each upright. (These ends become the bottom ends.)

3. Trim the six cut-off pieces from step 1 to exactly 24 inches each for the spanners.

4. Assemble the spanners and the uprights to make three 27×96-inch rectangular frames, as shown in the exploded-view diagram.

476

LUMBER CUTTING LIST

Size	Piece	Quantity
2 × 4		
1½'' × 3½'' × 96''	Uprights	6
1½'' × 3½'' × 29''	Spacers	2
1½'' × 3½'' × 24''	Spanners	6
Plywood		
⅝'' × 24'' × 96''	Shelves	4
Dowels		
¾'' × 30''	Shelf supports	12

Be sure to keep the bottoms of the uprights at one end of the frames.

5. Locate the studs in your wall where the shelves will be installed. Fasten the three frames, bottoms down, to three studs so that the frames are spaced 32 inches apart on center. Use 10d common nails. (Use alternative fastening methods if you have a masonry wall, or if the studs are 24 inches on center.)

6. Cut two pieces of 2 × 4 to 29 inches each for the spacers. Fasten these between the front uprights so the 32-inch on-center spacing of the uprights is maintained.

7. Cut 12 pieces of ¾-inch-diameter hardwood dowel to 30 inches each for the shelf supports. Round off one end of each dowel.

8. Rip two sheets of ⅝-inch A-C grade plywood along the center line to make four shelf boards, each 24 × 96 inches. (Or substitute four discarded hollow-core doors.)

9. Paint the shelf boards, dowels, and frames, as you desire.

10. To assemble the shelves, slide the 12 support dowels through the front uprights and into the rear uprights at the desired shelf heights. The rounded ends of the dowels should project. Now slide the shelf boards into the frames from one end so that they rest on the shelf supports. If there is insufficient room to slide the shelf boards in from one end, try this: Remove all the dowels. Set all four shelf boards into the frames by standing them upright, then laying them down horizontally on the floor. Now lift the top shelf into position and install shelf supports beneath it. Raise the next shelf into place, insert the supports, and so on, until all four shelves are installed.

FREE-STANDING SHELVES

SHOPPING LIST

Lumber
2 pcs. $1 \times 10 \times 8'$
1 pc. $1 \times 6 \times 5'$
4 pcs. $1 \times 4 \times 8'$
Plywood
1 pc. $\frac{3}{4}'' \times 1' \times 1'$ exterior grade
Dowels
2 pcs. $\frac{1}{2}'' \times 3'$
1 pc. $\frac{1}{4}'' \times 3'$
Hardware
4 pcs. self-adhesive foam $2\frac{1}{4}'' \times 3\frac{1}{2}''$
2 carriage bolts $\frac{5}{16}'' \times 2\frac{1}{2}''$
2 tee nuts $\frac{5}{16}''$

These shelves, created by the Rodale Design Group, stand freely anywhere in a room and do not require fasteners installed in the walls or ceiling. Adjustable blocks at the top of the unit tighten to exert pressure, securing the shelves firmly in place by pressing them between floor and ceiling. Pads at each end prevent the marring of surfaces. Disassembly is easy also, and storage is compact.

The plans for the shelves shown in the photograph were made to fit a room whose ceiling height measures 85 inches. In order to erect the shelves, the vertical supports were cut 2 inches shorter. Measure your own ceiling before beginning this project, and size accordingly the lumber you choose.

Our unit was made using No. 2 pine and is finished with clear lacquer. Only four shelves were included, even though positions for six shelves exist. Naturally, choices such as these are matters of personal preference. The plans are easily modified to suit your needs.

CONSTRUCTION

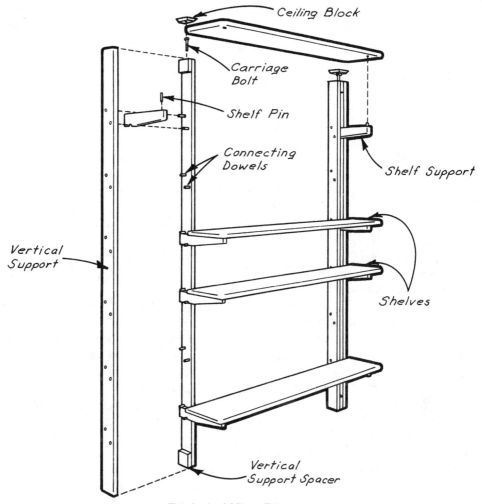

Ceiling Block

Carriage Bolt

Shelf Pin

Connecting Dowels

Shelf Support

Vertical Support

Shelves

Vertical Support Spacer

Exploded-View Diagram

1. Cut four pieces of 1×4 ($\frac{3}{4}'' \times 3\frac{1}{2}''$) stock to 83 inches each (or 2 inches less than the height of your ceiling) for the vertical supports. On one, mark the 12 positions where holes must be drilled for dowels that will lock the shelf supports in place (see step 3). Center the first hole $10\frac{3}{8}$ inches above the lower end of the vertical support

and $\frac{3}{4}$ inch from the front edge. Locate five additional holes on 12-inch centers above the first, as shown in illustration A.

2. Mark the centers for a second line of six holes $\frac{3}{4}$ inch from the rear edge of the vertical support, each centered $2\frac{3}{4}$ inches higher than the centers of the holes laid out in the previous step. Drill $\frac{1}{2}$-inch-diameter

479

LUMBER CUTTING LIST

Size	Piece	Quantity
1 × 10		
¾'' × 9¼'' × 48''	Shelves	4
1 × 6		
¾'' × 5⅛'' × 12⅜''	Shelf support blanks	4
1 × 4		
¾'' × 3½'' × 83''	Vertical supports	4
¾'' × 3½'' × 3½''	Vertical support spacers	4
Plywood		
¾'' × 2¼'' × 3½''	Ceiling blocks	2
Dowels		
½'' × 2⅜''	Connecting dowels	24
¼'' × ⅞''	Shelf pins	8

holes through the vertical support at the 12 points marked. Then use the support as a pattern for marking a matching set of holes through each of the other three vertical supports. Drill those holes as well.

3. Cut four pieces of 1 × 4 stock to 3½ inches each for spacers. Also cut 24 pieces of ½-inch-diameter dowel stock to 2⅜ inches each. Fasten the vertical supports together in pairs with one spacer at the upper end and another at the lower end. Insert the dowels through the sets of parallel holes and secure all dowels and spacers using carpenter's wood glue. Clamp the pieces while the glue dries, using scrap pieces of

1 × 4 stock as temporary spacers near the dowel joints. Remove these spacers after the glue is dry.

4. Drill a ⅜-inch-diameter hole 2½ inches deep into the center of the upper end of each assembled vertical support, for installing a height-adjusting bolt, as shown in the exploded-view diagram.

5. Use sandpaper or a chisel to trim the ends of the dowels flush with the sides of each vertical support. Then round-over all exposed edges on the supports using sand-

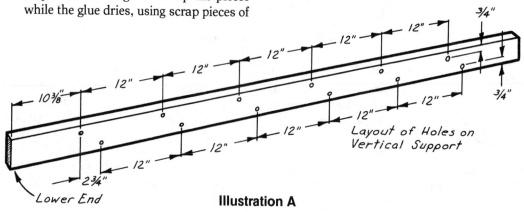

Layout of Holes on Vertical Support

Lower End

Illustration A

paper or a router equipped with a ¼-inch rounding-over bit.

6. Cut four pieces of 1 × 6 (¾″ × 5½″) stock to 12⅜ inches each for shelf support material. Trim each piece to 5⅛ inches in width, then center and drill a ⅝-inch-diameter hole through each piece 2⅝ inches from one end, as shown in illustration B. Next, center and drill ¼-inch-diameter holes ½ inch deep into both edges of each piece ¾ inch from the end opposite the one previously drilled, as shown in the same illustration. The latter holes are for shelf pins.

7. Rip each piece of shelf support material down the middle, cutting the ⅝-inch-diameter hole in half. Trim each resulting piece to the shape shown in illustration B. Then cut eight pieces of ¼-inch-diameter dowel to ⅞ inch each for shelf pins. Glue the pins in the holes drilled for them on what are now the upper edges of eight shelf supports.

8. Cut four pieces of 1 × 10 (¾″ × 9¼″) stock to 48 inches each for the shelves. Center and drill a 9/32-inch-diameter hole 1 inch from each end and 1⅛ inches from the front edge on the underside of each shelf. Make each hole ½ inch deep to receive the

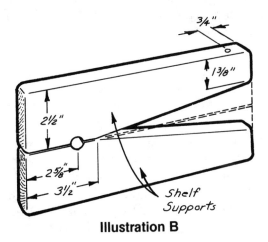

Illustration B

ends of the pins protruding from the tops of the shelf supports. Then cut a 1-inch radius on the corners of the shelves and round-over all sharp edges with sandpaper or a router equipped with a ¼-inch rounding-over bit.

9. Sand all shelves, shelf supports, and vertical supports, then apply finish, as desired.

10. Cut two pieces of ¾-inch exterior-grade plywood to 2¼ × 3½ inches each for ceiling blocks. Countersink a ¾-inch-diameter hole 3/16 inch deep into the center of one face on each block, then bevel the edges of the block toward that face, as shown in the exploded-view diagram. Sand both blocks and paint them to match the ceiling where the shelves will be installed.

11. Hammer a 5/16-inch tee nut into each hole in the top of the vertical supports. Thread a 5/16 × 2½-inch carriage bolt into each nut to serve as a height adjuster. Cover the top of each ceiling block and the bottom of each vertical support with self-adhesive foam.

12. To install the shelves, raise the vertical supports and place the ceiling blocks over the heads of the height-adjusting bolts. Plumb one support and secure it in place by tightening the adjusting bolt until the ceiling block is pushed firmly against the ceiling. Space the second vertical support 48¼ inches from the first, measuring from outside edge to outside edge, then adjust the bolt to lock the ceiling block into position. For good appearance, make sure both ceiling blocks are turned to match the profile of the vertical supports.

13. Insert the shelf supports at the heights desired, between the pairs of dowels inside the vertical supports. Lock the supports into position, as shown in the exploded-view diagram. Then mount the shelves on the supports, hooking the shelf pins into the holes drilled on the underside of each shelf.

LADDER-TYPE BIKE RACK

SHOPPING LIST

Lumber
2 pcs. $2 \times 4 \times 10'$
1 pc. $1 \times 6 \times 4'$
Dowel
1 pc. $\frac{5}{8}'' \times 3'$ hardwood
Hardware
1 pc. foam rubber $\frac{1}{2}'' \times 3'' \times 29''$
2 carriage bolts $\frac{3}{8}'' \times 4''$
2 tee nuts $\frac{3}{8}''$
$\frac{1}{2}$ pound finishing nails 6d

This bike rack is ideal for use in confined areas such as hallways and apartments. It also can be taken down easily for moving and can be adjusted to suit varying ceiling heights. Furthermore, it will not mar floors or ceilings.

The rack offers ample shelf storage space while easily holding up to four adult-size bikes. (Placed against a wall, the rack holds one or two bikes; moved away, there is room for two more.) Construction consists of dadoed uprights fitted with shelves. A top plate and a sill (lower plate) complete the ladderlike framework. The adjusting assembly is made from carriage bolts and tee nuts. Paint or polyurethane makes a nice finish.

CONSTRUCTION

1. Measure the height of the ceiling where the bike rack is to be installed.
2. Cut two pieces of 2×4 ($1\frac{1}{2}'' \times 3\frac{1}{2}''$) stock for the uprights, each to a length that is 5 inches less than the height of the ceiling.
3. Cut two pieces of 1×6 ($1\frac{1}{2}'' \times 5\frac{1}{2}''$) stock to 18 inches each for the shelves. More than two shelves can be built if you desire, but a minimum of two is required.
4. Position the two uprights side-by-side with their ends flush. At any convenient height, mark the positions of the shelves by hold-

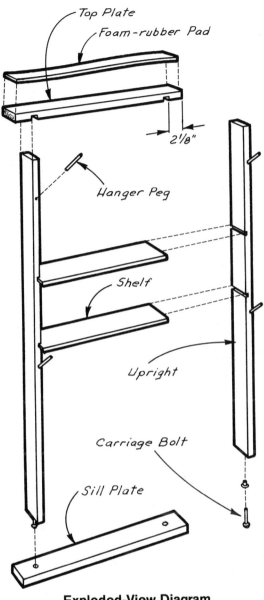

Exploded-View Diagram

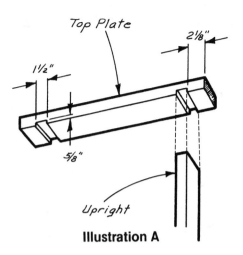

Illustration A

ing a square across both uprights at once and scribing ¾-inch-wide × ⅝-inch-deep dadoes across their inner faces. This will ensure that the shelves will be level.

5. Cut the shelf dadoes in the uprights and check the fit of the shelf boards. They should fit tightly.

6. Assemble the two uprights with the shelf

boards using carpenter's wood glue and 6d finishing nails. Check the assembly for squareness before the glue sets.

7. Cut two pieces of 2 × 4 stock to 24 inches each for the top plate and sill plate.

8. Center the top plate on top of the uprights and mark where the uprights fit against it. Cut dadoes 1½ inches wide × ⅝ inch deep across the underside of the plate to house the uprights, as shown in illustration A.

9. Fasten the plate to the uprights with wood glue and 6d finishing nails. Now hold the assembly in position. There should be about a 3-inch clearance between the top plate and ceiling.

10. Find the centers of the uprights by scribing an X from corner to corner across the end grain at the bottom of each upright, as shown in illustration B. Drill a ½-inch-diameter × 2-inch-deep hole into the bottom of each upright where the lines of each X cross. Insert a ⅜-inch tee nut into each hole, so the flange of the tee nut seats against the bottom of the upright; then thread a ⅜ × 4-inch carriage bolt into each tee nut and up into the hole.

11. Hold the sill plate centered against the carriage bolts and mark where the bolts touch the sill. Drill ⅜-inch-diameter × ⅛-inch-deep holes into the sill to accept the carriage bolt heads.

LUMBER CUTTING LIST

Size	Piece	Quantity
2 × 4		
1½″ × 3½″ × 96″	Uprights	2
1½″ × 3½″ × 24″	Top plate	1
1½″ × 3½″ × 24″	Sill plate	1
1 × 6		
¾″ × 5½″ × 18″	Shelves	2
Dowel		
⅝″ × 5½″	Hanger pegs	4

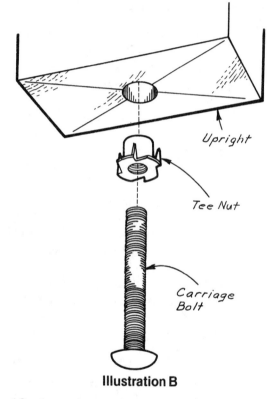

Illustration B

12. Cut a piece of foam rubber to ½ × 3 × 29 inches for a padding block. Fasten it to the upper surface of the top plate with wood glue.

13. Install the rack by positioning the sill on the floor in the approximate position that you want the bike rack. Stand the assembly on the sill with the carriage bolts in the sill plate holes. Plumb the rack and move it, if necessary, to get it in the exact spot. Tighten the rack into position by screwing the carriage bolts out with a wrench so they press against the sill (which in turn presses against the floor).

14. Position the bike hanger pegs by holding the first bike on the rack as high as you comfortably can. Make a mark on the uprights just below where the bike frame's horizontal tube touches them. Move the marks up or down if the pedals hit the shelves.

15. On each mark, drill a ⅝-inch-diameter × 2-inch-deep hole at a slightly downward angle into the front of the upright.

16. Cut ⅝-inch-diameter × 5½-inch dowels— two per bike—to use as bike hanger pegs.

17. Insert the bike hanger pegs in the first two bike holes.

18. Position the second bike below the first bike, allowing some clearance. As you did in step 15, drill two more hanger peg holes into the uprights, then insert the pegs.

19. Repeat steps 14 through 18 for the other side of the rack if additional bikes are to be stored.

20. Remove the bikes and gear from the rack and apply a finish to the wood. The project is then complete, unless you wish to add boxes or holes in the shelves to hold specialized gear.

TRI-ANGULAR BIKE RACK

SHOPPING LIST

Lumber
1 pc. 2 × 3 × 6'
1 pc. 5/4 × 4 × 8'
4 pcs. 5/4 × 4 × 6'
2 pc. 1 × 4 × 7'
1 pc. 1 × 2 × 6'
Dowels
3 pcs. ¾'' × 3' hardwood
Hardware
4 brass flathead wood screws #10 × 2¼''
5 brass roundhead wood screws #8 × 1½''
12 brass roundhead wood screws #6 × ⅝''
½ pound finishing nails 2d

Bicycles are a very efficient means of transportation, and fun besides, but only if they are kept convenient to use. Spending a lot of time getting ready for a short trip makes riding a bike something less than fun—and makes using your not-so-efficient car too convenient.

The triangular bicycle storage rack presented here offers a solution: It keeps everything neat, safe, and ready to roll. Not only will the rack hold two bikes (although it is also stable with just one), it also has shelves to store your helmet, gloves, shoes, and other bicycling gear.

Build the frame for the rack of 5/4-inch stock. This is actually about 1¼ inches thick and provides better stability and appearance than the more common ¾-inch stock.

CONSTRUCTION

1. Cut four pieces of 5/4 × 4 (1⅛'' × 3½'') stock to 72 inches each for the side pieces. Cut two pieces of 5/4 × 4 stock to 38 inches each for the bottom rails.

2. Cut the half-lap joints, as shown in illustration A. Assemble (without glue) the three pieces of each frame side to make sure the angles at the bottom corners are equal and

485

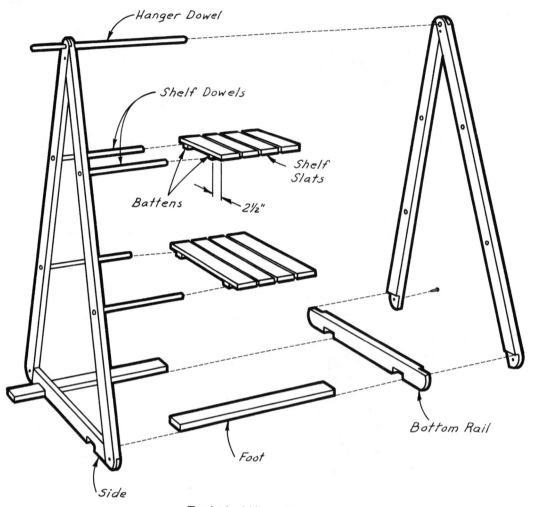

Hanger Dowel

Shelf Dowels

Shelf Slats

Battens

2½"

Foot

Bottom Rail

Side

Exploded-View Diagram

the joint at the top fits together tightly. Lay the dry-assembled sides on top of each other to make sure they are identical.

3. Now drill ⁵⁄₆₄-inch-diameter pilot holes at each joint, as shown in illustration A, and permanently assemble the frame sides with carpenter's wood glue and ⅝-inch #6 brass roundhead wood screws.

4. Drill ¾-inch-diameter holes in the frame sides for the dowels, in the positions shown in illustration B. Check the fit of the dowels after drilling the first hole since they

must be tight. For maximum accuracy use an expandable wood bit adjusted to the exact diameter of the dowel.

5. Round all six corners of the side frames with 1¼-inch radii.

6. Cut two notches, each 1½ inches deep × 2½ inches wide, in each of the bottom rails to accept the frame feet, as shown in illustration A.

7. Cut two pieces of 2 × 3 (1½" × 2½") stock to 29½ inches each for the feet.

LUMBER CUTTING LIST

Size	Piece	Quantity
2 × 3		
1½″ × 2½″ × 29½″	Feet	2
5/4 × 4		
1⅛″ × 3½″ × 72″	Sides	4
1⅛″ × 3½″ × 38″	Bottom rails	2
1 × 4		
¾″ × 3½″ × 25¾″	Lower shelf slats	4
¾″ × 3½″ × 14″	Upper shelf slats	4
1 × 2		
¾″ × 1½″ × 15¼″	Shelf battens	4
Dowels		
¾″ × 29½″	Bike hanger dowel	1
¾″ × 17½″	Shelf supports	4

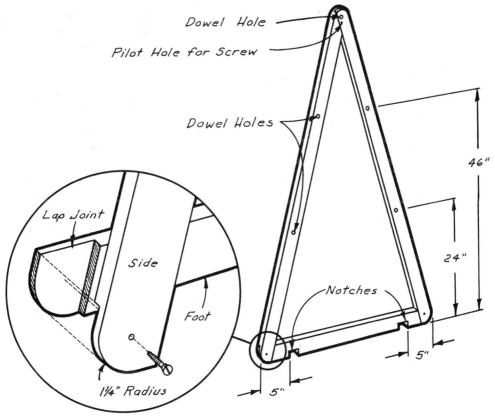

Illustration A

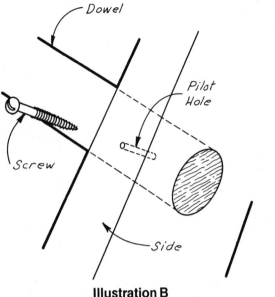

Illustration B

8. Cut one ¾-inch-diameter dowel to 29½ inches for the bike hanger dowel, and four pieces of ¾-inch-diameter dowel to 17½ inches each for the shelf dowels.

9. Insert the four shelf dowels through the holes in the frame until they fit flush with the outer face of each. Insert the bike hanger dowel through the upper hole so it extends 6 inches beyond the frame on both sides. Drill ¹⁄₁₆-inch-diameter pilot holes through the side frame and into the dowels. Secure the dowels with five 1½-inch #8 brass roundhead wood screws.

10. Tilt the assembly and align the feet so they extend past the frame sides by 6 inches in each direction. Drill ⅛-inch-diameter pilot hoels through the bottom of the feet and into the notches that house them. Secure the feet in the notches with 2¼-inch #10 brass flathead wood screws.

11. Cut four pieces of 1 × 4 (¾″ × 3½″) stock to 14 inches each for the upper shelf slats. Cut four pieces of 1 × 4 stock to 25¾ inches each for the lower shelf slats. Cut four pieces of 1 × 2 (¾″ × 1½″) stock to 15¼ inches each for the shelf battens.

12. Position the two groups of shelf slats on a flat surface. Arrange the slats in each group so they are evenly spaced and, together with their spacing, measure 15¼ inches across their width. Now position the shelf battens 2½ inches from the ends of each slat and nail the battens to the slats with 2d finishing nails. Sink the nail heads and fill the holes with wood putty.

13. Sand and finish all the parts of the rack. Install the shelves by laying them on top of the shelf dowels. No fasteners are required.

14. Hang the bikes from the dowel at the top and store all your gear on the shelves.

TRASH-CAN SHED

This attractive little shed provides an enclosure for two 22-gallon trash cans. Designed and built by the Rodale Design Group, the shed is meant to be attached to the wall of an existing structure, such as a house or garage, or against a back fence. Since the shed has neither a back nor foundation, you will have to devise a way to anchor it to the ground and enclose the back if you want it to stand alone. Each of the two trash-can holding units swings out of the shed on hinges attached to the sides. To open the shed fully, it must be located with 22 inches of free space on each side. The units rest and travel on casters, so the

SHOPPING LIST

Lumber
4 pcs. 2 × 4 × 8'
1 pc. 1 × 4 × 8'
Plywood
2 sheets ¾'' × 4' × 8' A-C grade
Roofing Material
12 square feet roofing material
Hardware
8 swivel casters 1½'' with screws
4 strap hinges 5'' with screws
¼ pound common nails 12d
½ pound common nails 8d
½ pound underlayment nails 1½''
1 pc. aluminum flashing 8'' × 42¼''
1 pc. drip molding 10'
1 quart exterior-grade primer
1 quart exterior-grade paint

ground beneath them and to each side of the shed should be reasonably firm and level to provide a smooth, rolling surface and to prevent excessive strain on the hinges. When the units are pushed back under the shed, the cans are not visible and are protected from the elements and from animals.

Our shed was finished with paint and shingles. We recommend using roofing material and exterior coating that match the structure to which the shed is attached.

CONSTRUCTION

1. Cut three pieces of 2 × 4 (1½'' × 3½'') stock to 46½ inches each for wall studs. Cut the upper end of each stud to slope 20 degrees toward the front, as shown in the exploded-view diagram.

2. Cut three pieces of 2 × 4 stock to 24½ inches each for the shed ceiling joists.

3. Cut three pieces of 2 × 4 stock to 26 inches each for the roof rafters. Cut the upper end of each rafter to a 20-degree angle and the lower end to a 70-degree angle. Both angles must slope to the inside of each piece, as shown in the exploded-view diagram.

4. Using 12d common nails, fasten one rafter to the upper end of each stud so the sloping top of the stud forms a continuous edge with the top of the rafter, as shown in the exploded-view diagram. Complete the triangular roof structure by fastening the three

joists under the angled bottom ends of the rafters and against the inside edges of the wall studs.

5. Cut one piece of 2 × 4 stock to 40¾ inches for the sill plate. Turn the wall studs on edge with their attached rafters up and nail the sill plate across the bottom ends of the studs using 12d common nails.

6. Cut one piece of ¾-inch A-C grade plywood to 34½ × 40¾ inches. Use the cutting diagram as a guide for cutting this and all other pieces of plywood. Lay the cut piece lengthwise across the inside of the three wall studs so its lower edge is flush with the bottom of the sill plate. Make sure the plywood is flush with the outside edge of the wall stud at each side, then fasten the plywood to the sill and the wall studs with 8d common nails. Before nailing the

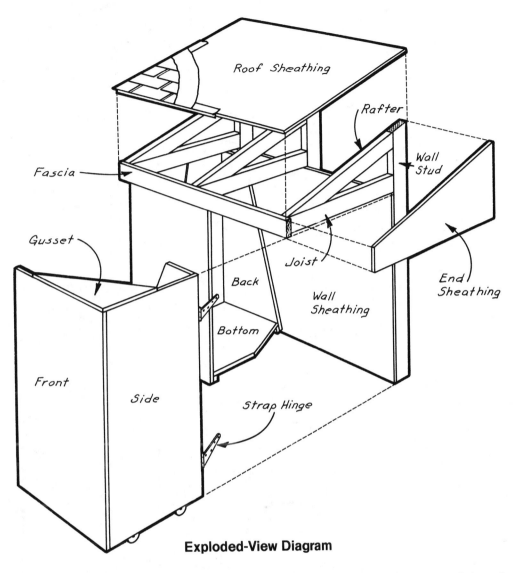

Exploded-View Diagram

plywood to the middle stud, check to make sure it is properly centered.

7. Cut one piece of ¾-inch plywood to 31 × 42¼ inches for the roof sheathing. Position the piece of plywood on the roof rafters so that its back edge is flush with the back of the wall studs and its ends overlap the rafters ¾ inch on each side. Fasten the sheathing to the ends of the studs and the upper edges of the rafters with 8d common nails.

8. Cut one piece of ¾-inch plywood to 18¼ × 28 inches for the blank from which to cut the two end sheathing pieces. Draw a diagonal line across the sheet to guide you in cutting two identical pieces, each 4 inches high on one side, 14⅛ inches high on the other side, and 28 inches across the

491

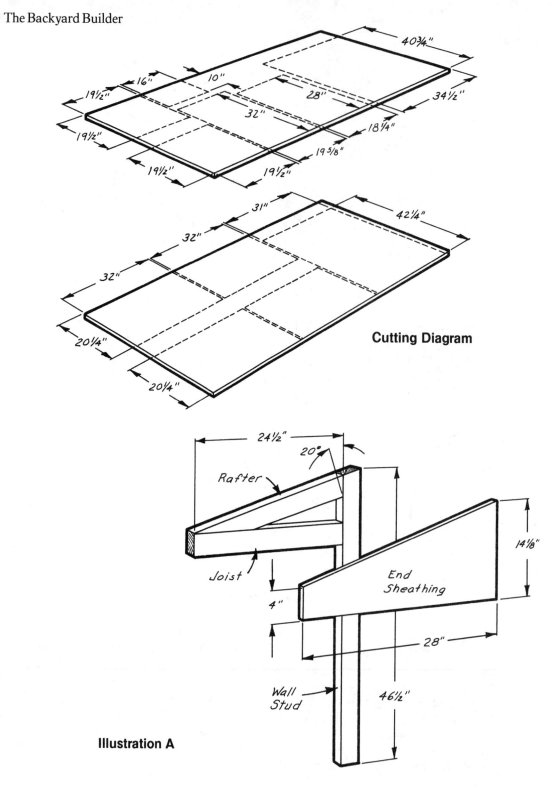

Cutting Diagram

Illustration A

LUMBER CUTTING LIST

Size	Piece	Quantity
2 × 4		
1½″ × 3½″ × 46½″	Wall studs	3
1½″ × 3½″ × 40¾″	Sill plate	1
1½″ × 3½″ × 26″	Roof rafters	3
1½″ × 3½″ × 24½″	Ceiling joists	3
1 × 4		
¾″ × 3½″ × 42¼″	Fascia	1
¾″ × 1″ × 19½″	Side cleats	2
¾″ × 1″ × 18¾″	Front cleats	2
¾″ × 1″ × 14¾″	Back cleats	2
Plywood		
¾″ × 34½″ × 40¾″	Wall sheathing	1
¾″ × 31″ × 42¼″	Roof sheathing	1
¾″ × 20¼″ × 32″	Can holding unit fronts and sides	4
¾″ × 19⅝″ × 32″	Can holding unit back blank	1
¾″ × 19½″ × 19½″	Can holding unit bottoms	2
¾″ × 18¼″ × 28″	End sheathing blank	1
¾″ × 10″ × 16″	Top gusset blank	1

bottom, as shown in illustration A. Remember to allow ⅛ inch for the saw kerf.

9. Fit one piece of end sheathing on each side of the shed roof. Hold the back edge of the sheathing flush with the back edge of the wall stud to which it will be attached, and the sloping upper edge of the sheathing flush with the underside of the shed roof. Fasten the sheathing to the rafters, joists, and studs with 8d common nails.

10. Cut one piece of 1 × 4 (¾″ × 3½″) stock to 42¼ inches for the eave fascia board. Fasten the board below the eave of the roof, across the front ends of the ceiling joists. The ends of the fascia board should be flush with the outside edges of the end sheathing, and the bottom edges of all the pieces should be flush as well. Fasten the fascia to the ends of the joists with 8d common nails.

11. Cut four pieces of ¾-inch plywood to 20¼ × 32 inches each for the fronts and sides of the can holding units.

12. Cut one piece of ¾-inch plywood to 19⅝ × 32 inches for a blank from which the backs of the can holding units will be cut. From the left side of the piece, measure 4 inches across the top and 15½ inches across the bottom. Then connect those two points with a diagonal line. Cut to the right of this line to form two identical pieces of the shape shown in illustration B.

13. Assemble the pieces cut in steps 11 and 12 into two units, one that will open to the left, the other to the right. In both units the side piece must overlap the back piece and be overlapped by the front piece, as shown in illustration B. Fasten the pieces of each unit together with wood glue and 1½-inch underlayment nails.

493

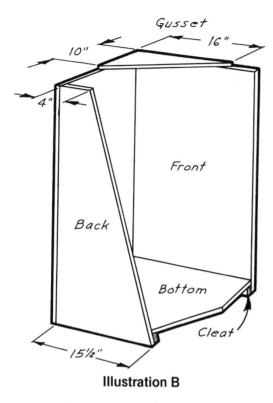

Illustration B

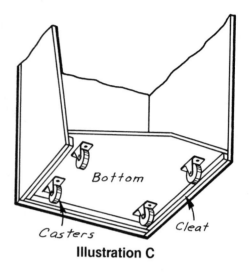

Illustration C

14. Cut one piece of ¾-inch plywood to 10 × 16 inches to form the blank for the top gussets. Cut this rectangle in half to form two right triangles. Fasten one of these triangular gussets to the upper edges of the front and side pieces to each can holding unit, as shown in illustration B, using wood glue and 1½-inch underlayment nails.

15. Cut one piece of 1 × 4 stock to approximately 40 inches in length. Then rip it into three 1-inch-wide pieces. From these rippings cut two pieces 14¾ inches each for back cleats, two pieces 18¾ inches each for front cleats, and two pieces 19½ inches each for side cleats.

16. Fit one side cleat into place on each can holding unit, making the bottom edges of the cleats and side pieces flush. Fasten the cleats to the side pieces with wood glue and 1½-inch underlayment nails.

17. Fit one front cleat and one back cleat in place on each can holding unit, as shown in illustration C. The front cleat butts against one end of the side cleat and the back cleat butts against the other end of the side cleat. Fasten these cleats to the front and back pieces with wood glue and 1½-inch underlayment nails.

18. Cut two pieces of ¾-inch plywood to 19½ × 19½ inches each for the bottoms of the can holders. From one corner of each piece, measure along the edge 9¾ inches to one side and 4½ inches along the edge to the other side. Connect the two points with a line, then cut away the triangular corner of each piece.

19. Attach the bottom pieces to the can holding units. The cut-away corners of each should be toward the rear and inside, as shown in illustration B. Fasten each bottom piece across the tops of the cleats installed in each unit, using wood glue and

1½-inch underlayment nails.

20. Paint the shed and can holding units with your choice of exterior-grade paint. Apply both a primer and finish coat.

21. When the paint is dry, fasten four 1½-inch swivel casters to the bottom of each can holding unit, as shown in illustration C. Fasten each unit to the shed with two 5-inch strap hinges, also as shown.

22. Attach the trash-can shed to the wall, fence, or other location you have selected, using appropriate fasteners, such as nails or lag bolts. To finish up, attach a drip molding to the edges of the shed roof, and seal the joint between the shed roof and the wall or other surface to which the shed is attached with a piece of aluminum flashing. Finally, cover the roof with shingles or with other roofing material of your choice.

PVC WOOD-SHED

Firewood needs some exposure to weather in order to season, but at the same time it must be sheltered sufficiently to avoid soaking up moisture from rain and snow. The Rodale Design Group developed the PVC woodshed to meet these needs. The slatted floor and open sides of the shed allow for air circulation, which gives the woodpile a chance to give off moisture. Meanwhile, the polyethylene cover shelters the wood from direct rain or snow.

The PVC woodshed is simple to construct and relatively inexpensive. Its interesting geometric form is sure to catch the eye of neighbors and passersby. The shed's major expense is the PVC pipe and the pressure-treated lumber that form the framework. However, these are durable materials and should provide many years of service. The polyethylene cover for the shed is quite inexpensive. If necessary, it can be easily replaced from year to year.

CONSTRUCTION

1. Cut three pieces of pressure-treated 4×4 (3½'' $\times$ 3½'') stock to 48 inches each for the end skids and center skids.

2. Cut three pieces of pressure-treated 2×4 (1½'' $\times$ 3½'') stock to 48 inches each, two for the intermediate skids and the third for the ridge board.

3. Cut two pieces of pressure-treated 2×4 stock to 66 inches each for the ridge supports. Obtain six pieces of 2×4, each 144 inches in length, for the floor slats.

4. Cut six pieces of 1×2 (¾'' $\times$ 1½'') stock to 48 inches each for the roof cover supports.

5. Bore a 1⅛-inch-diameter hole through the

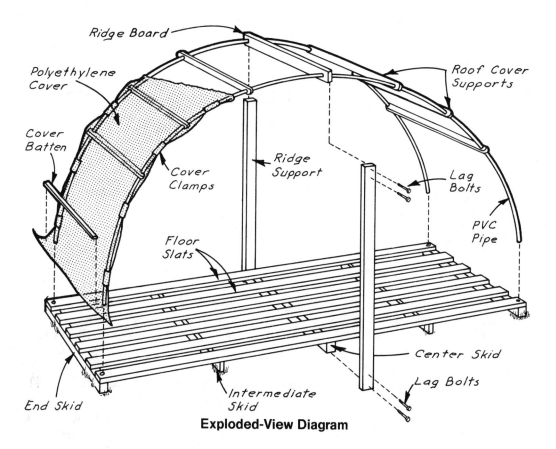

Ridge Board

Polyethylene Cover

Roof Cover Supports

Cover Batten

Cover Clamps

Ridge Support

Lag Bolts

PVC Pipe

Floor Slats

Center Skid

Lag Bolts

End Skid

Intermediate Skid

Exploded-View Diagram

ends of each cover support and also bore holes through the ends of the ridge board. Center each hole 1¾ inches from the end of each piece, as shown in illustration A. Afterward, cut a ¾-inch radius on the ends of each cover support.

6. Fasten the slats to the tops of the skids with 12d galvanized common nails. Make sure the slats and skids are evenly spaced, as shown in the exploded-view diagram. Avoid driving nails into the four corners of the shed base since holes must be drilled here for the pipe.

7. Bore a 1⅛-inch-diameter hole down through the center of each corner formed by the outside slats and end skids to receive the ends of the PVC pipe.

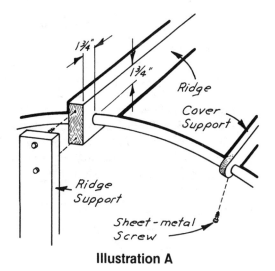

1¾"

1¾"

Ridge

Cover Support

Ridge Support

Sheet-metal Screw

Illustration A

497

LUMBER CUTTING LIST

Size	Piece	Quantity
4 × 4		
3½'' × 3½'' × 48''	End skids and center skids	3
2 × 4		
1½'' × 3½'' × 144''	Floor slats	6
1½'' × 3½'' × 66''	Ridge supports	2
1½'' × 3½'' × 48''	Intermediate skids	2
1½'' × 3½'' × 48''	Ridge board	1
1 × 2		
¾'' × 1½'' × 48''	Roof cover supports	6
⅜'' × ¾'' × 48''	Cover battens	2

8. Fasten the lower ends of the ridge supports to the ends of the center skid using two ¼ × 3-inch lag bolts with washers for each. Hold the ridge supports perpendicular to the shed floor while fastening.

9. Fasten the ridge board between the upper ends of the ridge supports using ¼ × 3-inch lag bolts with washers. Avoid the holes in the ends of the ridge, as shown in illustration A.

10. Cut two pieces of 1-inch-I.D. PVC pipe, each 18 feet in length. Push the pipe through the holes in the ridge until the length of pipe on each side of the ridge is equal.

11. Slip three cover supports onto the PVC pipe on each side of the ridge, then insert the ends of the pipe into the four corner holes in the floor. Spread the cover supports apart on 20-inch centers, measuring from the ridge, as shown in the exploded-view diagram. Fasten the supports in place by installing ½-inch #6 sheet-metal screws through the undersides of the supports into the pipe, as shown in illustration A.

12. Cut one piece of 6-mil polyethylene to 5 × 18½ feet for the shed cover. Center the cover over the shed frame and, using ¼-inch staples, staple it to the ridge board, cover supports, and the floor.

13. Cut a piece of 1 × 2 stock to 48 inches, then rip it into two pieces, each ⅜ × ¾ × 48 inches, for cover battens. Fasten the battens to the floor with 1 inch × 16-gauge wire nails, securing the ends of the cover.

14. Cut 20 pieces of 1-inch-I.D. polyethylene pipe, each 6 inches in length, for cover clamps. Slit the pieces of pipe along the length of one side so they can be pressed over the curved PVC pipes at the front and rear of the shed to function as clamps. Fasten the clamps over the polyethylene sheet at various points along each curved PVC pipe to hold the edges of the cover in place.

MINI-GREEN-HOUSE SHED

The Rodale Design group created this minished for gardeners who need a compact, outdoor storage area for garden supplies. The shed can provide shelter for bags of potting soil, peat moss, and other soil amendments, along with watering cans, clay pots, and small garden tools. The top of the shed is covered with a shiny aluminum cap so that it can serve as the base for a sunspace. A transparent window-well cover attached to a wooden frame sits on the base, creating a miniature greenhouse for starting seedlings and growing potted plants. Air holes drilled in the frame provide a small amount of

SHOPPING LIST

Lumber
5 pcs. $2 \times 4 \times 8'$
3 pcs. $1 \times 2 \times 8'$
Plywood
2 sheets $\frac{5}{8}'' \times 4' \times 8'$ T1-11
Hardware
1 window-well cover $16'' \times 44''$
30 panhead aluminum screws #4 $\times \frac{1}{2}''$
4 tee hinges $2''$ with screws
2 draw catches with screws
2 friction catches or barrel-bolt locks with screws
2 utility handles $4''$ with screws
1 pound common nails 12d
1 pound galvanized common nails 4d
1 box wire nails 18 gauge $\times \frac{1}{2}''$
1 pc. aluminum flashing $20'' \times 46\frac{1}{2}''$
1 tube silicone caulk
2 quarts polyurethane

ventilation to the greenhouse, but in really sunny weather the cover should be unlatched from the shed and blocked up to avoid overheating.

Our mini–greenhouse shed was built from construction-grade lumber and T1-11, a popular and relatively inexpensive textured plywood siding material. We finished the structure with a durable polyurethane. Alterations in materials and dimensions can, of course, be made according to individual needs and materials at hand.

CONSTRUCTION

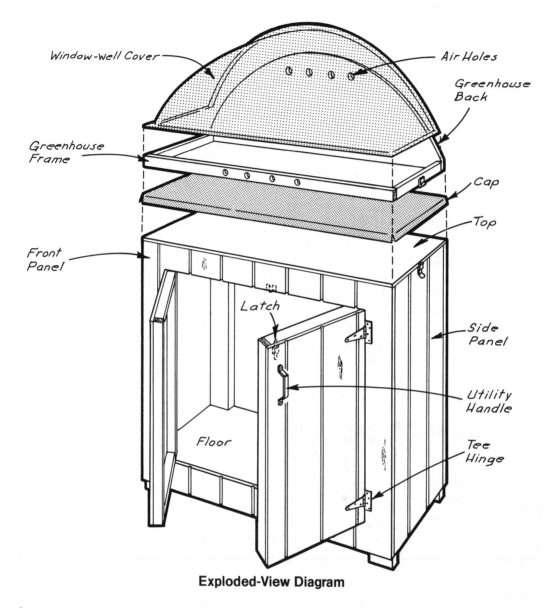

Exploded-View Diagram

1. Cut four pieces of 2×4 ($1\frac{1}{2}'' \times 3\frac{1}{2}''$) stock to $41\frac{1}{2}$ inches each for the corner posts. Also cut four pieces of 2×4 stock to $36\frac{1}{4}$ inches each for rails to suspend between posts across the front and rear of the shed. Cut six pieces of 2×4 stock to $13\frac{7}{8}$ inches each for joists to connect the front and rear sections of the post and rail structure. Fas-

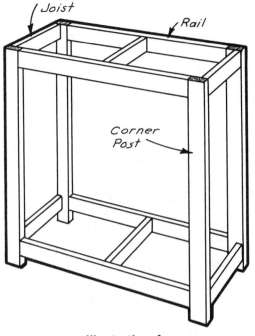

Joist

Rail

Corner
Post

Illustration A

ten these framing members together, as shown in illustration A, using 12d common nails.

2. Cut one piece of T1-11 plywood siding to 16⅞ × 43¼ inches for the shed floor. Use the cutting diagram as a guide for cutting this and all other pieces of plywood. Cut a 1½ × 3½-inch notch in each corner of the floor panel to make it fit around the corner posts. Fasten the panel smooth-side up to the floor framework. Use 4d galvanized common nails as fasteners when installing this and other pieces of plywood called for in subsequent steps.

3. Cut two pieces of T1-11 siding to 16⅞ × 39½ inches each for the side panels, and two pieces to 44½ × 39½ inches each for the front and back panels. Cut all four panels so that, when installed, the lines on their textured faces will be vertical, as shown in the exploded-view diagram. Fasten the side panels to the posts and joists on

LUMBER CUTTING LIST

Size	Piece	Quantity
2 × 4		
1½″ × 3½″ × 41½″	Corner posts	4
1½″ × 3½″ × 36¼″	Rails	4
1½″ × 3½″ × 13⅞″	Joists	6
1½″ × 2″ × 2″ × 3″ (approx.)	Reinforcing blocks	2
1 × 2		
¾″ × 1½″ × 44½″	Greenhouse frame front	1
¾″ × 1½″ × 16⅝″	Greenhouse frame sides	2
¾″ × 1″ × 31¾″	Door frame sides	4
¾″ × 1″ × 16½″	Upper and lower door frame members	4
Plywood		
⅝″ × 44½″ × 39½″	Front and back panels	2
⅝″ × 44½″ × 18½″	Greenhouse back	1
⅝″ × 18″ × 44½″	Shed top	1
⅝″ × 16⅞″ × 43¼″	Shed floor	1
⅝″ × 16⅞″ × 39½″	Side panels	2

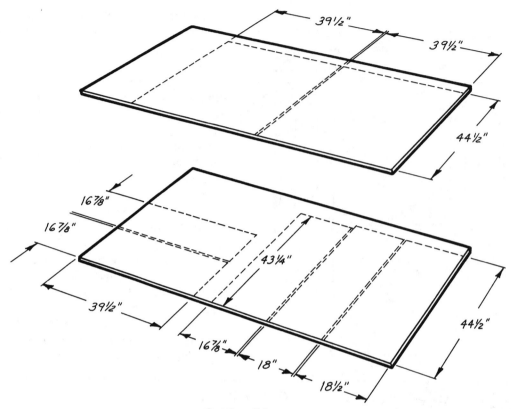

Cutting Diagram

the sides of the shed. Make sure the outside edges of the plywood and framing members are flush.

4. Lap the back panel over the edges of the side panels at the rear of the shed and fasten the panel to the framing members. Lay out a 36⅜ × 31⅞-inch rectangle 4⅛ inches above the lower edge and centered on the width of the front panel, as shown in illustration B. Cut the opening out carefully along the inside of the lines, then fasten the panel to the shed frame. Rip the cut-out piece down the middle to make two door panels.

5. Cut four pieces of 1 × 2 (¾″ × 1½″) stock to 31¾ inches each for the side members, and four pieces to 16½ inches each for the

upper and lower members of the door frames. Rip each piece to 1 inch in width, then arrange them on edge on the backs of the door panels, the side pieces lapped over the ends of the upper and lower pieces. Fasten the frame pieces to the door panels using 4d galvanized common nails.

6. Cut one piece of T1-11 siding to 18 × 44½ inches for the top of the shed. Fasten this panel, smooth-side up, to the top of the shed framework. Paint the inside and outside of the shed and doors with polyurethane, or finish as desired.

7. Cut one piece of aluminum flashing to 20 × 46½ inches for the cap of the shed. Slit the ends of the flashing so it can be folded all around its perimeter to create a

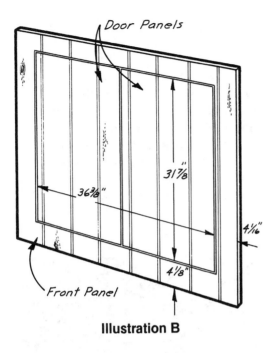

Door Panels

31⅞"

36⅜"

4 1/16"

4⅛"

Front Panel

Illustration B

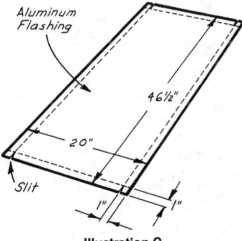

Aluminum Flashing

46½"

20"

Slit

1"

1"

Illustration C

1-inch-deep cap, as shown in illustration C. Fit the cap over the top of the shed and fasten it in place using ½-inch × 18-gauge wire nails.

8. Cut one piece of 1 × 2 stock to 44½ inches for the front member of the greenhouse frame, and two pieces to 16⅝ inches each for the side members. Also cut one piece of T1-11 siding to 44½ × 18½ inches for the back of the greenhouse. Scribe the rear radius of a 16 × 44-inch window-well cover on the textured face of the piece, then trim it along the scribed line.

9. Center and drill four ¾-inch-diameter air holes, spaced 5 inches apart along the length of the front member of the greenhouse frame. Drill a similar set of holes through the upper part of the back piece, as shown in the exploded-view diagram, to provide the minigreenhouse with ventilation.

10. Cut a pair of triangular blocks, each approximately 2 × 2 × 3 inches, out of scrap 2 × 4 material to reinforce the front corners of the greenhouse frame. Assemble the frame, fastening the front and back pieces to the ends of the side pieces, and the reinforcing blocks to the upper inside front corners, using 4d galvanized common nails. Apply the same finish to this frame as was used on the shed.

11. Put a bead of silicone caulk between the window-well cover and the frame. Then fasten the cover to the frame using ½-inch #4 panhead aluminum screws, spaced evenly around the rim. Install a draw catch on each side of the shed to hold the greenhouse in place, as shown in the exploded-view diagram.

12. Mount the doors on the shed using 2-inch tee hinges, as shown in the exploded-view diagram. Fasten a 4-inch utility handle and either a barrel-bolt lock on the outside or a friction catch on the inside of each door.

ARCHED GREEN-HOUSE

Tom Minnich of Archer City, Texas, built this inexpensive, yet durable, greenhouse mainly using PVC pipe and fiberglass-reinforced plastic panels. The greenhouse measures 8 feet in height. For a lower structure, you will have to shorten the lengths of the pipes that are bent to form the arches. You will also have to shorten the lengths of the uprights and door jambs. As for the foundation, if you live in an area where frost heaving is a problem (Minnich does not), the sills should be anchored below the frost level, either by setting them on a perimeter footing or on posts.

SHOPPING LIST

Lumber
1 pc. 2 × 4 × 10'
13 pcs. 2 × 4 × 8'
3 pcs. 1 × 4 × 8'
Hardware
22 fiberglass-reinforced corrugated plastic panels 2' × 8'
28' foam rubber 1'' × 1''
4 flathead wood screws #10 × 3½''
6 flathead wood screws #8 × 2½''
8 flathead wood screws #8 × 1¼''
12 flathead wood screws #8 × 1''
16 flathead wood screws #8 × ¾''
2 roundhead wood screws #10 × 3''

250 panhead sheet-metal screws #8 × 1½'' with neoprene washers
4 panhead sheet-metal screws #8 × 1''
7 lag bolts ⅜'' × 4''
6 lag bolts ¼'' × 4''
7 flat washers ½''
6 flat washers ¼''
2 butt hinges 3'' × 3''
1 hook-and-eye fastener 3''
1 pound galvanized common nails 12d
1 pound galvanized common nails 8d
11 pcs. PVC pipe 1½'' I.D. × 20'
8 pipe couplings 1½''
1 pint PVC cement

CONSTRUCTION

1. Dig a trench approximately 8 inches wide and 10 inches deep around the perimeter of the greenhouse area. The front trench should measure 14 feet in length and be located 8 feet from the house wall. Be certain to dig the end trenches parallel to each other, and at right angles to the front trench. Level the bottom of the trench, then fill with gravel to a depth of approximately 1 inch.

LUMBER CUTTING LIST

Size	Piece	Quantity
2 × 4		
1½'' × 3½'' × 96''	Sills	8
1½'' × 3½'' × 96''	Rail	1
1½'' × 3½'' × 96''	Side nailers	2
1½'' × 3½'' × 86''	Door jambs	2
1½'' × 3½'' × 72''	Rail	1
1½'' × 3½'' × 29½''	Door sill	1
1½'' × 3½'' × 29½''	Door header	1
1 × 4		
¾'' × 3½'' × 74''	Door rails	2
¾'' × 3½'' × 22''	Door cross pieces	2
¾'' × 3½'' × 22''	Window cross pieces	2
¾'' × 3½'' × 22''	Window rails	2

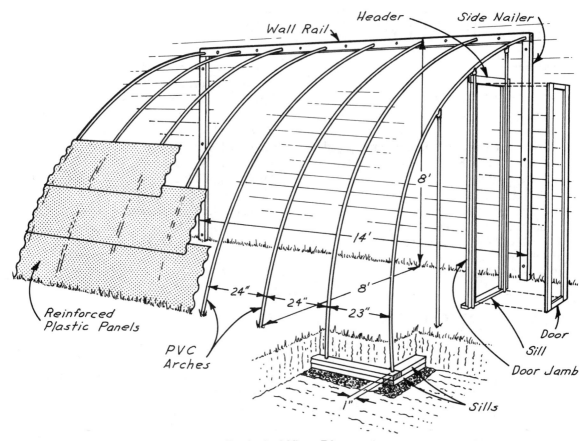

Labels in diagram: Wall Rail, Header, Side Nailer, Reinforced Plastic Panels, PVC Arches, Door, Sill, Door Jamb, Sills

Measurements: 8', 14', 8', 24", 24", 23", 1"

Exploded-View Diagram

2. Use eight pieces of 2×4 ($1\frac{1}{2}'' \times 3\frac{1}{2}''$) stock, each 96 inches in length, for the front and end sills, as shown in the exploded-view diagram. To construct the front sill, cut one piece into two 4-foot lengths, then lay each at opposite ends of an 8-foot piece to form an assembly 16 feet long. Place two 8-foot pieces end-to-end on top, so that the joints in both layers are staggered, then fasten the pieces together with 12d galvanized common nails. Trim to a final length of 14 feet. To construct the end sills, merely nail the remaining 8-foot lengths together in pairs.

3. Cut notches 1½ inches deep and 3½ inches

wide in the ends of each sill, as shown in illustration A. Then position the sills in the trench, overlap the notched corners, and fasten the sills together using 12d galvanized common nails.

4. Drill 1¾-inch-diameter holes through the top boards of each sill for the ends of the arches (see step 8). Space the holes at 24-inch intervals, as shown in the exploded-view diagram. (At the corners where the sills meet, locate the holes 1 inch from the ends of the boards.)

5. Cut one piece of 2×4 stock to 72 inches and position it end-to-end with one 96-inch length to form the 14-foot-long wall rail

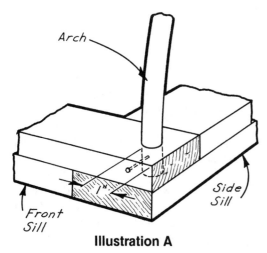

Illustration A

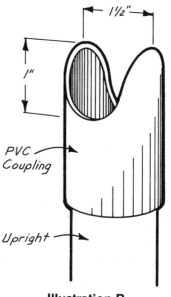

Illustration B

shown in the exploded-view diagram. Drill eight 1¾-inch-diameter holes through the pieces, spaced at 24-inch intervals. Position the first and last holes 1 inch from the outer ends of the boards. Midway between each pair of holes, drill an additional smaller hole—seven in all—⅜-inch in diameter, along the rail for mounting bolts.

6. Position the wall rail on the side of the house, 8 feet above ground level, parallel with the front sill. Be sure that the holes on the rail are aligned with the holes in the sill. Tack the rail to the house siding using 12d galvanized common nails, then drill ¼-inch-diameter holes into the siding using the ⅜-inch holes in the rail as guides. Fasten the rail to the house using seven ⅜ × 4-inch lag bolts fitted with ½-inch flat washers.

7. Cut eight pieces of 1½-inch-diameter PVC pipe to 14 feet each for the arches.

8. Push one end of each arch into the holes in the front sill. Drill ⅛-inch-diameter holes through the edge of the sill and into each arch, as shown in illustration A. Then drive an 8d galvanized common nail into each hole to lock the arches in place. Push the top ends of the arches into the holes in the wall rail and lock them into place using the same method.

9. Notch six 1½-inch PVC pipe couplings to the shape shown in illustration B to fit the arches.

10. Cut six pieces of 1½-inch-diameter PVC pipe for uprights to fit between the end sills and end arches. To find the correct lengths of the uprights, measure the distance each upright should span, then allow for the depths of the holes in the end sills. Two of the uprights should measure approximately 75 inches each, two others approximately 89 inches each, and the remaining two approximately 93 inches each.

11. Fasten a coupling onto one end of each upright, using PVC cement, then install the uprights in the holes in the end sills and fit the couplings around the arches. Use a level to bring the uprights plumb, then drill holes in the edges of the end sills and lock the uprights into place with nails, as described in step 8. Fasten the couplings to the arches by drilling through them and

installing 1-inch #8 panhead sheet-metal screws.

12. Use two pieces of 2 × 4 stock, each 96 inches in length for the side nailers, as shown in the exploded-view diagram. Position the nailers against the house wall, beneath the ends of the wall rail and on top of the end sills. Drill ¼-inch-diameter holes through the nailers, then, using these holes as guides, drill ³⁄₁₆-inch-diameter holes into the house wall. Fasten the nailers to the wall using ¼ × 4-inch lag bolts fitted with flat washers.

13. Cut two pieces of 2 × 4 stock to 86 inches each for the door jambs, and a third piece to 29½ inches for the header. Notch both ends of the header and one end of each jamb to form half-lap joints. Then fasten the three pieces, as shown in the exploded-view diagram, using 1¼-inch #8 flathead wood screws (two screws per joint, placed diagonally).

14. Position the door frame between the second and third uprights on one side of the greenhouse frame, as shown in the exploded-view diagram. Drill and countersink ⅛-inch pilot holes through the frame and into the upright, then fasten the frame to the uprights using 2½-inch #8 flathead wood screws.

15. Build a door by cutting two pieces of 1 × 4 (¾″ × 3½″) stock to 74 inches each for the rails, and two pieces to 22 inches each for the cross pieces. Cut half-lap joints in the ends of all the pieces, then fasten them together using four ¾-inch #8 flathead wood screws per joint. (For extra strength, install the screws in pairs from opposite sides.)

16. Hang the door inside the door frame using two 3 × 3-inch butt hinges. Mortise the hinges into the frame and door so that the door will swing inward when installed.

Fasten the hinges with 1-inch #8 flathead wood screws.

17. Cut one piece of 2 × 4 to 29½ inches for the door sill. Cut a 3½-inch-long notch 1¾ inches deep in each end so the sill will fit between the jambs. Fit the sill in place beneath the door, as shown in the exploded-view diagram, leaving ½-inch clearance between the upper surface of the sill and the lower edge of the door. Drill and countersink ⅛-inch pilot holes, then fasten the sill to the jambs using four 3½-inch #10 flathead wood screws.

18. Fill in the trench around the sills with gravel.

19. Enclose the greenhouse with 24 × 96-inch fiberglass-reinforced corrugated plastic panels. Install the material beginning at the top, next to the house wall. Place the first two panels square against the wall, overlapping the panels down the center and allowing the sides of the panels to project beyond the outer arches of the greenhouse frame. Then drill ⅛-inch-diameter holes through the panels into the arches, spacing the holes at every fourth corrugation peak, stopping 3 inches from the bottom edge. Fasten the panels with 1½-inch #8 panhead sheet-metal screws fitted with neoprene washers. Draw the screws snug but do not flatten the panels.

20. Place the third and fourth panels on the arches so that two corrugations lie under the set of panels previously attached. Drill through the panels into the arches as before, and fasten the panels with 1½-inch #8 panhead sheet-metal screws. Continue until the front of the greenhouse is enclosed.

21. Cut corrugated plastic panels to the shape of the greenhouse sides, and install them—with the corrugations horizontal—so they fit flat against the uprights and side nailers,

and tightly against the arched edges of the roof panels. Cut separate panels to fit across the door. Fasten the panels with 1½-inch #8 panhead sheet-metal screws, using the method described in the previous two steps. Afterward, attach a latch to the greenhouse door.

22. Cut 3-inch-long strips of 1 × 1 foam rubber for packing. Install the packing in the side walls and roof joints where the corrugations do not touch the outer arches of the greenhouse frame.

23. If desired, add a window on the side of the greenhouse not occupied by the door. To do this, cut a 22 × 22-inch section from the wall, between the second and third uprights. Save the section of plastic. Cut four pieces of 1 × 4 stock to 22 inches each for the window rails and cross pieces. Join the pieces using half-lap joints fastened with ¾-inch #8 flathead wood screws to make a 22-inch-square frame, as shown in illustration C. Position the frame in the window opening. Drill a 1-inch-diameter hole through

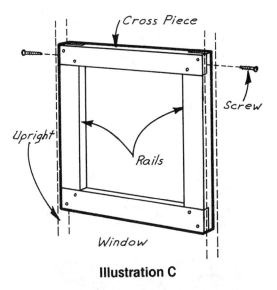

Illustration C

each of the two uprights, then into the frame, 1 inch from the top. Install a 3-inch #10 roundhead wood screw in each hole so that the window will pivot. At the bottom of the window frame, attach a 3-inch hook-and-eye fastener.

ATTACHED GREEN-HOUSE

Harvey Hebbe of St. Paul, Minnesota, designed and built this attached greenhouse, not only for growing plants but for supplying supplemental household heat during all but the coldest months of the year. The base of the greenhouse measures 8 × 9 feet at floor level, and at the highest point there is 8 feet of headroom.

Hebbe used salvaged glass for the sides and roof and also incorporated an elaborate homemade chain-drive mechanism for opening and closing the vent. We've modified his plans somewhat, suggesting clear acrylic instead of glass — at least for the roof — and substituting poles to prop open the vent in place of a mechanism. As an option, we also suggest insulating the foundation walls.

Although extensive instructions are given for this project, you should plan your own greenhouse very carefully before you begin to build. Most importantly: Design the foundation to extend below frost level, and take into account the availability of glazing in the sizes you will need.

SHOPPING LIST

Lumber
1 pc. 2 × 8 × 10' pressure-treated
2 pcs. 2 × 8 × 8' pressure-treated
4 pcs. 2 × 4 × 10'
37 pcs. 2 × 4 × 8'
1 pc. 1 × 8 × 10'
8 pcs. 1 × 2 × 8'

Hardware
1 door 27'' × 6'
2 sheets double-walled acrylic glazing
    ⅝'' × 4' × 8'
36 square feet safety glass (sized to fit
    end walls) ⅛''
24 stainless steel panhead screws
    #8 × 1''
12 lag bolts ¼'' × 2½''
10 lag bolts ¼'' × 1½''
6 anchor bolts ½'' × 6'' with nuts
6 flat washers ⅝''
12 flat washers ⅜''
neoprene washers
6 loose pin hinges 6'' × 6''
3 butt hinges 3'' × 3''
10 pounds galvanized common nails 16d

1 pound galvanized common nails 8d
2 pounds finishing nails 4d
2 pounds aluminum roofing nails 1''
1 roll aluminum flashing 1' × 30'
concrete blocks 8'' × 8'' × 16'', quantity
    as needed
8 cubic feet concrete for footer
mortar, quantity as needed
8 pcs. high-density extruded polystyrene
    1½'' × 4' × 8' (optional)
vermiculite or core-fill block insulation,
    quantity as needed (optional)
2 joist hangers 3'' × 3½''
1 pc. angle iron 1½'' × 1½'' × 95''
2 pcs. angle iron 1½'' × 1½'' × 3''
72 cubic feet gravel
6 tubes silicone caulk
2 10-ounce tubes waterproof construction
    adhesive (optional)
1 quart glazing compound
100 glazing points
5 gallons exterior waterproofing compound
    (optional)

CONSTRUCTION

To build the foundation:

1. Excavate the site for the foundation of the greenhouse, as shown in illustration A. Its depth will depend on the frost depth for your region. Pour a 5-inch-thick concrete footer 10 inches wide at the bottom of the excavation, around the intended perimeter of the greenhouse. The outer edge of the footer's front wall should measure 93 inches from your house wall, and the front wall itself should measure 110 inches in length.

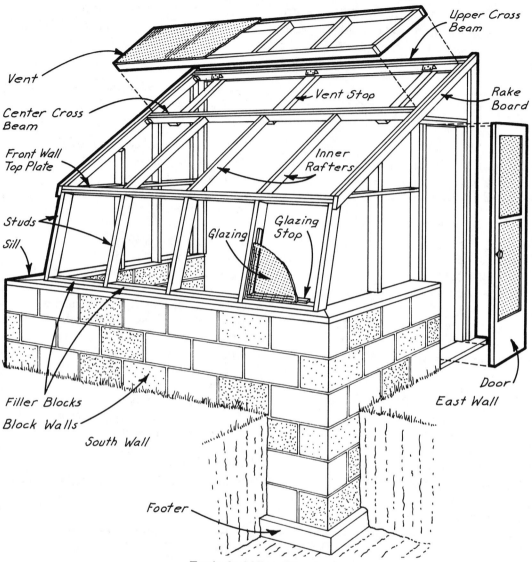

Vent

Center Cross
Beam

Front Wall
Top Plate

Studs

Sill

Upper Cross
Beam

Vent Stop

Rake
Board

Inner
Rafters

Glazing

Glazing
Stop

Filler Blocks

Block Walls

South Wall

Door

East Wall

Footer

Exploded-View Diagram

2. When the concrete in the footer has cured, lay block walls, centered over the footer, to a height of 24 inches above grade. Use 8 × 8 × 16-inch concrete blocks. The number you will need depends on the depth of the foundation. The greenhouse shown required 145 blocks. To allow for a doorway on the east side of the greenhouse, build the 35-inch-wide section closest to the house wall only to grade height, as shown in the exploded-view diagram. As you lay the walls, fill the block cavities with vermiculite or other loose insulation, if desired.

3. Pour concrete into the top cavities of the blocks and embed two ½ × 6-inch anchor bolts in each wall (none in the door area).

LUMBER CUTTING LIST

Size	Piece	Quantity
2 × 8		
1½″ × 7¼″ × 108″	Front sill	1
1½″ × 7¼″ × 92″	End sill	1
1½″ × 7¼″ × 57″	End sill	1
1½″ × 7¼″ × 35″	Door sill	1
2 × 4		
1½″ × 3½″ × 120″	Vent props	3
1½″ × 3½″ × 96″	Rake boards	2
1½″ × 3½″ × 96″	East wall rear stud	1
1½″ × 3½″ × 96″	East wall nailer	1
1½″ × 3½″ × 95″	Upper cross beam	2
1½″ × 3½″ × 95″	Front wall plate	1
1½″ × 3½″ × 94″	End rafters	2
1½″ × 3½″ × 92″	Center cross beam	2
1½″ × 3½″ × 91″	Vent rails	2
1½″ × 3½″ × 88″	Horizontal wall plate	1
1½″ × 3½″ × 77⅞″	West wall plate	1
1½″ × 3½″ × 72½″	Door frame	2
1½″ × 3½″ × 72½″	Door jamb	1
1½″ × 3½″ × 72″	West wall rear stud	1
1½″ × 3½″ × 72″	West wall nailer	1
1½″ × 3½″ × 55″	Inner rafters	3
1½″ × 3½″ × 44⅜″	East wall plate	1
1½″ × 3½″ × 40″	Vent stops	3
1½″ × 3½″ × 32½″	Vent rafters	5
1½″ × 3½″ × 31½″	Door headers	2
1½″ × 3½″ × 24″	Front wall studs	5
1½″ × 3½″ × 24″	End wall studs	3
1½″ × 3½″ × 24″	End wall stud extension	1
1½″ × 3½″ × 21⅞″	Front wall filler blocks	4
1½″ × 3½″ × 9″	End wall stud extensions	2
1 × 8		
¾″ × 7¼″ × 100″	Roof board	1
1 × 2		
¾″ × 1½″	Glazing stops	As needed

4. If desired, insulate the exterior of the greenhouse using sheets of 1½-inch-thick, high-density extruded polystyrene insulation.

Cut the panels to fit, then fasten them in place using waterproof construction adhesive. Fill the seams with adhesive as

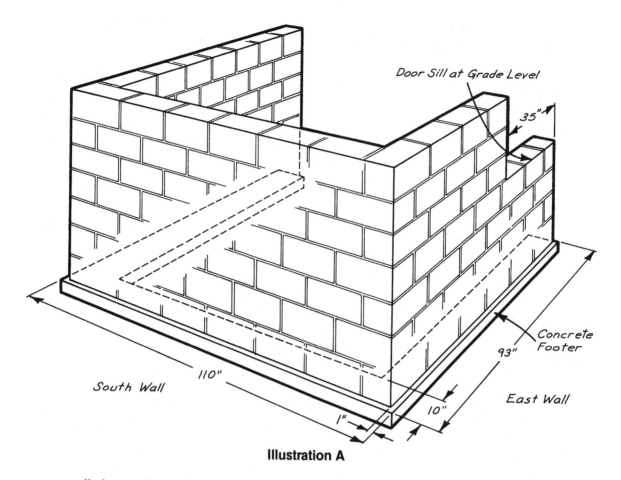

Door Sill at Grade Level

35"

Concrete Footer

110"

93"

South Wall

1"

10"

East Wall

Illustration A

well, then apply waterproofing compound over the insulation up to grade level. Apply a protective layer of stucco or siding material over the outside of the polystyrene to protect it. Add aluminum flashing to the top edge of the walls to shed water from the siding.

5. Backfill earth against the foundation walls, to grade level on the outside, and to 12 inches below grade on the inside. Then spread 12 inches of gravel inside the greenhouse for the floor.

To build the greenhouse frame:

1. Cut one piece of pressure-treated 2×8 ($1\frac{1}{2}'' \times 7\frac{1}{4}''$) stock to 108 inches for the front sill. Miter the ends to 45-degree angles. Drill $\frac{5}{8}$-inch-diameter holes through the sill so it will fit over the anchor bolts, then fit the sill in place and fasten it to the foundation wall by installing $\frac{5}{8}$-inch-diameter flat washers and nuts on the anchor bolts.

2. Cut two additional pieces of 2×8 stock to 92 inches each for the end sills. Miter one end of each to 45 degrees. Trim the unmitered end of one piece to 57 inches for the short east wall, and use the remaining 35-inch piece for the door sill. Drill holes in each sill (except the door sill) to accommodate the anchor bolts, then fasten these

sills to the foundation wall as you did the front sill in the previous step. The door sill requires no fasteners. It is held in place by the pressure of the door frame.

3. Use two pieces of $2 \times 4 (1\frac{1}{2}'' \times 3\frac{1}{2}'')$ stock, each 96 inches in length, for the east wall rear stud and nailer. Cut a 30-degree bevel across the face of the nailer at one end, and across one end of the stud, as shown in illustration B.

4. Cut two pieces of 2×4 to 72 inches each for the west wall rear stud and nailer. Cut one end of each piece to a 30-degree angle, as in the previous step.

5. Fasten the studs to the nailers, so that the beveled ends are flush, to form two posts. Use 16d galvanized common nails. Rest the east wall post flush to the inside of the door sill, and the west wall post flush to the inside of the wall sill. Plumb both posts. Then fasten the posts to the house wall, using nails or other fasteners appropriate to its construction.

6. Cut one piece of 2×4 stock to 88 inches for the horizontal plate. Bevel one long

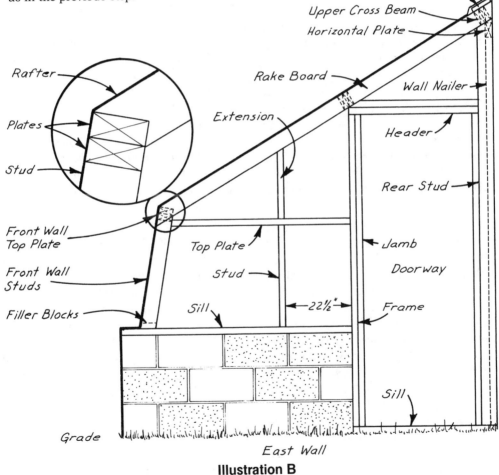

Illustration B

edge of the piece to 30 degrees, then fit the plate between the posts, with the beveled end up, and fasten it to the house wall.

7. Cut five pieces of 2 × 4 stock to 24 inches each for the front wall studs. Cut one end of each piece to a 10-degree angle. Also cut one piece of 2 × 4 stock to 95 inches for the front wall top plate.

8. Fasten the front wall studs, using 16d galvanized common nails, on 23⅜-inch centers, between the top plate and front sill. Use temporary braces to hold the wall at the 10-degree slant, as shown in illustration B.

9. Cut one piece of 2 × 4 stock to 95 inches for the second top plate, and fasten it on top of the first front wall plate—doubling its thickness—using 16d galvanized common nails.

10. Bevel one edge of a 10-foot length of 2 × 4 stock to 10 degrees to match the slant of the front wall. From this cut four shorter pieces to 21⅞ inches each for filler blocks. Fasten the blocks between the studs of the front wall, as shown in the exploded-view diagram, using 16d galvanized common nails.

To build the roof and vent:

1. Use two pieces of 2 × 4 stock, each 96 inches in length, for the rake boards. Cut a 30-degree angle in one end of each piece, as shown in illustration B. Fasten the beveled end of the rake boards to the top end of the rear studs using 16d galvanized common nails. Fasten the lower end to the ends of the front wall top plates so that the top edges of each piece are flush. Trim the bottom end of the rake boards to match the front wall slope, if desired.

2. Cut two pieces of 2 × 4 stock to 95 inches each for the upper cross beam. Position the pieces face-to-face with their ends flush and nail them together to make up the 3 × 3½ × 95-inch beam. Lift the upper cross beam into place between the rake boards and fasten it with 16d galvanized common nails.

3. Use a 95-inch length of 1½ × 1½-inch angle iron to brace the upper cross beam. Position the angle beneath the beam and against the horizontal wall plate, as shown in illustration B. Temporarily tack it in position with nails, then drill 5/16-inch-diameter holes through the angle, into both the beam and the plate, and permanently fasten the angle using 10 ¼ × 1½-inch lag bolts. Cut two additional pieces of angle to 3 inches each, and use them in the next step.

4. Cut two pieces of 2 × 4 stock to 94 inches each for the end rafters. Install them against the inside of each rake board using 16d galvanized common nails. Where the rafters meet the upper cross beam, fasten them with the pieces of angle cut in the previous step.

5. Cut two pieces of 2 × 4 stock to 92 inches each for the center cross beam. Fasten them together face-to-face, with their ends flush.

6. Position the center cross beam between the end rafters, as shown in the exploded-view diagram, centered 37½ inches from the inside of the top beam. Fasten it in place with two 3 × 3½-inch joist hangers.

7. Cut three pieces of 2 × 4 stock to 55 inches each for the inner rafters. Cut a notch, as shown in illustration B, in one end of each piece to fit over the front wall plate. Nail the rafters in place on 23⅜-inch centers.

8. Cut three pieces of 2 × 4 stock to 40 inches each for the vent stops. Position the stops against the undersides of the center and upper cross beams—one stop in the center and the others 12 inches from the ends, as shown in illustration C—then drill 3/16-inch-diameter pilot holes and fasten the stops to the beams using 12 ¼ × 2½-inch

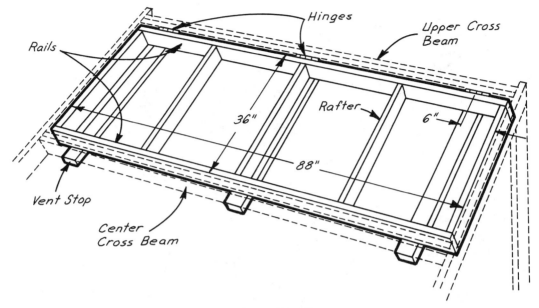

Illustration C

lag bolts fitted with ⅜-inch flat washers.

9. Cut two pieces of 2 × 4 stock to 91 inches each for the vent rails. Cut five additional pieces to 32½ inches each for the vent rafters. Fasten the rails and rafters together to form the vent assembly shown in illustration C.

10. Set the vent assembly on top of the vent stops, between the upper and center cross beams, leaving a ½-inch gap at each side between the assembly and the end rafters. Attach the vent to the upper cross beam using three 6 × 6-inch loose pin hinges, as shown in illustration C. Position one hinge in the center of the beam, and the others 12 inches from the ends.

11. Use three pieces of 2 × 4, each 120 inches in length, for vent props. Attach these using loose pin hinges to the underside of the lower vent rail, in line with the ends and center vent rafters. Use the props to hold open the vent. Disassemble them for storage in winter.

To build the end walls:

1. Cut three pieces of 2 × 4 stock to 72½ inches for the door frame and jamb, and two additional pieces to 31½ inches for the header and header plate, all as shown in illustration B. Bevel one end of the header plate to a 30-degree angle so it fits underneath the end rafter, also as shown. Then, cut notches in the ends of the header pieces so that they fit between the door frame and the wall nailer.

2. Install the door frame pieces and then the header and header plate, as shown in illustration B. Then install the jamb, also as shown. Use 16d galvanized common nails.

3. Cut three pieces of 2 × 4 stock to 24 inches each for the end wall studs. Use two studs for the west wall and one for the east wall. Also cut one piece of 2 × 4 stock to 77⅞ inches for the west wall plate, and an additional piece to 44⅜ inches for the east wall plate. Bevel one end of each plate so it butts against the front wall plate. Notch

517

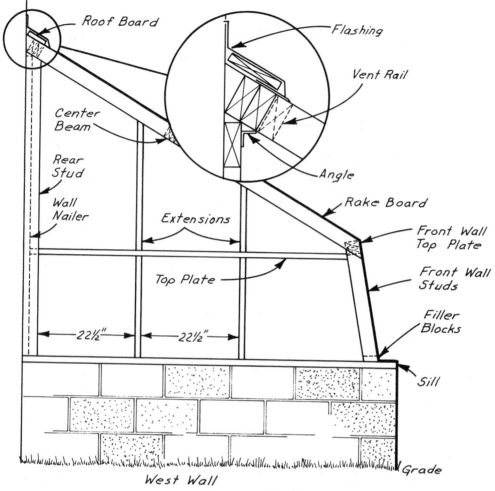

Roof Board

Flashing

Vent Rail

Center Beam

Rear Stud

Wall Nailer

Extensions

Angle

Rake Board

Front Wall Top Plate

Front Wall Studs

Top Plate

Filler Blocks

22½"

22½"

Sill

Grade

West Wall

Illustration D

the unbeveled end of the longer plate so it fits around the rear wall stud.

4. Nail the west wall plate to the front plate and wall nailer, and the east wall plate to the front plate and door frame. Then attach the west wall studs, on 24-inch centers measured from the rear wall nailer, between the end sills and the plates, as shown in illustration D. Fasten the east wall stud on 24-inch centers measured from the door frame, as shown in illustration B.

5. Cut three pieces of 2 × 4 for the end wall

extensions. Measure and cut these pieces to fit exactly between the end wall plates and the rake boards so that they are in line with the wall studs. The rough measurements for these pieces are two pieces at 9 inches, and one piece at 24 inches. The top end of each must be beveled also to fit under the rake boards.

6. Cut pieces of 1 × 2 (¾" × 1½") for the glazing stops, against which the end-wall glazing rests. Cut each stop to length individually, then fasten it to the framing

to form a ¾-inch-wide lip outlining the areas to be glazed, as shown in the exploded-view diagram. Cut and fit the pieces individually to fit around each area of glazing. Fasten each stop ¾ inch from the outside edge of the studs using 4d finishing nails.

To add the glazing, flashing and finishing:

1. Paint the greenhouse framing with a durable finish, such as two-part epoxy paint or marine varnish, designed to withstand constant moisture.

2. Cut one piece of aluminum flashing to 8×107 inches. Fasten it so that it is centered along the length of the upper cross beam, and so that the flashing extends over the top rail of the vent, as shown in illustration E. Use 1-inch aluminum roofing nails. Bend the ends of the flashing down to cover the ends of the rake boards. You need to miter the flashing to make it fit against the house wall.

3. Cut one piece of 1×8 ($¾'' \times 7¼''$) to 100 inches for the roof board, as shown in illustration D. Position it on top of the flashing, against the house wall and flush with the lower edge of the upper cross beam, centered so it overlaps the ends of the greenhouse evenly. Trim the board, if necessary, then fasten it to the upper cross beam using 8d galvanized common nails.

4. Cut a second piece of aluminum flashing to 10×100 inches. Bend it to the shape shown in illustration D. Then attach it over the roof board using 1-inch aluminum roofing nails. Fit the upper edge of the flashing under a course of siding on the house wall, or, if the wall is masonry, into a groove chiseled into the mortar. Caulk the seam using silicone caulk. Bend the ends of the flashing down to cover the ends of the roof board.

5. Attach ⅝-inch-thick double-walled clear acrylic glazing to the greenhouse roof and vent. First cut two pieces to $48 \times 55½$ inches to cover the roof. Drill ⅛-inch-diameter holes through the glazing and into the rafters, then fasten the glazing in place using 8d galvanized common nails fitted with neoprene washers. To cover the vent, cut two pieces to $35½ \times 45½$ inches each. Fasten these panels also using nails fitted with neoprene washers. Caulk the ends of the panels or use gaskets supplied by the manufacturer.

6. Cut two strips of aluminum flashing to 6×96 inches for the rake board flashing. Bend it to the shape shown in illustration E. The bends are a 90-degree bend at 3 inches, and a slight bend outward at ½ inch from one leg. Fasten it, also as shown,

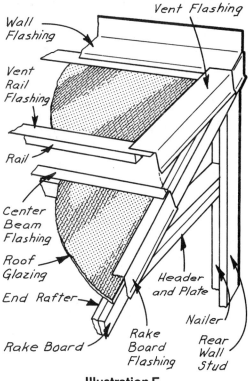

Illustration E

519

using 1-inch aluminum roofing nails. Then, cut one piece of flashing to 6 × 97 inches for the center cross beam. Bend the piece 90 degrees at 3 inches. Notch one leg of the piece to fit between the end rafters and fasten it to the center cross beam with 1-inch aluminum roofing nails.

7. Cut one piece of flashing to 4 × 97 inches to cover the bottom rail of the vent. Cut two additional pieces to 8½ × 33 inches each to cover the sides of the vent. The bottom rail piece is left flat. Bend the side pieces 90 degrees at 4½ inches and a slight bend ½ inch from the bottom edge of the 4-inch leg to fit the vents, as shown in illustration E.

8. Position the rail flashing so that it is over the bottom rail of the vent and also overlaps the center beam. Position the vent flashing on the vent glazing so that it overlaps the glazing, but also fits against the outside of the rake boards. Drill ⅛-inch-diameter holes every 8 inches through the flashing and glazing and into the grid frame. Apply silicone caulk to the underside of the flashing, then push the flashing in place and fasten it with #8 × 1-inch stainless steel panhead screws fitted with neoprene washers.

9. Measure and cut pieces of ⅛-inch-thick glass and install them in the end-wall openings, against the glazing stops. Use glazing points to hold the glazing in place, then seal around the outside with glazing compound.

10. Install a door, measuring 27 × 72 inches, in the door opening, using three 3 × 3-inch butt hinges.

11. Use silicone caulk to fill any remaining gaps. Add weather stripping around the door and vent.

GARDEN SLAT HOUSE

SHOPPING LIST
Lumber
4 pcs. 8″ diameter × 10′
2 pcs. 8″ diameter × 8′
14 pcs. 2 × 4 × 10′
56 pcs. 1 × 6 × 10′
Hardware
1 pound galvanized common nails 16d
1 pound galvanized common nails 10d
2 pounds galvanized common nails 8d
2 pounds galvanized common nails 4d

Mrs. Mary "Mart" McLaury enjoys the shade as much as the extra storage space her garden slat house provides. Summers in Fort Worth, Texas, where she lives, are hot. Neighbors and friends helped Mrs. McLaury erect the small shed, which is actually a simple pole structure covered with 1 × 6 boards for slats. Donated cedar posts and planks, plus a few 2 × 4s, were the only materials used.

Though the slat house provides ample protection from the sun, even more shade may be obtained by using the shed as a trellis for climbing plants such as melon vines, beans, ivy, or wisteria. Inside, you can add a potting bench, shelves, or racks for hanging garden tools. You won't want to store any equipment that can be damaged by moisture, however. Obviously, the garden slat house is not rainproof!

Our diagram and instructions for this project show a streamlined version of the slat house pictured, which is Mrs. McLaury's. In our adaptation, the doors are centered between the corner posts and all the slats are the same width. You don't need to follow our plans to the letter. If you have sal-vaged lumber to work with, by all means alter the dimensions given here to suit your needs. We don't mention paint or finish either. The cedar on Mrs. McLaury's slat house doesn't need any. If you're using pine or other softwood, exterior paint or stain will help protect the wood.

CONSTRUCTION

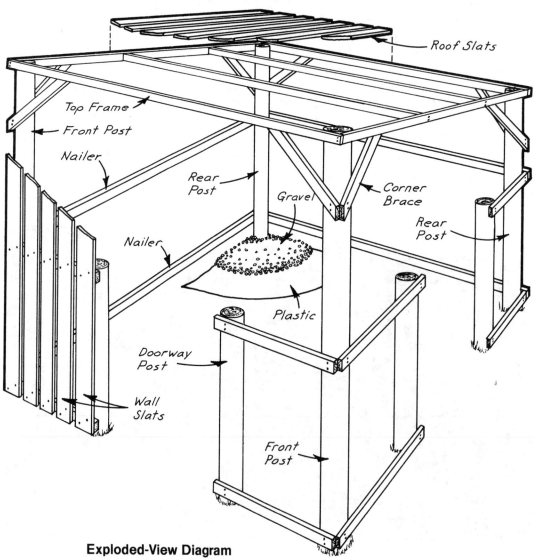

Exploded-View Diagram

1. Level an area approximately 12×14 feet for the construction site. If you desire maximum shading, orient the site so that when the slat house is built, the door openings will face north and east. Otherwise, prepare to build the house so its doors face your garden.

2. Cut two 10-foot lengths of 2×4 ($1\frac{1}{2}'' \times 3\frac{1}{2}''$) stock to 117 inches each, and two others to 108 inches each for the top frame pieces, which you will use as a guide to position the corner posts (see step 4). With 16d galvanized common nails fasten these together to make a 9×10-foot rectangular frame, as shown in the exploded-view diagram.

3. Lay the framework in the middle of the cleared area. Orient the frame according to the siting decisions you made in step 1,

then square the frame by measuring diagonally across the four corners. The frame is square when both measurements are equal.

4. Dig 18-inch-deep postholes for 8-inch-diameter posts (or larger, to suit posts that are different from those specified here). Locate the holes as closely as possible to the inside corners of the frame.

5. Move the top frame aside temporarily. Set the posts in the holes, the two 8-foot-long posts to the rear of the area and the two 10-foot-long posts to the front. Tamp the soil firmly around the base of each post to hold the posts securely in place.

6. With help from at least one assistant, lift the frame up and over the tops of the posts, then lower it until the top edge of the frame is flush with the tops of the posts. Fasten the frame in place around the outside of

LUMBER CUTTING LIST

Size	Piece	Quantity
Posts		
8'' diameter $\times$ 120''	Front posts	2
8'' diameter $\times$ 96''	Rear posts	2
8'' diameter $\times$ 60''	Doorway posts	4
2 $\times$ 4		
$1\frac{1}{2}'' \times 3\frac{1}{2}'' \times 120''$	Side wall nailers	2
$1\frac{1}{2}'' \times 3\frac{1}{2}'' \times 117''$	Top frame	2
$1\frac{1}{2}'' \times 3\frac{1}{2}'' \times 108''$	End wall nailers	2
$1\frac{1}{2}'' \times 3\frac{1}{2}'' \times 108''$	Top frame	2
$1\frac{1}{2}'' \times 3\frac{1}{2}'' \times 105''$	Roof slat supports	2
$1\frac{1}{2}'' \times 3\frac{1}{2}'' \times 24''$	Corner braces	8
$1\frac{1}{2}'' \times 3\frac{1}{2}'' \times 24''$	Doorway wall nailers	8
1 $\times$ 6		
$\frac{3}{4}'' \times 5\frac{1}{2}'' \times 120''$	Roof slats	15
$\frac{3}{4}'' \times 5\frac{1}{2}'' \times 94''$	Front wall slats	10
$\frac{3}{4}'' \times 5\frac{1}{2}'' \times 61''$ to 94''	Side wall slats*	20
$\frac{3}{4}'' \times 5\frac{1}{2}'' \times 61''$ to 94''	Side wall slats*	12
$\frac{3}{4}'' \times 5\frac{1}{2}'' \times 61''$	Rear wall slats	16

*Cut these pieces to fit the varying wall height.

the posts using 16d galvanized common nails driven through the outer face of the frame into the sides of the posts.

7. Cut two pieces of 2 × 4 stock to 105 inches each for the roof slat supports, and fasten them between the side pieces of the top frame using 16d galvanized common nails.

8. Use 15 pieces of 1 × 6 (¾″ × 5½″) stock, each 120 inches in length, for roof slats. Position these on top of the frame, running lengthwise, as shown in the exploded-view diagram. Arrange the slats with equal amounts of space between them, then nail the slats to the top frame and roof supports using 8d galvanized common nails. The 2 × 4 frame members won't hold much weight, so use a ladder to reach the pieces while nailing. Don't climb on the roof.

9. Cut two 10-foot-long posts in half for the doorway posts. Locate and dig four postholes, as shown in the exploded-view diagram, in line with and 24 inches from each corner post. Sink the doorway posts in the earth to a depth of 12 inches so that 48 inches of each post remain exposed.

10. Rake the ground area within the slat house to level it. Spread sheets of black plastic over the raked ground, and on top of the plastic, spread gravel or mulch to a depth of 2 inches. (This is the finished floor of the slat house. Preparing it at this stage of the project allows the remaining work to go more smoothly and also makes the task easier than it would be with the sides of the house already enclosed.)

11. Use two pieces of 2 × 4 stock, each 120 inches in length, for nailers on the solid side wall. Fasten one of the nailers 48 inches above ground level, and the other 2 inches above ground level. Use 10d galvanized common nails.

12. Cut two pieces of 2 × 4 stock to 108 inches each for end wall nailers. Fasten these across

the rear posts at the same height as the side wall nailers in the previous step. Use 10d galvanized common nails.

13. Cut eight pieces of 2 × 4 stock to 24 inches each for nailers for the doorway walls. Fasten these to the corner and doorway posts, also at 2- and 48-inch intervals above ground level, again using 10d galvanized common nails.

14. Cut eight pieces of 2 × 4 stock to 24 inches each for corner braces, then miter the ends of each piece to 45-degree angles. Fasten the braces between the corner posts and top frame using 10d galvanized common nails, as shown in the exploded-view diagram.

15. Now cut the slats. First, cut 10 pieces of 1 × 6 (¾″ × 5¼″) stock to 94 inches each for slats to fit on the front wall. Fasten these in place—vertical, evenly spaced, their top ends flush with the top edge of the frame—using 4d galvanized common nails, as shown in the exploded-view diagram.

16. Next, cut 12 pieces of 1 × 6 stock for the slats on the longer doorway wall. Because of the roof slant, these slats range in length from 94 inches at the front to 61 inches at the rear. Measure each slat by holding it in place, then cut it to length. Fasten the slats using 4d galvanized common nails. (Leave the doorway space open.)

17. Cut 16 pieces of 1 × 6 stock to 61 inches each, and nail these slats to the rear wall using 4d galvanized common nails.

18. Finally, cut 20 pieces of 1 × 6 stock to fit the solid wall. Use the same procedure for measuring and cutting as in step 16, then fasten the slats in place using 4d galvanized common nails.

19. Install shelves, a potting bench, or other built-in features inside the finished slat house, as desired.

POTTING SHED-SLAT HOUSE

This structure, designed and built by the Rodale Design Group, combines the functions of an enclosed potting shed, equipped with shelves, storage bins for soil mixes, and a work surface for dividing and potting plants, with a partially open slat house that provides shade for newly set-out seedlings on their way to permanent outdoor homes in a garden or yard. By moving young plants (still in containers or flats) progres-sively from the growing bed at the rear of the slat house to the one at the front, the plants may be allowed increasing amounts of sun and space to gradually prepare them for transplanting in the open.

Though the plans for the potting shed-slat house show specific dimensions and might appear to call for a high degree of precision in building, the pole-construction style on which the design of the structure is based actually lends itself to a good deal of approximating and rough cutting. "By-eye" fits are usually sufficient. Sophisticated car-pentry skills aren't necessary either. How-ever, you should be familiar with methods of setting posts plumb and level, using string to lay out overall construction lines, handling a portable circular saw, and ham-mering nails from many different angles

SHOPPING LIST

Lumber
6 pcs. 4 × 4 × 10' pressure-treated
2 pcs. 4 × 4 × 8' pressure-treated
8 pcs. 2 × 8 × 8' pressure-treated
2 pcs. 2 × 8 × 6' pressure-treated
3 pcs. 2 × 6 × 8'
11 pcs. 2 × 4 × 8'
2 pcs. 2 × 4 × 6'
2 pcs. 1 × 6 × 12' (optional)
2 pcs. 1 × 6 × 8' (optional)
Furring
22 pcs. 1 × 3 × 12'
Plywood
1 sheet ¾" × 4' × 8' CDX
1 pc. ¾" × 2' × 8' CDX
5 sheets ⅝" × 4' × 8' T1-11
Hardware
5 pounds galvanized common nails 16d
5 pounds galvanized common nails 8d
2 gallons exterior-grade stain

(quite a lot of toenailing is required). You'll also need a helper throughout most of the project, most often to assist in positioning large pieces and holding them while they are being fastened.

The materials used to construct our potting shed–slat house are durable and readily available. The posts are made of pressure-treated pine. Galvanized nails are used to prevent rust. The T1-11 siding chosen for the roof and sides of the shed adds strength as well as attractiveness to the structure. We finished our shed with a redwood-color exterior stain.

CONSTRUCTION

1. Lay out the location of the eight posts so that the potting shed will face south. Mark the position of the pair of posts on the south end first, then space the remaining posts as shown in the exploded-view diagram. Note that the second pair of posts is spaced 67 inches apart on center from the first, the third pair 75 inches on center from the second, and the fourth pair 43¼ inches on center from the third. Also, note that each pair of posts is set 89¼ inches apart on center.

2. Dig a hole for each of the eight posts to a depth of at least 6 inches below the frost line in your area. Put a few inches of gravel in the bottom of each hole to aid drainage.

Plan on setting all posts at least a foot deep no matter what the frost line.

3. Cut two pieces of pressure-treated 4 × 4 (3½" × 3½") stock to 50 inches each plus the length below grade to serve as the rear posts of the potting shed. Cut three notches, each 1½ inches deep and 3½ inches long, on one face of each rear post to receive the cross members, as shown in illustration A. Note that the first notch begins at the top of each post, the second notch 16 inches below the top, and the third notch 43 inches below the top.

4. Cut three pieces of 2 × 4 (1½" × 3½") stock to 92¾ inches each for the rear post cross members, which will serve as sup-

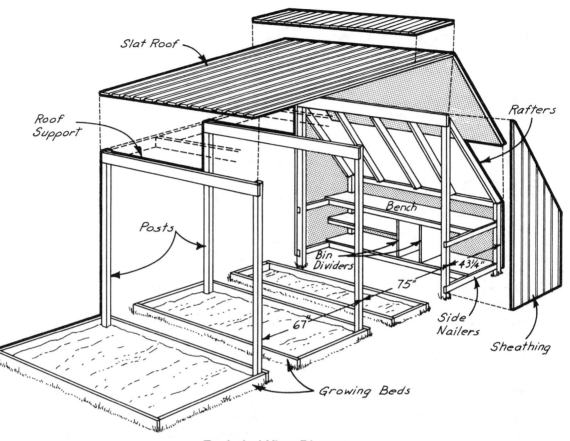

Slat Roof

Roof
Support

Rafters

Posts

Bench

Bin
Dividers

43¼"

75"

67"

Side
Nailers

Sheathing

Growing Beds

Exploded-View Diagram

ports for roof rafters, bench and lower shelf, and as nailers for the back sheathing. Place the rear posts in their postholes with their notches facing the back. Fit the three cross members into the notches on the posts and nail them in place with 16d galvanized common nails. Make sure posts and cross members are square with each other as you nail. Plumb the rear posts in both directions and make sure the cross members are level. Work some gravel under one post, as needed to make the structure level. Backfill both postholes with additional gravel, tamping firmly as you proceed.

5. Cut two pieces of pressure-treated 4 × 4

stock to 98 inches each plus the length below grade for the front posts of the potting shed. Cut three notches, each 1½ inches deep and 3½ inches long, in each potting shed front post to receive the roof support and side nailers, as shown in illustration A. Note that the notch for the roof support is on the front face at the top of each post. The notches for the side nailers begin 64 inches and 91 inches down from the top, respectively. These notches are located on the outside face of each post, which means one post must be notched on the right side and the other on the left side to make a matching pair.

6. Cut four pieces of 2 × 4 stock to 43¼

LUMBER CUTTING LIST

Size	Piece	Quantity
4 × 4		
3½″ × 3½″ × 98″ (plus length below grade)	Potting shed front posts	2
3½″ × 3½″ × 90″ (plus length below grade)	Slat house middle posts	2
3½″ × 3½″ × 84″ (plus length below grade)	Slat house front posts	2
3½″ × 3½″ × 50″ (plus length below grade)	Potting shed rear posts	2
2 × 8		
1½″ × 7¼″ × 95¾″	Growing bed frame sides	6
1½″ × 7¼″ × 63″	Front growing bed frame ends	2
1½″ × 7¼″ × 48″	Middle growing bed frame ends	2
1½″ × 7¼″ × 33″	Rear growing bed frame ends	2
2 × 6		
1½″ × 5½″ × 92¾″	Roof supports	3
2 × 4		
1½″ × 3½″ × 92¾″	Rear post cross members	3
1½″ × 3½″ × 89¾″	Bench and lower-shelf supports	2
1½″ × 3½″ × 65¼″	Middle rafters	3
1½″ × 3½″ × 62¼″	Side rafters	2
1½″ × 3½″ × 43¼″	Potting shed side nailers	4
1½″ × 3½″ × 43″	Middle shelf front support	1
1½″ × 3½″ × 40″	Middle shelf rear support	1
1½″ × 3½″ × 21″	Bin divider nailers	2
1 × 6		
¾″ × 5½″ × 142″	Face boards	2
¾″ × 5½″ × 92¾″	Roof cross members	2
Furring		
¾″ × 2½″ × 144″	Slats	22
¾″ Plywood		
¾″ × 24″ × 92¾″	Bench top and bottom shelf	2
¾″ × 24″ × 43″	Middle shelf	1
¾″ × 24″ × 26¼″	Bin wall and divider	2
T1-11 Plywood		
⅝″ × 48″ × 72″	Shed roof panels	2
⅝″ × 47⅜″ × 96″	Shed side panels	2
⅝″ × 46⅜″ × 48″	Shed rear panels	2

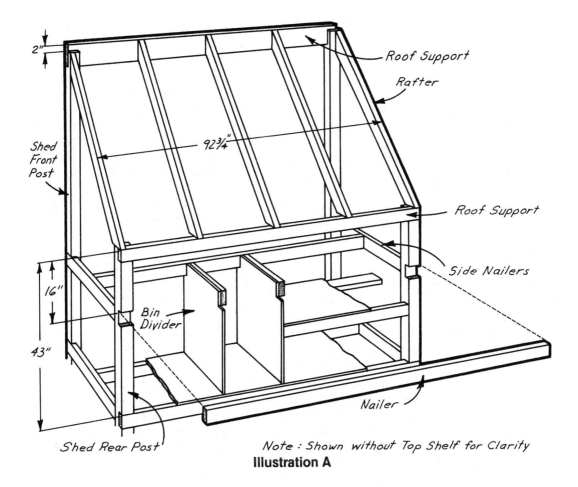

2"

Roof Support

Rafter

Shed Front Post

92¾"

Roof Support

Side Nailers

16"

Bin Divider

43"

Nailer

Shed Rear Post

Note: Shown without Top Shelf for Clarity

Illustration A

inches each for the potting shed side nailers. Fit the nailers into the notches cut for them on the posts. Square them to the posts, then fasten them in place with 16d galvanized common nails. Make sure the nailers are positioned so they will extend to the rear posts when the front posts are set in place. Note that the front posts will be set with their notched tops forward and their side nailers to the outside.

7. Cut one piece of 2×6 ($1\frac{1}{2}'' \times 5\frac{1}{2}''$) stock to 92¾ inches for the upper roof support of the potting shed. Place the front posts of the potting shed in their holes and

fasten the roof support beam to their notched tops with 16d galvanized common nails. Square the beam to the posts when fastening it in place. Plumb the posts to make the beam level, adding gravel to one hole as needed. Then plumb them in the other direction so the side nailers are level and butt up against the rear posts. Toenail the nailers to the rear posts with 16d galvanized common nails. Backfill around the posts with gravel, tamping firmly as you proceed.

8. Cut two pieces of pressure-treated 4×4 stock to 84 inches each plus the length

529

below grade for the front posts of the slat house. Cut a notch 1½ inches deep and 5½ inches long in one face at the upper end of each post to receive a roof support beam.

9. Cut one piece of 2 × 6 stock to 92¾ inches for the roof support beam to attach to the posts cut in the previous step. Place the front posts of the slat house in the holes dug for them. Fasten the roof support beam in place on the top front of the posts using 16d galvanized common nails. Make sure the beam is square to the posts before nailing. Plumb the front posts and beam of the slat house in both directions. Add gravel under one post as needed to make the beam level. Then backfill the postholes with gravel, tamping firmly as you proceed.

10. Cut two pieces of pressure-treated 4 × 4 stock to 90 inches each plus the length below grade for the middle posts of the slat house. Stretch string from across the tops of the roof supports to determine the slope of the slat-house roof. Drop the middle posts of the slat house into their holes, plumb them, and mark where the line touches their tops. Then remove the middle posts from their holes and cut them to final length. Cut a notch 1½ inches deep and 5½ inches long in one face of the top end of each post to receive a roof support.

11. Cut one piece of 2 × 6 stock to 92¾ inches for a roof support beam. Place the middle posts of the slat house in their holes with their notched faces forward. Fasten the roof support beam to the posts with 16d galvanized common nails, making sure the beam is square to the posts. Plumb the posts in both directions, making sure the beam is level and that the top of the beam is even with the line strung in the previous step. Backfill the postholes with gravel, tamping firmly as you proceed. Remove the string line.

12. Use 22 pieces of 1 × 3 (¾″ × 2½″) furring,

each 144 inches in length, for slats. Position the slats on the roof of the slat house so the upper end of each extends approximately ¾ inch onto the top of the upper roof support beam of the potting shed, and the lower end overhangs the front roof support beam of the slat house, as shown in the exploded-view diagram. Space the slats approximately 4½ inches center-to-center, beginning and ending flush with the sides of the slat-house roof. Fasten the slats to the roof support beams with 8d galvanized common nails.

13. Cut two pieces of 2 × 4 stock to 89¾ inches each to serve as the front supports for the bench and lower shelf of the potting shed. Fit one support between the two upper side nailers and the other between the two lower side nailers, with the front face of each positioned 24 inches from the back of the rear posts. Nail two 16d galvanized common nails through the side nailers into each end of each support.

14. Cut two pieces of 2 × 4 stock to 21 inches each for the nailers for the two vertical bin dividers under the bench. To position these nailers, measure from the outside edge of the upper nailer on the east side of the potting shed along the front bench support and square lines across the board at 33 and 49¾ inches. Make a large X on the left side of each line to indicate the location of one end of each nailer. Measure and mark the same points on the rear bench support to locate the other ends of the nailers. Fasten the nailers in place by driving two 16d galvanized common nails through the front and rear bench supports into each end of each nailer.

15. Cut one 4 × 8-foot sheet of ¾-inch CDX plywood in half lengthwise. Trim the ends to make two pieces, each 92¾ inches in length and approximately 24 inches in width (the saw here will have shaved off

$\frac{1}{16}$ inch or so). Cut a $3\frac{1}{2} \times 3\frac{1}{2}$-inch notch on both corners of one long side of each piece so it will fit between the rear posts. Fit one plywood piece between the posts on top of the bottom nailers to make the bottom shelf. Fasten the shelf to the nailers with 8d galvanized common nails. The other piece of plywood will be installed later (see step 27).

16. Cut one 24-inch-wide sheet of ¾-inch plywood into two pieces, each $26\frac{1}{4}$ inches in length, for the left wall of the bin and the bin divider. The right wall of the bin will be formed by the exterior sheathing to be installed later. Trim the remainder of the half-sheet to 43 inches in length and save it for use as the middle shelf of the potting shed. Notch both upper corners of the bin wall and the bin divider so they will fit between the front and back bench supports, as shown in illustration A. Cut each notch $1\frac{1}{2}$ inches across the width and $3\frac{1}{2}$ inches along the length of each upper corner. Position the left wall of the bin on the right side of the nailer provided for it. Fasten the top of the bin wall to the nailer with 8d galvanized common nails. Make sure the piece is vertical, then toe-nail or use a cleat to fasten its lower end to the shelf beneath it. The bin divider will be installed later.

17. Cut one piece of 2×4 stock to 40 inches for the rear support of the middle shelf. Position the support between the left rear post of the shed and the left wall of the bin. The top of the support should be $14\frac{3}{4}$ inches above the top of the bottom shelf and its outside face should be flush with the outside edges of the bin wall and the rear post. Fasten the support to the post and the bin wall with 8d galvanized common nails.

18. Cut two pieces of ⅝-inch-thick T1-11 plywood to $46\frac{3}{8} \times 48$ inches each for the

rear panels of the potting shed. Position the rear panels so the outside edge of each is flush with the outside edge of a rear post and their upper edges are flush with the upper edge of the top nailer connecting the rear posts of the shed. Fasten the panels to the rear posts and nailers with 8d galvanized common nails.

19. Cut the following pieces of 2×4 stock: two pieces to $62\frac{1}{4}$ inches each for the side rafters of the potting shed, and three pieces to $65\frac{1}{4}$ inches each for the middle rafters of the potting shed. Turn the rafters crown (convex) side up. Mark and cut both ends of each rafter, as shown in illustration B. Note that the rise of the roof is 12 inches for each $10\frac{5}{8}$ inches of run. This means the cutting angle at the upper end of each rafter will be approximately $41\frac{1}{2}$ degrees and that of the lower end will be approximately $48\frac{1}{2}$ degrees.

20. Nail the side rafters in place, one flush

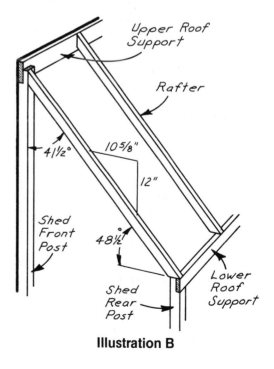

Illustration B

with the outside edges of each pair of front and rear shed posts. The top edge of each rafter should be flush with the top of the front posts at its upper end and flush with the outside of the plywood sheathing at its lower end. Attach the rafters to the posts with 16d galvanized common nails. Position the three middle rafters parallel to the side rafters, spaced 22¹³/₁₆ inches apart on center. Fasten the rafters in place with 16d galvanized common nails.

21. Trim two sheets of ⅝-inch-thick T1-11 plywood to 47⅜ inches in width, then mark and cut each sheet to the shape of the sides of the potting shed. Cut from the midpoint on the left side of one sheet to its full 96-inch height on the right side. Cut the other sheet from the middle of the right side to the top of the left side. Fasten the side panels to posts, rafters, and nailers with 8d galvanized common nails. The long side of each panel should be flush with the front of a post and the short side should overlap the rear panels. The diagonal edge of each should be flush with the top of a side rafter.

22. Cut two pieces of ⅝-inch-thick T1-11 plywood to 48 × 72 inches each for the shed roof. Position the roof panels side by side with their outside edges overlapping the side rafters by 1⅝ inches on each side. The upper end of each panel should rest on the upper roof support. The lower end of each panel should overhang the rear wall of the shed. Fasten the roof panels to the roof supports and rafters with 8d galvanized common nails.

23. Cut one piece of 2 × 4 stock to 43 inches. Turn it facedown and position it under the front part of the middle shelf so it can become a support for the front of the shelf, as shown in illustration A. Fasten the shelf to the support with 8d galvanized common nails.

24. Cut a 3½ × 3½-inch notch in the left rear corner of the middle shelf so it will fit around the left rear post of the shed. Position the shelf on the left side of the left wall of the bin, so the rear edge of the shelf rests on the rear nailer provided for it, flush with the rear sheathing. Fasten the back of the shelf to its nailer with 8d galvanized common nails.

25. Hold the middle shelf so its top surface is 15½ inches above the lower shelf. Fasten the middle shelf in place by driving 8d galvanized common nails through the left bin wall into the right end of the shelf support and through the left wall of the shed into the left end of the shelf support.

26. Position the bin divider to the left of the upper nailer provided for it. Fasten the upper part of the divider to that nailer; then, after checking to make sure it is vertical, toenail or use a cleat to fasten the lower end of the divider to the shelf beneath it.

27. Fasten the remaining sheet of ¾-inch plywood (cut in step 15) in place on top of the bench supports using 8d galvanized common nails to form the bench top.

28. Cut the following pieces of pressure-treated 2 × 8 (1½″ × 7¼″) stock: six pieces to 95¾ inches each for the sides of the growing bed frames, two pieces to 63 inches each for the ends of the front growing bed frame, two pieces to 28 inches each for the ends of the middle growing bed frame, and two pieces to 33 inches each for the ends of the rear growing bed frame.

29. Finish all wood members of the potting shed–slat house, including the growing bed frame pieces, with two coats of exterior-grade stain.

30. When the stain is dry, assemble the front growing bed frame around the front posts of the slat house with the back piece of

the frame just behind the posts, as shown in the exploded-view diagram. Fasten the sides to the ends with 16d galvanized common nails. Assemble the middle growing bed frame around the middle posts of the slat house with the back of the frame just behind the posts, also as shown in the exploded-view diagram. Fasten the sides to the ends with 16d galvanized common nails. Assemble the rear growing bed frame by fastening the sides to the ends with 16d galvanized common nails. Position this frame 16 inches behind the middle frame.

31. Sink each of the three growing bed frames 2 inches into the ground.

32. If heavy snow load is a problem in your area, reinforce the roof of your slat house by adding a 1 × 6 (¾″ × 5½″) face board on each side of the slat house roof along with 1 × 6 cross members halfway between the 2 × 6 roof support beams, as shown in the exploded-view diagram.

33. For additional weather protection, attach the T1-11 cut-off pieces from the shed roof to the rear of the slat house roof so they slightly overlap the upper edge of the shed roof.

A-FRAME WOOD AND STORAGE SHED

This attractive and interestingly designed storage structure is actually an A-frame shed on stilts. Garth Van Saun of Harrisburg, Pennsylvania, planned and built it using conventional building materials and techniques. The open space between the posts can store nearly four cords of wood. If desired, a concrete slab may be poured as a floor, after construction of the building has been completed. The shed itself—reached by means of a ladder—holds tools, supplies, and other paraphernalia. Van Saun says his children use

the room as a clubhouse, and it also makes a comfortable place to sleep on humid summer nights.

Pressure-treated lumber works best for the posts. Ordinary construction-grade stock may be used elsewhere. Normal roofing is applied. The roof's steep pitch sheds snow easily.

CONSTRUCTION

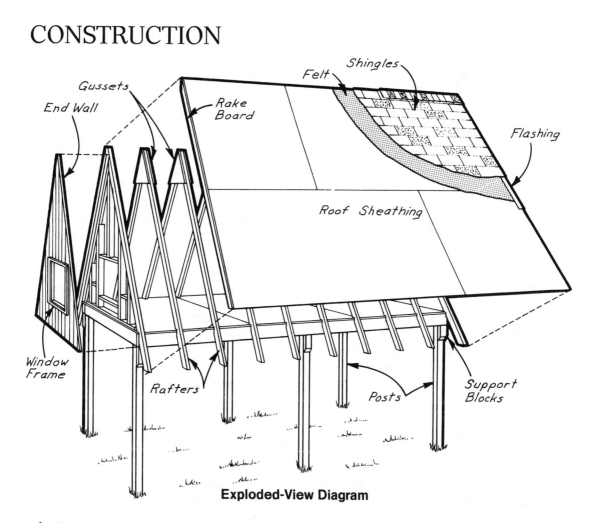

Exploded-View Diagram

1. Prepare the construction site by clearing and leveling a rectangular area measuring 8 × 14 feet. If you plan to pour a concrete pad under the shed, remove the sod as well. When orienting the site, keep in mind that a door will be located on one end wall of the shed and a window on the other.

2. Dig six postholes, each 36 inches deep, in the locations shown in illustration A. Place 6 inches of gravel in each hole to promote drainage.

3. Cut six pieces of 4 × 4 (3½″ × 3½″) stock to 96 inches each for the posts. If the lumber is pressure-treated, apply copper naphthenate wood preservative to the freshly cut ends of each. If the lumber is untreated, apply preservative to all surfaces.

4. Cut six pieces of 2 × 6 (1½″ × 5½″) stock to 72 inches each for the floor joists.

5. Fasten the six posts flush with the ends of three floor joists so that the post tops are flush with the top edges of the joists. Use 16d galvanized common nails.

6. Set the pairs of posts, with the floor joists attached, in the postholes. Place the end posts so that the joists attached to them

535

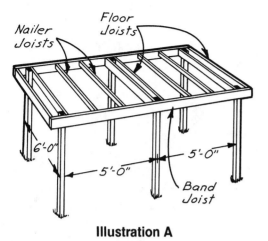

Nailer Joists

Floor Joists

6'-0"

5'-0"

5'-0"

5'-0"

Band Joist

Illustration A

face inward—toward the middle of the shed—as shown in illustration A. Special orientation is not necessary for the center posts.

7. Use two pieces of 2 × 6 stock, each 144 inches in length, for the band joists.

8. With the help of a friend, raise the band joists flush with the top of the posts. Then nail them in place making sure the posts are located properly and that they are vertical. The end posts should measure 10¼ inches on center from the ends of the band joists, and the center posts should measure 72 inches on center, also from the ends of the band joists. Use 16d galvanized common nails.

9. Plumb the bottoms of the posts, enlarging one or more of the holes, if necessary. Then fasten temporary bracing at angles from the posts to the ground to hold the structure firmly in position.

10. Mix and pour concrete into the six postholes to set the posts. Use one 60-pound bag of concrete per post. Recheck the posts occasionally while the concrete is curing to make sure that their alignment does not alter.

11. After the concrete has cured, fasten the

remaining 2 × 6 floor joists to the framing, one joist at each end, between the ends of the band joists, and the other two against the center posts, as shown in illustration A. Use 16d galvanized common nails.

12. Cut four pieces of 2 × 4 (1½″ × 3½″) stock to 75 inches each for nailer joists. Save the cut-off pieces for support blocking. Fasten the nailer joists on 16-inch centers between the floor joists, as shown in illustration A.

13. Cut six pieces of 2 × 4 stock (use the cutoffs from the previous step) to 16 inches each for the support blocks. Cut a 45-degree bevel across the wide face on one end of each piece. Fasten the blocks to the posts beneath the band joists, as shown in the exploded-view diagram, so the beveled ends point down and the square ends butt against the joists.

14. Cut three pieces of ½-inch exterior-grade plywood to 48 × 75 inches each for floor sheathing. Save the cutoffs. Position the sheathing on top of the joists to allow a ⅛-inch expansion gap between panels. Fasten the panels to the joists using 8d galvanized common nails.

15. Paint the floor and posts.

16. Use 20 pieces of 2 × 4 stock, each 96 inches in length, for the rafters. Trim stock lengths to exact dimensions, if necessary. Cut a 30-degree peak angle and a bird's-mouth joint in each rafter, as shown in illustration B. The bird's-mouth joints rest on the floor when the rafters are installed.

17. Cut 18 pieces of ½-inch plywood, using the cutoffs from the floor sheathing (see step 14), to make the gussets, as shown in the exploded-view diagram. Each side of these triangular pieces should measure 17 inches.

18. Position the rafters in pairs so that they form the roof peak angle, then, using 2-

LUMBER CUTTING LIST

Size	Piece	Quantity
4 × 4		
3½″ × 3½″ × 96″	Support posts	6
2 × 6		
1½″ × 5½″ × 144″	Band joists	2
1½″ × 5½″ × 72″	Floor joists	6
2 × 4		
1½″ × 3½″ × 96″	Rafters	20
1½″ × 3½″ × 75″	Nailer joists	4
1½″ × 3½″ × 70″	Framing plates	2
1½″ × 3½″ × 62⅜″	Framing studs	2
1½″ × 3½″ × 36⅜″	Framing studs	4
1½″ × 3½″ × 30″	Framing studs	3
1½″ × 3½″ × 23⅜″	Framing studs	4
1½″ × 3½″ × 16″	Support blocks	6
1½″ × 3½″ × 6″	Framing studs	4
1½″ × 1½″ × 96″	Rake boards	4
1 × 4		
¾″ × 3½″ × 30″	Door frame	2
¾″ × 3½″ × 30″	Window frame	2
¾″ × 3½″ × 28½″	Door frame	2
¾″ × 3½″ × 28½″	Door trim	4
¾″ × 3½″ × 28½″	Window sash frame	2
¾″ × 3½″ × 20″	Window frame	2
¾″ × 3½″ × 17″	Window sash frame	2
Plywood		
½″ × 48″ × 96″	Roof sheathing	4
½″ × 48″ × 75″	Floor sheathing	3
½″ × 48″ × 48″	Roof sheathing	4
½″ × 17″ × 17″ × 17″	Roof gussets	18
Plywood Siding		
⅝″ × 48″ × 71″	End wall siding	2
⅝″ × 20″ × 10½″	End wall siding	4

inch galvanized roofing nails, fasten the gussets to the peaks, as shown in the exploded-view diagram.

19. Hoist the trusses onto the floor, one at a time, and fasten them upright on 16-inch centers to the edges of the floor. Use 16d

galvanized common nails. Erect temporary braces to hold the trusses upright.

20. Cut the following pieces of 2 × 4 stock for the end wall framing: two pieces to 70 inches each, two pieces to 62⅜ inches each, four pieces to 36⅜ inches each, three

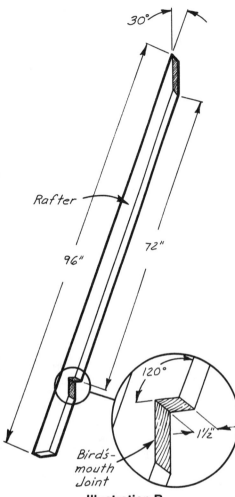

Illustration B

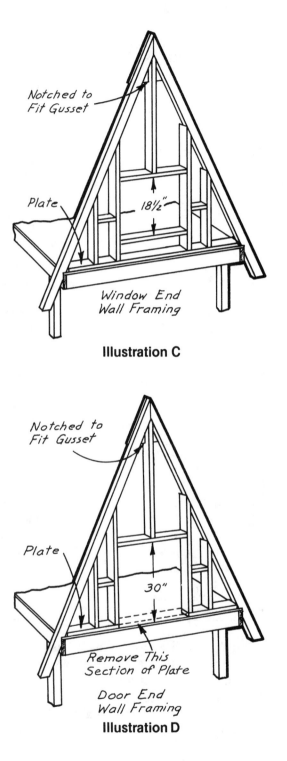

Illustration C

Illustration D

pieces to 30 inches each, four pieces to 23⅝ inches each, and four pieces to 6 inches each.

21. Trim the 70-inch pieces for plates to fit between the end rafters and floor, and install them as shown in illustrations C and D. Then locate the studs 16 inches on center to accommodate the roof sheathing (see step 23). Mark the angle of the rafters on the top of each stud, then trim the tops of the studs so that they fit under the end rafters. The top center stud must be

538

notched to fit the end rafter gusset. Now nail the studs in position using 16d galvanized common nails.

22. Cut away the section of plate that spans the door opening, as shown in illustration D.

23. Use six 4 × 8-foot sheets of ½-inch plywood for the roof sheathing. Cut two of the sheets to 48 × 48 inches each. Position the sheathing across the rafters, as shown in the exploded-view diagram, leaving ⅛-inch gaps between the panels for expansion. The edges of the plywood should extend 1½ inches beyond the end rafters. Align the sheets square to the rafters and flush with their bottom ends. Then, fasten the sheets to the rafters using 8d galvanized common nails.

24. Rip two pieces of 96-inch-long 2 × 4 stock down the middle to make the rake boards, each 1½ × 1½ × 96 inches. Fasten the rake boards to the outside faces of the end rafters using 16d galvanized common nails.

25. Obtain seven pieces of 1½-inch aluminum drip edge, each 8 feet in length. Fasten them to the edges of the sheathing, both the rake and eve, using 2-inch galvanized roofing nails. One piece of flashing must be cut in half to fit the roof dimensions.

26. Obtain one roll of 15-pound roofing felt and fasten it in overlapping rows across the roof using 2-inch galvanized roofing nails. Follow the manufacturer's suggestions to apply the roofing felt properly.

27. Obtain 200 square feet of roof shingles and fasten them to the roof following the manufacturer's suggestions.

28. Obtain two sheets of ⅝-inch exterior plywood siding to cover the end walls. Cut one sheet to 48 × 71 inches for the window end wall, as shown in the cutting diagram, and fasten it to the end wall framing using 8d galvanized common nails. (Use the second sheet of siding in step 31.) Cut

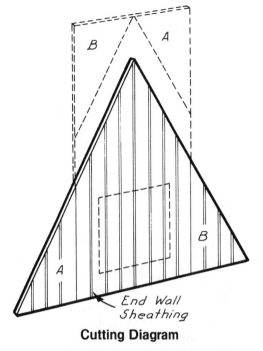

Cutting Diagram

two triangular-shaped pieces from leftover siding and use them to fill in the end walls.

29. Cut out the window area by first crawling inside the shed and drilling four holes through the siding, one in each of the corners of the window framing. Then, move outside again and cut away the window area siding using the four holes as guides.

30. Cut two pieces of 1 × 4 (¾″ × 3½″) stock to 30 inches each, and two pieces to 20 inches each for the window frame. Position the frame pieces on the studs so that the front edges extend ¼ inch past the siding. Fasten the pieces to the end wall studs, as shown in the exploded-view diagram.

31. Cut one piece of ⅝-inch plywood siding to 20 × 10½ inches for the door end wall, as shown in the cutting diagram, and fasten it to the end wall framing using 8d galvanized common nails. From pieces left over, cut two small triangular panels, also shown

in the cutting diagram, to fill in alongside the larger panel. Fasten them in place using 8d galvanized common nails.

32. Cut out the door area siding by first crawling through the window opening into the shed. Drill holes in the corners of the door framing, then cut the door panel from the outside using the holes as guides. Save the panel removed for use as the door.

33. Cut two pieces of 1 × 4 to 30 inches each, and two pieces to 28½ inches each for door framing. Position the framing so that ¼ inch extends past the siding; then, fasten these pieces to the door frame studs using 8d galvanized common nails.

34. Trim the door panel so that it fits easily into the trimmed-out door frame. In order for the vertical seam pattern of the door and end wall to match when the door is installed, you'll have to trim ¾ inch from each side of the panel, rather than trimming a wider strip from just one side. Then cut off 1½ inches from either the top or bottom edge of the panel.

35. Cut four pieces of 1 × 4 to 28½ inches each for door trim. Miter the ends to 45-degree angles. Fasten these pieces to the front of the door panel using 8d galvanized common nails. Bend the points of the nails to a 90-degree angle as they emerge from the wood, then hammer the shanks flat after the nail is completely driven so the points embed in the wood.

36. Fasten the door to the door frame using two 1½ × 3-inch butt hinges. Cut mortises into the door jambs and door edge, fasten the hinges using 1-inch #8 flathead wood screws, and hang the door. Install a 2-inch hook-and-eye fastener to hold the door closed.

37. Cut two pieces of 1 × 4 stock to 28½ inches each, and two pieces to 17 inches each, for the window sash frame, as shown in illustration E.

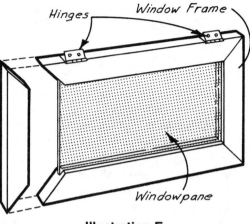

Illustration E

38. Cut a ¼-inch-deep × ¼-inch-wide groove in one edge of each sash frame piece to hold the sheet of 3/16-inch-thick acrylic sheet used for the windowpane (see step 40).

39. Miter the ends of the sash frame pieces to 45-degree angles. Fasten three of the pieces together using carpenter's wood glue and 8d finishing nails. Be sure to align the grooves accurately.

40. Cut one piece of 3/16-inch-thick clear acrylic sheet to 10⅜ × 21⅞ inches for the windowpane. (The pane is sized to allow for expansion in hot weather.) Slip the pane into the sash frame grooves, then fasten the last piece of window sash to the frame using 8d finishing nails.

41. Fasten the window frame to the top of the window opening so that the window hinges are on the top edge. Use two 1½ × 3-inch butt hinges. (Mortise the hinges into the frame, as in step 36, and fasten them with 1-inch #8 flathead wood screws.) Hang the window in place and install a 2-inch hook-and-eye fastener to the frame and siding to keep the window closed.

42. Caulk the seams between the siding and the door and window framing, then paint the remainder of the shed.

ROOT CELLAR

This root cellar was designed by members of the Rodale Design Group to fit into the side of an existing embankment, eliminating the need for stairs. Pressure-treated lumber and plywood were used throughout, except for the storage shelves where the preservative would come into contact with food. The cellar was insulated with slabs of solid insulation.

To keep the path open into the root cellar, retaining walls were installed, backed by chicken wire, to hold the soil until vegetation could get established. Adjacent studs in these walls were made to face at right angles to each other to alternate structural strength and soil retention capabilities.

SHOPPING LIST

Lumber
2 pcs. $2 \times 6 \times 10'$ pressure-treated
3 pcs. $2 \times 6 \times 8'$ pressure-treated
16 pcs. $2 \times 4 \times 10'$ pressure-treated
14 pcs. $2 \times 4 \times 8'$ pressure-treated
1 pc. $1 \times 4 \times 12'$
10 pcs. $1 \times 4 \times 8'$
Furring
5 pcs. $1 \times 3 \times 8'$
3 pcs. $1 \times 3 \times 6'$
Plywood
1 pc. $\frac{3}{4}'' \times 4' \times 5'$ pressure-treated
1 sheet $\frac{5}{8}'' \times 4' \times 8'$ T1-11
4 sheets $\frac{1}{4}'' \times 4' \times 8'$ pressure-treated
Hardware
5 pounds galvanized common nails 16d
3 pounds galvanized common nails 8d
1 pound galvanized common nails 4d
126 flathead wood screws #6 $\times 1\frac{1}{2}''$
$\frac{1}{2}$ pound galvanized staples $\frac{7}{8}''$
1 box wire staples $\frac{5}{16}''$
2 tee hinges 6'' with fasteners
1 barrel bolt 6'' with fasteners
4 pcs. steel reinforcing rods (rebar)
    $\frac{1}{2}''$ diameter $\times 16''$
1 pc. chicken wire (1'' squares)
    32 square feet
4 pcs. extruded polystyrene $1'' \times 4' \times 8'$
10 pcs. expanded polystyrene $2'' \times 2' \times 8'$
8 pcs. expanded polystyrene $1\frac{1}{2}'' \times 2' \times 8'$
1 pc. 6-mil polyethylene 120 square feet
50' flexible perforated pipe 4'' diameter
1 pc. rigid PVC pipe 4'' diameter $\times 8'$
1 PVC pipe elbow 4'' diameter $\times 90$ degrees
2 galvanized chimney caps 4'' diameter
1500 pounds crushed stone $\frac{1}{2}''$
1 quart exterior-grade stain

CONSTRUCTION

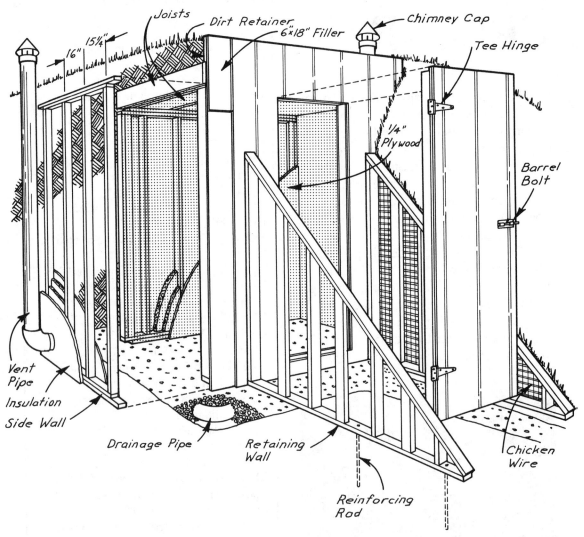

Joists
Dirt Retainer
6"×18" Filler
Chimney Cap
Tee Hinge
16"
15¼"
¼" Plywood
Barrel Bolt
Vent Pipe
Insulation
Side Wall
Drainage Pipe
Retaining Wall
Reinforcing Rod
Chicken Wire

Exploded-View Diagram

To build the root cellar:

1. Cut 22 pieces of pressure-treated 2 × 4 (1½″ × 3½″) stock to 60 inches each for wall studs. Also cut four pieces of the same material to 48 inches each and four pieces to 41 inches each, all for the side wall plates.

2. Square lines across the four shorter wall plates and place Xs next to the lines to mark the positions for the wall studs. Locate the first stud at one end of the plates, the second 15¼ inches on center from the first, and the third stud 16 inches on center from the second, as shown in

the exploded-view diagram. Mark a fourth stud position at the other end of the plates, then fasten studs between them using 16d galvanized common nails to form two wall sections. Use the same-size fasteners in joining 2 × 4 and 2 × 6 framing members in subsequent steps.

3. Double the bottom plate of each side wall section by fastening one of the longer plates to the original bottom plate, allowing its ends to extend an equal distance on each side of the wall. The second top plate will be added to each side wall after all four walls of the root cellar have been erected.

4. Cut 4 pieces of pressure-treated 2 × 4 stock to 60 inches each for the primary front and back wall plates. Also cut 3 pieces of the same stock to 53 inches each, 2 pieces to 6½ inches each, and 1 piece to 32 inches for the secondary front and back wall plates. Fasten 10 of the remaining wall studs into 5 L-shaped pairs for use at the ends of the front and back walls and on the hinge side of the door, as shown in illustration A.

5. Frame the back wall using two of the 60-inch wall plates. Place one of the paired studs at each end, turned so that the stem of its L is flush with the inside of the wall and the stud that forms the foot of its L is at the end of the plate. Fill the space between the paired studs with the three remaining studs, by placing the first 18¾ inches from one end of the wall and the others on 16-inch centers.

6. Frame the front wall with L-shaped-paired studs set between the ends of 60-inch wall plates, the same as the back wall. Place the final studs just outside the points 19⅞ inches from each end of the wall to create a 20¼-inch door opening. Be sure to place the paired studs on the hinge side of the opening with the stem of the L flush with the outside of the wall, as shown in illustration B.

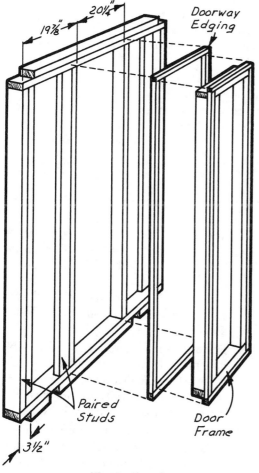

Illustration A

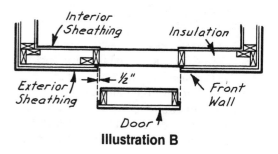

Illustration B

LUMBER CUTTING LIST

Size	Piece	Quantity
2 × 6		
1½″ × 5½″ × 60″	Roof headers	2
1½″ × 5½″ × 60″	Dirt retainer	1
1½″ × 5½″ × 45″	Roof joists	7
2 × 4		
1½″ × 3½″ × 96″	Retaining wall stud material (cut to fit)	4
1½″ × 3½″ × 96″	Retaining wall top plates	2
1½″ × 3½″ × 87″	Retaining wall bottom plates	2
1½″ × 3½″ × 60″	Cellar wall studs	22
1½″ × 3½″ × 60″	Front and back wall plates	4
1½″ × 3½″ × 59¼″	Door frame vertical members	2
1½″ × 3½″ × 53″	Front and back wall plates	3
1½″ × 3½″ × 51″	Shelf supports	3
1½″ × 3½″ × 48″	Side wall plates	4
1½″ × 3½″ × 41″	Side wall plates	4
1½″ × 3½″ × 32″	Front wall bottom plate	1
1½″ × 3½″ × 16½″	Door frame horizontal members	2
1½″ × 3½″ × 6½″	Front wall bottom plate	2
1 × 4		
¾″ × 3½″ × 40½″	Shelf boards	18
¾″ × 3½″ × 16″	Shelf boards	12

7. Fasten the 6½-inch-long plates on the underside of the front wall bottom plate, holding them back 3½ inches from each end of the wall. Then center the 32-inch plate between the two short ones and fasten it in place. Center and fasten one of the 53-inch plates on top of the front wall, and the other two above and beneath the primary plates of the back wall.

8. Cut two pieces of pressure-treated 2 × 6 (1½″ × 5½″) stock to 60 inches each for the roof headers and seven pieces to 45 inches each for the roof joists. Fasten the roof framework together with one joist between the headers at each end. Place a second joist just inside the points 3½ inches from the ends of the headers to provide nailers for the interior roof. Position the remaining joists in the usual way. Starting from one side, place a joist 15¼ inches on center from the preceding one and the rest on 16-inch centers, as shown in illustration C.

9. Dig a hole for the root cellar, preferably into the side of an embankment. Make the hole big enough to allow room for working on the outer walls and for installing drainage pipe around the walls' perimeter.

10. Dig a drainage ditch approximately 7 inches below grade, sloping it so that water will drain away from the root cellar. Line the bottom of the ditch with at least 3

Size	Piece	Quantity
Furring		
¾'' × 2½'' × 52½''	Back wall shelf rails	3
¾'' × 2½'' × 39''	Side wall shelf rails	6
¾'' × 2½'' × 16''	Front wall shelf rails	6
¾'' × 1'' × 85''	Doorway and door frame edging material (cut to fit)	4
¾'' Pressure-Treated Plywood		
¾'' × 48'' × 60''	Cellar roof top	1
T1-11 Plywood		
⅝'' × 48'' × 77¾''	Exterior front wall sheathing	1
⅝'' × 21'' × 60¾''	Exterior door panel	1
⅝'' × 6'' × 18''	Exterior front wall sheathing fillers	2
¼'' Pressure-Treated Plywood		
¼'' × 48'' × 65¾''	Interior back wall sheathing	1
¼'' × 41'' × 53''	Ceiling sheathing	1
¼'' × 40½'' × 65¾''	Interior side wall sheathing	1
¼'' × 40½'' × 42⅞''	Interior side wall sheathing	1
¼'' × 40½'' × 22⅞''	Interior side wall sheathing	1
¼'' × 19½'' × 30''	Interior door panel	1
¼'' × 19½'' × 29¼''	Interior door panel	1
¼'' × 16⅜'' × 65¾''	Interior front wall sheathing	2
¼'' × 6'' × 9''	Ceiling vent damper blank	1
¼'' × 5'' × 65¾''	Interior back wall sheathing	1

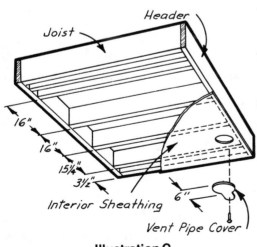

Illustration C

inches of crushed stone and install 4-inch-diameter, flexible perforated pipe. Cover the pipe with crushed stone. Use additional stone to create a solid base for the walls and a dry, level floor inside the root cellar.

11. Raise the side walls first, then the front and back walls, lapping the bottom plates. Make sure all walls are level and plumb, then link them with nails where the plates overlap and the studs butt together. Fasten the remaining 48-inch plates to the tops of the side walls and to the plate extensions from the front and back walls. Set the roof framework on top of the walls and nail it in place. Cut one sheet of pressure-treated ¾-inch plywood to 60 inches in

545

length and fasten it to the top of the roof.

12. Cut two pieces of 1 × 3 (¾″ × 2½″) furring to 85 inches each, then rip them into four pieces, each 1 inch in width, for use as doorway and door frame edging. Cut two of the pieces to fit on edge around the exterior perimeter of the doorway, ½ inch back from the opening, as shown in illustration B. Fasten the edging in place using 4d galvanized common nails.

13. Cut two sheets of 1-inch-thick extruded polystyrene each to 72¼ inches in length, to fit the exterior side walls of the root cellar. Fasten them in place using 4d galvanized common nails. Cut additional sheets of extruded polystyrene to cover the front and back exterior walls and the edges of the insulation just applied to the side walls. Fit the insulation around the door opening against the inside of the edge banding. Where pieces of insulation must be butted side by side, cut them to meet over nailers.

On the front wall, use only enough nails to hold the insulation until plywood sheathing can be mounted over it.

14. Cut pieces of 1½- and 2-inch-thick expanded polystyrene to fill all spaces between the wall studs and roof joists. Then cover the entire interior framework of the root cellar with a layer of 6-mil polyethylene for a vapor barrier, fastening it in place with 5/16-inch wire staples. Cover the vapor barrier with one layer of pressure-treated ¼-inch plywood, fastening it to the roof and wall framework using 4d galvanized common nails. (See the cutting diagram.) Also cover the exterior of the roof with 6-mil polyethylene to protect it from moisture.

15. Cut one piece of pressure-treated 2 × 6 stock to 60 inches for a dirt retainer. Set it on edge on top of the root cellar, aligned flush with the insulation. Use 8d galvanized common nails to toenail the dirt retainer in place until the front sheathing

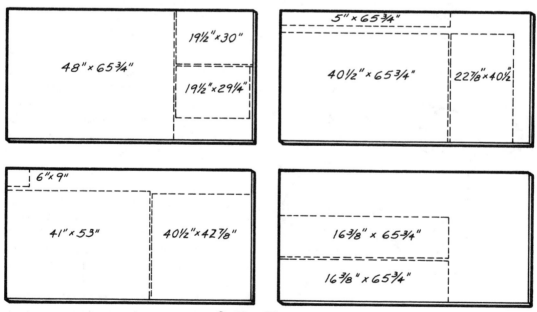

Cutting Diagram

can be mounted over it.

16. Cut one piece of ⅝-inch T1-11 plywood to 77¾ inches in length. Lay out a 21 × 60¾-inch rectangle 3⅛ inches above the bottom of the sheet and centered across its width. Cut carefully along the outside of the rectangle to create a door opening. Save the cutout for use as the front of the door. Place the larger plywood sheet up against the front of the cellar and align the edges of its opening with the edging that surrounds the wall opening. Mark and notch the lower edge of the sheet, where needed, to allow the retaining wall bottom plates to slide beneath the cellar front wall. Then, fasten the plywood to the front of the cellar and the dirt retainer using 8d galvanized common nails. Take the 18 × 48-inch piece of T1-11 cut off the end of the original sheet and rip two pieces, each 6 inches in width, for use as fillers. Fasten the fillers to the upper front corners of the cellar, as shown in the exploded-view diagram.

17. Cut the ¾ × 1-inch strips remaining from step 12 to fit on edge around the inside perimeter of the door panel. Fasten the edging to the panel using 4d galvanized common nails. Cut pieces of pressure-treated 2 × 4 stock to fit around the inside of the edging to create the framework of the door, as shown in illustrations A and B. Drive 8d galvanized common nails through the front of the panel into this framework to hold it in place.

18. Fill the space inside the door cavity with expanded polystyrene. Cover the inside of the door with 6-mil polyethylene. Then cut one piece of pressure-treated ¼-inch plywood to 19½ × 30 inches, and another piece to 19½ × 29¼ inches, as shown in the cutting diagram. Fasten them to the inside of the door frame using 4d galvanized common nails. Hang the door on the front of the cellar using a pair of 6-inch tee hinges. Install a 6-inch barrel bolt to hold it in place. Finish the plywood front of the root cellar with a coat of exterior-grade stain.

19. Cut a 4-inch-diameter hole near the floor in one of the root cellar side walls and a similar hole in the roof near the opposite side wall, to receive PVC vent pipes. Run one 4-inch-diameter PVC pipe through the wall a short distance outside. Put a 90-degree elbow on it and run more pipe vertically up to a point about a foot above the dirt retaining wall. Run another piece of 4-inch-diameter PVC pipe up through the roof to a similar height. Place a 4-inch galvanized chimney cap on top of each of the vent pipes. Cut a 6-inch-diameter disk out of ¼-inch pressure-treated plywood, leaving a pivot tab on one side, as shown in illustration C. Fasten the disk to the cellar ceiling where it can be moved from side to side to open or close the ceiling vent pipe.

To build the retaining walls:

1. Cut two pieces of pressure-treated 2 × 4 stock to 87 inches each for the bottom plates of the retaining walls. Insert the ends of these plates into the spaces provided for them in the bottom front plate of the cellar. Smooth the soil beneath so the plates rest solidly on the ground. Tack them temporarily to the cellar bottom plate.

2. Use two pieces of pressure-treated 2 × 4 stock, each 96 inches in length, for the retaining wall top plates. Cut the angle needed on the upper end of each (approximately 30 degrees) to fit against the front tip of the root cellar while its lower end rests on the front of a bottom plate. Tack the top plates in place temporarily.

3. Measure and cut four 2 × 4 studs to fit

on 12-inch centers along each retaining wall. Position the first stud of each wall flush against the front of the root cellar. Alternate the direction in which successive studs face, as shown in the exploded-view diagram. Be sure to mark the stud locations on both plates before removing them for assembling the walls. Drive a pair of 16d galvanized nails through the plate into each stud end.

4. Fasten 1-inch mesh chicken wire to the back of each retaining wall using ⅞-inch galvanized staples. Then raise the walls and fasten them to the front of the root cellar. Cut four pieces of ½-inch-diameter steel reinforcing rod (rebar) to 16 inches each. Drill a ½-inch-diameter hole through both plates near the front end of each retaining wall and drive a steel rod through into the ground to hold the wall in place. Drive a second rod through the bottom plate of each wall approximately 3 feet farther back, as shown in the exploded-view diagram.

5. Backfill around the root cellar and behind the retaining walls. When the grading is complete, plant a ground cover to hold the soil after the chicken wire has rusted away.

To make the storage shelves:

1. Measure the length of the back wall of the root cellar (approximately 52½ inches) and cut three pieces of 1 × 3 furring for rails to support shelves. Hold the upper edge of one rail 16½ inches below the ceiling and fasten it to the wall using 8d galvanized common nails. Fasten the other two rails on 16½-inch centers below the first, as shown in illustration D.

2. Cut six pieces of 1 × 3 stock to 16 inches each for rails to fit the front wall of the cellar. Fasten three of these rails on either side of the door opening at the same height

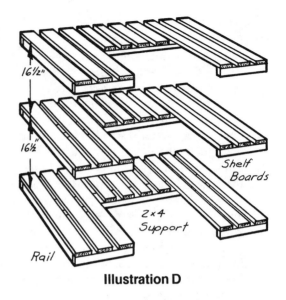

Illustration D

as the rails on the back wall. Then cut six pieces of 1 × 3 stock to approximately 39 inches each to fit across the side walls between the ends of the rails previously installed.

3. Cut three pieces of pressure-treated 2 × 4 stock to approximately 51 inches each to fit between the pairs of side wall rails just behind a point 16 inches from the back wall. Turn these supports face-up and align their upper surfaces with the top edges of the side wall rails. Toenail them to the rails and side walls using 16d galvanized common nails.

4. Cut 18 pieces of 1 × 4 (¾″ × 3½″) stock to 40½ inches each, and 12 pieces to 16 inches each for shelf boards. Place four short boards in the middle and three long boards on either side at each of the three shelf levels. Space the boards evenly and fasten them to the rails and 2 × 4 supports using 1½ inch #6 flathead wood screws. Insert and countersink two screws where each shelf rests on a support.

GARDEN SHED WITH WOOD-STORAGE AREA

This attractive shed was designed by the Rodale Design Group to fit the needs of a city or suburban dweller with a yard and garden to tend and a small amount of firewood to store. The shed's enclosed portion—approximately 60 square feet of floor space—affords plenty of room to house a lawn mower, wheelbarrow, assorted garden tools, plus other bulky items. Its interior is simple and functional. Shelves may easily be added to suit individual needs. The sheltered firewood area, open to allow plenty of air circulation, yet protected from

SHOPPING LIST

Lumber
4 pcs. $4 \times 4 \times 9'$ pressure-treated
2 pcs. $4 \times 4 \times 7'$ pressure-treated
20 pcs. $2 \times 6 \times 8'$
5 pcs. $2 \times 4 \times 12'$
21 pcs. $2 \times 4 \times 8'$
5 pcs. $2 \times 2 \times 8'$
1 pc. $1 \times 6 \times 6'$
Furring
40 pcs. $\frac{3}{4}'' \times 2\frac{1}{4}'' \times 8'$
Plywood
8 sheets $\frac{5}{8}'' \times 4' \times 8'$ T1-11
6 sheets $\frac{1}{2}'' \times 4' \times 8'$ CDX
1 sheet $\frac{1}{4}'' \times 4' \times 8'$ exterior grade
Roofing Material
1½ squares asphalt shingles
1 roll asphalt roofing paper 15#
Hardware
3 four-lite window sashes
    $1\frac{1}{8}'' \times 20\frac{3}{4}'' \times 25''$
60 flathead wood screws #$6 \times 1\frac{3}{4}''$
2 roundhead wood screws #$10 \times 1\frac{1}{2}''$
3 heavy tee hinges 8'' with screws
4 light tee hinges 2'' with screws
1 door latch
2 sash chains 12'' with screws
5 pounds common nails 16d
5 pounds common nails 8d
10 pounds galvanized common nails 8d
½ pound aluminum finishing nails 8d
¼ pound underlayment nails 1''
5 pounds galvanized roofing nails 1¼''
5 pcs. aluminum drip edge 10'
10 joist hangers
2 gallons exterior-grade stain
2 quarts exterior-grade latex paint

rain and snow by the roof, stores about a cord and a half of wood.

We think the exterior is more attractive than the usual backyard utility building. Textured plywood siding (referred to in the instructions by its lumberyard designation, T1-11) provides an elegant look for a moderate price. We stained the siding dark brown, then trimmed the door, windows, and corners of the building with furring lumber painted white. Leftover pieces of siding and trim were used to make window boxes that further decorate the structure.

Before undertaking this project, check on the materials available in your area. Windows you locate, for instance, may be a different size than the ones we used, or you may find that furring material in your area is sold in widths different from what we specify. Our design and instructions—though they do accurately describe the construction of the actual garden shed pictured here—should be viewed as sources for ideas and procedures. Alter the dimensions given or the materials used to suit your own needs.

CONSTRUCTION

To build the foundation:

1. Lay out the position of the six posts, as shown in illustration A. Dig the postholes to a depth at least 6 inches below the frost line in your area. Make the holes roomy enough to adjust the spacing of the posts. Put a few inches of gravel in the bottom of each hole to aid drainage. Plan on setting all posts at least a foot deep no matter what the frost line. Stand a 4 × 4 (3½″ × 3½″) pressure-treated post in each hole. Posts A and B should rise at least 84 inches above ground level, posts C and D at least 79 inches, and posts E and F at least 60 inches aboveground. If the ground is not level, erect the post at the highest spot first and adjust the height of the rest accordingly.

2. Plumb the six posts, making sure they are the proper distance apart. Brace them with pieces of furring stock that will later be used for the wood storage floor. Backfill the postholes, tamping the soil firmly around the posts.

To build the shed floor:

1. Cut a 1-inch-deep notch 1½ inches wide and 5½ inches long into the four shed posts at each point where a header or floor joist will fit. Notch the post set at the highest ground level first. Make the bottom of the notch in that post no more than 6 inches above the ground. Make all subsequent notches level with those. Note that the headers and outside joists should form a continuous surface with the outside edges of the posts so that exterior sheathing may be applied.

2. Cut two pieces of 2 × 6 (1½″ × 5½″) stock to 91 inches each for the shed floor joist headers. Holding the pieces together, mark them for joist locations on 16-inch centers, making the first location 13½ inches from one end to allow for the posts. Fasten the headers in the post notches, one header between posts A and C, the other between posts B and D. Use 16d common nails.

3. Cut two pieces of 2 × 6 stock to 87 inches

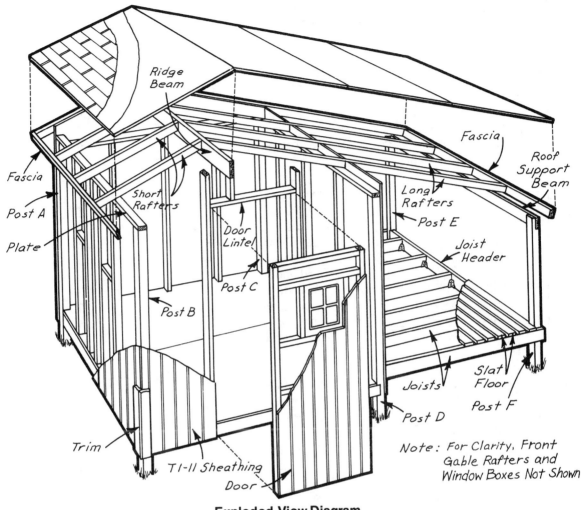

Fascia

Ridge
Beam

Fascia

Roof
Support
Beam

Post A

Short
Rafters

Long
Rafters

Plate

Door
Lintel

Post E

Joist
Header

Post C

Post B

Joists

Slat
Floor

Post F

Post D

Trim

TI-II Sheathing

Door

Note: For Clarity, Front
Gable Rafters and
Window Boxes Not Shown

Exploded-View Diagram

each for the outside floor joists. Fasten one joist between posts A and B, the other between posts C and D, using 16d common nails.

4. Cut five pieces of 2 × 6 stock to 89 inches each for the inside floor joists. Fasten these joists where marked between the headers using 16d common nails.

5. Cut five pieces of 2 × 6 stock to 14½

inches each for bridging between the floor joists. (Save cutting the final piece of bridging until all are in place; see next step.) Snap a line across the joists at their midpoint and install the bridging. To simplify nailing, install consecutive pieces on opposite sides of the center line, as shown in illustration B. Use 16d common nails.

6. Make sure the floor joists are pulled tight
(continued on page 554)

551

LUMBER CUTTING LIST

Size	Piece	Quantity
4 × 4		
3½″ × 3½″ × 84″ (plus length below grade)	Shed posts	2
3½″ × 3½″ × 79″ (plus length below grade)	Shed posts	2
3½″ × 3½″ × 60″ (plus length below grade)	Wood storage area posts	2
2 × 6		
1½″ × 5½″ × 96″	Roof support beam	1
1½″ × 5½″ × 92″	Ridge beam	1
1½″ × 5½″ × 92″	Wood storage joist headers	2
1½″ × 5½″ × 91″	Shed floor joist headers	2
1½″ × 5½″ × 89″	Shed floor inside joists	5
1½″ × 5½″ × 87″	Shed floor outside joists	2
1½″ × 5½″ × 71⅜″	Wood storage floor outside joists	2
1½″ × 5½″ × 66⅜″	Wood storage floor inside joists	5
1½″ × 5½″ × 14½″	Floor joist bridging	5
1½″ × 5½″ × 13″	Floor joist bridging	1
2 × 4		
1½″ × 3½″ × 142¾″	Gable ends	2
1½″ × 3½″ × 142″	Roof rafters	3
1½″ × 3½″ × 96″	Wall studs	2
1½″ × 3½″ × 96″	Fascia	2
1½″ × 3½″ × 92½″	Wall plate	1
1½″ × 3½″ × 92″	Wall plates	2
1½″ × 3½″ × 71¾″	Wall studs	5
1½″ × 3½″ × 68¼″	Wall studs	3
1½″ × 3½″ × 66¾″	Wall studs	3
1½″ × 3½″ × 46¾″	Gable ends	2
1½″ × 3½″ × 46″	Roof rafters	3
1½″ × 3½″ × 36″	Door lintel	1
1½″ × 3½″ × 20¾″	Window framing members	4
1½″ × 3½″ × 14¾″	Cripple stud	1
1½″ × 3½″ × 9″	Cripple stud	1
2 × 2		
1½″ × 1½″ × 73½″	Door vertical framing members	2
1½″ × 1½″ × 32¾″	Door horizontal framing members	6
1½″ × 1½″ × 25″	Door window framing members	2

Size	Piece	Quantity
1 × 6		
¾″ × 5½″ × 27″	Windowsills	2
Furring		
¾″ × 2¼″ × 95″	Wood storage area flooring	25
¾″ × 2¼″ × 77½″	Wall trim	4
¾″ × 2¼″ × 74″	Wall trim	4
¾″ × 2¼″ × 74″	Door trim	2
¾″ × 2¼″ × 40½″	Door trim	1
¾″ × 2¼″ × 25″	Window trim	4
¾″ × 2¼″ × 24¼″	Window trim	4
¾″ × 2¼″ × 22¼″	Window box trim	2
¾″ × 2¼″ × 18¾″	Window box trim	2
¾″ × 2¼″ × 10⅛″	Window box trim	4
¾″ × 2¼″ × 8″	Window box trim	4
¾″ × 2¼″ × 4″	Turn latches	2
¾″ × 1″ × 4″	Window filler blocks	2
½″ × ¾″ × 73½″	Door stops	2
½″ × ¾″ × 36″	Door stop	1
¼″ × ¾″ × 20¾″	Windowsill shims	2
T1-11 Plywood		
⅝″ × 48″ × 96″	Wall sheathing	4
⅝″ × 48″ × 82½″	Wall sheathing	1
⅝″ × 48″ × 77½″	Wall sheathing	1
⅝″ × 45¼″ × 82½″	Wall sheathing	1
⅝″ × 45¼″ × 77½″	Wall sheathing	1
⅝″ × 8¼″ × 19¾″	Window box bottoms	2
⅝″ × 8″ × 21″	Window box fronts	2
⅝″ × 8″ × 19¾″	Window box backs	2
⅝″ × 8″ × 8⅞″	Window box sides	4
½″ Plywood		
½″ × 48″ × 96″	Roof	4
½″ × 48″ × 96″	Shed floor	1
½″ × 44″ × 96″	Shed floor	1
¼″ Plywood		
¼″ × 35¾″ × 73½″	Door panel	1

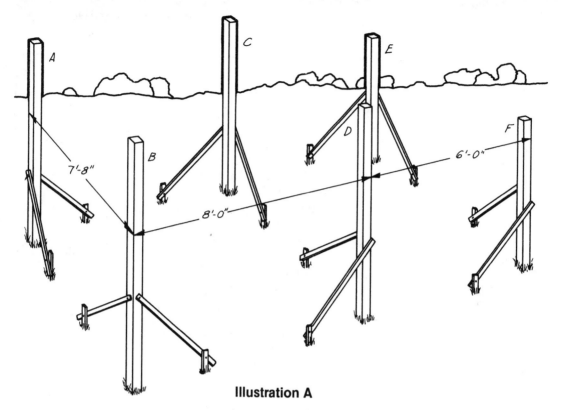

Illustration A

against the bridging, then measure the space between the last two joists. Cut one piece of 2 × 6 stock to that length for the final piece of bridging and fasten it in place.

7. Cut a 3½ × 3½-inch notch in the corners of one long side of a 4 × 8-foot sheet of ½-inch CDX plywood. Lay the plywood across the floor joists, good side up, fitting the notched corners around posts A and C. Fasten the plywood to the header and floor joists with 8d common nails.

8. Trim 4 inches off the width of a 4 × 8-foot sheet of ½-inch CDX plywood. Cut a 3½ × 3½-inch notch in each corner of the ripped side and install the sheet, good side up, over the remainder of the shed floor structure, fastening it with 8d common nails.

To build the shed end walls:

1. Trim posts A and B to a height of 71½ inches above the shed floor.

2. Trim posts C and D to a height of 66¾

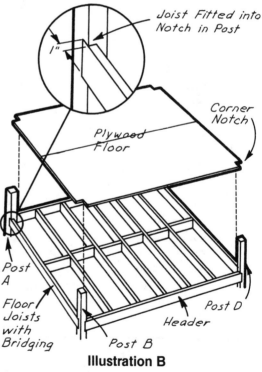

Illustration B

554

inches above the shed floor.

3. Cut two pieces of 2 × 4 (1½″ × 3½″) to 92 inches each for the wall plates. Fasten one plate to the tops of posts A and B and the other to the tops of posts C and D, as shown in the exploded-view diagram, using 16d common nails.

4. Cut one piece of 2 × 4 stock to 92½ inches for the plate between posts A and C. Fasten one end of the plate on top of the plate already resting on post C and toenail the other end into post A at the same height using 16d common nails. Now remove the braces from the shed posts installed previously (see step 2 of "To build the foundation").

5. Measure from the end of the plate on top of post A along the surface of the plate and mark points at 14½, 36¾, 46½, 53¾, and 76 inches. Make an X after each mark to indicate the locations of the tops of the wall studs. Lay out identical marks on the floor, directly beneath the plate to locate the bottoms of the studs.

6. Cut five pieces of 2 × 4 stock to 71¾ inches each for wall studs. Install all but the middle stud in the wall between posts A and B, nailing down through the plate into the top end of each stud and toenailing the bottom end to the floor using 16d common nails. Save the middle stud for installation after the window framing has been completed (see step 8 below).

7. Cut four pieces of 2 × 4 stock to 20¾ inches each for window framing members. Frame out the opening for the windows between the first and second studs at each end of the window wall, as shown in illustration C. Turn one framing member on edge and fasten it between the studs to form the header at the top of each window opening and make the outside face of each header flush with the outside edges of the studs. Fasten the headers in place with 16d

common nails. Fasten the other two framing members between the studs, leaving a space of 25⅞ inches between each lower member and its parallel header above, also as shown.

8. Nail the middle wall stud in place.

9. Cut three pieces of 2 × 4 stock to 68¼ inches each for wall studs between posts A and C. Locate the first stud immediately past a line scribed 23¼ inches from the outside corner of post A. Install the remaining studs on 24-inch centers. Fasten them in place between the plate and the floor using 16d common nails.

10. Cut three pieces of 2 × 4 stock to 66¾ inches each for wall studs between posts C and D. Measuring from the outside cor-

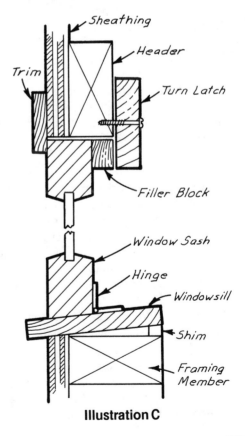

Illustration C

ner of post D, along the plate and the floor toward post C (as you did in step 5 above), make an X immediately past the 22½-, 46½-, and 70½-inch points to mark the positions of the studs. Fasten them in place with 16d common nails.

11. Apply a good quality exterior-grade stain to eight 4 × 8-foot sheets of ⅝-inch-thick T1-11 plywood siding.

12. Fasten one of the stained sheets of siding to the wall between posts A and C, holding the right edge of the sheet flush with the outside corner of post A and the lower edge of the sheet flush with the bottom of the floor joist header. Attach the sheet to the post, header, wall plate, and studs using 8d galvanized common nails.

13. Fasten another sheet of siding to post B and the header extending between posts B and D. Hold the left edge of the sheet flush with the outside corner of post B and the lower edge of the sheet flush with the bottom of the header. Secure the sheet with 8d galvanized common nails, leaving the last 16 inches of the lower right part of the sheet free to be cut out later for the door (see step 3 of "To frame the shed door").

14. Measure across the top of each sheet of attached siding, starting from the post edge and make a large X just past the 34¾-inch point on each sheet. Cut one piece of 2 × 6 stock to 92 inches for the ridge beam and position it on edge between the two sheets of siding at the points marked, so that the top of the beam lies flush with the tops of the sheets of siding. Drive three or four 8d galvanized common nails through each sheet into the ends of the ridge beam.

15. Measure the distance between the top of the wall plate that connects posts A and C and the bottom of the ridge beam (approximately 14¾ inches). Cut a short

stud (called a cripple) from 2 × 4 stock to that length and fasten it between the plate and the beam with 16d common nails.

16. Fit a second sheet of siding against each piece previously installed to complete the sheathing of the two walls. Fasten the siding using 8d galvanized common nails, but leave free the lower left half of the sheet covering the door area.

To frame the shed door:

1. From the inside of post B, measure 34 inches across the floor toward post D. Mark that point and place an X immediately past it. Continue measuring across the door area and place a mark at 71½ inches, followed by an X. Stand an 8-foot 2 × 4 against the inside wall at each place marked. Toenail each stud to the floor. Holding each stud plumb, nail 8d galvanized common nails through the sheathing into the studs.

2. Cut one piece of 2 × 4 stock to 36 inches for the lintel. Fasten this piece, using 16d common nails, between the wall studs erected in the previous step, keeping the cross member 74 inches above the floor.

3. Carefully cut out the wall sheathing in the space just framed. Save the pieces for use on the door.

4. Cut one piece of 2 × 4 stock to 9 inches. Fasten it, using 8d galvanized common nails, to the inside of the wall sheathing in the space between the top of the door frame and the ridge beam.

To frame the roof:

1. Mark posts E and F where they are level with the shed floor. Measure from that point 43 inches up each post to mark the bottoms of notches for the roof support beam to be suspended between those posts. Cut a notch 1½ inches deep and 5½ inches

tall across the outside of each post to receive the beam, as shown in the exploded-view diagram.

2. Use one piece of 2 × 6 stock, 96 inches in length, for the roof support beam. Fit the beam in the notches on the back of posts E and F, allowing 2 inches of the beam to extend beyond each post. Fasten the beam to the posts with 16d common nails. Then trim the top of the posts flush with the upper edge of the beam.

3. Cut three pieces of 2 × 4 stock to 142 inches each for roof rafters. Check the rafters for crowns and plan on installing them crown (convex) side up. Cut one end of each rafter at the angle necessary for it to fit flush against the ridge beam while resting on the plate connecting posts C and D and the beam connecting posts E and F. Cut bird's-eye notches on the underside of the rafters, if necessary, to make them rest against all three surfaces simultaneously. Be sure to cut the notches so that the top edges of the rafters will all be at the same level; otherwise, the roofing surface will not be even.

4. Locate the position of the three interior rafters by measuring along the roof support beam from the outside of the sheathing on either wall. Mark and place an X immediately after the 21⅞-, 45⅞-, and 69⅞-inch points. Mark the wall plates connecting posts A and B, and C and D in the same manner. Fasten the three long rafters in place using 16d common nails.

5. Cut three pieces of 2 × 4 stock to 46 inches each for the short interior rafters. Cut one end of each rafter to the angle needed to fit it flush against the ridge beam, then fasten the rafters in place with 16d common nails.

6. Cut two pieces of 2 × 4 stock to 142¾ inches each, and two additional pieces to 46¾ inches each, for gable ends.

7. Miter one end of each gable end so that

one long and one short board will fit together when positioned parallel to the rafters, on the outside of the wall sheathing. Apply the desired exterior-quality paint or stain to the gable ends. When the paint is dry, fasten the gable ends to the sheathing and shed roof support beam with 8d galvanized common nails. Trim the sheathing and the projecting wall studs flush with the tops of the gable ends and save the cut-off pieces of sheathing for later use.

To build the shed partition wall:

1. Cut two 4 × 8 sheets of ⅝-inch T1-11 siding to 77½ inches each for the shed partition wall. Rip one sheet to 45¼ inches in width. Position the ripped sheet on the outside of the wall between posts C and D, the ripped edge lapped over the edge of the wall sheathing previously attached to post C (see step 12 of "To build the shed end walls"). With the sheet pressed against the undersides of the rafters, mark the positions of the rafters, then take the sheet away and cut 3½-inch-deep notches in it so it will fit around the rafters when installed. Fasten the sheet in place between posts C and D with 8d galvanized common nails.

2. Position the unused sheet of siding cut in the previous step where it will lap the first sheet attached to the shed partition wall. Cut notches where needed to fit around rafters, then fasten the sheet in place with 8d galvanized common nails.

To build the window wall:

1. Cut two 4 × 8-foot sheets of ⅝-inch T1-11 siding to 82½ inches each for installation on the wall between posts A and B. Rip one sheet to 45¼ inches in width. With the ripped edge lapped over the sheathing attached to post B (see step 13 of "To build the shed end walls"), cut out notches

for rafters and tack this sheet in place following the procedure used previously in building the shed partition wall.

2. Lap the second sheet with the first, notch, and tack in place. Trace the window openings (each 25 inches tall × 20¾ inches wide) on the backs of the two sheets and remove them for cutting. Afterward, nail the sheathing in place with 8d galvanized common nails. (Note: You may find it just as easy to cut the window openings with the sheathing in place.) Save the cut-out pieces for use on the window boxes.

To finish the roof:

1. Use two pieces of 2 × 4 stock, each 96 inches in length, for fascia boards. Fasten one piece to the ends of the short rafters and the other piece to the ends of the long rafters, as shown in the exploded-view diagram. Use 16d common nails.

2. Cover the short side of the shed roof with one 4 × 8-foot sheet of ½-inch CDX plywood. Center the plywood lengthwise across the rafters and fasten it in place with 8d common nails.

3. Cover the long rafters of the shed and wood storage area with three 4 × 8-foot sheets of ½-inch plywood laid lengthwise across the rafters. Fasten them with 8d common nails.

4. Fasten an aluminum drip edge around the perimeter of the roof, then cover the roof with 15# asphalt roofing paper. Staple the paper to the plywood, then shingle the roof using 1¼-inch galvanized roofing nails to hold the shingles in place.

To build the wood storage area:

1. Cut two pieces of 2 × 6 stock to 92 inches each for the joist headers in the wood storage area. Center one header lengthwise along the shed partition wall with the bottom edge of the header positioned 4 to 6 inches above the bottom of the wall sheath-ing. Use 16d common nails where they will secure the header to corner posts and wall studs behind the sheathing.

2. Cut notches 5½ inches high and 1½ inches deep across the inside faces of posts E and F, for installing a header level with the one installed in the previous step. Fasten the other 2 × 6 header to the notched posts with 16d common nails.

3. Cut two pieces of 2 × 6 stock to 71⅜ inches each for the outside joists of the wood storage area. Lap one joist over the ends of both headers and the side of the post at each end of the wood storage area. Fasten each joist in place with 16d common nails.

4. Cut five pieces of 2 × 6 stock to 66⅜ inches each for the inside joists of the wood storage area. Lay out and mark the position of each of the five joists on the two headers. Space them on 16-inch centers, or merely evenly apart. Mount joist hangers on the headers, then suspend the joists between the hangers, fastening them in place by driving 1¼-inch galvanized roofing nails at an angle through the hangers into the joists.

5. Cut 25 pieces of unpainted furring stock (¾″ × 2¼″) to 95 inches each for the wood storage area flooring. Position the first piece of flooring across the joists ¼ inch from one header. Leave a ½-inch space between all subsequent pieces installed. Fasten the flooring to the joists with 8d galvanized common nails.

To build the windows:

1. Make two ¼-inch-wide rippings from ¾-inch-thick furring stock, each 20¾ inches in length. Glue and nail one ripping on the upper inside edge of the lower framing member of each window opening to serve as a shim for the sill, as shown in illustration C.

2. Cut two pieces of 1 × 6 (¾″ × 5½″) stock to 27 inches each for the windowsills. Notch each sill, as necessary, to fit inside a window opening. Prime and paint the sills with exterior-quality paint. When the paint is dry, fasten the sills in place with 8d galvanized common nails.

3. Select 13 pieces of furring stock, each 8 feet long, and paint them with exterior-quality paint. Set these pieces aside for use in trimming out the windows, door, and corners of the shed. Cut-offs from the longer trim pieces should be saved for use in trimming out the window boxes.

4. Cut four pieces of painted furring stock to 24¼ inches each for window trim. Center one piece across the top of each window opening, allowing it to overlap the opening ½ inch. Fasten the trim in place with 8d galvanized common nails. Fasten the other two trim pieces in place underneath the windowsills.

5. Measure the distance between the windowsills and the trim above the windows. Cut four pieces of painted furring stock to that length and fasten one piece on each side of each window opening so the outer edge of each piece is flush with the end of the horizontal trim piece above it. Use 8d galvanized common nails.

6. Cut a bevel on the bottom frame piece of each of the two window sashes to match the slant of the windowsills. Position each sash in a window opening so the front of the sash frame lies flush against the rear of top and side pieces of window trim. Join each sash to its sill with a pair of light 2-inch tee hinges, as shown in illustration C.

7. Cut two pieces of furring material to 4 inches each for turn latches to hold the windows in their closed positions. Fasten one latch to the back of the header above each window using a 1½-inch #10 round-head wood screw. Position the latches where they can be turned to allow the windows to open and shut. Glue a small filler block (¾ × 1 × 4 inches) to the back of each window, if needed, so the latch holds the window tightly shut, as shown in illustration C.

8. Attach a 12-inch sash chain to each window and adjacent framing member to support the window when opened.

To build the shed door:

1. Cut two pieces of 2 × 2 (1½″ × 1½″) stock to 73½ inches each for the vertical framework of the door.

2. Cut six pieces of 2 × 2 stock to 32¾ inches each for the horizontal members of the door frame.

3. Cut two pieces of 2 × 2 stock to 25 inches each for the door window framing members.

4. Arrange the pieces cut in the previous three steps into a 1½ × 35¾ × 73½-inch door frame with a space for a 20¾ × 25-inch window sash, as shown in illustration D. Glue the pieces of the frame to the back of the T1-11-sheathing cutout of the door opening (see step 3 of "To frame the shed door"). Secure the pieces in place on the sheathing with 1¾-inch #6 flathead wood screws.

5. Mark the opening for the window on the back of the door panel, making it ½ inch narrower on all four sides than the frame. Cut out this 19¾ × 24-inch rectangle and save the pieces for use on the window boxes.

6. Put a 20¾ × 25-inch four-lite window sash into the frame on the back of the door panel. Fasten it to the frame with 1¾-inch #6 flathead wood screws.

7. Cut one sheet of ¼-inch exterior-grade plywood to 35¾ × 73½ inches for the inside panel of the door. Cut a window opening

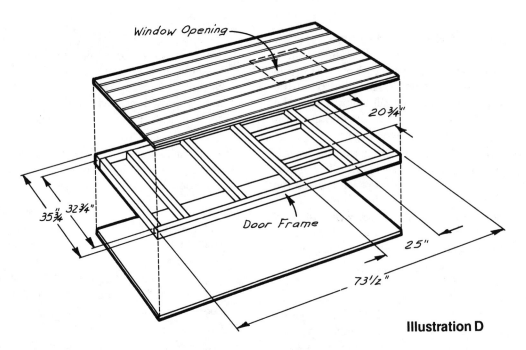

Window Opening

20 ¾"

35 ¾" 32 ¾"

Door Frame

25"

73 ½"

Illustration D

in this panel to match the opening cut in the outside panel. Fasten the panel to the back of the door frame with glue and 1-inch underlayment nails. Glue rippings of the appropriate size into the space between the window and the inner panel.

8. Fasten the door to the shed wall using three heavy 8-inch tee hinges. Install your choice of latch and lock for the door now, or delay this step until after you have mounted the trim around the door opening (see step 1 of "To fasten and build the window boxes").

9. Cut one piece of furring stock to 73½ inches, then rip it into three pieces, each ½ inch thick, for use as door stops. Cut one of the pieces to 36 inches and nail it to the underside of the framing member at the top of the door opening, where it will stop the door in the closed position. Fasten one long piece to the framing member at either side of the door opening to assist in stopping the door also in the closed position. Use 1-inch underlayment

nails to secure the three door stops to the framing members.

To fasten the trim
and build the window boxes:

1. Cut one piece of painted furring stock to 40½ inches for door trim. Center the piece over the door opening and fasten it to the sheathing and framework behind with 8d galvanized common nails.

2. Cut two pieces of painted furring stock to 74 inches each, also for door trim. Fasten one piece to the sheathing and framework on each side of the door using 8d galvanized common nails.

3. Cut four pieces of painted furring stock to 77½ inches each for wall trim. Position one piece at each corner of the window wall, one edge of the trim flush with the wall corner. Place a second piece where it overlaps the edge of the first while extending around the corner, as shown in the exploded-view diagram. Before fastening in place, cut the top of each piece to fit the underside of the roof and gable ends, while making the

lower end of each piece flush with the bottom edge of the wall sheathing. Fasten all four pieces in place with 8d galvanized common nails.

4. Cut four pieces of painted furring stock to 74 inches each for wall trim. Fit these pieces around the corners of the shed next to the wood storage area, lapping the trim on the eave walls over the trim attached to the wood storage wall. The pieces will have to be cut to fit around the header and joists found at these two corners. Fasten all pieces in place with 8d galvanized common nails.

5. Cut two pieces of T1-11 plywood scrap to 8 inches wide and 21 inches long each for the fronts of the window boxes, and four pieces to 8 inches wide and 8⅞ inches long for the sides of the window boxes. Cut two more pieces of T1-11 scrap to 8 inches wide and 19¾ inches long for the backs of the window boxes. And finally, cut two additional pieces to 8¼ × 19¾ inches each for the window box bottoms.

6. Assemble each window box as shown in illustration E. The front piece overlaps the side pieces, the back piece fits between the side pieces, and the bottom piece is installed inside them all. Fasten the boxes together with 8d aluminum finishing nails. Drill several holes in the bottom of each box for drainage.

7. Cut four pieces of painted furring stock to 8 inches each. Fasten the pieces to the front corners of each window box, as shown in illustration E, to cover the exposed end grain of the front piece. Use 8d aluminum finishing nails.

8. Cut four pieces of painted furring stock to 10⅛ inches each for the top trim of each window box side. Also cut two pieces to 22¼ inches each for top trim on the front of each window box, and cut two pieces to 18¾ inches each for top trim on the back

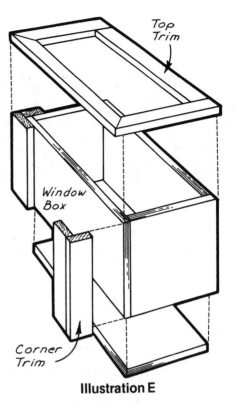

Illustration E

of each window box.

9. Miter the ends of the trim pieces, as shown in illustration E. Fit the trim pieces together around the top of the window boxes with the mitered ends of the side pieces meeting the mitered ends of the front pieces, and the back pieces butting against the side pieces. Fasten these trim pieces to the window boxes using 8d aluminum finishing nails.

10. Center one box under each window and fasten it to the wall sheathing with 1¼-inch galvanized roofing nails or other fasteners of an appropriate length. Bend over any fasteners that penetrate the inner wall of the shed.

11. Paint the fascia boards and exposed portions of the rafters with the same paint used on the wall trim. Touch up the trim as needed. Paint or stain the exposed wooden members of the wood storage area according to taste.

PROJECTS FOR HOUSEHOLD AND LAWN CARE

GARDEN TOOL CART

This handy garden tool cart will save hours of tool gathering and toting since it keeps all your tools together so you can take them to the garden at one time. You can also use the cart (empty) to move hay bales, firewood, and stones, and to do other small hauling chores. Small bins behind the rack offer ample space for seeds and smaller tools, and the cart's narrow width makes it easy to negotiate doorways.

564

SHOPPING LIST

Lumber
1 pc. 2 × 4 × 8'
1 pc. 1 × 3 × 2' hardwood
1 pc. 1 × 2 × 6'
Plywood
2 sheets ½" × 4' × 8' exterior grade
Dowel
1 pc. 1" × 3' hardwood or broom handle
Hardware
2 wheels 10" diameter × 1½"
1 steel rod ½" diameter × 31⅝"
16 flathead wood screws #6 × ½"
4 tee hinges 2" with screws
50 common nails 6d
12 common nails 2d
8 flat washers ½"
1 pint waterproof glue
1 quart exterior-grade primer/sealer
1 quart exterior-grade paint

We won't try to show you exact positions for placing tools in the cart since everybody's collection varies. Experiment a little, though, and you will undoubtedly find that you're able to pack all your tools in, probably with room left over as well for new tools you acquire. The sizes of the bins in the back of the cart can be altered to suit your needs.

The garden tool cart can be built with conventional materials, but an exceptionally strong and durable cart can be built with Wolmanized plywood, waterproof glue, and brass or aluminum fasteners. In all likelihood the extra cost will pay for itself in added life span. Wheels and axles can be salvaged from wagons or other carts. Wide wheels with large diameters are best; they will help keep the cart from bogging down in rough terrain.

CONSTRUCTION

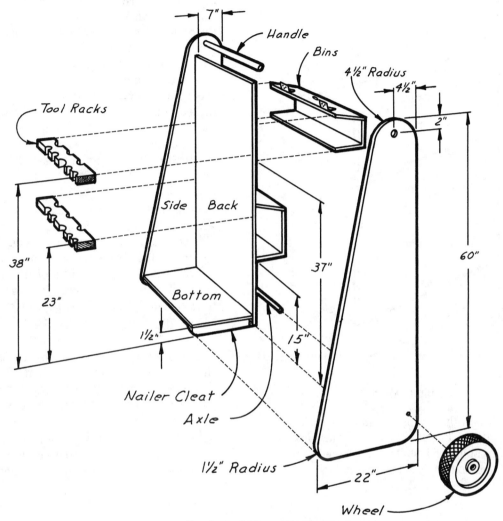

Exploded-View Diagram

1. Start by cutting the back, sides, and bottom pieces to the sizes shown in the exploded-view diagram and listed in the cutting list. Although the corners of the side pieces are shown rounded, leave them square at this time until the nailer cleats and bearing blocks have been installed. Note also that the front edge of the bottom piece is cut to a 13-degree angle to match the front slope of the sides.

2. Cut the three nailer cleats to size from 1 × 2 (¾'' × 1½'') stock. Ideally the bearing blocks should be cut from hardwood 1 × 3 (¾'' × 2½'') stock, but a softwood will work adequately for all but very heavy-duty carts.

3. Cut the parts for the bins, as shown in

565

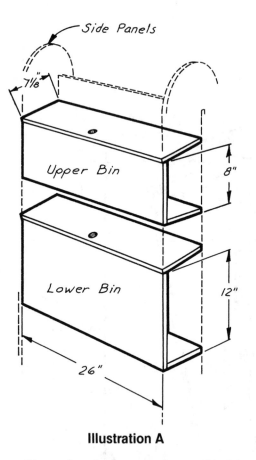

Side Panels

7⅛"

Upper Bin

8"

Lower Bin

12"

26"

Illustration A

illustration A, or cut and assemble bins later to match your needs. The bins can be built and installed after the sides, back, and bottom have been assembled.

4. Fasten the bearing blocks to the side pieces, as shown in illustration B. Locate the horizontal centerline of the bearing blocks on the centerline of the wheels you are using. If 10-inch-diameter wheels are used, as shown, then the bearing block centerline should be on the 5-inch mark. Use waterproof glue and 6d common nails to fasten the blocks in place. Drill axle holes through the side pieces and the bearing blocks to accept the axle and wheels you are using. Be sure that the bottom of the wheels are flush with the bottom of the sides when installed.

5. Drill handle holes in the side pieces, as shown in illustration B, or to the same diameter as the handle you are using. An old broomstick works well as a handle for the cart. Stack the two sides of the cart and drill through both pieces at the same time to match the handle holes perfectly.

6. Fasten the nailer cleats for the bottom panel to the side pieces with waterproof glue and 2d common nails. Position the side cleats flush with the bottom edges of the sides. Center the cleat for the back panel so that a 1¼-inch space remains on each side. The space allows the side panels to fit properly against the back panel.

7. Use a saber saw to round-over the top, front, and rear corners of the side panels

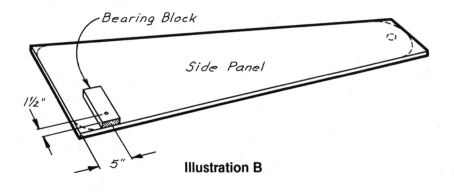

Bearing Block

Side Panel

1½"

5"

Illustration B

LUMBER CUTTING LIST

Size	Piece	Quantity
2 × 4		
1½″ × 3½″ × 26″	Tool racks	2
1 × 3		
¾″ × 2½″ × 6⅞″	Bearing blocks	2
1 × 2		
¾″ × 1½″ × 13¼″	Side nailer cleats	2
¾″ × 1½″ × 26″	Back nailer cleat	1
Plywood		
½″ × 22″ × 60″	Side panels	2
½″ × 26″ × 56″	Back panel	1
½″ × 14″ × 26″	Bottom panel	1
½″ × 12″ × 26″	Storage bin front	1
½″ × 8″ × 26″	Storage bin front	1
½″ × 7⅛″ × 25¾″	Storage bin tops	2
½″ × 6⅜″ × 26″	Storage bin bottoms	2
Dowel		
1″ × 27″	Handle	1

to make the cart easy to push around and to give the cart a finished appearance. As in step 5, stack the panels to achieve symmetrical results. Cut the top to a 4½-inch radius, the front to a 1½-inch radius, and the rear to a radius of 4 inches.

8. Assemble the sides and back of the cart with waterproof glue and 6d common nails. Fit the side nailer cleats against the ends of the back nailer cleat.

9. Install the bottom panel, using waterproof glue and 6d common nails. Drive the nails through the bottom panel and into the nailer cleats.

10. If parts for storage bins have not been cut, do so now (see step 3). These are located, as desired, in the back of the cart. First cut the bottoms, fronts, and tops of the bins to size, as shown in illustration A. Mark where each piece is to fit on the cart,

and drill 1/16-inch-diameter pilot holes through the cart's side panels into the bin pieces. Note: Do not install the pieces yet; paint them first (see step 11). Cut finger holes close to the front edge of each top piece, also as shown.

11. Make a rack, or racks, for large tools to be carried in the front of the cart. Use 2 × 4 (1½″ × 3½″) lumber. First place your tools in position in the cart, then hold the 2 × 4 against them and mark out notches on the 2 × 4 to accept the tool handles. Cut out the notches, then—after removing the tools from the cart—fasten the rack to the back and side panels with 6d common nails. You might also wish to install metal clips or shock cord instead of or to supplement the 2 × 4 rack. A visit to a hardware store may provide ideas. Before installing hardware, though, paint all the pieces made

so far with a good primer coat followed by at least two coats of exterior-grade paint.

12. When the paint has dried, install the parts of each bin on the back of the cart. Fasten the bin bottoms and fronts using waterproof glue and 6d common nails. Attach the tops with 2-inch tee hinges held by screws.

13. Attach any additional hardware.

14. Install the rod for the axle through the bearing blocks on the cart, and attach the wheels, with washers on either side. An axle is best cut from straight steel rod. Thread the ends so that the wheels can be held in place with nuts, or drill the ends to accept cotter pins. A third method is to use snap nuts; these may be pressed over the axle ends after the wheels are in place. After assembling the parts, test the cart with some moderately heavy weight to make sure the wheels do not rub against the sides of the cart. If they do, you may need to use a sturdier axle or obtain wheels with better bearings.

15. Finally, install the handle through the holes in the top of the cart and secure it with waterproof glue and small finishing nails driven into the handle at an angle so they also enter the side panels. It is best to leave the handle unpainted. Your cart is now complete and ready for many seasons of happy gardening.

HOSE-REEL CART

Here is a handy cart designed primarily for hauling and storing up to 150 feet of garden hose. Two features make it unique: It may be hung on a wall (from a special mounting bracket, as shown in illustration B), or, with the hose reel removed, the cart may double as a trash-can carrier. The hose-reel cart is easy and inexpensive to build. Two 8-inch-diameter wheels are recommended, but nearly any size will work as long as they can be mounted on a sturdy axle whose diameter measures at least $\frac{1}{2}$ inch. To ensure a long life for your cart, use exterior-grade plywood and waterproof glue, and apply several coats of exterior-grade paint or varnish as a finish.

CONSTRUCTION

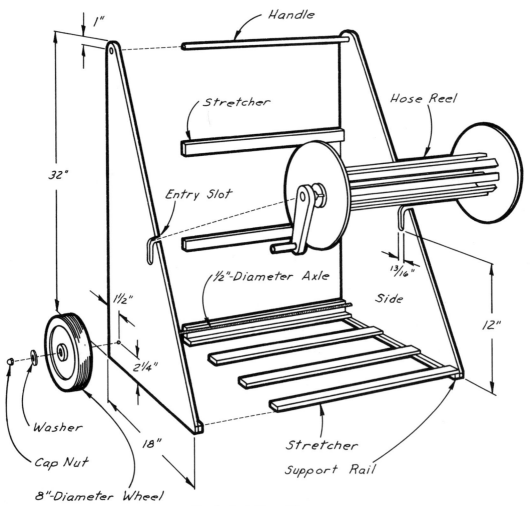

Exploded-View Diagram

1. Cut two triangular pieces of ½-inch A-C grade plywood, as shown in the exploded-view diagram, for the cart sides. Before rounding their top corners or drilling any holes, clamp the two pieces together.

2. With the side pieces clamped together, mark and then drill holes (see exploded-view diagram) for the handle dowel, reel axle, and cart axle.

3. Use a saber saw to round-over the top corners of the side pieces to a 1-inch radius. Also saw the entry slot for the reel axle.

4. Cut two pieces of 1×1 (¾″ × ¾″) baluster stock to 18 inches each for the cart sup-

570

LUMBER CUTTING LIST

Size	Piece	Quantity
1 × 6		
¾″ × 5½″ × 19″	Wall bracket back	1
1 × 2		
¾″ × 1½″ × 19″	Cart stretchers	7
¾″ × 1½″ × 19″	Wall bracket stretcher	1
¾″ × 1½″ × 17⅜″	Reel stretchers	8
Baluster Stock		
¾″ × ¾″ × 18″	Cart support rails	2
Plywood		
½″ × 18″ × 32″	Cart sides	2
½″ × 7″ × 12″	Wall bracket sides	2
½″ × 3″ × 8½″	Reel handle link	1
½″ × 14″ diameter	Reel sides	2
½″ × 3″ diameter	Reel lock	1
Dowels		
⅞″ × 20″	Cart handle	1
¾″ × 21⅜″	Reel axle	1
¾″ × 4″	Reel handle	1
¼″ × 3″	Reel lock dowel	1

port rails, and attach one rail flush with the bottom inside face of each side piece using waterproof glue and 6d finishing nails.

5. Cut seven pieces of 1 × 2 (¾″ × 1½″) stock to 19 inches each for the cart stretchers that make up the bottom and back of the cart. Glue two of the stretchers together at right angles to form the L at the lower rear corner of the cart, as shown in the exploded-view diagram. Bevel the edge of another stretcher to form the cart's lower front edge.

6. Attach the stretchers to the side pieces and across the support rails at desired spacings, using waterproof glue and nails.

7. Cut one piece of ⅞-inch-diameter dowel to 20 inches for the cart handle. Insert the handle in the holes drilled in the top corners of the side pieces and glue it in place.

8. Sand and finish the cart. (If you wish to sand and finish the entire project at once, postpone this step and the next one until after you have completed steps 10 through 23.)

9. Cut one piece of threaded steel rod to 24 inches for the cart axle. Insert it through the holes drilled in the lower corners of the side pieces, then attach the wheels, washers, and cap nuts.

10. Cut two 14-inch-diameter disks of ½-inch plywood for the reel sides. Scribe 6-inch-diameter circles on the inside face of each (for use in step 14). Then clamp both disks and drill a ¾-inch-diameter hole through

their centers to accept the reel axle (see step 15).

11. Cut one 3-inch-diameter disk of ½-inch plywood for the reel lock. Drill a ¾-inch-diameter hole through the center of the disk.

12. Rout or saw a groove ¼ inch deep × ¼ inch wide across the center of one face of the reel lock, as shown in illustration A.

13. Glue the reel lock—grooved face outward —to one of the reel sides. Be sure the holes are aligned.

14. Cut eight pieces of 1 × 2 stock to 17⅜ inches each for the reel stretchers. Place the outside edge of each stretcher on the scribed circles marked on the inside of the reel side disks, then glue and nail the stretcher in place by nailing through the plywood and into the ends of the stretchers, as shown in illustration A.

15. Cut one piece of ¾-inch-diameter dowel to 21⅜ inches for the reel axle. Drill a ¼-inch-diameter hole through the axle, 1½ inches from one end.

16. Cut one piece of ¼-inch-diameter dowel to

3 inches. Insert it in the hole drilled through the axle and glue it in place. When the axle is inserted in the reel (see step 19), this small dowel should fit in the grooved face of the reel lock.

17. Cut one piece of ½-inch plywood to 3 × 8½ inches for the handle link. Round-over one end of the link to a 3-inch radius, and the other end to a 1-inch radius. Drill two ¾-inch-diameter holes through the handle link, spaced 6 inches apart on center, as shown in illustration A.

18. Cut one piece of ¾-inch-diameter dowel to 4 inches for the reel handle. Insert it in the hole at the 1-inch-radiused end of the handle link, then glue and nail it in place.

19. Fit the handle link onto the end of the reel axle closest to the inserted dowel. Glue and nail the link in place. After finishing (see step 24), insert the reel axle through the holes in the reel sides.

20. Cut two triangular pieces of ½-inch plywood for the wall bracket sides, as shown in illustration B. As you did with the cart

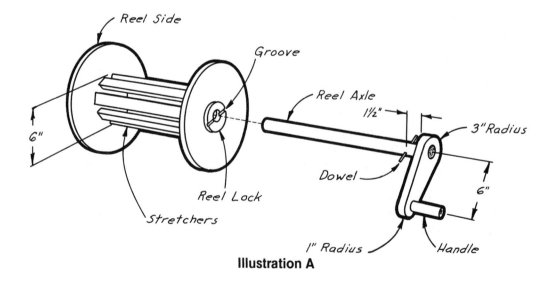

Illustration A

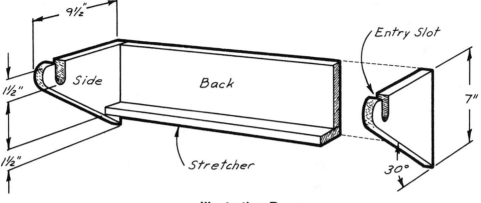

Illustration B

sides in steps 2 and 3, clamp the two bracket sides together, mark and drill a hole and entry slot to accept the cart handle, then round-over the front corners of the triangles.

21. Cut one piece of 1 × 2 stock to 19 inches for the wall bracket stretcher.

22. Cut one piece of 1 × 6 (¾″ × 5½″) stock to 19 inches for the wall bracket back.

23. Glue and nail the stretcher to the back to form an L, as shown in illustration B. Then fasten the bracket sides to the ends of the assembly, also with wood glue and nails.

After finishing (see next step), the bracket may be mounted on a wall using screws fastened through the bracket's back piece.

24. Sand and finish the mounting bracket, as well as all parts of the cart and reel, if necessary. Assemble the reel and axle and install the unit in the entry slots on the sides of the cart. The hose-reel cart is now ready to use. By engaging the ¼-inch dowel on the reel axle in the groove of the reel lock, the reel may be cranked by turning the handle. Disengaging the dowel from the groove allows the reel to run free.

TRASH-CAN DOLLY

SHOPPING LIST

Plywood
1 pc. ¾'' × 2' × 2' A-C grade
Hardware
3 heavy-duty pivoting casters 1⅝'' diameter
    with screws

You may find this trash-can dolly an enormous help in handling your trash containers. It's designed to fit inside the bottom flange of a 55-gallon steel drum and will also fit beneath most standard-sized galvanized garbage cans as well. The trash-can dolly is equipped with three pivoting casters for easy maneuvering. We bored a small hole in our trash-can dolly so it could be hung on the wall when not in use. For long life, use exterior-grade plywood and apply several coats of paint to the finished product.

LUMBER CUTTING LIST

Size	Piece	Quantity
Plywood		
¾'' × 22'' diameter	Top	1

CONSTRUCTION

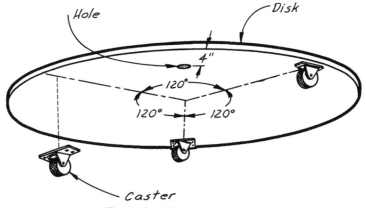

Exploded-View Diagram

1. Cut one 22-inch-diameter disk of ¾-inch A-C grade plywood for the top of the trash-can dolly.

2. Drill a 1-inch-diameter hole 4 inches from the edge of the disk, for hanging.

3. Space casters on the panel 120 degrees apart, equidistant from the hanging hole. Align the mounting flange of each caster ¼ inch from the top's outer edge.

4. Using the mounting flanges as guides, drill pilot holes for the casters' mounting screws, then remove the casters.

5. Sand and finish, as desired, both sides of the dolly. Be sure to seal all edges, including those of the hanging hole.

6. Mount the casters using the screws provided.

LEAF-BAG FRAME

SHOPPING LIST

Lumber
1 pc. 1 × 2 × 10'
Dowels
6 pcs. ½'' × 3' hardwood
Hardware
2 offset hinges ¾'' with screws
2 strap hinges 2'' with screws
2 loose pin hinges 1½'' × 1½'' with screws
1 box wire nails 18 gauge × ¾''
1 pint waterproof glue

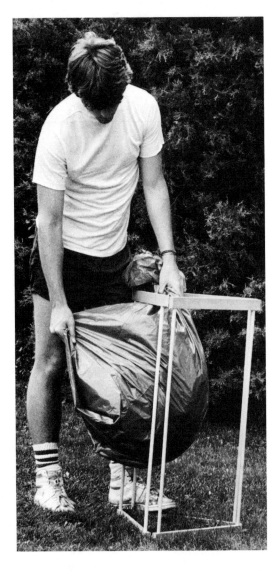

Autumn leaf collection can be made easier with the help of this simple leaf-

bag frame. A product of the Rodale Design Group, the frame has several useful features. Stood vertically, it will hold a 30-gallon leaf bag open for easy filling. Laid horizontally, it will hold the mouth of a bag open so you may rake leaves directly into it. The upright members of the frame are spread far enough apart so that a full bag of leaves can be removed through the side of the frame without having to lift the bag to an uncomfortable height. Finally, the combination of hinges used to hold the frame together enables it to be collapsed into a compact unit for storage. Merely remove the pins from the hinges at corner C, as shown in the exploded-view diagram, and fold the sides together. Since the hinges are of different sizes, each side can be folded one over the other.

The basic materials used in our leaf-bag frame are hardwood dowels and No. 2 pine. Any durable variety of wood may be substituted for the pine. We left our frame unfinished, but its wooden parts may be coated with exterior-quality paint, varnish, or wood preservative, if desired.

CONSTRUCTION

1. Cut four pieces of 1 × 2 (¾″ × 1½″) stock to 18 inches each for the long members of the frame's top and bottom sections.

2. Cut two pieces of 1 × 2 stock to 17¹³⁄₁₆ inches each for the short members of the sections.

3. Cut six pieces of ½-inch dowel to 26 inches each for the uprights.

4. Drill ½-inch-diameter holes on the lower edge of the top frame members and on the upper edge of the bottom frame members to receive the uprights, as shown in the exploded-view diagram. Center each hole 1 inch from both ends of each top and bottom frame member.

5. Fasten a pair of uprights in the holes of each matching pair of top and bottom frame members. Use waterproof glue and ¾-inch × 18-gauge wire nails to hold the uprights in place.

6. Attach the three sections of the frame together using a ¾-inch offset hinge at corner A, a 2-inch strap hinge at corner B, and a 1½ × 1½-inch loose pin hinge at corner C, as shown in the exploded-view diagram. Note that the shorter top and bottom frame members are located between corners B and C.

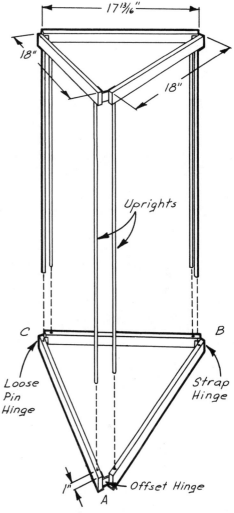

Exploded-View Diagram

LUMBER CUTTING LIST

Size	Piece	Quantity
1 × 2		
¾″ × 1½″ × 18″	Long top and bottom frame members	4
¾″ × 1½″ × 17¹³⁄₁₆″	Short top and bottom frame members	2
Dowels		
½″ × 26″	Uprights	6

WET BROOM

SHOPPING LIST

Hardware
1 16-inch heavy-duty street broom
4 flathead wood screws #6 × 1″
2 pcs. galvanized steel pipe ½″ I.D. × 20″
2 pipe straps ½″
3 galvanized steel pipe nipples ½″ × 6″
1 galvanized steel pipe coupling ½″
1 galvanized steel pipe tee ½″
2 galvanized steel pipe caps ½″
1 pipe valve ½″
1 garden hose adaptor ½″
1 roll Teflon tape

An ordinary street broom purchased from a hardware store was modified by the Rodale Design Group into this rugged wet broom, useful for scrubbing down garage floors, porches, sidewalks, and driveways.

The handle attaches to a garden hose and is made of heavy-duty galvanized pipe. A spigot valve mounted right on the handle controls the flow of water from where you are standing so that you don't have to keep running back and forth to the hose outlet to regulate the pressure or to turn the water off when the broom is temporarily not in use.

You will do well to search out the stiffest and sturdiest broom you can find. Our broom measures 16 inches across and features a hardwood head. The cross pipe underneath is sized to fit the broom. If the broom you obtain is different in size, you will have to alter the cross-pipe dimensions accordingly.

CONSTRUCTION

1. Obtain a 16-inch heavy-duty street broom. Remove and discard the handle, then re-drill one of the handle holes in the head to accept ½-inch-diameter pipe for the new handle (see step 5). Remove as much of the inner bristles as necessary to fit the bottom cross pipe to the underside, as shown in the exploded-view diagram. Test-fit the tee fitting to be used for joining the cross pipe to the handle (see step 4), and notch the underside of the handle hole so the fitting will seat flat against the broom head.

2. Assemble the cross pipe by fitting one

6-inch pipe nipple to each side of a ½-inch pipe tee, then covering the open end of each nipple with a pipe cap, as shown in the exploded-view diagram. Use Teflon tape on all pipe connections in this and subsequent steps.

3. Determine the angle at which the cross pipe will be mounted, then mark and drill three ⅛-inch-diameter holes through the underside of each nipple so water will shoot straight down onto the surface being washed.

4. Position the cross pipe on the underside of the broom head, then screw a 6-inch pipe nipple through the handle hole and into the top of the tee. Fasten the cross pipe to the broom head using two ½-inch pipe straps and four 1-inch #6 flathead wood screws.

5. To construct the handle, first attach a ½-inch pipe coupling to the 6-inch pipe nipple installed in the handle hole, then add a 20-inch length of ½-inch-I.D. pipe, followed by a valve, another 20-inch length of pipe, and a hose adaptor, all as shown in the exploded-view diagram.

Exploded-View Diagram

579

AUTO-CLEANOUT CADDY

SHOPPING LIST

Plywood
1 pc. ¾'' × 2' × 4' A-C grade
Hardboard
1 pc. ¼'' × 1' × 2'
Dowel
1 pc. 1'' × 3'
Hardware
½ pound finishing nails 6d
1 pint latex enamel

Has cleaning your car become more of a chore than it needs to be because of the time it takes to round up all the materials you need? This auto-cleanout caddy, a product of the Rodale Design Group, not only stores your car-cleaning supplies all in one place, but also provides a handy way of carrying them out to the driveway or car wash as well. Designed like a simple toolbox with four compartments, the caddy has space for a wide assortment of supplies. Into ours, we fit a roll of paper towels, a large sponge, a cleaning rag, a package of polishing cloths, a whisk broom, a spray can of glass cleaner, a spray bottle of disinfectant, a can of chrome cleaner, a can of paste wax, and a jar of tire and vinyl protectant—all with room to spare.

We made our auto-cleanout caddy from birch veneer plywood, but any grade or type of plywood will do. Small holes

and defects can be filled with wood putty before applying the final finish. Our choice for finish was a dark latex enamel.

CONSTRUCTION

1. Cut two pieces of ¾-inch A-C grade plywood to 12 × 12 inches each for the ends of the caddy.
2. Shape the end pieces as shown in illustration A. A 1¼-inch radius is used for all the curves. The narrow section at the top of each piece begins 7 inches from the bottom and is 2½ inches wide.
3. Drill a 1-inch-diameter hole through the center point of the radius at the top of each end piece, as shown in illustration A.
4. Cut a ⅜-inch-deep dado ¼ inch wide across

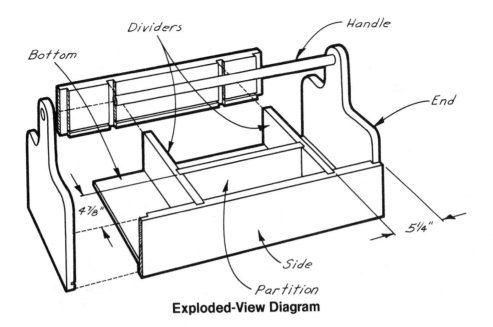

Exploded-View Diagram

one face of each end piece. Locate the outer edge of the dado ½ inch from the bottom, as shown in illustration A.

5. Cut two pieces of ¾-inch plywood to 4½ × 24 inches each for the sides of the caddy.

6. On one face of each side piece, cut a ⅜-inch-deep rabbet ¾ inch wide across each end, and a ⅜-inch-deep dado ¾ inch wide, beginning 5¼ inches from each end, as shown in illustration B. Also on the same face, cut a ⅜-inch-deep groove ¼ inch wide along the entire length of each piece, ½ inch from the bottom edge. These grooves should match the end-piece dadoes cut in step 4.

LUMBER CUTTING LIST

Size	Piece	Quantity
Plywood		
¾″ × 12″ × 12″	Ends	2
¾″ × 4½″ × 24″	Sides	2
¾″ × 3¾″ × 12¾″	Partition	1
¾″ × 3¾″ × 12″	Side-to-side dividers	2
Hardboard		
¼″ × 12″ × 23¼″	Bottom	1
Dowel		
1″ × 24½″	Handle	1

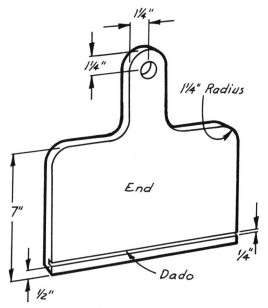

Illustration A

7. Cut two pieces of ¾-inch plywood to 3¾ × 12 inches each for the side-to-side dividers.

8. Cut a ⅜-inch-deep dado ¾ inch wide across one face of each divider, beginning 4⅞ inches from one end, as shown in the exploded-view diagram.

9. Cut one piece of ¾-inch plywood to 3¾ × 12¾ inches for the partition between the dividers.

10. Cut one piece of ¼-inch hardboard to 12 × 23¼ inches for the bottom.

11. Cut one piece of 1-inch-diameter dowel to 24½ inches for the handle. Lightly round-over both of the handle ends.

12. Assemble the caddy as shown in the exploded-view diagram. Fasten the pieces together with carpenter's wood glue and 6d finishing nails.

13. Set all nails flush or slightly below the surface of the caddy. Sand where needed and finish with two coats of latex enamel or other finish, as desired.

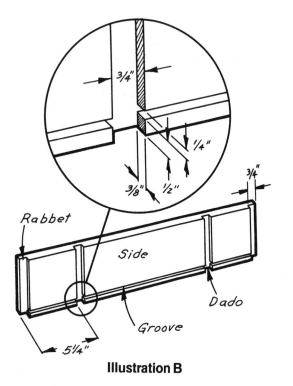

Illustration B

AUTO-TOOL CART

The Rodale Design Group pooled their thoughts on tune-up-day chores to develop this very strongly built auto-tool cart. It is designed both to hold heavy tune-up and

repair equipment and to roll easily from the garage out into the driveway for on-site access. Most of the storage space is in open trays and along the back of the cart, so that tools may be readily spotted and quick to hand, and also to help dispel the tendency to lay tools on the ground or near the engine "where they won't get lost." However, there is one large drawer, which has a capacity of 4 square feet, beneath the centralized work surface.

The cart is constructed of wood, plywood, and hardboard, materials that are inexpensive and easy for the average do-it-yourselfer to work with. Metal casters with

583

rubber tires are mounted underneath. Since these can be rather expensive to buy, you might try locating some used ones before starting to build the cart. We've recommended a particular combination of casters designed to provide the cart with maximum mobility, but any combination of casters—as long as they are all the same size—is perfectly satisfactory. Casters with larger rather than smaller diameters, however, will carry more weight and roll more easily, especially over rough surfaces.

CONSTRUCTION

1. Cut two pieces of 1 × 3 (¾″ × 2½″) stock to 60¼ inches each for the cart's rear uprights. Notch each piece 5¼ inches from one end, as shown in the exploded-view diagram. Make each notch 2½ inches long and ¾ inch deep. Then use a router to cut a ¼-inch-wide groove ¼ inch deep lengthwise along one face of each board, starting from the inside edge of the notch and ending 3½ inches from the far end of the board. Locate the groove, which is meant to house the cart's back panel, ¼ inch from the edge of the board, as shown.

2. Cut two pieces of 1 × 3 stock to 64½ inches each for the sloped uprights. Cut a 20-degree angle on the end of each that will become the bottom.

3. Lay the pieces out in pairs, one rear upright and one sloped upright in each. Overlap them at their upper ends and spread them 24 inches (outside edge to outside edge) at their lower ends. Make certain the sloped uprights are turned so that their angled ends are in line with the lower ends of the rear uprights. Also, overlap the pieces of one pair opposite the way you lap the other so that, when mounted on the cart, the sloped upright of each pair will overlap the outer face of its companion upright, as shown in the exploded-view diagram.

4. With the pieces in position, mark and cut them to form half-lap joints. Fasten the pieces of each pair together with carpenter's wood glue and ¾-inch #8 flathead wood screws. Then, for a finished look, cut a 1¼-inch radius on the lapped ends of each pair.

5. Cut two pieces of 1 × 4 (¾″ × 3½″) stock to 24 inches each for the frame's lower side pieces. Cut a ¾-inch-wide rabbet ⅜ inch deep along one edge of the length of each piece, and continue it across one end. These rabbeted edges will become the lower inside edges of the pieces. Be sure to rabbet the left end of one piece and the right end of the other so that the pieces can be installed with the end rabbets to their rear.

6. Cut one piece of 1 × 4 stock to 21¾ inches for the lower rear piece of the frame. Along the lower inside edge of the piece, cut a ¾-inch-wide rabbet ⅜ inch deep.

7. Cut one piece of 1 × 2 (¾″ × 1½″) stock to 21¾ inches for the lower front piece of the frame. Cut a ¾-inch-wide notch ⅜ inch deep into the upper half of each end of the piece so that, when assembled, it will fit between the front ends of the two side pieces, closing the rabbets.

8. Cut one piece of ¾-inch A-C plywood to 21¾ × 22⅞ inches for the bottom panel of the cart.

9. Now assemble all four lower frame pieces and the bottom panel, as shown in illustration A. Use wood glue and 4d finish-

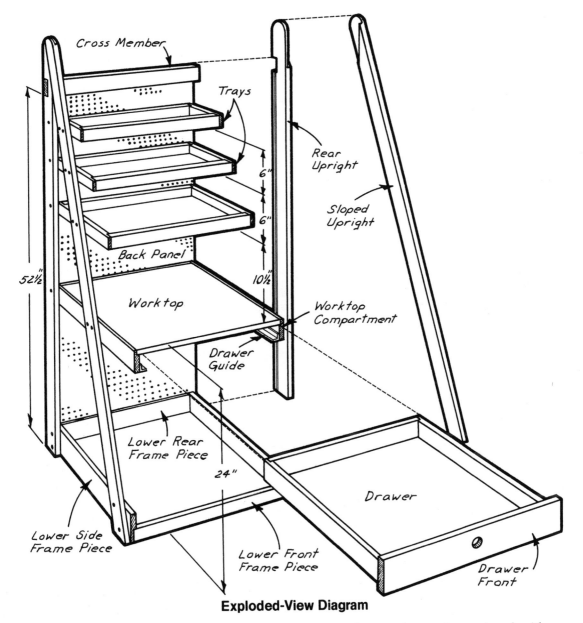

Cross Member

Trays

Rear
Upright

6"

Sloped
Upright

6"

Back Panel

52½"

10½"

Worktop

Worktop
Compartment

Drawer
Guide

Lower Rear
Frame Piece

24"

Drawer

Lower Side
Frame Piece

Lower Front
Frame Piece

Drawer
Front

Exploded-View Diagram

ing nails. When finished, rout a ¼-inch-wide groove ¼ inch deep across the upper edge of the frame's lower rear piece and across the ends of the frame's bottom pieces fastened to it, also as shown. Round-over all sharp edges of the finished unit, using sandpaper or a router equipped with a ¼-inch rounding-over bit.

10. Cut one piece of 1 × 3 stock to 24 inches in length for the upper cross member of the frame. Cut a ¼-inch-wide groove ¼ inch deep along the bottom edge of the piece,

LUMBER CUTTING LIST

Size	Piece	Quantity
1 × 4		
¾″ × 3½″ × 24″	Lower side frame pieces	2
¾″ × 3½″ × 22½″	Worktop compartment sides	2
¾″ × 3½″ × 22½″	Drawer front	1
¾″ × 3½″ × 21¾″	Worktop compartment back	1
¾″ × 3½″ × 21¾″	Lower rear frame piece	1
1 × 3		
¾″ × 2½″ × 64½″	Sloped uprights	2
¾″ × 2½″ × 60¼″	Rear uprights	2
¾″ × 2½″ × 24″	Cross member	1
¾″ × 2½″ × 21¾″	Drawer sides	2
¾″ × 2½″ × 19¾″	Drawer back	1
1 × 2		
¾″ × 1½″ × 21¾″	Tray fronts and backs	6
¾″ × 1½″ × 21¾″	Lower front frame piece	1
¾″ × 1½″ × 13″	Lower tray sides	2
¾″ × 1½″ × 10″	Middle tray sides	2
¾″ × 1½″ × 7″	Upper tray sides	2
¾″ Plywood		
¾″ × 21¾″ × 22⅞″	Frame bottom panel	1
¾″ × 21¾″ × 22⅛″	Worktop	1
¼″ Plywood		
¼″ × 19¾″ × 21⅜″	Drawer bottom	1
¼″ × 12¼″ × 21¾″	Lower tray bottom	1
¼″ × 9¼″ × 21¾″	Middle tray bottom	1
¼″ × 6¼″ × 21¾″	Upper tray bottom	1
Perforated Hardboard		
¼″ × 23″ × 49½″	Cart back panel	1

locating the groove ¼ inch from the outside edge of the piece so it is similar to the grooves cut in steps 1 and 9. Don't run this groove from end to end of the piece, though. It should start ½ inch from one end and stop ½ inch from the other.

11. Cut one piece of ¼-inch perforated hardboard to 23 × 49½ inches for the back panel of the cart.

12. Assemble the cart frame by fitting the back panel into the grooves in the uprights and in the frame cross members. Fasten the lower ends of the uprights to the bottom pieces of the frame (already joined to the frame's lower front and back in step 9) using two 1¼-inch #8 flathead wood screws at each joint, as shown in the exploded-view diagram. The ends of the

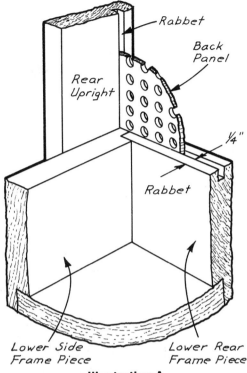

Rabbet

Back Panel

Rear Upright

¼"

Rabbet

Lower Side Frame Piece

Lower Rear Frame Piece

Illustration A

upper cross piece should fit into the notches in the uprights. Fasten them in place with one 1½-inch #8 flathead wood screw at each end.

13. Cut two pieces of 1 × 4 stock to 22½ inches each for the worktop compartment sides, and one piece of 1 × 4 stock to 21¾ inches for the compartment back.

14. Cut a ¾-inch-wide rabbet ⅜ inch deep on one end of each compartment side (to receive the back piece), and a similar rabbet on the upper inside edge of all three pieces to receive the worktop.

15. Cut one piece of ¾-inch plywood to 21¾ × 22⅛ inches for the worktop. Fasten the side and back pieces of the compartment around the worktop using wood glue and 4d finishing nails. When finished, round-over the upper and lower edges of the compartment back and sides, if desired.

16. Cut two pieces of ⅛-inch-thick ¾ × ¾-inch angle iron, each 21⅝ inches in length, for the drawer guides. Drill and countersink three holes in each drawer guide to accept ¾-inch #8 flathead wood screws.

17. Position the drawer guides on the insides of the compartment side pieces. The rear end of each guide touches the back of the compartment, and the bottom of each guide is flush with the bottom of each compartment side. Mark locations for mounting screws, then remove the guides and drill pilot holes. Fasten the drawer guides in place with ¾-inch #8 flathead wood screws.

18. Cut two pieces of 1 × 3 stock to 21¾ inches each for the drawer sides. On one end of each piece cut a ¾-inch-wide rabbet ⅜ inch deep to receive the drawer back. On the inside bottom edge of each piece (remember, you must make a left-hand piece and a right-hand piece), cut a ¼-inch-wide rabbet ⅜ inch deep to receive the drawer bottom.

19. Cut one piece of 1 × 3 stock to 19¾ inches for the drawer back. On the inside bottom edge cut a ¼-inch-wide rabbet ⅜ inch deep, similar to the rabbets in the bottoms of the drawer sides.

20. Cut one piece of 1 × 4 stock to 22½ inches for the drawer front. Cut two ¾-inch-wide stopped dadoes, each ⅜ inch deep, on the inside face of the piece, to receive the side pieces, as shown in illustration B. Locate the outside edge of each dado 15⁄16 inch from one end of the piece, also as shown. Begin each dado at the bottom edge of the drawer front and extend it 2⅝ inches.

21. Connect the two dadoes on the inside of the drawer front with a ⅜-inch-wide rabbet ⅜ inch deep along the bottom edge of the piece, to accept the drawer bottom.

22. Drill a 1-inch-diameter hole in the drawer front to create a finger pull. Center the hole

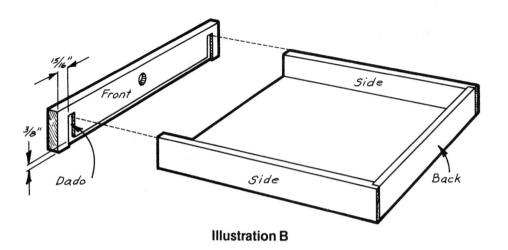

Illustration B

lengthwise along the piece and set it at the center or slightly above center on the width of the piece. Round-over the edges on both sides of the hole, along with all edges on the outer face of the drawer front.

23. Cut one piece of ¼-inch exterior-grade plywood to 19¾ × 21⅜ inches for the drawer bottom.

24. Assemble the drawer by fitting the pieces together, locking the bottom in the grooves. Use wood glue and 4d finishing nails.

25. Cut six pieces of 1 × 2 stock to 21¾ inches each for the fronts and backs of the three trays. Then cut two pieces of 1 × 2 stock to 7 inches each for the sides of the upper tray, cut two pieces of 1 × 2 stock to 10 inches each for the sides of the middle tray, and finally, cut two pieces of 1 × 2 stock to 13 inches each for the sides of the lower tray.

26. Cut a ¾-inch-wide rabbet ⅜ inch deep on each end of one face of all six tray sides to receive the front and back pieces.

27. Cut a ¼-inch-wide rabbet ⅜ inch deep on the inside bottom edge of all 12 tray pieces to accept the tray bottoms.

28. Cut one piece of ¼-inch plywood to 6¼ × 21¾ inches for the bottom of the upper tray. Cut a second piece of ¼-inch ply-

wood to 9¼ × 21¾ inches for the bottom of the middle tray. Cut a third piece of ¼-inch plywood to 12¼ × 21¾ inches for the bottom of the lower tray.

29. Assemble the three trays using wood glue and 4d finishing nails. Sand the completed frames and round-over all sharp edges.

30. Now sand the remaining solid wood parts of the auto cart and round-over all sharp edges. Coat the cart and all its parts with a clear lacquer or finish of your choice. Paint the worktop and the bottoms of the trays with a colorful enamel.

31. Fasten the worktop compartment and the three trays between the cart uprights using 1¼-inch #8 flathead wood screws. Position the upper surface of the worktop 24 inches above the bottom of the cart. Position the bottom of the lower tray 10½ inches above the worktop. Position the bottom of each of the other two trays 6 inches above the bottom of the tray immediately beneath it. Follow the screw pattern shown on the exploded-view diagram.

32. Mount casters, two fixed and two swivel, to the bottom of the cart. At least one of the casters should be lockable to prevent the cart from rolling when this is not desired.

SMALL-TOOL CARRIER

SHOPPING LIST

Plywood
1 pc. ½″ × 2′ × 4′ exterior grade
1 pc. ¼″ × 2′ × 4′ exterior grade
Hardware
1 flathead wood screw #8 × 1½″
2 flathead wood screws #8 × ½″
1 finish washer ⅜″
1 snap ring fastener ½″
1 pc. leather or nylon webbing 1″ × 30″
¼ pound finishing nails 6d
¼ pound finishing nails 3d
1 pc. soft copper tubing ½″ diameter × 30″
exterior-grade paint

Art Rakestraw of Chambersburg, Pennsylvania, built this practical carrier to hold his hand tools while performing home maintenance chores. The angled rear panel permits the carrier to rest firmly on the shelf of a stepladder, well back against the rails. A safety strap secured by an ordinary snap ring fastener prevents the carrier from falling should it be bumped or the ladder jolted. Two clever pockets are built into the sides of the carrier for storing handsaws. A panel drilled with holes of various sizes holds small tools, and bins in the lower part of the carrier are meant for nails, small cans of paint, and other items.

CONSTRUCTION

1. Cut the following pieces of ½-inch exterior-grade plywood: one piece to 14 × 18 inches for the rear panel, one piece to 7 × 13 inches for the bottom panel, two pieces to 4½ × 14½ inches each for the upper and lower front panels, and one piece to 8½ × 13 inches for the shelf bottom.

2. Cut ¼-inch-deep notches ¾ inch wide centered in the ends of the shelf bottom to accept the handle, as shown in the exploded-

589

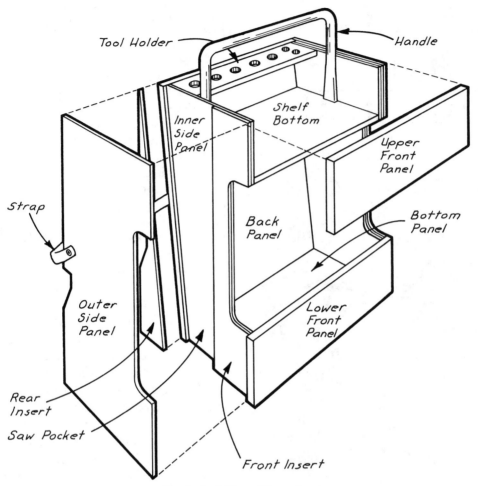

Tool Holder

Handle

Inner Side Panel

Shelf Bottom

Upper Front Panel

Strap

Back Panel

Bottom Panel

Outer Side Panel

Lower Front Panel

Rear Insert

Saw Pocket

Front Insert

Exploded-View Diagram

view diagram. Then, bevel one long edge to a 2-degree angle, also as shown.

3. Fasten the upper front panel to the square edge of the shelf bottom using carpenter's wood glue and 6d finishing nails. Align the pieces so the panel overlaps the shelf bottom, flush with its lower edge.

4. Bevel one long edge of the bottom panel to a 2-degree angle. Attach the lower front panel to the square edge of the bottom panel, aligning the pieces as in the pre-

vious step and using the same method of fastening.

5. Cut one piece of ½-inch-diameter soft copper tubing to 30 inches for the handle. Make 90-degree bends in the tubing 8½ inches from each end, as shown in illustration A. Flatten the last 5 inches of tubing at each end so that it will fit flat against the sides of the carrier. Drill and countersink ⅜-inch-diameter holes ½ inch from the ends of the tubing, as shown in illustration A.

LUMBER CUTTING LIST

Size	Piece	Quantity
½" Plywood		
½" × 14" × 18"	Rear panel	1
½" × 8½" × 13"	Shelf bottom	1
½" × 7" × 13"	Bottom panel	1
½" × 4½" × 14½"	Upper front panel	1
½" × 4½" × 14½"	Lower front panel	1
½" × 3½" × 13"	Tool holder	1
¼" Plywood		
¼" × 9½" × 18"	Outer side panels	2
¼" × 9" × 18"	Inner side panels	2
¼" × 3¾" × 18"	Front inserts	2
¼" × 1½" × 18"	Rear inserts	2

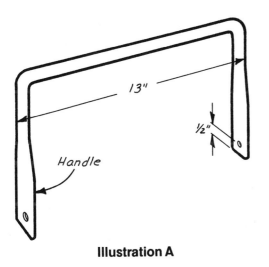

Illustration A

6. Position the handle in the notched ends of the shelf bottom, then drill ³⁄₁₆-inch-diameter pilot holes into the wood, using the holes drilled in the handle as guides. Fasten the handle to the shelf bottom using two ½-inch #8 flathead wood screws.

7. Cut two pieces of ¼-inch exterior-grade plywood to 9 × 18 inches each for the inner side panels, two pieces to 9½ × 18 inches each for the outer side panels, and two pieces to 3¾ × 18 inches for the front inserts. Then, cut two triangular-shaped pieces to 1½ × 18 inches each for the rear inserts.

8. Cut the inner panels to the pattern shown in illustration B, tapering the rear edge of each panel so one end is 2 inches shorter than the other.

9. Fasten the inner panels to the bottom panel, upper and lower front panels, and the shelf bottom, as shown in the exploded-view diagram, using wood glue and 3d finishing nails.

10. Fasten the front inserts to the inner side panels, using wood glue. Be sure that the front edges of each are flush.

11. Fasten the rear panel to the rear edges of the assembly, as shown in the exploded-view diagram, using wood glue and 6d finishing nails.

12. Fasten the outer side panels to the assembly so that their front edges are flush with

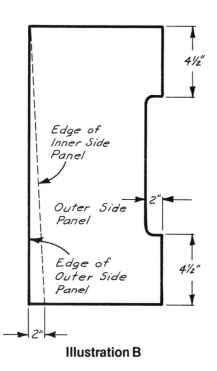

Illustration B

those of the inner side panels and inserts. The rear edges should overlap the sides of the rear panel. Use wood glue and 6d finishing nails.

13. Glue the rear inserts to the inner side panels, as shown in the exploded-view diagram, so that the rear edges of the pieces are flush. No nails are necessary.

14. If desired, cut away a portion of each side panel assembly, as shown in illustration B, to allow easier access to the lower part of the carrier.

15. Cut one piece of ½-inch plywood to 3½ × 13 inches for the tool holder. Drill ¾-inch-diameter holes through the holder to fit the handles of your screwdrivers, chisels, and other tools. You might need a few custom-sized holes as well. Position the holder in the top of the carrier and fasten it in place using 6d finishing nails.

16. Set the tool carrier on the fold-out shelf of your stepladder. If the carrier will not

fit well, cut a notch in the rear panel to fit the top of the ladder.

17. Paint the tool carrier using quality exterior-grade paint.

18. Obtain a 30-inch length of 1-inch-wide leather or nylon webbing for the safety strap. Drill a ⅛-inch-diameter pilot hole and fasten one end of the strap to the edge of the rear panel, 8 inches below the top, using a 1½-inch #8 flathead wood screw and a finish washer, as shown in illustration C. On the opposite edge of the rear panel, also 8 inches below the top, install the bottom half of a ½-inch snap ring fastener, also as shown.

19. Lead the strap behind the front legs of the ladder to the opposite side of the carrier and pull the strap tight. Mark the strap where it contacts the fastener installed in the previous step, then install the upper half of the fastener in the strap, as shown in illustration C. Trim off any excess strap material.

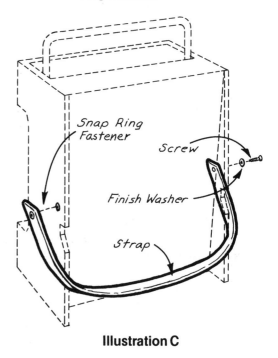

Illustration C

GENERAL-PURPOSE STOOL

This lightweight stool makes a welcome addition to anyone's collection of home and garden tools. It is based on a simple design and easy to build. The illustrations and photograph tell most of the story. Howard Anderson of Prattville, Alabama, is the designer. He has found the stool useful for all sorts of tasks ranging from changing light bulbs to providing comfortable seating while shelling beans. We're sure you'll also find many uses for this clever project as well.

SHOPPING LIST

Lumber
1 pc. $2 \times 2 \times 4'$
1 pc. $1 \times 8 \times 3'$
1 pc. $1 \times 6 \times 2'$
Hardware
3 flathead wood screws #10 $\times$ 3''
11 flathead wood screws #10 $\times$ 2''

CONSTRUCTION

1. Cut two pieces of 1×8 (¾'' $\times$ 7¼'') stock to 11¼ inches each for the stool legs.
2. Cut a V-shaped wedge from each piece to form the feet, as shown in the exploded-view diagram. Begin each cutout centered 5¾ inches above the bottom edge of the legs, and make each foot 1½ inches wide at its base.
3. Cut one piece of 1×8 stock to 16 inches for the seat. Align the seat flush with the

593

outside faces of the legs, and fasten it to the top edges of the legs using four 2-inch #10 flathead wood screws, which require a ⅛-inch-diameter pilot hole and 3/16-inch-diameter shank hole. Countersink the holes with a ½-inch-diameter bit.

4. Cut one piece of 1 × 6 (¾″ × 5½″) stock to 14½ inches for the center brace. Drill and countersink pilot holes and fasten the brace between the legs, centered beneath the bottom of the seat. Install two 2-inch #10 flathead wood screws through each leg and into the ends of the brace and two screws down through the top of the seat and into the brace's upper edge.

5. Cut one piece of 2 × 2 (1½″ × 1½″) stock to 36 inches for the back of the stool. Position the back vertically, centered over the V-notch of one leg, as shown in the exploded-view diagram. Drill and countersink three pilot holes through the back and into the leg and seat, then fasten the back in place using three 3-inch #10 flathead wood screws.

6. Cut one piece of 2 × 2 stock to 4 inches for the handle. Cut a ¾-inch-deep notch 1½ inches wide across the center, as shown in the exploded-view diagram, so the piece will fit over the back. Drill and countersink a pilot hole through both pieces, then

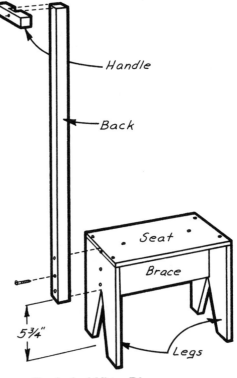

Exploded-View Diagram

install a 2-inch #10 flathead wood screw to fasten them together.

7. Fill all the screw holes with wood filler, then paint the completed stool, as desired.

LUMBER CUTTING LIST

Size	Piece	Quantity
2 × 2		
1½″ × 1½″ × 36″	Back	1
1½″ × 1½″ × 4″	Handle	1
1 × 8		
¾″ × 7¼″ × 16″	Seat	1
¾″ × 7¼″ × 11¼″	Legs	2
1 × 6		
¾″ × 5½″ × 14½″	Center brace	1

KITCHEN UTILITY TABLE

SHOPPING LIST

Lumber
1 pc. $2 \times 12 \times 4'$
1 pc. $2 \times 6 \times 3'$
2 pcs. $1 \times 3 \times 8'$
2 pcs. $1 \times 2 \times 8'$
Hardware
4 flathead wood screws #10 $\times$ 3''
4 flathead wood screws #10 $\times$ 2''
¼ pound finishing nails 6d

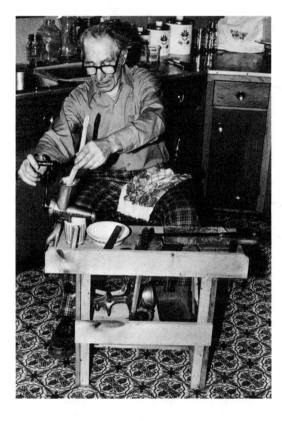

Art Rakestraw of Chambersburg, Pennsylvania, designed and built this small table to hold his juicing machine and grinder. A lower shelf holds extra equipment and attachments, and slots in the tabletop hold large butcher knives.

The top is made of heavy 2×12 construction-grade lumber. It is supported by built-up legs made of 1×2s and 1×3s. Sturdy and utilitarian, this table will take a lot of abuse, not just from holding the heavy grinder and juicing machine, but by serving as a chopping block as well. For durability and good looks, the top should be given a hand-rubbed finish of nontoxic oil or a coating of brush-on lacquer especially formulated for countertops and butcher blocks. The legs may be finished the same way, or be painted, stained, or left as is.

CONSTRUCTION

1. Cut four pieces of 1×3 (¾'' $\times$ 2½'') stock to 20 inches each for the front and back leg pieces.

2. Cut four pieces of 1×2 (¾'' $\times$ 1½'') stock to 20 inches each for the leg side pieces.

3. Assemble the finished legs fastening the wider boards to the edges of the narrower boards, using carpenter's wood glue and 6d finishing nails.

4. Cut two pieces of 1×3 to 18½ inches each

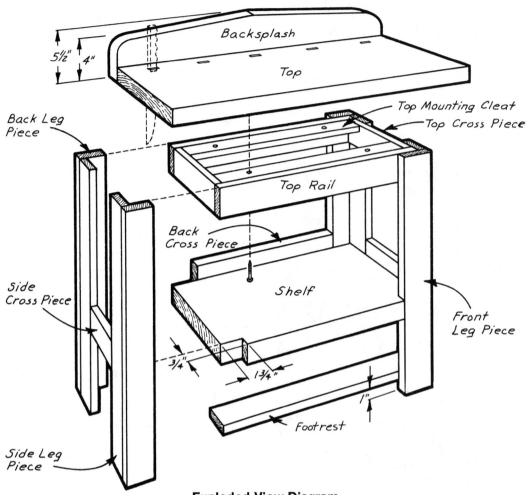

Exploded-View Diagram

for the top rails, and two additional pieces to 8 inches each for the top cross pieces.

5. Fasten the top rails to the top cross pieces to make the top frame. Use 6d finishing nails. The frame should measure 18½ × 9½ inches when assembled.

6. Cut two pieces of 1 × 2 to 17 inches each for the top mounting cleats. Fasten the cleats between the top cross pieces, using wood glue and 6d finishing nails, so the cleats are flush with the cross pieces and rails.

7. Attach the legs to the top frame using wood glue and 6d finishing nails, so the pieces are flush at the top edges, as shown in illustration A. Place the nails so they enter the mounting cleats and top frame pieces.

8. Cut one piece of 2 × 12 (1½″ × 11¼″) stock to 18½ inches for the shelf, then rip or plane the piece to measure 11 inches wide. Cut a ¾-inch-deep notch 1¾ inches long in each corner of one long side of the shelf so it will fit around the front legs.

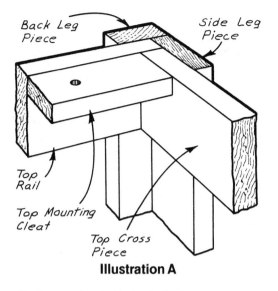

Back Leg Piece

Side Leg Piece

Top Rail

Top Mounting Cleat

Top Cross Piece

Illustration A

inches each for the side cross pieces. Fasten these pieces between the legs using wood glue and 6d finishing nails, so the bottom edges of the cross pieces are flush with the bottom surface of the shelf.

9. Fasten the shelf inside the legs using wood glue and 6d finishing nails. Position the shelf 6 inches from the bottom of the legs.

10. Cut one piece of 1 × 3 to 15 inches for the back cross piece, and two pieces to 6½

11. Cut one piece of 1 × 3 to 18½ inches for the footrest. Fasten this piece 1 inch above the bottom of the front legs, as shown in the exploded-view diagram, using 6d finishing nails.

12. Cut one piece of 2 × 12 to 28 inches for the top. Rip or plane one long edge so the piece measures 11 inches wide.

13. Cut one piece of 2 × 6 (1½″ × 5½″) to 28 inches for the backsplash. Choose one of the long edges as the top and plane it so it tapers from 5½ inches at the center to 4 inches at each end, then round off the top corners, as shown in the exploded-view diagram.

14. Fasten the backsplash to the rear (ripped or planed) edge of the top using wood glue

LUMBER CUTTING LIST

Size	Piece	Quantity
2 × 12		
1½″ × 11″ × 28″	Top	1
1½″ × 11″ × 18½″	Shelf	1
2 × 6		
1½″ × 5½″ × 28″	Backsplash	1
1 × 3		
¾″ × 2½″ × 20″	Front and back leg pieces	4
¾″ × 2½″ × 18½″	Top rails	2
¾″ × 2½″ × 18½″	Footrest	1
¾″ × 2½″ × 15″	Back cross piece	1
¾″ × 2½″ × 8″	Top cross pieces	2
¾″ × 2½″ × 6½″	Side cross pieces	2
1 × 2		
¾″ × 1½″ × 20″	Leg side pieces	4
¾″ × 1½″ × 17″	Cleats	2

and four 3-inch #10 flathead wood screws. Align the pieces first, then drill ⅛-inch-diameter pilot holes into both pieces. Drill ³⁄₁₆-inch-diameter shank holes in the back-splash only, and countersink the holes. Realign the pieces and install the screws.

15. Turn the top upside-down, and center the stand—also upside-down—on the top. Drill ⅛-inch-diameter pilot holes through the mounting cleats and into the top. Then drill ³⁄₁₆-inch-diameter shank holes through the mounting cleats only. Countersink the holes in the mounting cleats, and realign the stand with the top. Fasten the pieces together using 2-inch #10 flathead wood screws.

16. Make slots for knives by first drilling ³⁄₁₆-inch-diameter starter holes down through the top, where desired, then finishing the slots with a keyhole saw.

17. Apply a nontoxic oil or lacquer finish to the top and backsplash, and whatever finish you desire to the legs and other parts of the table.

MULTI-PURPOSE TABLE

SHOPPING LIST

Lumber
1 pc. 2 × 2 × 18″ (scrap)
4 pcs. 1 × 3 × 8′
Hardboard
1 sheet ¼″ × 4′ × 8′
Hardware
8 flathead wood screws #6 × ¾″
2 carriage bolts ¼″ × 3″
2 carriage bolts ¼″ × 2″
4 wing nuts ¼″
4 flat washers ¼″
1 box finishing nails 6d

This lightweight folding table takes up little space and is very handy to have around the house. It can serve as a general utility table, a painting and finishing table for use in the workshop, or a table on which to fold clothes in the laundry. During the summer, take the table outside for backyard cookouts, or put it in the back of the car and take it along on picnics and camping trips. Use it year-round as a display table at yard sales and flea markets.

The folding table is inexpensive and relatively simple to build. Construction materials are 1 × 3 lumber and tempered hardboard. Before undertaking the project, though, notice that one pair of legs has a stretcher on the inside and that the other pair has a stretcher on the outside. Also notice that additional notches are cut into the edges of two diagonally opposed legs and not in the other two. These features enable the legs to fit together compactly when the table is folded; however, since each leg is different, you must take care when building the table to label each piece according to the diagrams and to follow the step-by-step instructions precisely to avoid making mistakes. When finished, the pair of legs with the stretcher on the inside must be folded first.

Clear finish such as lacquer or polyurethane is a good choice for the table. Of course, you may wish to paint it instead.

Don't overload the table with heavy objects. Although its design is sound for general purposes, the folding table is not intended for heavy-duty use.

CONSTRUCTION

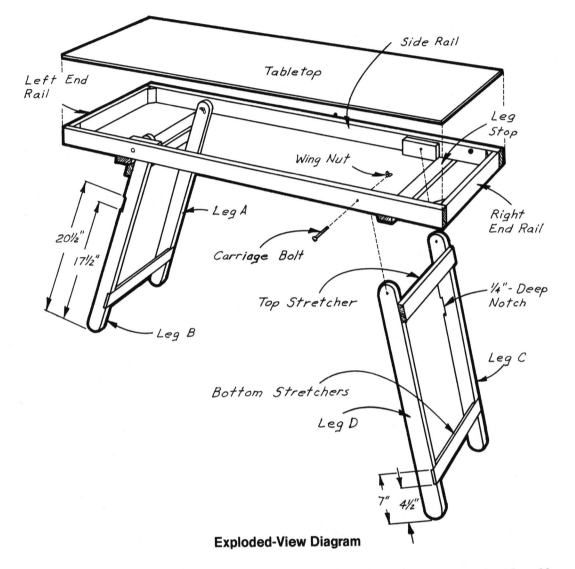

Side Rail

Tabletop

Left End Rail

Leg Stop

Wing Nut

Right End Rail

Leg A

20½"

17½"

Carriage Bolt

¼"- Deep Notch

Top Stretcher

Leg B

Leg C

Bottom Stretchers

Leg D

7"   4½"

Exploded-View Diagram

1. Cut two pieces of 1 × 3 (¾″ × 2½″) stock to 60 inches each for the side rails of the tabletop.

2. Cut two pieces of 1 × 3 stock to 16½ inches each for the end rails of the tabletop.

3. Arrange all four rails so the side rails over-

lap the end rails to create the 18 × 60-inch rectangular tabletop framework, as shown in illustration A. Fasten the side rails to the end rails in this position with carpenter's wood glue and 6d finishing nails.

4. Use a scrap piece of 2 × 2 (1½″ × 1½″)

LUMBER CUTTING LIST

Size	Piece	Quantity
2 × 2		
1″ × 1″ × 2½″	Glue blocks	4
1 × 3		
¾″ × 2½″ × 60″	Side rails	2
¾″ × 2½″ × 32″	Legs	4
¾″ × 2½″ × 18″	Leg stops	2
¾″ × 2½″ × 16½″	End rails	2
¾″ × 2½″ × 15½″	Top stretchers	2
Hardboard		
¼″ × 18″ × 60″	Tabletop	1
¼″ × 2½″ × 15½″	Bottom stretchers	2
¼″ × 2⅛″ × 5½″	Spacer blocks	8

stock approximately 18 inches in length to make glue blocks. First rip the piece at a 45-degree diagonal and discard the smaller of the two triangular pieces formed. Cut the remaining piece into four blocks, each 2½ inches in length. Square blocks may be substituted for triangular ones, if desired. Glue the blocks into the four corners of the tabletop frame, as shown in illustration A, to reinforce the joints and

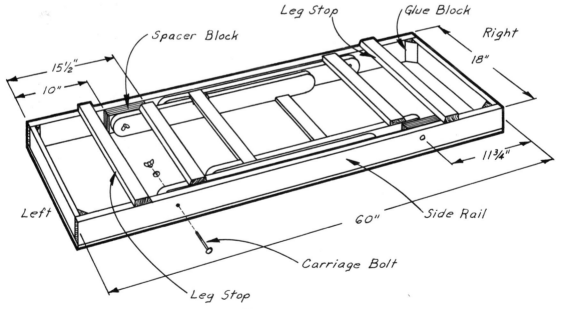

Illustration A

601

keep them square. Make sure the ends of the glue blocks do not protrude beyond the edges of the rails.

5. Cut a piece of ¼-inch hardboard to 18 × 60 inches for the tabletop. Glue the hardboard top to the rail framework, keeping all edges flush. Clamp the top to the rails while the glue sets. Use saw rippings or other long, thin pieces of scrap wood between the clamps, tabletop, and frame to evenly distribute the pressure of the clamps and to protect the work from clamp marks.

6. Cut four pieces of 1 × 3 stock to 32 inches each for the table legs. Label the legs A, B, C, and D for future reference. Also, select and mark a top and bottom end on each leg.

7. Using a compass, scribe a 1¼-inch radius on both the top and the bottom end of each leg. At the top end of each leg only, drill a ¼-inch-diameter hole through the center point of the radius. For easy layout in the following steps, do not cut the radius at this time.

8. Now measure from the bottom end of each leg along one edge and mark the leg at 4½ inches and 7 inches, as shown in the exploded-view diagram. Between these two points on each leg, cut a notch ¼ inch deep and 2½ inches long for the bottom stretchers, which will be installed in step 11.

9. Notches must be cut in legs B and C, as shown in the exploded-view diagram, so that the legs may fold flat. Lay out these notches by measuring from the bottom ends of legs B and C, along the edges opposite those previously notched. Mark legs B and C at 17½ inches and 20½ inches, as shown. Cut a notch ¼ inch deep and 3 inches long between these points on each of the two legs. Notch only legs

B and C. Do not notch legs A and D.

10. Finally, cut the 1¼-inch radii marked on both ends of each leg in step 7.

11. Cut two pieces of ¼-inch hardboard to 2½ × 15½ inches each for the bottom stretchers. Install one stretcher between legs A and B, and the other between legs C and D, as shown in the exploded-view diagram. Apply wood glue to the lower notches in each leg, where the stretchers are to be installed, then drill ³⁄₃₂-inch pilot holes and fasten the stretchers in place with two ¾-inch #6 flathead wood screws at each end.

12. Cut eight pieces of ¼-inch hardboard to 2⅛ × 5½ inches each. (Hardboard pieces aren't essential. Any scrap material may be used as long as the blocks are the correct dimensions.) Glue these pieces together in groups of four to form two spacer blocks, each block measuring 1 × 2⅛ × 5½ inches. Turn the tabletop facedown and mark a left and right end, to correspond with illustration A. Measure from the left end of the table along the upper edge of the side rail farthest from you and mark a point at 10 inches and one at 15½ inches. Do the same along the upper edge of the side rail nearest you, measuring this time from the right, but again marking points at 10 and 15½ inches. Now glue one spacer block on the inside of each rail between the points marked, as shown in illustration A.

13. Square lines across the width of both side rails 11¾ inches from each end of the tabletop. At the midpoint of each line, drill a ¼-inch-diameter hole through the rail (and spacer block if applicable) to receive the leg bolts.

14. Fit legs A and B into position on the left end of the tabletop so the bottom stretcher fastened between them faces toward the

center of the table. Attach leg A to the side rail with a ¼ × 2-inch carriage bolt. Attach leg B to the spacer block and rail with a ¼ × 3-inch carriage bolt. Secure both bolts with ¼-inch flat washers and ¼-inch wing nuts. Position legs C and D on the right end of the table, with the bottom stretcher facing toward the outside. Attach the legs to the table with carriage bolts, washers, and wing nuts, as you did legs A and B.

15. Cut two pieces of 1 × 3 stock to 18 inches each for the leg stops. Bevel one long edge of each leg stop to a 15-degree angle, as shown in illustration B.

16. Position the stops so that when the legs are opened, the stops will prevent the legs from splaying more than 15 degrees past vertical, as shown in illustration B. Apply wood glue to the stops and nail them in place using 6d finishing nails.

17. Cut two pieces of 1 × 3 stock to 15½ inches each for the top stretchers. Cut a 15-degree bevel along one long edge of each piece, as you did with the leg stops in step 15.

18. With the legs in their open position, mark where each top stretcher can be attached to the legs to fit snugly against a leg stop, as shown in illustration B. Fold the legs down, then glue the top stretchers in posi-

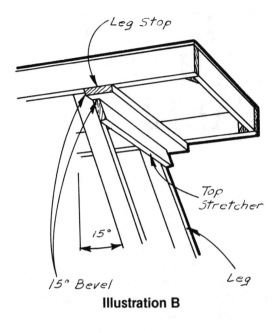

Illustration B

tion and fasten them with 6d finishing nails.

19. Unbolt the leg assemblies from the tabletop for finishing. Sand all parts of the table, rounding over all sharp edges. If the top ends of the legs fit too tightly against the underside of the table, sand them down, as needed. Apply a clear lacquer or polyurethane finish to the table, if desired, then reassemble.

FOLDING UTILITY TABLE

SHOPPING LIST

Lumber
2 pcs. 1 × 4 × 9'
2 pcs. 1 × 4 × 8'
Plywood
1 sheet ½'' × 4' × 8' A-C grade
Hardware
6 strap hinges 6'' with screws

Here is a sturdy, easy-to-build table that quickly folds out of the way for storage when not in use. A product of the Rodale Design Group, the table is ruggedly but simply constructed of No. 2 pine and plywood. Heavy-duty steel strap hinges join the tabletop and legs to the frame and allow for folding. The table pictured was left unfinished. However, you may wish to apply paint or polyurethane to the project for durable, long-lasting protection.

CONSTRUCTION

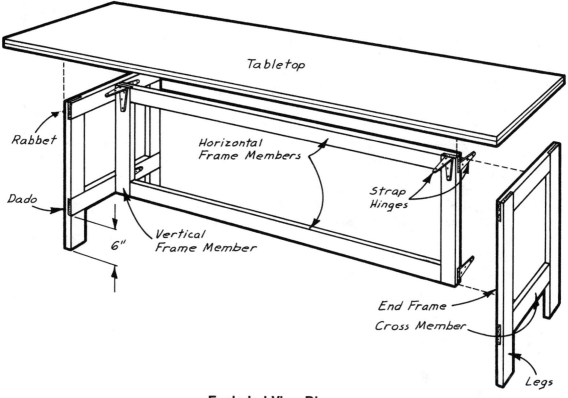

Exploded-View Diagram

1. Cut two pieces of 1×4 (¾″ × 3½″) stock to 72 inches each for the horizontal members of the table frame. Also cut two pieces of 1×4 stock to 23 inches each for the frame's vertical members.

2. Cut four pieces of 1×4 stock to 29 inches each for the legs. Also cut four pieces of 1×4 stock to 20 inches each for the end frame cross members.

3. Form half-lap joints by cutting ⅜-inch-deep rabbets 3½ inches wide across both ends of all pieces except the legs. On the legs, cut rabbets across one end, and dadoes—also ⅜ inch deep × 3½ inches

wide—across the other, beginning 6 inches from the unrabbeted end, as shown in the exploded-view diagram.

4. Join the horizontal and vertical members of the table frame together, and also the legs and cross members of the end frames, using carpenter's wood glue.

5. Attach the table frame to the end frames, as shown in the exploded-view diagram, using a pair of 6-inch strap hinges at each end. Be sure to attach all four hinges to the same side of the table frame.

6. Rip a 4×8 sheet of ½-inch A-C grade plywood in half to produce two sheets each

LUMBER CUTTING LIST

Size	Piece	Quantity
1 × 4		
¾'' × 3½'' × 72''	Table frame horizontals	2
¾'' × 3½'' × 29''	Legs	4
¾'' × 3½'' × 23''	Table frame verticals	2
¾'' × 3½'' × 20''	End frame cross members	4
Plywood		
½'' × 24'' × 96''	Tabletop	2

measuring 24 × 96 inches. Glue the two sheets together face-to-face for the tabletop. (When gluing, be sure that at least one good side of the plywood is exposed to serve as the table's top surface.)

7. Attach the tabletop to the upper horizontal member of the table frame, using a single 6-inch strap hinge at each end. Fasten the hinges to the same side of the table frame, on the side opposite the hinges installed in step 5.

8. If desired, sand the table and finish with paint or polyurethane.

RECYCLING UNIT

SHOPPING LIST

Lumber
1 pc. 5/4 × 2 × 10′
1 pc. 1 × 3 × 10′
3 pcs. 1 × 3 × 8′
Plywood
1 pc. ¾″ × 2′ × 4′ B-C grade
1 pc. ¼″ × 4′ × 4′ exterior grade
Hardware
6 flathead wood screws #6 × 2″
4 swivel casters 2″ with screws
3 butt hinges 1⅜″ × 2″ with screws
finishing nails 5d
wire nails 18 gauge × ⅝″
brushing lacquer

The Rodale Design Group designed this simple cabinet to make home collection of recyclable materials a convenient and tidy operation. Built of 1 × 3 pine and ¼-inch plywood, the unit contains two

compartments, each large enough to hold two standard-size shopping bags. The lid of the recycling unit is hinged for easy removal of full bags, yet features sliding panels as well for use when depositing material. Casters attached to the bottom of the unit allow easy movement of the unit from one location to another.

CONSTRUCTION

1. Cut four pieces of 1 × 3 (¾″ × 2½″) stock to 32 inches each for the side frame rails and six pieces to 20 inches each for the side frame stiles. Cut dadoes across the center of each rail and rabbet the ends of the rails and stiles both, to form half-lap joints, as shown in illustration A.

2. Choose two of the stiles cut in the previous step for center stiles. Cut a ¼-inch-wide groove ⅜ inch deep along the centerline of each, between the rabbeted ends, to accept the middle divider. Fasten the frames together using carpenter's wood glue.

3. Cut four pieces of 1 × 3 stock to 14 inches each for the end frame rails, and four pieces to 20 inches each for the end frame stiles. Rip the stiles to 1¾ inches in width, then rabbet the ends of both rails and stiles to form half-lap joints. Glue the pieces together to make the frames, as in the previous step.

4. Position all frames so that the rabbeted

607

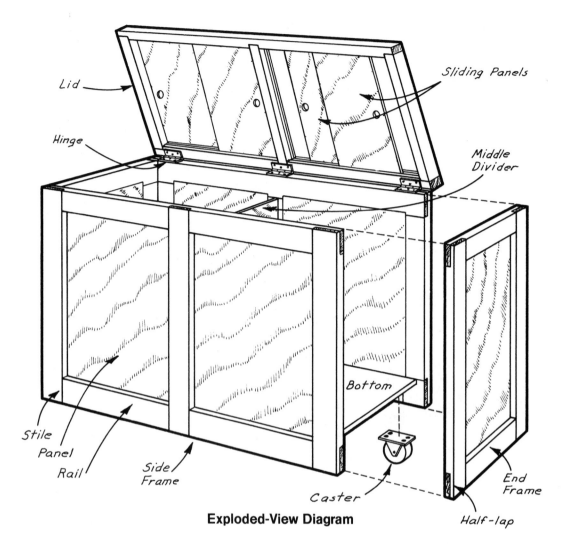

Lid

Hinge

Sliding Panels

Middle
Divider

Stile

Panel

Rail

Side
Frame

Bottom

Caster

End
Frame

Half-lap

Exploded-View Diagram

sides of their stiles face up, then use a router to cut a ½-inch-wide rabbet ¼ inch deep around the inside of all frame openings to receive the panels. Clean out the corners with a chisel.

5. Cut four pieces of ¼-inch exterior-grade plywood to 13⅛ × 16 inches each for the side frame panels, two pieces to 11½ × 16 inches each for the end frame panels, and one piece to 14¾ × 15 inches for the middle divider. Fasten the panels in the rabbets

cut for them, using wood glue and ⅝-inch × 18-gauge wire nails.

6. Fit the end frames and middle divider between the side frames, then fasten the frames together using wood glue and 5d finishing nails.

7. Cut one piece of ¾-inch B-C-grade plywood to 14 × 30½ inches for the bottom panel. Fit the panel between the frames just beneath the middle divider, so the upper face of the panel is flush with the

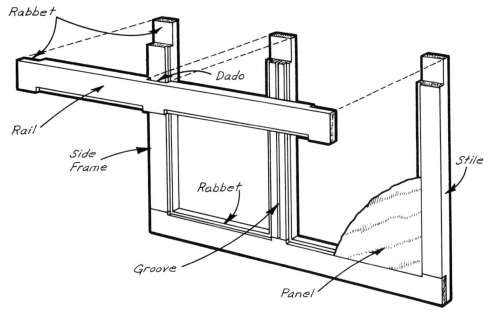

Illustration A

LUMBER CUTTING LIST

Size	Piece	Quantity
5/4 × 2		
$1\frac{1}{8}'' \times 1\frac{1}{2}'' \times 32''$	Lid side rails	2
$1\frac{1}{8}'' \times 1\frac{1}{2}'' \times 13\frac{7}{8}''$	Lid cross members	3
1 × 3		
$\frac{3}{4}'' \times 2\frac{1}{2}'' \times 32''$	Side frame rails	4
$\frac{3}{4}'' \times 2\frac{1}{2}'' \times 20''$	Side frame stiles	6
$\frac{3}{4}'' \times 2\frac{1}{2}'' \times 14''$	End frame rails	4
$\frac{3}{4}'' \times 1\frac{3}{4}'' \times 20''$	End frame stiles	4
¾'' Plywood		
$\frac{3}{4}'' \times 14'' \times 30\frac{1}{2}''$	Bottom panel	1
¼'' Plywood		
$\frac{1}{4}'' \times 14\frac{3}{4}'' \times 15''$	Middle divider	1
$\frac{1}{4}'' \times 13\frac{1}{8}'' \times 16''$	Side frame panels	4
$\frac{1}{4}'' \times 11\frac{1}{2}'' \times 16''$	End frame panels	2
$\frac{1}{4}'' \times 7\frac{7}{8}'' \times 13\frac{3}{4}''$	Lid panels	4

upper edges of the bottom rails. Fasten the plywood in place using 5d finishing nails.

8. Cut two pieces of 5/4 × 2 (1⅛″ × 1½″) stock to 32 inches each for the lid side rails, and three pieces to 13⅞ inches each for the lid cross members (select two for the ends and one for the center). On the inside face of each rail, cut a 1⅛-inch rabbet ⁵⁄₁₆ inch deep across the ends, and a dado of the same dimensions across the center, as shown in illustration B, to receive the ends of the cross members.

9. On the inside face of each end cross member, cut a ¼-inch-wide groove ⁵⁄₁₆ inch deep, ⁵⁄₁₆ inch from one edge. Cut a similar-size groove on each side of the center cross member, also ⁵⁄₁₆ inch from an edge, but locate the grooves diagonally opposite each other, as shown in illustration B.

10. Cut a pair of grooves, each ¼ inch wide × ⁵⁄₁₆ inch deep, on the inside face of each rail, as shown in illustration B. Locate each groove ⁵⁄₁₆ inch from an edge, also as shown.

11. Cut four pieces of ¼-inch plywood to 7⅞ × 13¾ inches each for the lid panels. Drill a ¾-inch-diameter hole centered along the length of each panel, 1 inch from an edge, for finger pulls, as shown in the exploded-view diagram.

12. Drill and countersink pilot holes for #6 wood screws through the lid rails at the six points where cross members will join, as shown in illustration B. Sand all pieces of the recycling unit, rounding over any sharp edges, as desired. Then apply two coats of a thin finish such as brushing lacquer (so the panels will slide easily).

13. Assemble the lid after carefully positioning the cross members so their grooves are staggered, as shown in illustration B. Fit the lid panels into the grooves and fasten the lid frame together using six 2-inch #6 flathead wood screws. Fasten the lid to the upper rail of the recycling unit's rear side frame using three 1⅜ × 2-inch butt hinges. Fasten 2-inch swivel casters on the bottom of the unit near each corner.

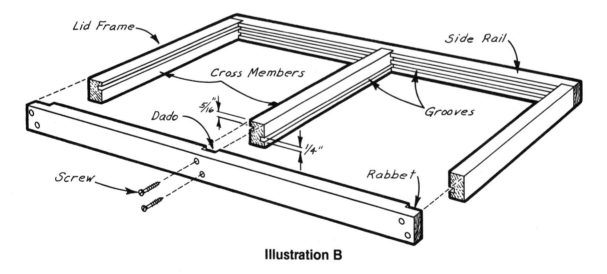

Illustration B

COLLAPS- IBLE WHEEL- BARROW

Simplicity underscores the design of this small wheelbarrow. Created by the Rodale Design Group, this easy-to-build cart is light in weight and features a hinged back and sides, which allow it to be folded into a compact unit for storage. The body of our wheelbarrow is made of ½-inch plywood and 1 × 6 pine. Since such a small amount of these materials is required, scraps left over from other projects may fill the bill and reduce the size of your shopping list.

SHOPPING LIST

Lumber
1 pc. 1 × 6 × 6'
Plywood
1 sheet ½'' × 4' × 8' exterior grade
Hardware
1 pc. steel conduit ¾'' diameter × 88½''
2 rubber wheels 6'' diameter
1 pc. steel rod ½'' diameter × 29⅝''
¼ pound cement-coated box nails 6d
10 flathead wood screws #8 × 1''
12 flathead wood screws #8 × ¾''
18 flathead machine screws 10-24 × ½''
2 thumbscrews ¼'' × 1½'' with ¼'' flat washers
4 carriage bolts ¼'' × 1½'' with washers and nuts
2 tee nuts ¼''
18 tee nuts 10-24
2 flat washers ½''
4 tee hinges 3''
2 strap hinges 2''
4 conduit clamps ½''
2 snap caps ½''
1 tube panel adhesive
1 quart exterior-grade enamel

We covered the wooden parts of our wheelbarrow with two coats of exterior-grade enamel. Other durable finishes will do as substitutes.

Use your collapsible wheelbarrow for lightweight chores around the yard and garden. Don't overload it. With only minimal care it should serve as a handy helper for many seasons.

611

CONSTRUCTION

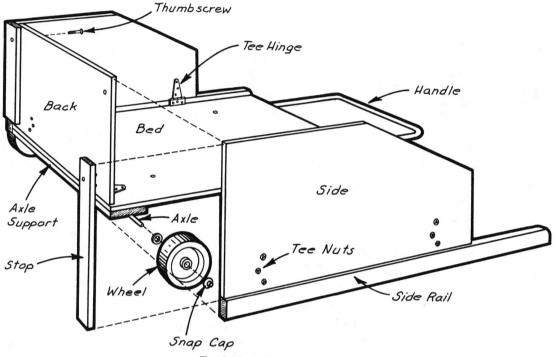

Exploded-View Diagram

1. Cut one piece of ½-inch exterior-grade plywood to 24 × 32 inches for the bed of the wheelbarrow. Also cut one piece of 1 × 6 (¾″ × 5½″) stock to 24 inches for the axle support. Then fasten the axle support across the width of the rear underside of the bed using panel adhesive. Make sure the outside edges of each are flush, then clamp the pieces while the adhesive sets.

2. Cut one piece of 1 × 6 stock to 32 inches, then rip it into two pieces, each 2 inches in width, for the side rails of the bed. Cut a ½-inch radius on what will become the top front corner of each rail, as shown in the exploded-view diagram. Center the side edges of the bed along the inside faces of the rails and fasten the rails to the bed

using panel adhesive and 6d cement-coated box nails.

3. Cut two pieces of ½-inch plywood to 11½ × 24 inches each for the wheelbarrow sides, and one piece to 12 × 23¼ inches for the back. Then cut each side piece to the shape shown in illustration A. Also cut one piece of 1 × 6 stock to 11½ inches, then rip it into two pieces, each 2 inches in width, for stops to hold the back of the wheelbarrow in the open position. Fasten the stops perpendicular to and across the width of the side pieces next to their square ends using panel adhesive and 6d cement-coated box nails. Put the stops on opposite faces of the side pieces to create a left and right side piece.

LUMBER CUTTING LIST

Size	Piece	Quantity
1 × 6		
¾" × 5½" × 24"	Axle support	1
¾" × 2" × 32"	Side rails	2
¾" × 2" × 11½"	Stops	2
Plywood		
½" × 24" × 32"	Wheelbarrow bed	1
½" × 12" × 23¼"	Wheelbarrow back	1
½" × 11½" × 24"	Wheelbarrow sides	2

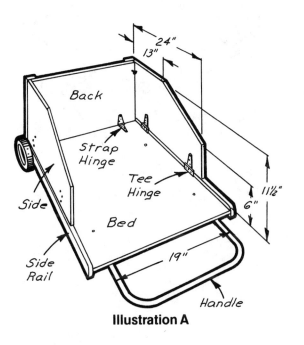

Illustration A

4. Cut one piece of ¾-inch conduit to 88½ inches for the wheelbarrow handle. Start a bend approximately 4½ inches on each side of the midpoint on the conduit, and continue both bends by pressing the conduit against a 10-inch-diameter stationary object until the two legs of the handle are parallel and approximately 19 inches apart, as shown in illustration A. Drill a ¼-inch-diameter hole through the handle at points 6 and 20 inches from the end of each leg to receive fastening bolts.

5. Center the handle on the underside of the wheelbarrow bed, so the end of each leg is flush against the axle support. On the underside of the bed, mark the position of the four holes in the handle. Remove the handle and drill ¼-inch-diameter holes through the bed to match the holes. Fasten the handle to the bed using four ¼ × 1½-inch carriage bolts, washers, and nuts.

6. Sand all wooden parts of the wheelbarrow, smoothing all sharp edges and corners. Coat all pieces with an exterior-grade enamel, or finish as desired.

7. Attach the side pieces to the inner faces of the side rails using four 3-inch tee hinges, as shown in the exploded-view diagram. Fasten the rectangular sections of the hinges to the side rails using ¾-inch #8 flathead wood screws, and fasten the tapered tongues to the side pieces using ½-inch 10-24 flathead machine screws and 10-24 tee nuts. Drill ¼-inch-diameter pilot holes for the tee nuts and drive them into the back faces of the side pieces before inserting the screws.

8. Fasten the back piece of the wheelbarrow

613

to the bed using 2-inch strap hinges. Locate the hinges on the inner faces of the bed and back pieces approximately 6 inches from each end of the back piece. Fasten the hinges to the bed using 1-inch #8 flathead wood screws, and to the back using ½-inch 10-24 flathead machine screws and 10-24 tee nuts. Install the tee nuts as in the previous step.

9. Position the sides and back of the wheelbarrow in their open positions, the back resting on the stops attached to the sides. Drill a 5/16-inch-diameter hole ¾ inch from each side and 3 inches below the top of the back. Drill through the stops behind it. Drive a ¼-inch tee nut into the hole on the underside of each stop. To secure the sides and back in the open position, insert ¼ × 1½-inch thumbscrews with ¼-inch flat washers through the holes in the back and into the tee nuts in the stops. Hold the back piece firmly against the stops and tighten the thumbscrews until snug.

10. Cut one piece of ½-inch-diameter steel rod to 29⅝ inches for the axle. Place a ½-inch flat washer on each end of the axle, fol-

lowed by a 6-inch-diameter rubber wheel. Secure the wheels on the axle with ½-inch snap caps. Center the axle across the axle support beneath the wheelbarrow, 2 inches from its outside edge. Fasten the axle to the axle support using ½-inch conduit clamps and 1-inch #8 flathead wood screws. Place clamps approximately 3 inches and 10 inches from each end of the axle support, alternating the direction of the clamps, as shown in illustration B.

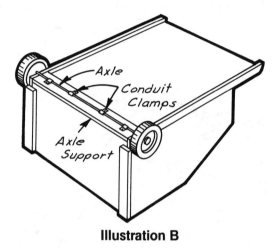

Illustration B

LOW-LOADER WHEEL-BARROW

If you have ever tried to lift a heavy rock into a conventional wheelbarrow, you'll immediately appreciate the low-loader wheelbarrow. Its body rests squarely on the ground for easy loading and unloading with very little lifting. All you have to do is roll or push objects onto it. Once underway the low-loader is easy to maneuver since the load stays close to the ground, well-balanced because of its low center of

gravity. The low-loader wheelbarrow is a great help when it comes to moving rocks around, and it is also handy for moving firewood, heavy packages, or earth. A large, side-opening box could be made (though we haven't tried it) — sized to fit the bed of the wheelbarrow — for carrying leaves and other loose material.

This project requires welding and tube bending. The 14-gauge, 1-inch-diameter steel conduit used for the frame can be bought at most electrical supply stores. If you do not have a large tubing bender or a welding outfit, take the conduit and the diagrams to a welding shop and have them do the work for you. The labor expense should be much lower than what a new wheelbarrow would cost. Another possibility is to rent a tubing bender and only job out the welding work.

While the frame is being made, you can complete the bed of the low-loader, which is made of ¾-inch exterior-grade plywood. You could have the welding shop attach a metal bed instead if you feel its extended life would be worth the added expense.

615

The wheel you'll need can be salvaged from your present wheelbarrow, or you can buy a new wheel at a hardware store. A 16-inch-diameter pneumatic balloon tire with an extended hub works best and will easily carry heavy loads over rough terrain.

You should obtain the wheel before having any work done on the frame. Advise the welding shop of the wheel's axle diameter so they can drill the wheel gussets accurately for you.

CONSTRUCTION

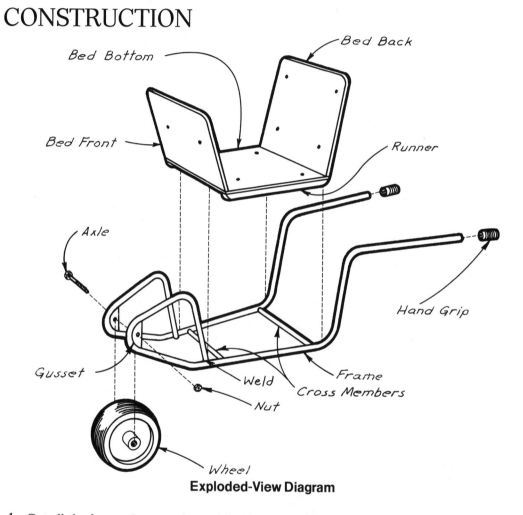

Bed Bottom

Bed Back

Bed Front

Runner

Axle

Hand Grip

Gusset

Weld

Frame Cross Members

Nut

Wheel

Exploded-View Diagram

1. Cut all the frame pieces to size and bend the two side pieces to the angles shown in illustration A. Start with the sharp bend (labeled A), then make the wheel gusset bend (labeled B), and continue with the bed and handle bends until the handles are formed.

2. Lay one side piece on top of the other to

LUMBER CUTTING LIST

Size	Piece	Quantity
2 × 4		
1½″ × 1¾″ × 22½″	Runners	2
Plywood		
¾″ × 22½″ × 24″	Bed bottom	1
¾″ × 13½″ × 24″	Bed rack	1
¾″ × 12″ × 24″	Bed front	1

check the alignment of the two pieces. Adjust the bends in each, if necessary, until the two pieces are identical. The side pieces must match perfectly or the frame will be twisted when the cross members are added.

3. Weld the wheel ends of the side pieces where they contact the bed area, as shown in the exploded-view diagram, then trim off any excess conduit protruding below the frame.

4. Weld the cross members in place behind the wheel ends, at right angles to the side pieces.

5. Make identical wheel gussets out of ¼-inch steel plate, as shown in the exploded-view diagram. For accuracy, after cutting out the pieces, stack them together and drill the axle hole for each in one operation.

6. Position the wheel gussets to the frame side pieces very carefully. Mark the positions so that the axle will remain straight, then tack-weld the gussets to the frame. Check the alignment of the axle holes with a length of rod, or with the wheel and axle. Reposition the gussets, if necessary, and then weld them permanently.

7. Install the wheel and axle in the gussets, move around to the rear of the frame and grasp the handlebar ends as if you were going to use the wheelbarrow. If the handles feel too low or too high, alter their bends to suit. Then paint the frame, unless you are having a metal bed installed. Remove the wheel and axle before painting.

8. Cut out the bed pieces from ¾-inch exterior-

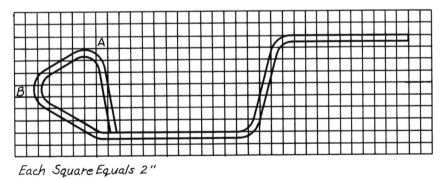

Each Square Equals 2″

Illustration A

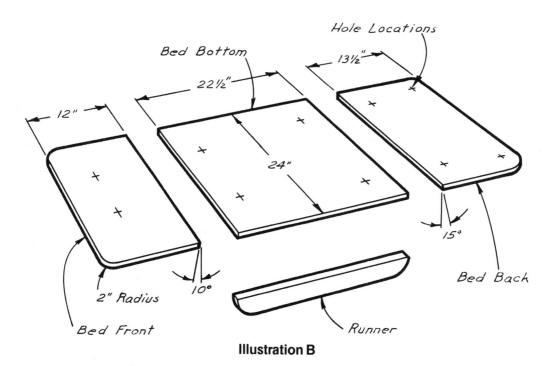

Illustration B

grade plywood, as shown in illustration B.

9. Position the bottom piece on the frame, center it, and mark where it contacts the rear bend of the side pieces. Chisel these areas, if necessary, so the bed will lie flat. Now drill a ⅜-inch-diameter hole through the plywood and frame, at one of the positions indicated in illustration B. Insert a ¼ × 2-inch carriage bolt through the bed and frame piece. Drill a second hole, insert a bolt, then move on to the third, and so forth. Inserting each bolt before drilling the next hole guarantees the bed will stay centered across the frame.

10. Fasten the front and rear bed pieces as in the previous step. To accommodate the

bend in the side pieces, you may have to chisel part of the rear piece where it joins the bottom.

11. Add runners to the underside of the bed's bottom piece. These may be made by ripping a 2 × 4 (1½″ × 3½″) along its centerline. Round-off the corners, if desired, then fasten the runners to the bed using 1½-inch #10 wood screws.

12. Apply several coats of finish to the plywood bed and runners. Add 1-inch-I.D. bicycle-type hand grips to the handle ends, and reinstall the wheel if you have not already done so. Your low-loader is now ready to roll.

HEAVY-DUTY GARDEN CART

SHOPPING LIST

Hardware
1 discarded garden cart with handle
2 bicycle wheels 20″ with axles and nuts
1 pc. flat mild steel ⅛″ × 1″ × 2′
2 pcs. angle iron 1½″ × 1½″ × 3′
4 pcs. angle iron 1½″ × 1½″ × 32″
rust-resistant paint

When E. Gardner Brownlee of Florence, Montana, decided to resurrect his "Radio"-brand garden cart after its wheels gave out from heavy use, he did so by adding a solid angle-iron frame and large-diameter bicycle wheels. Now his heavy-duty cart hauls everything from concrete to hay and, chances are, it will never need rebuilding again!

Welding is required, along with a discarded cart and handle. Brownlee's cart body measures 22 inches wide. The bicycle wheels are 20-inch-diameter, heavy-duty wheels designed for motocross use.

CONSTRUCTION

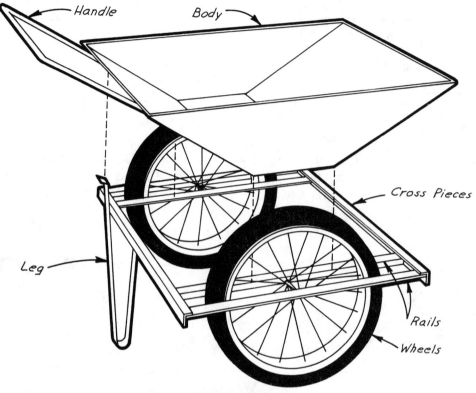

Handle Body Cross Pieces Leg Rails Wheels

Exploded-View Diagram

1. Cut four pieces of 1½ × 1½-inch angle iron to 32 inches each for the frame's rails. Cut two additional pieces to 36 inches each for the cross pieces.

2. Fit two rails between the cross pieces, one under each end, as shown in the exploded-view diagram. Square the corners, then tack-weld the pieces in position.

3. Fit and tack-weld the remaining two rails parallel to those installed in the previous step, also under the cross pieces but 4 inches from the cross piece ends.

4. Center and drill a 5/16-inch-diameter hole

through the midpoint of each rail, making sure all holes align. Cut away the metal below each hole, as shown in illustration A, to form notches for the axles.

5. Test-fit two 20-inch-diameter bicycle wheels in the notches, and also try the body of the discarded garden cart (along with its handle) between the inner rails of the frame, as shown in the exploded-view diagram.

6. Make adjustments to the frame, if necessary (you will have to break the tack welds). Then, when all components of the cart fit

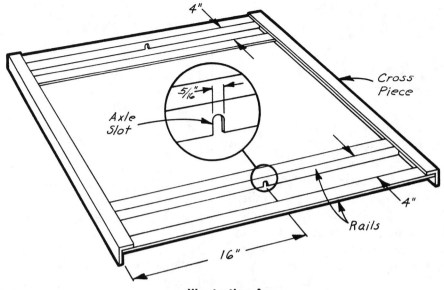

4"

Cross
Piece

5/16"

Axle
Slot

Rails

4"

16"

Illustration A

properly, remove the wheels and cart body and permanently weld the frame members together.

7. Replace the cart body in the frame and permanently weld it at several points of contact. Fit the bicycle wheels in their notches, but do not tighten the axle nuts.

8. Cut a strip of ⅛ × 1-inch-wide flat mild steel stock to approximately 24 inches for the support leg. Bend it into a U-shape and form tabs on each end, as shown in the exploded-view diagram. Locate the

proper position for the leg on the rear of the cart body (when in place, the cart should be supported level), then weld the leg in place.

9. Remove the bicycle wheels once again. Thoroughly grind all welds smooth, clean and sand the cart and frame, then apply rust-resistant paint.

10. After the paint has dried, reattach the wheels and tighten the axle nuts. Now the cart is ready to use.

GARDEN TRAILER

Here's a multipurpose garden trailer —a product of the Rodale Design Group— that can meet a variety of outdoor needs. It is made to be hitched to the back of a car, truck, or garden tractor. The trailer has a steel chassis and rides on two tubeless tires. It has a stake body, so its sides and ends can be quickly removed for loading and unloading heavy items, or for using the trailer as a flatbed. The 9-square-foot floor is large enough to carry trash cans, bales of hay, and other bulky items. The garden trailer can also be used to transport small loads of firewood, manure, or compost.

Construction is easy (most parts bolt together), but a small amount of welding and heavy-duty drilling through steel is necessary. You may want to have these tasks done for you at a machine shop or garage. The cost will be minimal. We chose to finish our trailer by painting the metal chassis, the sides, and floor panels a bright red. For contrast, we applied a clear lacquer to the body stakes and the outer frame of the floor.

SHOPPING LIST

Lumber
2 pcs. $2 \times 4 \times 8'$
1 pc. $1 \times 4 \times 8'$
1 pc. $1 \times 4 \times 6'$
Plywood
1 sheet $\frac{3}{4}'' \times 4' \times 8'$ A-C grade
Hardware
2 wheels with tubeless tires 4.80/4.00-8
2 pcs. square steel tubing $1'' \times 1'' \times 39''$ ($\frac{1}{8}''$ wall)
1 pc. steel bar $\frac{3}{4}''$ diameter $\times 39''$
2 pcs. steel bar $\frac{3}{4}''$ diameter $\times 1'$
2 pcs. steel plate $\frac{1}{4}'' \times 1'' \times 9''$
40 flathead wood screws #8 $\times 1\frac{1}{4}''$
6 carriage bolts $\frac{3}{8}'' \times 3''$ with washers and nuts
16 carriage bolts $\frac{3}{8}'' \times 2''$ with washers and nuts
2 flat washers $\frac{3}{4}''$
2 cotter pins $\frac{1}{8}'' \times 1''$
1 spray can of metal-adhering paint
1 quart exterior-grade enamel

CONSTRUCTION

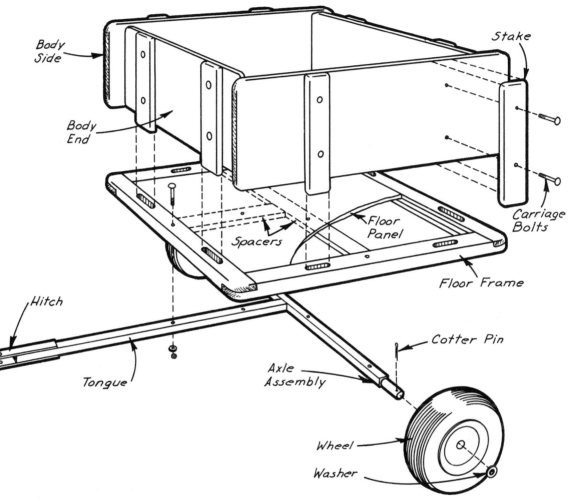

Body
Side

Body
End

Spacers

Hitch

Tongue

Stake

Carriage
Bolts

Floor
Panel

Floor Frame

Cotter Pin

Axle
Assembly

Wheel

Washer

Exploded-View Diagram

1. Cut two pieces of 1-inch-square steel tubing (⅛-inch wall thickness) to 39 inches each, one for the tongue section and one for the axle section of the chassis frame. Then cut one piece of ¾-inch-diameter steel bar to 39 inches, and two pieces to 12 inches each.

2. Insert the longer bar inside the tongue sec-

tion of the chassis frame so that the ends of both are flush, then weld the bar to the tubing. Drive the two shorter bars into the ends of the axle section until only 3½ inches of each bar protrudes from the tubing. Weld these bars in place, then drill a ⅛-inch-diameter hole centered 3/16 inch from the outer end of each to accept cotter pins, as shown in illustration A.

623

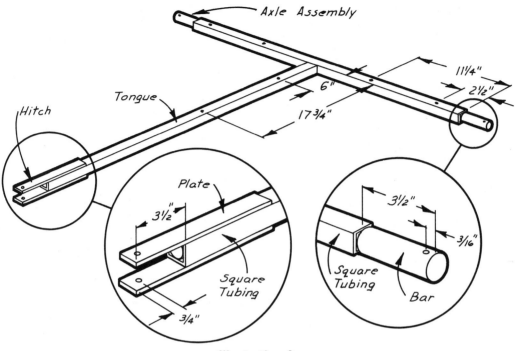

Illustration A

3. Cut two pieces of ¼ × 1-inch steel plate to 9 inches each for the hitch assembly. Weld one piece to the top and the other to the bottom of the front end of the tongue assembly, so each section of the hitch extends 3½ inches past the end of the tongue, as shown in illustration A.

4. Drill a ⅜-inch-diameter hole centered ¾ inch from the front end of each section of the hitch to accept a hitch pin. Then drill two more holes of the same dimension through the tongue assembly, the first centered 6 inches from the rear end of the tongue and the other 17¾ inches from the rear, as shown in illustration A. Drill a similar set of holes through the axle section of the chassis frame. Center one hole 2½ inches from each end of the tubing and another 11¼ inches from each end; then weld the tongue assembly perpendic-

ular to and centered on the axle assembly, also as shown.

5. Cut one piece of ¾-inch A-C grade plywood to 32 × 35 inches for the floor of the trailer. Then cut one piece of 1 × 4 (¾″ × 3½″) stock to 30 inches for a floor-to-axle spacer, and another piece to 14⅜ inches for a floor-to-tongue spacer.

6. Cut two pieces of 2 × 4 (1½″ × 3½″) stock to 37 inches each for the ends of the floor frame, and two pieces to 40 inches each for the sides. Cut two slots centered on the width of each piece. Make each slot ¾ inch wide and 3½ inches long, beginning and ending with a ⅜-inch radius, as shown in illustration B. Center the radius for the beginning of each slot 8⅞ inches from the ends of each side piece and 8⅜ inches from the ends of each end piece, also as shown. Lightly round-over

LUMBER CUTTING LIST

Size	Piece	Quantity
2 × 4		
1½″ × 3½″ × 40″	Floor frame sides	2
1½″ × 3½″ × 37″	Floor frame ends	2
1 × 4		
¾″ × 3½″ × 30″	Floor-to-axle spacer	1
¾″ × 3½″ × 14⅜″	Floor-to-tongue spacer	1
¾″ × 3½″ × 13½″	Body stakes	8
Plywood		
¾″ × 32″ × 35″	Floor panel	1
¾″ × 12″ × 40″	Body sides	2
¾″ × 12″ × 31⅝″	Body ends	2

the sharp edges around each slot.

7. Cut a 1-inch-wide rabbet ¾ inch deep along the length of the upper inside edge of each floor frame piece to accept the floor panel. Then cut a 3½-inch-wide rabbet ¾ inch deep across both ends, on the lower face of each end section, and a rabbet 2½ inches wide and ¾ inch deep on the upper face of each side section of the floor frame, also across both ends.

8. Half-lap the ends of the floor frame pieces to form a rectangle with a continuous rabbet along its upper inside edges. Check to be sure the floor panel fits into the rabbeted part of the rectangle, then fasten the frame and panel together using carpenter's wood glue and 1¼-inch #8 flathead wood screws. Insert the screws from the underside of the frame into the plywood panel and the half-lap joints. Radius the four

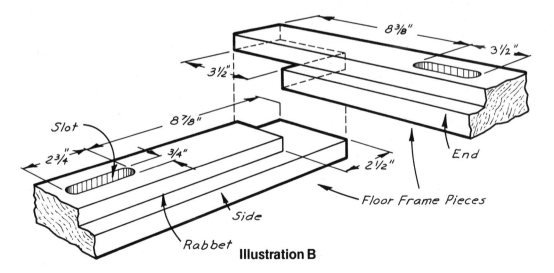

Illustration B

corners and round-over all sharp edges along the sides of the floor frame.

9. Fasten the floor-to-axle spacer to the underside of the floor panel with wood glue and 1¼-inch #8 flathead wood screws, positioning it lengthwise between the side sections of the frame, 14⅜ inches from the frame's front section, as shown in the exploded-view diagram. Then use similar fasteners to install the floor-to-tongue spacer between the center of the frame's front section and the other spacer.

10. Position the chassis frame on top of the inverted trailer floor with the axle and tongue assemblies centered over their respective spacers. Mark the location of the six holes in the chassis frame on the spacers. Remove the chassis and drill a ⅜-inch-diameter hole through the spacers and floor panel at each of the six points marked, to receive carriage bolts.

11. Cut eight pieces of 1 × 4 stock to 13½ inches each for the body stakes. Drill a ⅜-inch-diameter hole centered 3 inches from the top end of each stake and a second hole of the same size centered 6 inches farther along. These holes will receive the carriage bolts that will fasten the stakes to the body sides.

12. Round-over all sharp edges on the eight body stakes, cutting a radius along the side edges sufficient to allow the stakes to slide in and out of the slots in the frame of the trailer floor.

13. Cut two pieces of ¾-inch plywood to 12 × 40 inches each for the body sides, and two pieces to 12 × 31⅝ inches each for the body ends. Cut a radius on all four corners of each piece and round-over all other edges to minimize splintering and to blend with the appearance of the other parts of the trailer body.

14. Arrange two stakes on the outside face of each body side and end, aligned so the top ends of the stakes are flush with the upper edges of the body sides. Space the stakes 5½ inches from the ends on each body end piece, and 8⅞ inches from the ends on each side piece. Make sure that, if mounted in these positions, all stakes will fit into the slots in the floor frame. Adjust stake positions, if necessary; then, using the bolt holes in the stakes as guides, drill similar-size holes on through the body side and end pieces. (Fasten the assemblies after finishing the pieces; see step 16.)

15. Fill all voids in the wooden parts of the trailer, then sand and finish all parts, as desired. Use metal-adhering paint on the chassis and exterior-grade paint or varnish on all wooden parts.

16. Assemble the trailer using ⅜ × 3-inch carriage bolts with washers and nuts to hold the body to the chassis, and ⅜ × 2-inch carriage bolts with washers and nuts to fasten the stakes to the body sides and ends. Mount a set of 4.80/4.00-8 wheels with tubeless tires on the axles, followed by ¾-inch flat washers, and lock them in place with ⅛ × 1-inch cotter pins.

TRACTOR CART

You'll never have to worry about overloading this tractor cart! Michael Kirchner of Haymarket, Virginia, designed it to easily hold up to 800 pounds in its 18-cubic-foot bed. Kirchner uses it for hauling firewood, stone, and other heavy loads.

The undercarriage is heavily braced with angle iron and large bolts. Two large wheelbarrow wheels carry the load and act as shock absorbers.

A portable drill guide is advisable for

SHOPPING LIST

Lumber
4 pcs. 2 × 12 × 8'
3 pcs. 2 × 6 × 8'
4 pcs. 2 × 2 × 10'
Plywood
1 sheet ⅝'' × 4' × 8' exterior grade
Hardware
1 trailer hitch (to fit tractor)
2 wheelbarrow wheels 18'' diameter with ⅝'' axle hole
1 pc. angle iron 1½'' × 1½'' × 80''
4 pcs. angle iron 1½'' × 1½'' × 6¾''
2 pcs. angle iron 1½'' × 1½'' × 6''
2 pcs. steel rod ⅝'' diameter × 14½''
36 lag bolts ¼'' × 3'' with flat washers
30 lag bolts ¼'' × 1½''
4 hex head machine bolts ⅜'' × 1'' with nuts
88 carriage bolts ¼'' × 3½'' with nuts
12 carriage bolts ¼'' × 2'' with nuts
136 flat washers ⁵⁄₁₆''
6 flat washers ⅝''
4 lockwashers ⁵⁄₁₆''
4 cotter pins ⅛'' × 1''

drilling the many holes required for this project. If you have the facilities and are a careful planner, many of the pieces may be predrilled using a drill press instead.

CONSTRUCTION

1. Cut two pieces of 2 × 12 (1½'' × 11¼'') stock to 48 inches each for the side rails, and two pieces to 16 inches each for the wheel blocks. Trim both sets of pieces to the shapes shown in illustration A.

2. Cut four pieces of 2 × 6 (1½'' × 5¼'')

stock to 37 inches each for the cross pieces, four pieces to 11¼ inches each for the wheel braces, and one piece to 14 inches for the tie.

3. Cut 12 pieces of 2 × 2 (1½'' × 1½'') stock to 5½ inches each for corner blocks.

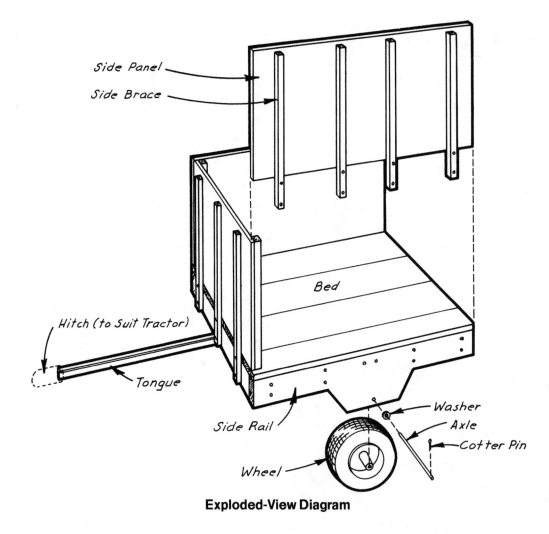

Side Panel

Side Brace

Bed

Hitch (to Suit Tractor)

Tongue

Washer

Axle

Cotter Pin

Side Rail

Wheel

Exploded-View Diagram

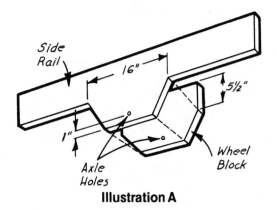

Side
Rail

16"

5½"

1"

Axle
Holes

Wheel
Block

Illustration A

4. Position a corner block flush with the ends of each cross piece and wheel block, as shown in illustration B. Drill ¼-inch-diameter holes through each pair of pieces, centered on the blocks, then fasten the blocks to the cross pieces using ¼ × 3½-inch carriage bolts fitted with flat washers and nuts.

5. Position the wheel braces against the wheel blocks and rails by centering the braces across the widths of those pieces, as shown in illustration B. Then drill four ¼-inch-

LUMBER CUTTING LIST

Size	Piece	Quantity
2 × 12		
1½″ × 11¼″ × 48″	Bed planks	4
1½″ × 11¼″ × 48″	Side rails	2
1½″ × 11¼″ × 16″	Wheel blocks	2
2 × 6		
1½″ × 5¼″ × 48″	Bed plank	1
1½″ × 5¼″ × 37″	Cross pieces	4
1½″ × 5¼″ × 14″	Tie	1
1½″ × 5¼″ × 11¼″	Wheel braces	4
2 × 2		
1½″ × 1½″ × 30½″	Panel braces	11
1½″ × 1½″ × 24″	Panel corner blocks	2
1½″ × 1½″ × 5½″	Corner blocks	12
1½″ × 1½″ × 5″	Tongue spacer	1
Plywood		
⅝″ × 24″ × 48″	Side panels	2
⅝″ × 24″ × 38¾″	Front panel	1

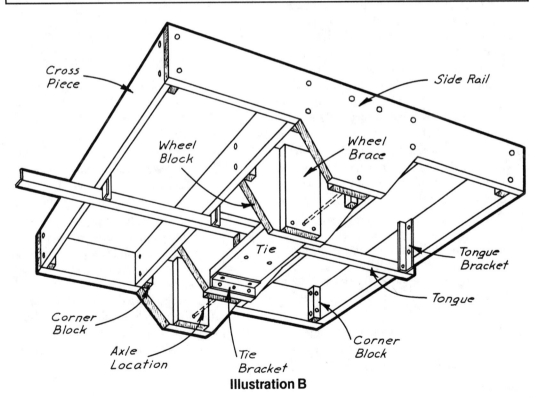

Illustration B

629

diameter holes through each pair of pieces and fasten the braces to the blocks using ¼ × 3½-inch carriage bolts, flat washers, and nuts. Do not permanently tighten the bottom four bolts at this time (see step 14).

6. Drill ⅝-inch-diameter axle holes through the rails and wheel blocks, centered 1 inch from the bottom edges of each, as shown in illustration A.

7. Attach the wheel blocks between one pair of cross pieces, 10 inches from the ends of the cross pieces and flush with their top edges, as shown in illustration B. Be sure the corner blocks on each cross piece face each other. Drill ¼-inch-diameter holes through the cross pieces and corner blocks attached to each wheel block. Then fasten all the pieces together using ¼ × 3½-inch carriage bolts, flat washers, and nuts.

8. Assemble the cart frame by placing the rails across the ends of the cross pieces, as shown in illustration B. Drill ¼-inch-diameter holes through the rails and corner blocks attached to each cross piece. Then fasten the rails and cross pieces together using ¼ × 3½-inch carriage bolts, flat washers, and nuts. Notice that the inner cross pieces are each located 14½ inches from the end of the frame.

9. Cut one piece of 1½ × 1½-inch angle iron to 80 inches for the tongue of the cart. Cut four additional pieces to 6¾ inches each for the tongue brackets.

10. Position the tongue brackets ¾ inch to one side of the cart frame's centerline, as shown in illustration B. Drill 5/16-inch-diameter holes through the cross pieces and brackets, then fasten the brackets with ¼ × 2-inch carriage bolts, flat washers, and nuts.

11. Position the tongue so that one side lies flat against the tongue brackets, then drill 7/16-inch-diameter holes and fasten the tongue to the brackets with ⅜ × 1-inch hex head machine bolts, lockwashers, and nuts.

12. Cut one piece of 2 × 2 stock to 5 inches for the tongue spacer.

13. Cut two pieces of 1½ × 1½-inch angle iron to 6 inches each for the tie brackets.

14. Position the tie brackets flush with the ends of the tie (cut in step 2). Drill 5/16-inch-diameter holes and fasten the brackets to the ends of the tie using the same bolts installed in step 5 to hold the wheel braces to the wheel blocks.

15. Center the tie between the wheel blocks, then slip the tongue spacer between the tongue and tie. Drill 5/16-inch-diameter holes and fasten the tie to the tongue with ¼ × 3½-inch carriage bolts, flat washers, and nuts.

16. Align the tie brackets attached to the ends of the tie against the wheel blocks. Drill 5/16-inch-diameter holes and fasten the tie to the wheel blocks with ¼ × 2-inch carriage bolts, flat washers, and nuts.

17. Using the holes in the wheel blocks as guides, drill a ⅝-inch-diameter hole through each tie bracket to complete the axle holes in the cart frame.

18. Obtain two pieces of ⅝-inch-diameter × 14½-inch steel rod for the axles. Slide them through the axle holes to check their alignment. If necessary, enlarge misaligned holes slightly to achieve a proper fit.

19. Obtain two 18-inch-diameter wheelbarrow wheels. Slide the axles out of the frame, position the wheels as shown in the exploded-view diagram, then slide the axles back through the axle holes and wheels to fasten the wheels in place on the frame. If needed, use ⅝-inch flat washers as spacers to keep the wheels centered between the frame members.

20. Fit ⅝-inch-diameter flat washers on the ends of the axles, drill ⅛-inch-diameter holes, and use ⅛ × 1-inch cotter pins to fasten the axles in place.

21. Cut four pieces of 2 × 12 stock and one piece of 2 × 6 stock to 48 inches each for the bed planks.

22. Position the planks on top of the cart frame, flush with its edges. Rip the last plank to achieve a perfect fit, flush with the rail. Drill ¾-inch-diameter holes ⅜-inch deep into the planks, centering the holes over the cross pieces. Then drill ³⁄₁₆-inch-diameter holes through the planks and into the cross pieces. Enlarge the holes to ¼-inch-diameter where they pass through the planks, then fasten the planks to the cross pieces using ¼ × 3-inch lag bolts fitted with flat washers.

23. Cut two pieces of ⅝-inch exterior-grade plywood to 24 × 48 inches for the side panels. Cut one additional piece to 24 × 38¾ inches for the front panel.

24. Cut 11 pieces of 2 × 2 stock to 30½ inches each for panel braces. Cut two additional pieces to 24 inches each for panel corner blocks.

25. Position the braces against the rails and front cross piece of the cart frame, as shown in illustration C. Drill ¼-inch-diameter holes through the pieces, then fasten the braces to the frame members using ¼ × 3½-inch carriage bolts, flat washers, and nuts.

26. Position the panels against the braces so the panels rest on the bed planks of the cart, as shown in illustration C. Drill pairs

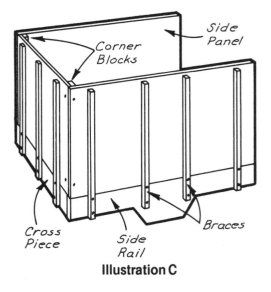

Illustration C

of ³⁄₁₆-inch-diameter holes through the panels and into each brace. Enlarge the holes to ¼-inch diameter where they pass through the plywood, then fasten the panels to the braces using ¼ × 1½-inch lag bolts fitted with flat washers.

27. Position the corner blocks against the inside of the front and side panels, as shown in illustration C. Drill ¼-inch-diameter holes through the panels and blocks, then fasten the pieces together using ¼ × 1½-inch lag bolts with flat washers.

28. Apply copper naphthenate wood preservative or paint to the entire cart. Then attach a trailer hitch to the tongue to fit your tractor.

DATE DUE		